THE MEANING AND END OF SUFFERING FOR FREUD AND THE BUDDHIST TRADITION

Gordon E. Pruett

UNIVERSITY
PRESS OF
AMERICA

LANHAM • NEW YORK • LONDON

British Cataloging in Publication Information Available

Library of Congress Cataloging in Publication Data

Pruett, Gordon E., 1941-
    The meaning and end of suffering.

    Includes bibliographical references and index.
    1. Suffering—Religious aspects—Buddhism.
2. Freud, Sigmund, 1856-1939.   3. Four Noble Truths.
4. Suffering.   I. Title.
BQ4235.P78   1987   294.3'422   86-26735
ISBN 0-8191-5758-9 (alk. paper)

To Wilfred Cantwell Smith

Acknowledgements

I would like to acknowledge with gratitude the help and cooperation of those people who have eased and helped to expedite the many tasks associated with this extended project. For aid and assistance in connection with the substantial research required I wish to thank the staff of the Bodleian Library, Oxford University, and Professor Gary Tubb, Chair of the Department of Sanskrit and Indian Studies, Harvard University. My special thanks are due Susan Goldwitz of Northeastern University's Department of English for reading and correcting the very long and complex manuscript. I wish to thank also Cheryl Morse and Nancy Shapiro of Northeastern (at the time of their work on this project) for their assistance in transcribing parts of the manuscript to computer. In this respect Michael Lipton, Chair of the Department of Philosophy and Religion, Northeastern University, offered invaluable assistance as my guru in the world of word processing and electronic printing. I wish to thank the College of Arts and Sciences, Northeastern University, and its former Dean, Richard Astro, for financial assistance with permission fees, and the Department of Philosophy and Religion for financial assistance in transcribing portions of the book onto computer. The College and Northeastern University also awarded me sabbatical leave in 1981 and 1983, without which this book could not have been written. Finally, my deep indebtedness to the many family and friends who lovingly forced me to render my thoughts coherently is hereby acknowledged; and my obligation to Wilfred Cantwell Smith, who listened to my words about the book itself and whose life- long task is the major inspiration for this work, is also gratefully acknowledged.

I would like to thank the following publishers for permission to reprint portions of the relevant works: Routledge & Kegan Paul PLC, for quotations from The Pali Text Society's Translation Series; Sigmund Freud Copyrights Ltd, The Institute of Psycho-Analysis and The Hogarth Press for permission to quote from *The Standard Edition of the Complete Psychological Works of Sigmund Freud* translated and edited by James Strachey; from *Collected Papers*, Vols. 1, 2, 4 and 5, by Sigmund Freud, Authorized Translation under the supervision of Joan Riviere, published by Basic Books, Inc. by arrangement with the Hogarth Press Ltd. and The Institute of Psycho-Analysis, London (Reprinted by permission); Alfred A. Knopf, for excerpts from *Moses and Monotheism*, by Sigmund Freud and translated by Katherine Jones (1955); from *Introductory Lectures on Psychoanalysis* by Sigmund Freud, translated and edited by James Strachey, copyright (c) 1966 by W. W. Norton & Company, Inc., copyright (c) 1965, 1964, 1963 by James Strachey, copyright (c) 1920, 1935 by Edward L. Bernays, used with the permission of the Liveright Publishing Corporation; from *Beyond the Pleasure Principle*

Contents

Notes on Style

It may be helpful to the reader to know that I have made two decisions concerning style that give this book its unique appearance. First, I have retained British spelling and, on occasion, punctuation when justified by the texts I am using. The Pāli Text Translation Series is of course a British product, and it seems entirely appropriate to employ that usage here. Further, since I have used both American and British editions of the works of Sigmund Freud, I have retained the appropriate spelling and punctuation in each case.

Second, since this work is intended for an audience wider than Pāli Text specialists, and thus includes those who are unfamiliar with Pāli grammar, I have decided to pluralize Pāli nouns by using "s," following English rules, so that the reader will not be distracted from the flow of the argument.

ABBREVIATIONS

Abbreviations used in the footnotes in this book are as follows:

Pāli Texts

A = *The Book of the Gradual Sayings (Anguttara-Nikāya)*, I-V, translated by E. M. Hare and F. L. Woodward, for the Pali Text Society (London and Oxford: 1932-1937)

D = *Dialogues of the Buddha (Dīgha Nikāya)*, I-III, translated by T. W. and C. A. F. Rhys Davids, (*Sacred Books of the Buddhists*, II-IV, edited by T. W. Rhys Davids; London: Oxford University Press, 1899-1921)

M = *The Collection of Middle Length Sayings (Majjhima-Nikāya)*, I-III, translated by I. B. Horner, for the Pali Text Society (London: Luzac & Co., Ltd., 1954-1959)

S = *The Book of the Kindred Sayings (Saṃyutta-Nikāya)*, I-V, translated by Mrs. Rhys Davids, Suriyagoda Sumangala Thera and F. L. Woodward, for the Pali Text Society (London: Oxford University Press, 1917-1930)

U = *Udāna: Verses of Uplift, and Itivuttaka: As It was Said, The Minor Anthologies of the Pāli Canon, Pt. II*, translated by F. L. Woodward, with an introduction by Mrs. Rhys Davids (*Sacred Books of the Buddhists*, VIII, edited by T. W. Rhys Davids; London: Oxford University Press, 1935)

SN = *Woven Cadences of the Early Buddhists (Suttanipāta)*, translated by E. M. Hare (*Sacred Books of the Buddhists*, XV, edited by T. W. Rhys Davids; London: Oxford University Press, 1945)

Th = *Psalms of the Early Buddhists II. Psalms of the Brethren*, translated by Mrs. Rhys Davids, for the Pali Text Society (London: Oxford University Press, 1937)

Dh = *The Minor Anthologies of the Pāli Canon, Pt I: Dhammapada*, translated by Mrs. Rhys Davids (*Sacred Books of the Buddhists*, VII, edited by T. W. Rhys Davids; London: Oxford University Press, 1931)

The Writings of Sigmund Freud

SE = *Standard Edition of The Complete Psychological Works of Sigmund Freud*, edited by James Strachey et. al., I-XXIII (London: Hogarth, 1953-1966)

CP = *The Collected Papers of Sigmund Freud*, edited by Joan Riviere, (New York: Basic Books, 1959)

IL = "Introductory Lectures on Psychoanalysis," SE XV, XVI

NIL = "New Introductory Lectures on Psychoanalysis," SE XXII

Introduction

The reader may be wondering why this book has been written; to such wonderment he or she is more than entitled. Therefore a few explanatory remarks are in order. I think, also, that a few suggestive remarks are in order; for I seek here not simply to justify this essay and the time required both to read and to write it, but also to say, with not very much modesty, that I hope it is the first step–however tentative–in a new (and very old) journey along a path toward understanding the nature of human life as (what I like to call) the religious enterprise.

The first, and still introductory, remark, is that the book is about suffering chiefly. There are significant questions and insights raised by bringing together two such historically disparate traditions as the psychoanalytic and the Buddhist; but these are, in my view, secondary, however significant they may be. If the reader will bear this in mind the perspective I have adopted in general and particular matters will, I think, remain clear. In other, and negative, terms, it was never my intention to say that Buddhism is psychoanalysis (manqué or any other way) or that psychoanalysis is Buddhism (manqué, etc.). It certainly is my intention to analyze the nature of suffering, its origins, scope and end.

On the other hand, the implication of the study that the truth of suffering is universal is essential to my argument. I shall pursue this matter to its conclusion below.

Let me raise, then, what I think is a useful question in this context: On what grounds would it be held that while the Buddhist tradition is clearly religious, the psychoanalytic is clearly not? At first glance, this would seem in fact to be the case. Freud's analysis of religious life, of religion (and cognate Weltanschauungen) as neurotic symptoms, as projections of wishes, as dominated by the pleasure principle, as willful ignorance of Ananke ("Harsh Necessity"), and as significant hindrances to Science and Reason, would seem to give us a straightforward answer. Psychoanalysis is virtually the opposite of religion. Of course for Freud there are no exceptions in the historical record. Not only the Semitic traditions but the other two great classes, the primitive religions and the religions of the East, fall easily into the general category of religion since they share the characteristics I have described. In contrast, psychoanalysis holds a correspondence theory of reality, is open to change, seeks to break the grip of the repressed material upon which religious structures are grounded–in short, to move beyond the illusion of religion. We know all of this.

My response to this apparently serious challenge to my notion of psychoanalysis' role in the religious enterprise–I obviously hold that it is a positive and creative one–is twofold. First, it will be evident that the clearly "religious" tradition here, the Buddhist, does not see itself as Freud sees it, and is evidently in agreement with Freud's critique con-

1

cerning all those characteristics of human life that he places under the "religious" rubric.

Second, and I think somewhat more significantly, Freud is working with a concept of religion and religions—and therefore with a concept of science and its cognates—that does a radical disservice to religious traditions in general and the Buddhist in particular. That concept is not his alone. It is indeed a significant portion of the intellectual baggage of his, an earlier, and a later day. This concept is the notion of religion as a reified, objective and static cultural artifact as seen from the outside by individuals who do not share the faith of those whose tradition is in question. Such a view has a history.* It is a *parvenu* reading of religious history that emerged at precisely the time of the rise of so-called "Modern Science." The connection is not accidental. For Europeans "Modern Science" came to stand for an understanding of nature, man and—for a time—God based on mature, sober and honest reflection that was unflinching in the face of correction, courageous in speculation, humane, liberal and in general open to growth. "Religion," as all the world knows, came to stand for dogmatic, childish, scholastic and authoritarian institutions, arguments and politics that only a fool or a knave could possibly accede to. I mean to include both the "philosophical" and polemic implications in this contrast, for they are there. The rise of "Religion" as defined in this way cannot be separated from its polemical context.

But it was not always this way. The history of the term suggests that pre-modern usages of *religio*, in its various forms, were several and certainly susceptible to change. In general they tended to retain their etymological connotation of "obligation"; but they came increasingly to focus on what was the truth of the universe and of God as seen by one whose piety, that is, whose commitment of heart, soul and mind, was serious, mature, integrated and entire. The notion of "religion" had much more to do with faith than with belief—that is, much more to do with the openness of the individual to God's truth, the truth of the universe, the *Dhamma*. Religion in the later, Freudian (*inter alia*) sense, had everything to do with belief in propositions that could only be sustained by self-deception or outright intellectual dishonesty.

Moreover, for those interested in pursuing the history of culture and of the nature of the self the notion of the history of religion meant two different things, according to whether one followed the earlier or later notion of the term. For the earlier (Latin, Greek and European language) writers, the history of "religion" meant the history of attempts to celebrate rightly the founding acts of the community (ritual, liturgy), and/or to come to a knowledge of the truth that was not limited to its historical, symbolic, manifestations. For those concerned, as Freud was,

---

* See *Excursus*: **Freud's Conception of Religion**, below.

2

to explain religion as a clear example of primitive, that is to say neurotic and childish, thinking or experience, religion occurred in distinct and fixed forms characterized precisely by those neurotic–or at least bizarre–elements. One could speak of these forms in a general sense–Religion–and one could speak of them severally–religions–, each with a name attached by Western "observers."

The benefits of such a method for defenders of Science are obvious. The contrasting views of the world, science and religion, make religion the perfect "straw man" who could be made to say or do anything the outsider chose to make it, or them, say or do. In Freud's case, they (it) all believed in the personification of the Father whose characteristics were exactly the characteristics of the Father–he later spoke of the Parents–as seen in the context of the Oedipal crisis. There were no exceptions. Since this is what they (it) believed, and since we know that the Oedipus complex must be annihilated in the process of maturation, religious peoples are arrested in their development, caught in the web of an illusion of their own making, and qualify easily as the world's largest collection of neurotics.

Freud's defense of Science and Logos must be understood as the counterpart to his attack on Religion. When he defends science he defends courageous acceptance of a universe that is no nursery; his hero is Leonardo. When he attacks religion, he attacks illusion based on wishes and projections. Science is concerned only to understand the nature of life and in Freud's case human life; religion seeks to maintain the illusion of the nursery, to avoid confrontation with reality, to maintain the pleasure principle even if it is necessary to postpone satisfaction in the bosom of the family to a life after death.

A complete critique of the conception of religion that I have described will require something approaching an examination of all religious traditions to show that they are dynamic, not static, clearly concerned with the nature of reality, with the truth, leading toward liberation from illusion and self-deception, based firmly upon experience, critical of their own past and open to new expressions for the universal truth which they love. I must let my presentation of the Buddhist tradition stand for all other traditions in these respects; but I do so confidently. The conclusion of such a view must be that the reified "Religion" and "Religions" that Freud and his peers, and many today, hold to be the true one is in fact a perversion and a parody. On the contrary, the older notion of *religio*, with its dynamic nature, its openness to new expressions of faith (of which belief is one and only one), is, from the historical perspective at least, the only proper one.

If this be so, then it must also be the case that any expression of what is true must perforce be part of a religious tradition, regardless of its specific mode of expression, the difference (from one period to another) in its means of expression, and regardless of the differences between and among

3

the traditions with respect to their expressions of the truth. Freud himself, in commenting on Empedocles' cosmology, acknowledges as much. In that conclusion he expresses the true nature of the history of religious traditions, rather than in his attack upon "Religion."

In sum, then, while we may learn much from Freud in his treatment of religion concerning the nature and origins of suffering, we learn also that his comments must be severely qualified; if there were only "Religion" of the sort he describes, his judgement could be accepted at face value. There is not, and it cannot.

I shall proceed now to a discussion of the religious nature of both traditions. Here that earlier notion of "religious" is crucial (and I will cease, for the most part, to use the noun "religion," for reasons that I hope are evident). The signal issue is this: how does this commitment to what is true and ultimate find expression that can serve to make our life fully human, so that we may become what we are? It is hard for me, at least, to conceive of a more important question; and it is equally hard to conceive of human life, seen either individually or collectively, without, if not an answer, at least a serious striving toward an answer to this question. This striving, I would suggest, is precisely what we mean by human life. That is to say, this religious question, which I suggest is *the* question, is universal both in the sense that every individual who ever lived confronts it in one form of another and in the sense that it is the most general context in which human life is lived.

I am claiming, of course, that the religious enterprise understood in this way—and I honestly cannot conceive of another way that is consistent with the history of human life, including mine—is the critical element in the life every person who has ever lived and will ever live. In this sense everyone is religious.

But it may be objected that there are so many different ways of putting the truth, so many paths to it, so many different cultural expressions. Moreover this diversity exists not only between but within cultures and societies—and not only within societies but between individuals, and even within individuals. If there is a fact in the history of humankind it is the fact of diversity on precisely this matter of how the commitment to what is true can find expression in our lives.

There can be only one response to this objection: the answer to the religious question is never abstract but always personal. If personal it must be diverse. If diverse it must be dynamic. No single expression, no single striving, no single tradition can be said to be right in any abstract sense. There is no abstract sense, for the question arises from particular and historical experience. If it did not so arise it would not be human. Thus the diversity of expression is proof of the personal basis on which the religious enterprise is constructed. Further, however, no person lives *de novo*. Rather, he is who and what he is because of the tradition in which

4

he lives. And that tradition is precisely the prior struggles to pursue the religious enterprise. He pursues the enterprise on the foundation laid before him, and he changes it in light of his own experience. The dynamic appropriation and alteration of past answers and strivings in the religious enterprise is the reason why there is a history of human life and culture. Does this mean that all traditions are "right"? Yes, but only if they are seen as committed to incorporating the truth in their own lives–and we have some bizarre (bizarre to whom?) instances of that endeavor.

In the end I am arguing that the religious enterprise is universal and that by definition–in its nature–it is a striving to make human life what it is, an effort to gain and live the truth. If I am right, then, it is an easy step to the conclusion that both the Buddhist and psychoanalytic traditions are religious enterprises.

This essay is about suffering; I should also say that it is for that reason about truth. The Buddhist tradition speaks of the Universal Noble Four-fold Truth of Suffering. The Truth of Suffering is, for both traditions, the whole truth of human life–and there is no other so-called "truth" with which we need concern ourselves ultimately, as both Freud and Gotama insist. To understand fully and to live in the light of the Truth of Suffering is, then, and finally, to move from darkness to light, from bondage to freedom, from ignorance to knowledge, from a lie to the Truth. Done is what must be done. As the Indian tradition has taught us, the path one takes to the summit of the mountain may have any number of qualities. What matters is that it is a path to the summit, and that it is the summit only that matters ultimately. The metaphor applies well to our two paths. Freud adopts the language, symbols and structures of electricity, fluid mechanics and homeostatic balance. Gotama employs the language and symbols of Indian cosmology, ethics and spiritual disciplines. But it is clear that their goal is the same, a saving enlightenment in, of and by each of us of our true nature, and the liberation that is the consequence.

Finally, what does this study suggest about what some still call the study of religion, or what I would call the study of the religious enterprise? I think we should conclude that the religious enterprise is the most significant form of the study of human life, for two closely related reasons. First, it takes as its subject the most significant of subjects. In fact, in the terms of this essay, it takes suffering as its most significant issue, which has no peer. Second, the student of humanity is by necessity personally involved in that study. This conclusion spells the end of the pseudo-objectivity under whose tyranny we in the study of humankind have labored for almost as long as we have denied the true nature of the religious enterprise. And this is the only honest form of study, for it demands the whole-hearted and, yes, pious, commitment of the student. The consequence of such a view of the religious enterprise is not

5

only an honest knowledge of oneself, as well as others, but precisely that compassion that both Buddhist and analyst see as the *summum bonum* of human relationships. In raising the issue of the nature of suffering I and all others who do so recognize no "methodological" boundaries between us as the students and the "objects" of our study. This, surely, is the true basis for the human and universal community. Wilfred Cantwell Smith once wrote that in order for a statement to be true it must be known to be true to the person who makes it, to the person about whom it is made, and to the standards of rigorous intellectual honesty. He spoke not simply of the study of religious traditions, to which this principle obviously is applicable, but of all statements of significance–that is, all statements about human life, since there are no other significant statements. Thus religious studies (to use a less odious phrase than the "study of religion") must be about the nature and destiny of humankind, entered into–fearfully, for the most part–in a spirit of compassion, honest inquiry and absolute integrity, for the purpose of knowing and living by the truth. This is very different from the study of religion or religions, a task that rests upon a number of historically and morally questionable assumptions. Rather, religious studies is itself the religious enterprise. We should not be studying religion, we should be pursuing the truth.

The implications for the present structure of the University, with its departments and disciplines, are profound and, at least in our present context, revolutionary. But I look forward to the day when neither I nor anyone else must write a brief explanation such as this one, when it will be evident that the psychoanalytic tradition is "Buddhist," that is devoted to enlightenment (as the term meant originally, before it came to be an adjectival designation of a "religion," "Buddhism") and the Buddhist tradition is "psychoanalytic," that is, committed to a full understanding of the range, nature and destiny of the human experience. It will be on or about that same day that our understanding of faith as the universal capacity to know the Truth in whatever form tradition, ours and others, expresses, knows and employs it will be established universally. To that day this present work looks forward.

The Truth of Suffering

Preamble

If one examines and follows carefully the Buddhist tradition concerning the Four Noble Truths of suffering it is evident that they must be taken together. That is to say, they are interdependent. For no one claiming to have the insight of which the Buddha speaks can see these truths–of suffering, of the cause of the suffering, of the end of suffering, of the cause of the end of suffering–as other than co-originative, co-dependent.

This conclusion Nāgārjuna[1] drew to its logical end when he equated *saṃsāra* and *nirvāṇa*, eternal ill with eternal bliss, through *śūnyata*, "emptiness."[2] Following what I understand to be an authentic Buddhist tradition Nāgārjuna rejects the concept of the Truths as separate steps related by means of cause and effect. Rather, the Truths and their component parts are subjected to the same analysis to which they subject the self, the world, transmigration, creation, beings, identity, and the concept

---

[1] This is the first of many references to the work of the great Indian Buddhist Nāgārjuna, probable father of the Mādhyamaka School of the Buddhist tradition, who wrote in Sanskrit some years after the death of Gotama. By more or less general consent he occupies, by virtue of his interpretation of the received tradition, a critical position in the development of the Buddhist tradition between the Theravāda and Mahāyāna Schools. That is one of two reasons for giving special attention to his work in a treatment otherwise limited to the earlier Pāli tradition; for I wish to suggest that the differences between the two Buddhist traditions are less important than the core of the tradition they share. Nāgārjuna's work, in other words, is well known as fundamental to the development of the Mahāyāna tradition; but, as I hope will be clear, in no significant way does he depart from the tradition of the *Āgamas*. In short, the testimony of Nāgārjuna suggests to me, and I hope to the reader, that the presentation of the Buddhist tradition found here is appropriate to both Theravāda and Mahāyāna Schools.

The second reason for including some of Nāgārjuna's observations is not historical but interpretive. As the text to which this note is appended says, one's understanding of the *Dhamma* is complete only when the absolute dependence of all four of the Noble Truths upon each other is fully realized. Perhaps more than any other thinker in the tradition, Nāgārjuna drives this point home. It is a point that, in my view, is absolutely essential to the understanding of suffering. Nāgārjuna offers considerable and exceptional aid in the endeavor to understand suffering, and I feel that it should be accepted.

[2] *Nāgārjuna: A Translation of his Mūlamadhyamakakārika*, by Kenneth H. Inada (Tokyo: The Hokuseido Press, 1970), with an introductory essay, 153-159.

7

of causality.[3] To do otherwise would amount to a denial of the empty (*śūnya*) nature of the *Dharma* and to make it a factor of existence.[4]

As we shall see, this temptation to separate the Four Noble Truths into four distinct assertions which might be independently considered runs contrary to what is asserted about the nature of suffering by both the Buddha and Freud. To state the matter briefly here–and at length later–when Freud identifies illness as neurosis (or psychosis) he is stating both the fact of suffering and, in explicating and defining neurosis, the cause of suffering. Further, in describing the best analytic procedure his words about raising what is unconscious into the conscious or converting hysterical misery into ordinary unhappiness suggest that to know the cause of suffering is to know the cause of the end of suffering, and thus to know both the truth of suffering and the truth of the end of suffering.

Similarly, and particularly in the analysis of the *paṭiccasamuppāda* series, the series of co-dependent origination, the Buddha does not distinguish between the relationship of the component parts of the series in describing the cause of suffering and the cause of the end of suffering. The relationship of the elements remains the same whether it leads to suffering or to the end of suffering. The dependent nature of the Four Truths reflects their origin in ancient Indian medicine as the classic statement of diagnosis and cure.[5] It should also be evident that the Buddha's understanding of the universal problem of suffering is, therefore, not original (an issue to be raised at a later point). The usefulness of this analytic approach is evident also in the fact that the Buddhist texts employ it in connection with all manifestations of suffering, not simply the best known, *dukkha*. For example, it may be applied to each of the five component "heaps," or *khandhas* (body, consciousness, feeling, perception, recurrent forms (*sankhāras*)). It may be applied also to birth and death.

Nevertheless, despite the interdependence of the Four Truths, I will treat the question of suffering with the aid of these two great traditions by addressing each truth in order. There is a very good reason for this, namely, that I wish to approach the subject not from the point of view of the enlightened person, the *Arahant* or *Tathāgata*, or of the analyst seasoned in the insights and pitfalls of a training analysis, but from the point of view of someone who suspects that something is wrong, who is not quite sure what it is that is wrong, and is not entirely sure he wants to find out. In other words, the issue of suffering is to be approached from the perspective of the one who suffers most of all, that is, the one who

---

[3] *Cf.* Inada, *passim.*

[4] *Cf.ibid.*, 153-159.

[5] *Cf.* Lama Anagarika Govinda, *The Psychological Attitude of Early Buddhist Philosophy and its Systematic Representation according to Abhidhamma Tradition* (London: Rider & Co., 1961), 72, *et passim.*

has only the slightest notion of the disease, who is not even convinced that he is ill. It is to such a person that both Gotama and Freud spoke, and through such a person to that vast "untaught manyfolk" who are convinced of their own health. The issue of suffering must be approached from the starting point of ignorance. The outstanding characteristic, then, of the prospective patient is that he is very nearly completely unaware that he is ill; and until that fact of illness is made clear to him it is pointless to explain why he is ill, and how he may become well. It is not simply a question of his ability to participate in the process of release from illness, but of his willingness to participate. Therefore, the first issue before us must be the truth of suffering.

Before turning to that question I wish to raise the "problem" of how we may listen to both Freud the twentieth-century scientist and neurologist and the Buddha of ancient India on the question of suffering. The "problem" does not lie in the subject matter of suffering; for it is supremely clear that both hold that human existence is suffering in origin and nature. Nor is the "problem" in their general response to the fact of suffering; for they both wish to analyze its causes and thus to find a way to the release from suffering—and not just for themselves but for all people. The "problem" lies in the difference in language—and clearly I mean something more than tongues. In turn, their languages reflect their traditions; and our summary of those traditions reflects our tradition. Let us accept our interpretive setting as a "constant" in our attempts to understand Freud and Gotama, and certainly Freud and Gotama together. There is no question here of using our reading of either or both of these traditions as the benchmark for deciding what each means, and which is right, if either—or both, or neither. Rather, I see the "problem" in this way, that we are heirs to the scientific language of our modern world or to the grand and magnificent, ancient, tradition of primordial wisdom that India has nurtured so long and so well. One effect of this study will be a certain jarring of the interpretive nerves as the boundary area between the two languages appears—or as they meet. And, rather like the id's reaction to external stimuli (according to Freud's structural theory), we don't like it at first. Yet we must strengthen the ego in its task of representing the truth in its various forms—and in the same way the "problem," which is nothing more or less than a symptom of infantile narcissism, may be transformed into a mature understanding of the nature of the truth which is not simply a reflection of our wishes. The overcoming of the "problem" is a work of culture. It is a problem, of course, because it hinders us in grasping the saving truth about our suffering and, ultimately, our release from suffering.

9

The Reality of Suffering

In the early Buddhist texts *dukkha* is the word for suffering. It is translated in various ways: "ill," "anguish," "woe," "suffering." However it is translated it is the presentation in a single concept of the nature of reality. It is the first of the Four Noble Truths for the simple and profound reason that without a recognition of the nature of reality as *dukkha* there is no hope of release: "It is through not understanding and grasping the four Ariyan Truths...that we have had to run so long, to wander so long in this weary path of transmigration [*saṃsāritaṃ*]."[6] *Dukkha* is that which dies and is reborn, rises and falls: "...it is simply Ill [*dukkha*] that rises, Ill that doth persist, and Ill that wanes away. Nought beside Ill it is that comes to pass, Nought else but Ill it is doth cease to be."[7]

"Birth is anguish, and old age...and disease...and dying...grief, lamentation...suffering...tribulation..., despair...if one does not get what one wants."[8] All the ills we feel are simply manifestations of the fundamental truth of *dukkha*.

Consider one overcome by ill, in mind forspent – he grieves, mourns, laments, beats his breast and becomes bewildered; or roams abroad in search of who knows a spell or two to end his ill. Ill yields bewilderment and search....[9]

In a word, he lives in dread, fearful.[10] One who is ignorant of the truth of the reality of *dukkha* finds neither peace nor satisfaction: "just as a stick, when thrown up into the air, falls, now on its butt, now on its middle, now on its tip, even so beings, hindered by ignorance, fettered by craving, run on, wander on, pass on from this world to the next, and thence back again to this world."[11] For those who simply follow the delights of their senses, seeking only pleasure where suffering is the only reality, it is like one approaching a precipice, ignorant of its presence: "they fall down the precipice of rebirth, of old age, of death...of despair," and they are not released.[12]

Although the sufferer is ignorant of the nature of his plight, in his state there are nevertheless concerns very close to his heart–false concerns. He "runs to and fro,"[13] beset with questions that cause him considerable anguish: "Did I live in times gone by? Or did I not? What was I in times gone by? How was I then? Or from being what did I

---

6 D II, 96.
7 S I, 169-170.
8 M I, 60-61.
9 A III, 295.
10 S I, 52.
11 S V, 371-372.
12 S V, 379.
13 S I, 52-53.

become what?"[14] Or of the future he demands, "Shall I be reborn in a future time, or shall I not? What shall I become in the future: How shall I become in the future? Or, being what, shall I in the future become what?"[15] And, most immediately, he cries "Am I indeed? Or am I not indeed? What indeed am I? How indeed am I? This person that is I, whence came he, whither will he go?"[16] As is evident the very identity of the sufferer is in the balance. Lesser matters also perplex and confound him: "Alas! what shall I eat, and where indeed? How ill I've slept! Where shall I sleep today?"[17]

Like the stick that lands now on its side, now its top, now its bottom, the one who suffers has no orientation, no peace, no identity. Moreover, he is ignorant of his situation to the extent that he does not understand that his actions are in fact pointless and misguided, like the bouncing stick. He *does* concern himself with such questions–who was I, who am I, who will I be?–that signify that he is suffering. They have no other function, as we shall see, than this.

Furthermore, the nature of this suffering is not physiological but what we shall call, at least for the moment, psychological. It is true that physical conditions arise from this psychical state; but the nature of the disease is to be understood in the reality of suffering where suffering means the pain that comes from not knowing, from fundamental ignorance. Indeed, what chiefly characterizes the description of suffering we shall pursue is the state of ignorance. The neurotic and psychotic simply do not understand that they are suffering or why; and the ignorant person (*puthujjana*) pursues his own pleasure in blissful ignorance of the inevitable suffering that awaits him. More, they resist suggestions that they are launched on a path of self-destruction; for they actively desire to follow the path of gratification. The state of suffering I am describing, then, might be called a state of "mind"–a phrase I use only to stress the truth that suffering is not simple physical pain but the crisis of human existence perceived at its most fundamental level, namely, of self-knowledge. The ignorance that surrounds this suffering is therefore appropriately profound.

---

[14] S II, 22.
[15] *Ibid.*.
[16] *Ibid.*.
[17] SN, 141.

I

Freud and the Truth of Suffering

Neurosis

A neurotic, says Freud, is incapable of enjoyment and efficiency.[18] He struggles against reality.[19] "We have long observed that every neurosis has as its result, and probably therefore as its purpose, a forcing of the patient out of real life, and alienating of him from reality."[20] This conflict with reality nourishes several neurotic circumstances. There is, of necessity, a state of frustration; for the ill person has encountered a situation in which he is unable to obtain what he wishes from the world beyond his feelings. This is of course a very common situation; but Freud notes a distinguishing mark of neurotic frustration: it is frustration that arises from the *loss* of a loved one or desired object; "[t]he subject was healthy so long as his need for love was satisfied by a real object in the external world; he becomes neurotic as soon as this object is withdrawn from him without a substitute taking its place. Here happiness coincides with health and unhappiness with neurosis...."[21] To this type, says Freud, the vast majority of human beings belong, and this suggests (here and throughout his work) that to study the neurotic is to study every person.[22]

The neurotic conflict with reality takes a second form, for which the cause lies, as it were, not in the demands of the external world *per se* but in the inability of the self to meet those demands. This situation has one of two causes, which are not readily distinguished by simple observation, but which exist nonetheless: there may come about a change in the external world; or a change in the psychic balance may occur (again, this term "psychic balance" presupposes an investigation into the causes of suffering which has not yet been presented, but it is a term whose *prima facie* meaning suggests the direction in which we are going). As to the second sort of alteration of circumstances, and really the more interesting of the two, Freud argues that it presupposes an internal, psychical history

---

[18] IL, SE XVI, 454-455.

[19] For the moment, since our issue is the reality of suffering rather than its causes, I would like to leave aside the question of what Freud means by "reality" except to say that he does mean the world active beyond and external to the emotional life of a neurotic. *Cf.* IL, SE XVI, 429-430, 454-455, *et passim*.

[20] "Formulations on the Two Principles of Mental Functioning," SE XII, 218.

[21] "Types of Onset of Neurosis," SE XII, 231-233.

[22] *Ibid.*

of the sufferer that contains threatening elements of its own.[23] It cannot be shown that neurosis is the inevitable consequence of any shift in environment or external circumstances, a point Freud grants. Rather, it is the consequence of a shift away from the only set of circumstances which the self identified previously as real: "It is true that reality does not here frustrate every kind of satisfaction; but it frustrates the one kind which the subject declares is the only possible one."[24] Moreover, he continues,

> Nor does the frustration come immediately from the external world, but primarily from certain trends in the subject's ego. Nevertheless, frustration remains the common factor of the two types and the more inclusive one.[25]

Freud suggests yet other types of neurosis. A third is a consequence of simply failing to mature beyond the childish demands for instant satisfaction from the body and the external world. The neurotic characteristic of this condition arises from the fact of growing older, a condition which alters and intensifies the demands of the world upon the child-self which has never matured. A fourth sort arises from an abrupt and radical physical change resulting in severe stress to the psychic system (Freud suggests menopause and puberty as examples).[26]

In discussing the "Onset of Neuroses" Freud simply opens the door to the subject of suffering, suggesting that for at least some sick people, designated here as neurotic, the conflict between themselves (and here, at least for the moment, I mean themselves as wanting and desiring beings) and an obstinate, intractable world produces frustration and illness. This illness has marks, symptoms, that are obvious to the physician and obscure to the patient. To this matter of the symptoms of neurosis and their nature I shall presently turn. Now, however, I think two things should be made quite clear about what insight Freud is giving us: (1) the neurotic is simply an ordinary person whose universal conflict with reality has gotten out of hand (it is, says Freud, a quantitative problem); and (2) the illness from which the neurotic suffers cannot be treated by medicines, surgery, or biological remedies; and this is so because it is not a disease of the body, although it may have somatic consequences. Taken together, these two insights enable us to address the issue of suffering psychoanalytically, since the issue of suffering is universal and spiritual, that is to say, irreducible.

When a loved object is removed or lost, and no substitute is found, neurosis can arise. This is a universal possibility, argues Freud, for anyone runs the risk of losing a loved object. It is a condition of existence, of

---

23 *Ibid.*, 233.
24 *Ibid.*, 234.
25 *Ibid.*.
26 *Ibid.*, 235-237.

necessity, *Ananke*, whose power no one appreciated and respected more than Freud.[27] The conditions for illness, for suffering, are endemic; it is a question of whether one can stand the tension, the pain of stress between desire and the frustration of that desire by external conditions. There is, then, "no qualitative distinction between the determinants of health and those of neuroses, and...on the contrary, healthy people have to contend with the same tasks [as neurotics] of mastering their libido–they have simply succeeded better in them."[28]

As we shall see, one of the most significant discoveries to emerge from Freud's investigation of the dreams of his patients was that there was no way of distinguishing between the dreams of neurotics and those of healthy people. Their content yielded to the same interpretations. The difference between health and neurosis was to be observed in the fact that dreams were the only symptoms of healthy people, while neurotic symptomatology was more extensive. This fact Freud explained, once again, in quantitative rather than qualitative terms:

> Thus a healthy person, too, is virtually neurotic.... The distinction between nervous health and neurosis is thus reduced to a practical question and is decided by the outcome–by whether the subject is left with a sufficient amount of capacity for enjoyment and efficiency. It probably goes back to the relative sizes of the quota of energy that remains free and not of a qualitative nature.[29] ✓

Indeed, it was precisely the qualitative identity of neurotic illness and nervous health and the quantitative nature of the difference that encouraged Freud to believe that, at least in principle, neuroses were curable.[30]

Freud's reputation among his medical peers was not good, as is widely known; and in the opposition to his work he found another indication of the proximity of neurosis and health. His critics resisted the

---

[27] *Ibid.*, 231-233, *cf.* IL SE XVI 429-430.
[28] "Onset," 235-237.
[29] IL, SE XVI, 457.
[30] *Ibid.*. We shall see, in investigating the cause of the end of suffering, that the Buddhist tradition found the metaphor of the refining of gold to be a suitable expression of the method and nature of the cure of suffering. In this metaphor it exposes its agreement with the analytic approach of Freud on the question of the possibility of cure and on the method. The essential nature of the suffering person was such that he could be freed from suffering without the destruction of that nature. This, I believe, is the significance of Freud's emphasis upon the quantitative analysis of neurosis, of his early espousal of libido-theory, and such optimism as he expressed for psychoanalysis as a therapy, and even a cure. We shall return to this subject again.

notion of infantile sexuality in a manner and for a reason that tallied exactly with neurotic behavior. Freud argued that everyone represses memories of childhood experiences, notably those relating to their feelings for parents. This repression is marked in the almost literal sense by a "point" which, if encountered, resisted further examination. Indeed, the presence of such resistance was a crucial indicator of the type and nature of neurosis with which the analysis must contend. The presence of resistance in the learned community to the theory of infantile sexuality simply revealed to Freud how close normality and neurosis were to one another. For resistance to the theory did not rest upon objective, scientific, criteria but upon factors found without exception in the aetiology of all neuroses.[31] It seems Freud had an unanswerable rejoinder to his critics, since their opposition to his theory of repressed infantile sexuality was proof positive of that theory. My point here, however, is that the behavior of "normal" professionals and that of neurotics cannot in principle, in quality, be distinguished.

The issue of the relationship between the aetiology of neuroses and the emergence of the great social institutions and of civilization itself awaits development at a more appropriate place in this and other sections. However I want to note in passing that Freud was clear on the point of that relationship: it existed and was both root cause and explanation for the social institutions. Thus the behavior that society describes as normative, that it enforces in its religion, its moral codes, its law and justice and order, must be understood as a necessary if temporary imposed solution to the conflict of the self which is poignantly manifested in neurosis. Indeed, that "normality" is a constant source of trouble for the suffering self.

Thus the neurotic is simply an ordinary, healthy person for whom the basic elements of mental life have been thrown out of balance. The distinction between "neurotic" and "healthy" is for Freud quantitative; I put the emphasis here not on the difference between them but on the similarity, indeed the identity, of the neurotic and the normal. When, therefore, we address ourselves to the question of suffering we must begin with the recognition that the suffering of which we speak is in principle universal, that there is no one for whom it is impossible, and that by understanding it we understand not simply the state of illness but the state of health.

Now the second insight I mentioned above was that the suffering was not biological, or not only biological. In raising this issue there is a great deal at stake, nothing less than the question of the nature of human life. It is certainly true that Freud has been accused of reducing the life

---

[31] *Cf.* "The Question of Lay Analysis: Conversations with an Impartial Person," SE XX, 208-213.

of the mind, its feeling, thought and will, to a series of electrical charges (cathexes) and/or to hardly-describable ancient instincts whose biological heritage explains entirely their nature. But it is worth remembering that in dealing with the question of the psychical or mental life and the suffering of neurotics and psychotics Freud stated clearly that what concerned him was not biological in nature. He was of course referring on all occasions, implicitly or explicitly, to his fundamental view of the reality of the unconscious mind, to its ability to have thoughts, to influence and to act–in short, to psychical reality. But, more specifically, to various audiences whom he seemed–rightly at times–to perceive as hostile, he insisted that his experience as a doctor had convinced him that there were illnesses that were mental, psychical, in nature, and that they would respond only to appropriate psychical treatment.[32]

It must have been a surprised audience who heard Freud describe his subject, neuroses, as not susceptible to biological treatment, in that relevant part of his *Introductory Lectures*. The audience doubtless came to hear his views on what were called *"Actual"* neuroses, which meant present or contemporary somatic ailments found in people suffering from what the psychiatry of the day defined as neurotic behavior. Instead, Freud announced:

> What characterizes psycho-analysis as a science is not the material which it handles but the technique with which it works. It can be applied to the history of civilization, to the science of religion and to mythology, no less than to the theory of the neuroses, without doing violence to its essential nature. What it aims at and achieves is nothing other than the uncovering of what is unconscious in mental life. The problems of the 'actual' neuroses, whose symptoms are probably generated by direct toxic damage, offer psycho-analysis no points of attack. It can do little towards throwing light on them and must leave the task to biologico-medical research.[33]

A biological medicine was, then, inappropriate to the diseases of the mind. When the specific issue of the qualifications which an analyst must have was raised in "A Question of Lay Analysis" Freud argued that medical training in the traditional sense was not the essential preparation; indeed, the attitude of the medical profession towards psychoanalysis constituted a hindrance to the development of that field. What was essential, he stated, was what he called "self-analysis," that is the analysis of the analyst, what is called today a training analysis.[34] Freud's view on this

---

[32] "The Claims of Psycho-Analysis to Scientific Interest: Part II. The Psychological Interest of Psycho-Analysis," SE XIII, 165-175.
[33] IL, SE XVI, 389.
[34] Cf. "Lay Analysis," SE XX, *passim*, and "Analysis Terminable and

matter, one essential to our understanding of the human mental life, is that one can hardly be of help to a neurotic patient if he has not worked through the neurotic elements of his own psychic life.

Dreams

No one can claim to be free of the constituent elements of neurosis, for they are the very elements of our mental lives and our sense of our self. Freud was unswerving and unshaken in this conclusion after he had recognized the significance of dreams as the window on the operation of the unconscious life of man.

The mere presence of dreams suggested to Freud the extraordinary plasticity of mental life. Sleep is our goal every night; and in it "we throw off our hard-won morality like a garment, and put it on again next morning. This stripping of ourselves is not, of course, dangerous, because we are paralyzed, condemned to inactivity, by the state of sleep."[35] But the contents of the mind are not replaced or discarded in the change from waking to sleeping but rather revealed without the guardian devices that obscure them to our wakeful consciousness. Those contents are revealed in dreams just because dreaming is the operation of the unfettered mind.

> The ego, freed from all ethical bonds, ...finds itself at one with the demands of sexual desire, even those which have long been condemned by our aesthetic upbringing and those which contradict all the requirements of moral restraint. The desire for pleasure –the "libido," as we call it–chooses its objects without inhibition, and by preference, indeed, the forbidden ones.... Lusts which we think of as remote from human nature show themselves strong enough to provoke dreams. Hatred, too, rages without restraint.[36]

Unrestrained, then, the mind, the inner self, seems utterly immoral, sensuous, and egoistic. Yet there seems also little point in condemning what is obviously a vital function, namely sleep, because of its repugnant content (repugnant, of course, for very good reason):

> But you must not blame the dream itself on account of its evil content. Do not forget that it performs the innocent and indeed useful function of preserving sleep from disturbance. This wickedness is not part of the essential nature of dreams. Indeed you know too that there are dreams which can be recognized as the satisfaction of justified wishes and of pressing bodily

---

Interminable," SE XXIII.
[35] "Thoughts on War and Death: I. The Disillusionment of the War," SE XIV, 286.
[36] IL, SE XV, 143.

needs....[37]

The content of dreams reveals what Freud regards as the essentially sexual nature of human development. The content of dreams is in Freud's handling always a version of the child's early sexual history, especially of the emergence of the inevitable conflict of feelings Freud came to call the Oedipus complex. That this history is one of conflict suggests to us that although the unrestrained mind of the sleeper is enormously egoistic and sensuous it is not wholly unrestrained. Freud defended this conclusion on the basis of clinical experience and his study of ancient myths, legends, and archaic literary themes. All of these shared with the reported dreams of his patients the unmistakable signs of distortion. He gained the distinct impression that a series of imagined, dreamed occurrences had been altered by some agency and for a reason of great significance. This explained the disjointed structure of dreams (and stories of the gods), their sudden shifting of persons, times, places, and climaxes so that one could hardly follow their "plot" at all. Freud concluded that there must be differences between the reported dream (which he called the "manifest dream") and the hidden dream ("latent dream").[38] He attributed the distortion of the latent dream to "dream work" (*Traumarbeitung*); and the agency of dream work he called the censor, which he identified as a work of the ego in carrying out its mission of protecting the psychic apparatus from the exigencies of external reality.[39] Further, the distortion carried out by dream work could be seen to be in direct proportion to the "immorality" of the dream-wish; distortion "becomes greater the worse the wish that has to be censored."[40] But the degree of censorship was variable as well, so that dream distortion "becomes greater the more severe the demands of the censorship at the moment."[41] The content of dreams, then, indicated that a part of the self was in conflict with another part; and that at least one part of the self, as revealed in dreams, had no moral concerns or rational judgement whatsoever. (Some years after the publication of the *Introductory Lectures*, in *Ego and Id*, Freud chose the Latin term "id" to designate this part of self.)

The dream work transforms the latent dream into the manifest dream by several methods. It may suppress a dream entirely, or fragment or fuse elements of it. Second, under the influence of censorship, it may displace

---

[37] *Ibid.*.

[38] *Cf.* "Dreams and Telepathy," SE XVIII, 197, 220.

[39] *Cf. The Ego and the Id*, tr. Joan Riviere, *The International Psycho-Analytical Library*, No. 12, ed. Ernest Jones (Leonard and Virginia Woolf at Hogarth Press, and the Institute of Psycho-Analysis; London, 1927), 16.

[40] IL, SE XV, 143.

[41] *Ibid.*.

the focus of the dream not by replacing any component part but by shifting the "psychical accent" to a more remote element and away from one that is significant but threatening in the latent dream. Third, dream work distorts the latent dream by transforming the "thought" or "idea" of the dream into visual images and by imposing upon the latent dream the structure of the manifest dream. Finally, contrary relationships may be rendered in the form of identities, and opposites made to imply each other.[42]

The transformation of thought in dream work is regressive, argues Freud. The history of thinking[43] begins with sense impressions or, more properly, "mnemic residues of such impressions," which are the first stages of thought. It is only later that words are attached to impressions, and still later that thoughts are attached to words.[44] Dream work reverses this order, that is, it "submits thoughts to *regressive* treatment and undoes their development; and in the course of the regression everything has to be dropped that had been added as a new acquisition in the course of the development of the mnemic images into thoughts."[45]

"Dream work" explains not only the distortions evident in dreams, but also those present in archaic systems of thought and literature. In other words, what is characteristic of dreams, namely the distortion, the condensation, transformation, displacement, and so forth, is also characteristic of "[a]ncient systems of expression by speech and writing, and they involve the same difficulties...."[46] The point here is not that dreams are derived from archaic literatures, nor the reverse, but that both in some way reveal the nature of mental operations in a manner very much more transparent than obtained by ordinary observation or conscious thinking. The implications are profound. There is not only an unconscious mind, or part of the mind, but also, it is universal and it functions at both individual and collective levels (although as we shall see Freud did not believe that there was a social psychology that was not at the same time and in all respects an individual psychology).[47]

---

[42] IL, SE XV, 171-180.

[43] Thinking occupied Freud for the major part of his theoretical writings, and was finally identified in the *New Introductory Lectures* as a trial discharge of libidinal energy enabling the psychical apparatus to test the possibly hostile external world at little risk.

[44] Incidentally, although it is not clear from the passage in question here–from the *Introductory Lectures*–whether Freud means an ontogenetic or phylogenetic development, a more general reading tells us that he means both–a point to be taken up later.

[45] IL, SE XV, 180-181.

[46] IL, SE XV, 180.

[47] This is the burden of *Group Psychology and the Analysis of the Ego.*

The understanding of the function of dreams reveals the fact of the unconscious and its contents.

The prehistory which the dream work leads us back to is of two kinds—on the one hand, the individual's prehistory, his childhood, and on the other, in so far as each individual somehow recapitulates in an abbreviated form the entire development of the human race, phylogenetic prehistory.[48]

And yet we are ignorant, in our conscious state, of this content and of this architectonic process in our selves and in others. It is not, one must concede, simply a question of not having enough information. In the early days of his research into the aetiology and treatment of neuroses Freud set some store by the method of getting the patient to admit to the truth of past traumas that had been repressed, a kind of abreaction. But he soon discovered that it was not enough for the patient to "know" in some obvious sense the causal factors of the disease; it was essential that the patient participate in their transformation from an unconscious to a conscious state. However, the patient resisted such a therapy. The ignorance was, then, a "willed" ignorance, a "deliberate" amnesia in fact, carried out with the assistance of the ego although not entirely through its power.

Of course we, the patient, have not wholly forgotten our childhood. There are certain memories that come to us from time to time; and among neurotics these are suspiciously strong and recurrent. Freud noted, as did his patients, that the memories seemed absurdly insignificant, as insignificant as they were persistent. Freud dubbed these "screen memories" for they obscured more than they revealed. Yet their existence proved, like jokes, dreams and slips of the tongue, to be a window into the unconscious mind, most of whose operations have not simply been forgotten but repressed, deliberately forgotten.

Dreams, like jokes, slips of the tongue, and screen memories, which are so characteristic of what Freud called the "psychopathology of everyday life," suggest two worlds in conflict, that of the conscious, civilized, restrained world of the waking hours, and a pleasure-seeking, utterly selfish, extremely energetic portion of the self making its wishes known at night during the essential activity of sleep. Again, this is not a description of illness over against health, but of the state of the human life. We must conclude then that that life is above all a state of conflict between what Freud calls the ego, the agency of highly organized mental structures ("acquisitions of human evolution made under the impact of human history"), and the "unserviceable" impulses that are "ever ready to assert power beyond the protective barriers of substitute structures."[49]

---

[48] IL, SE XV, 199.
[49] "Preface to Reik's *Ritual: Psycho-Analytic Studies*," SE XVII, 259-

This struggle explains the instability of the superstructure of the mind, dreams, and neuroses. It is a universal struggle, not only in the sense that each individual lives and dies by it but also in the sense that all the products of culture are in some way effects of this psychic cause. The highest aspirations of the human spirit—poetry, religion, philosophy, the desire for achievement—all owe their existence to this fundamental struggle. The artist, the philosopher, the mystic, the cultural hero share with the hysteric and the obsessional neurotic these causes and driving forces.[50]

As dreams demonstrate, the conflict is based in childhood. It is the initial conflict between what is desired and what can be obtained, the conflict of frustration. If we are to understand the origin, nature and content of dreams, we must understand that they are, above all, expressions of original wishes, original desires (what Freud came to call "libido"). In understanding dreams, as I have tried to suggest, we shall also then understand the nature of the conflict that defines our selves. Dreams are egoistic, psychotic and narcissistic; that is to say, they are entirely self-centered, they take no account whatever of the external world, they are the expression of wishes unqualified by experience, and have no commitment to the stability of the conscious self. This situation is precisely that of children:

> children love themselves first, and it is only later that they learn to love others and to sacrifice something of their own ego to others. Even those people whom a child seems to love from the beginning are loved by him at first because he needs and cannot do without them—once again from the egoistic motives. Not until later does the impulse to love make itself independent of egoism.

> It is literally true that *his egoism has taught him to love.*[51]

"*What is unconscious in mental life is also what is infantile,*" Freud asserts. Thus what the dream accomplishes is a regression to childhood and thereby to the elementary state of human mental life:

> dream work not only translates our thoughts into a primitive form of expression; but it also revives the characteristics of our primitive mental life—the old dominance of the ego, the initial impulses of our sexual life, and even, indeed, our old intellectual endowment, if symbolic connections may be regarded as such.[52]

All dreams, concludes Freud, are children's dreams. The dream works with childhood's mental impulses and mechanisms. They are, then,

---

261.
[50] *Ibid.*.
[51] IL, SE XV, 203-204.
[52] *Ibid.*, 211-212.

22

dreams of wish-fulfillment. In fact we can be more discriminating about the types of dreams. There are wish-fulfillment dreams, but there are also anxiety-dreams and punishment-dreams, among others. For example, Freud cites non-dream material from an old fable (he is of course entirely justified in doing this to make a point about dreams since the essential material is the same) about a couple given three wishes. The woman wishes for fried sausages, the man wishes they would hang from her nose because she was stupid, and then he must spend the third wish to have them removed.

> The fried sausages on a plate were the direct fulfillment of the wish of the first person, the woman. The sausages on her nose were the fulfillment of the wish of the second person, of the man, but was [also] a punishment for the woman's foolish wish.... There are many such punitive trends in the mental life of human beings; they are very powerful, and we may hold them responsible for some of the distressing dreams....[53]

The wish, then, whether for a tasty morsel, for punishment, or arising out of anxiety is the primary element of the dream. In the dream, moreover, the wish is fulfilled.[54] The dream has no respect for external reality; and hallucination holds no terrors for its work.[55] This suggests the essential narcissism of dreams. In his essay on narcissism[56] Freud described a mental process according to which love, or desire, could be directed toward the self rather than to the external world. In applying the notion of narcissism to dreams it was immediately evident that the chief actor is always the self, and that dreams are unfailingly egoistic: "We now readily understand that this is due to the narcissism of sleep."[57] Narcissism, a condition of complete self-centeredness, was a characteristic of both dreams and the condition Freud designated psychosis (although he considered only the latter to be pathological). Psychotics suffered from a virtually complete lack of external orientation, for their mental conflict had reached the stage at which it raged within the confines of the self without any reference to external conditions. Neurosis, by contrast, was a condition of uncontrolled conflict between the ego and the id, and thus retained some orientation to external reality, however strained.[58]

---

[53] *Ibid.*, 219.

[54] *Ibid.*, 224.

[55] *Ibid.*, 213.

[56] "On Narcissism: An Introduction," SE XIV.

[57] "Metapsychological Supplement to the Theory of Dreams," CP IV, 138.

[58] Psychosis was at first seen by Freud as inextricably related to the condition of narcissism, but later he drew a distinction between narcissistic neuroses and psychoses. A further emendation of his original position

Sleep was "psychotic" in its utter indifference to external reality; but the condition was not dangerous for it persisted, in "healthy" people, only during sleep and was dissipated upon waking. But again we see that the issue here is not primarily illness but the nature of the human self. In its dream state it is narcissistic, neurotic and psychotic; and not only in its dream state is it narcissistic or neurotic but also in its culture, its ancient heritage, its philosophy, its poetry, its art.[59]

If, one may ask, the dreaming self is in such fundamental conflict with the waking self, with the conscious life, what is the self? Is it the conscious ego? Is it the id? Is it both? Are we justified in referring to a unity at all? Is the concept of a system, or even of a closed process, more appropriate to what is emerging? Since at this point I am chiefly concerned with presenting Freud's notion of suffering as a truth I must simply state these questions in anticipation of the treatment of the truth of the cause of suffering. Nonetheless, a beginning can be made by raising the question of who is the responsible moral agent in the content of the dream work. Freud noted that the censor operates on the dream material and produces a manifest if distorted version of the true dream. It is, indeed, the task of the analyst to undo the work of the censor for the purpose of locating the reason for the distortion. But the censor has already been presented with material to censor; and we must now ask whence it comes and who is responsible for its content.

Is the dreamer responsible for the "evil impulse" of his dreams? Freud's answer is forthright, if, at first, confusing:

Obviously one must hold oneself responsible for the evil impulses of one's dreams. What else is one to do with them? Unless the content of the dream (rightly understood) is inspired by alien spirits, it is a part of my own being.[60]

There is both good and bad content—"good" and "bad" according to social standards—in all dreams.[61] While in terms of strict logic such assertions may obscure more than they reveal there is no doubting the accuracy of their report as far as feelings are concerned. For while one may not find the ego guilty of immoral thoughts, it is also true that those thoughts are the responsibility of the dreamer. The paradox is clear: the dreamer

---

is only hinted at (see "Splitting of the Ego in the Process of Defence," SE XXIII, and "Fetishism," SE XXI) in his investigation of cases in which rejection of external reality did not result in psychosis, but rather in a "splitting of the ego."

[59] *Cf.* NIL, SE XXII, 7-30 for an overview of dream interpretation and its relationship to analysis.

[60] "Some Additional Notes on Dream-Interpretation as a Whole: B. Moral Responsibility for Dreams," SE XIX, 133-134.

[61] *Ibid.*.

is responsible for the content of dreams, for clearly no other being could possibly be responsible. Yet the dreamer's ego censors, resists, the dream, striving mightily to make it acceptable lest the true story be known and the dreamer somehow threatened. Can the blame be put on the id, that "mindless" resource of the basic wishes? It can; and yet the ego is part of the id, and thus also blameworthy.[62]

What then? If, because of the elemental dependency between ego and id, we cannot isolate an agent who is responsible for either good or evil deeds but find only a congeries of forces (some conscious, some not) that are responsible for all, are we left having to acknowledge (1) the non-existence of a separate agency for either good or evil, and (2) the paradoxical assignment of responsibility for *unconscious* impulses to an opposing conscious process? Indeed, both statements are correct. As Freud puts the matter,

> Moreover, if I were to give way to my moral pride and tried to disregard the evil in the id and need not make my ego responsible for it, what use would that be to me? Experience shows me that I nevertheless *do* take that responsibility, that I am somehow compelled to do so. Psychoanalysis has made us familiar with a pathological condition, obsessional neurosis, in which the poor ego feels itself responsible for all sorts of evil impulses of which it knows nothing, impulses which are brought up against it in consciousness but which it is unable to acknowledge.[63]

What is here described is not abnormal. On the contrary this condition of the suffering of the dreamer is the most general condition.[64] What we call good behavior rests, then, upon the same foundation as what we call bad behavior, that is, the conflict between the virtually irrepressible demands of the thoughtless instincts and the ever-threatened ego's desperate attempt to keep them under control. Dreams tell us all of this. It is pointless to wish for an alternative–that wish itself is an expression of the conflict, as we shall see in investigating the role of morality and religion in the life of the psychic conflict. This is the truth of suffering:

> The ethical narcissism of humanity should rest content with the knowledge that the fact of distortion in dreams, as well as the existence of anxiety-dreams and punishment-dreams, afford just as clear evidence of his *moral* nature as dream-interpretation gives of the existence and strength of his *evil* nature. If anyone is dissatisfied with this, would like to be 'better' than he was created, let him see whether he can attain anything more in life

---

[62] *Ibid..*
[63] *Ibid..*
[64] *Ibid..*

than hypocrisy or inhibition.[65]

Symptoms

I have suggested that the truth of suffering, a truth of which we are ordinarily ignorant, was recognized by Freud in his analysis of dream work and the content of dreams. The interpretation of dreams is both possible and necessary only in light of the fundamental fact of conflict as the basic nature of the self, of conflict of which the self is ignorant, and conflict that in its nature tends toward instability of the self leading toward the various forms of mental disease, or circumstances in which the conflict rages out of control. What Freud discovered was that the causes of human life are the causes of illness.

Dreams are symptoms, evident (to the disciplined observer) indications of trauma, disease, instability, and illness. As dreams, of course, they are benign symptoms. Other symptomatic phenomena are not. The dreams of the neurotic and the "healthy person" may be identical in structure and content; but the evident and sustained behavior of the neurotic stands out unmistakably. Freud's famous case histories, such as the "Wolf Man," the "Rat Man," "Little Hans," "Anna O." and others[66] reveal in solid detail the presence of unmistakable symptoms, such as animal phobias– intense fear of rats, wolves and horses. The phobias, and all symptoms, are psychological facts in that they are evident characteristic beliefs or patterns of behavior. But they, like dreams, are distortions of a psychical reality, marking its existence but obscuring its nature. They are evidence of suffering. How do they arise?

As Freud's case studies showed, symptoms appear to be idiosyncratic. However, in light of the general understanding of the aetiology of neuroses Freud regarded symptoms as indications of universal significance. No fundamental distinction could be assumed.[67]

Thus it is possible to identify basic elements of symptom formation. One must begin with the clear understanding that symptoms signify some other process and are not meaningless aberrations in behavior patterns. Symptoms are related to some critical event in the past history of the person. The patient is, as Freud put it, fixated on that event.[68] Further, the patient will not recognize his symptomatic behavior for what it is.

---

[65] *Ibid.*, 134.

[66] "Notes upon a Case of Obsessional Neurosis (1909)," SE X, 153-249 ("The Rat Man"); "Analysis of a Phobia in a Five-year-old Boy (1909)," SE X, 5-149 ("Little Hans"); "From the History of an Infantile Neurosis (1918 [1914])," SE XVII, 7-122 ("The Wolf Man"); "Case Histories: Fräulein Anna O.," SE II, 21-47.

[67] IL, SE XVI, 271.

[68] In terms of Freud's theory of development a fixation is established at any point in the earliest stages of psychical development at which

The fundamental and, one might say, willful ignorance of the symptom of neurosis is the result of a deliberate blocking or repressing. Moreover, the primary event to which the symptom is to be traced is unacknowledged—indeed, it is rejected—and the symptom emerges as a substitute for that event itself and its effects. The symptom both obscures and reveals the fact of illness; it is with the symptom that the path of cure begins. While it is true that symptoms disappear when their cause is known, this is no simple consequence of the discovery of the traumatic event. One cannot cure the patient, says Freud, simply by telling him that this event or that caused his illness. Rather, some internal psychic change[69] must take place which brings about the end of the neurotic conflict in the self—or at least reduces the conflict to a manageable level—and thus the end of the symptom.[70]

Symptoms, then, are in essence substitutive conditions, replacing the memories and experiences of traumatic events. The replacement is carried out unconsciously, and the true cause of symptoms is hidden from the patient. Summarizing what it is that symptoms replace, Freud concludes:

> ...a comparative study of the determining causes of falling ill leads to a result which can be expressed in a formula: these people fall ill in one way or another of *frustration*, when reality prevents them from satisfying their sexual wishes.... It is only thus that symptoms can be properly viewed as substitutive satisfactions for what is missed in life.[71]

We shall see that Freud understood neurosis to be the result and manifestation of a conflict between desire and external reality. Symptoms show that this is the case, for they emerge as a result of and as substitutions for frustrated desires that have been denied by the external world. If one cannot have what one truly wants from others and from the world, then, decrees the psychical apparatus and the pleasure principle—or the id, which has no desire or need to adjust—one shall have it from oneself. A symptom is formed to take the place of the inaccessible external goal. Symptoms both abandon and oppose external reality, for they arise out of a previous frustration of desire. They are carefully oblivious to the world: "In place of a change in the external world these [symptoms] substitute a change in the subject's own body: they set an internal act in place of an

---

entrance to the conscious is denied to an instinct or, more accurately, to the "psychical (ideational) representative of the instinct." "Repression," SE XIV, 148.

[69] What Freud called repeating, *cf.* "Remembering, Repeating and Working Through ...," SE XII, 151-152.

[70] *Cf.* IL, SE XVI, 273-284.

[71] *Ibid.*, 300.

external one, an adaptation in place of an action."[72] It is noteworthy that the symptom carries out its work of replacement in the same manner observed in dream work, that is, through condensation and displacement–a fact which suggests to us that the operation of the unconscious is of a piece, whether operating through dreams or symptoms.

The emergence of symptoms is linked to events which, for reasons of his own, the person wishes desperately to hide. In treating the question of anxiety Freud drew the connection between the emergence of symptoms and the causes of anxiety. A brief discussion of this matter will suffice here since I want to return to the general question of anxiety below. Anxiety arises to signify the need for flight and is therefore related to the process of defense. In distinguishing between flight from external and flight from internal danger Freud argues that in the latter case symptom formation constitutes a defense against an internal threat. This internal threat, however, is– finally–a threat of castration by the parent of the child, fear of which is the cause of the emergence of such symptoms as animal phobias (in the cases of the Wolf Man and the Rat Man). What has happened is that the internal source of anxiety has been displaced onto an external symbol, such as horses, rats or wolves.[73] The relationship between the animal phobias and neurotic compulsion and fear of the conscience (or super-ego) presumes our examination of the Oedipus complex; but in each case the emergence of symptoms constitutes an unmistakable sign of neurosis.[74]

The presence of symptoms means that unconscious feelings and desires are being diverted from the conscious. It means also that the conflict inherent in the relationship between the unconscious and the conscious has reached threatening proportions, and that the repression of unacceptable material is causing great distress in the patient. The material must therefore be of enormous significance for the patient; and the fact that it is being repressed indicates the profundity of the conflict and the high priority to which the activity of repression has been assigned by the mind. As I have already noted, the material repressed is material revealed in the interpretation of dreams, the material of childhood desires and the memories of their frustrations and transformations. Freud held that knowledge of this material is the sum and substance of psychoanalysis:

---

[72] *Ibid.*, 366.

[73] Sigmund Freud, *The Problem of Anxiety*, tr. Henry Alden Bunker (New York: The Psycho-Analytic Quarterly Press, 1936; W. W. Norton & Co., 1963), 87.

[74] We should bear in mind that Freud's treatment of symptoms depended greatly upon his work among neurotics, rather than psychotics–who he often said he believed to be virtually untreatable–and especially with cases of hysteria.

Strictly considered—and why should this question not be considered with all possible strictness?—analytic work deserves to be recognized as genuine psycho-analysis only when it has succeeded in removing the amnesia which conceals from the adult his knowledge of his childhood from its beginning (that is, from about the second to the fifth year). This cannot be said among analysts too emphatically or repeated too often.[75]

And again, he argued, for example, that the reconstruction of past events are of great therapeutic effect so long as the events penetrate the screen shielding those events of early childhood: it is of special importance in analysis of the patient's own forgotten sexual activity as a child and also of the intervention by the adults which brought it to an end."[76]

But the induction of these memories is strenuously resisted. The agency of repression, if it has done its work well, will be got round only with difficulty. For these early events are at one and the same time the most crucial and the most hidden of the mental life. Freud contrasts the life of the repressed material with the growth of a village into a town:

When a village grows into a town or a child into a man, the village and the child become lost in the town and the man. Memory alone can trace the old features in the new picture; and in fact the old materials or forms have been got rid of and replaced by new ones.[77]

The mind, however, works differently:

Here one can describe the state of affairs, which has nothing to compare with it, only by saying that in this case every earlier stage of development persists alongside the later stage which has arisen from it; here succession also involves co-existence, although it is to the same materials that the whole series of transformations has applied. The earlier mental state may not have manifested itself for years, but none the less it is so far present that it may at any time again become the mode of expression of the forces in the mind, and indeed the only one, as though all later developments had been annulled or undone....
...[T]he primitive mind is, in the fullest meaning of the word, imperishable.[78]

---

[75] " 'A Child is Being Beaten': A Contribution to the Study of the Origin of Sexual Perversions," SE XVII, 183.

[76] "Lay Analysis," SE XX, 216.

[77] "Thoughts: I," SE XIV, 285-286.

[78] Ibid.. Cf. "Claims," SE XIII, 184, Civilization and its Discontents, tr. and ed. James Strachey (New York: W. W. Norton & Co., 1961), 16ff..

Repression

Repression is an operation of the mind that prevents it from taking on the forms and appearance of its primitive state. As in anxiety the self is attempting to flee; but flight from an internal danger is literally not possible. Thus repression is employed instead. "Repression," says Freud, "is the preliminary stage of condemnation, something between flight and condemnation."[79] Repression seems to be unrelated to pain caused by external stimuli, or indeed to internal somatic discomfort such as that caused by hunger. It arises, rather, only when a "sharp cleavage" between unconscious and conscious mental activity has occurred: "*The essence of repression lies simply in turning something away, and keeping it at a distance, from the conscious.*"[80] At one point Freud thought of repression as the work of a censor acting in one of two capacities. It may prevent unconscious thoughts from entering into the preconscious—here the characteristic intermediate stage between unconscious and consciousness of his earlier thought—or may expel unwanted unconscious thoughts from the pre-conscious. It is as though there were three adjoining rooms: a large entrance hall (with the unconscious thoughts); a smaller room guarded by the censor (the pre-conscious); and a third room rather like a receiving room (the conscious). All mental phenomema originate in the large entrance hall, and from there they do or not proceed to the receiving chamber according to the decision of the censor.[81]

The process of repression has two stages. First, a primal repression occurs when the repressed material, which is in fact the "ideational representative" of the impulse or instinct desiring satisfaction, is denied access to consciousness. That denial results in a fixation, a point of persistent tension between the instinct and the conscious to which the mental activity returns again and again. The second stage Freud calls repression proper. This "affects mental derivatives of the repressed representative, or such trains of thought as, originating elsewhere, have come into associative connection with it. On account of this association, these ideas experience the same fate as what was primarily repressed. Repression proper, therefore, is actually an after-pressure."[82]

As with dreams, slips of the tongue, and symptoms the patient is quite unaware of the activity of repression. This is true despite the fact that the chief agency of consciousness, the ego, is probably the repressing

---

[79] "Repression," SE XIV, 146.

[80] *Ibid.*, 147.

[81] Freud suggests one exception to this procession of thoughts, a mental act that does not exist "to begin with in an unconscious stage and phase." "The exception...must no doubt be the case of external perception." IL, SE XVI, 295-298.

[82] "Repression," SE XIV, 148.

30

agent as well.[83]

A major goal of analysis is in fact the replacement of repression with judgement, or condemnation.[84] In accomplishing this end the unconscious is made accessible to the conscious and the therapeutic process can proceed in earnest; for repression interferes with only one aspect of the psyche, the access to the conscious of impulses which are judged unacceptable by the ego.[85]

Repression is most effective when the material repressed is most objectionable and threatening. On the other hand, argues Freud, that which is repressed has a greater chance of breaking through to the conscious in its most distorted form, that is, when it least resembles the psychical actuality of the unconscious. It is in fact this distorted material that is revealed, more or less openly, in analytic free association. This open reporting of distorted elements of the repressed material–for example, screen memories, indirect and unintentioned references in the form of slips of the tongue, jokes–becomes increasingly forced and difficult as the material reported comes to resemble more closely the psychical actuality of the patient's mind. At this point the repressing mechanism comes into play and resistance is encountered. The difference between what gets into the conscious and what is repressed, however, is often very small and always idiosyncratic. Freud suggested that this may explain why the same material may comprise both the content of repressed material and, with a slight modification, the highest civilized values.[86]

The process of repression is mobile, adjusting its operation to meet the strength of the repressed material in its drive toward expression. According to Freud's libido theory, the energy of the drive to expression is countered by the energy of the repressing mechanism. A change on either side may affect the repression work, notably when the repressed material is very energetic and the repressing mechanism too operates with equal and counter-vailing vigor.[87]

The success of the repression can be evaluated in terms of two elements found in the repressed material. Freud distinguished between the history of the idea connected with the repressed material and the "quota of affective energy" or "quantity of cathected energy" associated with it. The repression is successful only to the degree that both elements are superseded. In various neuroses we see examples of successful repression of one and not the other. For example, in the case of hysteria anxiety and animal phobias the demand for the love of the father may be replaced by,

---

[83] *Cf.* NIL, SE XXII, 57-80.
[84] *Ibid.*.
[85] "Repression," SE XIV, 149.
[86] *Ibid.*, 149-150. His study of fetishism is the basis for this suggestion.
[87] *Ibid.*, 151-152.

for example, the fear of wolves. In this case the ideational content of the repressed material has been effectively suppressed. However, the distress associated with the repression is unacceptable and produces the phobia. The affective energy has not been repressed but appears in the guise of a symptom. Since all repressions are attempts to avoid pain, or unpleasure, as Freud says, the repression must be said to have failed. On the other hand, in the case of hysteria the opposite is true, for the affective energy has been reduced but a long chain of substitutive formations emerges, culminating in a symptom.[88]

Repression might seem to have succeeded in the case of obsessional neuroses. What is repressed is, in the first place, the hostile or sadistic feelings for a loved one. At an early stage repression does work very well. The distress associated with the hostility disappears, as well as the idea, or feeling, of hostility. What appears in place of these is "increased conscientiousness," which would hardly seem to be a symptom. Indeed, in civilization it is a mark of maturity and cause for respect. However, argues Freud, the repression is brought about by a reaction-formation, that is the formation of a substitute that exists only as a reaction to the repressed material, and is therefore dependent on it and expressive of it in however distorted a manner. This reaction formation—increased conscientiousness—amounts to a substitute by replacement of the rejected idea. The situation worsens as behavior associated with the reaction formation is established, that is, a pronounced social anxiety, moral anxiety and continuous self-reproach. These may be acceptable forms of behavior in society, but they are symptoms nonetheless. The neurosis then develops, producing phobias, prohibitions, and symptoms of flight as the repression of affective elements continues to falter. On the other hand the idea related to the repressed material, hostility to loved ones, continues to be successfully repressed. In the obsessional neurosis, then, the repression both fails and is prolonged in "sterile and interminable struggle."[89]

The material that is repressed is characteristic of its id-nature, for

---

[88] Ibid., 152-158.

[89] Ibid., 157; cf. ibid., 152-158. Freud considered the theory of repression to have been an original one presented by him until Otto Rank showed him a passage from Schopenhauer's The World as Will and Idea "in which the philosopher seeks to give an explanation of insanity. What he says there about the struggle against accepting a distressing piece of reality coincides with my concept of repression so completely that once again I owe the chance of making a discovery to not being well-read. Yet others have read the same passage and passed it by without making this discovery, and perhaps the same would have happened to me if in my young days I had had more taste for reading philosophical works." Although he is confirmed in his confidence about his contribution, Freud also forgoes "all claim to priority in the many instances

it has no sense of time or place, and returns whenever the repression process allows it to by its weakness. This issue of the return of the repressed touches not only upon neurosis but, as we shall see, upon the products of civilization, and upon the whole human mental life. In the treatment of patients, however, the return of the repressed is both a crucial step in therapy and an indication of the distorting operations of the mind. For example, when an analyst suggests to the patient an interpretation, that is to say a construction, of the causes of his condition the patient usually responds in a manner that suggests that he has not understood or accepted the construction offered but rather one that is closely related to it. This puzzling behavior yields to an explanation; the patient's view of the matter is distorted, and is thus "off-center," somewhat askew. The patient's view is also, argues Freud, a delusion about the nature of his illness. But this response is to be understood as the return of the repressed; it discloses a piece of historical reality which has been suppressed, but in a distorted fashion.[90]

This phenomenon suggests an explanation for a type of behavior that is only indirectly perceived but crucial to culture and religion. In the latter the notion of prophecy as a foretelling of the future shares with the construction phenomenon in therapy a sense of delusion and hallucination that is nevertheless very close to the truth about the past that has been repressed. The repressed material returns in a protective distorting guise—a glimpse into the future, a hearing of the word of God, the announcement of the moral or legal code. What emerges is the repressed material, revealed in a manner that obscures its true content. For this reason Freud placed his entire discussion of religion, morality, and group psychology within the context of neurotic behavior. The facts of repressed material and the tendency of the repressed to return enable us to understand the true source of our history—the conflict of our unconscious desire with our conscious prudence. We may succeed from time to time in repressing those desires; but they will not evaporate, disappear or be consumed. They must eventually find expression.

> Just as our construction is only effective because it recovers a fragment of lost experience, so the delusion owes its convincing

---

in which laborious psychoanalytic investigation can merely confirm the truths which the philosopher recognized by intuition." "On the History of the Psycho-Analytic Movement," SE XIV, 15-16. *Cf.* also "Analysis," SE XXIII, 245ff., and "Resistances to Psycho-Analysis," SE XIX, appendix, where Freud offers similar comment on the link between the philosophy of Empedocles and his theory of the instincts; and *cf.* "An Autobiographical Study," SE XX, 59-60, where Schopenhauer's intuition is again noted.

[90] "Construction in Analysis," SE XXIII, 268-269.

power to the element of historical truth which it inserts into the place of the rejected reality....

If we consider mankind as a whole and substitute it for the single human individual, we discover that it too has developed delusions which are inaccessible to logical criticism and which contradict reality. If, in spite of this, they are able to exert an extraordinary power over men, investigation leads to the same explanation as in the case of the single individual. They owe their power to the element of *historical truth* which they have brought up from the repression of the forgotten and primaeval past.[91]

In his discussion of the return of the repressed Freud concludes that we can no more insist upon a distinction between individual and collective experiences of this return than we can upon any supposed distinction between the neurotic and the healthy person.

Moreover, the repressed material is infantile and based on real experience; indeed it is an expression of real experience: "The part of a person's psychical material which has remained infantile and has been repressed as being unserviceable constitutes the core of his unconscious." It is this material which "lies in wait for a change to become active and makes use of its opportunities if the later and higher psychical structures fail to master the difficulties of real life."[92] That frustration which so clearly characterizes the tendency toward neurosis stems from past events:

I prefer this way of representing the matter because it has a secret content. For it hints at the probability that the internal impediments arose from real external obstacles during the prehistoric periods of human development.[93]

While it is not yet our concern to explain exhaustively the causes of neurosis it is worthwhile to note that throughout his investigation Freud recognized the need to deal with the question of disposition toward fixation, and therefore repression, which characterized the structure of mental life, and, on the other hand, to take into account infantile (or primitive, in the case of societies) experience and historical traumatic events. The relationship between the two causative elements, one of which might be called external, the other internal, was described by him as a "complemental series": "You can declare, as a schematic abbreviation, that libidinal fixation represents the predisposing, internal factor in the aetiology of the neuroses, while frustration represents the accidental, external one."[94]

---

[91] *Ibid.*.
[92] "Claims," SE XIII, 184.
[93] IL, SE XVI, 350; *cf.* 346.
[94] *Ibid.*, 346.

Freud, in opposition to Charcot, argued that the origins of neurosis, for example hysteria, lay not in the experience by a child of seduction by an adult who was his parent, but in the fact of the fantasy about the seduction. There was, he argued, a psychical reality, revealed in the fantasy, in addition to any other relevant "practical reality."[95] But the relationship is not mutually exclusive; some neuroses have external occasions to which the disposition to break through repression responds. But neurosis is not necessarily dependent upon such occasions, although all neuroses are linked to frustration. The situation may be seen as a spectrum of conditions: at one end there are those who because of the sort of development their ego has followed were bound to fall ill virtually without regard to circumstances, and at the other end there are those who would have escaped illness had circumstances been different.[96]

What is true of the individual is of course true of the group as well. External conditions—Freud once called them "purely chance experiences"—may leave fixations behind them for individuals, and for groups:

Constitutional dispositions are also undoubtedly after-effects of experiences of ancestors in the past; they too were once acquired, without such acquisitions there would be no heredity. And is it conceivable that acquisitions such as this, leading to inheritance, would come to an end precisely with the generation we are considering?[97]

Whatever the difficulties besetting Freud's concept of the inheritance of acquired characteristics he simply could not assign the entire aetiology of neuroses to internal causation; nor could he regard external stimuli and experience of the external world as discontinuous.

Perversions

The themes of intra-mural conflict in the mental life, of ignorance of this conflict on the part of the patient—and us all—and the truth of suffering which lies behind and is the cause of dreams, symptoms and the neuroses may be seen in the examination of sexual perversions. That examination begins with the fact of infantile sexuality and the denial of it. The denial of infantile sexuality, characteristic as much of the opposition to psychoanalysis as of the behavior of patients in therapy, is civilization's primary task, as well as the clue to its discontent. Education (Freud writes *Erziehung*, or "upbringing," rather than simply "schooling") cannot succeed unless it tames and restricts the sexual instinct. This task applies most obviously to that period of sexual activity attached to puberty, reproduction and what Freud calls the "primacy of

---

[95] "History," SE XIV, 17-18.
[96] IL, SE XVI, 339-347; *cf.* 362.
[97] *Ibid.*, 361.

the genitals." The urge to reproduction must be subjected to "an individual will which is identical with the bidding of society." This sexual activity must be postponed until a certain degree of intellectual maturity has been achieved, or else the work and future of civilization itself are in peril.[98]

This is clear to any student of the history of culture. But according to the psychoanalytic view of human nature sexuality and its problems are by no means limited to reproductive needs. Sexual perversions are a ready clue that other types of sexuality exist; and the fact that they are called "perverse" is an important clue to the truth that civilization's concern with sexuality is not simply to create an economic balance between reproduction and work but actively to deny the significance and existence of any other interpretation of sexuality. The study of sexual perversions is inextricably tied to the study of infantile sexuality. Their presence and significance suggest a far broader understanding of sexuality as well as of the profound conflict between the conscious and the unconscious, the civilized and the instinctual. The readiness of psychoanalysis to pursue these matters naturally attracted the scorn of the learned:

> You will no doubt have heard, ...that in psycho-analysis the concept of what is sexual has been unduly extended in order to support the theses of the sexual causation of the neuroses and the sexual meaning of symptoms.... We have only extended the concept of sexuality far enough to be able to comprise the sexual life of perverts and of children. We have, that is to say, given it back its true compass. What is called sexuality outside psychoanalysis relates only to a restricted sexual life, which serves the purpose of reproduction and is described as normal.[99]

But such a broad compass of sexuality suggests that the urge for reproduction must be derived from earlier stages of sexual behavior which, perforce, appear in different guises, and which have little if any concern for reproduction. Indeed, it is very likely that at the earliest stage of "sexuality" we shall be unable to distinguish between the urge for reproduction and any of the other elements present. The perversions, by their nature, suggest that is so.[100]

These perversions are permitted to a degree in normal life, for example, kissing or biting; they display no necessary relationship to intercourse and conception. This lack of relationship is more strikingly apparent in the more obvious perversions. Perversions, then, should be understood as seeking another aim of sexuality than reproduction, and as vestigial remnants of that other aim which, in some cases, have been incorporated

---

[98] IL, SE XVI, 311-322.
[99] Ibid., 319.
[100] Cf. ibid., 320-321.

36

in, or grafted onto, reproduction by cultural practice. Reproduction, in turn, has become the only acceptable justification for sexuality, so that all sexual activity must conform to the aims of reproduction or suffer the stigma of being designated as perverse. Perversions are so called because they do not lead to reproduction. Their existence, however, suggests that the significance of sexuality extends far backward from adult urges to procreate to the formative years and experiences of children.[101]

There is an empirical issue to be raised here. If language and culture demand that sexuality be linked to reproduction, can we meaningfully use the notion of sexuality outside that context? What would it mean to refer to the sexuality of infants, if they are—and indeed they are—totally disinterested in reproduction? Freud replies:

> ...we call the dubious and indefinable pleasurable activities of earliest childhood sexual because, in the course of analysis, we arrive at them from the symptoms after passing through indisputably sexual material. They need not necessarily themselves be sexual on that account—agreed![102]

But a useful analogy may be drawn from horticulture:

> Suppose we had no means of observing the development from their seed of two dicotyledonous plants, the apple-tree and the bean, but that it was possible in both cases for us to trace their development backwards from the fully developed individual plant to the first seedling with two seed-leaves. The two seed-leaves have a neutral appearance. They are just alike in both cases. Am I then to suppose that they are really alike, and that the specific difference between an apple tree and a bean is only introduced into the plants later? Or is it biologically more correct to believe that this difference is already there in the seedling, although I cannot observe any distinction in the seed-leaves? But we are doing the same thing when we call the pleasure in the activities of an infant-in-arms a sexual one.[103]

Our concern at the moment is with sexual perversions and their significance; like infantile sexuality, they signify the enormous breadth of sexual activity in the development of the mature adult. The fact that perversions are so called signifies the compass of the conflict between that early sexuality and the later control of it by the socially-adapted ego. Therefore it is not surprising to find that sexual perversions are distorted forms, just as dream work distorts latent content, as symptoms obscure the repressed material and replace it, and as the repressed material returns in misdirected and altered form. Freud explores this phenomenon

---

[101] *Ibid.*, 322-323.
[102] *Ibid.*, 324-325.
[103] *Ibid.*.

in his treatment of the relatively common fantasy that a child is being beaten.[104] The fantasy is a distortion of experience drawn from the Oedipal period and revived in a form favorable for the return of the repressed. The fantasy distorts the material—which is essentially a fantasy about love of a child for its parents, with an attendant ambivalence—in a manner that allows it into the conscious so that it can be reported, usually by free association. The sexual content is quite evident to the analyst.

The stages of distortion may be identified. They incorporate themes of sadism, that is, the beating of the child in the most obvious version of the fantasy, and masochism, a less apparent aspect of the fantasy partially disguised by the joining of opposites—a common form of distortion in both dreams and fantasies.

It is this transformation of the sadistic elements of the fantasy into masochistic elements that illumines the fact and nature of distortion and therefore the presence of material that needed to be altered. Masochism—an issue to be taken up shortly—was understood to be a manifestation of Oedipal influences that had been taken into the mental structure in the form of the super-ego and the ego-ideal. In the child-beating fantasy Freud discovered that masochism was a reversal of sadism and found in that reversal the distortion associated with the perversion:

> The transformation of sadism into masochism appears to be due to the influence of the sense of guilt which takes part in the act of repression. Thus repression is operative here in three ways: it renders the consequences of genital organization unconscious, it compels that organization itself to regress to the earlier sadistic-anal stage, and it transforms the sadism of this stage into masochism, which is passive and again in a certain sense narcissistic.[105]

Once more the apparent aberration, the symptom, the perversion or deviation, is a distorted representative of the powers of the unconscious self and reveals the conflict that defines the self. In the child-beating fantasy we have an indication of the need to repress unsuitable infantile material. This repression, says Freud, must be successful. The boundary restraining sexual impulses appropriate to the child must be defended so that the genital organization of the adult may remain intact—that is what we mean by health.[106] When repression fails symptoms arise, notably in the form of regression; infantile sexuality is, then, the chief factor in the formation of symptoms. As we shall see this is tantamount to asserting

---

[104] " 'A Child,' " SE XVII.
[105] Ibid., 194; cf. 191-195.
[106] Ibid., 203f..

that "the Oedipal Complex is the nuclear complex of neuroses."[107]

Anxiety

Perversions and fantasies of perversions, like symptoms, indicate the presence of suffering; but these indications are lost on the one who suffers, however evident they may be to the analyst. In principle that conclusion applies to all of us. However, it is also true that a sense of dis-ease, or unrest, is experienced by patients and all others from time to time in the form of anxiety. The presence of anxiety signifies distress and is indeed distressful in itself.

Once again, a close examination of the nature and causes of anxiety shows evidence of distortion and conflict. In general, anxiety serves a vital function, that of initiation of a state of preparedness for physical danger. It is a highly useful defense which is to be found throughout the history of the race. Freud traces anxiety back to the experience of birth, the prototype of the effects of mortal danger.[108] The link between the state of anxiety and the moment of birth–when that is understood primarily as separation from the mother–is considered critical by Freud.[109] It suggests a fruitful line of thought leading to a connection between neurotic anxieties and what we call "real" anxieties.

Neurotic anxieties are manifest in what may be termed "free-floating apprehensions" on the one hand, and in what Freud called "bound cathexes" on the other, that is, zoophobias, animal phobias, or anxiety that has a highly specific and peculiar object. Further, in children it is evident that anxiety is directly related to separation from the mother. Adult anxiety hysteria is not different in essence, since it is an extension of the childhood anxiety. However, it has been subjected to more intensive repression consistent with the development of the sexual stages and the primacy of the genital organization.

This view of anxiety–with its elements of separation from the mother, childhood sexuality, displacement of anxiety onto other objects such as animals in phobias–was never abandoned by Freud; but his theoretical presention of the metapsychological issues did change. In the *Introductory Lectures* he identified the separation from the mother as the real frustration of a libidinal need. That need then sought some other expression in the form of a symptom. In other words, anxiety is the affective characteristic of the return of repressed libido to a fixation. It is a by-product of discharge of frustrated libido.[110] Neurotic anxieties and phobias, therefore, were to be distinguished from other anxieties because the former had

---

[107] *Ibid.; cf.* 199-200.
[108] IL, SE XVI, 392-397.
[109] *Ibid.*, 397.
[110] *Ibid.*, 410.

an internal source, and were not what might be regarded as responses to genuine threats but were, as one might say, neurotic responses.[111]

This interpretation was altered significantly in later writings, first in Freud's extended essay on anxiety. The early interpretation, according to which phobias were the result of the transformation of libido into anxiety and therefore had an internal source, is rejected in favor of the view that phobias are the consequence of real external threat, and that, very likely, all anxieties were the result of external threats. He could, then, explain the fact that in the case of Little Hans' fear of horses and the Wolf Man's wolf phobia it was only necessary for them to avoid horses and wolves to solve their immediate problem. The danger is, as we shall see, not avoided as simply as that, but this view does suggest that the matter is more complex than simple frustrated longing for re-union with the mother. For that desire for union involved a fundamental danger which the self must be on guard against.

> On a previous occasion I ascribed to phobias the character of a projection, since they substitute for an internal instinctual danger an external perceptual one. Such a process has the advantage that from an external danger protection may be gained through flight and the avoidance of the perception of it, whereas against a danger from within, flight is of no avail. This statement of mine is not incorrect, but superficial. For the instinctual demand is not in itself a danger, but is so only because it entails a true external danger, that of castration. So fundamentally we have in the phobias, after all, merely the substituting of one external danger for another.[112]

In phobias, then, anxiety is now understood as a distress signal which will cause the ego to take action and avoid situations in which it and the whole self are threatened. Little Hans feared horses; they made him anxious, and he avoided them. His anxiety served to warn him of danger. This danger, as Freud discovered, was not from the horses but from what they meant to Hans, the threat that his father would castrate him as punishment for Hans' love for his mother.[113] The danger was two-fold: separation from the mother and castration by the father. This, Freud argued, meant that anxiety had a pattern centered on separation from a loved object. If that were so, the simple act of birth could not in itself be the cause of anxiety in the first instance. The foetus is completely narcissistic and does not know the mother as object; and therefore it could hardly be anxious about separation.[114] Birth itself did not lead

---

[111] *Ibid.*, 379-411; *cf. Anxiety*, 39-40.
[112] *Anxiety*, 62.
[113] *Ibid.*, 29ff..
[114] *Ibid.*, 67-68.

to anxiety; and it was very unlikely that there is a such a thing as birth trauma *per se*, although situations of privation may seem to the infant to be analogous to the birth experience, since both are danger situations.[115]

Initially–and here Freud means "initially" in the history of the individual *and* of the race–anxiety was castration anxiety, the fear of the boy that his penis, which he enjoys, would be cut off, and that he could no longer engage in infantile sexual relations with the mother. The form of this anxiety in girls appeared as fear of removal from their mother's love. This separation-castration anxiety takes forms appropriate to the stages of infantile sexual development. For this reason the emphasis of other interpreters, such as Otto Rank, on the birth trauma concept is misleading. This anxiety first takes the form of helplessness, then fear of the loss of objects, then fear of castration and finally fear of the superego. This final phase remains virtually unchanged in the history of the adult. Castration anxiety is the fear of an external danger, just as helplessness and deprivation encourage anxiety in light of possible external dangers. Castration anxiety should then be seen as an anxiety that can take appropriate forms.[116]

In the latter half of his career Freud insisted on the external causes of neurotic anxiety. Anxiety is the consequence of real and general human experience. The distinction between neurotic anxiety and "real" anxiety blurs greatly if we understand that what neurotics fear really could have happened to them, and perhaps did happen to others in the past. Freud believed that in the history of the race small boys had every right to be fearful of castration by their jealous fathers:

> [the boy] has some grounds [for believing that he will be castrated], for people threaten him often enough with cutting off his penis during the phallic phase, at the time of his early masturbation, and hints at that punishment must regularly find a phylogenetic re-inforcement in him. It is our suspicion that during the human family's primaeval period castration used actually to be carried out by the jealous and cruel father upon growing boys, and that circumcision, which so frequently plays a part in puberty rites among primitive peoples, is a clearly recognizable relic of it. We are aware that here we are diverging widely from the general opinion but we must hold fast to the view that fear of castration is one of the commonest and strongest motives for repression and thus for the formation of neuroses. The analysis of cases in which circumcision, though not, it is true, castration, has been carried out on boys as a cure or punishment for masturbation (a far from rare occurrence in

---

[115] *Ibid.*, 76.
[116] NIL, 81-89; *cf. Anxiety*, 88-90, *Civilization*, 82.

41

Anglo-American society) has given our conviction a last degree of certainty.[117]

The conflict in anxiety is between the infantile sexual impulses and the forces that seek to control that impulse lest the person suffer punishment from the world, in the form of the Oedipal figures and super-ego models. Thus anxiety is peculiarly an ego defense and an ego phenomenon. As we have seen it is the responsibility of the ego to prevent the conflict between the instinctual desires and the exigencies of external life from breaking out into the open—for it knows the result very surely indeed. The ego, then, is the seat of anxiety. In the course of its growth it has acquired three masters: the instinctual desires of the id, the inexorable pressures of the external world, and the more recently acquired super-ego.[118]

The general causes of anxiety, then, are three: biological, phylogenetic, and psychological. Human biology dictates a short intra-uterine period and a longer extra-uterine development. The influence of the external environment is correspondingly great and elicits an early discrimination between that part of the organism which must respond to external pressures—the ego—and that which constitutes the desires of the infant. Thus "the value attached to the object who alone can offer protection from [external] dangers and effect a substitution for the intra-uterine life which has been lost, is enormously augmented."[119]

Second, human phylogeny is such that there is a serious interruption in the maturation of the human sexual life at about the fifth year, and is thus unique in the animal realm. This fact mandates a diphasic onset of sexuality, and is the most significant (phylogenetic) element in the aetiology of the neuroses.

Third, anxiety must be traced psychologically to the fundamental and continuous conflict between the ego and id due to the response of the ego to the environment. The fact is that the ego is less able to deal with the uprisings of the instincts than with the external environment:

Itself intimately connected with the id, the ego is able to stave off an instinctual danger only by putting restrictions upon its own organization and by tolerating symptom formation as a substitute for its crippling of the instinct.[120]

Finally, therefore, there is no reason for regarding real anxiety as in any significant sense different from neurotic anxiety. There is an apparent difference: a real danger is a threat from an external object, a neurotic danger from an instinctual demand. But this instinctual demand, insofar

---

[117] NIL, SE XXII, 86-87.
[118] *Cf. Ego and Id*, 85.
[119] *Anxiety*, 99-100.
[120] *Ibid.*.

as it is a piece of reality such as the threat of castration, is founded on reality, just as a "real" danger is founded on experience. The ego protects itself from the instinctual demand in the same way that it reacts to an external danger;

> but...in consequence of an imperfection of the psychical apparatus this defensive activity eventuates in neurosis. We have become convinced also that instinctual demands often become an (internal) danger only because of the fact that their gratification would bring about an external danger–because, therefore, this internal danger represents an external one, one which has become internal for the ego but which is nonetheless the result of an experienced situation of helplessness.[121]

Anxiety, then, acts as yet another sign that the mental conflict which is general in human life constitutes a general truth of suffering, not simply an indication of neurotic suffering. Or, to put the matter in another way, the mental life is in principle conducive to neurosis by reason of its nature. Anxiety makes this truth evident in the same way and for the same reasons as dreams, symptoms and slips of the tongue. The ego must protect itself by repression; but in consequence of repression it may become distressed beyond its ability to suffer. It must draw the relevant instinctual impulse into its organization. When it cannot do so it feels weakened.[122] Anxiety is a signal of weakening. But it also enables the psychic apparatus to function in the face of unavoidable traumas which leave their mark forever, and is thus a valuable defense as well as a neurotic symptom.[123]

Fetishism

Freud's study of fetishes led him to conclude that the threat of castration could be avoided, that is, displaced. The fetish acted as a substitute for the penis, whose future was so much in doubt. Freud pointed out on numerous occasions that the empirical evidence that convinces the small boy that castration is no idle threat is the fact that girls have no such organ. For the fetishist the replacing of that missing organ is achieved by substituting another and arbitrarily chosen part of a woman to act as penis, and thus to relieve the anxiety in the face of the threat of castration. The fetishist denies stark reality; at the same time he solves a major psychic crisis.

> We can now see what the fetish achieves and what it is that it maintains. It remains a token of triumph over the threat of castration and a protection against it. It also saves the fetishist

---

[121] *Anxiety*, 115-116; *cf.* 117, *Ego and Id*, 87.
[122] NIL, SE XXII, 89-90.
[123] *Ibid.*, 93-95.

from becoming a homosexual, by endowing women with the characteristic which makes them tolerable as sexual objects. In later life, the fetishist feels that he enjoys yet another advantage from his substitute for a genital. The meaning of the fetish is not known to other people, so the fetish is not withheld from him; it is easily accessible and he can readily obtain the sexual satisfaction attached to it. What other men have to woo and make exertions for can be obtained by the fetishist with no trouble at all.[124]

Fetishism is therefore neurotic in the sense that a symptom is substituted for external reality. But it has psychotic characteristics as well, in that it denies completely the existence of a certain, and very important, sector of that external reality. As we shall see, Freud had begun to revise his view on psychosis toward the end of his career on this particular point in his treatment of fetishism. Contrary to his earlier expectation that such denial of external reality could only result in complete breakdown of the ego structures and render a patient untreatable, he observed that in fetishism a phenomenon he called the "splitting of the ego" occurred, which enabled the ego to continue its difficult task of organizing the mental apparatus. In other words his view of psychosis and the situation of the neurotic and all of us with respect to external reality appeared increasingly complex, more so than his more monolithic view that if the self could not adjust to external reality, it would be destroyed.

Narcissism

In narcissism Freud discovered what he regarded as the primary threat to any adjustment therapy, that is, to responding in a useful manner to the exigencies of external reality. Like dreams, fetishes, perversions, slips of the tongue, and symptoms in general it finds various expressions. Freud's initial view of the narcissistic personality was expressed in terms of psychosis; for he believed that if the ego took itself rather than an external object as the goal of its love it was simply denying external reality and was therefore untreatable. Psychosis, narcissism and sleep were in principle identical in this respect. Later he distinguished between narcissistic neuroses and psychosis, for reasons I will discuss shortly.

Here I wish only to suggest briefly what Freud intends by the concept of narcissism (the topic is discussed in considerable detail below). As the name implies, narcissism (after the Greek figure Narcissus, who drowned in a pool because of love of his own reflection he saw there) means love of the self, by the self, or, more precisely, love of the ego–in place of love of an object. Freud distinguished between two paths leading to the choice

---

[124] "Fetishism," SE XXI, 154.

of a love object (and in terms of Freud's notion of desire, or libido, as the driving and defining power of the self, there was no possibility of this desire not finding an object):

A person may love:–
(1) According to the narcissistic type:
    (a) what he himself is (*i.e.* himself),
    (b) what he himself was,
    (c) what he himself would like to be,
    (d) someone who was once part of himself.[125]

The alternatives for "self-love," then, include not only the person as he sees himself, but also that part of himself which Freud called the "ego-ideal." This linking of the elements of the super-ego and narcissism is extremely important in explaining the distress of the self, notably the distress of the ego. For the conflict between the ego-ideal, especially in its form as super-ego/conscience (introjected into the mental structure from the experience of the Oedipal period) and the ego is seen by Freud to endanger the ego far more than the simpler neurotic symptom formation in the attempt to suppress and redirect desires away from the external world. For in psychotic behavior the conflict is wholly within the self, and is due to the more destructive consequences of narcissism.

The alternative to the narcissistic path to finding an object is the love for one who is not oneself. Freud calls this the anaclitic, or attachment type. The objects here are, first and foremost, the woman who feeds the infant, the man who protects it, and the substitute figures who succeed them.[126] The distinction between the narcissistic and anaclitic types is not analogous to a distinction between sickness and health. Narcissism as self-love in a general sense is essential for ego health. The relationship between love for others and love for oneself may be understood in this way: if love is what Freud calls "ego-syntonic," that is, conducive to the health of the ego, it allows a dynamic relationship between loving and being loved.

Loving in itself, in so far as it involves longing and deprivation, lowers self-regard; whereas being loved, having one's love returned, and possessing the loved object, raises it once more.[127]

Loving is therefore an activity which is to be judged like any other work of the ego, that is, in terms of a non-destructive relationship between the libido of the id and the limitations of the external world. In this optimal view narcissism is ego-syntonic in that it is the necessary complement to loving one who is other than oneself.

---

[125] "Narcissism," SE XIV, 90.
[126] *Ibid.*.
[127] *Ibid.*, 99f..

Freud's treatment of feminine sexuality is intimately related to the concept of narcissism. He draws a clear distinction between the types of libidinal attachment characteristic of each sex.

Complete object love of the attachment type is, properly speaking, characteristic of the male. It displays the marked sexual overvaluation which is doubtless derived from the child's original narcissism and thus corresponds to a transference of that narcissism to the sexual object.... A different course is followed in the type of female most frequently met with, which is probably the purest and truest one. With the onset of puberty the maturing of the female sexual organs, which up till then have been in a condition of latency, seems to bring about an intensification of the original narcissism, and this is unfavourable to the development of a true object-choice with its accompanying sexual overvaluation. Women, especially if they grow up with good looks, develop a certain self-contentment which compensates them for the social restrictions that are imposed upon them in their choice of object. Strictly speaking, it is only themselves that such women love with an intensity comparable to that of the man's love for them. The importance of this type of woman for the erotic life of mankind is to be rated very high.[128]

The difference between men and women enunciated here is not, again, the difference between sickness and health but between two ego-syntonic assignments of libidinal energy. This is an important point because, although narcissistic disorders are central to Freud's conceptualization of analysis, they should not be confused with the ego-syntonic narcissism he finds characteristic of feminine development.[129]

The situation is altered when loving has, for any reason, become attached to an act of repression, that is, when the loving desire has been prevented from entering the conscious, and the libidinal impulse is repressed. Under these conditions the libidinal activity is felt as a "severe depletion of the ego" which requires withdrawal from objects.

The return of the object-libido to the ego and its transformation into narcissism represents, as it were, a happy love once more; and on the other hand, it is also true that a real happy love corresponds to the primal condition in which object-libido and ego-libido cannot be distinguished.[130]

Narcissism as a "sickness," then, is related to the infantile history, in which a *primary* narcissism first existed before being replaced with object

---

[128] *Ibid.*, 88-89.
[129] See further discussion of feminine sexuality below.
[130] *Ibid.*, 99-100.

love that incorporated the external world. However, the conflict between the infantile desire and the demands of experience may re-emerge in a *secondary* narcissism. Primary narcissism gives no place to ego development, with its necessary relationship to external objects. Self-love and object-love in this primary state cannot be distinguished. "The development of the ego consists in a departure from primary narcissism and gives rise to a vigorous attempt to recover that state."[131] The recovery attempt is successful only at the expense of the ego's relationship with external reality. What is particularly threatening in the narcissistic case is that the ego is in fact suffused with libido, and thus takes no account of reality.

This fact brought Freud again and again to the unhappy conclusion that narcissism was psychotic and therefore unresponsive to the sort of treatment that was so promising in the cases of transference neuroses. In these cases it was possible, because of the patient's continued relationship with external reality—however distorted—, to recreate, repeat, and work through the neurosis, especially through the patient's work of transferring his neurotic feelings from an individual, usually father or mother, to one who was present, the analyst. But narcissism prevented this transference. For example, schizophrenics were virtually untreatable for this reason. In his essay "The Unconscious" Freud concluded:

> Indeed, the capacity for transference...presupposes unimpaired object-cathexis. In schizophrenics, on the other hand, we have been obliged to assume that after the process of repression the withdrawn libido does not seek a new object, but retreats into the ego; that is to say, that here the object-cathexes are given up and a primitive objectless condition of narcissism is re-established. The incapacity of these patients for transference..., their consequent inaccessibility to therapeutic efforts, the repudiation of the outer world characteristic of them, the manifestations of hyper-cathexis of their ego, the final outcome in complete apathy—all these clinical features seem to accord excellently with the assumption that object-cathexes are relinquished.[132]

The danger of narcissism, in Freud's view, lay in the fact that, although *self-regard* was essential to health, denial of objects and external reality was dangerous to the organism. Analysis had as its goal the strengthening of the ego for precisely this reason. Narcissism, then, posed a fundamental threat despite its necessary position in the psychic economy. It was, essentially, a return to the utter selfishness of childhood, the source of conflict with external reality. The truth of suffering for Freud

---

[131] *Ibid.*.
[132] "The Unconscious," CP IV, 128-129.

may be summarized in part as the truth of man's inability to live with both his desires and his frustration; and yet he has no alternative. He must live with both. Narcissism simply presents a way of ending the frustration by directing it inwards–and backwards. Therefore it is obviously the fundamental threat, however endemic, to mature life.

This conclusion may be applied to the race as an whole as well as to the individual. Freud observes that the narcissism of the race has recently suffered three major blows, each directly related to the scientific revolution of the modern age. Two of these were well known to Freud and his peers: the discovery that the earth was not the center of the universe "but only a tiny fragment of a cosmic system of unimaginable vastness;" and man himself was but a recent member of the animal family, of an "ineradicable animal nature." But

> human megalomania will have suffered its...most wounding blow from the psychological research of the present time which seeks to prove to the ego that it is not even master in its own house, but must content itself with scanty information of what is going on unconsciously in its mind.[133]

Here Freud, as he did so frequently, extended what he learned of the dynamic forces of the psyche of the individual into the general realm of human culture. The symptoms are centered around a delusion that is closely allied to that fundamental ignorance of which the symptoms already considered are clear indicators to the discerning student. Addressing the ego, Freud declares,

> Turn your eyes inward, look into your own depths, learn first to know yourself! Then you will understand why you were bound to fall ill; and perhaps, you will avoid falling ill in the future.[134]

Although Freud acknowledges that Schopenhauer had already pointed to the dangers of the instincts–which Schopenhauer called the "Will"–if they are underestimated, psychoanalysis has demonstrated two threats to the narcissism of the race, namely the "psychical importance of sexuality and the unconsciousness of mental life," at the level of the individual, and has urged him "to take up some attitude towards these problems."[135]

While narcissism threatens healthy realism, that is, a realistic acknowledgement of the need to balance desire against reality, it also provides, on occasion, a means of ignoring or superseding the perceived reality in a manner that may be beneficial, in that it enables the self to resist being overwhelmed by reality. Freud believes that this function of narcissism underlies humor. He contrasted humor with jokes and the

---

[133] IL, SE XVI, 284-285.
[134] "A Difficulty in Psycho-Analysis," SE XVII, 142, 143.
[135] Ibid., 143-144.

comic. Humor "has something of grandeur and elevation which is lacking in the other two ways [in jokes and the comic] of obtaining pleasure from intellectual activity. The grandeur in it clearly lies in the triumph of narcissism, the victorious assertion of the ego's invulnerability." In this mode the ego refuses to be distressed by reality and its traumas; indeed, it sees them as occasions for gaining pleasure. Humor "is not resigned; it is rebellious." It flaunts the victory of pleasure over reality and frustration.[136]

This very proclamation is, of course, what brings narcissism so close to psychopathology; and humor, in its narcissistic tendency, can look very much like psychosis:

> These last two features–the rejection of the claims of reality and the putting through of the pleasure principle–bring humour near to the regressive or reactionary processes which engage our attention so extensively in psychopathology. Its fending off of the possibility of suffering places it among the great series of the methods which the human mind has constructed in order to evade the compulsion to suffer–a series which begins with neurosis and culminates in madness and which includes intoxication, self-absorption and ecstasy. Thanks to this connection, humour possesses a dignity which is wholly lacking, for instance, in jokes....[137]

What all this suggests is that narcissism is both essential to the balance of the ego's relation to reality and at the same time an almost irresistible threat to the organism's acceptance of reality. Freud never underestimated the threat of narcissism, despite the heroic words concerning its manifestation in humor. He rejected the argument that since harmless sleep is narcissistic in nature it was claiming too much to say that narcissism was a source of neurosis or psychosis. On the contrary, narcissism implies the possibility that the satisfaction of desire in self-love may not be reversed, and the self can lose all touch with objects. Nor does he accept the notion that narcissism identifies the interests of the ego with the desire to discover objects of instinctual impulse. It may appear that this is so, since the suffusion of the ego with libido seems to be a syntonic effect. But closer study of narcissism shows that this view is inconsistent with the history of narcissism:

> It seems that an accumulation of narcissistic libido beyond a certain amount is not tolerated. We may even imagine that it was for that very reason that object-cathexes originally came about, that the ego was obliged to send out its libido so as not

---

[136] "Humour," SE XXI, 162-163.
[137] *Ibid.*.

49

to fall ill as a result of its being dammed up.[138]

Furthermore, in linking pathogenic narcissism to the infantile differentiation between object-love and self-love we must conclude that the narcissistic neuroses have origins very far back in the history of the person, farther back than those evident in either hysteria or obsessional neuroses; that is to say, the narcissistic conflict is pre-Oedipal. One consequence is that the narcissistic illnesses are extremely difficult to treat since they cannot draw upon object-identification in the manner of the transference neuroses.[139] The ideal ego (ego-ideal) was itself established as a means of returning to the primary narcissistic state of which the self had been deprived by many disturbances, especially the ego-censor, the conscious, and the Oedipal relations, which effect identification with model figures. In short the conflict signified by narcissistic illness is not simply between the desires of the id and the needs of the ego but between a state in which there was no ego and one in which there is one. It constitutes a regression to virtually the initial stage of desire, prior to the establishment of a conflict with the external world.[140]

The significance of narcissism lies chiefly in the fact that it shows that human suffering is not simply a conflict between unconscious desires and an external world, but rather between the unconscious desires themselves. If, prior to the discovery of narcissism (Freud points out that we do not discover narcissism except as an implication of mental illness), Freud had established the existence of the unconscious, the weakness of the ego, and the struggle between the world and the desires of the self, it was not until he realized that the ego itself could become an object of libido that he began to identify the extent of the conflict within the self. This lead him to alter his description of the nature of the instincts, so that he drew the line of conflict at the difference between eros and thanatos, the instincts for attachment and withdrawal. The ego itself was, then, to be seen as a seat of conflict, rather than a unified agency. Man emerged as conflict, and remained in conflict, in suffering we may say, and as such was he to be defined. The self was, then, not an entity over against the world, but a dynamic interplay of forces and states constantly endangered by one or more of the powers in the conflict. What the discovery of narcissism contributed to psychoanalysis was a clue to the nature of ego-structure, just as the study of instincts revealed the nature of the id. What it revealed was that the ego, like the id, was properly understood only as dynamic forces in interdependent relationship.[141]

---

[138] IL, SE XVI, 420ff..

[139] *Ibid.*, 420-422.

[140] *Ibid.*, 422-429.

[141] Pictorial representation of the structure of the self, then, is not possible. *Cf. Civilization*, 16-18.

It was not until Freud had proposed his revision of the theory of instincts, especially in *Beyond the Pleasure Principle*, that his description of the phenomenon of masochism was completed. As narcissism suggested that the self could be an object of love, masochism made it quite clear that it could also be the object of hate. In ordinary, that is to say "normal," behavior we are only dimly aware of either of these possibilities of love and hate. We do perceive vaguely that love turns into hate and hate into love. However, in the context of psychoanalytic thought that vague feeling suggests a more precise and general conclusion about the life of the instincts, that we "normally" perceive instinctual drives as fused. For example, sadism and masochism occur as separate phenomena only when they are defused in the neurotic symptoms of people who demand punishment of themselves for acts whose occurrence cannot be ascertained, and whose guilt is by no means evident.

Masochism takes various forms. The first, in chronological order of the development of the infant–and therefore the antecedent of other types–, is what Freud calls a "primal erotogenic" masochism, and is identified with the death instinct.[142] According to this view the original masochism is eventually transferred to an object beyond the self; but a residuum remains, the erotogenic masochism proper, which both has become a component of the libido and has the self as its object.

> This masochism would thus be evidence of, and a remainder from, the phase of development in which the coalescence, which is important for life, between the death instinct and Eros took place. We shall not be surprised to hear that in certain circumstances the sadism, or instinct of destruction, which has been directed outwards, projected, can be once more introjected, turned inwards, and in this way regress to its earlier situation. If this happens, a secondary masochism is produced, which is added to the original masochism.[143]

To this primal erotogenic masochism, which is in fact an introversion of the death instinct, or primary sadism directed against the self, we may add the notion of feminine masochism. This is a name Freud gives to the type of masochism that is actually a perversion incorporating what he persisted in calling "feminine" traits.[144]

Third, Freud observed a "moral" masochism. In the second type, and therefore by extension in the first, the pleasure found in masochism

---

[142] "The Economic Problem of Masochism," SE XIX, 164.
[143] *Ibid.*, 164; *cf. Civilization*, 66.
[144] "Masochism," SE XIX, 165f.. *Cf., e.g.*, "Narcissism," SE XIV, and NIL, SE XXII for traits such as the desire for copulation, binding, castration, and being rendered helpless.

is directly related to the role of a loved one, with clearly defined Oedipal implications. In moral masochism, however, while the Oedipal content is readily evident it has been qualified; for here the specific role of the loved one has fallen away, and the masochism is related solely to the suffering itself. In this instance we confront the fact that neurotics, especially those of the obsessional sort, desire to be punished. This interpretation more clearly describes the condition than the more customary expression that their suffering is due to an unconscious sense of guilt. That this is so is made evident by the clinical observation that the patient's neurotic symptoms tended to disappear when he had placed himself in a punishing situation, when, for example, he entered into an unhappy marriage or disaster befell him.[145]

This need to be punished is in some sense self-imposed. In the structure of the psychic apparatus, the structure of ego, id and super-ego, it is the super-ego that imposes sadistic punishment upon the ego, giving the appearance to external observation of masochistic tendencies and symptoms. The super-ego is the direct heir of the Oedipus complex. In the state of health the super-ego assumes the role of conscience and internalized authority, representing the interests of civilization and external reality to the ego. In the case of illness, however, the super-ego's essentially sexual nature, evident in its Oedipal origin, reappears. One must distinguish at this point, argues Freud, between "moral masochism" and those cases in which the person is morally inhibited to an excessive degree. In the former case the ego submits to the sadism of the conscience, or the super-ego. In the latter case the ego itself is masochistic, that is to say, it actively solicits the punishment of the super-ego. It is easy to confuse the two types since the former makes its character known readily while the latter is quite secretive. Neurotic symptoms found in obsessional neurosis seem at first to be appropriate to the case of moral masochism, but this is not always so. The case of excessive moral inhibition has in fact nothing to do with morality, but is a resexualization of the Oedipus complex. It is a desire to be beaten, to be punished by the father figure in response to imagined (or real, as we shall see) deeds for which the person knows he should be punished. Here the conscience is not in fact present, but has vanished into masochism. The place of the conscience is taken by the sadistic super-ego. The patient, in order to fulfill the sadism of the super-ego, must provoke the punishment of Destiny, that is, the ultimate parental punishment.[146]

The natural threat of the external world, as *Ananke*, can thus be joined with the sadism of the super-ego. This strengthened sadism is complemented by the masochism of the ego. The effects are the same in

---

[145] "Masochism," SE XIX, 165-166.
[146] *Ibid.*, 170.

the patient's response as if he were being punished by the world for past misdeeds. In fact, he is seeking that punishment; for otherwise his guilt, lingering from the Oedipal period and newly resexualized for cause, would not be incorporated into the "reality structure" of his emotional development. It would appear meaningless, and the neurotic knows, above all else, that it is *not* meaningless.

It is only in this way, I think [writes Freud], that we can understand how the suppression of an instinct can–frequently or quite generally–result in a sense of guilt and how a person's conscience becomes more severe and more sensitive the more he refrains from aggression against others....[147]

This in turn means that the need for punishment does not stem from pre-existent ethical norms having been breached; rather, the situation is quite the other way around. One begins with the desires of the self; and it is their vicissitudes that provoke creation of the (derivative) system of ethics.

The first instinctual renunciation is enforced by external powers, and it is only this which creates the ethical sense, which expresses itself in conscience and demands a further renunciation of instinct.[148]

Moral masochism is moral, then, only in the latter instance. For our ethical sense is the product of the vicissitudes of the instincts, of our having been forced by external exigency to renounce and repress them. The ethical sense provides a content of cause and effect that distorts the original case but still provides a context of meaning for our guilt. It is, nonetheless and for all that, moral; and it operates with respect to the instinctual base out of which it arises only insofar as those instincts are fused, to the extent that the death instinct is not separated from eros and directed, in the form of the super-ego, against the ego, awakening the masochism of the ego which has been there from the beginning. The best of all possible worlds, therefore, is one in which the instincts of life and death remain joined or fused together. Only thus can the ego live within the boundaries of a conscience which it must serve.

Psychosis

As we have already noted, Freud's analytic approach to hysteria, obsessional and conversion neuroses suggested that they were in principle susceptible to treatment precisely because they were conflicts between the desires of the self and the need on the part of the ego to control the discharge of those desires in a hostile world. By contrast, the narcissistic neuroses suggested another conflict in which the issue had been joined

---

[147] *Ibid..*
[148] *Ibid..*

53

before the struggle between the ego and the world arose, at the point where it was necessary to end the state of auto-erotism, or primary narcissism, of the infant. Narcissism was in fact a determined attempt to return to that state. The narcissistic self cares not a whit for the world. This state of affairs was conducive to the development of psychosis. Freud was very skeptical about the treatment of psychosis for the reasons suggested in treatment of neuroses. Once again, the pivot of his argument was whether the conflict could be defined as one between the self and the world or wholly within the self. Psychoanalysis, he said, is really useful only in the first instance. But this was not his final word.

Freud was indebted, as he pointed out in his *Introductory Lectures*, to Karl Abraham's research on *dementia praecox*, a psychosis, for the conclusion that libido is directed toward the self as well as objects. When libido is directed solely toward the self the result is megalomania.[149] This condition is of course narcissistic. The characteristics of this self-directed desire were directly analogous to normal erotic life with respect to any love-object. Narcissism, which Freud called "the universal and original state of things, from which object-love is only later developed, without narcissism necessarily disappearing on that account," is therefore linked directly to a psychotic condition.[150]

Following the publication of *The Ego and The Id*, Freud expanded his discussion of psychosis as a crisis of the self which has lost contact with reality, thereby distinguishing it from neurosis. The genetic difference between a neurosis and a psychosis is that *"neurosis is the result of a conflict between the ego and its id, whereas psychosis is the analogous outcome of a similar disturbance in the relations between the ego and the external world."*[151] The clinical manifestation of psychosis was radical or acute hallucinatory confusion; either the world was not perceived at all, or the perception of it had no effect whatsoever upon the patient's choices. Normally, Freud thought, the ego directs the responses of the psyche using, first, present perceptions which are always renewable, and second, the "store of memories" of earlier perceptions which have become the possession of the ego, *i.e.* an "internal" world. However, in psychosis–for example in *amentia*–

[n]ot only is the acceptance of new perceptions refused, but the internal world, too, which as a copy of the external world, has up till now represented it, loses its significance.... The ego creates, autocratically, a new external and internal world; and there can be no doubt of two facts–that this new world is constructed in accordance with the id's wishful impulses, and the motive of

---

[149] IL, SE XVI, 415-416.
[150] *Ibid.*.
[151] "Neurosis and Psychosis," SE XIX, 149.

this dissociation from the external world is some very serious frustration by reality of a wish–a frustration which seems intolerable. The close affinity of this psychosis to normal dreams is unmistakable. A precondition of dreaming, moreover, is a state of sleep, and one of the features of sleep is a complete turning away from perception of the external world.[152]

Like sleep, then, there are psychotic elements in our mental life, and certainly in the course of any person's behavior. The demands of reality upon the ego are, from time to time, simply insupportable for most of us. Whether this situation leads to psychosis, says Freud, depends very much upon economic considerations, that is "the relative magnitude of the trends which are struggling with one another."[153] A "splitting" of the ego may occur under these conditions, in which the ego may allow and suffer encroachments upon its unity. The "inconsistencies, eccentricities and follies of man," would, then, be the result of such splitting, revealing "more than one mind" to the observer. They would appear, he argues, in a form similar to sexual perversions because, like the acceptance of sexual perversions such as fetishism, they obviate the need for repression.[154]

This experience of the loss of reality, however, is implied even in the neurotic conflict between the id and the ego. At first the ego represses the demands of the instincts. But if the repression effects an unsupportable distress a decreasing sense of reality becomes evident, and the neurosis moves in the direction of psychosis. It does so when precisely that piece of reality whose suppression has been the work of the ego is lost, and in whose place the symptomatic substitutions occur. It is not yet psychosis; but a piece of reality has in fact been lost, and repressed.[155] The condition becomes psychotic when another reality altogether is constructed. Instead of fleeing, as in neurosis, the psychotic builds a world which his instincts will allow him to inhabit. In both instances the id refuses to adapt itself to *Ananke*, harsh reality.[156]

Neurosis avoids, psychosis rebuilds. Yet we note in the restructuring work of psychosis a valuable tool of civilization. Indeed, Freud argues[157] that neurosis and psychosis provide two opposing but complementary elements of the ideal man:

> We call behaviour "normal" or "healthy," if it combines certain features of both reactions–if it disavows the reality as little as does a neurosis, but if it then exerts itself, as does a psychosis,

---

[152] *Ibid.*, 150-151.

[153] *Ibid.*, 152f..

[154] *Ibid.*.

[155] "The Loss of Reality in Neurosis and Psychosis," SE XIX, 183.

[156] *Ibid.*, 184f..

[157] *Cf.* "Libidinal Types," SE XXI.

to effect an alteration of that reality. Of course, this expedient, normal behaviour leads to work being carried out on the external world; it does not stop, as in psychosis, at effecting internal changes. It is no longer *autoplastic* but *alloplastic.*[158]

The internal alteration of the world carried out by psychosis works with the "store of memories" which was the possession of the ego, that internal world which replicated in the mental life the external model from which it was derived. However psychosis is not content with remodeling the present house, but adds new material which it derives from other sources, constantly expanding and decorating the mental quarters. This new material is derived not from observation, perception and reception of stimuli from external reality but from delusions and hallucinations. Further, it is known that this construction of the psychotic world view is marked by anxiety. We have seen that anxiety is both a sign of the forward movement of instinctual impulse and a defense against that impulse and its consequences. The impulse that is the cause of the anxiety has already undergone repression, as we noted, and thus threatens continually to return, to the detriment of the ego.

The presence of anxiety in the psychotic's world-building activities indicates, then, that his delusions and hallucinations are strongly linked to repressed material which is regarded as dangerous and requires repression. Freud concludes, "probably in a psychosis the rejected piece of reality constantly forces itself upon the mind, just as the repressed instinct does in a neurosis, and that is why in both cases the consequences too are the same."[159] In sum, the difference between neurosis and psychosis may be seen in the question of whether the ego remains faithful to its fundamental task of representing reality to the id, or whether it yields entirely to its true originating source, the id. If the latter is the case, the ego cannot represent reality, however feebly, cannot seek to assess the consequences of discharging impulses in the real world, but seeks to build a world that has but one master, the id.[160]

While both neurosis and psychosis "reserve" a domain "which became separated from the real external world at the time of the introduction of the reality principle," in psychosis the fantasy intends to replace the whole of the objectionable reality, and in neurosis the fantasy attaches itself to a piece of reality, which in time becomes "symbolic" of the fantasy. It is not only a question of the loss of reality but of a "substitute" for reality.[161] For the psychotic the substitution consists entirely of the fantasy, while for the neurotic the fantasy attaches to a piece of real expe-

---

[158] *Ibid.*.
[159] *Ibid.*, 186.
[160] *Ibid.*, 186-187.
[161] *Ibid.*, 187.

rience, giving it the status both of symbol and of anchor–however poorly set–in the world.

Freud's conclusion concerning the difference between neurosis and psychosis, that in psychosis the ego was cut off from external reality, was reviewed and partially altered by him in light of his work on fetishism. Fetishism establishes a means of denying external reality, here the highly threatening absence of the penis in women, by substituting another, "token," penis which in fact is not a penis to anyone but the fetishist. According to this view of psychosis the fetishist must be psychotic. However, Freud knew that fetishism does not have the signs of psychosis in those who practice it. Furthermore, he had come to know of cases that should have been psychotic but were not, in which the death of a father had been categorically denied–the father had in fact died–by someone who was clearly not psychotic, that is, was not cut off from reality in general. Further analysis of these cases showed that the death of the father was *both* accepted *and* denied, as though two "currents" existed in the patient's mind. We have here, said Freud, an indication that there are two attitudes which exist side by side: "[t]he attitude which fitted in with the wish [the wish that the father had not died] and the attitude which fitted in with the reality." In other words, a split had taken place in the ego. Nevertheless, Freud's fundamental understanding of the nature of psychosis remained in place, that in a psychotic situation the attitude consistent with the reality was absent.[162]

But a splitting of the ego that made it possible to deny significant sectors of reality and not become psychotic was observed. Freud took up this issue again in his unfinished and posthumously published paper, "Splitting of the Ego in the Process of Defence." The paper examines the case of a boy who displaced his fear of castration as punishment for masturbation onto a fetish, which served as a replacement for the presumably lost female penis–a state of affairs he takes as a warning against masturbation. (In this case he could not bear to have his little toes touched.) The implication here is that a highly significant reality has been denied for erotic reasons, and the distortion of circumstances has been carried to a radical conclusion, that is, the boy finds a fetish. However, since the boy continued to masturbate, one must conclude that an instinctual desire is being satisfied regardless of a threat from the external world (the complex of father-castration-evidence of female anatomy), and at the same time a symptom characteristic of neurotic avoidance has formed, the appearance of a fetish. Freud was drawn to try to explain these phenomena in terms of a splitting of ego-functions–one working for the id (masturbation), one working for the external world (the fetish, a distorted representation of reality). It seemed possible for the ego both to deny external reality and

---

[162] "Fetishism," SE XXI, 155-156.

to represent it in a manner that would substitute a symptom which, however much it obscured the reality, also revealed it in the manner of all symptoms.[163]

But in the end we must respect Freud's fundamental position on the psychosis: that it is a much more serious illness than neurosis precisely because it rests upon a radical denial of external reality, and seeks to substitute its own world of delusion and fantasy to the detriment of the balanced ego structure.[164]

Mourning and Transience

The separation of the ego from the external world assumes special poignancy when the beloved is removed forever from its grasp. Since this is the most common of all human moments, the fact that it is painful, and perhaps even conducive to self-destruction, makes this separation utterly significant for the truth of suffering. The death of those whom we love is so fraught with distress that our immediate response is rejection. This rejection may eventually take the form of some notion of immortality; in any event it is in essence the denial of death. It is therefore also denial of the ultimate transience of all things. In reflecting on this crucial issue Freud moved along a number of paths. He raised the general question of the rejection of death and transience inherent in religion and in beliefs in immortality, in mourning, and in the neurosis of melancholia.

In a brief and powerfully simple essay, "Transience," which begins with a report of a conversation with a poet just before the outbreak of the Great War, Freud writes:

> But this demand for immortality is a product of our wishes too unmistakable to lay claim to reality: what is painful may nonetheless be true. I could not see my way to dispute the transience of all things, nor could I insist upon an exception in favour of what is beautiful and perfect. But I did dispute the pessimistic poet's view that the transience of what is beautiful involves any loss in its worth.[165]

On the contrary, the very evanescent nature of things enhances the enjoyment of them, just as the blossom which disappears overnight is seen for that reason to be the more beautiful. But more important was the evident fact that the significance of these transient things lay in their role in our emotional lives. The fear of separation, transience, and the pain of death would never arise if this were not so:

---

[163] "Splitting," SE XXIII, 275-278.

[164] Cf.: NIL, SE XXII, 136-157; Moses and Monotheism: Three Essays, SE XXIII, 76; An Outline of Psychoanalysis, tr. James Strachey (New York: W. W. Norton & Co., 1949), 62, 63, 108, 114.

[165] "Transience," SE XIV, 305.

...since the value of all this beauty and perfection is determined only by its significance for our own emotional lives, it has no need to survive us and is therefore independent of absolute duration.[166]

The pessimistic poet was unable to focus clearly on the central issue of transience and mourning, namely the emotional crisis of the self. The plants and the people are not in themselves significant except insofar as they are loved—and we are not significant to them except insofar as they love us.[167] Freud thus identifies the suffering that is attached to transience with the emotional life, and not with anything else. It is the activity of libido, whether attached to objects or whether it takes the ego itself as an object, that determines the presence of distress at the passing of all things. Thus, later in the same essay, when Freud summarizes the situation during and after the Great War, as the fond hopes and institutions of pre-war Europe lay in ruins, he assigns the cause of the sense of profound dismay not to the fact of their destruction but to our commitment to them as indications of our worth, our self-esteem, that is to say, our narcissism. They had no other significance. Their loss was in fact a loss of illusion.

In contrast, Freud calls mourning the mature acknowledgement of death and transience. This state is to be distinguished from melancholia, to which we shall shortly turn. Mourning is nothing less than the healthy recognition of transience through the act of mourning the death of a particular loved one. Thus the world that remains retains its value despite the undeniable truth that it, too, is perishable. Those who take this view of things can enter into a state of mourning because they "seem ready to make a permanent renunciation."[168] When mourning comes to its "spontaneous" end and consumes itself, renouncing the object that is lost, the libido is free once again either to find another object or to return to itself. One may love again; and we shall fall ill if we fail to love. A civilization, like a person, can be rebuilt or replaced—though it too is transient. Yet love can continue, and that is what must happen if we are to live.

The fact of death is fundamental. Yet we are extremely reluctant to learn it. Freud pointed out that our attitude toward death is quite complex. For example, the death of an enemy is greeted with glee, of a loved one with grief. Yet the relationship with the loved one has always been ambivalent, an expression of fused instinctual impulses. Freud saw in the history of the individual and of the race both love and hate directed toward loved ones, in the first instance the parents. The rise of the

---

[166] *Ibid.*, 306.
[167] *Ibid.*, 307.
[168] *Ibid.*.

notion of life after death—whether in the form of belief in spirits, ancestor-worship, gods or the immortality of the soul—amounted to a denial of the death of a loved one. When the fact is denied, there can be no guilt; and the essential child-parent relationships can continue in some form.[169]

But of course this denial of death or, more commonly, the fear of death, is finally explicable in terms of the aetiology of the neuroses, rather than as a learned reaction; for the unconscious, like primitive man, ac-knowledges nothing of death. Only the ego suspects that death could be its fate if it does not maintain repression, even in the form of symptoms and neuroses if necessary. For the fear of death is in fact the fear that we shall be destroyed by those closest to us. When they die, we are relieved; yet we are guilty of wishing them dead. They protected us and served as models for us, and thus we loved them. We grieve, then, because we are guilty.

But our intelligence and our conscious feelings reject straightaway any ambivalence toward those whom we love and who have died. The unconscious truth comes to us distorted, if at all, and we insist upon hav-ing loved them always. Our conscious view is, taken alone, not a healthy one; for it asserts an emotional state that never existed. Moreover, since it denies the truth of ambivalent feelings, it prevents us from accepting the irrevocable fact of death. Nature, however, says Freud, has carried out a fusion of love and hate in the unconscious for the purpose of keeping the possibility of love ever present and makes it possible for us to escape our self-deception by loving again.[170] Further, we are probably living beyond our psychological means—an economic expression useful to Freud throughout his work—when we do not give death the "place in reality" it actually owns. It is both pointless and ignoble to ignore death; for one must, finally, accept the truth. An illusion is no help if it makes life harder for us. The illusion of immortality attempts precisely that, as it manifests neurotic wishes. "To tolerate life remains, after all, the first duty of all living beings.... If you want to endure life, prepare yourself for death."[171]

Yet it is evident that not all are prepared to renounce belief in the imperishability of all things and enter mourning—and then love again. Rather melancholia, the neurotic response to death and transience, is more common. Freud's metapsychological explanation of melancholia, in which the ego itself is the object of sadism and can lead to suicide in its final stage, returns to the notion of libidinal attachment, or cathexis. Mourning frees libido for attachment either to another love object or to

---

[169] "Thoughts on War and Death: II. Our Attitude Toward Death," SE XIV, 291-295.
[170] Ibid., 299.
[171] Ibid., 299-300.

the ego itself. In the case of both mourning and melancholia, the discovery of the loss of the love object requires the person to withdraw all libido from this object. The distress of both mourning and melancholia is due in part to an extreme reluctance to abandon the attachment; "it may be universally observed that man never willingly abandons a libido-position, not even when a substitute is already beckoning to him."[172] Reluctance may turn into a struggle of such intensity that the ego's relationship with reality is threatened by its attempt to cling to the object, even by hallucination. In the case of mourning reality wins out, and the loved object is released.[173]

In the case of melancholia there is a different result. Instead of withdrawal of libido from one loved object and transference to another, or instead of withdrawal of libido into the ego prior to redirection, the withdrawn libido is attached to the ego in such a way as to identify the ego with the abandoned object. The ego now becomes an object of criticism and attack, as though it were the abandoned object. Such an object is regarded with considerable ambivalence: "the conflict between the ego and the loved person [is] transformed into a cleavage between the criticizing faculty of the ego and the ego as altered by identification."[174] By its nature melancholia tends toward destruction of the ego. Yet from the first the primal libidinal situation is that of narcissism. How is the narcissistic commitment of libido to the ego, which would protect the ego at all costs, overcome in melancholia? How could it be that one would contemplate, to say nothing of execute, the act of suicide? This, nevertheless, is the fact for this illness. In the event, narcissism is not overcome; rather in melancholia the ego becomes the object of ambivalent feelings arising from the loss of the loved one. It attracts the animus properly directed toward the lost object. The situation is analogous to the state of being in love, in which the ego is depleted by the extension of its libido to the loved object. In both cases, being in love and melancholia, the object is stronger than the ego but for, of course, very different reasons.[175]

In other terms, melancholia is a condition in which the lost love-object is not released but maintained—at great cost—in the economy of the self. It is a delusion and a neurosis. Both melancholia and mourning signify the distress and suffering asociated with transience and the fact of death in the emotional life of the ego. Neither annihilates transience and suffering; but whereas melancholia falsely denies death and is thus an illness, mourning acknowledges it and is therefore not an illness. The truth of suffering is the first step on the path to release from suffering;

---

[172] "Mourning and Melancholia," CP IV, 154.
[173] Ibid..
[174] Ibid., 159.
[175] Ibid., 162-163.

and the failure, usually willful in an unconscious sense, to acknowledge that truth is surely part of the cause of suffering.

Transference

The causal relationship between the recognition of the truth or fact of illness and its cure is especially clear in Freud's analysis of the phenomenon of transference. My aim here is to show the phenomenon as a neurosis, but it will be seen that it is also the crux of the therapeutic program. Indeed, as Freud often remarks, if transference is not possible therapy is very likely impossible.[176]

The announcement of the analyst to the patient of the fundamental rule of therapy, that the patient must say whatever comes into his mind, is often greeted with silence. That, however, is a response; for it is a repetition of his mental history, or at least a beginning of it. He is both resisting the command to reveal what is in his mental life, that is, to see it consciously, and thus also identifying the point at which the analyst must begin his work. Analysis can proceed only so long as the patient is compelled to remember, to repeat, to work through his mental history, thus bringing what is unconscious into consciousness.

In this therapeutic process, however, remembering eventually becomes more and more difficult. Resistance is increasingly evident, and remembrance is replaced by repetition, that is, a form of living through again the events that are crucial to the present emotional condition. But this process is difficult, even painful; for the patient does not wish to repeat those events, despite any theoretical knowledge he may have about the need to do so. The resistance to returning becomes greater the closer one is to the repressed material, as we have seen. Resistance, therefore, is an essential tool in the hands of the analyst; for it marks the point of departure in the central stage of the analysis.[177]

When resistance has been encountered, the analyst can be certain that the transference phenomenon is likely to occur in the near future of the treatment. Resistances, as Freud describes them, are attempts to maintain the state of emotional affairs in which the ego has managed to repress libido and frustrate its satisfaction. It acts like a defense mechanism for the ego, lest the repressed material rise and threaten the entire organism. Thus resistances mark the repressed libidinal material which is the most powerful and sensitive element of the neurosis. As the analysis proceeds to investigate the neurotic symptoms and approaches the unconscious root cause of this substitute behavior the resistance strengthens perceptibly: "a region is entered in which the resistance is so strong that a compromise must be made between its demands and those of analy-

---

[176] Cf., e.g., IL, SE XVI, 437-447.
[177] "Remembering," SE XII, 150-151.

sis."[178]

It is at this point [says Freud]...that transference enters on the scene. When anything in the complexive material (in the subject matter of the complex) is suitable for being transferred on to the figure of the doctor, that transference is carried out; it produces the next association, and announces itself by indications of a resistance–by a stoppage, for instance. We infer from this experience that the transference-ideal has penetrated into consciousness in front of any other possible associations *because* it satisfies the resistance.[179]

However, although the resistance is successful in the sense that the material is still protected in its "native setting," so to speak, in the inner self, nevertheless that material is transferred to the consciousness by attachment not to the self but to the analyst. By this transition what was unconscious is now become conscious. This pivotal point in the therapy brings the repressed material into the open so that it can be overcome, that is to say, so that it no longer operates as repressed but as expressed material. The treatment instantly becomes more pertinent. Every such conflict, says Freud, must be found out in transference.[180]

Transference signifies neurotic behavior, even delusion; for the attachment to the analyst of the emotions repressed within the self means that the patient will ignore the true identity of the physician, a piece of reality, and substitute another piece of reality holding a much higher emotional "charge." Transference is part of the neurosis. It is also as complex as neurotic behavior is in general. The transference phenomenon, for example, will probably be a highly positive experience at first for the analyst. The positive, loving feelings which in reality attach to another person crucial to the emotional life of the patient now attach to him. The physician should of course beware, warns Freud, of responding to such emotional attachment–this is the phenomenon of counter-transference. But more important for the analysis is the fact that so long as the transference remains positive and productive it has not yet reached the stage at which the most repressed material is made conscious. Friendly feelings, says Freud, are invariably erotic.[181] It is no different with positive transference. What makes the analysis proceed so swimmingly is in fact the same erotic drive that is at the source of the neurosis and at the heart of the repressed material. We must now return to the link between resistance and transference. If the transference is positive, why is it linked to resistance? For transference would not take place if it

---

[178] "The Dynamics of Transference," SE XII, 102.
[179] *Ibid.*.
[180] *Ibid.*, 105; *cf.* IL, SE XVI, 286-291, 294.
[181] *Ibid.*, 105.

did not satisfy a resistance, and a "hiding" of the emotional life. The answer is that the positive transference is a function of the resistance; and therefore it is only when the transference becomes negative, when the patient takes a patently hostile view of the analysis and the analyst that transference becomes valuable for therapy. It is also helpful to the analysis if the transference is positive but understood as an expression of repressed erotic impulses. In the successful analysis the repressed material becomes conscious through this transference of it–as a satisfaction of resistance at first and then as a defeat of resistance–to the person of the doctor. Freud suggests that then it may be possible to begin to "remove the transference by making it conscious," and to separate the negative or positive feelings which are repressed erotic impulses from the person of the doctor. The analysis proceeds, very likely, to its conclusion, to the benefit of the patient.[182]

The importance of transference and resistance for the theory and therapy of psychoanalysis cannot be overestimated. It suggests the nature of the neurotic diseases, a means of cure, and the role of the analyst virtually all at once. In an early history of the psychoanalytic movement Freud wrote that the theory of psychoanalysis was developed in order to explain just these two striking and unexpected facts.[183] Thus Freud was easily able to identify his opponents by their failure to recognize their objections to his theories, notably those having to do with the repressed material *par excellence*, infantile sexuality, as resistances. So the doctors and the scientists, on the one hand, insisted that the mental diseases arose from biological, somatic causes; and on the other philosophers argued that one should find mental phenomena only in the conscious mind, and that the notion of unconscious ideas was a contradiction in terms.

What in fact was happening in this academic debate was what was happening in analysis, namely that the patient offered resistances to exposing the repressed material. However in the case of both doctors and philosophers, and society in general, the resistance was intended to carry out the work of the ego in repressing the instincts and their persistent struggle for satisfaction. Resistance to analysis amounted to active rejection of the offer to participate in curing oneself, much as the patient is increasingly reluctant to address himself to his past. Society, and the conscious but neurotic patient, care little about the cost of this repression, only that it be successful. Society's resistances indicate that it will force the individual to live beyond his psychological means, to repress his libidinal power no matter what the cost. The result is neurotic symptoms. But, as we have seen, the ego will tolerate these symptoms rather

---

[182] *Ibid.*; *cf.* IL, SE XVI, 437-447.
[183] "History," SE XIV, 16-17.

than risk the discharge of instinctual impulses.[184]

---

[184] "Resistances," SE XIX, 213-219, 221.

Individual and Collective Suffering

The focus of this presentation of Freud's first truth, the truth of suffering, has been the mental life and condition of the individual. This is only proper, since the symptoms and illness with which Freud was concerned manifested themselves in the lives of individuals whom he treated. But he could not fail tó investigate in depth the influence of the external world, and especially the cultural context with its institutional and moral pressures. That investigation led him to consider in more abstract terms the artifacts, institutions, and general structures of civilization in light of what he had learned from his patients. He concluded that the illnesses of the individual were also to be found at large in society. He meant that the social forces and institutions which form the pillars and caryatids of our civilized superstructure were to the discerning eye manifestations of the fundamental underlying conflict between the conscious and the unconscious that defines human existence. There was, as he made clear in *Group Psychology and the Analysis of the Ego*, no social motivation or instinctual impulse that was not also individual. The study of society was in truth the study of social psychology–and even that expression is not very helpful. There are, he said, only two sciences: (1) psychology (pure and applied); (2) natural science.[185] We shall now explore what Freud believed about the institutions of society in exemplary areas. But it should be quite clear that what he is describing in each instance is distress, suffering, discontent. He was not won over by either the Enlightenment notion that man is essentially good and his institutions evil, or the communistic notion that institutions are essentially good and it is the pernicious drive for individual freedom that encourages corruption and oppression.[186]

As suggested, Freud was acutely sensitive to the effects on the mental economy of civilization's restrictions on behavior, that is, on the discharging of instinctual impulses. The individual must repress his sexuality, with the exception of activity obviously related to reproduction. Moreover, civilization required that the individual live "beyond his psychological means" in the name of ethical behavior. But ethics, argues Freud, initially has nothing to do with the matter. Ethics arose in response to instinctual conflict, as a secondary "explanation" for the repression of instincts effected by the ego.

Ethics is a "therapeutic attempt," an endeavor to accomplish something which has not yet been achieved by means of any other cultural activities. Indeed, the demands of ethics replicate in severity the demands of the individual super-ego, against which psychoanalysis is often forced to struggle, as in cases of melancholia. So it is for the cultural

---

[185] NIL, SE XXII, 179; *cf. Civilization*, 86ff..
[186] *Cf. Civilization*, 59ff..

super-ego.

It, too, does not trouble itself enough about the facts, the mental constitution of human beings. It issues a command and does not ask whether it is possible for people to obey it. On the contrary, it assumes that a man's ego is psychologically capable of anything that is required of it, that his ego has unlimited mastery over id.... If more is demanded of a man, a result will be produced in him or a neurosis, or he will be made unhappy. The commandment, "Love thy neighbour as thyself," is the strongest defence against human aggressiveness and an excellent example of the unpsychological proceedings of the cultural super-ego.[187]

The ethical structures of civilization serve largely, then, to provide a context for the sadism of the super-ego and the masochism of the ego. Civilization may believe that proper behavior arises from the self-evident truth of ethical systems. Even as it compels behavior it believes that its "good" is also "true." But the resulting behavior has nothing to do with the good or the true, although certain self-restraints seem to have been imposed. The results of both collective and individual systems of repression (although, indeed, only one is really operating on the mental life of the self) are ambiguous:

> only a particular concatenation of circumstances will reveal that one man always acts in a good way because his instinctual inclinations compel him to, and the other is good only in so far and for so long as such cultural behaviour is advantageous for his own selfish purpose.[188]

But in general we shall not be able to tell the difference.[189] We must look beyond the ethical standards, customs and structures of society for an explanation of our behavior and our illnesses. Freud is very straightforward about where we should go: to the analysis of the self and the psychic economy. "The contrast beyond Individual Psychology and Social or Group Psychology, which at first glance may seem to be full of significance, loses a great deal of its sharpness when it is examined more closely."[190] More specifically, the distinction between the study of the individual's relationship with his parents, his brothers and sisters, his physical and his narcissistic experiences may be accepted: "but the contrast between social narcissistic mental acts...falls wholly within the domain of Individual

---

[187] *Ibid.*, 89-90.
[188] "Thoughts: I.," SE XIV, 283-284.
[189] *Ibid.*.
[190] *Group Psychology and the Analysis of the Ego*, tr. James Strachey, *The International Psycho-analytical Library*, no. 6, ed. Ernest Jones (London: International Psycho-analytical Press, 1927), 1.

Psychology, and is not well calculated to differentiate it from a Social or Group Psychology."[191]

In analyzing the structure of groups Freud addresses the theory that there is a dynamic characteristic of group structure and behavior that is absent from the dynamic of the self. Turning to representative groups, church and army, he illustrates that this is a dubious notion, and that indeed the dynamic of the group is not simply an exact replica of the dynamic of the self in relation to its parts and the external world, but another version of that dynamic.[192] What, then, of the wide-spread belief that in both church and army, and indeed all groups, the relationship of the individuals therein to each other is a uniquely determined equality under the headship of the leader? It is an illusion; and one upon which everything depends. The leader "stands to the individual members of the group of believers in the relation of a kind of elder brother; he is their father surrogate."[193] Indeed, the problem for any group is how to equip itself with the attributes of the individual, "which are extinguished in the individual by the formation of the group. The surrender to the group of the individual's own peculiar inhibitions upon his instincts must, then, be compensated for; the group must take on precisely the characteristics of the individual's inhibitions. It does so in the person of the leader."[194] The leader occupies the father's place in the economy of the individual. He serves, then, as the ego-ideal with which the individual identifies himself; he molds his own ego after the fashion of the one that has been taken as a " 'model.' "[195]

The Oedipal language suggests libidinal ties among the members of the group and with the father-surrogate which are productive of the same emotional states noted in individual psychic organization:

> We already begin to divine that the mutual tie between members of a group is in the nature of an identification [of the ego with the Oedipal object], based upon an important emotional common quality; and we may suspect that this common quality lies in the nature of the tie with the leader.[196]

This libidinal attachment shares many elements with the psychologically fascinating state of being in love. Freud defines this state metapsychologically by saying that libido flows out of the ego to the object to such an extent that even that reserve of narcissistic affection kept for the ego

---

[191] *Ibid.*, 2.
[192] *Cf. ibid.*, 3, 42ff. *et passim*; *The Future of an Illusion*, tr. and ed. James Strachey (New York: W. W. Norton & Co., 1961), 69ff..
[193] *Group Psychology*, 42, 43.
[194] *Ibid.*, 31-33.
[195] *Ibid.*, 63; *cf.* 102.
[196] *Ibid.*, 66; *cf.* 54.

is projected on to the loved object. This projection takes the form of sexual overvaluation, although in most less intimate instances the sensual aspect is made to appear "spiritual," and the object is said to be valued for its intrinsic merits rather than its sensual charm; but there is reason to suspect that this is a distortion of the lover's feelings.[197]

In group ties, then, the idealization and overvaluation of the leader and the depletion of the ego's self-regard resemble very closely the state of being in love. Yet the situation is not one of distress but of satisfaction. Freud explains this by arguing that the feelings directed toward the object, or the group leader, are the feelings normally associated with the ego, and therefore have not ceased to be narcissistic but rather seek in this round-about way to satisfy their aim by loving the ego in the form of the externalized ideal. This is especially so if the ideal had been sought and missed.[198]

Hypnosis provided Freud with another analogy of the group libidinal tie, especially with respect to the question of the ego-ideal. In the group and in being in love, the ego has been replaced, or displaced, by an object. That object serves as the ego-ideal; and since it is an object it attracts libido normally reserved for the ego and accordingly depletes and replaces the ego. This is, in short, ego surrender. In hypnosis a similar replacement of the ego-ideal has taken place, in the person of the hypnotist. As with the group libidinal tie and being in love, there is the same humble subjection, "...the same absence of criticism," towards the hypnotist as towards the loved object. The hypnotist has taken the place of the ego-ideal.[199] On the other hand, what distinguishes the libidinal nature of group ties from both being in love and hypnosis is that the group adds to the replacement of the ego-ideal by the object/leader the identification with other individuals. This is made possible originally by these individuals having the same relation to the object. Thus the libidinal ties of the group are the original and definitive sources of the concepts of fraternity and equality.[200]

Freud's understanding of the nature of group ties is of course entirely controlled by his view of the Oedipus complex and of the concomitant theory of the origins of the group, which we shall investigate elsewhere. What is significant is that group ties are libidinal in nature, they are extensions of, distortions of and variations on the ambivalent relationship between the child and the parent, and are recapitulations of the individual's psychic history as well as that of the race. From the very beginning of history there was the "Superman whom Nietzsche only expected from

---

[197] *Ibid.*, 74; *cf.* "Narcissism," SE XIV, 76.
[198] *Group Psychology*, 74; *cf.* 75f..
[199] *Ibid.*, 77.
[200] *Ibid.*, 125.

the future."[201] The members of the group required that he love them equally but he requires no love at all, for his libido is entirely satisfied in the consummate narcissism which is his prime, and primal, characteristic. The demand for equal love in the group is a distortion of the past, an "idealistic remodelling" that transposes equal fear of the father into equal love by him.[202]

This conflict in misty pre-history is repeated by the ego just as it is played out in the history of groups—and for exactly the same reasons. For the relationship between the ego and its ideal, which was developed out of the ego's history, is in principle the same relationship, for good or ill, whether the scene is played between the ego and an external object or within the dynamic of the ego itself. In other words, the dynamic is the same both for relations between the ego and the world and within the ego itself.[203] The difference between these options is illustrated in the difference between the church and army; in the latter case the barrier between the soldier and the general is maintained although the libidinal tie exists and operates in the manner described. In the case of the (Christian) church the believer must in the end identify himself with Christ, so that the libidinal relationship is played out within the context of the ego, in loving Christ as Christ loved him, and in loving others as Christ loved them. Despite the distinction, however, one matter is clear: the group's coherence depends upon the fact that it is a version and an extension of the primal child-parent relationship.[204]

Freud amplified his analysis of neurosis with respect to both group and individual in *Moses and Monotheism* on the basis of his earlier analysis of group libidinal ties. The cause of neurosis is pre-eminently libidinal; that is to say, it is the struggle between the sexual desires of the infantile period and the repression effected by the ego. In *Moses and Monotheism* Freud presents what some regard as a bizarre explanation for the emergence of the Hebrew-Jewish-Christian tradition, and indeed for Western religion as an whole (nor did he omit Eastern religions). If, however, we focus our attention upon the psychoanalytic significance of his argument his position on social behavior and culture gains more clarity.

The entire story of *Moses and Monotheism* is that of the return of the repressed. The repressed material in question is, as one can imagine, highly convoluted and distorted by the time it appears in the historical record—which functions as a defense mechanism of the ego in the context of social identity. The repressed contents that we are accustomed to investigating in the history of the individual must now be illustrated in

---

[201] *Ibid.*, 77ff..
[202] *Ibid.*, 94-95.
[203] *Cf. ibid.*, 103.
[204] *Ibid.*, 111.

the history of Western civilization. Freud states quite clearly his belief that the contents of the mental life investigated in *Moses and Monotheism* are attributable to an archaic heritage shared by all. This heritage consists not merely of symbols apparent to a comparative study of linguistic usages and dream symbols but of the legacy of historical, "actual," circumstances and events. We speak not of symbolization only, but of memory of an event. Freud argues that the content of neuroses in general cannot be explained solely by reference to traumatic experiences of the individual. They must be due in part, he insists, to phylogeny; and that can only mean that the Oedipal themes of childhood, so prominent in the neuroses, were residues of actual historical events. If that is the case, then it follows that there is no fundamental difference between neuroses, based on the Oedipal experience, in the group and in the individual. They are the same thing.[205] In sum, says Freud, "[i]n my opinion there is an almost complete conformity in this respect between the individual and the group: in the group too an impression of the past is retained in unconscious memory-traces."[206]

Given the identification between individual and group we shall not be surprised to discover that the discontents of civilization are precisely those of the individual, and respond to the same diagnosis and therapy–if they respond at all. The significance of this conclusion has long been recognized in the context of the discussion about social ills and reform–and bitterly opposed. But if one is to understand Freud's notion of suffering rightly, this collapse of the distinction between individual and social psychology can only mean that all suffering is individual suffering; and to take any other view, such as that man suffers because of the world about him, the society which he constructs, the forces which wear him down–that if left to his own devices he would simply cease to suffer–contradicts what we know about our own feelings, and, very likely, is a delusion whose intentions are all too clear. Society's ills are not causes of our ills; they are expressions of them. The discontent of civilization is our discontent, as individuals. To whom else, to what else, would they belong?

Civilization

We should not, then, be surprised to learn that the hero of civilization is the one whose inner conflicts do not dissolve but rather are the cause of his "heroic" behavior. The civilized person, in short, epitomizes his discontent by and in his heroism. Such is the conclusion of Freud's first examination of the figure of Moses (quite literally a figure), that of the "Moses" of Michaelangelo. Moses is seated, facing left, his beard drawn towards his right side by the right forefinger, which is pulling in turn a part of the left-handed side of the beard well over to the right. The

---

[205] *Moses*, SE XXIII, 92-102.
[206] *Ibid.*, 94.

Tables of the Law are upside down, resting on one of their corners. Moses' left foot is up on its toes. The figure is in an arrested act of conflicted movement.

Freud describes this arrested movement as the end of a motion occasioned by three successive events which mark one of the supreme moments of Moses' life, the return from Sinai with the Tablets of the Law. First, Moses has become aware of the blasphemy and idolatry (the worship of the golden calf) being perpetrated by the Israelites at the moment when he is about to reveal the Law to them. Second, in extreme anger he has seized his beard with his right hand but in the process risks dropping, and almost does drop, the Tablets. Third, at the very last moment, aware of the danger to the Tablets, he squeezes the falling Tablets to his side with his right arm, just managing to arrest their descent. As a secondary effect only the longest and uppermost finger of the right hand remains in contact with the beard.

In short, Moses has been depicted at the instant in which he masters his rage and becomes the hero of culture, the role in which he is known to us. Freud is aware that this interpretation is not wholly consistent with scripture. The passage in question[207], however, is rife with conflation, overlapping, and contradiction and is a formidable challenge to interpretation. In the much later *Moses and Monotheism* Freud suggests that this confusion is in fact the sort of distortion that is virtually deliberately carried out by the written record, and constitutes a mechanism of defense, a repression of the unacceptable material. The genius of Michaelangelo, however, reveals not only a Moses different from that of the received record but a superior one. Michaelangelo's Moses does not smash the Tablets in rage, as the scriptural record reports, but saves them by a tremendous effort of self-control:

> In this way he has added something new and more human to the figure of Moses; so that the giant frame with its tremendous physical power becomes only a concrete expression of the highest mental achievement that is possible in a man, that of struggling successfully against an inward passion for the sake of a cause to which he has devoted himself.[208]

To be sure, this is heroic. But these heroic qualities betray what for the rest of us, to say nothing of the heroes, constitutes a struggle between our rage or lust and the consequences of its satisfaction. Civilization is a product of this conflict; and as such it can be nothing other than a neurosis factory. The history of civilization begins at a point identical to the beginning of the individual. Freud uses the phrase "omnipotence of thought" (*Die Allmacht der Gedanken*) to describe the earliest mental

---

[207] Exodus 32.
[208] "The Moses of Michaelangelo," SE XIII, 233; *cf.* 221-236.

and emotional state of mankind. It is a state [209] in which reality is not only confused with but identified with human desires. This is of course a collective expression of primal narcissism. As with the individual, however, the race soon discovers that attempts at satisfaction of its desires must take into account the obstructions placed in the way of these desires by external reality and adapts itself accordingly.[210] The progressive control of the environment characteristic of civilization is in fact intended to secure a successful adaptation of the relationship between the world and the desires of the self in order to satisfy those desires. This requires a gradual and systematic suppression of the omnipotence of thought.

An historical progress becomes evident, moving from a primal narcissism to the limiting notion of external powers such as spirits or gods. The paraphernalia of religion emerge, only to be replaced, Freud profoundly hopes, by the unclouded vision of reality afforded us by science.[211] Yet side by side with this evolution lives the heritage of unfulfilled desires. Satisfaction cannot be immediately gained; and therefore it must be postponed—it can never be finally and fully denied. Religion and morality provide this measure of satisfaction in the promise of an afterlife in which there is pleasure for those who practiced unpleasure for so long.[212]

In brief, the great social institutions are attempts to solve the problems so evident in the case histories of neurotics. Freud writes:

> Our knowledge of the neurotic illnesses of individuals has been of much assistance to our understanding of the great social institutions. For the neuroses themselves have turned out to be attempts at *individual* solutions for the problem of compensating for unsatisfied wishes, while the institutions seek to provide *social* solutions for these same problems.[213]

But as the social institutions attempt to solve these problems they also exacerbate them; for, as in the "Moses" of Michaelangelo, it is clear that the solutions must always reduce to suppression. The neuroses, says Freud, are asocial in nature; and it is the task of civilization to socialize man, and drag him out of the isolation of his illness. It does so using the very powerful tool of guilt, which is so wide-spread a characteristic of the neuroses. So long as the human community adopts only the form of the family, the conflict between aggression and love

is bound to express itself in the Oedipus complex, to establish

---

[209] *Totem and Taboo: Resemblances Between the Psychic Lives of Savages and Neurotics*, tr. A. A. Brill, new edition (New York: Dodd, Mead and Co., n.d.), *passim*.

[210] "Claims," SE XIII, 186-187.

[211] *Cf. Illusion*, 75ff..

[212] "Claims," SE XIII, 186-187.

[213] *Ibid.; cf. Illusion*, 11-13.

the conscience and to create the first sense of guilt. When an attempt is made to widen the community, the same conflict is continued in forms which are dependent on the past; and it is strengthened and results in a further intensification of the sense of guilt. Since civilization obeys an internal erotic impulsion which causes human beings to unify in a closely-knit group, it can only achieve this aim through an ever-increasing reinforcement of the sense of guilt. What began in relation to the father is completed in relation to the group.[214]

In so enforcing guilt and repression civilization must inevitably be a causal element in the aetiology of the neuroses. The forces that operate within the ego to bring about restraint and repression owe their origin to compliance with civilization's demands. This compliance is a factor in neurotic cases: constitution and a set of childhood experiences which, in another case, "would invariably lead to a neurosis will produce no such result where this compliance is absent or where these demands are not made by the social circle in which the particular individual is placed. The old assertion that the increase in nervous disorders is a product of civilization is at least a half truth."[215] What was at one time an external repression of instinctual demand has become an internal one, and is inherited from the demands of civilization in the form of internalized controls on desires.[216]

It is through the process of sublimation that the instinctual demands, unaccceptable to and repressed by the forces of civilization, may emerge in acceptable and culturally creative forms. There is of course no question of annihilating these instincts; for there is no such thing as the human emotional life—and therefore no such thing as human life—without them. Rather, Freud argues that the high road of civilization is that of sublimating and transforming these impulses into the creative cultural activities we cherish.[217] Psychoanalysis reveals the "previous contributions to the

---

[214] *Civilization*, 79-80.

[215] "Claims," SE XIII, 188-190.

[216] *Cf. Illusion*, 14.

[217] Genital sexual love is a source of enormous satisfaction; this discovery provided the prototype of all human happiness. It also makes man dependent in the most dangerous way upon a chosen love-object. But there are cultural heroes who have transformed genital love into a form in which the loving itself replaces the object of love; the instinct is transformed into an impulse with an *"inhibited aim."* "What they bring about in themselves in this way is a state of evenly suspended, steadfast, affectionate feeling, which has little external resemblance any more to the stormy agitations of genital love, from which it is nevertheless derived. Perhaps St. Francis of Assisi went furthest in thus exploiting love for the

formation of character" made by the perverse and asocial instincts. If they are not repressed but rather "diverted from their original aims to more valuable ones by the process known as 'sublimation'" those creative achievements we have honored in the past will be repeated.

> Our highest virtues [he says] have grown up, as reaction formations and sublimations, out of our worst dispositions. Education [*Erziehung*] should scrupulously refrain from burying these precious springs of action and should restrict itself to encouraging the processes by which these energies are led along safe paths.[218]

Admittedly this view of sublimation is the most optimistic face Freud ever put on civilization. He did accept both the need for civilization and the possibilities it held out for whatever happiness man could achieve in the face of the titanic struggle that defined him. He plumped for civilization, without doubt. But at no point did he lose sight of the fact that civilization was in the end an expression and extension of that primary conflict. Civilization "is a process in the service of Eros, whose purpose is to combine single human individuals, and after that families, then, races, peoples and nations, into one great unity, the unity of mankind. Why this has to happen, we do not know; the work of Eros is precisely this." But man's aggressive instincts oppose those goal with force and persistence; even "necessity," *Ananke*, will not bind us together. We will persist in our aggression in response to thanatos. "And now, I think, the meaning of the evolution of civilization is no longer obscure to us; it must present the struggle between Eros and Death, between the instinct of life and the instinct of destruction, as it works itself out in the human species. This struggle is what all life essentially consists of, and the evolution of civilization may therefore be simply described as the struggle for the life of the human species. And it is this battle of giants that our nurse-maids try to appease with their lullaby about heaven."[219]

Thus it is unrealistic to be disillusioned by the vicissitudes of civilization. In reflecting on the Great War and the tide of disillusionment Freud

---

benefit of an inner feeling of happiness." This, Freud says, is the highest stage of love according to one ethical view. And further, "what we have recognized as one of the techniques for fulfilling the pleasure principle has often been brought into connection with religion; this connection may lie in the remote regions where the distinction between the ego and objects or between objects themselves is neglected." This readiness for universal love is said by some to be the highest stage of mankind. Freud offers two objections to this view: first, "a love that does not discriminate seems to me to forfeit a part of its own value, by doing an injustice to its object; and secondly, not all men are worthy of love." *Civilization*, 49f.; *cf.* 44.

[218] "Claims," SE XIII, 190.
[219] *Civilization*, 69.

found that most people had thoroughly misunderstood the true nature of "civilized" behavior. It was generally assumed that people would eschew evil acts either because they were well-born or well-educated. Their destructive instincts would either not arise or be eradicated. This quaint notion Freud derided:

> In reality there is no such thing as "eradicating" evil. Psychological–or, more strictly speaking, psychoanalytic–investigation shows instead that the deepest essence of human nature consists in instinctual impulses which are of an elementary nature, which are similar in all men and which aim at the satisfaction of certain primal needs. These impulses in themselves are neither good or bad. We classify them and their expressions in that way according to their relation to the needs and demands of the human community.[220]

Men are not gentle creatures who want to be loved,

> and who at the most can defend themselves if they are attacked; they are, on the contrary, creatures among whose instinctual endowments is to be reckoned a powerful share of aggressiveness. As a result, their neighbour is for them not only a potential helper or sexual object, but also someone who tempts them to satisfy their aggressiveness on him, to exploit his capacity for work without compensation, to use him sexually without his consent, to seize his possessions, to humiliate him, to cause him pain, to torture and to kill him. *Homo homini lupus.* Who, in the face of all his experience of life and history, will have the courage to dispute this assertion?[221]

It is obvious that the primitive selfish and cruel wishes are precisely the ones civilized people deplore. Such impulses have been subjected to a long process of development before they appear in the life of the adult, that is, of adjustment, refinement, suppression and sublimation of these desires in the face of the demands of external reality. Some of these changes are very deceptive indeed; egoism becomes altruism, hate becomes love, cruelty becomes piety. Such a transformation of the instincts appears to be successful on the whole, although from time to time the ambivalence of feelings, in which the same person can be both loved and hated, despised and cherished, breaks through. The fully civilized, fully formed "character," then, cannot in truth be reduced to pure categories of "good" and "bad." Rather the issue is whether the process of education, of civilization, has succeeded in distorting and controlling the eternal instinctual impulses so that they do not cause the destruction

---

[220] "Thoughts: I.," SE XIV, 281-282.
[221] *Civilization*, 58.

either of the self or of others.[222]

The role of love is essential in this process of transformation. We are all as egoistic, self-loving, and resistant to the world as our dreams reveal us to be. But it is a cultural work to alter this situation. This is done by taking advantage of the inherent need and desire of the organism to attach itself to an object and to be loved by that object. The initial instance and manifestation of this inherent desire is very evident in the development of children. Here is the primary cultural act. We are civilized by our need for love, taken in its widest sense. "By the admixture of *erotic* components the egoistic instincts are transformed into *social* ones.[223] In addition to this inherent need for love of which civilization can take advantage, the attachment of the self to the world (as opposed to narcissistic retreat) is in part effected by the demands of the environment: "[c]ivilization has been attained through the renunciation of instinctual satisfaction, and it demands the same renunciation from each newcomer in turn."[224] This external compulsion would not achieve the success it obviously has if it were not in the end an element of the self, with the irresistible power of an internal compulsion.[225] Further, just as this introjection of external compulsion is a characteristic feature of the individual's development—with its crucial Oedipal stage—so it is a feature of the history of mankind. Moreover, Freud urges that we not underestimate the influence through heredity itself of the primal external compulsion, which he firmly believes to be an historical episode of surpassing significance.[226]

In order to live, we must love. In order to be civilized, however, we must deceive ourselves, especially about the motives for our behavior. It is a high price we pay for civilization, nothing less than psychological hypocrisy. But in Freud's view the price is probably worth the gain: "...the maintenance of civilization even on so dubious a basis offers the prospect of paving the way in each new generation for a more far-reaching transformation of instinct which shall be the vehicle of a better civilization."[227] Such optimism never succumbs to the illusion of the altruistic society, however; there is no basis for disappointment in society because rather than falling lower than we feared we have not risen so high as we believed.[228]

As a physician Freud was sometimes sympathetic to the person who

---

[222] "Thoughts: I.," SE XIV, 281-282.

[223] *Ibid.*, 282-283.

[224] *Ibid.*.

[225] *Ibid.*.

[226] *Ibid.*; cf. *Civilization*, 44, *et passim.*

[227] "Thoughts: I.," SE XIV, 284-285.

[228] *Ibid.*; cf. 287: "Reasons are as plenty as blackberries." The issues raised above concerning the role of civilization with respect to the conflict with the instincts are discussed at, *e.g.*, IL, SE XV, 22-23, SE XVI, 354-

found the conflict with reality too great to bear. He was, in a seemingly hard-hearted fashion, aware that the path of education (*Erziehung*) was an arduous one, and many fell by the way: Necessity, *Ananke*, "has been a strict educator and has made much out of us. The neurotics are among those of her children to whom her strictness has brought evil results; but that is a risk with all education."[229] But there are occasions when reality must to some extent be denied. It is not the physician's role, Freud points out,[230] to take the side of traditional morality over against the needs of the patient. And at times he must actively support the symptom he has encountered:

> You must not be surprised to hear that even the physician may occasionally take the side of the illness he is combatting. It is not his business to restrict himself in every situation in life to being a fanatic in favour of health.... If we may say, then, that whenever a neurotic is faced by a conflict he takes flight into illness, yet we must allow that in some cases flight is fully justified, and a physician who has recognized how the situation lies will silently withdraw.[231]

This conclusion is not the same as the view that holds, over Freud's strenuous objection, that the neurotic's problem lies in his having been too tightly controlled by civilization and that the cure lies in letting him yield to his impulses. This was a popular—for obvious reasons—interpretation of psychoanalysis. On the contrary, Freud wrote, a treatment of neurotics based on a fuller sexual expression

> could not possibly play a part in analytic therapy—if only because we ourselves have declared that an obstinate conflict is taking place in [the neurotic] between a libidinal impulse and sexual repression, between a sensual and an ascetic trend. This conflict would not be solved by our helping one of these trends to victory over its opponent.

The analyst will simply encourage injurious consequences should he support either the traditional introjected morality, which is the agency of repression, or the irrational sexual impulses that are being repressed.

> We see, indeed, that in neurotics asceticism has the upper hand; and the consequence of this is precisely that the suppressed sexual tendency finds a way out in symptoms. If, on the contrary, we were to secure victory for sensuality, then the sexual repression that had been put on one side would necessarily be replaced

---

355.
[229] IL, SE XVI, 354-355.
[230] *Cf. ibid.*, 434-435.
[231] *Ibid.*, 382.

78

by symptoms. Neither of these alternative decisions could end
the internal conflict; in either case one party to it would remain
unsatisfied.[232]

Civilization is not honest with itself about its motives, any more
than the individual whose distress it manifests is. Psychoanalysis is perfectly well aware of this; indeed, it is the analytic perception of the grand
disparity between stated and hidden intention that gives analysis its im-
petus. Thus it does not abet civilized dishonesty but makes very sure
the patient knows the truth. What patients do with this hard-won truth,
says Freud, is entirely up to them:

> if, having grown independent after the completion of their treat-
> ment, they decide on their own judgement in favour of some
> midway position between living a full life and absolute asceti-
> cism, we feel our conscience clear with their choice. We tell
> ourselves any one who has succeeded in educating himself to
> truth about himself is permanently defended against the danger
> of immorality, even though his standard of morality may differ
> in some respect from that which is customary in society.[233]

In sum, the analyzed patient follows the middle path between conformity
to possibly destructive and in any case essentially dishonest social norms
and unqualified grasping after instinctual gratification. He is civilized
enough, but more.[234]

Freud's conceptualization of the link between mental illness and civilization was extended and deepened, as with much of his thinking, by his
formulation of two basic concepts: the structural theory, which described
the relationship between ego, id, and super-ego; and the revision of his
theory of the instincts from a simple dichotomy between ego and sexual
instincts to the more complex and profound one of the conflict between
eros and thanatos, the instincts of love—really, attachment—and death,
that is, retreat, rejection, and morbidity. A full treatment of this aspect
of his notion of suffering belongs to the following section concerned with
the causes of suffering. However, with respect to civilization and its role
in suffering a few comments may be enlightening.

In contrasting the death instinct with the instinct for attachment
Freud claimed, to the chagrin of many supporters and the glee of many
detractors then and now, that inherent in the human life was a tendency,
an irrational instinct, toward death, toward refusing to engage external
reality in any form. If, one may ask, this tendency exists at the instinctual
level—there could be no more profound and irresistible level than this—how
does one explain the drive for improvement, even perfection, so evident

---

[232] *Ibid.*, 432-433.
[233] *Ibid.*, 434-435.
[234] *Cf.* "Resistances," SE XIX, 220f..

in human culture? Is this not a contradiction of a fundamental element of human nature? For surely a "death" instinct would concern itself solely with the breaking down of relations and reversing the process of growth.

As might be expected, Freud finds the concept of a drive toward perfection to be another example of that distortion of motives so convenient to the interests of civilization on the one hand, and a symptom, or at least evidence of the existence of another and hidden process, on the other. It is, he says

> difficult...for many of us to abandon the belief that there is an instinct towards perfection at work in human beings, which has brought them to their present high level of intellectual achievement and ethical sublimation which may be expected to watch over their development into supermen. I have no faith, however, in the existence of such an internal instinct and I cannot see how this benevolent illusion is to be preserved. The present development of human beings requires, as it seems to me, no different explanation from that of animals.[235]

The Tables are about to be turned. What appears as an untiring striving for perfection

> can easily be understood as a result of the instinctual repression upon which is based what is most precious in human civilization. The repressed instinct never ceases to strive for complete satisfaction, which would consist in the repetition of a primary experience of satisfaction....[236]

That is to say, satisfaction of instincts requires driving backwards to the stage of ultimate satisfaction. This backward-moving instinctual impulsion is what Freud means when he discusses the death instinct. For it is a movement back to that initial stage of primary narcissism at which the conflict and tension with the external world characteristic of the growing organism has not yet begun. To this stage of ultimate pleasure the self wishes to return, and it will not be denied. Civilization, characterized by striving and vigorous activity, is in fact the product of a conflict between the goal of this death instinct and the objects that stand in its path.

> No substitutive or reactive formations and no sublimations will suffice to remove the repressed instinct's persisting tension; and it is the difference in amount between the pleasure of satisfaction which is *demanded* and that which is *actually achieved* that provides the driving factor which will permit of no halting at any

---

[235] *Beyond the Pleasure Principle*, tr. James Strachey, with an introduction by Gregory Zilboorg (New York: Liveright, 1928; Bantam, 1959), 76-77.

[236] *Ibid.*.

position attained, but, in the poet's words, *"ungebändigt immer vorwärts dringt."* ["unchained it drives ever onward."] The backward path that leads to complete satisfaction is as a rule obstructed by the resistances which maintain the repressions. So there is no alternative but to advance in the direction in which growth is still free–though with no prospect of bringing the process to a conclusion or of being able to reach the goal.[237]

Just as we think, mistakenly but for discoverable reasons, that civilization is evidence of a drive for improvement and perfection, we also believe that our ego is the locus in our selves of those efforts at establishing what is conscious to us, and that it is in our ego that our reason and our free choice operate. It is man's ego, we believe, that separates him from his animal ancestors; for it is through its quality of consciousness that human civilization has progressed faster and farther than any other species. However, psychoanalytic investigation indicates, as Freud argued in *The Ego and the Id*, that the ego is not a unity of consciousness standing in well-defined opposition to the unconscious desires of the rest of the self. Rather, the ego was only a certain portion of the id. The id must be seen as the whole mental self, modified in certain aspects by its contact with the external world. The ego is nothing but the most significant and initial area of contact. We should think of the ego as serving three masters, the id, of which it is a part, the external world, with which it must be in constant relationship for the sake of the id, and the superego. Thus the ego was not comprehendible as a monolithic reservoir of consciousness; on the contrary, Freud concluded that it was a reservoir of libido and the seat of anxiety. Thus the ego had to be thought of as containing both conscious and unconscious elements; and both what was morally exemplary and morally repugnant should be regarded as arising from the unconscious. From the perspective of the present issue one should not simply equate what was conscious with what was civilized.[238]

A better conceptualization of the ego is that when, as a particular function of the id, it represented the conscious world to the id it was simply an extension of the id. Ego did not oppose id, any more than, in truth, civilization opposed sexual drives–although this is the usual form of our conceptual presentation.[239] Yet a conflict certainly arises. It takes a form so similar to obedience to the moral injunctions of society that we are inclined to equate the two and to describe such obedience solely in terms of cultural norms, as though people behaved morally because it was somehow "right" to do so. However, although appearance lends credibility to this interpretation, the conflict (thus "obedience") of which

---

[237] *Ibid.*.
[238] *Ego and Id*, 33.
[239] *Ibid.*, 34.

we speak is potentially threatening and even destructive for the ego itself. The role of civilization is taken over by the super-ego, which, it should be recalled, is a part of the mental life introjected as a result of the "dissolution" of the Oedipus complex. Here is Freud's description of the conflict that misleads us into identifying the resultant behavior as moral:

From the point of view of morality, the control and restriction of instinct, it may be said of the id that it is totally non-moral, of the ego that it strives to be moral, and of the super-ego that it can by hypermoral and then becomes as ruthless as only the id can be. It is remarkable that the more a man checks his aggressive tendencies towards others the more tyrannical, that is aggressive, he becomes in his ego-ideal. The ordinary view sees the situation the other way round: the standard set up by the ego-ideal seems to be the motive for the suppression of aggression. The fact remains, however, as we stated it: the more a man controls his aggressiveness, the more intense become the aggressive tendencies of his ego-ideal against his ego. It is like a displacement, a turning round upon the self. But even ordinary normal morality has a harshly restraining, cruelly prohibitory quality.[240]

The illness that arises when this conflict can no longer be controlled is melancholia, in which the ego is reduced to a possibly fatal weakness by the super-ego. The morality of civilization must be seen in light of this possibility; and we must therefore conclude that it has the instinctive basis of its original condition, the complex of repression of infantile sexual instincts. Seen in this light the role of civilization in the aetiology of the neuroses is unmistakable and undeniable.[241]

Libidinal Types

In view of the interdependence of civilization and the individual neurotic tendencies one would expect that individuals of one psychic condition–or disposition–would emerge as highly beneficial to civilization; such an individual, it could be argued, would be one in whom repression had been most successful and in whose character the boundary line between the unconscious drives and the conscious civilized behavior was most difficult to breach. In fact, civilization is a more complex entity than one seeking only control of instincts; and accordingly the individuals who have contributed most to civilization are similarly complex. Freud examined them in a essay he entitled "Libidinal Types," a title that reveals the irrefrangible link between character and libidinal activity (indeed, there are no other means of differentiating character, since character is itself the product of libidinal vicissitudes).

---

[240] *Ibid.*, 79-80.
[241] *Ibid.*, 80, 81.

He identifies three types: the erotic; the obsessional; and the narcissistic. The erotic type, as implied by its name, is "devoted to love," that is, it desires above all else, and at any price, the love of others. It fears above all the loss of that love. Second, the obsessional type, although it fears the loss of love and appreciates the love of others, is concerned primarily to achieve the approval of the super-ego. Accordingly it suffers more than the other two from an active fear of the conscience and is ever attentive to its hypermoral demands. Such people are "true, pre-eminently conservative vehicles of civilization." Third, and in sharp contrast to the others, is the narcissistic type. Here the characteristic tension between ego and super-ego is missing; indeed, if one acknowledged only the narcissistic type he would have little ground for recognizing the function of a super-ego at all. "The subject's main interest," Freud explains, "is directed to self-preservation; he is independent and not open to intimidation." Loving is preferred to being loved; and a large amount of aggressiveness is at this person's disposal because it has not been depleted in attachment to objects other than himself. Surprisingly, at least at first glance, Freud holds that this person is essential to civilization; for he is a good leader, upsets the present state of affairs and therefore frequently stimulates cultural development.[242]

These types are rarely found in pure states. The compounds are more frequently seen. Double compounds are, then, the erotic-obsessional, the erotic-narcissistic, and the narcissistic-obsessional. The erotic-obsessional type is characterized by heavy dependence on the super-ego, seen particularly in obedience to exemplars and loved ones. In the erotic-narcissistic compound we find a commitment to the unification of opposites and the constant creation of new conditions. It is, incidentally, in connection with this type that we learn that aggressive behavior is not inconsistent with narcissism, but rather almost always is found in conjunction with it. Third, the narcissistic-obsessional compound appears in individuals with strong consciences and vigorous commitment to the Good, which frequently takes them beyond the limitations of accepted behavior. They too, then, are culturally valuable. They also may be said to strengthen the super-ego; and thus they resolve at least one major problem of civilization, how to avoid the super-ego's threats to the ego without losing the sense of conscience which makes repression and resultant moral behavior possible.

Each of these types is found in civilization, and each may be seen as contributing to its health. Further, it is noteworthy that the purer the type the less useful it is to civilization; and conversely the compounds provide types more obviously essential to the complex of civilized functions. If we were to simplify greatly and conclude that civilization requires

---

[242] "Libidinal Types," SE XXI, 217-218; cf. *Civilization*, 30-31.

both growth and stability, we would find that it is powerfully dependent in both of these needs upon the dispositions of libido among individuals. If we grant this conclusion, it must be true that the most valuable libidinal type for civilization is that compound which incorporates all three types, the erotic-obsessional-narcissistic. Indeed, says Freud, this is the ideal "normal" type in which the diverse elements of libidinal disposition are brought into harmony. Civilization benefits most from just this compound. On the other hand we may explain illness in part by noting the tendency of the less complete types, and in particular the non-compounded types, to threaten civilization, and to appear as illnesses.

In the economy of the mind there is a marked tendency towards the sacrifice of one or two of these trends for the benefit of the others. This defusion probably is parallel to the defusion of instincts which, for example, resexualizes the Oedipal feelings and leads to melancholia. It is beneficial to individuals and civilizations alike, then, for these libidinal vicissitudes to be fused or bound together. But the presence of neurotic and psychotic persons indicates that neither civilization nor individuals are very successful in this task.[243]

Before leaving the notion of libidinal types we should observe that they are not necessarily illnesses but tendencies which, if unrestrained, lead to illnesses. It is an insight into the life of the mind to recognize that the ideal, or normal health, is not the absence of conflict but the economy of conflict, a state in which the eternal libidinal and instinctual forces strike a homeostatic balance of tension. This state implies a tendency toward instability that requires constant adjustment—adjustment in which success is unlikely and virtually impossible.[244]

Guilt

The control of the individual's behavior in the context of civilization is greatly enhanced by his sense of guilt and closely allied to the notion of conscience. It has been the view of many moral philosophers, among them Kant, that man possesses an inherent sense of what is good and that it is within his reason's ability to discover and employ it. He is thus enabled to compare the acts of himself and others against this ideal standard and assess their ethical content. The role of the sense of guilt in this argument arises from the knowledge of what is good, on the one hand, and of the performance of deeds that are not, on the other. Interestingly, Freud too holds that we know what is good and believes that the sense of guilt follows from this knowledge.[245] But whereas the idealist means by "good" a universal ethical standard, with its categorical imperative,

---

[243] *Ibid.*, 218-220.

[244] *Cf. Civilization*, ch. II, and *Ego and Id*, ch. III, for other discussions of libidinal types.

[245] *Cf.* "Masochism," SE XIX, 167.

84

Freud means the universal emotional experience of having been denied satisfaction of one's desires and of having been threatened with severe sanctions for attempting to satisfy those desires. Indeed, the sense of guilt has an historical basis; for in the beginning was the deed, the deed of yielding to instinctual desires to possess the love-object, and in doing so destroying whatever, or whomever, stood in the way.

We have interpreted the first rules of morality and moral restrictions of primitive society as reactions to a deed which gave the authors of it the conception of crime. They regretted this deed and decided that it should not be repeated and that its execution must bring no gain.[246]

That deed was the killing of the primal horde-father by the sons so that the women of the horde could be taken from the father. Freud is in no doubt that this actually happened. The sense of guilt we all bear and suffer from is derived partly from this event. We, like the sons, are sorry for this act and erect barriers and rules that will prevent it from happening again. Totemism and its attendant rule of exogamy are, in Freud's argument, early manifestations of this guilt translated into socio-religious norms and law. But we continue to this day to see the consequences of regret for this deed; although it has not happened for a very long time it is still true as it was then, that we *wish* to commit it. In the life of the self there is virtually no difference between wishing a deed to happen and its actually happening (as in the story of the three wishes). Therefore we should expect to find remnants of that primal sense of guilt. "This creative sense of guilt has not become extinct from us. We find its asocial effects in neurotics producing new rules of morality and continued restrictions, in expiation for misdeeds committed, or as precautions against misdeeds to be committed." But upon examination they are guilty of no deeds. "Only psychic realities and not actual ones are at the basis of the neurotic's sense of guilt." This, indeed, is a fundamental characteristic of neurotic behavior in general, namely that psychic reality is more powerful in its effect than the other kind.[247]

Guilt arises not from having committed a deed that is bad but from having wished to commit that deed. It is common to call the response to having committed a deed that we regret[248] remorse. Or perhaps one should now refer to "true" guilt, that is, guilt associated with conscience. Freud described a two-stage development of guilt. Each is related to feelings about the parent. In the first stage, one is "guilty" only when one is caught; that is, the very young child, and some adults, feel this

---

[246] *Totem*, 264.
[247] *Ibid.*, 264.
[248] It must be pointed out that that deed has an ambivalent relationship to what is called "bad." *Cf. Civilization*, 71.

primitive guilt only when punishment by a superior power becomes a real threat. The threat is, in fact, a loss of love, followed by its inevitable consequence of punishment. In the second stage, the authority of the parent is no longer external but internal, and takes the form of the "super-ego." The super-ego is, above all, omniscient; for, as part of the psychic structure, it is fully aware of the wishes, and not merely the deeds, of the individual. There is now no distinction between what is done and what is wished; and the individual is as guilty for one as for the other. He may expect to suffer the consequence of the loss of love in either case. Therefore even if one has not committed an act of aggression in obedience to his instincts, the fact of his wish remains, and he is guilty. Instinctual renunciation is not enough, for the wish persists and "cannot be concealed from the super-ego."[249]

But we should not forget the link, Freud argues, between phylogeny and ontogeny. Was there a deed for which we should feel guilt, in the sense of remorse, for something actually done? Yes: the killing of the primal father was precisely that deed. The remorse that followed

> was the result of the primordial ambivalence of feeling towards the father. His sons hated him, but they loved him too. After their hatred had been satisfied by their act of aggression, their love came to the fore in their remorse for the deed. It set up the super-ego by identification with the father; it gave that agency the father's power, as though as a punishment for the deed of aggression they had carried out against him, and it created the restrictions which were intended to prevent a repetition of the deed. And since the inclination to aggressiveness against the father was repeated in the following generations, the sense of guilt, too, persisted, and it was reinforced once more by every piece of aggressiveness that was suppressed and carried over to the super-ego.... Whether one has killed one's father or has abstained from doing so is not really the decisive thing. One is bound to feel guilty in either case, for the sense of guilt is an expression of the conflict due to ambivalence, of the eternal struggle between Eros and the instinct of destruction or death.[250]

The psychic reality is not without power to determine action. On the contrary, it overcomes the evident situation of reality. There arises a condition in which individuals behave as though they were guilty of some misdeed and must bear the consequences when in fact they seem to be either innocent or successful. Freud investigates these conditions in his case histories and also in literary sources. For example, in Shakespeare's

---

[249] *Ibid.*, 74.
[250] *Ibid.*, 79; *cf.* 70ff..

MacBeth Lady MacBeth begins to behave neurotically as a direct consequence of her success in gaining control of the throne. This remarkable
development has been the subject of much commentary. But while it is
clearly an occasion for analytic treatment Freud confesses that he finds
the obstacles too intimidating; the obscurity of Shakespeare's intention,
the differences between the time scale of the historical situation and that
of the play defy clear interpretation. He turns with more success to Ibsen's *Rosmersholm*. The play is clear enough. Rebecca West, adopted
daughter of Dr. West, lives with him and his wife, Beata, at Rosmersholm. After a time Rebecca and Dr. West have an affair. For both it
is an experience of liberation. Beata commits suicide; and Dr. West is
confounded as to the reason, for he believes that the obvious one, the
affair between himself and his adopted daughter, was a secret from his
wife. In time a marriage is arranged between Dr. West and Rebecca
and the pinnacle of success for Rebecca is within reach. A brother of the
deceased Beata comes to Rebecca, however, and announces (like a "perspicuous analyst," Freud writes) that he can prove that Rebecca is the
biological daughter of her husband-to-be. Rebecca goes quite mad.[251]

Rebecca's success, seen in the context of the psychological themes at
work, has come about as the result of an action–a psychical act, a wish–
of hers, namely, accomplishing the death of her father's wife. And as a
direct result of that wish she is about to obtain what she has sought all
along, the love of her father. The proof that she is her father's daughter
is essential for the plot and for the audience. But according to the psychoanalytic truth of the play Rebecca has never been anything but her
father's daughter, and has never sought any goal other than his love–for
which she was willing to kill, or wished to kill, and for all intents and
purposes did kill. Her madness reveals the crushing load of guilt for her
crime. She was guilty. She knew she was guilty, and paid the penalty.[252]

Rosmersholm presents a pellucidly clear literary example of the nature and origin of guilt to Freud. Guilt is a consequence of libidinal
attachment on the one hand and deliberate repression of that attachment on the other. He wrote, "[p]sycho-analytic work teaches that the
forces of conscience which induce illness in consequence of success, instead of, as normally, in consequence of frustration, are closely connected
with the Oedipus complex, the relation to father and mother–as perhaps,
indeed, is our sense of guilt in general."[253] A variation, for example, on
the Oedipal theme is the neurotic situation in which one may actually
commit a crime in order to fix a cause for the sense of guilt in the external

---

[251] "Some Character Types Met with in Psycho-Analytic Work," SE
XIV, 316-331.
[252] *Ibid..*
[253] *Ibid.*, 331.

world. The guilt of which we speak is the original guilt, the desire for the parent of the opposite sex. The act of crime thus is a consequence of this sense of guilt, rather than a cause.[254]

A sense of guilt, then, is a manifestation of a struggle that took place originally between the parent and the child and subsequently was introduced into the operation of mental life. It is the super-ego, the legacy of the Oedipal relationship, that threatens the ego with the consequences of allowing the primal desire to be fulfilled. This super-ego is therefore a representative of the external world, and of a particularly important part of it, the parent of the opposite sex. It was born when essential features of the id's original objects were incorporated into the growing person's psychic structure. These features were the strength, power and oversight of the parents.[255]

The categorical imperative of Kant, one may say, inherits the Oedipus complex. Whether one wishes to call this reality of the conscience and the super-ego a psychical reality or a universal, transcendent reality makes no difference to the experience of the person. The agency of the conscience, in fact the agency of parental authority acting within the self, is real. It has real power, for it is the most strongly felt of all manifestations of reality.[256] Reality and the id are therefore merged. The guilt from which the obsessional neurotic and the rest of us suffer is then real, as real as the rules that have been broken and the threats that are made. Indeed, if we properly understand the nature of guilt as a response to reality it will be seen that the reality in question is the most general possible. The last figure in the series of representatives of authority, and therefore reality, which begins with the parents and which includes our teachers, heroes and all exemplary and authoritative figures, is the dark power of Destiny which only the fewest of us are able to look upon as impersonal. Even when guidance of the world is seen to be in the hands of Providence, or God or even Nature, one cannot avoid the conclusion that at bottom these remotest of powers are seen as the original parental couple. With them our first ties were formed. In the end our relationship with reality is formed by guilt; we respond to it as guilty persons, and this is entirely proper for such is the case.[257]

Religion

Since the purpose of this work is to investigate the nature of suffering as understood by the psychoanalytic perspective of Freud and the Buddhist tradition, the Freudian idea that religion is neurotic in nature

---

[254] Ibid., 332-333.
[255] "Masochism," SE XIX, 167.
[256] Ibid..
[257] Ibid., 166-168; cf. IL, SE XVI, 331-332.

and its paraphernalia the symptoms of neurosis is a matter of special interest. Freud assigns religion to what I am calling his truth of suffering. That people are religious is itself a symptomatic condition; and therefore analysis of religion may and should proceed along the lines of analysis of a neurosis. Further, just as a neurotic may be said to be cured, that is, to have been made aware of the fact that he was deluding himself and should now proceed to live according to the conscious choices of his strengthened ego, so someone who was religious would be considered cured if he were to unmask religion and see it for what it really is. In other words, Freud does not simply believe that religion is factually wrong; he believes that it is an illness to which the only healthy response is replacement with reality. These general conclusions are well-known in the popular tradition, and will be illustrated and explained below. One further question arises immediately—and I intend only to pose it at this time and answer it later. It is this: if this is Freud's view of religion, what, in the context of this work, should we make of Buddhist perceptions—which, of course, I am arguing, Freud shares—of the truth of suffering? Freud himself believed that all Eastern religions were in essence ancestor worship. This conclusion, as will be easily recognized, enabled Freud to fit them neatly into his Oedipal interpretation of religions of the world in general. But on this point he is simply wrong—that is, he is misinformed, deliberately reductionistic, and, perhaps above all, completely at ease in making generalizations about a subject of which he knows very little (a situation which, as one of the great thinkers and scientists of the world, he would never allow in any other circumstance). I wish to take note of one futher point: Freud's understanding of religion in general is that it is quintessentially belief in a God who acts as Father. Thus according to him the people who believe such a thing, *i.e.* all religious people, must be neurotic, since such a belief shows beyond doubt that the resolution of the Oedipus complex has not taken place for them. If one accepts this notion of religion as belief in the Father-God as the right one—that is, as the accurate and incisive view of what religion in fact is and has been—then Freud is clearly correct. However, what Freud describes, while a neurotic situation, is not a religious goal and never has been. It is the major burden of this work to show what a religious view of the issue of suffering is, and what it offers. To accomplish that task I have turned (some would say, ironically) to Freud himself, for there is no question but that his contribution to the universal issue is some version of a universal solution; and I have turned to the Buddha for the same reasons, and, I believe, with the same justification for hope that I shall find the same universal answer. The fact that, at least in my understanding, the Buddha (or the Buddhist tradition—a distinction implying an issue that need not, and must not, obstruct us here) and Freud both grasp the truth that human life is suffering, and that there is a cause for it and its relief, is surely more significant than

Freud's misguided attack on religion—or rather, his attack on what he and other scientists regarded as religion. More significant surely is his attention to the question of suffering.

Finally, it is highly significant that among the causes of suffering, and among the indications of the truth of suffering, as understood in the Buddhist tradition, is the notion of false views, or false understandings of the nature of reality. This interpretive concept includes such notions as a fixed and stable soul, and a God who causes all effects. This is clearly a critique of precisely the sort of thinking that Freud called religion. That is, if this phrasing is not too confusing and/or offensive, both Freud and the Buddha attack religion, for the purposes of identifying it as a truth of suffering and eliminating its causes. But, as I hope to make clear, the very work upon which each is engaged is religious in nature.

As we have already seen, religion in its primitive and modern forms figured prominently in Freud's treatment of most issues related to suffering. In treating the discontents of civilization he draws together the behavior of neurotics and the nature and function of religion in the social context. Furthermore, there is a relationship of identity between social and individual psychology. The emergence of culture, then, must be understood in terms of the psychological history of the individual. The place of religion in cultural development, as everyone would agree, is at least superficially highly creative. In *Totem and Taboo* Freud explored the origins of religion from the point of view of the tendency to neurosis in light of the conflict that defines human life. He noted three successive cultural stages in the history of mankind: animistic; religious; and scientific (in so dividing history he was simply imitating many of his nineteenth-century peers). He distinguished them in this way:

> In the animistic stage man ascribes omnipotence to himself; in the religious he has ceded it to the gods, but without seriously giving it up, for he reserves to himself the right to control the gods by influencing them in some way or other in the interest of his wishes. In the scientific attitude towards life there is no longer any room for man's omnipotence; he has acknowledged his smallness and has submitted to death as to all other natural necessities in a spirit of resignation.[258]

Or, at least, one hopes. But that hope is somewhat misplaced; for, as Freud points out continually, the primitive belief in the omnipotence of thought never entirely disappears, any more than our essential narcissism.[259] Yet, as civilization's very existence demonstrates, vigorous attempts were mounted to suppress the omnipotence of thought and replace it with the so-called reality principle. I want to postpone the discussion of

---

[258] *Totem,* 147.
[259] *Ibid..*

the reality principle until a later section; but it must be introduced here briefly in order to illustrate Freud's understanding of religion. Religion is seen as a way of dealing with the conflict between the pleasure principle and the reality principle, the conflict between the desire to gratify instinctual impulses without regard for the consequences and the recognition on the part of the ego that these impulses may not be gratified in their own way. The conflict often leads to neurosis. Freud describes the function of religion in this conflict as the postponement of immediate gratification, for which the justification is the belief in an after-life. That after-life, as a brief review of the scriptures and traditions of the world clearly shows, promises to the deserving a reward that is a fulfillment of their desire for pleasure. One may ask, as many have, if this is a response of the reality principle, how is it different from the pleasure principle? Freud points out that in fact religion does serve the pleasure principle by the institution of this myth. This is not the view religion has of itself. On the contrary (Freud's) "religion" believes that it has conquered the pleasure principle in favor of the Good, the True, and the omnipotence of Providence. But this is an illusion.[260]

It boots little, furthermore, to defend religion as a unique feeling, the "oceanic feeling" of the writer Romaine Rolland, who sees in this "feeling of an indissoluble bond, of being one with the external world as a whole," the root cause of the "whole need for religion."[261] The very idea of the absence of a distinction between the self and the world fairly reeks of narcissism, of the infantile pleasure principle. The ego, as psychoanalysis has taught, maintains, for its very existence, a sharp and clear demarcation with the external world (to this state there is a very important exception, namely the state of being in love). However, the origins of religion are to be found in the infant's experience of helplessness and its consequences. No "oceanic feeling" can survive the realities of life. Its real attraction, therefore, and thus that of religion, is consolation, the hope that the world is a nursery. But this longing is simply grist for Freud's mill, in which he grinds religious claims down to their constituent libidinal parts.[262]

Before leaving the question of the oceanic feeling, let us pause to note Freud's view on one of the oldest disciplines directed to disengagement from the world, yoga. He writes of a friend who experimented with the method (he does not say at what level). The friend suggests that "new sensations and coenaesthesias [sic] in oneself, which he regards as regressions to primordial states of mind that have long ago been overlaid," emerge; and they rest upon a physiological basis shared with mys-

---

[260] "Two Principles," SE XII, 223-224.
[261] *Civilization*, 12.
[262] *Ibid.*, 11-19.

ticism.[263] Yoga, Freud concludes, is "the extreme form" of the attempt to "master the internal sources of our needs." It seeks to kill off the instincts. "If it succeeds, then the subject has, it is true, given up all other activities as well–he has sacrificed his life; and, by another path, he has once more only achieved the happiness of quietness."[264] This is certainly a famous case of misunderstanding–to put the matter charitably–and just how wrong Freud is in this, another judgement of the religious traditions, will be seen.

Religious beliefs and structures are distorted remnants of both a real historical past and of the individual's crises of development. As for the real past, "God the Father once walked upon earth in bodily form and exercised his sovereignty as chieftain of the primal human horde until his sons united to slay him. It emerges...that this crime of liberation and the reactions to it had as their result the appearance of the first social ties, the basic moral restrictions and the oldest form of religion, totemism."[265] In *Totem and Taboo* Freud describes the primal conflict of the sons with the father over control of the women of the tribe. The sons in collusion rise up and kill the father. But guilt follows, and they establish both a means of controlling what they know to be their own most fundamental wishes and a means of reminding themselves of what they have done, thereby stirring up the feelings of guilt. The first means were exogamy and social rules in general, and the second was totemism, the substitution of a (subsequently) sacred object for the father who was killed. This object is revered, but also eaten. The ambivalent feelings toward the father are thus recapitulated in the usages surrounding the totem. According to Freud it is at this point that religion *per se* emerges; for man invented a supernatural figure now inaccessible but still omnipotent, who bears the burden of the ambivalent feelings of the children.[266]

Freud sees the aim of religion as threefold: (1) the provision of a cosmogony, or instruction in the nature of the world's origins; (2) the offering of consolation and protection, chiefly through the device of theodicy, a justification of suffering which always depends upon God's actions; and (3) the ordering and defining of rules and prohibitions concerning the gratification of desires. These three goals describe both the operation of religion and the effects of the libidinal relationship between parents and child. They also contradict quite obviously what Freud perceives to be the realities of human existence. They constitute an illusion that replaces the empirical fact of the unfairness of the world and the meaninglessness of suffering, and panders to our need for structure and meaning.

---

[263] *Ibid.*, 19.
[264] *Ibid.*, 26.
[265] "Preface," SE XVII, 262-263.
[266] *Cf. Totem, passim*, and NIL, SE XXII, 158ff..

In other words, religion exists because we simply refuse to face the fact of existence—that it is mean, nasty, harsh, brutish and short—and insist upon a worldview that enables us to deal with our longing by projecting it into heaven. We wish to have our desires fulfilled; and we wish to be protected from them at the same time. Religion provides the perfect vehicle for this course; and that is simply because it was invented for that purpose.

Religion transforms the forces of nature, first into personal beings and then into one personal being, God. They, and then He, are not our equals. This action suggests both an infantile and phylogenetic prototype.[267] The progression from polytheism to monotheism follows a logical development, Freud argues. For as Nature, or Fate, was finally understood to respond only to its own internal and ineluctable rules, the gods retired farther into the background. Their one remaining function was to provide compensation for the sufferings and privations of existence; and the demand that they fulfill this function transmuted them into the single, father, God.

This, then, is the present function of religion. Despite the evidence of our senses and memories of many life-times, we cling to the notion that there is a higher purpose to existence than our daily perceptions permit. We cling also to the concept of a benevolent Providence "which is only seemingly stern and which will not suffer us to become a plaything of the over-mighty and pitiless forces of nature. Death itself is not extinction, is not a return to inorganic lifelessness, but the beginning of a new kind of existence which lies on the path of development to something higher." Further, all good is rewarded and all evil punished—if not in this life, then in the next. The terrors, sufferings and deprivations of this life are temporary; and the qualities of goodness and justice, however contradictory, are inherent in the nature of the Supreme Being in whose charge the whole is. Most significantly, man's relationship with this Being is precisely the relationship that he would wish with his own father, to be his only beloved child, his Chosen People.[268]

These ideas are illusions. What Freud means by "illusion" is different from what we mean by "error." Aristotle believed that vermin arose from dung; that is an error. But Columbus' belief that he had arrived in the East Indies is an illusion—precisely because it is a conclusion based upon wish rather than empirical fact. So it is with religious ideas. As for their empirical base, there is none. Religious ideas are not defended in the same manner as other ideas, that is, with empirical verification or, at the very least, the rational possibility of verification. They are defended on the bases that they were handed down by our forefathers, that our

---

[267] *Illusion*, 24.
[268] *Ibid.*, 26-27.

forefathers have already transmitted accompanying proof, and that it is forbidden to question the truth of these ideas. However, the fact is that when we accept religious ideas—which Freud defines as "teachings and assertions about facts and conditions of external (or internal) reality which tell one something one has not discovered for oneself and which lay claim to one's belief"[269] —we are only seeking "fulfilments of the oldest and strongest and most urgent wishes of mankind;" the power of belief lies in the strength of those wishes.[270]

What those wishes are is clear enough:

> ...the benevolent rule of a divine Providence allays our fear of the dangers of life; the establishment of a moral world-order ensures the fulfilment of the demands of justice, which have so often remained unfulfilled in human civilization; and the prolongation of earthly existence in a future life provides the local and temporal framework in which these wish-fulfillments shall take place.... It is an enormous relief to the individual psyche if the conflicts of its childhood arising from the father-complex—conflicts which it has never wholly overcome—are removed from it and brought to a solution which is universally accepted.[271]

But, says Freud, "ignorance is ignorance," and no claim for the benefits of such illusions can overturn that fact.[272] In point of fact our religious ideas are exactly what we wish them to be, that there is a benevolent Providence, an after-life, and a moral order in the universe.[273] In accepting the illusion of religion mankind loses most of its chance for adaptation to the real world; for religion "imposes equally on everyone its own path to the acquisition of happiness and protection from suffering. Its technique consists in depressing the value of life and distorting the picture of the real world in a delusional manner—which presupposes an intimidation of the intelligence. At this price, by forcibly fixing them in a state of psychical infantilism and by drawing them into a mass delusion, religion succeeds in sparing many people an individual neurosis. But hardly anything more." In the end, even religion, along with other paths "which may lead to such happiness as is attainable by men," cannot keep its promise. If the believer must fall back finally upon God's inscrutable decree, he is simply admitting that unconditional submission to that inscrutable God is the true foundation of his belief. He might have saved himself his circuitous route through belief in its promise of happiness.[274]

---

[269] *Ibid.*, 37.
[270] *Ibid.*, 47.
[271] *Ibid.*, 47-48.
[272] *Ibid.*, 51.
√ [273] *Ibid.*, 52, 53.
[274] *Civilization*, 31-32.

This critique can be applied to all world views, or *Weltanschauungen*, that propose a meaningful, coherent, and even just universe. It holds equally, however, for those that see the universe as in principle meaningless. Just as Freud rejected the notion that because the analyst does not enjoin traditional morality he therefore supports complete libidinal freedom, so it does not follow from the critique of philosophical or religious systems that it makes no difference what assessment one makes of the world. The supporters of nihilism have, Freud opines, let the theory of relativity go to their heads. They seem to think that if knowledge of the absolute truth is impossible one may believe, and thus do, anything he likes. But this is in practice quite ridiculous. It makes a difference, Freud points out, whether a bridge is built of concrete or cardboard. The nihilist may reply that there is no necessary link between theory and practice. But at this point the argument of the nihilist becomes irrelevant to one who must live in the world, which threatens punishment for ill-considered acts.

Another example of a world view, one which insists on the possibility of a just universe, is Marxism. Freud's critique of Marxism owes much to his conclusion concerning social and individual psychology. Marx argued that human behavior is largely explicable as an expression of economic conditions and struggle. It seems unlikely, Freud contends, that economic forces alone could determine each human endeavor, especially our artistic, intellectual, religious and social activities. But further, Marx owes much more to the sort of projection of illusion we are accustomed to seeing in religious thought than to any clear understanding of human experience. The establishment of the communistic society, in which each gives according to his ability and receives according to his needs, is a working out of the desire for equality and the illusion that the leader loves his followers equally.

What is more obvious is that man is narcissistic, aggressive, an egoist in all his deeds. Communism errs in attributing all evil to the ownership of property and to its attendant maldistribution of power. It argues that "if private property were abolished, all wealth held in common, and everyone allowed to share in the enjoyment of it, ill-will and hostility would disappear among men. Since everyone's needs would be satisfied, no one would have any reason to regard another as his enemy; all would willingly undertake the work that was necessary." This, Freud concludes, is an illusion, a belief based on wishing that it were so. "In abolishing private property we deprive the human love of aggression of one of its instruments, certainly a strong one, though certainly not the strongest; but we have in no way altered the differences in power and influence which are misused by aggressiveness, nor have we altered anything in its nature. Aggressiveness was not created by property." If private property were removed, aggression would remain, and simply seek other forms, such as sexual ones.[275]

Upon closer examination it becomes clear to Freud that we are in fact talking about another religion. The behavior of the Bolsheviks suggests this conclusion, especially their dogmatic stance, their enforcement of rules and prohibitions, and their expectation of the coming kingdom of absolute equality. That it is an economic kingdom makes no difference; for their expectation too flies in the face of the economic facts of experience. That is not of concern to them, notes Freud. It is not experience but hope which drives them. Moreover, they are free in their own minds to carry out whatever tasks seem to them necessary to establish this kingdom in whatever manner they choose. It is for the common ultimate good.

Marxism falls into the critical category of religion for these reasons.[276] The root of Freud's objection to religion and all other "false views" is that they obscure the truth which they also reveal. If they were recognized as symptoms that would be one thing; but the historical fact is that they are treated as higher truths. Their power to obscure what Freud believes to be the real truth is immense; and it is to Freud's rueful recognition of this point that we must attribute the length and strength of his attack on religion. And there can be no questioning of the fact of this attack, nor of his conviction that religion is a symptom and thus an illusion. Moreover, his concern with the power of religion is evident wherever he contrasts it with science. His approval of science appears in clear perspective if we understand it to be central to his notion of the end of suffering; thus religion, as a truth of suffering, stands forth as the great opponent among cultural artifacts to scientific freedom. Religion provides comfort, explanation, rules. Science provides none of these things, except perhaps some strong theories with respect to cosmogony. Science seems helpless at times against the dogmatism and certainty of religion; and it clearly raised Freud's ire to think that the still, small voice of *logos* had to contend with the tintinnabulation of the neurotic throng of beliefs.[277]

He writes:

In summary, therefore, the judgement of science on the religious *Weltanschauungen* is this. While the different religions wrangle with one another as to which of them is in possession of the truth, our view is that the question of religious beliefs may be left altogether on one side. Religion is an attempt to master the sensory world in which we are situated by means of the wishful world which we have developed within us as a result of biological and psychological necessities. But religion cannot achieve this. Its doctrines bear the imprint of the times in which

---

[275] *Ibid.*, 59-60; *cf.* 62, 90.
[276] NIL, SE XXII, 158-182.
[277] *Ibid.*, 161-163.

96

they arise, the ignorant times of the childhood of humanity. Its consolations deserve no trust. Experience teaches us that the world is no nursery.[278]

Freud offers an illuminating discrimination concerning religion: the ethics of religion need to be separated from religious belief. For while the restrictions on our wishes are essential, the religious context of an illusory belief in God is altogether improper.

> The ethical demands on which religion seeks to lay stress need, rather, to be given another basis; for they are indispensable to human society and it is dangerous to link obedience to them with religious faith.[279]

And what is the danger in this alliance with religious faith? While ethical limitations are essential, religion is not a "permanent acquisition" in the evolution of mankind but "a counterpart to the neurosis which individual civilized men have to go through in their passage from childhood to maturity."[280] Religion's power lies therefore in its affective basis, which dogmatic insistence upon belief effectively screens from most people.[281] Science, with its correspondence theory of reality, is in fact threatened by religion; and the attack must be repulsed.[282]

Indeed, contrary to his critic's position in *The Future of an Illusion*, Freud believes that civilization runs a risk in its dependence on religion.[283] If we begin with the fundamental fact of civilization, the prohibition of murder, we shall see, following the psychoanalytic argument, that civilization exists to restrict what is both an individual and collective instinctive trait. What has happened is that this prohibition has been associated with God as the Giver of the Law. We do not publish this psychological explanation of the cornerstone of civilization, it should be noted, but rather simply announce it as the will of God. Thus what has a perfectly rational (both historical and ontogenetic) origin which would easily be understood is tied to the inscrutable nature and will of God.[284]

However,

> Since it is an awkward task to separate what God Himself has demanded from what can be traced to the authority of an all-powerful parliament or a high judiciary, it would be an undoubted advantage if we were to leave God out altogether and

---

[278] *Ibid.*, 168-169.
[279] *Ibid.*.
[280] *Ibid.*.
[281] *Ibid.*, 169-170.
[282] *Ibid.*, 170-171.
[283] *Illusion*, 57.
[284] *Ibid.*, 57ff..

honestly admit the purely human origin of all the regulations and percepts of civilization.[285]

But we should pause; is such a reasonable expectation justified? The prohibition against killing was made necessary by the psychological and historical fact of the wish to kill, especially to kill the father. Therefore the religious demand with its unmistakable and adamantine bond to the father is justified. Men knew that they had killed their father, and responded, guiltily, by pledging to do his will and by restricting their own passions lest they too became victims. The warehouse of religious ideas includes wish-fulfillments but also important historical recollections.[286]

This discovery alters our understanding of what we may expect from civilization, and clarifies the emergence of religious ideas. They are linked to neurotic behavior. We know that every human child must pass through a phase of neurosis. For instinctual demands, unserviceable to rational interests, require repression.[287] Most of these neuroses are overcome simply by growing up, while others are susceptible to psychoanalytic treatment. The analogy between the individual and the collective is irresistible. Mankind too suffered neurotic states, and for the same reasons: "in the times of ignorance and intellectual weakness the instinctual renunciations, indispensable for man's communal existence, had only been achieved by it by means of purely affective forces."[288] The precipitates that emerged carried on long after their use was essential. Religion, then, would thus be the "universal obsessional neurosis of humanity;" it was born in the Oedipal relations with the father. If this is so, says Freud, then our present turning away from religion constitutes the mid-point in the end of the Oedipal crisis for humanity. The prognosis for the end of this obsessional, infantile neurosis, namely religion, is good.[289]

Thus, while religion preserves a psychoanalytic/historical fact of human life, it nevertheless must be treated as a neurosis; and like a neurosis it has the time of its beginning and the time of its ending: "...the time has probably come, as it does in an analytic treatment, for replacing the effects of repression by the results of the rational operation of the intellect. We may foresee, but hardly regret, that such a process of remoulding will not stop at renouncing the solemn transfiguration of cultural precepts, but that a general revision of them will result in many of them being done away with. In this way our appointed task of reconciling men to

---

[285] *Ibid.*, 68.

[286] *Ibid.*, 69, *cf.* 68f..

[287] *Ibid.*, 70.

[288] *Ibid.*..

[289] *Ibid.*, 70f.. Freud took the position that the Oedipus complex was in the end annihilated, and by extension, and for the same reasons, the end of religion is inevitable. *Cf.* "Dissolution," SE XIX.

civilization to a great extent will be achieved."[290]

Freud's most extensive case study of religious beliefs as neurotic symptoms was undertaken toward the end of his career in *Moses and Monotheism*. It is a remarkable essay for three reasons: (1) Freud evidently had a great deal of trouble organizing it (as it stands it is three essays, with long sections of repetition); (2) it shares with other treatments of religion, notably *Totem and Taboo*, a remarkable absence of attention to the historical record as generally understood; (3) there is a striking lack of concern about (2). This may perhaps be accounted for by the fact that Freud's conclusion concerning the link between religion and neurosis was derived from treatment of patients, on the one hand, and on the other his refusal to admit any causes for social behavior that were different from individual behavior. One effect of this approach was to render his position impervious to historical criticism that did not accept these views. Finally, as can be inferred from the discussion thus far, Freud perceives the historical record in the same light that he perceives social institutions in general and the activity of the conscious ego in particular, namely, as a version of the instinctual conflict distorted by repression and symptom formation. *Moses and Monotheism* betrays all of these concerns.

The issue for the work is the emergence of monotheism and its link to Moses. Freud's account relates that monotheism emerged first in Egypt under the brief but seminal rule of Akhenaton, for whom the Egyptian Moses was a governor. When the seventeen-year reign of Akhenaton collapsed and the ancient regime was reinstated Moses was forced to flee, with his entourage, who were Levites. He joined tribes called "Hapiru" (whose possible role as the original Hebrews is suggested by the tablets found at Tell el-Amarna). The entire group made its way toward Canaan.

The practice of circumcision had been general among the Egyptians; and Moses, who assumed a position of leadership in this new company, insisted that it be taken up as a mark of holiness for his followers.

At this point it seems that a second narrative begins, also centered on the Moses name/figure. In this narrative the God of Moses is not Aten but Yahweh; and Moses is the son-in-law of Jethro the Midianite. Yahweh's worship is centered at the volcano at Horeb; and of Aten, the sun-god of the first Moses, nothing is known. The fact that the two narratives are combined in the record suggests that two groups, each following a different tradition, were joined. But at some point in this process the original Moses, the Egyptian, was killed; and the monotheism of the worship of Aten is conflated with the worship of the volcano god Yahweh. There is some evidentiary support for this view, according to Freud, in the fact that the two earliest narratives call their gods by

---

[290] *Ibid.*, 72-73.

99

different names, "Jahway" and Adonai. Adonai is, possibly, a corruption of Aten. This merging of traditions also explains the acceptance of the Egyptian Moses-figure as the main leader in exchange for the acceptance of Yahweh as the one true God. All Moses stories are now assigned to one figure. Further, circumcision, which was unknown to the Horeb group, is now made a general requisite. On the other hand, Yahweh is the god of the pillar of smoke by day and fire by night in the Exodus narrative, suggesting the volcano god's eventual ascendancy.

Remnants of the Egyptian tradition remain in distorted form. The Levites, originally part of the Egyptian Moses' entourage, came to occupy an anomalous place among the twelve tribes of Israel; this fact betrays the distortion of their true past in the conflation of the traditions. Another half-buried clue to the Egyptian tradition is the absence of a belief in an after-life in the Hebrew religion. This is a striking characteristic, for the surrounding traditions were enthusiastic in their examination of the after-life, and made it virtually the center of their ritual and theology. If we recall, argues Freud, that the Aten tradition of Akhenaton had rejected the notion of an after-life we see that part of the tradition remains alive in the subsequent Hebrew theology.

Why all this distortion? For in order to discover this narrative, Freud, or indeed anyone who attempts the task, must rearrange the order received in the tradition and must pick up the smallest clues, which occur as very slight anomalies, and ferret out their true meaning. In a very important example of what must be done, Freud states that the infamous episode of the idolatry of the golden calf, with its details of Moses breaking the Tablets of the Law and executing the idolaters, actually betrays the true but hidden event, the slaying of Moses himself. In another case, the record is very choppy on the question of circumcision. The institution of circumcision is assigned to Yahweh who requires it of Abraham, Isaac and Jacob. The original link between circumcision and the Egyptian heritage, then, has been deliberately expunged. That this is so may be seen in the strange passage in which Moses himself is circumcised. Yahweh sets out to kill Moses because he has not been circumcised. Moses is saved by the quick action of his wife, who performs the operation in great haste.

In sum, the younger tradition of Horeb actively suppressed the Egyptian heritage, translating and incorporating it into the tradition whose followers, Freud is certain, are responsible for the death of Moses. But the repression is not completely successful. Some 800 years after the death of Moses the prophetic tradition of Israel emerges. In its proclamation of an ethical monotheism we see the re-emergence of the Egyptian theology with its emphasis on *Ma'at*, justice, and its opposition to priestcraft, superstition and sacrifice. This ethical monotheism arose, as we know, in opposition to the worship of the Baals, which was powerfully established in the Kingdom and supported by the aristocracy and the kings.

As Freud subsequently argues, this re-emergence marks the beginning of a development which leads to the rise and fall of Jesus of Nazareth and the crucial work of Paul.[291]

The truth of this tale for Freud depends wholly upon its psychoanalytic content. It clearly conflicts with the written record. That record, however, seeks to homogenize the conflict between the two sources of monotheism in Israel, and chiefly to obscure the fact and implications of the death, or murder, of Moses. In Freud's reading, however, there are clues in great number that this record is the result of a repression. We have noted several; but perhaps the most significant for Freud's argument is the fact of the re-emergence of the Egyptian tradition 800 years after the death of Moses. In psychoanalytic terms it marks the end of the period of the suppression of infantile sexuality and the second onset of the development process. The period of latency seeks to represent its interests as the truth, and these are typically found in the written record—if we may speak of the history of civilization in this psychoanalytic manner. By contrast, there is the oral tradition which, in such traditions as Greek, German and Finnish epic literature, tells an almost entirely different story from what Freud calls the official record. For example, Homer draws upon a tradition of a great Mycaenian civilization of which there is hardly a trace found in the official record. It is of course significant that it is the poet who discovers these traces; for the poet, like all artists, draws upon unconscious sources rather than conscious ones, upon imagination rather than "facts." In so doing he will be closer to the psychological truth—and in Freud's view, therefore, to the historical truth.

The tale of *Moses and Monotheism* is, then, an allegory of a uniquely Freudian type. It is an historical narrative; this actually happened, Freud does not doubt. It is a psychological narrative as well. History and psychology follow paths that are more than parallel: they are as identical as the difference between phylogeny and ontogeny will allow them to be. For clarification let us turn for a moment to the tale of the self in its development.

The issue is the aetiology of the neuroses. It is assumed that a trauma is a *sine qua non* of neuroses. A trauma has the following characteristics: it occurs before the age of five; it is sexual and aggressive in nature; and it is subject to amnesia. Symptoms emerge as a consequence of this trauma. The effects of trauma may be either positive or negative. The person may wish to repeat the experience. In this case a fixation develops. Or the person may desperately wish to avoid any repetition of the trauma. In this instance phobia and inhibition arise. Either response to the trauma is compulsive; and if the effects of the trauma are not checked they will

---

[291] *Moses*, SE XXIII, 7-53.

create a part of the mental organization that will become inaccessible to the rest and go its own way, threatening the general economy of the mental life. These independent elements take on the quality of being real; and since they are closer to the self than even the effects of external reality they may actually challenge and replace that reality, a condition leading to neurosis and psychosis. These results do not occur in every case. Both constitutional and experienced (sic) factors are involved, and illness requires a certain imbalance involving each of them to a critical degree. Some traumas do not result in neuroses. But here, and in all neurotic behavior, we are dealing, says Freud, with some trauma that has a suitably compulsive effect; and therefore it is useless to attempt to decide which events are or are not traumatic in themselves. It is their effect that makes the difference.

These traumas and their effects pass through a period of latency. They are forgotten and subjected to a more or less effective amnesia. But at puberty, the second stage of the diphasic onset of sexuality, they re-emerge and in patients take the form of psychopathic behavior. This is the "return of the repressed." The defensive mechanisms of the latency period break down, only to be replaced by others which are in fact signs of the disease. If the general mental organization is sufficiently weakened, as for example in a sustained enfeeblement of the ego-organization, psychosis, or detachment from reality, may occur.[292]

This developmental history is directly transferrable to the course of the history of religion. The tale of *Totem and Taboo* is essentially the same: trauma, repression, latency, and partial return of the repressed. Assuming (with Darwin and Atkinson) that the primal social group was a horde ruled by a dominant male figure, Freud tells his story of how the sons rose up and killed the father, and ate him. Overwhelming guilt ensued. They established the rites and rules of totemism to sustain their guilt and prohibit repetition of their actions, notably in the prohibition of incest. There followed a matriarchal society in which some of the power drawn from the father was assigned to the mother. This stage gave way to a patriarchal period; and finally worship of gods replaced totemism altogether. In the end, in the final stage of religion, the primal father reappears as God the Father. The original ambivalent feelings toward the primal father also reappear in the fear and the love of God. The unlimited dominion of God is recognized; He is omnipotent, omniscient and omnipresent. But the clues to his history remain in the frequently anomalous behavior on the part of religious people today. Noteworthy here are circumcision and the Lord's Supper. Both instill power in ways that reflect the primal traumatic relationship between parent and child.[293]

---

292 *Ibid.*, 72-78.
293 *Ibid.*, 80-84.

Early trauma, defense, latency, outbreak of neurotic illness, and partial return of the repressed—

Such is the formula which we have laid down for the development of a neurosis. The reader is now invited to take the step of supposing that something occurred in the life of the human species similar to what occurs in the life of individuals; of supposing, that is, that here too events occurred of a sexually aggressive nature, which left behind them permanent consequences but were for the most part fended off and forgotten, and which after a long latency came into effect and created phenomena similar to symptoms in their structure and purpose.

We believe that we can guess these events and propose to show that their symptom-like consequences are the phenomena of religion.[294]

If we return to the story of Judaism, Moses, and monotheism we may now ask, when and why did the neurosis toward which this case study must inevitably lead arise? The outbreak occurs in the conflict created by Christian developments among the Jews, and is most poignantly represented in the life of Paul. The salient characteristic of this neurosis is an overwhelming sense of guilt. As one would expect, guilt is the primal guilt related to the killing of Moses and ultimately the wish to destroy the primal Father God. It was on the central doctrine of original sin that Paul based his interpretation of Christ, his Christology, and therefore his understanding of the *raison d'être* of Christian life and teachings. He carried the sense of guilt beyond the figure of Moses to the figure of God Himself. That primal murder was recapitulated in the death of Jesus; and the guilt which was attributed could not be restricted to Jews, although it was Paul's Mosaic heritage that made the truth of what had happened utterly clear.[295]

As in the case of the Hebrew prophets Christianity marked a return of the repressed; for it acknowledged the trauma of the primal murder in its acceptance of the innate justice of the death of the Son. The institutions of Christianity regressed from this stage of the triumph of monotheism as they became increasingly concerned with the life after death, magical ceremonies, and a lightly veiled polytheism in the cults of the saints and Mary. But at the heart of Christianity is a confession of guilt and a celebration of the victory of the Son who died because he ✔ had killed the father. The guilt was absolved.[296]

Judaism, Freud said, became a fossil; but its history clearly demonstrates the cultural significance of the aetiology of the neuroses. Freud

---

[294] *Ibid.*, 80.
[295] *Cf. ibid.*, 86-87.
[296] *Ibid.*, 86-88; *cf.* 122-137.

seizes upon what is in his view the outstanding trait of Judaism and the ancient Hebrew religion, its spiritual (*geistig*) quality, as a striking clue to the nature of religion. The central tenet of Moses' religion was the proscription of the worship of idols. God was to be grasped intellectually, as a spirit. The effect was to give Jews a sense of belonging and of superiority; for they engaged in the intellectual pursuits—logic, abstraction, pure thought, reason—as an extension of their intellectual religion.[297] The pride of the Jews is therefore linked directly to the function of the super-ego; for the intellectual commitment replaces the gratification of the instincts. The ego feels rewarded for accomplishing this repression and replacement. The Jewish God is not a god of sexual power and fertility but of the ethical ideal, and therefore exalted beyond the struggle of the self and its desires. However this may be, it is circumcision that betrays the real struggle. As a substitute for castration it indicates the archaic fact, that the threat of castration is the effective barrier against attempts to gratify one's desires; and whoever accepted circumcision, as all male Jews must, were thereby signifying their submission to the father and the restraint upon their own behavior. The ethical ideal stems then from the same crisis of infantile sexuality that is to be found in all cultural settings.[298]

The ethical commands so characteristic of Judaism represent the return of the repressed, Freud concludes. That repressed material is the killing of Moses, the historical trauma of the race which is both an allegory and a repetition of the psychological truth of the desire to kill the father. Ambivalence toward the father figure centers on Moses, and, of course, his God. On the one hand it is Moses and Yahweh who lead the Jews out of slavery in Egypt and bring them to the promised land under Yahweh's special protection. On the other hand this God imposes ethical standards of behavior that are remarkable in the cultural context for their purity. The imposition of these laws plays the same role and has the same effect as the establishment of the totem; for the laws are needed to prevent from happening again what has already taken place historically and psychologically. The laws are needed because men are guilty already. The history of the Jewish law strengthens the conclusion that it functions to stir up and sustain the sense of guilt. The law became increasingly complex, burdensome, and difficult to obey. Like the obsessional neurotic seeking some cause for the guilt he feels so keenly, the Jews seem, in Freud's view, to have gone in search of some cause for their guilt, while at the same time denying the true cause of the guilt. Confession of guilt was impossible. Unlike Christians, who admitted their guilt for having killed the father and had been forgiven for it in the wiping out of original

---

[297] *Ibid.*, 111-115.
[298] *Ibid.*, 116-122.

sin, the Jews never admitted their guilt and thus brought down the rage of Christians against them.[299] Whatever the historians' and theologians' judgements of this conception of Judaism have been, Freud rests his case on the psychoanalytic truth of his claim. That case stands or falls on the point that the return of the repressed material is accomplished by distorted representation of that material. The religious belief in God as omnipotent, all-good and ethically pure, who requires what is just, is precisely the distorted representation of the repressed material, the veritable proof of Freud's pudding. Another significant aspect of the distortion in the case of the Judaeo-Christian tradition is the compulsive, that is, dogmatic, insistence upon the belief that Jesus who is the Christ, the Messiah, died so that we would not be punished for our actions—and thoughts. In refusing this message, Freud insists, the Jews refused to acknowledge their guilt, and that is why they are so unhappy. Paul's message, too, is a distortion of the original act, but like all symptoms it reveals what it obscures. It does so by substituting an hypothesis or theology of original sin for the original historical and psychological act.[300]

The belief in God sustained by religious folk is an illusion, the result of a distortion of the historical and psychological experience of love and hate between parent and child. They are not in touch with God but with a neurotic, distorted, truth about the history of their desires. If they continue to be religious they deceive themselves and the truth is not in them. Freud is not above ironic praise for the believers.

> How enviable, to those of us who are poor in faith, do those enquirers seem who are convinced of the existence of a Supreme Being! To that great Spirit the world offers no problems, he himself created all its institutions. How comprehensive, how exhaustive and how definitive are the doctrines of believers compared with the laborious, paltry and fragmentary attempts at explanation which are the most we are able to achieve! The divine Spirit, which is itself the ideal of ethical perfection, has planted in men the knowledge of that ideal and, at the same time, the urge to assimilate their own nature to it. They perceive directly what is higher and nobler and what is lower and more base.... All of this is laid down so simply and so unshakably. We can only regret that certain experiences in life and observations in the world make it impossible for us to accept the premiss of the existence of such a Supreme Being.[301]

This quotation is useful because it summarizes some important as-

---

299 *Ibid.*, 122-137.
300 *Ibid.*.
301 *Ibid.*, 122-123.

pects of Freud's attitude toward and, more significantly, definition of, religion. First, Religion is belief in a Supreme Being. Second, it is a belief in a set of absolute ethical standards by which one may mark one's path of action. Third, it is dogmatic and absolutist in nature; that is, religion has as a *premiss* "the existence of such a Supreme Being." Finally, this general view is offered by one who is envious, he says, of the certainty provided by religion–knowing very well, perhaps as well as or better than anyone, that such a worldview is a delusion, an illusion and distortion of experience. Lest it be thought that Freud's conclusion on the nature of religion is either deliberately or inadvertantly ethno-centric, we should note that he found no fundamental differences among the religions of the world. He admits some ignorance about them. But his remarks on Islam, which he calls the *Mahommedan* religion (it very clearly is not), are illustrative.

> The founding of Mahommedan [*sic*] religion seems to me like an abbreviated repetition of the Jewish one, of which it emerged as an imitation. It appears, indeed, that the Prophet intended originally to accept Judaism completely for himself and his people. The recapture of the single great primal father brought the Arabs an extraordinary exaltation of their self-confidence, which led to great worldly success but exhausted itself in them. Allah showed himself far more grateful to his chosen people than Yahweh did to his. But the internal development of the new religion came to a stop, perhaps because it lacked the depth which had been caused in the Jewish case by the murder of the founder of their religion.[302]

And that is all he has to say about Islam. Noteworthy are (1) the brevity of the discussion in a work devoted to the rise of religion, (2) the fact that this is the *only* "discussion" of Islam in the whole of the Freudian corpus, (3) the conclusion on this superficial basis that there was no growth in Islam after some undetermined time in the far distant past, (4) the curious notion that Allah was "grateful" to his people–a view that only someone who had never read the *Qur'an* could hold–, and (5) the generally condescending tenor of the entire discussion, if that is the word for a paragraph of unsubstantiated and uninformed reference. Freud intends to shore up his case for the universality of his interpretation of religion. Thus all religions are instances of belief in a Supreme God who is actually the murdered father, and all one need know about traditions outside the Judaeo-Christian is whatever suffices to support this conclusion. This paragraph is illustrative of Freud's treatment of other traditions; thus we must conclude that he does not believe that it is necessary to know anything about those traditions but only to assert that they do not contradict

---

[302] *Ibid.*, 92-93.

his thesis.

If one were exercised—as I think any Muslim should be and would be—about Freud's treatment of Islam, let him consider the following discussion of the so-called Eastern Religions:

> The apparently rationalist religions of the East are in their core ancestor-worship and so come to a halt, too, at an early stage of the reconstruction of past.[303]

As for the so-called primitive religions,

> [i]f it is true that in primitive peoples to-day the recognition of a supreme being is the only content of their religion, we can only regard this as an atrophy of religious development and bring it into relation with the countless cases of rudimentary neuroses which are to be observed in the other field.[304]

Insofar as religion is an indication of the truth of suffering it is important to clarify what Freud intends about religion (and, for him, religions) as neurotic behavior or an indication of suffering. It is equally important to clarify what he means when he uses the terms "religion," "belief" and cognate and related words. Briefly, his critique of what he calls religion—that is, the belief in an illusory supreme being whose nature and existence resolve all the conflicts of our lives—is one which is very compelling. But Freud as the historian of religious traditions is simply wrong. The doctrine of religion as acceptance of an illusion is characteristic of a concept of religion that Freud, if he did not invent it, inherited from the world of the West in the nineteenth century. It was a concept that not only bore no relationship to the world's traditions but served effectively to obscure them, and to prevent any useful understanding of those traditions. Further, the religion Freud and his peers attacked was one in which the central element was belief, that is to say, acceptance of a proposition. Since this proposition was patently false to Freud, the religions were patently false. His task, then, was to explain why they had persisted through all these millenia; and his answer is recorded in *Totem and Taboo, Civilization and its Discontents, The Future of an Illusion,* and *Moses and Monotheism.*

The reality is quite different. On the question of the Buddhist view of the nature of God and any absolute, the matter is crystal clear: the acceptance of a supreme God whose nature and existence resolve all the conflicts of our lives is an illusion. It is based on wishful thinking and the impulse for satisfaction. I would suggest, although I have chosen not to pursue this matter in a form more general than the Buddhist and Freudian perspectives on suffering, that, indeed, this position is central

---

[303] *Ibid..*
[304] *Ibid..*

to all religious traditions. The critique of the Father-God would seem to be an essential step in the direction of liberation. The cultural heroes who reflect this truth are numerous indeed. I propose, then, that the religion Freud attacks is (a) of a peculiar invention bearing no significant relationship to the experience of the religious traditions of our world or to the individuals engaged in and molded by them, (b) a religion worthy of attack, as, for example the Buddhist tradition agrees.*

The Occult

In connection with this analysis of religion as a symptom of neurotic suffering Freud addressed the traditional and (one must say) persistent claims concerning the occult, the uncanny and telepathy. Understandably, claims of supernatural knowledge, extrasensory perception, and perhaps above all any notion of immortality appeared to Freud in the same light as religion. This is especially true with respect to wish-fullfilment and the ambivalence toward death.

It is true [he said] that the statement "all men are mortal" is paraded in text-books of logic as an example of a general proposition; but no human being really grasps it, and our unconscious has as little use now as it ever had for the idea of its own mortality.[305]

The cultural significance of this belief in immortality is obvious:

Religions continue to dispute the importance of the undeniable fact of individual death and to postulate a life after death; civil governments still believe that they cannot maintain moral order among the living if they do not uphold the prospect of a better life hereafter as a recompense for mundane existence.... [N]ot a few of the most able and penetrating minds among our men of science have come to the conclusion, especially towards the close of their own lives, that a contact [with departed beings] is not impossible.[306]

This primitive belief/wish in the life after death–and the possibility of communication over the border of death–is still with us. It is strong, and ready to rise to the surface at the merest provocation.

What has happened to that repression which civilization imposed to subdue the omnipotence of thought? It is still there, for the educated man avers stout disbelief in occult notions. But while he may now reject as improbable the notion of direct contact with spirits and ancestors, there remains his religious piety. The old relationship with the dead was highly ambivalent; and the religious piety into which that ambivalence

---

* See *Excursus*: **Freud's Conception of Religion**, below.
[305] "The Uncanny," SE XVII, 242-243.
[306] *Ibid.*.

has been molded still betrays its emotional origins.[307] In the feeling of the uncanny the infantile wish-world is more strongly suggested, in that an uncanny event is first and foremost a wished-for event. The boundary between what is real and what is psychical has been crossed again, and, indeed, effaced: the omnipotence of thought is revealed once more.[308]

The feeling of the uncanny proceeds, argues Freud, from two sources: (a) the omnipotence of thought, the conviction that what is wished for will come true, with its attendant consequences (note the cases of animism and primitive thought in general); and (2) infantile repressed complexes, such as the fear of castration. The "truth" of the uncanny experience is established in two stages. In the first stage the experience of the uncanny is tested against material reality. In the second stage the material reality is replaced by the psychical reality, so that the uncanny experience is seen as a "real" experience; but its "uncanny" nature reveals the history of the conflict between psychical and material reality. It is, furthermore, significant that if the material common to reports of uncanny experiences were to be expressed in the form of literary fiction the uncanny effects would not be achieved. When reported as an experience the material we call uncanny is threatening and frightening to us. But when that material—and Freud is in no doubt that the material is the same—is the subject of fiction, we are not frightened. On the contrary, we are drawn to it; we can treat it as real without fear of its consequences.[309]

While the experience of the uncanny finds its place is his psychic economics, the occult, with its claims to superhuman powers, simply angers Freud. For example, the notion that one can have dreams that foretell the future is too patently wish-fulfillment to require further examination:

> I must confess that upon this point [of prophetic dreams] my resolution in favour of impartiality deserts me. The notion that there is any mental power, apart from acute calculation, which can foresee future events in detail is on the one hand too much in contradiction to all the expectations and presumptions of science and on the other corresponds too closely to certain ancient and familiar human desires which criticism must reject as unjustifiable pretensions.[310]

Moreover the occult looks altogether too much like the religions of ancient times to be allowed a separate judgement. As with those religions one sees in the occult the same dogmatic claim to supernatural power which

---

[307] Ibid..

[308] Ibid., 244.

[309] Ibid., 246-252.

[310] "Dream Interpretation as a Whole: C. The Occult Significance of Dreams," SE XIX, 135-136; cf. "Psychoanalysis and Telepathy," SE XVIII, 177-181.

thinly veils the archaic emotional conflict in the self. Its claims may safely be rejected.[311]

Before leaving this topic there is an interesting aspect to Freud's discussion we should explore briefly, his conclusions concerning telepathy. Telepathy is the single phenomenon among the so-called supernormal powers to which Freud is willing to give serious consideration. In his *New Introductory Lectures* he reviews cases relevant to the claims for telepathy and, in each case, finds grounds for acceptance of thought-transference. The conditions for this transference are not as predictable (and, frankly, saleable), as his patients believed; but they are extant and identifiable. Further, the material of the transference phenomenon is now quite familiar: it is always an expression of infantile sexual conflict and its results, and it is always repressed material.

The common theme among the cases cited [312] is that, properly interpreted, telepathic dreams and prognositications are distorted reports of the wishes of the reporter transferred to another agent, such as a relative or fortune-teller. In this interpretation the striking "truth" of the information received telepathically, however distorted, must be accounted for; in each of these cases there was enough truth to demand some explanation.[313] In the case of one woman, a fortune-teller was reported to have forecast that she would be married and have two children by the time she was 30. At the time the prediction was made the woman was childless and 27. At the time of the narration, she was 43, still childless, and seriously ill, in analysis. According to Freud, she had hoped for children in order to replace her husband with her father (in the form of a child) to whom she was greatly attached. This had not happened. The most striking element of the tale, however, is that what the foretune-teller foresaw had happened, in almost exactly the way described, to the patient's mother, who had had two children by the time she was 32. Freud concluded:

> ...there was then no better explanation of the whole, unequivo-
> cally determined chain of events than to suppose that a strong
> wish on the part of the questioner–the strongest unconscious
> wish, in fact, of her whole emotional life and the motive force of
> her impending neurosis–had made itself manifest to the fortune-
> teller by being directly transferred to him while his attention was
> being distracted by performances [the presumably meaningless
> ritual] he was going through.[314]

---

[311] NIL, SE XXII, 31ff..

[312] *Cf.* "Dreams and Telepathy," SE XVIII, 197-208, 208-220; "Psycho-analysis and Telepathy," SE XVIII, 181-185, 185-193; "Dream Interpretation: C.," SE XIX, 135ff..

[313] "Dream Interpretation: C.," SE XIX, 136.

[314] *Ibid.*, 138.

Thought transference of this kind would seem to occur easily when an idea was passing from the primary to the secondary process. But more research was needed.[315]

While this is as far as Freud felt he could go, two points are worth noting: (1) not surprisingly, the content of telepathic episodes consists wholly of manifestations of conflict in the developmental stages of the child's life; (2) the feelings and emotions surrounding the conflict in some way as yet unexplained lend themselves to transmission to other people under the proper circumstances. These circumstances are pertinent to both the recipient and the "transmitter." On the one hand, the recipient must be peculiarly receptive to such emotional power; and on the other the level of emotional conflict must be of such power that it dominates all or virtually all other qualities and characteristics of the emotional and intellectual state of the "transmitter."

Other, non-affective, sorts of material probably are not transferred by thought; but Freud suspects that

in spite of [telepathy's] being so hard to demonstrate, it is quite a common phenomenon. It would tally with our expectations if we were able to point to it particularly in the mental life of children. Here we are reminded of the frequent anxiety felt by children over the idea that their parents know all their thoughts without having to be told them–an exact counterpart and perhaps the source of the belief of adults in the omniscience of God.[316]

Art

Freud's opposition to religion is in sharp contrast to his views on art. At first this seems surprising, for both are based on illusions, both are symptomatic of neurosis. But art, as has been suggested already, allows us to admit our infantile emotions without being overwhelmed by them.[317] The artist is able to help us face our guilt, our rage and our remorse, and in so doing provides an unusually successful therapy by bringing the unconscious into the conscious through the medium of a cultural artifact. Religion, on the contrary, simply increases the pressure of the repressed material. But art, and the artist, are peculiarly benign in Freud's analysis of culture:

An artist is originally a man who turns away from reality because he cannot come to terms with the renunciation of instinctual satisfaction which it at first demands, and who allows his erotic and ambitious wishes full play in the life of phantasy.

---

[315] Ibid..

[316] NIL, SE XXII, 31-56.

[317] See above, Freud's treatment of Rosmersholm, and his comments on the uncanny.

He finds the way back to reality, however, from this world of phantasy by making use of special gifts to mould his phantasies into truths of a new kind, which are valued by men as precious reflections of reality.[318]

As in all the categories of discontent with which civilization is beset, art is symptomatic of neurosis. The artist is no more able than anyone else to completely repress his frustrated desires. What distinguishes him from others is his life of fantasy. Unlike other neurotics, he is on the one hand seemingly farther removed from reality by virtue of the depth of his commitment to his fantasies, and on the other closer because he is able, by virtue of his gifts, to find his way back. It is a circuitous path; but this simply assures him his special, even heroic, stature in the world of men;

> Thus in a certain fashion he actually becomes the hero, the king, the creator, or the favourite he desired to be, without following the roundabout path of making real alterations in the external world. But he can only achieve this because other men feel the same dissatisfaction as he does with the renunciation demanded by reality, and because that dissatisfaction, which results from the replacement of the pleasure principle by the reality principle, is itself part of the reality.[319]

Art provides a significant "half-way" point between the reality that frustrates wishes and the world of imagination, where "primitive man's strivings for omnipotence are still in full force." But it is a conventionally accepted reality, this art, despite its power to represent the frightening view of our real wishes before our believing eyes.[320] Art offers satisfaction that replaces the renunciations of culture, and more than anything else reconciles us to our sacrifice to civilization.[321] Freud, like so many, is unable to provide us with a complete explanation of those magical powers of creation that set the artist apart from others, though certainly, as Freud's masterful essay on Leonardo da Vinci shows, psychoanalysis reads the universal tale of wish and repression, writ large, in the artist's life. But it is precisely this power to transform too plain passions into beautiful things that sets the artist apart.

> He represents his most personal wishful phantasies as fulfilled; but they only become a work of art when they have undergone a transformation which softens what is offensive in them, conceals their personal origin and, by obeying the laws of beauty, bribes

---

[318] "Two Principles," SE XII, 224.
[319] *Ibid.*.
[320] "Claims," SE XIII, 188.
[321] *Illusion*, 18; *cf. Civilization*, 26.

112

other people with a bonus of pleasure.[322]

However miraculous this transformation to beauty, the link between the artist's childhood and his life-history on the one hand and his works on the other "is one of the most attractive subjects of analytic examination."[323] Freud's attraction to the art of several genres and media—plastic, visual, literary—testifies to the special view he held of the artist. The artist enables the audience to view and experience its own conflicts in an aesthetic framework. In art, the omnipotence of thought is retained in a modified conscious mode.

> In art alone it still happens that man, consumed by his wishes, produces something for the gratification of these wishes, and, this playing, thanks to artistic allusion, calls forth effects as if it were something real.[324]

The way of art leads, albeit curiously, from fantasy to reality. The artist wants fame, power, and the love of women. He cannot have them in reality, and looks for the consummation of his goals in his fantasy. Artists, as the world knows, are notorious neurotics; for their mechanisms of repression do not work for so long as they do for the rest of us. But it is also true that they are able to turn to their fantasy world, to the world of the day-dream, and express its contents in some medium in such a way as to remove the repelling personal aspects and present the themes found there in universal form. Their success in this endeavor permits the more repressed among us to enjoy those fantasies without suffering the consequence of enacting them. A large yield of pleasure is obtained in art, and we are all grateful to the artist. What the artist cannot achieve in his own life is attained indirectly through the honor bestowed upon him by a grateful and delighted public.[325]

Fantasy

Art is an expression of fantasy. Freud took a life-long interest in fantasy. He defines it for the first time in psychological terms, and places it squarely within the context of the aetiology of the neuroses, that is to say, in the context of infantile sexuality, repression and neuroses. There is, he says,

> a general tendency of our mental apparatus, which can be traced back to the economic principle of saving expenditure [of energy], which seems to find expression in the tenacity with which we hold onto the sources of pleasure at our disposal, and in the difficulty with which we renounce them.

---

[322] "Claims," SE XIII, 187; *cf.* NIL, SE XXII, 158ff..
[323] "Claims," SE XIII, 187.
[324] *Totem*, 150-151.
[325] IL, SE XVI, 375-377.

With the introduction of the attachment to the world and the need to attend to its demands–that is, the reality principle–one activity was split off.

[I]t was kept free from reality-testing and remained subordinated to the pleasure principle alone. This activity is *phantasying*, which begins already in children's play, and later, continued as *day-dreaming*, abandons dependence on real objects.[326]

Fantasy is a remnant, if an active one, of the mental activity characteristic of the wish-fulfilling world of the id. It is a testimony to the strength of the desire to maintain that activity that, despite the demands of reality, fantasy continues as a mental activity. Indeed, Freud's discovery that patients' fixations and symptoms were due to imagined rather than actual events (*i.e.* empirically verifiable events, or events verifiable in principle) was a pivotal point in his development as a theorist. Upon discovering that a patient's tales of seduction were fantasies, his initial decision was to ignore them as insignificant and to find out what "really happened." But Freud soon realized that, at least from the patient's point of view, there was no such distinction to be drawn; what was imagined psychically really happened to the patient. In the psyche, as he pointed out frequently, there is a low valuation of reality and the distinction between it and fantasy.[327] The proper approach was, then, to ignore the distinction, follow the patient's lead, and treat the fantasy as a reality. "It remains a fact," he wrote, "that the patient has created these phantasies for himself, and this fact is of scarcely less importance for his neurosis than if he had really experienced what the phantasies contain. The phantasies possess *psychical* as contrasted with *material* reality," and "*in the world of the neuroses it is psychical reality which is the decisive kind.*"[328]

The fantasying operation is therefore a direct result of a psychical reality, and, very likely, not the one the patient knows or describes.[329] The psychical reality is the reality of a frustrated wish. The patient's course of cure must eventually bring him face to face with the reality of his wishes; in the course of the treatment the patient will return to those childhood wishes he has so effectively disguised.[330]

The question of the psychical reality of the fantasy poses another:

---

[326] "Two Principles," SE XII, 222.

[327] IL, SE XVI, 368.

[328] *Ibid.*.

[329] See below, concerning the child-beating fantasy, for an example of this observation.

[330] This process of disguise, and therefore of uncovery, or archeology, is again an allegory of the race: "every nation disguises its forgotten prehistory by constructing legends." *Ibid.*.

are events the causes of psychic trauma? Freud insisted that one could not predict with utter certainty that some events would produce neurosis, nor that certain mental dispositions would always yield to neurosis. Yet a link between the peculiar disposition of one's mental life and history on the one hand and the environmental factors on the other was apparent. Freud suggested that a "complemental series" could be discerned. In the *Introductory Lectures* he concedes that he had not succeeded in pointing to any difference in the consequences, "whether phantasy or reality has had the greater share in these events of childhood."[331] However we may surely speak of a complemental relationship. But we can go even farther. He reminds his audience that there must be a source for these fantasies. Assuredly, the source lies in the instincts:

> but it has still to be explained why the same phantasies with the same content are created on every occasion. I am prepared with an answer which I know will seem daring to you. I believe these *primal phantasies*, as I should like to call them, are a phylogenetic endowment. In them the individual reaches beyond his own experience into primaeval experience at points where his own experience has been too rudimentary.

> [I]t seems to me quite possible that all the things that are told to us to-day in analysis as phantasy—the seduction of children, the inflaming of sexual excitement by observing parental intercourse, the threat of castration (or rather castration itself)—were once real occurrences in the primaeval times of the human family, and that children in their phantasies are simply filling in the gaps in individual truth with prehistoric truth. I have repeatedly been led to suspect that the psychology of the neuroses has stored up in it more of the antiquities of human development than any other source.[332]

Here, in terms as clearly formed as any in his extensive writings, is Freud's answer to the question of the relationship between ontogeny and phylogeny. I have used the word "allegory" to describe this relationship, and perhaps now it is clear why it seems appropriate if it was not before. The content of the mind was originally filled with experience; and the shift to civilization sealed over that experience, repressing it, making it imaginative. Thus each child repeats in his emotional, sexual development the history of the race. That the content is known to us through fantasy is the proof of Freud's point, that we could not imagine what we had not experienced, and that what we experienced would not be manifested as *fantasy* if it were still permitted.

---

[331] *Ibid.*, 370f..

[332] *Ibid.*, 370-371; *cf.* "[The Wolf Man,]" SE XVII, 57-60, 95-97.

But fantasies do not readily give up their meaning. As with the other signs of civilization's discontent, the symptoms of neurosis (and the distortions of dreams in dream-work), what appears in the telling is a version of the truth carefully and artfully tailored to obscure as much as to reveal. Freud pursues this aspect of the fantasy-life in his essay " 'A Child is Being Beaten.' " This is a common masturbatory fantasy whose major element is the beating of a child. This fantasy must have a pleasure-goal which may not and cannot be satisfied in the real world and therefore is satisfied in an imaginary world. But this satisfaction must be accomplished in such a way that the ego is not threatened by external punishment. Thus the content of the fantasy will both satisfy a wish and do so safely by deflecting or displacing the effect of the wish from the ego.[333]

The fantasy "a child is being beaten" is clearly related to sexual satisfaction, masturbation and sadism and is therefore classified as a perversion fantasy. The fantasy has three stages—a fact evident at first only to the analyst as a result of thorough examination. The earliest form of the fantasy is an account of the loved parent of the opposite sex of the patient beating a sibling. The meaning here is evident, that is, the patient's love for the parent and hate for the sibling rival.

This stage indicates only partial sadistic pleasure, since the patient is not the one doing the beating. The second phase of the fantasy substitutes the patient for the sibling in the first stage. Here sadism is converted into masochism.[334] For the patient is now being beaten by the parent. In this stage the role of guilt is important, for the wish in the previous stage for the beating of the sibling and the (implied) sexual relationship with the parent has now been turned upon the patient, and he is being punished for his earlier wish. This second stage is also a regression, according to the theory of the development of sexuality, from the stage of genital primacy (seen in the first stage in the fact that the patient and parent have a positive love-relationship implied by the beating of the sibling) to the prior stage of anal-erotic sexuality, which is usually sadistic in appearance; but the guilt carried over from the first stage has given the sadism a masochistic appearance. In the third stage, the "public" or reportable stage of the fantasy, the patient is nowhere to be seen, and the beater is any person with authority, such as a teacher or another parent-

---

[333] A fantasy is not necessarily neurotic. It is, says Freud, a half-way point between reality and fixation, or disconnection from the real world; but the presence of a persistent fantasy marks for the person the possibility of neurosis, should the fantasy become the basis for action "in the world." *Ibid.*, 373-375.

[334] This conception of masochism as a conversion of sadism was later altered by Freud in *Beyond the Pleasure Principle.*

like adult figure. However, it is evident to the analyst that the one being beaten in this stage of the fantasy is in fact the patient, now disguised. Further, the sexual excitement attached to the fantasy is unmistakable. The one being beaten in this last stage always seems to be male. Freud concludes that while the reason for this is obvious in the case of male fantasies, the female fantasy requires further explanation: women wish to be men, for men are the heroes of these fantasies, although they are being beaten. The beating is in fact a sexual satisfaction for the patient, regardless of sex (recall the first stage).[335]

This fantasy has two other interesting characteristics: first, girls remember only the first and third stages; second, boys remember only the second and third stages. In examining the child-beating fantasies of boys Freud noticed that although the three stages of transformation are followed, as in the girls' fantasy, the first stage means "I am being loved by my father," the second stage means "I am being beaten by my father" and the third stage means "I am being beaten by my mother." The first stage is not remembered, says Freud, because of its homosexual implications. This danger is eliminated in the third stage, when the mother replaces the father. As in the girls' fantasy it is the third stage that is the surface or public version of the fantasy. Finally, while the girl is a spectator at the sexual act, the boy is always a participant.[336]

The child-beating fantasy is thus a story in need of sorting out, so to speak, but one that leads directly to a psychic truth, the love between parent and child. That it is a masked and repressed love is evident in the fact that what is reported is both a fantasy and perversion. But behind the psychic truth is an historical truth. For example, in discussing the role of fantasy in the art of Leonardo da Vinci Freud focuses on a "childhood memory" of the artist and its significance for his work. The fantasy of the vulture in the cradle appears at first to be a memory. But it soon becomes clear that elements of fantasy that emerged long after childhood had passed were significant in this vulture theme; indeed, the theme is transposed from this later fantasy back to childhood. The "memory," then, has been "altered and falsified" in a manner common to the memories of childhood. This falsified memory is then put in the service of later trends, so that it is very difficult to distinguish the memory from the fantasy.

This process, argues Freud, is a replication of, or is replicated by–a significant ambivalence–,

> the way in which the writing of history originated among the peoples of antiquity. As long as a nation was small and weak it gave no thought to the writing of its history.... Then came

---

[335] " 'A Child,' " SE XVII, 179-191.
[336] *Ibid.*, 198-199.

117

another age, an age of reflection: men felt themselves to be rich and powerful, and now felt a need to learn where they had come from and how they had developed. Historical writing, which had begun to keep a continuous record of the present, now also cast a glance back to the past, gathered traditions and legends, interpreted the traces of antiquity that survived in customs and usages, and in this way created a history of the past.[337]

But these two developments inevitably clashed; for a true picture of the past was, for a variety of reasons, undesirable and, indeed, now impossible. The memory of the country had emphasized certain developments at the expense of others, so that the intents and wishes of the now historically sensitive peoples came to the fore. The first kind of history reflects, then, and is comparable to, man's conscious memory of the events of his maturity, while the memories that he has of his childhood correspond to the account of a nation's earliest days, one compiled later and for "tendentious reasons."[338]

But despite distortion the reality of the past is also revealed. If it were possible to undo the distortions the real events of the past would be revealed, and stand forth regardless of the intentions of the historians. This is also true for the childhood memories and fantasies of an individual.[339] The fantasy, then, obscures and reveals the truth of our psychic history, both as individuals and as a race.

---

[337] *Leonardo da Vinci and a Memory of His Childhood*, tr. Alan Tyson (New York: W. W. Norton & Co., 1964), 33-34. Leonardo wrote:

It seems that I was always destined to be deeply concerned with vultures; for I recall as one of my very earliest memories that while I was in my cradle a vulture came down to me, and opened my mouth with its tail, and struck me several times with its tail against my lips.

The vulture theme may be seen in Leonardo's "St. Anne with Two Others." "Leonardo," SE XI (1910), 82, *et passim*.

[338] *Ibid..*

[339] *Ibid..*

Summary

It has been my intention in these preceding sections which are concerned with the nature of neuroses, symptoms and the discontents of civilization to illustrate Freud's understanding of what the Buddha calls The Truth of Suffering. Some of this material will be examined again as we turn to the causes of suffering as Freud understands them, and the causes of the end of suffering. But I think a few summary points may be usefully advanced.

First, the notion of suffering is of course psychological for Freud.[340] This is clear in his argument for the identity of so-called Social Psychology and Individual Psychology. As a topic in itself this identity occupied his attention at several points in his writing. But it also is clearly implied in his treatment of the psychology of the individual as ontogeny, of the psychology of the group as phylogeny, and his belief that the former is a recapitulation of the latter. This means that history is extremely significant, for there are real events behind the psychical history of the individual; but these real events have their own ultimate significance in psychical experience rather than in social institutions. The social institutions are, then, effects of these psychical causes.

Second, it is equally clear that the suffering in question is in a very profound sense self-imposed. Exactly how this self-imposition of suffering works is Freud's major contribution to the "Second Noble Truth," that of the cause of suffering. We shall see that his metapsychological investigations lay out the alternatives for the self in light of various forces that are opposed and of which the self consists. But it should already be quite evident that suffering is internally caused, and that its goal and source are to be found in the internal dynamic of the self. Now it is true that the external world plays a part so important that no one could possibly miss it. It is one of the masters of the ego; and it is contact with that external world that calls for differentiation between ego and id. But the external world is what Aristotle would call a material cause rather than a final cause; for the suffering to which Freud is so sensitive is in fact a result of the reaction of the self to the world. It is the self that determines the force and form of that reaction, that establishes the resistances, fixations and repressions. We should, then, understand the nature of suffering of which Freud writes so sensitively in the terms of those adjustments and responses.[341]

---

[340] But my dissatisfaction with this category will soon be evident.

[341] Of scientific interest in the external world Freud says:

> finally, the problem of the nature of the world without regard to our percipient mental apparatus is an empty abstraction, devoid of practical interest.

Illusion, 92.

119

Third, the truth of suffering is universal and ineluctable. If we accept Freud's general conclusion that the life of the emotions, or the mental life, is the result of the same conflict of forces in all individuals, then it must be true that every person grows up in conflict. Some manage this conflict better than others. But no one avoids the conflict, which is between the conscious and the unconscious worlds. Moreover, we should not think that a self enters a conflict situation, whether out of choice, accident, careless, ignorance, greed or stupidity. Rather, the conflict is what defines the self. We are, as so many have said, the conflict. There is no self that is not this titanic tension among the forces of creation, adjustment and destruction. Neurosis, then, is not so much an aberration of human behavior as it is an occasion in which reality or the id has got the upper hand for the time being in the conflict. It is, as we shall see, the work of analysis not to end the conflict but to encourage the weaker side against the stronger, the weaker side in most instances being the ego. That Freud is convinced that this picture is correct is evident in his attitude toward narcissism and psychosis. In each case one side of the conflict so dominates the other that any attempt at restoration of balance seems doomed. Psychosis is, indeed, a complete victory for one side. So also, in the opposite direction, is melancholia. What the analyst hopes to achieve—and his hopes for cure seem to be justified almost solely in this area—is to strengthen the claim of the weakened side, usually the ego, so that the tension of the conflict may be made more equable. Thus the significance of the notion of homeostasis lies not in Freud's apparent insistence on a static existence but in his appreciation of the fact that the very reality of which we speak, the self, is itself forces in conflict.

Fourth, the truth of suffering is a truth of self-deception, of false and misleading understanding. In every instance of investigation in this part the factors of distortion, illusion and self-deception are crucial. The fact is that we are determined to represent the world to ourselves in a manner contrary to the reality of our own wishes, which are, consequently, rendered obscure. We construct, whether through history, art, religion, custom or law, cultural artifacts to which we submit but which are something other than they appear to be. The artifact obscures the reality of our infantile wishes, converts them into something acceptable to the conscious, and at the same time reveals to the discerning eye the truth of its origin. That discerning eye is, of course, not the eye of the believer, the writer of history, the artist, but of another. When self-deception is replaced by judgement the situation is radically altered. But in the "given" situation false view, illusion, and wishful thinking obtain.

Fifth, the truth of suffering is a truth of desire, of instinctual, impulsive, striving for gratification. If it were not true that our fundamental nature is egoistic, sensual and irrational, suffering simply would not exist. Again, it is not the case that a self exists which from time to time expe-

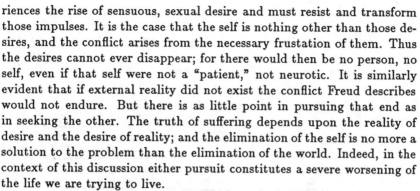

riences the rise of sensuous, sexual desire and must resist and transform those impulses. It is the case that the self is nothing other than those desires, and the conflict arises from the necessary frustation of them. Thus the desires cannot ever disappear; for there would then be no person, no self, even if that self were not a "patient," not neurotic. It is similarly evident that if external reality did not exist the conflict Freud describes would not endure. But there is as little point in pursuing that end as in seeking the other. The truth of suffering depends upon the reality of desire and the desire of reality; and the elimination of the self is no more a solution to the problem than the elimination of the world. Indeed, in the context of this discussion either pursuit constitutes a severe worsening of the life we are trying to live.

The truth of suffering as the truth of the conflict between desire and reality is related to Freud's profoundly personal notion of suffering. He rejects idealism, which holds that the only reality is intellectual and/or emotional; for the origins of the neuroses take us back to an historical past, and the fantasies have reality embedded in them. Nor is he a realist, believing that the aetiology of the neuroses must be the result of the action of external forces; psychical reality is not to be distinguished from material reality, and is not the less real for that. The unconscious is a reality, one usually more significant than material reality. Freud accepts neither of these views, as he does not accept nihilism, which only superficially seems to be a middle course. Rather, both instinct and trauma, both disposition and environmental occasion, both desire and external reality are interwoven in the suffering of mankind. It would be a mistake, and certainly an under-valuation of the Freudian insight, to call him either an idealist or a realist in the sense I have described. In the end the crux is the emotional life of the invidual as he faces the crises of growth and their consequences; this is who we are, and it is this pattern, this conflict, that Freud understands to be our selves. This conflict is the Truth of Suffering.

121

Excursus: Freud's Conception of Religion

As I have suggested, despite the aptness of Freud's critique of religion as a symptom of neurosis and therefore, in the terminology of this comparative study, part of the truth of suffering, he is surely misleading in his formulation of the nature of religion. The proof that this is so is evident when he identifies the historical religious traditions *in toto* as systems of (neurotic) belief. In order to draw this conclusion he must presume that the essential element in all religions and religion is belief in God–God as possessing the quality of existence and God as the founder of the ethical tradition that is present in all cultures. Further the religion that is essentially belief in this God may be isolated and designated with a noun. It is a thing–"Religion." As a thing it is in essence static. While it is true, in Freud's view, that there was some development in the history of Religion, it simply followed a path analogous to the development of the sexual and emotional stages of the individual. The fundamental elements of ambivalence toward the Father-God, the omnipotence of thought, the return of the repressed, and the obsessional neurosis of guilt were all there in their time; and there never has been nor ever will be any change in these elements. Religion, in short, is a static cultural artifact acting as distorting symptom-substitute for the emotional reality of the individual's life. My point here is not that Freud is wrong about the nature of religion as he describes it but that what he has called religion does not correspond to the historical experience of man as *homo religiosus*. That experience has not been static, for example; and it certainly has not been primarily about belief as an intellectual operation in which one accepts propositions for the wrong reasons.

Why is it that Freud defines religion in the way that he does? There are questions here pertaining to the historical context of the use of religion, its history as a term.*

By the time Freud employed it, "Religion"–and the issue I raise here is not affected in the slightest by Freud's use of German: the term in German in his work is *"Religion"*–owned a long and varied history. Its Latin history in the West passed through several stages of meaning. It probably meant "being bound," or "obliged," in its earlier stages, and remnants of that meaning still attend to it. Cicero and Lucretius suggested two significant usages of the term, the former an urbane and pragmatic view of the benefits and vices of performing certain rites and taking general account of the gods, the latter a metaphysical, ontological view of hidden and enormously powerful forces which bind and change the universe. The later Christian notion reflected at first the crucial role of the Church, so

---

* I am indebted to the work of Wilfred Cantwell Smith in what follows. See especially his *The Meaning and End of Religion* (New York: Macmillan, 1963).

122

that the *religio* of the Christian *ecclesia* was to be distinguished–certainly in intention and ultimately in form–from the *religio* of any other tradition. *Religio* here meant not belief but the whole range of practice, discussion, planning, organization, worship, plastic representation, and rules and customs that was characteristic of those who were in the *ecclesia*–as opposed to those who were not. There was no doubt that others had their *religio*–it flew in the face of clear observation to conclude otherwise. But "they" had "theirs," "we" had "ours."

As the Christian movement gained power, notably that of Rome, and systematic intellectual structure, notably that of Greece, the conceptualization of *religio* was also affected. For Augustine, with his Platonic idealism, *religio* meant the ideal relationship with Christ, cleansed of earthly limitations and taints, and was therefore a goal to be aspired to–certainly not a condition one could see every day. This conception remains for the most part the dominant one for a millenium, and is sustained by Ficino (Marsiglio of Padua). In the meantime, and consistent with the nature of the medieval church, the term *religio* and its cognates came to designate the life of self-denial and service, of celibacy, poverty and obedience. To be a "religious" meant that one had formally and permanently accepted a style and content of living that would set him or her apart from the common works of the day in order to achieve the high goal of life in Christ. It was, in short, a designation of intention and striving peculiarly tied to a social institution, monasticism. The term still retains this meaning within the Roman tradition, whose structure continues to be essentially monastic.

And even up until the period of the Reformation we still search in vain for the concept of religion that corresponds with Freud's. The Reformation revived in part the ancient Christian notion of *religio*. Zwingli, for example, discusses "true religion" and "false religion"–but what he is talking about is such a matter as the proper and the improper ways to celebrate the Lord's Supper. Again, Calvin's archetypal Protestant work, misleadingly entitled in English *Institutes of the Christian Religion*, does not even raise the question of the nature of an entity called Religion. Rather, Calvin is concerned to expose in all its variety the life of piety in thought, word and deed, which is oriented towards Christ. There is no suggestion of a religion, certainly not of a Christian religion.

Two and one-half centuries later the situation has changed considerably. It is readily seen that Religion is the subject of spirited discussion. The hunt is on for the "essence" of Religion. The central issue of an area of study called the Philosophy of Religion is whether the propositions of religion are to be regarded in the same light as those of science, and whether they can be defended and attacked in the same manner. For the most part the learned of the day hold that they can, and they do. The centers of learning, especially those in Germany such as Tübingen,

123

have launched an area of study called *Religionswissenschaft*, the scientific study of religion. Its main tenets are two: (a) no epoch is peculiarly close to God; (b) things and events must be described just as they happened. Religion is the subject of this study. The religion that is studied, however, is an entity, characterized by peculiar beliefs, static in essence, and institutional in form. The beliefs and practices are samples to be analyzed, their histories to be explicated by the disinterested scientist. The religion examined in this manner does not, as one might suspect, come off very well. Its beliefs are irrational–except, as Freud would note with interest, the rational-ethical contents–, its practices "primitive" (where "primitive" refers not to chronology but to phylogeny), its participants ignorant, deluded and/or simply incomprehensible, at least without reference to some atavistic predilection for the supernatural.

How did this state of affairs come to be? A most significant cause is evident in the religious history of Europe during the events of the Reformation through to the end of the Thirty (or Eighty) Years War. The emergence of opposed political units among (and between) Protestant and Catholic Europeans was widely characterized by a use of religious practices and doctrines for the purposes of identifying one's friends and one's enemies. Books are published describing the Religion of the Dutch, of the English, of Catholics. These tomes were not written by the friends but by the enemies of these people. Their appearance signifies one essential element in the notion of religion as Freud knew and denigrated it: religion is a term and a concept one uses chiefly about one's opponents, or at least about those other than oneself, whose cultures, traditions and lives differed from and even, apparently, contradicted one's own. In short, the term "religion" as Freud knew it emerged from a polemical context. It is fair to say, I believe, that it has never escaped entirely from that context; and it has never ceased to be a valuable weapon in the armory of the external critic.

It is of course utterly consistent with the polemic usage of the term to observe that what it describes seems to imply a view of the world at odds with what surely are each individual's aspirations as a human being. Religion has fixed beliefs, according to its describers. It denies freedom in favor of obedience. It is opposed to change. It is intolerant of other views. It is irrational. It is primitive. At times it is even silly. The students of religion in the nineteenth century were faced, as they saw it, not with the question of how the traditions of their ancestors had come to the liberating and universal truths which they passed on and how we as their heirs would employ them in our new situation to the benefit of all people; rather, their question was, how could people, whom we had previously thought to be exemplary, certainly rational, come to believe such silly and idiotic things? Thus were born the theories of the origin of religion.

124

Second, Religion emerged not only in a polemical context but as a system of propositions the acceptance or rejection of which was what marked a person as religious, or not, and, perhaps even more important, indicated what kind of religion he had, as they say, "bought into." In a period whose character is quite clear by the end of the seventeenth century until very nearly the present day this is the theme (with variations) of the notion of Religion. Religion was first and for the most part still remains "something" other people "have," although, if forced to explain one's own tradition, one may have recourse to discussing "my" religion. (I will only need to do this in conversation with an "outsider," someone who does not seem fully to understand my world view and who very likely does not share it.) The theme of religion is played out by the *Religionswissenschaftlicheschule*, and in extensive and brilliant enquiries by such thinkers as Hegel, Marx, Feuerbach and, of course, Freud—that is, the concept of "Religion itself," the underlying and presumably universal subject of religious people, that which they all share, whatever that is. It is well known that such an approach to Religion *per se* requires a Kantian or idealist world view which presupposes an Ideal that the various traditions approximate. It is highly significant that this "Religion" is believed to be primarily philosophical in nature, whose chief expression is belief, and whose chief exponents are systematic philosophers.

The third major element of religion as Freud employed it is implied in the other two, the concept of the religions of the world. If Religion *per se* exists and is universal it must be the case that all forms are approximations of the Ideal, but they approximate the Ideal in the same way. Indeed, the students of the history of religion opined that this is the case. They were convinced that there was a standard by which Hinduism, Buddhism, Shintoism, Muhammadanism (*sic!*—indeed, one should add *sic!* after each of these terms), Sikhism, Bonism, Judaism and of course Christianity could be measured to ascertain the success of their approximation. One need only collect items of belief in the most convenient manner and draw up a list of them for each of these religions. The most successful versions would be those approximating most exactly the fullest manifestation of the Ideal and the least successful would be the least systematic and theological—here "theological" in the sense of the application of reason to "belief," belief already being some sort of proposition.

The study of religion was, then, the study of belief systems of the cultures of man. Before this comparative analysis could be carried out, however, the religions of the world had to be invented—for they surely did not exist before. The terms "Buddhism," "Hinduism," "Sikhism," "Muhammadanism," and so forth, simply did not exist—in any European language or, more significantly, in any other cognate form of those terms in any language—until the West discovered and set out to identify, report, and test the religions of the world. The religions of the world, in short, are Western inventions, and therefore served the purpose of a Western agenda. In the period I am referring to (post-Reformation to the present) the outstanding, and for some only, characteristic of religion was its philosophic-propositional content and its corresponding apologetic form. If Religion *per se* were universal, then the religions of "non-Western" cultures had to be invented to bolster the claim for the universality of true belief, usually belief in God. It is not surprising that to Christian eyes and ears those other traditions did not approximate the full systematic expressions of belief; but from the more primitive expressions of belief in a High God to the sophisticated arguments of a Śaṁkara, or a Ghazālī, religion was now by definition an approximation to an Ideal whose sum and substance were intellectual proposition and argument, which was called belief.

Freud's view of religion fits, inevitably, into this three-part framework. He was also aware of the role of religion in the lives of his patients. And the presence of the established church in Austria and elsewhere, as well as what one acquaintance of mine called the "question you never ask in Vienna," (*i.e.*, whether one is a Jew) played crucial roles in his view of religion. Although I would like very much to understand the role of the Judaeo-Christian tradition in the personal life of Freud better than I do, I suspect that the best understanding lies in the direction of the application of the analytic approach Freud directs toward Religion to his own situation. The mix of these elements results in Freud's case in a notion of religion as a fixed system of truth which, when viewed from without, could only be an illusion, a helpful, therapeutic illusion, especially for those who needed all the help they could obtain, but an illusion nonetheless. Freud's frank identification of his work with that of science meant for him that only weak neurotics needed religion, and the heroes of the intellectual advance of man were scientists, that is to say, the opponents of religion. We must bear in mind what Freud probably thought when he wrote such things (he wrote them frequently). He meant that any person who would risk his intellectual heritage for the sake of a better understanding of human life must perforce reject any system of dogmatic belief that insisted that its members prove their loyalty by believing in a puppeteer God to whom they gave all responsibility for their thoughts and actions, before whom they cowered in fear and, paradoxically, loved because he forgave them for whatever they did. Whenever Freud denigrates religion this is what he has in mind. Naturally, in discussing "non-Western" traditions he makes no allowance for differences, for there were none in his view. The same *sacrificium intellectum*, the same mindless obedience, is required, whether by Allah or the ancestors who Freud assumes are the essential figures in all Eastern traditions. As I point out in a following *Excursus*, Freud's knowledge and understanding of (at least) the Buddhist tradition is a thing of fancy. His use of the nirvana

126

principle is proof of this conclusion; and his reduction of the Buddhist tradition, along with all the other Eastern traditions, to ancestor worship is a very strong indication that he does not have a sufficient historical understanding on which to rest his conclusions concerning religion.

But the most striking thing for me and, I would think, for anyone who has reviewed Freud's writings on religion, is that his conviction far outweighs his evidence. In cruder terms, one has the impression that here again any stigma is good enough to beat a dogma with; we find a man of critical faculties virtually without peer addressing a subject of enormous historical, emotional and intellectual significance with a dash and abandon more worthy of tabloid journalism. I conclude here by underscoring my point: the religion that Freud attacks is worthy of attack. This is not surprising since it was invented for that purpose, to be examined and attacked (or defended). It is a religion of propositions, and it is a static system. What it is not, however, is relevant in any direct way to the religious history of mankind, and to the issues that have concerned that history. At best, the religion Freud discusses is an aberrant development of Western history, contributing mightily to its intellectualization and "secularization." It certainly bears no relationship to any other tradition apart from being an academic mold into which modern Western philosophy sought to squeeze the great cultures of the world.

Freud's view of religion is both inadequate and wrong; but Freud's contribution to the religious history of humankind, notably in the modern era, is profound. That is the issue in this present work. His contribution lies in an area that is indisputably central to the religious life of persons: the area of suffering. It is Freud the student and physician of the suffering who, fortunately, shines forth, shadowing the misguided critic of "Religion."

The Buddha and the Truth of Suffering

The Universal Nature of Suffering

Among the ways in which the Buddha urged his followers to think of the nature of their experience was by conceptualizing it as suffering. The term, as I have noted above, is *dukkha* which is translated variously as "anguish," "ill," "suffering," "woe" (reflecting the usages of the different periods from Edwardian to the present in the translations I have used).

> [B]irth is anguish, and old age...and disease...and dying, ...grief, lamentation, ...suffering, ...tribulation, ...despair, ...if one does not get what one wants...; in short, the five groups of grasping are anguish [the *khandhas*, the "heaps" of which the self is composed].

> What is...the uprising of anguish? That craving which is connected with again-becoming, accompanied by delight and attachment, finding delight in this and that, namely the craving for sense-pleasures, the craving for becoming, the craving for annihilation [*kāmataṇhā, bhavataṇhā, vibhavataṇhā*]....

> What is the stopping of anguish? Whatever is the stopping with no attachment remaining, of that self-same craving, the giving up of it, the renunciation of it, the release from it, the doing away with it–this...is called the stopping of anguish.[342]

The course leading to the stopping of anguish is the Eight-fold Path and the coming to the True *Dhamma*, the true teaching.

If we put aside for the moment technical issues of translation and historical reference, one central theme is readily evident in this passage, the relationship between suffering and desire. A second striking point is the range of suffering; it is universal, from life to death and beyond. When Māra the tempter, whose world, as we shall see, is that dangerous one of sensory perception and sensuous delight, asks the *Bhikkhunī*, or Sister, Vajira, who is the creator of a being, she replies that Māra has wandered into a false opinion, for there is no being to be discerned. We must beware lest the language deceive us. Rather:

> ...it is simply Ill that arises, Ill
> That doth persist, and Ill that wanes away.
> Nought beside Ill it is that comes to pass,
> Nought else but Ill it is doth cease to be. [343]

Further, one "overcome by ill" leads a life of constant striving and stress.

---

[342] M I, 60-61.
[343] S I, 169-170.

Consider one overcome by ill... –he grieves, mourns, laments, beats his breast and becomes bewildered; or roams abroad in search of one who knows a spell or two to end his ill. Ill yields bewilderment and search....[344]

The characteristics of the life of *dukkha* include a desperate sense of being lost, a strong desire to find some cure for this sense of bewilderment and profound distress. There is some awareness of being ill; but his ignorance is so profound that the sufferer thinks a bit of medicine or magic will take care of the matter. The matter is far more serious; the discomfort, the sense of bewilderment, the stress are indications of the presence of a suffering more profound than its symptoms. The illness is the result of living in the world, indeed the result of living at all. Ill ranges from old age to rebirth–to give its scope one of many possible expressions. Ill is "such delight in activities that lead to rebirth, that lead to old age, to death, sorrow, grief, woe, lamentation and despair." Those who delight in these activities are said to "compose a compound [*sankhāra*] of activities that conduce to rebirth...," old age, death, sorrow and so forth. They fall into rebirth, old age, death. They are not released from this suffering (*dukkha*).[345] These "activities" will be discussed in a later section; but it is noteworthy here that they are activities done willingly by persons seeking a false goal; and the consequences are not brought about by external factors but as a result of "delight" in activities.

The truth of suffering is not grasped; and without knowledge of the truth of suffering the human experience is undirected, disoriented, susceptible to the forces of existence. "[J]ust as a stick, when thrown up into the air, falls, now on its butt, now on its middle, now on its tip, even so beings, hindered by ignorance, fettered by craving, run on, wander on, pass from this world to the next and thence back again to this world."[346] But it is the intending self, the self that acts, that creates this wandering, inefficient, distressful life. The acts performed are the cause of the consequences, and therefore the blame for the distress lies with the self:

I declare, monks, that of intentional deeds done and accumulated there can be no wiping out without experiencing the result thereof, and that too whenever arising, either in this same visible state or in some other state hereafter. I declare, monks, that there is no ending of Ill as regards intentional deeds done and accumulated without experiencing the results thereof.[347]

Thus the distress of this life and those following is the result of actions

---

[344] A III, 295.
[345] S V, 379.
[346] *Ibid.*, 371-372.
[347] A V, 189.

130

taken now. As a robber may stop himself from stealing by reflecting on the effects of the deed, so each should know the effects of evil action: "Evil in the future life is the fruit of bodily offence. Evil is the fruit of offence by work, by thought, in the future life. If I offend in deed, in word, in thought, should not I, when the body breaks up, after death be reborn in the Waste, the Way of Woe, the Downfall, in Purgatory?"[348]

Yet transience and the infinite flux of cause and effect are the very nature of man, rather than permanence of body, mind, or feeling. As the Buddha takes leave of his followers at his *parinibbāna*, his death, Sakka declares of the Buddha, and of all,

they're transient all, each being's part and powers,
Growth is their very nature and decay.
They are produced, they are dissolved again;
To bring them all into subjection—that is bliss.
349

Ignorance of the truth of suffering sustains the bewildered "running along" of the self.[350] Of the self, here understood as physical form, or *rūpa*, the texts say that it is "worn out, ...of diseases a nest, brittle...a rotting congeries; truly a dying end hath (this) life [*jivitaṃ*]."[351]

All men are and do is transient, says the *Dhammapada* (*sankhāra anicca*); all that men think and do is *dukkha*.[352] Yet the truth is not known to them. Indeed, they believe that their strivings, desires and cravings are painful because they are unfulfilled, and that when they are fulfilled their distress will end. Meanwhile they live in dread.

What is it that doth cause a man to be?
What is it of him that runneth to and fro?
What is it undergoes life's endless round?
What is it brings him fear and mighty dread?
Craving [*taṇhā*] it is that causeth man to be;
His thought [*cittaṃ*] it is that runneth to and fro;
The 'person' undergoes life's endless round [*saṃsāraṃ*];
Suffering is his fear, his mighty dread.[353]

In stating the bare fact of the truth of suffering, of *dukkha*, it is of course already evident that we must be concerned with more than the distress of the individual. The Buddhist traditions are very sensitive to the presence of this distress, and describe it in a psychoanalytically sophisticated metaphor of the bouncing stick. Yet the *dukkha* the individual feels

---

348 A I, 43-44.
349 D II, 175-176.
350 *Ibid.*, 96.
351 Dh, N. 148, p. 53.
352 *Ibid.*, N. 277, 278, p. 93.
353 S I, 52.

is also a "metaphysical" truth; by nature existence is *dukkha*. As Sister Vajira instructs Māra, it is *dukkha* alone that rises. Thus to address the issue of the individual's suffering is to address the nature of existence.

"Things to be Put Off": *The Marks of Suffering*

In the systematic presentation characteristic of the *Āgamas* the category of "things to be put off," abandoned, or renounced occurs frequently. These are the elements of the life of suffering. For example, one of the most significant rubrics is the renunciation of the senses *insofar as they identify our perceptions as though they were ultimate reality*. I shall address this issue of the relationship between suffering and the role of the senses in much greater detail below. Here I only wish to make the point that the senses play a central role in the Buddhist understanding of the truth of suffering. Thus the *Majjhima Nikāya*'s description of the "Thirty-six Modes" summarizes the attitude of these texts toward the senses and their renunciation. The "Thirty-Six Modes" are functions of the senses; in the Buddhist tradition there are six senses, for the mind is understood to be a sensory organ (the Pāli word here is *mano*; and one must take care not to confuse this use of "mind" with the use attached to *citta*, to which we shall come in a later section. Confusion is possible, for the same English term is frequently used to translate both Pāli terms). There are six joys of worldly life, six of renunciation, six sorrows of each, and six equanimities of worldly life and of renunciation. The six joys of worldly life are derived from pleasant sense impressions from the six senses or from remembering past sense impressions that are pleasant. But the six joys of renunciation arise from knowledge of the true nature of these impressions: "when one has known the impermanency of material shapes themselves, their alteration, disappearance and arrest," and when one understands this impermanence, then joy arises. This pertains to the eye, which perceives shapes, and to the ear, which hears sounds, the nose, which smells odors, and so forth. The six sorrows of worldly life arise "either from not attaining or beholding the non-attainment of" the present or past sense-impressions which would give delight (as above) and this results in sorrow for all the six sense-fields. The six sorrows of renunciation arise when impermanency, alteration, disappearance and arrest with respect to the six sense-fields are known, and a desire for deliverance from this arises. From that desire arises the "sorrow of renunciation." The six equanimities of the world refer to the experience of the average person (who plays an important role in the Buddhist didactic tradition since he is contrasted with the enlightened person). "When a foolish, errant average person has seen a material shape with the eye, there arises the equanimity of an uninstructed average person who has not conquered his defilements, who has not conquered fruition [of his works], who does not see the peril–equanimity such as this does not go further than material

132

shape." This is then the "equanimity" of the world, as applied to all the senses, and simply means the failure to understand the deceptive nature of sensation and perception. By contrast, the equanimity of renunciation arises when the impermanence, alteration, and so forth, of the sense fields are realized through perfect wisdom (*paññā*): "Equanimity such as this goes further than a mental state. Therefore it is called equanimity connected with renunciation."[354]

The truth of suffering is further elucidated in the various listings of bondages and things to be "thrown off." These pertain both to the monastic and the lay life. Thus the one who wishes to become an *Arahant* (the last and highest stage of monastic discipline) must throw off the five bondages of the heart (here heart is *citta*). He must throw off the state of not being dispassionate in the matter of sensual experience, and in the matter of objective form. He must renounce eating "his belly full," consuming as much as he wants, rather than only what he needs. He must throw off seeking the Brahma-life, that is, the status of the gods; and in so doing must avoid torpor and not striving.[355]

A more general mark of suffering is anger. The following poetry describes with great sensitivity the psychic state of anger with special respect to its role in sustaining ignorance, self-deception and illusion.

When anger-bound
Man Dhamma cannot see;
A man in wrath finds pleasure in bad deeds
As in good deeds; yet later, when his wrath
Is spent, he suffers like one scorched by fire....
...A man in anger will his father kill,
In wrath, his very mother will he slay,....
Thus ruin runs in wake of wrath, and they
Who act in wrath, perceive not that their deeds,
Destroying life, bring death unto the self.
356

This powerful and insightful summary of the nature and effects of anger suggests the seriousness with which the Buddhist tradition regarded the life of the emotions, especially as a seat of motivation. The sufferer suffers from his own rage, which is directed at others and at himself. Rage, or anger, is here highly aggressive and destructive. It is also directed precisely at those objects of love closest to him, his parents and himself. Yet the poet teaches that the wrath-bound person, however willingly he is bent on destruction, does not know what he is doing. Thus ignorance attends wrathful behavior, and, indeed, is a condition of its existence.

---

[354] M III, 265-268.
[355] A V, 13-16.
[356] A IV, 61-62.

133

Another such general mark of the sufferer is ill-will. The ignorant sufferer regards others with repugnance, because he believes they threaten him; and his response to them is, to his own mind, a defense against them. Ill-will, it is said, is conceived in the following thoughts: someone has done me harm; he is doing me harm; he is going to do me harm; he has done harm to one dear to me; he is doing harm to one dear to me, etc.; he will do harm, etc.; he has done good to one who is not dear to me; he is doing good, etc.; he will do good, etc. "Thus one is groundlessly annoyed."[357] Upon examination it is seen that these feelings of fear and apprehension have no ground in reality; but the mind of the sufferer does not permit such an interpretation.

Further, he who wishes to find release must abandon mental states which are hindrances: lust, malice, delusion, wrath, grudges, depreciation, spite, selfishness, wrongful envy. These states cannot be remedied simply by correcting speech or bodily action. They must be rejected by insight "on seeing them." They are, therefore, not states that are easily recognized by the sufferer as integral to his intentions and actions. His state is that of ignorance; and it is not until he is made aware by insight that he has acted from these motives that he can put them off. The character of these states, then, is that they are unconscious; and it is only through the transforming of the mind by the gaining of insight that they may be put away. But that transformation has, of course, not taken place in the sufferer; and therefore he continues to act out of lust, malice, delusion, and wrath without realizing the truth of the matter. Nothing in his conscious mind will prevent him from so acting. This is one of the chief meanings of the Buddhist notion that one is bound, that is, bound by ignorance of the nature of one's actions. The degree of ignorance is profound, contravening even the stated and conscious goals of those who act out of these motives. Sakka, ruler of the gods, asks the Buddha what fetters bind gods, men and the superhuman beings such as the Āsuras, Nagas, Gandhabbas and all other great classes of beings; for it seems that they all profess high intentions, "that, without hatred, injury, enmity, or malignity, we might live in amity." The Buddha replies:

By the fetters of envy and selfishness, ruler of gods, are they bound–gods, men, etc... [profess] to live in amity–they do nevertheless live in enmity, hating, injuring, hostile, malign.[358]

The bondage of the world, and thus its suffering, is assigned to a number of interlinking causes. This matter is central to the Buddhist notion of causality, which finds its classic expression in the so-called Series of Co-dependent Origination, or the paṭiccasamuppāda series.[359] There

---

[357] A V, 102.
[358] D II, 310.
[359] This will be a major issue in our next section.

are more general expressions of this causal interpretation of the bondage of the world. In a typical example it is said that the world is, first of all, dominated by "name," that is, countless numbers of the perceived things. It is plagued by thoughts (*cittena*) and desire (*taṇhā*). It is enchanted by pleasure (*nandi*). It is enslaved by death and age. It is pestered and goaded by desire and craving. It is rooted and grounded in suffering. It is held prisoner by wishes (*icchāya*).[360] It will be seen here that what for Western philosophy are three separate categories have been blended together as though they were inter-related: the category of physical and emotional feelings; of biological growth and decay; and the epistemological issues of the external world in the concern with name. The bondage of the world, its state of suffering, is therefore referred to all three categories but in such a way that they are linked together in an unbroken chain. As we shall see in discussing the causes for the end of suffering, the cure is as comprehensive as the disease. It is the whole of one's existence, and of the world, that is bound; and the whole must be released.

In the Pāli texts we find the material of the tradition organized according to ascending or descending numbered groups, probably for the purpose of memorization and recitation; and in these groups we find several lists of things to be thrown off or renounced. Their psychological content is unmistakable. For example, from the "nines" of the *Dīgha Nikāya*[361] there are nine things to be eliminated: pursuit caused by craving; gain caused by pursuit; decision caused by gain; desire and passion because of decision; tenacity because of desire and passion; possession because of tenacity; avarice because of possession; watch and ward because of avarice; and "many a bad and wicked state of things arising from keeping watch and ward on possession;—blows and wounds, strife, contradiction and retort, quarrelling, slander and lies."[362] The nine things to be eliminated are related by the cause and effect chain so characteristic of the presentation of the tradition. This is, however, no mere mnemonic device, but an indication of a powerful conviction that no state or entity, whether mental or material, is independent of its cause or its effect; in pursuing any of these negative characteristics one is led inexorably to its cause and effect, and so to the other causes and effects. Also, when the chain is reversed the opposite effect is gained.

Other marks of suffering are described as the "five fetters of the lower worlds," which must be thrown off: the error of the notion of a permanent individual entity; doubt; wrong judgement as to rules and rituals; sensuality; and malevolence. There are also five fetters of the

---

[360] S I, 54-57.
[361] D III, 204ff..
[362] *Ibid.*, 263.

upper worlds: lust after rebirth in higher worlds of Form (*rūpa*-worlds); lust after rebirth in the still higher worlds of non-Form (*arūpa* worlds); conceit, excitement, and ignorance. Thus all the various worlds of the Buddha tradition have fetters from which one must be released. This signifies that the reality of suffering is not limited to the historical world of the Buddha but is cosmic. It is nevertheless, still, firmly centered on emotional states, such as *taṇhā*, desire, and *rāga*, lust.[363]

There are, further, the five bondages of the mind (*citta*):

herein, brethren, when a brother has not got rid of the passion for sense-desires, of desire, fondness, thirst, fever, craving for them, he being thus, his mind does not incline towards ardour, devotion, perseverence, exertion. In the same way when a brother has not got rid of the passion...craving for his own person...for external objects.... ...if a brother has eaten as much as his stomach can hold.... ...and if a brother has adopted the religious life with the aspiration of belonging to some one or other of the deva-groups, thinking:–By these rules or by these rites or by these austerities or by this religious life I shall become a greater, or a lesser deva; he being thus, his mind does not incline towards ardour, devotion, perseverance, extertion.[364]

It is not my intention here to rehearse the immense body of material that describes the bondages and fetters of the self but rather to suggest that the state of suffering is describable as a state of bondage that is not due to external but to what we may call internal fetters. Conversely and accordingly, the release from this bondage is a matter of transforming the general state of the self and reversing the trends characteristic of bondage. Thus we find the "four knots" to be untied, to wit, the "body-knots" of covetousness, of malevolence, of inverted judgement as to rule and ritual, and of the inclination to dogmatize. And one must put off the four graspings, that is the laying hold of sensual desires, of error, of rules and rites, of the soul-theory. Finally, there are four classes of individuals, three of whom suffer. A certain individual torments himself and is devoted to self-mortification; another torments others and is devoted to torturing them; a third torments both himself and others; and the fourth is devoted neither to tormenting himself or others but to living free of the desire to torment or be tormented.[365]

Transience and Care

The state of suffering is a state of transience. A fundamental insight of the Buddhist tradition into the nature of suffering is that we suffer

---

[363] *Ibid.*, 224-230.
[364] *Ibid.*.
[365] *Ibid.*, 214-224; *cf.* 207-214.

because we crave; we desire that which we can never obtain, and thus live in perpetual frustration. Knowledge of this truth is tantamount to release from it. Yet the state of man is one of care about that which is transient in its nature. "What is it that doth cause a man to be?" asks the Teacher. It is desire.[366]

Suffering, then, is inextricably linked with *taṇhā*, with desire. This craving takes a multitude of forms, one of which we may call "care," that is, the concern about the immediate future. Implied by this care is anxiety, that is, a powerful feeling of fear, of danger, of insecurity. This anxiety is tied to past experience; for what is feared is that the imagined state of loss (a state already imagined) will emerge in fact. Thus caring entails the past, the present and the future. By logical extension the life of the sufferer is not limited to the arising and dying of this particular body; and therefore the care and anxiety of the sufferer also extends back and forward beyond his present life. However, it is more useful for our understanding to think of the division of care and anxiety into past, present and future as the division into this instant, instants which we imagine from the past, and instants we imagine for the future. The reason for preferring this formulation will be discussed later. Here the issue is the range and nature of care in the context of transiency.

Gotama describes the Ariyan disciple as one who by wisdom, or right insight (*paññā*), has "well seen even as they really are" the causal relations between things. One effect of this wisdom is that he is not anxious about his past. Never will he run back to the past, thinking, " 'Did I live in times gone by? Or did I not? What was I in times gone by? How was I then? Or from being what did I become what?' " Nor will it ever happen that he will run toward times to come, thinking, " 'Shall I be reborn in a future time, or shall I not? What shall I become in the future? How shall I become in the future? Or, being what, shall I in the future become what?' " Nor will he stop and turn to himself and ask, of his present moment, " 'Am I indeed? Or am I not indeed? What indeed am I? How indeed am I? This person that is I, whence came he, whither will he go?' " But these questions, and the care and anxiety they betray, are typical of the suffering self. Ignorant, concerned, he queries his past, future and present for any clues about what his ultimate fate is. It is noteworthy that the Ariyan disciple is contrasted with such a person not by his sure and certain knowledge of the answer to these questions, but by his utter lack of concern about them. It is the absence of the care and anxiety about these matters that typifies his understanding. This is not to say that the Ariyan is ignorant. On the contrary he is precisely described as one who by wisdom sees things as they really are. Thus the ignorance that concerns us here is not ignorance about the answers

---

[366] S I, 52-53.

137

to these anxious questions but ignorance about their significance. Their prominence is a sign that one is ignorant, and as yet unaware of the truth of suffering. Thus the suffering one asks, pointlessly, " 'Alas! what shall I eat, and where indeed?/ How ill I've slept! Where shall I sleep today?/ Whosoe'er trains and leads the homeless life,/ Must oust these thoughts that lead to discontent [vittakke paridevaneyye].' " [367] What is described here could be called a state of obsession (papañca) with the past, present and future. The contrast with the Ariyan suggests that such concern is pointless but highly characteristic of the ordinary and fettered "average person."

Desire and Pleasure

This obsessive behavior is caused by desire. The concept of desire permeates the Buddhist analysis of suffering. The link between desire and pleasure is essential to this analysis (taṇhā and kāma). Pleasure is identified with sensation, and thus with bondage to the world. It is said: " 'When six prevail arises the world,' the master said,/ 'When six prevail comes intimacy [channa]: Six are the attachments of the world:/ When six prevail the world's oppressed....' " [368] The "six" are of course the five senses of the body and the mind. When man concerns himself with what is pleasant and unpleasant he is bound to the world: "From trust in such there ariseth up desire [chando]:/ Man sees in forms becoming and decay [bhava, vibhava]/ And shapes his theories about the world." [369] However, the quality of pleasure tells us nothing of what is real; indeed it tends always to delude us. The realm of sensation is the realm of Māra, the tempter and the deceiver; the pleasures of the senses (kāma taṇhā) are mightily deceptive in their nature. Thus beings not yet free from attachment to pleasures of the senses find one sensation pleasurable only because it is less painful than another; so a leper will find the touch of fire pleasant because it is a change of his sensation. But these discriminations are all deceptive; for in truth all sense pleasure is painful, "exceedingly hot and afflicting." But the deluded do not know this, and pursue pleasure, or the diminution of pain, unaware of their true condition. [370] Those who seek satisfaction of their desires cannot succeed; even the princes who "with goodly treasures, ample wealth,/ And broad domains, ever in sense-desires/ Insatiate, envy each others' goods." [371]

The question arises whether the fault lies with the object in the world or with the sense organ. It is reasonable to suppose, for example, that

[367] SN 11, 141.
[368] Ibid., 27.
[369] Ibid., 128.
[370] M II, 186-187.
[371] S I, 23f..

either alone cannot be the cause of suffering; for neither the eye nor the object is *per se* conducive to attachment.

Is the eye the bond of objects [*cakkhu rūpānaṃ saṃyojanaṃ*], or are the objects the bond of eye? Is the tongue the bond of savours, or are savours the bond of the tongue? Is mind the bond of mind-states, or are mind-states the bond of the mind?

...The eye is not the bond of objects, nor are objects the bond of eye, but that desire and lust [*chandarāga*] that arise owing to these two. That is the bond. And so with tongue and mind....
...[I]t is the desire and lust that arise owing to savours and tongue, mind-states and mind.[372]

The cause of suffering is in this passage clearly and exclusively related to desire; the speaker, Sāriputta, asserts that if it were otherwise, that is, if desire were not the cause of ill, then the life of righteousness for the utter destruction of *dukkha* could not be proclaimed. In other words desire is the root of suffering that must be attacked. If the cause were in the objects of the world or in the physiological functioning of the body the end of suffering would not be possible. The *Tathāgata* (or the Buddha), the one who is freed, has an eye which sees objects; but the Buddha does not suffer ill, for in that eye is no desire and lust. "Wholly heart [*citta*] -free is the Exalted One."[373] This point is very significant for us. Sensation and perception are not in and of themselves the causes of suffering. This observation, furthermore, pertains to any conclusion we may draw about objects as well. According to Buddhist epistemology the sense-field includes the object perceived as well as the sense perception; thus neither perception nor object in and of itself is a cause of suffering. They enter into the realm of suffering only in conjuction with desire and lust. The key to the nature of suffering lies, then, in the emotional and mental life of the individual. It is for this reason that Sāriputta asserts that if it were not so the Ariyan life would be impossible. I do not think this means that there is some other inaccessible cause of suffering but that the Ariyan life is possible because desire is one of the causes, or the only cause which is accessible. Rather, Sāriputta's assertion means that desire is the only cause of suffering in conjunction with perception and the sense-field, and that the righteous life is a way not of altering the world or perception but of transforming desire; therefore if desire were not the cause of ill, in conjunction with the sense-field, the righteous life would not lead to the end of suffering.[374]

---

[372] S IV, 101f..

[373] *Ibid.*, 101-102.

[374] One of the more remarkable summaries of the connection between the world of sensation, desire and suffering is offered in the *Udāna*:

In a poignant example of the central place of desire in connection with the truth of suffering, a story is told of one Bhadragaka, a headman. The issue in question was whether suffering was greater for some than for others according to the strength of their desire and longing. Some, like Bhadragaka, found that the pain and death of some people distressed them more than that of others. The explanation for the difference is straight-forward and revealing: "Whatso ever Ill arising has come upon me in the past, –all that is rooted in desire [*chanda*], is joined to desire." And so also for the future: "Desire is the root of ill [*chando hi mūlaṃ dukkhassāti*]." The pointed example of the general truth is this: Bhadragaka admits that he would be greatly overwrought by the sorrow and death of his wife or of his son Ciravāsi. He is asked quite simply, "When you did not see, not hear Ciravāsi's mother, did you fear desire or longing or affection for her?" "No." Indeed, the reverse was true. This was the Teacher's response to the question of how *dukkha* came to be; and the connection with desire is very plain and emphatic.[375]

Greed, Hate and Illusion

As we shall see the general conceptualization of desire is divisible into component parts that reveal the subtlety and sophistication of the early Buddhist texts with respect to human desires and the unconscious. For example, they identify a desire for self-destruction as well as a desire for self-preservation, and for destruction of the other as well as love for the other. In examining further the nature of suffering as a fundamental truth the Buddhist tradition was keenly aware of the role of motives and set itself the task of discriminating among them. One of the classic formulations is the threefold division of motives into lust (or greed, or attachment), malice (or aggression, desire for the destruction of the other), and ignorance, or delusion.[376] These three concepts, although described in different Pāli terms, are usually found together. This is a

This world, become ablaze, by touch of sense afflicted,/ Utters its own lament. Whate'er conceit one has,/ Therein lies instability. Becoming other,/ Bound to becoming, yet in becoming it rejoices./ Delight therein is fear, and what it fears is Ill./ For abandoning becoming this Brahma-life is lived." U, 39.

[375] *Ibid.*.
[376] Western readers may be surprised to find "ignorance" or "illusion" in a list of motives. However, the Buddhist tradition finds that there is an important element of desire or willfulness in human ignorance. That is, we desire to be ignorant of the truth for our own reasons. Further, the Freudian analysis of symptoms and repression suggests the state of "ignorance" seen in the Buddhist tradition, replete with the willful, desiring quality of resistance and the obscuring of the truth. Ignorance is in

140

significant point, for it suggests that the life of the emotions consists in these three interdependent qualities, and therefore should be understood as a dynamic relationship among them. (The usual terms are *lobha, dosa, moha,* or *rāga/dosa/moha,* for greed, hatred and illusion, respectively. *Chanda, paṭigha* and *avijjā* are other terms widely used—*chanda,* "desire," or "lust;" *paṭigha,* "hatred," "repulsion;" *avijjā,* "ignorance," "delusion.")

One who acts from these motives will kill, steal, seek another's wife, tell lies, and lead another "into a state that is to his loss for a long time."[377] These motives are said to be unprofitable—*akusala*—that is, not conducive to release from suffering but on the contrary conducive to the arising and maintenance of suffering. It is said that lust, malice and ignorance are the three roots of "demerit."[378] One who speaks out of these unprofitable motives is seen to be inopportune, untrustful, irrelevant, "one who speaks contrary to the *Dhamma,*" "one who speaks contrary to the discipline." Such a person will cause distress and grief to others. He will cause the innocent to suffer unjustified punishment, imprisonment, loss of wealth, abuse and banishment, on the grounds that "might is right." "When confronted with the truth he denies it, does not understand it. When confronted with a lie he makes no effort to untangle it, saying, 'this is baseless, this is false.' "[379]

Ānanda, the great teacher and close associate of the Buddha, speaks of lust, malice and ignorance together as the causes of suffering. Thus one who is overwhelmed by them loses control of his mind—or heart (here *citta*)—and plans things which trouble himself and others, and so experiences mental suffering and dejection.[380] Such a person practices immorality in deed, word and thought. "He is blind, unaware, and possesses not wisdom, and [is] vexatious."[381]

The causal relationship between the evil deed and the intention of the doer is, furthermore, a central issue in this three-part analysis of motivation. The causes of doing an evil deed, the Buddha says, are lust (*lobha*), malice (*dosa*), delusion (*moha*), not paying proper attention, and wrongly directed thought.[382] It is said that there are four motives for evil deeds: partiality (*chanda*), enmity (*dosa*), stupidity (*moha*) and fear

---

fact illusion, as Freud said; it is the hope that the situation is as I want it to be whether it is so in truth. That we all act out of such a hope in thought, word and deed should be evident.
[377] A I, 176.
[378] *Ibid.,* 182-183.
[379] *Ibid.,* 183.
[380] *Ibid.,* 196.
[381] *Ibid..*
[382] A V, 61.

(*bhaya*).[383] These motives really amount to a depravity of the mind, the *citta*. So long as they are the motives of the mind evil deeds result.[384] They are the "Three Obstacles" to achieving release from suffering.[385] In further discussion we shall see that they arise in forms identical to the dispositions of the self and thus consititute in a very important sense the nature of the bound self.

"Ordinary Folk" and the Self

The state of suffering as we have seen can only be explained satisfactorily in terms of desire. We must, however, also find a complementary understanding of the self. It would seem that there must be a self that desires, is frustrated and suffers. That is indeed the view of the ordinary person and a central issue in the truth of suffering. The "untaught manyfolk," as one of the translations of *puthujjana* has it, regard the body as the self, regard the self as having a body, regard the body as being in the self and the self in the body. The "ordinariness" of this conclusion is noteworthy; for one who identifies body with self will perforce be ignorant of the truth of suffering. Thus one who so confuses self for body is really everyman before his realization of any of the Noble Truths. In this state of ignorance he will be prey to despair and distress when change and decay affect the body which is identified with the essential self. This same confusion and subsequent distress and suffering arise from the false identification of self with feelings, with perception, with *sankhāras*, the "activities" or general and continuing co-ordinated operations of mind and body (we shall return to a more detailed study of each of these concepts) and even consciousness. These five elements, the *khandhas*, or "heaps," constitute what is referred to as the "self," or "phenomenal self"; and as we shall see the identification of them separately or collectively as the essential self is a fundamental cause of suffering. It is precisely the mistake made by ordinary persons.[386] They, unlike the Ariyan disciple, are

> fettered by the bonds of body [*etc.*], bound to the inner and the outer, [as] one who has not sighted the beyond [*apāra-dassī*], who is born bound, who dies bound, one who from this world goes to the world beyond.[387]

The texts present a stylized contrast between the *puthujjana*, the ordinary, foolish person and the Ariyan disciple in their analysis of the mind or heart, the *citta*. " 'This mind, monks, is luminous, but it is defiled

---

[383] D III, 174.
[384] M I, 119-120.
[385] D III, 214-224.
[386] S III, 105.
[387] *Ibid.*, 140-141.

by taints that come from without. But this the uneducated manyfolk understands not as it really is. Wherefor, for the uneducated manyfolk there is no cultivation of the mind, I declare.' "[388] What the untaught manyfolk do not realize is that if they are not careful of the way in which the *citta* confronts the external world it will lose its luminousness, and therefore its liberated state. They are, in their ignorance, careless of the danger of defilement.

Yet the cleansing of *citta* is possible, and is indeed a goal for which one must strive; and thus it must be the case that the Ariyan disciples were themselves "untaught manyfolk" until the process of purification of the *citta* was undertaken. Moreover, the *citta* in and of itself is not transformed or corrupted, but rather tainted, and that taint or blemish can be removed. The state of untaught manyfolk is not irreversible. This is the meaning of one of the major metaphors of the tradition concerning the process of purification of the *citta*, that of the refinement of gold. Gold is refined in the following steps: (1) gross impurities, *e.g.* dust, gravel, are washed away, by an apprentice; (2) fine impurities, such as fine sand or grit, are removed by a dirtwasher or his apprentice; (3) trifling impurities like black dust are cleansed away by the dirtwasher; (4) the gold is placed in a crucible and melted by the goldsmith or his apprentice, but it does not yet run or flow; (5) the gold is blown until it is fine enough to flow out of the crucible. It is then flawless: "It is pliable, workable, glistening, no longer brittle; it is capable of perfect workmanship."[389]

The *citta* is refined in its development toward the state of *adhicitta*, the higher consciousness, by eliminating (1) the gross impurities of deed, word and thought, (2) moderately gross impurities, such as sensual reflections (*kāmavitakka*) and malicious and cruel thoughts (*vyāpāda, vihiṃsā*), and (3) minute impurities, such as reflections about one's relatives, district, and reputation.[390] The import of the metaphor is that what must be removed are impurities that have not corrupted the essential *citta* but, like the foreign elements in gold, have prevented it from reaching its state of pure pliability, so that it can be shaped into the ideal form, and achieve the highest possible consciousness. It is true that so long as one remains in the state of *puthujjana* this process cannot be begun; but as the gold-refining metaphor indicates, once one realizes that the gold is tainted one may set about the business of refining it.

The ordinary person's experience of the world is construed in terms of the deception of the senses. Just as the ordinary manyfolk falsely identify the self with any or all of the *khandhas*, so they search for pleasure and seek to avoid pain, thinking that this is the way to happiness.

---

[388] A I, 8.
[389] *Ibid.*, 231-232.
[390] *Ibid.*.

143

In fact it is the way to suffering. As with all the sense-fields, "visual consciousness arises because of eye and material shapes, the meeting of the three is sensory impingement; an experience arises conditioned by sensory impingement that is pleasant or painful, or neither pleasant nor painful." The ignorant person delights in a pleasant feeling, laments a painful feeling, and is confused by a feeling that is neither pleasant nor painful.[391]

Such is the arising of anguish, *dukkha*. It is noteworthy that the attachment to pleasant feelings, the rejection of painful feelings, and the confusion about feelings that are both pleasant and painful are linked directly to the three-fold nature of motivation that leads to suffering, *lobha*, *dosa*, and *moha*, lust, malice and ignorance. The connection lies in the observation that the response to sensation is to be understood as emotional rather than rational. The ignorant one, in short, is guided entirely in his experience of the external world by his feelings; and it is in the nature of feelings that they provide motivation that inevitably leads to suffering. Moreover, it should be noted that these three responses are described here in terms of "latent tendencies," *anusayas*; this suggests a predisposition in the self toward each of these three categories of response. They are understood here not to be (only) learned but to be inherent in the nature of the feeling-response, the self. They are, as we might say, natural.

The Buddhist treatment of the destiny and nature of both *puthujjana* and Ariyan transcends limitations of the present physical body. The ordinary person is contrasted with the Ariyan disciple with respect to the sort of expectations he may have for his future "lives." Even the ordinary person may achieve a certain level of advance in his spiritual life. Here is the itinerary for the ordinary person's journey towards higher consciousness:

> ...a certain person, by utterly transcending consciousness of form
> [*rūpasaññā*], by paying no heed to the diversity of consciousness
> [*nānatta-*], regarding space as infinite, reaches up to and abides
> in the sphere of infinite space. He enjoys it, longs for it and finds
> happiness therein. Established therein, given thereto, generally
> spending his time therein, and not falling away therefrom, when
> he makes an end he is reborn in the company of the Devas who
> have reached the sphere of infinite space.... Therein the ordinary
> man [*puthujjano*] stays and spends his lifetime according to the
> life space of those Devas [20,000 cycles].[392]

Then he will be reborn in purgatory, or in the world of animals or in the realm of ghosts! His destiny is in contrast with an Ariyan disciple

---

[391] M III, 334ff..
[392] A I, 245-246.

who will not go beyond the realm of infinite space nor regress from it but will pass away in that very state (*parinibbāyati*); or, with one who transcends the realm of infinite space and abides in the sphere of infinite consciousness, there to pass away; or, with one who transcends the realm of infinite consciousness to the sphere of *ākiñcañña*, or "nothing at all exists," and passes away there.[393]

Khandhas and the Self

The truth of suffering takes the form of a psychological ontology in the theme of the five *khandhas*. I use this phrase "psychological ontology" with reluctance because, as we shall see, it is contrary to the letter and spirit of the tradition to create categories of philosophical discourse since they tend toward reification, and toward a weakening of the major position of analysis, the notion of co-dependent origination. Nevertheless the *khandhas* serve as a useful representation of the relationship between what is perceived as the phenomenal self, the real nature of that self and the central issue of suffering.

A man who has never heard a lute demands that one be brought so that he may hear the sound of it. "Bring me the sound," he demands. He is told that the lute speaks because it is composed of diverse parts, *e.g.* the handle, the strings, the frame, *etc.*. Then the man smashes the lute, burns the pieces and scatters the ashes.

A poor thing [he says] is what you call a lute, my man, whatever a lute may be. Herein the world is exceeding careless and led astray.[394]

The metaphor is applicable to each of the five *khandhas*: body, feeling, perception, the activities, consciousness. In none of this is a self to be found.[395]

Thus there is the sound of a lute; but it is not to be found in any essential form, rather, only in the compoundedness of the lute. Similarly, there is no "I," no self, but only compounds, none of which is the self, and all of which together comprise the phenomenal self. But like the lute, which when destroyed—when its compounded structure is broken down— has no sound, the *khandhas* are impermanent, capable of destruction, and there is then no self. Yet in the human condition of suffering we assign to each and all of the *khandhas* the title and essence of self; and universal distress is the result. The body (and the other *khandhas*) is impermanent. What is impermanent is suffering. What is suffering is without self. What

---

[393] The life spans of the devas in each world increase apace, with 40,000 cycles for the realm of infinite consciousness, and 60,000 for the realm of "nothing at all." *Ibid.*.
[394] S IV, 29f..
[395] *Ibid.*, 129-130.

145

is without self is not mine, I am not that, not of me is this self. This is the situation as it "really is," and as it is seen in the perfect wisdom with which the monk sees. One who, deluded, identifies self with body, with consciousness, with feeling, with perception, with the activities, is constantly guessing at his past, his present and his future. The whence and whither of his feelings, body, and so forth are his constant concern; and in this state of distress and ill he will for ever remain, bound by his ignorance, his grasping, his craving for the life of the self.[396]

Thus the ordinary folk identify self with body, feeling, perception, consciousness, and/or the activities. In the instance of the identification with body this is the experience of the untaught manyfolk:

> Now when it has come to anyone to think "I am," there comes to pass a descent of the five feeling-faculties of seeing, hearing, smelling, tasting, and touching. Mind [the sixth faculty] is the result, mind states are the result, the ignorance element is the result. Touched by the feeling born of contact with ignorance, there comes to the untaught many-folk (the view), "I am"; there comes (the view), "things will have body"; the view, "things will be bodyless"; there comes the view, "things will be conscious"; etc.; the view "things will be unconscious"; the view, "things will be neither conscious nor unconscious."[397]

This speculation continues until the distress associated with the sense-fields and the identification of self with body, and the other *khandhas*, is fully arisen. For the body is not permanent but impermanent and unstable. In this body is desire and lust (*chandarāga*) which is suffering; so too for all the other *khandhas*.[398] There is indeed nothing in the world to which one may cling that is or serves as the self. Indeed, so to grasp any element, such as body, or consciousness, or feeling, is to enter immediately into suffering. For example, on the central question of how one ceases to be "reborn," that is, ceases to continue to become, the Ariyan disciple reflects on the question, and realizes that there is nothing to which he may cling without this clinging resulting in continued becoming. He thinks:

> Suppose I were to grasp and cling to body, to feeling, etc.. Conditioned by that grasping of mine could be coming-to-be; conditioned by that coming-to-be would birth be shaped; conditioned by birth would decay and death, sorrow, woe, grief, lamentation, and despair be shaped. Thus would come about the arising of this whole mass of woe.[399]

---

[396] S III, 39-40.
[397] *Ibid.*, 40-41.
[398] *Ibid.*, 54-55, *cf.* 41-42.
[399] *Ibid.*, 79-80.

Here is one formulation of the series of co-dependent origination. The *khandhas*, in this case, are linked to becoming, that is, the ongoing of the past life, to woe, suffering and death. The starting point here—and it will be seen that any of the elements of the series may serve as a starting point, although ignorance is the most favored initial element—is grasping (*upādāna*). For it is obviously not sufficient to assert that the "self" consists of the five compounds in order to show their link with suffering. There must be a grasping after the self in the forms of the *khandhas*. When one so grasps, the result is the suffering, *etc.*, of the remainder of the series.

Each of the *khandhas* is a contributing element in the arising of suffering according to the series of co-dependent origination. The Buddha is approached by one who has in his mind the question of how one breaks the final link in the causal chain of suffering, that is the *āsavas*, the connection caused by attachment to the most subtle and highest ideals. The Buddha recognizes the thought before it is spoken and replies. The untaught manyfolk, he says, regard the body as the self. Now this act is a *sankhāra*, an activity,

> and in this activity—nourished by feeling that is born of contact with ignorance, there arises craving; thence is born that activity. Thus...that activity is impermanent, willed [*sankhāto*], arisen from a cause.[400]

The same analysis is proposed for the other *khandhas*. If the compounded nature of each *khandha* is grasped and understood then one realizes that any identification of any form or compound or action with self, and *vice versa*, is the root of suffering, and endeavors to put an end to such identification. The same analysis must be applied to the notions that the self possesses body, or consciousness, or feeling, *etc.*, and to the notions that the body is in the self, or the self in the body.[401]

The relationships just described are said to be causal since no state or being arises without a cause. The notion of self, or what is called the "conceit 'I am,'" does not arise alone but (in one formulation) because of body, feeling, perception, activities, and consciousness.[402] The suffering of the untaught manyfolk arises from their belief in the self as body, or the body as self. Thus as a man swept away by a mountain stream clutches at grasses, reeds and creepers, and is destroyed, so the untaught manyfolk regard the self as body, as having body, as being in body, and the body as being in the self. When the body dies they come to their end; and so it is with the other *khandhas*.[403] The age-old search for any indivisible

---

[400] *Ibid.*, 80ff..
[401] *Ibid.*, 80-84.
[402] *Ibid.*, 89.
[403] *Ibid.*, 116.

147

reality is judged to be conducive to suffering. Everything is compounded and unstable. In a revealing anecdote the Buddha picked up a tiny pellet of cowdung, saying, "Even the getting of a selfhood [attabhāva] as small as this, brother, is not permanent, stable, eternal, by nature unchanging, like unto the eternal, so that thus it will stand fast. If the getting of a selfhood so small as this, brother, were permanent, stable, eternal...then the living of the holy life for the best destruction of suffering would not be set forth."[404]

The truth of the impermanence of the khandhas is eternal, that is to say it applies to all moments, past, present and future. There never was a time in which a permanent self existed, and there never will be. Thus the frantic concern for the status of one's existence in the past, present and future is based on ignorance and the desire for the self. The suffering, ignorant person foolishly concerns himself with such questions as "what was my shape, my consciousness, my perception, my feeling, my activities or habitual tendencies, in the past? What are they now? What will they be in the future?" The answers he gets will bring pleasure or unpleasure; but it matters little which he obtains, for the whole is an illusion based on the idea that there is a self possessing or being in shape, feelings, consciousness, perception, and habitual tendencies. So long as one attaches to these "heaps" the notion of self one will suffer.

That one who believes in the self is deluded is well illustrated in the simile of the blind man who was deceived into thinking that a coarse and grimy cloth was finest silk. When he regained his sight through the medical cure he sought he realized that he had been defrauded. So runs the experience of one was ignorant but was then brought to the Dhamma, the truth.[405]

False Beliefs

The truth of suffering implies a false view of suffering. The role of diṭṭhi, "view," or "opinion," is addressed at length throughout the early Buddhist writings. Its treatment is consistent with the central place accorded delusion, ignorance, and even stupidity in the hearts of men. False beliefs are dangerous for two reasons: (1) they are false, that is to say, to hold them is to believe something that simply is not true; and (2) so long as one holds them he will not strive for the truth. These false views, or mere opinions–which is their true status when compared with the Dhamma–are attractive. They gratify the wishes of the believers; if it were otherwise they would not be accepted. Furthermore, the presence of false views leads inevitably to contention among people; and this contention, if viewed from the perspective of the Dhamma, is debilitating and conducive to ill. Thus false views themselves are numbered among

---

[404] Ibid., 12.
[405] M II, 190.

the most serious instances of suffering by the early traditions. Into the usual welter of opinions such as determinism, nihilism, eternalism, and others, the Buddha introduces his own position: "I quarrel not with the world, brethren. It is the world that quarrels with me. No preacher of the Norm [Dhamma], brethren, quarrels with anyone in the world."[406] The Buddha is not interested in quarrels about opinons or philosophy because what he declares is what has been true eternally. He does not proclaim a novelty but an old truth brought back. The Buddha speaks of the world of the wise whose Dhamma he proclaims:

> That which is not upheld, brethren, in the world of sages [loke paṇḍitānaṃ], of that I declare "It is not." What...is upheld in the world of sages, of that I declare "It is so." And what...is not upheld...: That body is permanent, stable, eternal, not subject to decay [etc.].[407]

This Dhamma is the basis of certain knowledge. Anything more or less is irrelevant and, therefore, false and misleading. One who knows this Dhamma is freed: "There are no knots for him loosed from surmise; There are no errors for the wisdom-freed."[408] But those "who both surmise and view [diṭṭhi] accept, they warfare in the world at odds with folk."[409]

The tradition reports a plethora of views and widespread confusion and contention among all peoples about the fundamental issues of the human life. In the context of this confusion and dogmatism the Buddha stands out in splendid wisdom, possessed of the sense of proportion that arises from knowledge of what is true, what is false, what is irrelevant, and what is proper in its time. For example, among the many tales of confused and worried people coming to the Buddha for answers to their questions is that of a warrior who asks whether it is true, as he has heard, that he who exerts himself in battles and is then captured, tortured and killed by others will therefore be reborn in the company of the Devas of Passionate Delight. The Buddha refuses to answer at first. Finally yielding, he tells the warrior that life is not so rosy as he thinks. The destiny of the warrior is, rather, this:

> In the case of a fighting-man who in battle exerts himself, [and] puts forth effort, he must previously have had this low, mean, perverse idea, "Let those beings be tortured, be bound, be destroyed, be exterminated, so that they may be thought never to have existed." Then, so exerting himself [he] is captured, tortured and killed by others [who] make an end of him. When the

---
[406] S III, 117.
[407] Ibid..
[408] SN, 126.
[409] Ibid..

body breaks up he is reborn in the Purgatory of Quarrels.[410] But the sting is in the tail. For the warrior, having just learned that his happy expectations for reward were unfounded, is then told that the view he held, in addition to being false, is also by its nature conducive to even greater suffering in the scale of rebirth; for the view is a perverted view, that is, one leading to actions that are conducive to ill, and thus is itself a causal factor. That being so, the warrior will be reborn either in purgatory or will take the body of an animal. The warrior is understandably distraught, the story goes, and the Teacher points out that he was, after all, reluctant to respond. However, the warrior's complaint is directed not at the Buddha but at the false view he had held so firmly. He laments at the thought that he had been deceived or so long.[411] This tale ends with the warrior taking the refuge of the *Sangha*. Its general import suggests that the truth of suffering takes the issue of false views very seriously indeed, and teaches that perverted view has its rightful place in the world of suffering. This is not a case of simply having got it wrong; rather, a false view is a basis for action–with its own precedent cause–which is part of the arising of that "whole mass of ill."

In the matters of the origin and destiny of the self, or the question of *kamma/karma* and *saṃsāra*–the relationship of deeds to moral consequences–, there had always been beliefs. The Buddha's position on these issues was designated The Middle Way; for he held no mere opinions of either extreme but only the truth he knew from the sages, which was in turn corroborated by experience. In contrast the philosophers either went too far or not far enough, driven as they were by desire and not by wisdom, not seeing things "as they really were." When asked, for example, whether those who teach that all pleasure, pain and mental states are due to previous acts were correct the Buddha responds that they go too far. He does acknowledge what is known to all; that there is unpleasantness originating from bile, phlegm, wind, changes of seasons, stress of untoward happenings, sudden attacks from without, and also from ripeness of one's *karma*, as is generally acknowledged by the world to be true.[412] That is to say, a dogmatic position on the effects of actions is untenable. It is true that one is subject to discomfort and pain arising from various sources and causes, as the examination of one's experience will readily verify; and it is true that one can view these happenings as the fruition of previous acts. This is not a philosophy, however, but a conclusion drawn from experience, not a dogma, not something believed, but a useful observation about the nature of experience. What the Buddha understood to be true, the *Dhamma*, was true not because it was

---

[410] S IV, 216-217.

[411] *Ibid.*.

[412] *Ibid.*, 155-156.

believed, but because it was verified without exception in the life of man. The *Dhamma*, in short, was not a belief or the object of belief, it was not an opinion, or a position taken. It was a statement of reality—and the reality itself.

However, those accompanying the Buddha frequently misunderstood what he intended. The texts contain many accounts of dialogues in which the Buddha or one of the disciples patiently clarifies one or more of the teachings for one who is confused, who has heard a false version of the *Dhamma*, or who wishes to attack the teachings. For example, Gotama hears a report that he is said to hold a certain view concerning the "beginning of things," here specifically related to the state of affairs for a group of beings called "debauched-in-mind" (*manopadosikka*) and "debauched-by-pleasure" (*khiḍḍāpadosikka*). The account of the teaching that the Buddha is supposed to have proclaimed is this: both classes of beings fell into lives that were "impermanent, transient, unstable, short-lived, and deciduous." However, it might have happened that one of these beings left one or the other of those states, lived as a householder, then became a recluse, and then reflected upon his past using the power of recollecting his previous birth (a power acquired in his life as a recluse). And he might say to himself:

> Those worshipful spirits who are not debauched-by-pleasure, they have not, for ages, passed their time in the mirth and sport of sensual lusts. Hence is their self-control not corrupted. Hence they decease not from their estate, but are permanent, constant, eternal, unchanging, and will so remain for ever and ever. But we who were pleasure-debauched, we did pass our time for ages in the mirth and sport of sensual lusts, whereby our self-control became corrupted, so that we deceased from that estate, and are come to this form of life, impermanent, transient, unstable, short-lived, deciduous. Thus was appointed the beginning of things which ye declare as being due to a debauch of pleasure.[413]

And so it was also for those beings called "debauched-in-mind." This straight-forward cause-effect accounting is typical of the dogmatic positions on *kamma* and *saṃsāra*, the relation between actions and destiny. The Buddha denies that he taught this view of the "origin of things." This suggests that the classic doctrine of *kamma* and *saṃsāra* finds no place in the teaching of the Buddha. What the Buddha says is that he did not teach such a view; rather he taught that "[w]henever one attains to the stage of deliverance [*vimokha*] entitled the beautiful, one is then aware ''tis lovely!' "[414]

---

[413] D III, 28-32.
[414] *Ibid..*

151

The tradition reports the Buddha's warning concerning perverted view: "Monks, I know not of any other single thing so apt to cause the arising of evil states not yet arisen, and if arisen, to cause them more-becoming as perverted view." Perverted view leads to rebirth in "the Waste, the Way of Woe, the Downfall, Purgatory."[415] The perverted view leading to such disastrous consequences is the false view of self identified with the *khandhas*, and the concomitant elements of desire and the sense-fields. But false view is a danger even for those whose striving is virtually complete. One must not make the mistake of replacing one set of doctrines or opinions with another. The means must not be confused with the end, the symbol with the thing symbolized, the appearance with the reality. What is ultimate must be approached, and one must not lose sight of the goal while making the ascent: "Monks, do ye dwell with mind well established in the four stations of mindfulness [*satipaṭṭhāna*]./ But let not that be to you the Deathless [*i.e. nibbāna*, here *amata*]."[416]

This cautionary advice is directed then even to the *Dhamma* itself. In a dialogue chiefly concerned with the arising and uprooting of perplexity and doubt–themselves hindrances to right understanding–Gotama describes the stopping of doubt and perplexity and the arising of wisdom. Then he states, through the customary rhetorical question, what success in this endeavor means:

If you, monks, cling to, treasure, cherish, foster this view [*diṭṭhi*], then, ...would you understand that the Parable of the Raft is *dhamma* taught for crossing over, not for retaining? [No].... But if you, monks, do not cling to, do not treasure do not cherish, foster this view, then, monks, would you understand that the Parable of the Raft is *dhamma* taught for crossing over, not retaining? [Yes].[417]

Thus the truth itself must always lie on the further shore; and the view, however correct, however full a comprehension of the *Dhamma*, is nevertheless still a view, a means, an expression. Failure to draw the distinction, which means failure to understand the frailty and illusory character of all formulations (or, more positively, the referential quality of all symbols) is worse than being wrong, for it leads to suffering.

Nevertheless the propensity for formulating and answering questions abstracted from experience, and for constructing systems of an absolute nature–so that we can at least trust something or someone other than ourselves–is persistent and, seemingly, ineradicable. The early texts tell us time and again of those who want answers to the question, "Does the *Tathāgata* exist after death, after the final *nibbāna*, or not?" This

---

[415] A I, 27-28; *cf.* 247-248.
[416] S V, 161.
[417] M I, 315-316.

and similar questions are the famous unexplained points, those issues to which the Buddha did not give absolute answers but rather attacked the questions themselves as reflective of false view. The usual formulation of these questions was that of a four-fold inquiry: Does the *Tathāgata* exist after death? or not? Does the *Tathāgata* both exist and not exist after death? Does the *Tathāgata* neither exist nor not exist after death? The comprehensive nature of the so-called quatrilemma—it is certainly more comprehensive than a dilemma—would seem to promise a clear response to a highly significant question. For the *Tathāgata* is the one who has "come through," who possesses the absolute wisdom, who has attained *nibbāna*. Is it the same person who lived previous lives, or a different? Does he exist or not, or both, or neither? Since presumably the *Tathāgata*-nature is the goal toward which all strive, an answer would surely be forthcoming on a matter of such importance. The Buddha replies to all such enquiries, and to the concern and distress implied in them, that those who truly follow the Ariyan path are simply not bothered by such issues. They are "view-issues," *diṭṭhigata*, that is, they are meaningful only in the context of a rhetorical and philosophic conversation. Each position depends upon its opposite; and the defenders and attackers depend upon each other to sustain interest in the matter. But that sort of thing is quite separate from the goals of those who strive. The unlearned become greatly exercised over these questions. What they do not comprehend is that such concern is itself part of what must be overcome. It is part of the truth of suffering. They do not understand the truth of view, the rising of view, the end of view, and the cause of the end of view. For such a person "view grows; and he is not freed from birth, old age, death, from sorrows, griefs, ills, tribulations: he is not free from ill, I say." He is unlike the seeker of the Ariyan truth, who is not concerned, does not "fall to quaking" about these things. But for the unlearned such questions as the existence of the *Tathāgata* are questions arising from craving, from perception and illusion, and are eventually a source of remorse.[418]

The pursuit of answers to abstract questions contrived for the sake of satisfying deluded concerns about an illusory self is one of the "unprofitable" activities (*akusala*). (It is contrasted sharply and consistently with the profitable (*kusala*) pursuit of self-control and wisdom). These questions are of course very well-known:

> Monks, reason not ill, unprofitable reasonings [*cintā*], such as Eternal is the world or Not Eternal is the world: Finite is the world or Infinite is the world: Life is the same as body, or Life and body are different: The *Tathāgata* exists after death or The *Tathāgata* exists not after death, or He both exists...neither exists....

---

[418] A IV, 39-40.

Because...these reasonings are not concerned with profit, they conduce not to Nibbāna.

Reason thus: This is Ill, this is the arising of Ill, this is the ceasing of Ill, this is the practice that leads to the ceasing of Ill.[419]

This perennial questing after misleading and irrelevant matters is only frustrating. The Buddha informs Koṭṭhita, who wishes to know whether the six "spheres of contact," that is the activity of contact of the sense-fields, remain intact or are annihilated upon release–an apparently crucial question concerning the ontology of the self that has attained *nibbāna*. The Buddha first proclaims the four-fold denial, that one cannot say that the spheres are extant, not extant, both...or neither. Then, he continues, "...in saying that there is something left one makes difficulty where there is none," and so also for the other three elements of the four-fold denial. "So long...as there is going to the six spheres of contact, for just so long is there a going to difficulty [*papañca*]. But...by the passionless ending without remainder of the six spheres of contact there is calming down of difficulty."[420] The reality of the passionless ending transcends the issue of whether the spheres of contact exist. Concern for that issue is therefore a characteristic of one who is ignorant, still in the "difficulty" of the six spheres, their causes and effects.

Despite the attempts of some followers and most opponents to place the teachings within a philosophical school the texts are adamant in their insistence that none of the schools is truly reflective of those teachings, and that to identify the teaching of the Exalted One with any of them is a practice of perverted view. One can find such evidence as one seeks for the determinism, the indeterminism, the nihilism or the eternalism of the Buddha. But none of these world views, or any others, is held by him.

For example, determinism, the view that all activities are caused by prior conditions, and, therefore, the actor is not responsible for his actions, is denied by both plain and indirect statement as we have already seen. The belief that the cause of all actions is a Supreme Being to whom all causal relations must ultimately be traced is also rejected. If one were to follow this doctrine, there would be no need for either action or inaction. But "the truth is quite otherwise, for all things arise from a cause." Those who teach this doctrine, like those who teach determinism, are both bewildered and irresponsible. They are evidently bewildered else they would not construct such a system but would rather know what is true; and they are irresponsible and teach irresponsibilty, for according to their doctrine no one is responsible for his actions, and thus all actions are indifferent from a moral perspective. A third option, indeterminism,

---

[419] S V, 354.
[420] A II, 168-169.

154

is also denied. It is not a tenable position that all is uncaused; for this is contrary to our most direct experience, however grand it may sound as an argument.[421]

Māra's work is best done through false views, especially the false views concerning the nature of the self. There are these views of the self, that it is eternal, or that it is annihilated (*sassata-diṭṭhi*, *uccedaditthi*, respectively). It is significant that these two views are the third and fourth conceits by which one becomes a slave of Māra. The other two are *taṇhā*, desire, and *diṭṭhi*, "view" in general. Māra, it will be recalled, has as his kingdom the realm of sense and sense pleasures. The conceits surround the sensing self and aid him in his entrapment. Thus "I am" is a conceit. "This am I," "I shall be, "I shall not be," are conceits. "Embodied I shall be," "Disembodied I shall be," are conceits. "I shall be conscious," "Unconscious shall I be," and "Neither conscious nor unconscious shall I be" are all conceits. They are all views, all beliefs. These beliefs, teaches the Buddha, are wavering and vain. They arise out of lust, and are an imposthume (abcess) and a barb, and lead into Māra's trap.[422]

Thus none of the established beliefs is confirmed by the Buddha. Indeed the questions are condemned, and are as misguided as the answers, whatever they be. Any belief-notion, in short, is part of the truth of suffering. The Buddha consistently refuses to answer these questions of belief for fear of misleading his interrogators. Indeed the entire issue of whether Gotama would remain in the world of history and set the wheel of the *Dhamma* in motion for his time was fraught with difficulties. Māra himself urged him not to and instead to enjoy the fruits of his successful search for release from suffering. It was precisely on the thorny issue of how to answer the great philosophical issues of the time, and any time, that the ship of Gotama's mission was perpetually threatening to founder–and that is still the case today. Nevertheless the constant refusal to answer the questions of belief must be understood as in and of itself a function of wisdom. The Buddha reveals this wisdom on several occasions. For example, the question is put to him, is there a self or not? The Buddha refuses to say that there is a self or to say that there is not a self. If he replied in the affirmative it would appear that he held an eternalist view, that the self in whatever form was a permanent *ens*. However, this contradicts the fundamental truth of the transiency of all things, especially the self–the teaching of *anicca*. If he replied in the negative it would appear that he held, with the annihilationists, that all is destroyed. This, he asserts, would confuse his questioner, leading him to hold the absurd position that formerly he had a self and now he

---

[421] A I, 157-159.
[422] S IV, 134-135.

does not.[423]

The world has been seduced into believing that either things must exist or they must not; and all its judgements follow from this view. This seemingly reasonable position is in fact highly misleading and conducive to suffering. For to understand one's life in this way leads inevitably to "grasping after systems." It is in the nature of the search for the right doctrines that one becomes perplexed, bewildered, and beset by doubts. Worse, he attempts to mold his actions to fit the answers to his questions, thus compounding his ills. As every thinker knows it is only by denying the evident reality of its opposite that any system can be sustained. Yet experience itself indicates that this dogma of opposition/affirmation contradicts life itself. The one who sees things are they really are

> does not hold with the non-existence of the world. But he, who with right insight sees the passing away of the world as it really is, does not hold with the existence of the world. After systems, imprisoned by dogmas is this world.... [T]he man who does not go after that system-grasping [diṭṭhupādāna], that mental standpoint, that dogmatic bias, who does not grasp it, does not take up his stand upon it, [does not think]: "It is my soul!"[424]

Such a one knows that that which arises is just dukkha, and that which passes away is just dukkha. He is not perplexed. "Knowledge herein is his that is not merely another's." There are these two extremes, then: that everything exists, or does not exist. But each is false. The way of the Tathāgata, the Middle Way, is what is taught by the Buddha. In contrast, those who are mislead by false and perverted views are bound to death and suffering.[425]

The same is true for the polarity of becoming and annihilation. Those who believe in the continual becoming of the world are blind to its running down and destruction; and those who see only the running down of the world are blind to its arising and becoming. In holding either of these views, teaches Gotama, one is bound, attached to those views, averse to the others, and thus confused. He grasps after the system, and is hindered from seeing things as they really are. He comes to delight in what are in fact the impediments to his release, and is bound to birth, aging, dying, grief, sorrow, suffering, lamentation, despair.[426] Those who misunderstand the denial of the permanence of self believe they are right in asserting the truth of annihilation, and cite the teachings of the Dhamma in their favor. But Gotama, who is told that he is thought of as a nihilist because he denies becoming [vibhava], responds,

---

[423] Ibid., 281-282.
[424] S II, 13.
[425] Ibid..
[426] M I, 87-88.

but as this, monks, is just what I am not, as this is just what I do not say, therefore these...recluses misrepresent [me].... Formerly I, monks, as well as now, lay down simply anguish and the stopping of anguish [*dukkha*].[427]

There is no pleasure for the Buddha in the idea that he is supported by some in his teaching, nor sorrow in the idea that he is opposed by others. The truth of his teaching does not depend upon its being accepted or rejected, for the *Dhamma* transcends systems of belief with which men have concerned themselves at all times.[428]

Opponents and those who held wrong views approached the Buddha and his followers for advice and argument in a state of bondage to their beliefs. Thus they were vulnerable to suffering and in need of correction. Yamaka, for example, held the belief that insofar as a monk had broken the *āsavas*, the last ties of attachment to anything at all, he did not "become" when the body breaks up after he perished. This belief is addressed by Sāriputta, who sets Yamaka a series of questions as to whether the body is permanent or impermanent, whether the *Tathāgata* is body, perception, feeling, consciousness, or activities, in the body, or in any of the other *khandhas*, in possession of a body, or any of the other *khandhas*. The reply is negative to each query. Thus, since in this very life a *Tathāgata* is not to be regarded as existing in truth, it is improper to assert that the body does not "become" after death. The proper response to the question of the ultimate disposition of the body is that the body, like the other *khandhas*, is impermanent, and what is impermanent is *dukkha*, which has ceased.[429]

The early texts describe at some length the conflict between the Buddha and his followers and the influential group known to us as Jains. The Jains are important in the exposition of the truth of suffering because their system, however rigorous, was regarded as a perverted view. Whether the *Āgamas* give an accurate report of Jain beliefs is probably an issue for debate; but what the Jains are reported to have believed serves as a useful foil for understanding the teaching concerning false views. The Jains are said to hold that each and every act and condition is the result of a prior act. They strenuously seek to avoid evil actions because they produce evil results, and good actions are encouraged because they produce good results. The rigor of their application of this principle led them to follow a style of life of extreme self-denial, and of performing good works. There are also references to their belief in an Overlord, or Supreme Being, who is the initial or first cause.

It is said that the Jains deny all happiness, and concern themselves

---

[427] M I, 180.
[428] *Ibid.*.
[429] S III, 94-96.

solely with replacing evil actions with good works. The Ariyan way does not deny rightful happiness.[430] In the Jain view the salvation of the individual depended entirely upon his actions and their consequences. It is a mark of their (purported) misunderstanding of the Buddha that they held that he opposed striving. Thus one Sīha, a disciple of the Nigaṇṭha order of the Jains, wished to approach Gotama for the sake of discourse, but he is turned away by his leader, Nigaṇṭha, since Gotama taught inaction, the opposite of their discipline. In fact what Gotama rejected was the Jain belief in a system, a "Religion," rather than the truth itself.[431]

The role of false view is central to the truth of suffering. False view is a corruption, a distortion and a delusion. Again, it is not a question of having got the wrong answer, but of asserting that reality and the self are thus and so, and haring off in the wrong direction, toward untold and eternal misery. Furthermore, false view refers not only to specific views, or opinions, on various subjects, but also to a class of suffering. Thus to hold a view, or to hold to a belief of any stripe, as true is itself conducive to suffering. It boots little, the Buddha is arguing, what view you hold; the nature of that act is such that it is conducive to suffering. What is being done is something like idolatry: the confusion of representation for reality, a confusion of the part for the whole. Further, it is not a simple kind of confusion, such as holding a road-map upside-down. It is a fundamental error which in itself is productive of the whole chain of states, conditions and actions which leads to death and suffering.

In sum, these are the views that destroy: that in the impermanent there is permanence; that in the Ill there is not Ill; that in the not self there is self; that in the foul there is fair. "Such [persons bound by

---

[430] M III, 10-11.

[431] At times the contrast between the Buddha's wisdom concerning what was significant and what was not contrasts humorously with the notions of the earnest seekers and believers who approached him. One Udāyin, it is reported, found it hard to understand Gotama's statement that the past and the future should be left to themselves and were not a matter for concern according to Gotama. The true *Dhamma* states the arising and decline of all things thus: If this is, that comes to be; from the arising of this, that arises; if this is not, that does not come to be; from the stopping of this, that is stopped. Udāyin holds what seems to be a different view. This view is that there is no "lustre" (*vaṇṇa*) superior to "this," for it is the highest lustre. Which "this" possesses such a "lustre?" asks Gotama. This than which there is no higher lustre, was the reply. The Buddha responds that an investigation into the nature of truth conducted in the manner that this dialogue suggested would proceed for a very long time indeed. M II, 229-230.

these views] wander on the path of view perverse,/ Creatures of mind distraught, of mind unsound."[432]

Suffering and Co-dependent Origination

Suffering, *dukkha*, has an ongoing, continuous nature which arises from the impermanence of existence. The concept of the *khandhas* as the "self" bears testimony to this truth. The impermanence is dynamic; but it possess a certain "structure," if one can use any term at all at this point without betraying the *Dhamma*. The difficulty of terms is persistent and permanent in the Buddhist tradition, as in all traditions; and one understands why the great Buddhist analyst Nāgārjuna could say that *saṃsāra*, ordinary existence, was empty and thus like *nirvāṇa*, in order to break out of the threatening confinement of terms. Nevertheless, the risk taken by Gotama in preaching included the possibly misleading use of terms; yet it is because of these terms that we are able to grasp anything at all of the *Dhamma*. The question of the ongoing and dependent nature of suffering is a case in point. For the tradition understands and analyzes the nature of suffering in "causal" terms.

The central presentation of this truth takes the form of the co-dependent origination series, the *paṭiccasamuppāda* series, which explains how condition x leads to condition y, and how x without y does not arise. It will be seen that the use of the term "causal" is fraught with difficulties in light of the doctrine of *anicca*; for none of these "causes" or "effects" is in any way independent. In one metaphor it is like two reeds which cannot stand alone but only by leaning upon each other. Such is the nature of the existence of any of the causes and effects in the *paṭiccasamuppāda* series. (At this point I wish only to illustrate the nature of the relationship between various elements of suffering. A more detailed examination appears below.)

There are several versions of the origination series. Here is one of the most widely used: from ignorance activities (*sankhāra*) arise; from activities consciousness arises; from consciousness name-and-shape (*nāmarūpa*) arises; from name-and-shape sense (*saḷāyatana*, the six senses) arises; from sense sense contact (*phassa*) arises; from sense contact feeling arises; from feeling craving arises; from craving grasping arises; from grasping (*upādāna*) becoming (*bhava*) arises; from becoming birth arises; from birth old-age-and-death, grief, lamenting, suffering, sorrow, and despair arise. Such is the uprising of *dukkha*.[433]

The reversal of this series leads to the ending of suffering. The fading away of ignorance leads to the fading away of activities, the ending of activities leads to the ceasing of consciousness, consciousness to the ceasing of name-and-shape, and so forth to the end of the series. To move

---

[432] A II, 60-61.
[433] S II, 1-2.

beyond our immediate concern, let us note that it is characteristic of the Buddhist treatment of the truths concerning suffering that the cause of suffering is intimately related to the cause of the end of suffering. Thus the series depicts the interrelationships between the elements of suffering for the purpose of showing both their uprising and their cessation. This implies the very significant truth that the end of suffering is not effected from any point or by any agency beyond the congeries of the elements of suffering themselves.

Each of the elements in the series is itself subjected to analysis. What is birth? It is community, rebirth, reproduction, the *khandhas*, and acquisition of the sense-fields.[434] Becoming is becoming in pleasurable worlds, becoming in Form-worlds, and becoming in Formless-worlds. Grasping means grasping of desires (*kāma*), opinion (*diṭṭhi*), rule and ritual (*sīlabbatupādāna*), and of belief in a soul (*attavādupādāna*). Craving refers to craving for six groups of things, that is, the things perceived by the senses. Feeling means the feeling arising from sense contact. Contact is what in English one might call the "actual" contact of the eye with the objects of sense, to form the sense-fields. Those are the objects of the senses, the six senses of eye, ear, nose, tongue, body and mind. Moving ever closer to the beginning of this version of the series we come to name-and-form, or *nāmarūpa*. This element is commonly analyzed at greater length than the others because it summarizes the body, or "identity," as it were. It is most frequently the first *khandha* analyzed, and is the first *locus* of the error of identifying the self. In this analysis a distinction is drawn between name and form, or shape. Feeling (*vedanā*), perception (*saññā*), will (*cetanā*), contact, and work of mind (*manasikāra*) are called name. The four great elements (air, earth, fire and water) and the shape are derived from them. Consciousness means the consciousness attached to the operation of the senses, *e.g.* eye-consciousness, ear-consciousness. The activities are the activities of word, mind and deed (*vacī, citta, kāya*). And finally ignorance, *avijjā*, is ignorance concerning *dukkha*, its rise, and its cessation to its end.[435]

---

[434] S II, 1ff..

[435] S II, 1-5. Elsewhere ignorance is said to be dependent upon the "cankers," the *āsavas*, an element of the individual that will occupy our attention later; but it appears to refer to a very deep and fundamental tendency. It is the last of the bonds from which the monk must break free. Ignorance is said to arise from a tendency to ignorance. The uprising of the cankers is the uprising of ignorance, the stopping of the cankers is the way to release. Cankers are three (or four) in number: the canker of sense pleasure (*kāmāsava*), of becoming (*bhavāsava*) and of ignorance (*avijjāsava*) (and *diṭṭhāsava*, of speculation). However, the relationship between ignorance and the *āsavas* appears to have a reversible link; for

As an account of the origin of suffering the *paṭiccasamuppāda* series in whatever form is remarkable (to Western minds) for its easy transition from psychological or emotional to perceptual to metaphysical categories. But, as the treatment of the false views should warn us, such categorization, however venerable, does not address the nature of suffering successfully. That is, however, the purpose of the *paṭiccasamuppāda* series. That which arises and ceases is suffering and nothing but suffering. It is only suffering which arises and declines, comes and passes away. The origin of suffering is the origin of all things, the "created order," individuals, past, present and future. Nothing is to be found outside the ill of the series, and it accounts for and represents all things. The series is nothing less than the universal truth of the arising and cessation of suffering. When it arises there is suffering, when it does not there is no suffering. Thus the customary division of experience into external, internal, past, present and future, psychological and physical, social and individual, is simply a false view. The reality that the series presents, implies and declares as the only truth is the truth of *dukkha*. All other categorizations and interpretations are secondary and derivative.

If we understand it properly it is evident that the series may begin and end at any point, and may be reversed from any point back to the chosen point of origination. One may begin with birth and see that because of birth death arises. One may begin with contact and understand that the work of the mind ensues, followed by consciousness, the activities, and so forth. As there is no first cause or ultimate end–the contrary would contradict the insight of *anicca*–there is only a nexus of co-dependent origination for the whole of the mass of suffering and for each of its elements. One example of the nature of the series may be found in the analysis of *dukkha* as arising from will. "That which we will, brethren, and that which we intend to and that wherewithal we are occupied:–this becomes an object for the persistence of consciousness. The object being there, there comes to be a station of consciousness. Consciousness being stationed and growing, rebirth of renewed existence takes place in the future, and birth, decay-and-death, grief, lamenting, suffering, sorrow and despair come to pass. Such is the uprising, etc..″[436]

The application of the principle of co-dependent origination to suffering is appropriate for any of the elements of suffering, without necessarily incorporating them all. For example here is another application: thought of sense desires (*kāmavitakka*) arises from a causal basis (*nidāna*), as do ill-will and cruelty. How do they so arise? From sense desire arises sen-

---

it is also said, "From the uprising of ignorance is the uprising of the cankers, from the stopping of ignorance is the stopping of the cankers." M I, 63-67; *cf.* M I, 61-62, 63-67, D II, 81, 84, 91, *et passim.*
[436] S II, 45.

suous perception; from sensuous perception (*kāmasaññā*) arise sensuous aims (*kāmasankappa*); sensuous desire (*kāmachanda*) arises from sensuous aims; sensuous yearning (*kāmapariḷāha*) arises from sensuous desire; sensuous questions (*kāmapariyesanā*) arise from sensuous yearning . The *puthujjana*, pursuing a sensuous question, engaged in a malevolent quest, practices wrong and cruel conduct in thought, word and deed.[437]

In short the principle of co-dependent origination is applicable in the most general manner to the fact of suffering. It is an explanation both of its arising and of its cessation as an whole. But the varieties of its application exist in response to specific facts of suffering as well. If, for example, one asks how suffering arises in the body, the series may begin with name-and-form. Or, if the question is whether the true and eternal self is feeling, or craving, or becoming, the series may begin there. If death is seen as the quintessence of suffering and its nature is questioned, one may begin with death. The *Dīgha Nikāya* suggests the following order (among others) for the series, beginning with name-and-form: name-and-form gives rise to consciousness (*viññāṇa*), consciousness to name-and-form, name-and form to contact, contact to sensation, sensation to craving, craving to grasping, grasping to becoming, becoming to birth, birth to old age and death, old age and death to grief, lamentation, ill, sorrow and despair. This is the uprising of the whole body of ill.[438] Thus if there were no birth "after the several kinds of every one of these classes of beings [*i.e.* human, divine, goblins, *etc.*]" there would be no old age and death. If there were no becoming there would be no birth. If there were no grasping, there would be no becoming. If there were no craving there would be no grasping; and if there were no sensation, there would be no craving. At this point in this particular example the series moves in a different direction from what we have seen, following craving. Thus

> craving comes into being because of sensation, pursuit [*pariyesanā*] because of craving, gain [*lābho*] because of pursuit, decision [*vinicchayo*] because of gain, desire and passion [*chandarāgo*] because of decision, tenacity [*ajjhosānaṃ*] because of desire and passion, possession [*pariggaho*] because of tenacity, avarice [*macchariyaṃ*] because of possession, watch and ward [*ārakkho*] because of avarice, and many a bad and wicked state of things arising from keeping watch and ward over possessions:— blows and wounds, strife, contradiction and retort, quarrelling, slander and lies.[439]

> Our present interest in the *paṭiccasamuppāda* series is in the fact

---

[437] *Ibid.*, 105-106.

[438] "*nāmarūpa paccayā viññāṇaṃ, viññāṇa p. nāmarūpaṃ, ...,*" *etc.*. D II, 52.

[439] *Ibid.*, 55.

of its existence; for it purports to expose the nature of suffering and therefore the truth of suffering in terms of co-dependent origination and not in terms of external agencies, evil, a doctrine of original sin, or any elements that are extraneous and therefore non-existent. The series' role is to explain the truth that nothing but suffering arises and nothing but suffering ceases. The suffering, *dukkha*, of which it speaks is universal and comprehensive in nature, applying not only to the most "personal" forms of suffering, such as grief and lamentation, but also to the arising of sensation in general, the role of form, and the consciousness and activities of the "self."

That it includes ignorance is of course highly significant, for this implies that it is just as true to say that one would not suffer if ignorance did not arise as it is true to say that one would not suffer if death, or sensation, or suffering did not arise. Ignorance of the Four Noble Truths, for example, is itself a causal factor of *dukkha*. Finally, the series must be understood to be universal, applicable to the whole of existence, past, present and future, individual and collective. More, it is not merely applicable but rather is the definition of that existence in its parts and in its sum. The series, then, intends to show that the truth of suffering is a universal truth, and that there are no exceptions to it, no states beyond its being, for it encompasses, defines, and is our existence.

II

The Truth of the Cause of Suffering

As every analyst of the condition of human suffering affi[rms?] [there] is no suffering without a cause. What the Buddhist tradition a[nd others] share is the insight that the cause is not external to the suffer[ing] itself; therefore in the analysis of the truth of suffering one will surely find the cause of suffering. As we shall see, the analysis also must reveal the cause of the end of suffering, and even a glimpse of what that state of freedom from suffering might be.

Freud's Analysis of the Causes of Suffering

Sigmund Freud's analysis of the truth of suffering leads necessarily to an understanding of the causes of suffering. In this part we shall begin with his most significant contribution to the understanding of the human condition, the idea of the unconscious. This idea is so pervasive in his work that it could be said to represent his whole insight at a glance. As he pointed out both directly and indirectly throughout his writings (notably in the *Introductory Lectures*) the entire case for the existence of psychological truth rested upon the notion of the unconscious. If this were not accepted, the entire world view must be denied. But for Freud the existence of the unconscious was incontestable; for it offered the only rational explanation for the neuroses and related phenomena. As I have tried to show, such phenomena exist solely and simply because of a conflict between unconscious ideas and conscious behavior. Furthermore, this conflict is not characteristic only of neurotics but the very definition of human experience.

Freud's work with such seemingly aberrant behavior as slips of the tongue, jokes and, most important, dreams pressed him to the conclusion that the unconscious existed. Moreover, as we have seen, these phenomena were as characteristic of neurotics as of "normal" persons. In the case of such disorders as hysteria, *dementia praecox*, obsessional neuroses and others, Freud argued that in light of the fact of the unconscious, we must replace the traditional physiological aetiology with a psychological one, for the compelling reason that the causes of these conditions were not physiological but psychological.[1]

The Unconscious

The existence of the unconscious meant (and was implied by) the presence of "latent conceptions." Freud's work (as well as that of Bernheim, Janet, and Breuer) in the area of hypnosis suggested very strongly that a realm of the mind existed, complete with its own logic and content, that was accessible to another person only by altering the control

---

[1] "Claims," SE XIII, 165-175.

ɹich the conscious ordinarily maintained. The nature of the latent ideas revealed during hypnosis was not understood at first: "we were accustomed [Freud writes] to think that every latent idea was so because it was weak and that it grew conscious as soon as it became strong." But it became clear that there were some latent ideas that were excluded from the conscious. Freud therefore drew a distinction between two sorts of latent ideas: "latent ideas which become strong when brought into the conscious foreconscious, *i.e.* preconscious, were one sort of latent idea, while the term *unconscious* proper was to be reserved for those ideas which were significant in the neuroses. That is, 'unconscious' designates not only latent ideas in general, but especially ideas with a certain dynamic character, ideas keeping apart from consciousness in spite of their intensity and activity."[2] He wrote in *The Ego and the Id*, "...the state in which the ideas existed before being made conscious is called by us *repression*, and we assert that the force which instituted the repression and maintains it is perceived as *resistance* during the work of analysis. We obtain our concept of the unconscious, therefore, from the theory of repression. The repressed serves us as a prototype of the unconscious."[3]

Here, then, is Freud's initial description of the mental structure (it was to be altered somewhat in light of two other additions to his theory of the psyche, the structural theory, and the theory of the instincts as presented in *Beyond the Pleasure Principle*): the mental structure consists of the conscious, the unconscious, and a sort of "fore court"–Freud's own metaphor–called the "pre-conscious," which served as the entry-way for unconscious latent ideas into the conscious. Some latent ideas were admitted to the conscious, while others were barred. The difference between pre-conscious ideas and unconscious ideas is that the latter are admitted to the conscious only with effort and difficulty. The admission is accompanied by a strong feeling of repulsion; admission is resisted, quite strenuously at times, by "living forces which oppose themselves to [their] reception." This is not the case for pre-conscious ideas. The distinction is clearly accounted for by the content of the unconscious ideas, as clinical experience showed. Freud formulated the following rule concerning the admission of unconscious ideas into the conscious:

Unconsciousness is a regular and inevitable phase in the processes constitituting our psychical activity; every psychical act begins as an unconscious one, and it may either remain so or go on developing into consciousness, according as it meets resistance or not. The distinction between foreconscious [*i.e.*, preconscious] and unconscious activity is not a primary one, but

---

2 "A Note on the Unconscious in Psycho-analysis," SE XII, 260-262.
3 *Ego and Id*, 12.

comes to be established after repulsion has sprung up.[4]

There is a third use of the term "unconscious" which Freud employed throughout his writings, one which underwent less revision than the other usages, namely the Unconscious, *Die Unbewusste*. In this usage Freud epitomizes his own world view, incorporating more than the latent ideas of the mental life. The Unconscious is the active, driving hidden power of human life, its link with the past, the source of its growth and death, the self-grounded challenge to live or die which arises from within and cannot ever be ignored. How it works was a critical issue for Freud; but one senses that its existence was the more crucial discovery. His discovery of the universal nature of the truth of the Unconscious led Freud away from mere neurology to formulate what some called a philosophy, some a theology, that is, a concept of human existence as a meaningful whole. ✓ With the confidence of his mature understanding of the Unconscious he could explore the ancient, powerful symbols of *Ananke*, Necessity, *Moira*, Fate, *Eros*, Love, and *Thanatos*, Death. The Unconscious is in brief Freud's statement of the fate and destiny of man, not simply a chunk of the brain, or the explanation for a type of behavior.[5]

Let us return to the conflict between conscious and unconscious. Freud suggested that unconscious content (as opposed to pre-conscious content) is more likely to be repressed the closer it moves to the conscious. To put this point in other terms, unconscious material that threatens strongly to irrupt into the consciousness is that which is most vigorously repressed, as is the case in neurotic symptoms. Distortion too comes into play: for as repressed material moves closer to the conscious the greater is the distortion, and the more effective the repression. Freud observed this pattern in a clinical setting many times, and was confirmed in his notion that unconscious ideas were repressed for reasons having to do with a conflict between the conscious and the unconscious. The task of the analyst would either be brought to an unsuccessful conclusion when the material was effectively repressed or would proceed along lines that enabled the patient to see that repression was taking place, thereby also showing the patient that there was material to be repressed.[6]

That this material existed was the great discovery of Freud's work on dreams. While hypnosis suggested that the mind could hold latent ideas, dreams suggested that these ideas had their own content, logic, and structure in the unconscious setting. This content was revealed only in dreams for most people, but was present in more aberrant modes as well. It was egoistic, narcissistic, even psychotic in nature, as we have seen. It was never available in clear form to the waking person, and

---

[4] "Note," SE XII, 264.
[5] *Cf. ibid.*, 266.
[6] "Repression," SE XIV, 149-150.

therefore could be said to be inaccessible to the conscious mind. Yet it constituted an extremely important sector of human experience for all its hidden nature and repressed subject-matter. Dreams were wishes that were fulfilled. They shared this quality of the "Omnipotence of Thought," Freud argued, with primitive animism, obsessional neuroses, and myths and legends of ancient (and modern) times.[7] The wish is of course unconscious. That does not mean that the dreamer is not doing the wishing; indeed, one could be certain that the dreamer is the "true person," who in sleep carries out his real wishes, wishes he would neither attempt to fulfill or even acknowledge while awake, but wishes which are his nonetheless, and for which he is responsible.[8] What he is dreaming in fact is distorted through the activity of dream work and the censor. It is this distorted version which the interpreter of dreams must begin with. But it is a distortion, and this fact leads again to the conviction that there is an unconscious which exists and operates in constant conflict with the work of repression.

In the case of neurotics this same conflict has simply come closer to breaking out, that is, closer to a severe imbalance between the forces involved, threatening the health of the individual. Symptom formation, as we have seen, is a substitution of certain types of distorted behavior instituted for the purpose of preventing repressed material from being brought into the conscious and thus influencing conscious behavior. The ego, as already noted, would prefer to live with a symptom of neurosis rather than to allow repressed material to emerge. The symptom, then, both reveals and obscures the crisis between the unconscious and the conscious. The mere existence of symptoms, says Freud, is conclusive proof of the unconscious; they are not simply "degenerate" forms of behavior, as the psychiatry of the day believed. Symptoms are directly related to an event in the past, upon which the person is fixated. However, the person is incapable during the time in which the symptoms continue of recognizing that this sort of behavior is symptomatic in nature. This failure on the part of a patient to recognize his behavior as a symptom is in Freud's view incontrovertible proof of the existence of the unconscious. For the cause of this ignorance is the unconscious mental activity which both prevents acknowledgement of fixation in the patient's conscious and develops symptoms which substitute for the event itself and its effects. Clinical experience showed also that once the cause for the symptoms is known to the patient, the symptoms *automatically* disappear. This occurs not as a result of simply telling the patient what the unknown event is but through an internal psychic change brought about with the extended participation of the patient. (We shall address this

---

[7] Cf. IL, SE XV, 219.
[8] Cf. above, and *ibid.*, 224.

matter below). In short, the presence of a symptom is a sign of the existence of the unconscious, and an indication of the nature of its force
in any particular neurosis. It is also the major clue to the ending of the
neurosis.[9]

The significance of the unconscious cannot be overstated. In defining
the nature of cure, if that is the proper word, in psychoanalysis, Freud
drew what became a famous conclusion:

> What we must make use of must no doubt be the replacing
> of what is unconscious by what is conscious, the translating of
> what is unconscious into what is conscious. Yes, that is it. By
> carrying what is unconscious on into what is conscious, we lift
> the repressions, we remove the preconditions for the formation
> of symptoms, we transform the pathogenic conflict into a normal
> one for which it must be possible somehow to find a solution.[10]

The healthy person has "rather less that is unconscious and rather more
that is conscious in him than he had before."[11] The conflict between the
conscious and the unconscious seems always to be between the driving
force of the unconscious and the attempts by the conscious ego to reg-
ulate and control this force.[12] The unconscious accepts no limitations
on its activity. That this fact, obvious to us who have inherited Freud's
insights, should be utterly unknown, even rejected outright, in our conscious thought and our world view, is important. Yet the fact is, says
Freud, that there is this part of us which simply will not be limited in its
desires. It has no sense of mortality or morality.[13]

The nature of the unconscious is such, however, that despite every
attempt to control and channel its awesome energy, it will out. We have
seen already the effects of such irruption, in the form of distorted symptoms and, indeed, in the form of civilized sublimations.[14] One has the
image of a precariously but strategically placed boulder which, alone,
prevents the mountain side from sliding down into the valley. That is
the position of the conscious over against the unconscious. From time to
time small chips, pebbles, or stones slip past and clatter to the floor of the

---

9 *Ibid.*, 273-284.

10 *Ibid.*, 435.

11 *Ibid.*; *cf.* "Lines of Advance in Psycho-analytic Therapy," SE XVII,
159.

12 Freud eventually concluded that the ego was not coterminous with
what is conscious; but here the emphasis is clearly upon those operations
of the ego that attempt to delimit the influence of the unconscious, or
the id, as Freud termed it in his later writings.

13 "The Uncanny," SE XVII, 242-243.

14 Another remarkable—remarkable in view of Freud's commitment to
science—example of such irruption is that of telepathy.

valley. Sometimes the entire mass of the mountain moves ever so slightly with a roaring sound disproportionate to the distance of its motion but proportionate to its mass and weight. So long as the boulder remains in place, all holds steady. That, at least, is the image one has when one thinks of the conscious as the healthy part of man, and the unconscious as the mindless, destructive part.

Towards the close of his career Freud summarized once again the notion of the unconscious, this time from the perspective of all of his theoretical and clinical writings:

> The oldest and best meaning of the word "unconscious" is the descriptive one; we call a psychical process unconscious whose existence we are obliged to assume—for some such reason as that we infer it from its effects—, but of which we know nothing. In that case, we have the same relation to it as we have to a psychical process in another person, except that it is in fact one of our own. If we want to be still more correct, we shall modify our assertion by saying that it is being activated *at the moment*, though *at the moment* we know nothing about it. This qualification makes us reflect that the majority of conscious processes are conscious only for a short time; very soon they become *latent*, but can easily become conscious again.[15]

Thus the unconscious is an architectonic principle of life, an "area"—though this metaphorical expression is of limited use—of mental activity obeying its own rules, and possessed of its own content. The rest of the mental life, as we shall see, really amounts to what is built up as a consequence of the inevitable conflict between the unconscious and *Ananke*, external reality. It should be borne in mind that what we call unconscious becomes so only when the conscious arises. As Freud implies, without the conflict and contrast we would have no name for it at all. Yet it is the primordial state of ourselves, whose existence has been very carefully masked, very grudgingly revealed. I wish to leave the matter here, acknowledging the enormous significance of Freud's "discovery" of the unconscious. It was nothing short of a new anthropology; and for our purposes it must be described as an insight into the nature of suffering, and therefore into both its cause and cure.

The Instincts

If the unconscious is the transcendent element of Freud's psychoanalysis, the notion of the instincts is the immanent. Indeed, it is difficult to conceive of a more immanent concept than that of instinct. As we have seen and shall again see, the content of the unconscious appeared to Freud to be unmistakably sexual. Further, the sexual drive was, obviously, biological and not rational in origin and nature. If we attempt to

---

[15] NIL, SE XXII, 70.

understand human behavior by taking the unconscious and its contents seriously, it soon becomes evident that behavior is effectively molded by instinctive demands. Sexual demands, Freud argued, are not so simple as, say, demands for food. They both imply and stimulate behavior that is not solely in the service of procreation; the existence of the perversions makes this clear. The understanding of the sexuality of human beings is essential to comprehending their entire relationship with others and their sense of themselves. Biology, says Freud, presents to the child an extension of sexuality the working out of which will occupy him consciously or unconsciously for his entire growth period and for long periods afterward. Sexual instincts are imposed upon the individual's mental economy after a complicated series of developments. It is through the study of the neuroses that this development and its inevitable conflict are known. The conflict is instinctual in nature; Freud's theory of the instincts, regardless of its form, is always a theory of primal conflict.[16]

The discontents of civilization, as we have seen, arise not so much from our failure to achieve what is in us but in our overestimating, overvaluing, our conscious intentions.[17] The human nature consists of elementary instinctual impulses that are universal, and seek always satisfaction of primal needs. [18]Civilization demands a long process of development before these sexual instincts are allowed to become active as reproductive activities. The other, less civilized, aims of the sexual instincts must be altered, sublimated, or repressed. But civilization is rarely entirely successful in this venture. The ambivalent nature, or the ambivalent appearance of the instincts as they seek satisfaction, is a convincing clue to this truth. The clearest example of the tentative nature of repression and attempts at redirection of the instincts is the ambivalence of love and hate, though there are, of course, others. Freud concludes that

> It is not until all these "instinctual vicissitudes" have been surmounted that what we call a person's character is formed, and this, as we know, can only very inadequately be classified as "good" or "bad". A human being is seldom altogether good or bad; he is usually "good" in one relation and "bad" in another, or "good" in certain external circumstances and in others decidely "bad". It is interesting to find that the pre-existence of decidedly "bad" impulses in infancy is the actual condition for an unmistakable inclination towards "good" in the adult.[19]

These bad instincts are of course the sexual ones that have not yet

---

16 "Claims," SE XIII, 180-181; *cf. Civilization*, 65.
17 *Cf.* "Transience," SE XIV, 305-307.
18 "Thoughts: I.," SE XIV, 281f..
19 *Ibid.*.

been, or perhaps never are, brought under the hegemony of the genital sexual activity in the service of reproduction. Freud points to two factors working to transform these "bad" instincts into "good" ones, namely internal and external forces. The internal factor consists of the influence brought to bear by the human need to be loved, in its widest sense: "By the admixture of *erotic* components the egoistic instincts are transformed into *social* ones."[20] Our egoistic instincts may be transformed so that they are "good" instincts insofar as they allow us to love others so that we may in turn be loved by them. The external factor in the transformation of "bad" instincts is the "force exercised by upbringing," that is, *Erziehung*, which "represents the claims of our cultural environment, and this is continued later by the direct pressure of that environment."[21] This external compulsion is successful only insofar as it becomes internal, as a working part of the psyche of the individual. This role is taken up by the super-ego, as we shall see shortly. It is worth noting in passing, for discussion later, that the compulsion of civilization, incorporated in the life of the psyche, was, in Freud's view, originally an external compulsion in fact and history. For example, the Oedipus complex, with its fear of the parent that is inevitably translated into submission to social control, arose out of an actual event the "facticity" of which cannot be denied. For Freud the actuality of that event is crucial to human psychological development, and to the development of the neuroses.[22]

The control of the instincts and their transformation into acceptable behavior is the task and challenge of civilization. It succeeds only with the help of psychological hypocrisy; for the natural state of man is uncivilized (although he cannot remain in this state and survive). The success of civilization constitutes a demonstrable triumph of self-deception on a grand scale. It is the psychoanalyst who knows the true depth of this hypocrisy and its cost in mental health. But for all the ambivalence that Freud himself shows toward civilization, he prefers it to the natural state that leads only to destruction and admits that the hypocrisy of civilization, however deceptive or conducive to illness, is the only way to the survival of the species.[23]

The notion of the vicissitudes of the instincts is significant in Freud's understanding of the cause of suffering. The pure state of instincts is virtually inaccessible to us, except perhaps in the very first moments of life and in advanced psychotic states.[24] It is much more common to

---

[20] *Ibid.*, 282f..

[21] *Ibid.*.

[22] *Cf. ibid., passim.*

[23] *Cf. ibid.*, 284-285, and "Thoughts: II.," SE XIV, 299-300; *cf.* IL, SE XVI, 353-354, for the story of two girls and their conflict over sexuality and civilization.

[24] Freud refers in later writings to the "pure culture" of the death

observe instinctual behavior in a transformed, modified and ambivalent state; this is accounted for by the activity of repression carried out by ego forces.[25] As we have already observed, the development of the ego is a direct result of conflict between the external reality within which the organism must live and the mindless and inconsiderate instincts of which the organism is in part composed. Some restraint must be imposed or the organism will die. The restraint takes the form of repression. But this repression is a uniquely psychological phenomenon. If the threat to the organism were from without, rather than from within, flight would be the instant and appropriate response. But in the case of the instincts' conflict with the external world, the danger from the external world is an effect rather than a cause of the threat; for it is the determination of the instinct to achieve satisfaction regardless of the consequences that constitutes the threat.[26] Flight is therefore replaced with repression of the desire. And, "[a]t some later period, rejection based on judgement (condemnation) will be found to be a good method to adopt against an instinctual impulse."[27]

Thus repression is an important but mediate stage in coping with the issue of instinctual conflict with external reality. Freud suggests further a primal repression, a first phase of repression, which denies the psychical representative of the instinct entrance into the conscious.[28] This repression gives rise to a fixation, a critical point in the psyche's history to which the energy of the instinct remains attached and which is indicated by neurotic symptoms. The repression is directed at all representatives of that material which may not be admitted into the conscious.[29] Yet this repression, which is in most cases effective, is successful only with respect to one element of the mental life, the conscious. In what Freud calls the unconscious, or id, the instincts continue to live, move and have their being undisturbed. As Freud often remarked, the id has no sense of time or change.[30]

---

instinct in melancholia, cf. BPP.

[25] For the moment I shall address the issue of the nature of instinctual vicissitudes without reference to the alteration in the theory of the instincts which Freud advanced in *Beyond the Pleasure Principle* and subsequent writings, *i.e.* the eros-thanatos view of the instincts. It is perhaps worth bearing in mind that even then Freud retained the distinction between ego and sexual instincts as a topographical distinction even though he abandoned it as an economic one.

[26] *Cf. Anxiety*, 87 ff..

[27] "Repression," SE XIV, 146.

[28] *Ibid.*, 148.

[29] *Ibid.*.

[30] *Cf. ibid.*, 149.

As is obvious from any study of Freud's concepts of libido and cathexis (on these see below) his interpretation of instincts and repression is presented largely in terms of energy, of positive and negative charges, in other words in the language of electromagnetism. Although at times he seems to mean this language literally, speaking as though the instincts were electrical forces, I believe that he will be misunderstood if this is the conclusion one draws. Rather, he uses a central metaphor of the day, replete with the image of shifting and changing processes related to each other in terms of energy, force fields and impersonal power to convey his view of the human psyche. After all, Freud (of all people) believed that there was more happening than met the eye. The language of electromagnetism offered a metaphor that readily conveyed the notion of hidden but determining power (it also had legitimacy in the scientific community, absolving Freud of the charge of mysticism). Yet I wish to stress what I believe to be the case, that he uses the language metaphorically. Metaphorically, he nevertheless conveys what he intends about instincts and repression, that they are forces in conflict; and it is the conflict he wishes to comprehend.

Repression, then, is the ego's response to the strength of the instinctual charge. Repression is mobile, that is, it is a constant expediture of energy confronting an opposite, instinctual expenditure of energy. A change on either side affects the repression. Further, as we have noted, the stronger the instinctual desire or impulse the stronger the "charge" needed to repress it, and conversely a weakly cathected, or energized, instinct will attract only a weak repression. This quantitative analysis of repression suggests that we should distinguish between the ideational content of what is repressed and the amount of energy, or "energy quota," attached to the instinctual material that is to be repressed. This distinction is important because although the "idea" of repressed material may be suppressed the energy attached to it may continue to have significant effects. The evidence for this is found in the case histories of phobias and hysterical anxieties. Here the original idea of libidinal attachment to the parent is repressed, but the energy associated with it emerges in the forms of fear of wolves or rats and other neurotic phenomena. On the other hand, as we noted earlier, the conversion hysteria will repress the affective energy quota but must form a long series of substitute formations related to the idea until a symptom is fully formed. The obsessional neurosis is the textbook case of this vicissitude.[31]

We do not grasp the extent or nature of instincts until they emerge in a repressed and altered state–a point whose significance is fully grasped only in Freud's introduction of the death instinct (thanatos). The quantitative analysis of instincts therefore is an inference from the analysis

---

[31] *Ibid.*, 152-158; *cf. Anxiety*, 87.

of repression and symptoms. This quantitative approach, using the concept of cathexis and counter-cathexis, energy and counter-energy, was an integral part of Freud's notion of the psyche as an economic entity that sought a state of absolute balance, or homeostasis. The image is that of the Newtonian perpetual motion machine, in which expenditure and income of energy tend toward a state of equivalence in the best of times, and which threatens to destroy itself by overbalancing in the worst. The case of psychosis, the detachment from external reality, represents the worst situation, in which one of the two major elements is omitted and the mechanism threatens to destroy itself. This economic understanding is also evident in the central concepts of the pleasure principle and the reality principle, to which we shall turn soon. Here I simply point out that Freud's theory of the instincts was represented in a quantitative metaphor drawn from electromagnetic imagery in a manner consistent with and necessary to his general understanding of the mental life as an economic enterprise whose pivotal point was the matter of pleasure. Feeling is the most important issue for Freud, that is, how the person feels—not only in his conscious but in all elements of the psyche. Feeling is, however, convertible, for purposes of explanation, into electromagnetic-quantitative language, allowing Freud to render feeling in an objective manner. But, as I have said, I believe it to be a misrepresentation of Freud to conclude that he took the metaphor literally, for all his commitment to its usefulness.

Sexuality

One may ask, as many of Freud's contemporaries, followers, and students asked, whether when Freud wrote of instincts, notably the sexual ones, he meant just what he said. Was human civilization powered by its sexuality? Freud's response, which must be understood in the context of the polemic we have already glimpsed, was an emphatic yes. He rejected irrevocably any suggestion that in addition to the sexual intent of man, which produced both his artistic greatness and his neurotic diseases, there was any other creative resource. The attempt to spare religion and ethics from an analysis of their instinctual foundation was, Freud argued, misguided from the perspective of psychoanalysis, and guided only too clearly by narcissistic desires.[32] The entire symphony of human experience is a rich and varied development on the theme of the instincts. This did not mean, as it seemed to the biologists who heard and hear Freud, that human life was reducible to biology and organic behavior, to stimulus and response. Man was of course a biological organism. But that was not all he was. On the other hand the philosophers' objection to the no-

---

[32] "History," SE XIV, 62; *cf.* "Two Encyclopedia Articles: (A) Psychoanalysis," SE XVIII, 235-254, and "Two Encyclopedia Articles: (B) The Libido Theory," SE XVIII.

tion of unconscious ideas, that is, to the instinctual demands, was equally misplaced. Though hardly guilty of reductionism they did commit the error of overvaluation of the conscious mental life. Ideas of the conscious were directly related by heritage to the ideas of the unconscious, to the instincts, not to the supposed ideal categories of Western philosophy. A good deal of the issue between the biologists on the one hand and the philosophers on the other lay in what was meant by "sexual." As Freud argued one missed the significance of the sexual instincts if one limited the treatment of them to reproductive, genital activity. "Sexuality," rather, referred properly to the entire system or set of desires for satisfaction and gratification with which the individual was of necessity equipped from the beginning. These desires passed through an extensive period of growth and development whose results were found not only in the reproductive sexual activity, which civilization permitted and encouraged, but in the entire life of the psyche. There was, in short, nothing in the life of the psyche that was not in some way a manifestation of the history of sexual development.[33]

The instincts, then, are the basis of civilization, and of its discontents. The instincts and civilization, we may say, imply each other; they present a profound example of a symbiotic relationship.

We believe that civilization has been created under the pressure of the exigencies of life at the cost of the satisfaction of the instincts; and we believe that civilization is to a large extent being constantly created anew, since each individual who makes a fresh entry into human society repeats this sacrifice of instinctual satisfaction for the benefit of the whole community. Among the instinctual forces which are put to use the sexual impulses play an important part; in this process they are sublimated—that is to say, they are diverted from their sexual aims and directed to others that are socially higher and no longer sexual. But this arrangement is unstable; the sexual instincts are imperfectly tamed, and in the case of every individual who is supposed to join in the work of civilization, there is a risk that his sexual instincts may refuse to be put to that use. Society believes that no greater threat to its civilization could arise than if the sexual instincts were to be liberated and returned to their original aims.[34]

But society by itself could not hope to restrain instinctual desires if the individual did not in some effective way participate in the task of repression. Thus Freud suggests that there is in fact an inner, personal conflict between the mindless demands of the sexual instincts and the de-

---

[33] "Resistances," SE XIX, 213-219; Cf. "Difficulty," SE XVII, 137f..
[34] IL, SE XV, 22-23.

176

mands of the instincts he calls self-preservative, or ego-instincts.[35] These self-preservative instincts are apparent only in moments of conflict, that is, when they stand in some manner against the demands of the sexual instincts. These self-preservative instincts, however, appear very often to be sexual in essence; and then what we see is a conflict between types of sexual instincts.

The pathogenic conflict is...one between the ego-instincts and the sexual instincts. In a whole number of cases, it looks as though there might also be a conflict between different purely sexual trends. But in essence that is the same thing; for, of the two sexual trends that are in conflict, one is always, as we might say, "ego-syntonic," while the other provokes the ego's defence. It therefore still remains a conflict between the ego and sexuality.[36]

A clearer statement of the situation is that rather than two sets of instincts there is in fact but one instinctual force, which operates in two different ways, one for the preservation of the ego, that is, "ego-syntonic," the other in a manner that threatens the ego. It would then also be true that at times the two orientations of the instincts would not be in conflict, that is, not be pathogenic. This is indeed the case, says Freud. In the development of neuroses the ego is threatened by instinctual impulses, and has taken a defensive stand. It must be seen, argues Freud, that the ego always seeks harmony in the house of the mind. The activity of the sexual instincts may result in fixations with which the ego is willing to live. The ego may be perverse or infantile in this response, but it is no longer in conflict with the sexual instincts. The neurosis emerges when the ego refuses to accept activity of the instincts and lays down a repression.[37] But even in the case in which the ego does not introduce repression it is nevertheless threatened in its relationship with the external world—hence Freud's designation of that condition as perverse or infantile.

While one may grant the conclusion that sexual instincts are inherited and at least in that sense "instincts," that is innate dispositions to satisfaction, one may ask what is meant when it is claimed that ego-syntonic instincts, or a disposition to repress and control sexual instincts are inherited. As we have already observed education leads to the repression and sublimation of instincts; but this would hardly seem to be a phenomenon properly designated instinctual. In fact Freud holds that both the sexual and the ego instincts are heritages; and in explaining this point he raises again the crucial issue of the inheritance by the individual

---

[35] This is the earlier version of the instinct theory.
[36] Ibid., 350; cf. 413.
[37] Ibid., 351-353.

of the effects of past actions, actions which in and of themselves are historical, "real," external. In general, Freud believes that the development of the individual is a brief recapitulation of the development of the race—the Darwinian "ontogeny recapitulates phylogeny" applied to "mental" and "emotional" development.

The development of the individual's sexuality involves both a biological inheritance (to the point, Freud says, of being illuminated by a study of the evolution of the present placement of genitalia through the descent of the species) and an acquisition of behavioral patterns. The former inheritance surely refers to the sexual instincts. The latter, it would seem, must refer to ego-syntonic instincts. But, says Freud, the fact is that the ego-syntonic instincts are inherited as well. Of both classes Freud writes,

> ...this phylogenetic point of view is partly veiled by the fact that what is at bottom inherited is nevertheless freshly acquired in the development of the individual, probably because the same conditions which originally necessitated its acquisition persist and continue to operate upon each individual. I should like to add that originally the operation of these conditions was creative but that it is now evocative.[38]

It may be necessary to acquire ego-syntonic instincts, but they are nevertheless deservedly called instincts, for they are inherited just as surely as the sexual instincts. What causal conditions may be cited for this claim?

Freud asserts that ego-syntonic instincts have the same status as the biological instincts with respect to the nature of human life, and at the same time unlike the sexual instincts must be learned; and when learned they become part of the biological, individual ontogenic inheritance of man. Freud explains:

> ...there is no doubt that the prescribed course of development can be disturbed and altered in each individual by recent external influences. But we know the power which forced a development of this kind upon humanity and maintains its pressure in the same direction to-day. It is, once again, frustration by reality, or, if we are to give it its true, grand name, the pressure of vital needs—Necessity (Ananke).[39]

The self-preservative instincts respond to the inexorable demands of necessity; and this is hardly surprising, for Ananke is their mother and thus the source of their essential structure and their behavioral patterns, like all mothers. They respond to Necessity (Freud writes "Reale Not," hard or real necessity) easily, for only in this way can they gain what they

---

[38] Ibid., 354-355; cf. Civilization, 46(n).
[39] Ibid., 354-355.

wish. By contrast the sexual instincts are much harder to educate; they do not belong to this family: "[s]ince they are attached like parasites, as it were, to the other bodily functions, and find their satisfaction auto-erotically on the subject's own body, they are to begin with withdrawn from the educative influence of real necessity, and they retain this charac-teristic of being self-willed and inaccessible to influence (what we describe as being 'unreasonable') in most people to some respect all through their lives."[40] They persist in even the best-behaved persons in the forms of dreams and, especially, fantasies.

What is the source of these persistent impulses, whether ego-syntonic or sexual in nature? They are the legacy of a phylogenetic development. The "primal phantasies" of seduction of children and castration were once real occurrences in the primaeval times of the human family.[41] The in-stinctual activity of the human person is nothing less than an extension and repetition of the prior, primaeval, experience of the race.[42] There-fore, the instincts owe at least as much of their existence to the prior experience of the race during its social evolution as to any biological disposition. As we have already seen Freud does not finally resolve the issue of which source is the more significant, not because he cannot but because he is convinced that the model of a complemental series is a more satisfactory representation than any clear choice of one side over the other.[43]

I have introduced Freud's conviction that the instincts are as much caused by actual events in the past history of the race as by biologi-cal structures more recognizable to us as "instincts" in order to present a broad and comprehensive view of his initial theory of the instincts. There is no doubt that he believed in the "inheritance of acquired characteris-tics," as it were, with respect to both the ego and sexual instincts. This accords well with his general views on ontogeny and phylogeny, which he developed at great length from *Totem and Taboo* to *Moses and Monothe-ism*, and with his determination to provide a history, a real history, of hidden events on the basis of psychoanalysis. It does not accord well with what he can discover of relevant events in pre-history with respect, for example, to the origin of religion. I wish simply to raise a point which I shall investigate at some length later in this part, namely the question of what Freud thought he was doing in discussing the influence of pre-sumably unknown and unremembered events that occurred well prior–to understate the situation for the moment–to the experience of the person or case in question on the mental state and or distress of that person.

---

[40] *Ibid.*, 356-357.

[41] *Ibid.*, 370f..

[42] *Ibid.*.

[43] *Cf. ibid.*, and "[The Wolf Man]," SE XVII, 57-60, 95-97.

What did he have in mind when adducing as causal elements in the aetiology of neuroses the prehistory of the human race and the specific trauma of parental love, exemplified in the Oedipus complex? Freud obviously thought he was describing some actual events which, presumably, could have been observed by a contemporary whose memory, unlike that of the racial historians, had not been distorted by repression of unacceptable material. Further, he clearly believed that these events made a lasting impression upon the *inherited mind of individuals*, and would continue to do so; and he believed that civilization and its discontents were mightily influenced by these happenings.

The general conclusion of scholars on this aspect of Freud's thought is that there is no evidence to support his archeology, and that he has created it to sustain his own conclusions about the aetiology of neuroses, the theory of the instincts, and the structural theory—to support them with history and science, so to speak, in addition to the evidence gleaned from his own clinical experience. Indeed, when sailing out into the deep ocean of grand theory Freud is much less respected as a captain of soul's ship than when he is negotiating the lagoon whose rocks, shoals and ridges he himself has mapped out so well. For the moment, let us accept the truth of the judgement; Freud has no empirical evidence upon which to base his reconstruction of the past of the race. Why, then, did he insist upon doing so? It is truly a remarkable sight, this vision of the chief hermeneut of the individual's mind insisting with all the considerable rhetorical power at his disposal that the elements of the Oedipus complex, the love-hate relationship between boy and father, are based on "things," events and circumstances that actually happened in the past, and not in the child's past, not in the father's past, not in the grandfather's past, but in a past so obscured that its existence, of which Freud insists we must be certain, must be inferred, and then only by careful uncovering in analysis.

I suggest that he proceeded in this manner for two reasons. The first seems to be a straightforward conclusion which might be drawn by any interpreter of literature and history. People use the language of their time, even if, like the genius Freud, they bend and warp it so that it leads to a new language. The language Freud uses is the language of von Helmholtz, of reality, hard and irreducible stuff. He uses it to discuss something that is anything but hard. Even in the use of the electromagnetic metaphor the language of the time is understood by most to mean that there is something there, however infinitesimal. Freud is confronted with a problem the ramifications of which are enormous, and which we are perusing at several levels. The problem is that of the complemental series. Freud knows that mental conditions are caused by internal forces, which he sets out to describe in all their multivalent manifestations. But he is equally certain that external forces come into play; and unless those

180

became part of the psyche at some point they would not be influential in the way that they obviously are. These forces, moreover, must come from the past, if we view, as we must, the situation from the perspective that is the result of previous conditions; and they will create a new situation if we look forward to possible conflicts among those elements we already observe in action. The situation cannot be explained, in short, in terms of the present internal structure of the patient only; that is simply a condition of the moment. There must be some explanation of how past conditions arose and brought about the present. Freud's answer to this was that there must have been a trauma, that is, an actual event.

Now he does not take a simple view of what a "trauma" might be. He is fully aware, for example, that neurotics speak of past traumas as though they actually happened when, as far as can be determined by anyone, they did not. Further, some traumatic situations seem not to have produced neurotic behavior in some people, while in others the illness is very serious. Freud's "complemental series" proposes that the disposition of individuals to neurosis is not always equal, just as the external conditions productive of neurosis are not always equal. But there is still an event just as surely as there is a disposition. As for the historical content of trauma, that is, whether an "event" exists, as we have seen Freud argues that for a neurotic, as for primitives and religious people in general, the principle of the omnipotence of thought obtains. That is to say, what they wish is what comes true; or they are very much afraid that it will come true and they take steps to prevent it; or they take steps to act as though it had come true. There is, in short, in the mind of the neurotic no difference between a psychical and a real event. What is wished is as real as what is empirically experienced. Thus, in short, there is still an event. In sum, for Freud there had to be an event; and if it is the case that a neurotic is suffering for his unacceptable wishes, there must have been a time when these were not simply wishes but wishes which were preliminary to deeds, and deeds for which "he" was punished. The Oedipus story then is not only a story, but a fact,[44] like an artifact of whose existence the archeologist is convinced but which is discovered only after years of painstaking clearing away of obscuring and protecting sediment. The language of Freud's day demanded that these causes lie in real events. Any other explanation simply could not be countenanced; at that point Freud would have been charged, as he was in fact charged by some, with being a mystic.

Second, I suggest that Freud proceeded to his conviction concerning phylogeny and ontogeny with respect to the influence of past events because he simply could not fully account for the status of the mental life of the individual solely within the confines of that individual's existence,

---

[44] *Cf.* NIL, SE XXII, 81-89.

that is, that individual's bodily and mental development. His insistence upon the primal acts in conjunction with the individual history flew in the face of accepted theory; and his use of the language of the day bent it to the point of fracture. Fully aware, as we have seen, of how reluctant his audience would be to accept his proposals, he pressed ahead with them regardless. This suggests, at least to me, that beyond the realistic language we may discern Freud's conviction that the suffering of the individual is in part due to previous acts that, although not assignable to the present person, are nevertheless his, for which he is responsible. In discussing the moral responsibility for dreams we have already seen that one may be responsible for his acts in a mode that is other than conscious. This conclusion is of a piece with Freud's interest in the prior acts of the race and their recapitulation in the individual. Freud is convinced that the cause of suffering extends beyond the immediate intentions of the individual, and that, at least in principle, these causes may be extended infinitely, both forward and backwards. We shall re-examine this matter presently.

Let us return to the issue of the instincts, and especially their vicissitudes. In the development of his theory of the instincts Freud's interest in the changes, to use a broad term, through which the instinctive impulses passed, was persistent. Indeed, it was the general but still curious phenomenon of the ambivalent feelings children have for their parents that suggested much of his theoretical contribution. His developmental theory of the libido, to which we shall turn presently, was a means of describing systematically the order of changes through which instinctive desires passed as they were transformed under the influence of the growing ego. The ambivalence of the instincts suggested that their satisfaction was not a simple matter of success or failure but rather of diversion, detour and distortion, of inversion in the manner of the dream work and the content of dreams. Instincts emerged very often in forms of their opposites: sadism became masochism; scoptophilia became exhibitionism; and love became hate.[45] In his analysis of the child-beating fantasy, the relationship between sadism and masochism exemplifies the history of instinctual gratification. The fantasy itself, as it is reported, is sadistic; but upon further examination in the process of analysis a clearly masochistic theme is apparent. The child who is being beaten, in the case of girls, or being loved, in the case of boys, is the one having the fantasy. What is seen then is that it is possible for an instinct to regress to an earlier stage of satisfaction under certain psychic conditions. This implies that instincts achieve their satisfaction in various ways according to the stage of development. This process, furthermore, is reversible; and when reversed there is a danger of severe neurosis arising from conflict

---

[45] "Instincts and Their Vicissitudes," CP IV, 60ff..

with the ego. The fact that the child-beating is reported as a fantasy, and, like the dreams of all people, had undergone a certain amount of displacement and thus distortion, indicates that a tendency to regression is present, that is, regression from sadism, which is associated with a more "advanced" sexual stage (advanced toward the acceptable primacy of the genitals and reproductive sexuality), to masochism, which is an inferior degree of organization of the libido, of the sexual impulse. The fantasy is, therefore, both a perversion and an indication of the earlier stages of sexual organization.[46]

Psychoanalysis is not neutral, however, on the subject of development. It is extremely important that the genital organization of the instincts be firmly established, and that sexual power not operate in any other manner than as sexuality. If this should happen the repressing work of the ego may be turned against the ego itself. This is the case in melancholia, when the super-ego is resexualized and takes the role of the active father against the threatened child, represented in the ego.[47]

The complexity of the transformation of instincts in the development of the life of the libido requires interpretation. There is little question of the significance of elements of behavior to Freud as he pursued his analytic work. Yet behavior came to mean something in the analytic sense only when the trail of transformations and distortions and changes could be traced. In general Freud described the development of the life of the libido, or the sexual instincts, as beginning with an oral expression, moving to an anal expression, then to genital expression and through the resolution of the Oedipus complex to the sexual life of the mature, socialized adult under the hegemony of the genital organization and the reproductive definition of sexuality. At each of these stages, however, elements are left behind and suppressed as the subsequent stage is entered. This is most obviously the case in the repression of sexual activity peculiar to earlier stages in the stage of genital hegemony. Freud raises the question of what happens to these vestiges of the earlier stages in his essay "On Transformation of Instinct as Exemplified in Anal Erotism."[48]

To answer the question the title implies Freud draws upon the only reliable source of information, the behavior of neurotics in whom the repression of material peculiar to an earlier stage has produced neurotic symptoms, and in whose behavior regressive characteristics become evident. At the anal stage erotic desires take the form of identification of feces, baby and penis. This is the case for both boys and girls. However in the case of the boy the feces become a penis, which is then the focus of genital primacy for the boy, and the new stage is introduced. In the

---

[46] " 'A Child,' " SE XVII, 191-195.
[47] Ibid., 203-204.
[48] SE XVII.

183

case of girls, the evident contrast between the absence of a penis and the identification of feces with a penis leads to desire for a penis. This desire takes the form of a wish for a baby. The link between the wish for a baby and the feces-orientation of this stage lies in the belief among children at this stage that babies are born from the bowels: thus the equation of feces, penis and baby. A further element of this transformation, applicable to boys, is the discovery that girls have no penises. Freud's view is that the boy concludes that although he has a penis it is possible to lose it. The reluctance of boys, then, to part with their feces, and the (from their point of view) ironic praise received when they do give up their feces, form essential masculine aspects of anal erotism. This is followed by a focus upon the genitals proper and the resolution of the Oedipal conflict. The hegemony of the genitals is reached in girls when their wish for someone with a penis supersedes their wish for a baby, although the latter wish does not disappear but is transformed.[49]

What Freud describes here is a *transformation of instinct*; and the account reflects generally Freud's view of development. On the one hand it may be said that the transformation takes place in all individuals as a result of interaction between the instinctual desires and the demands of external reality. On the other it may be said that the transformation is caused by elements inherent in the instincts themselves, as the case just noted seems to indicate. The critical Oedipal period appears to bring these two tendencies, the one external and the other internal, into a relationship of integration. For the external limitations on the instincts are represented by other people, notably the parents in the first instance; and yet those same other people are themselves objects, union with whom defines the satisfaction of sexual desires. The introjection, to use Freud's word, of the parental authority figure into the ego itself in the form of the super-ego, and the concomitant identification of the self with the ego-ideal represented in the introjected super-ego, effect the integration of external limitation and internal desire. This integration is achieved only after a period of development, and is fraught with possibilities of disruption, as the psychoanalytic case histories amply testify. But in Freud's view the resolution of the Oedipus complex is absolutely necessary for a full and mature adult emotional balance. In fact he refers not to the resolution of the Oedipal conflict, but to its dissolution, that is, its eradication. This, then, is the normal consequence of the transformation of the instincts. When this does not happen, or when the regression to a resexualized super-ego is experienced, the resulting situation is highly threatening to the ego, and the entire balance of the psyche is lost (as in melancholia).[50]

My point here, however, as it is in the discussions below of libidinal

---

[49] "Transformations," SE XVII, 127-129, 130-133.

[50] This process is that of the fusion of the instincts, although Freud does not address this issue of the dangers of defusion until he alters his

development and the Oedipus complex, is that the transformation and vicissitudes of the instincts form a series of changes whose causes are not limited to *either* external or to internal changes, and whose other steps are implied at each point–thus the transformation of anal eroticism implies the genital stage, and *vice versa*. The issue may also be seen from the perspective of ego psychology. For the task of the ego is to serve three masters, the id or internal instinctual impulses, the external world, and the super-ego, which is allied to each of the other two. The ego itself is not an entity in the ontological sense at all but precisely the intersection of these opposing forces.[51] In sum, what is of interest to Freud and psychoanalysis is a process that may move in one direction and back, that may be fixated or arrested along the way, that tends to incorporate both internal and external influence, and that has no absolute point of termination or inception. The activity in and of the process is seen clearly in, *inter alia*, the transformation of instincts.

Our knowledge of the life and history of the instincts comes chiefly from the analysis of the behavior of neurotics. But this is not fortuitous; that is to say, our knowledge of the conflict between instinct and self and world arises from the inevitable nature of this conflict. It is in the nature of the self to pursue and consequently to suffer from this conflict. When one says, as many do, that Freud thought we were all sick, this is the grain of truth. We are all ill in the sense that the conflict leading to neurosis and psychosis is simply an extension of the very nature of our human life. It was this conclusion that lay behind Freud's famous dictum that with the help of psychoanalysis we can probably succeed in replacing hysterical misery with ordinary unhappiness, and not in much else. The instincts are both almighty and creative. It is to them that Freud turns to explain the very power of life–although exactly what they are he, or we, do not know. The crisis of the instincts arises when civilization, and we as individuals, attribute, as indeed we must, to our conscious, our ego, our rational self–all extensions of instincts–power they do not properly possess, and act as though they, and not the desires of our true instinctual selves, were omnipotent. The result is illness.[52]

Freud's view of instinct as impulses charged with quota of energy never changed with respect to his conception of the economy of the mind. His notion of the pleasure principle remained similarly unchanged, for virtually the same reasons, namely that the life of the psyche was definable as a conflict between opposing forces, of instinct and stimulus. This is his summary in the *New Introductory Lectures*:

An instinct, then, is distinguished from a stimulus by the fact

---

theory of the instincts in *Beyond the Pleasure Principle*.
[51] Cf. *Ego and Id*.
[52] "Difficulty," SE XVII, 142-143.

that it arises from sources of stimulation within the body, that it operates as a constant force and that the subject cannot avoid it by flight, as is possible with an external stimulus. We can distinguish an instinct's source, object and aim. Its source is a state of excitation in the body, its aim is the removal of that excitation; on its path from its source to its aim the instinct becomes operative psychically. We picture it as a certain quota of energy which presses in a particular direction.... ...[It is] correct to speak of instincts with active and passive aims; for an expenditure of activity is needed to achieve a passive aim as well. The aim can be achieved in the subject's own body; as a rule an external object is brought in, in regard to which the instinct achieves its external aim; its internal aim invariably remains the bodily change which is felt as satisfaction.[53]

An instinct is, at this (later) stage in Freud's thinking, either an impulse toward attachment, eros, or an impulse toward dissolution, thanatos.[54]

The new theory of the instincts seems to suggest a line of thought less biological than the earlier notion of instinct. My own view on this matter is that this is not necessarily so. One must remember that the instincts Freud concerned himself with were sexual instincts; and in his understanding the sexual instincts were to be distinguished qualitatively from others, especially with regard to their transformation. The transformation of instinct applied only to them. Further, the range of their application was much broader both in qualitative and quantitative terms. With respect to the latter they applied to all stages of human development in unique and complex ways; but hunger, for example, has a much more monolithic nature, with but few, if obvious, ramifications.[55] Further, Freud insisted that while the sexual instincts were, obviously, biological, they were not only biological; if that were not the case then, clearly, the need for a psychoanalytic, or mental, explanation, diagnosis and treatment of neuroses simply would not arise. The conflict and discontents of civilization were sexual in nature, but in Freud's argument, and in the history of civilization, it must be understood that sexual does not mean merely reproductive or genital phenomena but rather any tendency toward satisfaction of wishes; that is to say, it means desire in the broadest sense. It is not unreasonable according to Freud to discuss art, religion, law or ethics in the same context as anal eroticism and sexual perversions. They are all manifestations of this almighty power which is and should

---

[53] NIL, SE XXII, 96.

[54] I shall turn to these themes after I have addressed issues related to the general role of instincts, pleasure, libido and sexuality, since these are closely related.

[55] Cf. "Difficulty," SE XVII, 137-139.

be called sexual.

Finally, on this point, the introduction of the phylogenetic aspect of the life of the instincts is enormously significant. Freud's claim is that the ego-syntonic or ego-preservative instincts are inherited acquired characteristics whose roots lie in actual experience beyond "conscious" history. The issue here is not whether this claim can be empirically verified but what Freud intended by such an argument. One thing is quite clear from his emphasis on the *acquisition* of instincts, that his notion of instinct is not purely biological, but what he can only call "psychological." The supposed gap between the earlier and the later theories of the instincts does not, I submit, really exist. The notion of eros and thanatos is simply an extension of the early theory of the sexual instincts as psychological and elemental tendencies, never biological only, defining the human life, based on modifications made necessary by the discovery of narcissism and further work on the nature of masochism. That is, when Freud realized that the ego can itself be the object of libido it became necessary to re-enter the investigation of the structure of the ego in order to account for its dual libidinal activity.[56] Freud insists on the primordial and originating nature of sexuality. All of the highest feelings of man go back invariably to erotic sources. He writes,

> And we are thus led to the discovery that all the emotional relationships of sympathy, friendship, trust, and the like, which can be turned to good account in our lives, are genetically linked with sexuality and have developed from purely sexual desires through a softening of their sexual aim, however pure and unsensual they may appear to our conscious self-perception....[57]

The analyst may make good use of this truth in overseeing the transference of emotional ties to himself, but only if he realizes that the positive emotional ties have this original erotic source.[58] The elemental emotional truth, then, is sexuality; but it must be understood that by sexuality Freud means the entire process of development, not simply the permissible genital hegemony. Reproduction is a triumph of civilization, and a distortion of sexuality; the persistence of perversions and infantile sexuality reveal to the careful analyst the psychic truth of the matter.[59] There is no alternative; what we observe here is sexuality, regardless of form, illuminated by knowledge of a developmental series, and marked by transformation and vicissitudes.[60]

---

[56] *Cf.* NIL, SE XXII, 102-111, *Civilization*, BPP, *passim.*
[57] "Transference," SE XII, 105.
[58] *Ibid..*
[59] IL, SE XVI, 322-323.
[60] *Cf. ibid.*, 324-325.

Freud incorporated his conclusions concerning sexuality and the instincts in the more general framework of the pleasure principle and the reality principle. It should now be evident that the conflict that defines the condition of human suffering is between what the organism wishes to do in order to satisfy its desires and the experienced limitations placed upon that activity by the very nature of external reality. Thus in order to provide a comprehensive account of the basic conflict Freud suggested that there were two principles of mental functioning directing (at least in his earlier theoretical works) the operations of the ego-syntonic instincts and the sexual ones. These two principles were the pleasure and reality principles respectively. Our knowledge of both depends upon our ability to explain neurotic behavior; and in all neuroses it is the reality of the external world that is rejected. The role of the external world was therefore crucial to the essential conflict.[61]

Freud called the older activity of the self the "primary process," "[t]he residues of a phase of development in which they were the only kind of mental process." The "governing principle" of this primary process is the pleasure principle, or what Freud referred to as the *Lust-Unlust Prinzip.* "These processes strive towards gaining pleasure; psychical activity draws back from any event which might arouse unpleasure."[62] Thus the basic primary principle is established. It is important to note of this, Freud's original understanding of the nature of the pleasure principle, that the primary process—we are of course speaking of the sexual instincts, what Freud would later call the id—would resist any stimuli regarded as unpleasurable. The original and, presumably, most pleasant state was a state of absolute rest, a state of the complete absence of external stimuli. To this state the primary process wishes to return. The only disturbances in this primordial state were seen to be internal. The satisfaction of these impulses was achieved by simply hallucinating, or imagining the desired effects. The same thing still happens in dreams.

However, experience in the world led to persistent failure to satisfy the internal desires. In response the organism formed a "secondary" process whose function was to ascertain conditions in the external world and to "endeavor to make a real alteration in them." This would be done for the purposes of satisfying the original desires. The formation of the conscious or secondary process is, therefore, in the service of the pleasure principle. Freud states, "[a] new principle of mental functioning was thus introduced; what was presented in the mind was no longer what was agreeable but what was real, even if it happened to be disagreeable. This

---

[61] "Two Principles," SE XII, 219.
[62] *Ibid.*.

188

setting up of the *reality principle* proved to be a momentous step."[63] Thus the conscious apparatus reported sense data as well as indications of pleasure or unpleasure. Further, the secondary process instituted a procedure for retaining and becoming familiar with data of the external world whenever "an urgent internal need" arose. This was the function of attention. Also, a system of "notation" was introduced so that traces of past experience and acquired data could be retained. This was a function of consciousness, and part of it is what we call memory.[64] Thus the traditional categories of the mental life–reason, memory and emotion–emerge in this order: emotion, reason, memory; and the two latter categories are clearly servants of emotion. Further, repression, which had been instituted in response to the work of the secondary process's discovery that not all desires could be fulfilled, was superseded by "an *impartial passing of judgement*, which had to decide whether a given idea was true or false–that is, whether it was in agreement with reality or not–the decision being determined by making a comparison with memory traces of reality."[65]

The health of this mental apparatus depended upon its ability to report accurately the condition of the external world and to limit and channel the instinctive impulses when appropriate. Since Freud depicted these impulses in electromagnetic terms he conceived of their limitation, repression and rechanneling in terms of motor discharge, that is, the discharge of energy of the instinct in a manner that permitted action but not destruction of the organism. Thinking was therefore a very important operation of the secondary process. Freud defined thinking as a trial discharge of energy that would discover the consequences in the external world of discharging the energy of the instinct but without endangering the organism if the desire in question should result in a threat. Thus thinking "was endowed with characteristics which made it possible for the mental apparatus to tolerate an increased tension of stimulus while the process of discharge was postponed. It is essentially an experimental kind of acting, accompanied by displacement of relatively small quantities of cathexis together with less expenditure (discharge) of them."[66]

Thinking is, according to Freud, an evolved phenomenon actually in the service of the pleasure principle. It arises out of the contact between the instinctual desires and the limitations of reality and enables the mental apparatus to relieve, in his language of energy, the pressure of desire

---

[63] *Ibid.*, 219-220.

[64] *Ibid.*, 220-221.

[65] *Ibid.*.

[66] Freud suggests that this process was originally unconscious, and took on the appearance of consciousness only when it became connected with verbal residues. *Ibid.*, 221; *cf.* NIL, SE XXII, 75-76, 89-90.

to a useful extent without threatening the organism itself. Thinking, then, arises out of desire and contact to become the most useful creative function of consciousness.

Under the influence of the pleasure principle thinking enabled the organism to make tentative but useful steps into the real, external world. On the other hand fantasy allowed the mental life to remain in part unaffected by the demands of necessity. It was a form of thought-activity kept free from reality testing, subordinated only to the pleasure principle. Day-dreaming was an extension of this thought activity, as was children's play.[67] As we have seen Freud links fantasy, children's mental life, the omnipotence of thought of primitives and day-dreaming with the aetiology of the neuroses and in serious cases of refusal of reality, with psychosis.[68] He does so in order to show that the conflict between the pleasure principle and the reality principle is an essential form of the primal conflict of which human development is composed. Neurotics and normal persons are identical with respect to the presence of this conflict. But civilization depends upon the triumph of the reality principle; and that difficult struggle is virtually endless.

He writes,

> The supersession of the pleasure principle by the reality principle, with all the psychical consequences involved,...is not in fact accomplished all at once; nor does it take place simultaneously all along the line.[69]

Following his earlier distinction of ego from sexual instincts, Freud notes that the sexual instincts in their early manifestation, that is, early in the biography of the individual, do not find their satisfaction frustrated until the demands of the external world are recognized. This process takes some time; before its conclusion they obtain satisfaction in the subject's own body.[70] But the instincts then alter their tactics by searching for an *object* that can satisfy their aims. At a point soon after this object is identified–the object is usually a parent–the period Freud called latency sets in; the second objective (as opposed to subjective) phase of the pleasure principle is thus delayed until the onset of puberty.[71] The pleasure principle struggles with the reality principle; yet the reality principle seems to be in fact a pleasure principle that has learned some hard lessons from reality testing. It does not cease to seek satisfaction. The

---

[67] IL, SE XVI, 368; "Two Principles," SE XXII, 222.

[68] IL, SE XVI, 373-375; but fantasy is a mid-way point between neurosis and reality.

[69] "Two Principles," SE XII, 222.

[70] *Cf.* IL, SE XVI, 314-315.

[71] "Two Principles," SE XII, 222; *cf.* "Instincts," CP IV, 77-78, and "Narcissism," SE XIV, 83, 88-89.

sexual instincts, as we have seen, are resistant to education to reality. Yet it is clear also that the mental apparatus develops an ego to cope with this conflict between pleasure and reality.[72] Thus the mental apparatus as an whole is extremely sensitive to reality and reality testing. But to what end? Clearly, it tests reality in order to discover the most efficient means to satisfaction, and must therefore be said to be in the service of the pleasure principle.[73] In his essay on the two principles, and in the later work *Beyond the Pleasure Principle*, Freud holds this view, although at other times he seems to regard the reality principle as one independent of, if opposed to, the pleasure principle.[74]

It seems rather better to think of the mental apparatus as always seeking satisfaction, that is, obeying the pleasure principle; but in the course of its development it must of necessity create ever more complicated and sophisticated means of diverting reality from obstructing its satisfaction.

> Just as the pleasure-ego can do nothing but wish, and work for a yield of pleasure, so the reality-ego need do nothing but strive for what is *useful* and guard itself against damage. Actually the substitution of the reality principle for the pleasure principle implies no deposing of the pleasure principle, but only a safeguarding of it. A momentary pleasure, uncertain in its results, is given up, but only in order to gain along a new path an assured pleasure at a later time.[75]

Simply put, the purpose of life is determined by the "programme of the pleasure principle."[76] Its power is unquestionable; yet it cannot fully succeed; all the regulations of the universe contradict it.[77] Our own constitution threatens the satisfaction of the pleasure principle, for we are so constructed that extended and uninterrupted pleasure very soon becomes only a mild feeling of contentment, and intense pleasure is derived only from contrast, the sharper the better. The pleasure principle is not necessarily devoted to happiness. On the other hand, unhappiness has a clear relationship to pleasure. We suffer, Freud argues, for three causes: the decay of our body; the implacable demands of external reality; and our relations to other people. These sources are irresistible; and thus the pleasure principle, which drives against them, is moderated and redefined. We think ourselves happy to have escaped a degree of unhappiness, to have survived. We learn not to seek pleasure but to avoid

---

[72] *Cf. Ego and Id*, 29-30, 31.
[73] *Cf.* IL, SE XVI, 356-357.
[74] *Totem*, 150.
[75] "Two Principles," SE XII, 223-224.
[76] *Civilization*, 23.
[77] *Ibid.*.

pain. The paths laid out by worldly wisdom toward this goal are different from the more primitive, basic, routes to obtaining pleasure. The suffering caused by other people may be avoided by avoiding them. As for the external world one may try avoidance with little success or, with more success, come together with others to impose controls upon nature, guided by science.[78] But "the most interesting methods of averting suffering are those which seek to influence our own organism. In the last analysis, all suffering is nothing else than sensation; it only exists in so far as we feel it, and we only feel it in consequence of certain ways in which our organism is regulated."[79]

Various facets of civilization approach the problem of the pleasure principle differently; this is problematic, since the limitation, if not the overwhelming, of the pleasure principle is very much in the interests of civilization (if only for reasons arising from the principle itself). Religion postpones pleasure to another world in return for repression and sublimation; and morality and law draw indirectly upon this same injunction. Education—again *Erziehung*—seeks to instill the paths of sublimation in the young heart and mind. Art channels the sexual and pleasure instincts into expressions of beauty by which we may all work through, in that technical Freudian sense, the conflict between our desires and the limitations of necessity.[80] Science provides the best hope for defeating the pleasure principle, for it substitutes the pleasure of discovery and truth for the pleasure of instinctual satisfaction;[81] and herein lies the clue to a general reality principle with which Freud feels secure. The history of civilization begins with the unquestioned domination of the pleasure principle—as does the history of the individual. Each, for identical reasons, creates a host of structures, institutions, to prevent hindrances to satisfaction from persisting. But this stop-gap measure only postpones the inevitable confrontation with reality. Since the pleasure principle will not down, there is but one solution: "[men] turn away more and more from their original belief in their own omnipotence, rising from an animistic phase through a religious to a scientific one."[82]

Freud is, not surprisingly, highly sensitive to the dangers of the pleasure principle. That this is the driving principle of human existence for him simply lends emphasis to his analysis of human life as suffering and the pleasure principle as the cause of suffering. There are those who never renounce the pleasure principle. Like Richard III, whose humpback seemed to him to prevent him from loving and being loved and

---

[78] *Ibid.*, 24.
[79] *Ibid.*, 25.
[80] "Two Principles," SE XII, 224.
[81] *Ibid.*, 223-224.
[82] "Claims," SE XIII, 186-187.

therefore gave him license to seek pleasure through murder, they regard themselves as exceptions.[83] So also in connection with narcissism Freud regards pleasure that is not modified by reality as conducive to illness. His economic theory of libido describes the pleasure principle in terms of charges and discharges of energy; and thus unpleasure is the result of a damming up, as he puts it, of libido—the electromagnetic metaphor now turned hydrostatic. In the case of narcissism the libido is dammed up in the ego, and causes unpleasure. The unpleasure to which he refers is really the illness of narcissism in its pathogenic form. Pleasure can be obtained, and it will be obtained. The issue is whether it will be obtained in an ego-syntonic manner. Narcissism is both a natural tendency of libido to remain in and attach to the self for its satisfaction and a danger that leads directly to illness. Object-love, or the reality principle, the attachment to external reality is the cure for this illness. Pleasure is obtained and the pleasure principle satisfied, but through love of another. Illness may be averted only in this way.[84] The pleasure principle, to repeat, is never overcome; it simply learns to cope with the external world and to avoid conflict with the ego, with the ego's help, in what is called normal development. It is the neurotic, however, who reveals what the pleasure principle can do when it does not mature. Again, this description of health is at one with the aims of civilization, whatever its discontents.[85]

The pleasure principle should be understood as a principle of economy, that is, a principle of countervailing forces. In the language of Freud's time the mind was an entity influenced by and operating under the pressure of internal and external forces, reacting rather in the way the human body adjusts its internal air pressure to that in the environment. The forces involved, however, are emotional—a world of difference. Summing up the notion of the pleasure principle he wrote:

> It seems as though our total mental activity is directed towards achieving pleasure and avoiding unpleasure—that it is automatically regulated by the *pleasure principle*. We should of all things like to know, then, what determines the generation of pleasure and unpleasure; but that is just what we are ignorant of. We can only venture to say this much: that pleasure is *in some way* connected with the diminution, reduction or extinction of the amount of stimulus prevailing in the mental apparatus, and that similarly unpleasure is connected with their increase. An examination of the most intense pleasure which is accessible to human

---

[83] *Cf.* "Character Types," SE XIV, 311-315.
[84] "Narcissism," SE XIV, 85; *cf.* IL, SE XVI, 410-419, and *Ego and Id*, 25.
[85] IL, SE XVI, 311-312.

beings, the pleasure of accomplishing the sexual act, leaves little doubt on this point. Since in such processes related to pleasure it is a question of what happens to *quantities* of mental excitation or energy, we call considerations of this kind economic.... We can say that the mental apparatus serves the purpose of mastering and disposing of the amounts of stimulus and sums of excitation that impinge on it from outside and inside.[86]

The task of the ego-instincts is, on the contrary, to educate the pleasure-ego to the point where it will allow a certain amount of unpleasure. This introduction of the reality principle is nevertheless still in the service of the pleasure principle.[87]

In the revised version of the theory of the instincts, which we shall explore presently, Freud continued to speak of the distinction between ego and sexual instincts in terms of the topography of the mental apparatus, but substituted for them the distinction between the instincts of love and death, eros and thanatos, as his new economic explanation. This change meant that Freud no longer distinguished the ego, as a conscious entity, from the instincts, as an unconscious force, but knew the ego to be composed of both conscious and unconscious elements. He no longer distinguished between ego and sexual instincts but between instincts of attachment and of repulsion. Nevertheless, the pleasure principle still obtained as the fundamental economic statement on the nature of the psyche, which was still understood to be striving for pleasure, still opposed by the exigencies of life.

This is to say that Freud insisted on a dualism in the life of the instincts, represented in the vicissitudes and transformations of the instincts. It is true, he states, that love and hate are very closely related, and are even interchangeable, as clinical observation shows. They may be transformed into one another. But they are not the same thing. What they do have in common is that they are alternative ways by which an energy or force may discharge itself; if it cannot do so through love it will do so through hate. Thus in some homosexual relations the original form of attraction was hate and aggression. But when it became evident that such a relationship had no future with respect to gratification it was transformed, through a form of identification related to the Oedipus complex and its history, to a love relationship. (This sort of transformation is by no means limited to homosexual instincts.) Further, this account presumes that there is a neutral force that is available to both love and hate, and which makes no qualitative distinction between them and requires only discharge through whatever is the more available channel, according to the pleasure principle. Freud calls this force "desexualized

---

[86] *Ibid.*, 357.
[87] *Ibid.*.

194

eros," by which he means the tendency toward resolution by attachment that has lost its evidently sexual characteristics. It proceeds out of the narcissistic reservoir of libido in the ego—and it must be recalled that Freud understands the ego to be a "surface" of the id, complete with the id's characteristics as well as its own derived from contact with the outside world. The distinction between love and hate is maintained but they are seen to be equally available channels for the discharge of this desexualized eros.[88]

In obedience to the pleasure principle the id cares not at all how this discharge takes place. That is only an issue for the ego, which has two other masters in addition to the id, the external world and the super-ego. The ego, in obeying the pleasure principle in its own manner, directs some of this discharged energy toward ends that will enable the organism to survive rather than destroying itself in conflict with external reality. That is its own mode of obedience to the pleasure principle.[89]

The title of Freud's work *Beyond the Pleasure Principle* seems to imply that the hegemony of the pleasure principle was called into question in his mature thought. This is only partly true. It is more accurate to say that the notion of pleasure or satisfaction has been altered. If what he now means by pleasure is a satisfaction of some desire, the same may be said of both eros, the tendency in the self toward attachment, and of thanatos, the tendency toward dissolution. For the relationship between the two instincts was one in which the drive toward death required satisfaction but was resisted by the drive toward attachment and rebirth. Both were drives toward pleasure in the sense indicated above. On the other hand what Freud has now described is a profound and irrevocable state of internal conflict between two symbiotic forces. The balance of the psyche is not solely between the conscious and the unconscious but between the instincts defined in terms of their inherent aims. Furthermore the role of the external world has been altered in this revision of theory: attachment to the world is now seen as a resistance to the tendency toward death.[90]

Freud's re-examination of the pleasure principle in *Beyond the Pleasure Principle* begins with the curious phenomenon—curious at least in light of his previous understanding—of the repetition syndrome. He noted a tendency of some of his patients to enter persistently into unpleasureable situations. The direct experience of unpleasure did not prevent this sort of behavior.[91] He was drawn to the conclusion that he had come upon

the track of a universal attribute of instincts and perhaps of

---

[88] *Ego and Id*, 61-63.
[89] *Ibid.*, 63-65; *cf.* "Lay Analysis," SE XX, 202-204.
[90] *Ego and Id*, 66.
[91] *Cf.* BPP, 25-26, 40, 41.

organic life in general which has not hitherto been clearly recognized or at least not explicity stressed. *It seems, then, that an instinct is an urge inherent in organic life to restore an earlier state of things* which the living entity has been obliged to abandon under the pressure of external disturbing forces; that is, it is a kind of organic elasticity, or, to put it another way, the expression of the inertia inherent in organic life.[92]

He noted that this so-called tendency, the death instinct, replaces the pleasure principle in the sense that it is an inherent tendency that seeks something other than pleasure, since its manifestation lies in the unconscious drive toward unpleasure. But it does not replace the pleasure principle as it would if it were not a drive for satisfaction. It manifestly is just such a drive. In other words it is correct to conclude that the revised theory of the instincts constitutes a redefinition of the pleasure principle rather than a replacement of it.

If pleasure meant the avoidance of unpleasure masochism was inexplicable:

...if mental processes are governed by the pleasure principle in such a way that their first aim is the avoidance of unpleasure and the obtaining of pleasure, masochism is incomprehensible. If pain and pleasure cannot be simply warnings but actually aims, the pleasure principle is paralysed—it is as though the watchman over our mental life were put out of action by a drug.[93]

On the basis of the eros-thanatos distinction Freud then suggests that there exists in the economy of the mind a principle of stability, to which he assigns the name "Nirvana principle." It is clear that he chose this name because he (mistakenly) conceived nirvana to be a state of the complete absence of stimuli and of utter morbidity. That is, the nirvana principle is a description of the tendency of an organism toward complete separation and non-attachment. The nirvana principle is now closely related to the pleasure principle; but it is a negative relationship. Freud claims that the nirvana principle and the pleasure principle are two different principles. The former is a tendency toward non-attachment, the latter toward attachment. The pleasure principle, he argues, has emerged as a result of the modification of the nirvana principle in living organisms.[94] He summarizes the relationship between the nirvana principle, the pleasure principle, and the reality principle in this way:

The *Nirvana* principle expresses the trend of the death instinct; the *pleasure* principle represents the demands of the libido; and

---

[92] *Ibid.*, 67-68; *cf.* "Analysis," SE XXIII, 243.
[93] "Masochism," SE XIX, 159.
[94] *Ibid.*, 160-161.

the modification of the latter principle, the *reality* principle, represents the influence of the external world. None of these three principles is actually put out of action by another. As a rule they are able to tolerate one another, although conflicts are bound to arise occasionally from the fact of the different aims that are set for each other—in one case a quantitative reduction of the load of the stimulus, in another a qualitative characteristic of the stimulus, and lastly a postponement of the discharge of the stimulus and a temporary acquiescence in the unpleasure due to tension. The conclusion to be drawn from these considerations is that the description of the pleasure principle as the watchman over our life cannot be rejected.[95]

In short, the pleasure principle is never replaced in Freud's thought as the primary statement of human motivation. Thus when he identified the id as the fundamental element of the mental apparatus, more fundamental than the distinction between consciousness and unconsciousness and the source of all desire, he linked it with the pleasure principle. The id, he wrote, is concerned only with satisfaction, which is a synonym for pleasure. "The economic or, if you prefer, quantitative factor, which is intimately linked to the pleasure principle dominates all [the id's] processes. Instinctual cathexes seeking discharge—that, in our view, is all there is in the id."[96]

In the end the pleasure principle remains the major explanatory category. The following quotation is among the very clearest statements of Freud's position on the issues of the pleasure principle, the task and crisis of the ego, the nature of the id and the role of external reality. It is, so to speak, his creed (the role of thinking is noteworthy):

> The relation to the external world has become the decisive factor for the ego; it has taken on the task of representing the external world to the id—fortunately for the id, which could not escape destruction if, in its blind efforts for the satisfaction of its instincts, it disregarded that supreme external power. In accomplishing this function, the ego must observe the external world, must lay down an accurate picture of it in the memory traces of its perceptions, and by its exercise of the function of "reality-testing" must put aside whatever in this picture of the external world is an addition derived from internal sources of excitation. The ego controls the approaches to motility under the id's orders; but between a need and an action it has interposed a postponement in the form of the activity of thought, during which it makes use of the mnemic residues of experience.

---

[95] *Ibid.*.

[96] NIL, SE XXII, 74.

197

In that way it has dethroned the pleasure principle which dominates the course of events in the id without any restriction and has replaced it by the reality principle, which promises more certainty and greater success.[97]

I would qualify the statement by querying whether the pleasure principle has in fact been replaced, for it seems rather to have been modified into a more sophisticated version of itself, as Freud himself pointed out on other occasions. The ego is in fact in the service of the pleasure principle, as he maintained in most of his writings.[98] Indeed, the construction of the mechanisms of defense is in the service of the pleasure principle;[99] even the perception of reality will be sacrificed if it entails unpleasure.[100]

Libido

There are several concepts in Freud's analysis of the self that are explanations of the pleasure principle, among them instincts and libido. It is not in fact possible to discuss any of the three notions of pleasure principle, instinct and libido without implying the other two—and this interweaving of conceptualizations of mental aims and activity is a significant and inescapable aspect of Freud's thought. Nevertheless I have attempted to isolate the notions of instinct and pleasure principle in order to follow Freud's own example and treat the question of suffering analytically—knowing, of course that what are represented are abstractions. The problem inherent in this approach is perhaps nowhere more evident than in the issue of libido. Freud adopts this term, the Latin for desire or lust, as a central single expression of the most significant force in human life. All of our ties of affection, trust, and friendship, as well as those we are accustomed, being civilized, to calling sexual are libidinal in nature. This is the essence of what is called group psychology. But this psychology, as we have seen, is no different from individual psychology; and individual psychology arises from libido:

> Libido is an expression taken from the theory of emotions. We call by that name the energy (regarded as a quantitative magnitude, though not at present actually measurable) of those instincts which had to do with all that may be comprised under the word "love." ...[W]e do not separate from this—what in any case has a share in the name "love"—on the one hand, self-love, and on the other, love for parents and children, friendship and love for humanity in general, also devotion to concrete objects and to abstract ideas.[101]

---

[97] *Ibid.*, 74-76.
[98] "Analysis," SE XXIII, 235.
[99] *Ibid.*.
[100] *Ibid.*, 237.
[101] *Group Psychology*, 37ff.; *cf.* "Articles: (B)," SE XIV, 257-258.

It should be evident already that Freud thinks of libido as a force, a flow of energy. The references to the "flow" and "damming up" of libido are many. He also refers to it as a charged or discharged force. The notions of fixation, cathexis and decathexis are electromagnetic in origin.[102] Libido can be "invested" in things, perhaps in thought,[103] and certainly in objects and in the self. In a less mechanical metaphor Freud refers to libido as "our capacity for love."[104]

This capacity for love is never without an object, even if that object is the self. It is the success or failure of libido's attachment that affects so many of the elements of the emotional life—mourning and melancholia, group identity, narcissism, the Oedipus complex, and others. Each of these is worthy of examination on its own, and that is a task I have been undertaking. What they have in common, namely the ebb and flow of libido, our capacity for love, is more difficult to comprehend on its own. As with the other aspects of the psychic life it is only when we penetrate below the surface appearance that we glimpse the forces at play. We can, indeed, only infer the operation of something like libido. Yet, with the aid of a metaphor that was at times electromagnetic, as in the case of cathexes, and at others hydrostatic, as in the case of dammed up and flowing libido, Freud strung the history of the mental life along the chain of this capacity for love. It is of course instinctual in nature, that is, it is inherited, is present from the first. The conceptualization of the instincts is hardly to be distinguished from that of libido. But the concept of libido is used by Freud, after his interest in narcissism developed, as a description of the capacity for love of self as well as love of objects.[105] The interests of libido and those of the ego were to be distinguished in his thought prior to this development.[106] He had recognized that in the neonate libido was autoerotic, that is the infant loved itself and found satisfaction in autoerotism.[107] However a secondary narcissism developed, as a form of neurotic—and indeed psychotic—behavior, as a consequence of libido being dammed up in the ego. This allowed Freud to observe that libido may take as its object not only external objects [108] but the ego itself. Libido was then to be understood as flowing back and forth between object choices, either of the anaclitic or the narcissistic type.[109] These assignments, moreover, appeared to be mutually exclusive, in that the

---

[102] "Onset," SE XII, 233, 235.
[103] *Totem*, 149-150.
[104] "Transience," SE XIV, 306-307.
[105] *Cf.* "Narcissism," SE XIV, 76.
[106] *Cf.*, *e.g.*, "Onset," SE XII, 233.
[107] "Narcissism," SE XIV, 76-77.
[108] *Cf. Ego and Id*, 65.
[109] *Cf.* "Narcissism," SE XIV, 85f..

more libido was invested in objects, the less was invested in the self.[110] Moreover, libido is capable of flowing backwards, of regressing to an earlier stage of development.[111] This occurs in accordance with the stages of sexual development which Freud's developmental theory describes. Libido, then, is a force which can be fixated, can flow and ebb, can seek relief of pressure, and can be discharged. It can attach itself to others or to its own form, the ego.[112]

Freud envisions the libido as passing through several stages of expression, or satisfaction. The libido is an inherited and irreducible force; and as a force (in the electromagnetic terminology of psychoanalysis) it requires "discharge," or satisfaction. The initial satisfaction is gained in the oral stage, that is, by obtaining nourishment through sucking on the mother's breast. Freud identifies the feeling of satisfaction at this stage (as well as all subsequent stages) as sexual. As the infant matures satisfaction may be gained autoerotically, without dependence on another object. This is primary narcissism, represented for example by sucking one's own thumb and thereby attaining satisfaction solely through one's own action rather than at the whim of another. The following stage is that of the assignment of libido to the mother, rather than to her nipple; and at this point the pressure for libidinal satisfaction is somewhat reduced. The next stage, which immediately precedes the organization of the libido under the genital hegemony, is the anal stage, or as Freud more frequently denominates it, the anal-sadistic stage.[113] It is at this point that the child asserts a degree of mastery. Sexual interest is active rather than passive and the distinction between male and female sexuality begins to emerge.

During the subsequent stage of the hegemony of the genitals the civilization of the sexual instincts is accomplished. This is the Oedipal

---

[110] Cf. IL, SE XVI, 416-419, and Group Psychology, on being in love and hypnosis.

[111] Cf. IL, SE XVI, 362, and Ego and Id, 57-58.

[112] Cf. "Difficulty," SE XVII, 137-139.

[113] The anal eroticism of young persons, that is their fascination with their own excretory functions, is transformed into character traits familiar to us as parsimony, a sense of order and cleanliness. (Civilization, 43-44). The implications for this stage for civilization are obvious; indeed, says Freud, "we have seen that order and cleanliness are important requirements of civilization, although their vital necessity is not very apparent, any more than their suitability as sources of enjoyment." (Ibid., 44, cf. 39f..) What is striking is the similarity at this point between the libidinal development of the individual and the process of civilization (Ibid.). In his view, the development of civilization is a special process, "comparable to the normal maturation of the individual...." (Ibid., 44-45.)

period, in which there arises recognizable sexual desire for the parent of the opposite sex and the threat of punishment for that desire by the parent of the same sex, and the resolution of the conflict in the form of the introjection of the super-ego into the ego structure is accomplished. This final stage is characterized by libidinal activity in a number of different forms, only one of which is acknowledged by society as sexual. But libidinal ties are essential to all forms of human relationships, even those with or within the self. This last libidinal mode is a precarious one, as the aetiology of the neuroses suggests, and can under the proper conditions (both internal and external) become unbalanced in a number of different ways, each of which is characterizable as some form of misallocation of libido, signified by symptom formation.[114]

This history of libidinal transformation is identical with the history of the transformation and vicissitudes of the instincts. The conflict between libidinal force and self-preservative or retrogressive instincts (depending upon the stage of Freud's view of instinct theory) causes the transformation of libido in the context of the vicissitudes of the instincts.

The difference between men and women, or one should say between boys and girls, was the subject of a number of Freud's essays. For him that difference was never merely anatomical; indeed he held that one could not explain the difference in merely organic or biological terms any more than one could explain neuroses in those terms. The difference is a libidinal one, and therefore a psychological one. It was not the anatomical absence of a penis that drove feminine psychology in its particular direction but rather the feelings the girl experienced in response to the discovery. An analogous conclusion applies to boys. In general Freud thought that the feminine character was passive and narcissistic as a result of the sense of loss or incompleteness. The libidinal development of the girl follows the same path as the boy's until the anal-sadistic stage. It is then, as we have seen, that the focus of libidinal interests shifts to the genitals. Prior to this point the chief sexual attachment, as in the case of the boy, is to the mother. The discovery that, like the boy, sexual stimulation is possible by manipulation of the genitals and that, unlike the boy, the girl does not possess a penis but a clitoris leads to a sense of loss and inferiority. Now the girl's libidinal interest turns away from her mother, who is similarly deprived, to the father. As we have already seen, the homology between penis and baby is established; the girl wishes to have a baby because the baby is homologous to the penis she lacks. The mother is rejected. The delineation between the girl's libidinal development and the boy's now becomes very clear for the first time. The Oedipal crisis is resolved for these reason much more swiftly for boys than for girls. Indeed, the dissolution of the complex is not really accomplished until the girl has

---

[114] *Cf.* NIL, SE XXII, 97-102, and IL, SE XVI, 328-330.

borne a male child. That child is the penis that has been wished for.[115]

Feminine neuroses are thus largely defined in terms of ambivalence toward the mother figure, just as masculine neuroses are defined in terms of ambivalence toward the father figure. Female neurotics frequently exhibit symptoms indicating a regression to the phase of libidinal attachment centering on clitoral satisfaction, that is, the stage prior to the discovery of the absence of a penis. (Freud suggests that this regression is the cause of female homosexuality.) Further, the libidinal development of girls explains what Freud sees as the absence of a sense of justice in women, and of their passive and narcissistic outlook on life. The decisive phase for this mature personality is the pre-Oedipal period. It is here that the mature male-female relations are instituted on the basis of the fundamental difference between the sexes with respect to libidinal attachment.[116]

As is the case throughout, the emphasis in Freud's analysis lies in the nature and fulfillment of desire. The difference between men and women is precisely the difference in the development and history of their desire. That is the crucial point with respect to Freud's views on feminine psychology. It would be a mistake—one that is regularly made—to view Freud's observations in this area as recommendations for particular types of social organization or as the basis for defense of the inferior status of women so traditional in the history of the race. He made it quite clear that he had no desire to legislate morality, and indeed, he rejected the notion that society was a cause of behavior. It was, rather, an effect. His intention is to indicate that women are different from men and that the difference lies in the libidinal development. He offers or defends no program of social organization on the basis of his findings. Rather he seeks to understand and perhaps to cure the suffering of people. This can be done only when one understands the cause of their suffering. It is in these terms, I believe, that his observations on feminine psychology should be understood.

The proper understanding of libido is not, says Freud, a "dynamic" one so much as an economic one; for example, in the formation of neuroses the issue is always whether there is too much libido to maintain the balance of the psyche. If so, unpleasure will result, and adjustments will be made which may lead in turn to symptom formation.[117] Thus in the case of phobias one can observe what amounts to an improper assignment of libido. Neurotic anxieties are frequently made manifest in "free-floating apprehension" on the one hand and bound cathexes, phobias, on the other. The anxiety is properly understood as one of

---

[115] NIL, SE XXII, 112-113.
[116] *Ibid.*.
[117] IL, SE XVI, 375; *cf.* 387.

separation from the mother. But in neuroses the libido has attached itself to a substitute expression rather than to the proper object, the mother. This is especially true of children; but adult anxiety hysteria is simply an extension of this misallocation of libido with the difference that adult powers of repression are stronger. The affective characteristic of anxiety remains the telltale mark of a misplaced libidinal cathexis.[118] What is at the heart of anxiety, therefore, is a conflict between ego and libido; for the ego attempts to prevent the direct assignment of libido to its object by repression and symptom formation, which is seen in anxiety hysteria.[119]

Freud rejected attempts by others, notably Jung, to retreat from the dualism of the instincts. Jung had suggested that the whole of the instinctual life was reducible to libido, with the result that the theory of conflict within the life of the self was unwarranted. While Freud placed great emphasis upon the autoerotism of the neonate, he also insisted that the ego developed into a representative of the external world within the self; and he also argued that the self-preservative, or ego-syntonic, instincts were inherited and both phylogenetic and ontogenetic in origin.[120]

It is conflict from which our experience of disease and discontent arises. Libido would not be recognized nor understood were it not for the struggle between ego and libido to which the neuroses introduced us. Libido may be said, then, to be the cause of all neuroses—although it could equally well be said that the external world is such a cause. "We after all know," says Freud, "that it is a characteristic feature of the libido that it struggles against submitting to the reality of the universe, to Ananke."[121]

In the revised theory of the instincts the role of libido remains essentially unchanged. It continues as the capacity to love, and now it is the force that drives toward association. It is eros, the force that thrusts against the tendency toward morbidity. Its demands are represented by the pleasure principle over against the nirvana principle; and the reality principle is a modification of those demands.[122] The older theory of the instincts had distinguished between ego and libido. But the phenomenon of narcissism showed that the ego itself was a reservoir of libido and additionally an object of libido. Therefore the ego-libido distinction was replaced by the eros-thanatos distinction. Libido seeks alliance and union for the building up of life; and thus the sexual instincts are the true life

---

[118] *Ibid.*, 410.
[119] *Cf. ibid.*, 397-410.
[120] *Ibid.*, 413; *cf.* "Articles: (A)," SE XVIII, 252.
[121] IL, SE XVI, 429-430.
[122] "Masochism," SE XIX, 160-161.

instincts.[123]

In sum, libido in Freud's thought never ceases to mean our capacity to love. It is a force of attachment, behaving rather more like a liquid than a gas in that it seems to have limited volume and unlimited mobility. It can behave electromagnetically and be characterized as charged and discharged, with bound and mobile charges. Most important, it seeks satisfaction in the world beyond itself as well as in itself. In this it will not be refused. In conflict with the world it is modified, but still seeks its goal. Its retreat from the world is in Freud's view a sign of illness. It is in the end the force of life as well as the source of the neuroses. It is at the heart of the cause of suffering because it is at the heart of the cause of living.

Regression

The neuroses are closely related to earlier forms of libido, as in the case of fixations. Similarly, it is the tendency of the libido under certain circumstances to regress that reveals its history and disrupts the precarious balance achieved after the completion of the Oedipal period.[124] Dreams, as we have seen, reveal to analysis the childhood of persons, specifically the elements of their childhood sexual development. In dreams the dreamer regresses. But this situation is not threatening but rather a contribution to obtaining essential sleep.[125] What dreams show is that previous stages of libidinal development never disappear and in principle may always be returned to and experienced again. The primitive mind is, says Freud, imperishable.[126] As in dreams, so neuroses and psychoses are characterized chiefly by regression to infantile libidinal allocation. In fact the strength of the residues of that allocation and the persistence of these earlier libidinal ties are significant clues to the disposition to illness.[127]

The libidinal balance must be seen as precarious, under constant pressure from the demands of external reality in conflict with those of libido. This conflict, as I have said before, really defines what is meant by Freud when he talks about the self.

The Oedipus Complex

The end (in the senses of the *terminus ad quem* and the goal) of libidinal development, as well as the crisis *par excellence* of the self as it attempts to deal with its desires and the world around it, is what Freud called the Oedipal conflict. The term is drawn from the play of the Greek

---

[123] NIL, SE XXII, 107.
[124] *Cf.* IL, SE XVI, 346.
[125] *Ibid.*, 180-181, 171-180.
[126] "Thoughts: I.," SE XIV, 285-286.
[127] "Claims," 184.

dramatist Sophocles, *Oedipos Tyrannos*. It refers to the main character who, unknowing, marries his real mother and kills his real father and is subsequently sent into exile and blinds himself.

The literary origin of Freud's phrase is significant. Freud and many others found such a theme to be critical to the interpretation of the notion of tragedy with specific respect to the motives of the main characters–motives that are hidden from the characters themselves. Thus the three thematic elements of love for the parent of the opposite sex, fear of the parent of the same sex while identifying with them, and ignorance of these motives in the consciousness of the character constitute a universal psychological unit. A fourth element in the Oedipal dramatic situation, the desire for punishment (and creation of conditions to simulate or even effect punishment), resembles the obessional neurotic's unconscious search for punishment. Art, as in the works of Sophocles and Ibsen, brings truths to the consciousness out of the unconscious, and does, in part, the work of the analyst by revealing the emotional truths that conscious behavior has obscured. Rebecca, in *Rosmersholm*, goes mad–truly mad in terms of the play, only imaginatively mad for the audience, the actors and the playwright.[128]

A second reason for pointing to the literary origin of the Oedipus complex is to note that since it is drawn from literature, that is from the work of imagination and symbol, it should be a metaphor. This was not Freud's intention. Rather he insisted that the elements of the Oedipus complex arose not only in the emotional life of the child but also in the history of mankind, and in more or less the terms of the Oedipus myth.[129] Just as children actually have sexual desires for the parent of the opposite sex, actually fear punishment–for empirically good reason, says Freud, in light of female anatomy–, so there "must have been" a time in the past when the desire for the parent of the opposite sex led to overt action of unmistakable intent and to punishment of an irrevocable kind. Further, the historical event is as much responsible for the libidinal transformation within the individuals themselves. In short, the Oedipal period is a recapitulation, on the one hand, and a result, on the other, of actual events. The dramatic truth of *Oedipus Tyrannos* and of *Rosmersholm* simply represents to us, under conditions that are both revealing and therapeutic, an historical reality. Art imitates life.

I have already suggested that while it is difficult to take Freud at his word on the issue of the historical reality of the origins of the Oedipus complex on the basis of the knowledge we have from other sources, we must take seriously his insistence that the conditions of the development of the individual cannot be limited to the immediate experience or even

---

[128] "Character Types," 316-331.
[129] *Cf. Civilization*, 78-79.

the lifetime of that individual. Past actions have present consequences; and this truth must guide us in interpreting Freud and the Oedipal interpretation of sexual development.

The fact of the Oedipus theme is revealed, once again, in the interpretation of dreams. The ego, free in sleep from the limitations of external reality, chooses objects of sexual activity that are strictly forbidden to it when awake, specifically a man's mother and sister, a woman's father and brother. Also, the dreamer longs to destroy those who in waking life he is supposed to love and respect. The antithesis of the waking person, the dreamer expresses powerful desires in sleep which, obviously, he restrains with great energy when awake. What we see in dreams is the emotional life of the child; and the child is father to the man. Even in sleep these Oedipal desires are partially censored through the work of dream distortion.[130] However restrained, the power and depth of these desires is not to be denied. Freud notes that he is by no means the first person to observe and reflect on these themes of the criminal wishes, and in addition to Sophocles and Ibsen cites a translation by Goethe of a dialogue by Diderot: "If the little savage were left to himself in all his foolishness and adding to the small sense of a child in the cradle the violent passions of a man of thirty, he would strangle his father and lie with his mother."[131] These wishes are "natural;" their appearance in the dreams of all people and in the analyzed behavior of neurotics suggests that everyone has them and must somehow deal with them. They are the most mature expressions of the conflict between desire and necessity which dominates and defines our lives.[132]

The Oedipal conflict is also the source of neuroses. Neurosis is the product of libidinal desires and their conflict with reality; that is precisely what lies at the heart of the Oedipal conflict. The Oedipal conflict brings to a climax the long period of development of libido and instinct and their integration into and modification by the external world, which is represented first and most significantly by the parents. It is the point at which love, or libido, takes as its object a representative of the external world and at the same time limits its own desires in light of a learned understanding of the consequences of this action. The super-ego, or the ego-ideal, is the introjected representative of the external world; it is not faceless and harsh necessity but the loved and hated parent with whom the person identifies. The self-restriction of the Oedipal wishes, therefore, becomes the defense of civilization through the limitation of libido and the end of the overt conflict between desire and reality. The conflict now takes on a veneer, a covering of conscious deliberation and concern for the

---

[130] IL, SE XV, 143.
[131] IL, SE XVI, 337-338.
[132] Ibid., 338.

206

consequences of behavior. The overcoming of the Oedipus complex, Freud concludes, "coincides with the most efficient way of mastering the archaic, animal heritage of humanity."[133] It was precisely by the overcoming of the complex that the Oedipal wishes were transformed into the first social ties and the first and basic moral and religious strictures which constitute the foundations of civilization.

There is no guarantee that the resolution of the Oedipus complex (really the dissolution of the complex) leads to what we regard as normality. One possible result of the forces at conflict is that of homosexuality. Freud explored the homosexual transformation of the Oedipal struggle in his work on Leonardo da Vinci. Leonardo is uniquely interesting to Freud, and to us, because his biography is psychoanalytically revealing despite the fact that his father plays virtually no historical role in it; Leonardo's libidinal development occurs without benefit of an actual father. The ultimate consequence in Leonardo's case is homosexuality. Leonardo, Freud argues, identifies himself with his mother, rather than his father; but Leonardo's love for his mother must be repressed. He puts himself in her place, identifies with her, and "takes his own person as a model in whose likeness he chooses the new objects of his love. In this way he has become a homosexual."[134]

This identification is a regression to auto-eroticism. The objects of his love are now only substitute figures and revivals of himself in childhood, whom he loves as his mother loved him. This form of erotism is of course narcissistic.[135]

At the same time, and for the same reasons, Leonardo's aberrant Oedipal experience yields an uncivilized attitude toward authority. Free of the father image, his ego does not fear the social representatives of authority, but seeks its own satisfaction on its own terms. Authority holds no terror for him, for it does not have that base in his psyche that gives all authority its ultimate power. He becomes therefore the first modern natural scientist, relying not upon the authority of the ancients but solely upon observation and logic. Nature itself, which for him is not authoritative but simply the world as it is—just there—, is the final truth, and the source of all truth. In this he was simply recognizing what he had "known" from childhood, that the true and, here, only object of love was the mother, *mater terra*. It was for others to be compelled by the *paterfamilias* to obedience. Leonardo therefore represents a freedom from the Oedipal tyranny that is truly enviable.[136]

---

[133] "Preface," SE XVII, 262f.; *cf.* "Resistances," SE XIX, 220-221, and "Lay Analysis," SE XX, 206-213.
[134] *Leonardo*, 50.
[135] *Ibid.*.
[136] *Ibid.*, 72-73.

For Leonardo, then, God the father, the maker of laws, does not exist. Leonardo's creativity easily replaces that of God, and Leonardo suffers no guilt for replacing a non-existent authority. What Leonardo does recognize—and here he clearly speaks for Freud—is *Ananke*, the ultimate and terrible truth of harsh necessity, nature in her inexorably puissant, overwhelming majesty. His mature wisdom breathes resignation to the laws of nature, and freedom from dogmatic religion.[137]

I have spoken of the transformation of the Oedipus complex; but this is somewhat inaccurate. For unlike the other stages of sexual or libidinal development the Oedipus complex does not pass over into another stage but rather marks with its conclusion the transformation of sexuality itself. Thus the proper name for the alteration of the Oedipus complex is annihilation. There are both ontogenetic and phylogenetic reasons for this. With respect to the individual, the fact is that in ordinary development, despite his wishes, the boy does not fulfill his desire for loving his mother, nor the girl her father. Indeed, when such things do happen they are immediately recognizable as aberrant behavior, and have always been so understood since the imposition of the laws against incest. The Oedipal relation must pass away in order to make way for the next stage of human growth, which is demanded by education, for the good of the individual and the race.

Furthermore, experience indicates to the child that such desires are incapable of fulfillment and even dangerous. The origins of the complex for the boy are found in experience in the enjoyment of his penis through masturbation, or more indirectly through bedwetting. This enjoyment is made the central focus of his fantasy that he may have sexual relations with his mother. Prohibitions and threats, including threat of castration or some other mode of loss of his penis for masturbation, do not as a rule prevent this activity. What does bring it to an end, argues Freud, is the boy's discovery of female anatomy, that is the absence of a penis. This empirical fact brings home as nothing else can the meaning of the threats against him. He understands the threat to be a response to his wishes; and the only way to remove the threat is to stop wishing. At the same time the boy wishes to be loved by his father; but his discovery of the peculiarity of female anatomy convinces him that if his father is to love him he must, again, lose his enjoyment of his penis. In short, whichever sexual object is sought the threat of castration prevents its direct satisfaction. There is but one escape from the danger, and that is to bring the wishes for love of the mother and of the father to an end.[138] The relationship with his father now undergoes a change for the boy. He

---

[137] *Ibid.*, 74-75; *Cf.* "Masochism," SE XIX, 166-168.
[138] *Cf.* "The Dissolution of the Oedipus Complex," SE XIX, 173-177, and NIL, SE XXII, 86-87.

has discovered the difference between the sexes; and he identifies himself with his father rather than his mother, while at the same time forswearing any desire for his mother. This control is established in the form of the emergence of the super-ego, that is the portion of the ego (introjected into the psyche) that is the image of the father, the ideal which the boy strives to imitate, the internal voice of restraint and condemnation, and, finally, the internal basis of his ability to choose certain courses of action over others. It is the super-ego, the father's authority now taken into the psyche, that indicates which types of libidinal attachment are permissible and which are not.

Thus the end of the Oedipus complex is not a repression in the sense that other restraining judgements carried out by the ego are; it is the destruction of a complex. It also places the individual on the borderline between the normal and the pathological; and it is the dissolution, the destruction of the complex that makes normality possible.[139] But when the super-ego, the heritage of the Oedipus complex, is resexualized, the only possible consequence is illness. In speaking of anxiety in the neuroses Freud traced all anxiety back to a point of fear of an external danger, the danger of castration. In the instances of the phobias of children, the phobia operates as a substitution to be related to the fear of castration, or punishment for one's illicit wishes–wishes now known to be illicit by virtue of education.[140] In the case of melancholia the super-ego is resexualized, drawing upon its old alliance with the id, and sets about the destruction of the ego in a revival of the castration complex:

This super-ego can confront the ego and treat it like an object; and it often treats it very harshly.... Mental health very much depends on the super-ego's being normally developed–that is, on its having become sufficiently impersonal. And that is precisely what it is not in neurotics, whose Oedipus complex has not passed through the correct process of transformation. Their super-ego still confronts their ego as a strict father confronts a child; and their morality operates in a primitive fashion in that the ego gets itself punished by the super-ego.... ...[N]eurotics have to behave as though they were governed by a sense of guilt which, in order to be satisified, needs to be punished by illness.[141]

As the phobia is a substitute object of fear, a substitute for the father, so the fetish is a substitute object of love. The fetishist endows women with characteristics which amount to a penis, thus denying the reality of

---

[139] *Cf.* NIL, SE XXII, 57-80, and "Dissolution," 173-177.
[140] *Anxiety*, 62, 29ff..
[141] "Lay Analysis," SE XX, 223-224; *cf. Outline*, 121-122.

castration.[142] However useful to the neurotic such a circumvention is, it remains a circumvention, made necessary by the failure of the dissolution of the Oedipus complex.

The cultural ramifications of the Oedipal experience are definitive for Freud, as I have already suggested, in religion, art, and social authority. In religion, according to Freud's definition, the role and nature of God the father is simply—and purely—a projection of the Oedipal characteristics of the human father. He provides protection, punishment and guidance. He is the originator of all things and the eternal judge. Belief in this God is an extension of the Oedipal experience and is therefore an expression of the emotional history of the individual, rather than an insight into the nature of reality.[143]

The Oedipal experience is, as I have stressed, also an historical reality for Freud. His insistence upon the fact of the primaeval conflict between sons and fathers over control of the women of the group, the killing, eating and guilty deification of the father never wavers.[144] Religion was the symptom of a neurosis, a substitute for the incomplete dissolution of the Oedipus complex. In the particularly useful instance of the Judaeo-Christian tradition the repressed material relating to the killing of Moses—itself an historical version of the original killing of the father—returns in distorted and displaced form to alter and then determine the behavior of the Hebrews, Jews, and Christians. The entire scenario is that of a neurosis.[145] The other religions of the world yield to the same analysis.[146]

Thus the edifice of civilization rests upon the foundation of a conflict whose climax is the struggle within the psyche to both limit and fulfill undeniable desire. The Oedipus complex, and its feminine counterpart the Electra complex, is the central point in charting the cause of suffering. This is true because it is at this point that the implications of desire are manifested in such a way as to require transformation of that desire into a life-sustaining form which grants both satisfaction of the desires and protection from them. The balance is precarious, and threatens continually to slip into illness. The suffering of the mentally ill is caused by the desire which defines the life of every person, and at no point is this more evident or critical than at the Oedipal stage.

Narcissism

The discovery that the ego could be the object of libidinal attachment lead Freud from the dualism of consciousness and unconsciousness to the dualism of love and death; and the discovery of pathogenic narcissism led

---

[142] "Fetishism," SE XXI, 154; *cf.* "Splitting," 275-278.

[143] *Cf.* NIL, SE XXII, 158-182.

[144] *Cf. Totem*, and *Moses*, SE XXIII, 80-84.

[145] *Moses*, SE XXIII, 86-88, 88-92.

[146] *Ibid.*, 92-93, 92-102 *et passim, e.g.* 122-137.

him ultimately to question whether a psychoanalytic cure that depended upon the patient's adjustment to the external world could be applied to all neuroses.[147] Pathogenic narcissism was a signally important discovery; for it meant that the entire dynamic of the self could be played out wholly within the dialectic of the self. It also meant that the attachment of the psyche to the external world, specifically through the work of the ego, could be a dubious and tentative enterprise for anyone.

Freud uses narcissism as a description of a primary stage of libidinal development—which he also calls autoerotism—and as a description of a neurotic condition[148] to be distinguished from transference neuroses and psychoses.[149] As we noted earlier the crucial point in any analysis is the accomplishment of the transference of libidinal attachment from the representatives of the patient's past to the (very present) physician. This puts the patient in touch with the external world, releases him from bondage to his feelings, and gives the physician an opportunity to contribute to the strengthening of the ego in its work of living in the world. Narcissism stands directly athwart that path, as Freud understood it; for the libidinal attachment in narcissism is not to an object but to the self.[150] Pathogenic narcissism is a regression to a prior libidinal state.[151] It is characteristic not only of individuals but of the human race as an whole (consistent with Freud's rejection of any distinction between individual and group psychology).

The narcissistic self is concerned only with satisfaction of the instinctual impulses and cares not at all for the limitations imposed by, or even the libidinal objects available in, the external world. It cares only for its own feeling of satisfaction and not at all for the exigencies of necessity. But even when external objects are found for the libido, this narcissistic focus in never completely abandoned.[152] Indeed, the metaphor of the flow of libido away from and toward the ego shows that narcissism is a station to which libido is rarely permanently fixed but which it never abandons. The state of being in love, "so remarkable psychologically, and the normal prototype of the psychosis," interested Freud because it illustrated so well the action of libido with respect to the polarity of narcissism and object-love.[153] The highest development of object-libido is the state of being in love, in which the libido is almost completely with-

---

[147] Cf., e.g. IL, SE XVI, 420-422, 437-47, 455, and "The Unconscious," CP IV, 128-129.

[148] "Narcissism," SE XIV, 88; IL, SE XVI, 415-416.

[149] "Neurosis and Psychosis," SE XIX, 152.

[150] Cf. "Narcissism," SE XIV, 75.

[151] Ibid..

[152] Totem, 148-149; cf. Outline, 23.

[153] "Narcissism," SE XIV, 88-89, Civilization, 65; cf. Group Psychology.

drawn from the ego and invested in the loved object. When this object is rejected the flow of libido is reversed. Freud extended this economic conception of libidinal activity to explain certain types of behavior:

We have discovered, especially clearly in people whose libidinal development has suffered from disturbance, such as perverts and homosexuals, that in their later choice of love-objects they have taken as a model not their mother but their own selves. They are plainly seeking *themselves* as a love-object, and are exhibiting a type of object-choice which must be termed "narcissistic." In this observation we have the strongest of the reasons which have led us to adopt the hypothesis of narcissism.[154]

The difference in sexual development between men and women serves to illustrate further the primordial nature of narcissism and the critical aspects of the transformation of narcissistic love into object-love. For male children the love for the mother is characterized by the same "over-valuation" of the object seen in the previous autoerotic, primary narcissistic stage. However, a transference has occurred from the stage of libidinal attachment to the self to that of the object. That is to say, the state of being in love is derived from the state of loving the self. This transformation, Freud argues, is characteristic of male libidinal development. It is otherwise in the case of girls. Instead of the transference to the attachment or anaclitic type of libidinal development there is seen an intensification of the original narcissism which is "unfavourable to the development of a true object-choice with its accompanying sexual over-valuation...."[155]

Narcissistic libidinal attachment takes more than one form; this love of self is directed not only toward the self that is but the self that ought to be. The concept of an ego-ideal, that is, an element of the psyche that serves as both model and standard for any choice of action, is in fact derived from narcissistic attachment. A person may love not only himself but also the self he would like to be. This ideal ego possesses first and foremost the perfections sought in primary childhood narcissism. When in the course of growth he is disturbed by the influence and admonitions of others and develops his own critical judgement he still seeks that narcissistic infantile perfection in the formation of the ego-ideal.[156] This aspect of what comes to be the super-ego is thus charged with the task of ensuring the narcissistic satisfaction of the psyche by overseeing the activities of the actual ego and judging them in that light. The conscience, Freud concludes, is just such an agency.[157] It is quite significant that

---

[154] "Narcissism," SE XIV, 87-88.
[155] *Ibid.*, 88-89.
[156] *Ibid.*, 94.
[157] *Ibid.*, 95.

212

the faculty of assessing and judging the behavior of the ego arises from a narcissistic urge in the psyche and not from any knowledge of what is "in fact" good behavior. This is entirely consistent which Freud's general position that the knowledge of what is good, as for example in the notion of a categorical imperative, derives from the libidinal history of the individual. The categorical imperative, he says, is the heritage of the Oedipus complex.

Among those disorders Freud designated as narcissistic (for example dementia praecox, paranoia, and persecution complex) the suffering arises from within the psychic structure, specifically from the ego-ideal, or what Freud later called the super-ego. For example, the persecution complex is a condition in which one feels he is being persecuted unremittingly, although to an untrained observer this claim is indefensible. Freud noted that the persecutor is a person of the same sex who can be represented by other people. He concluded that the complex was a defense mechanism of the ego raised in response to homosexual feelings.

Thus narcissistic disorders tell us more about the psychology of the ego than we can learn from transference neuroses (Freud distinguished between transference and narcissistic neuroses on the grounds that the former were conflicts between the ego and the id and the latter between the ego and the super-ego).[158] In persecution mania the person is indeed being persecuted unmercifully, but from within, by the super-ego (here ideal ego). The ego-ideal has turned against the ego and attacked it for hindering the narcissistic satisfaction which is the goal of the super-ego.[159]

Here the implications of narcissism begin to emerge. The structure of the psyche includes: a source of instinctive impulses insensitive to the limitations of external reality, that is, the id; the part of the psyche that is in direct contact with the external world, the ego; and a part of that ego which, as an inheritance of the Oedipal experience, represents to the ego the standard for its behavior but also enhances primary infantile erotism, which has every possibility of conflict with the ego. This structure exposes a conflict which exists alongside and is at times orthogonal to the conflict between self and world. It is a conflict *within* the self, made possible and at times necessary by the ability of libido to be attached to the ego and the complementary need for it to be withdrawn from the ego. The assignment of libido always obeys the pleasure principle; and thus when either the world or the ego ceases to be the object of pleasure it is replaced by the other. The super-ego oversees this assignment consistently from the point of view of satisfaction of narcissistic impulses. Thus at times an object choice may be anaclitic rather than narcissistic in the narrower

---

[158] *Cf.* "Neurosis and Psychosis," SE XIX, 152.
[159] IL, SE XVI, 422-429.

sense; but the object choice is always narcissistic in the broader sense of satisfying the selfish and egoistic needs of the psyche. What the theory of narcissism suggests is that the satisfaction of these needs may be carried out at the expense of the ego itself. The ego must then cease to represent the external world to the id, and begin to represent the super-ego. That is to say, the ego will lose its contact with reality.

This account helps to explain the apparently implausible case of melancholia. Here the threat to the self by the super-ego is very possibly mortal. How does this threat accord with the theory of narcissism? We know that the volume of narcissistic libido available in the face of a threat to life is enormous. How, then, can the ego "connive at its own destruction?"[160] The answer is that it can do so when the ego becomes an object of aggression. This state arises when the aggressive impulses usually directed at others are re-directed toward the self, so that the ego is in an antipathetic subject-object relationship with the super-ego. The super-ego represents, as we have seen, the narcissistic forces of the self; and in melancholia the ego represents the limitation to the satisfaction of these impulses and is the object of aggression. Freud concludes:

> Thus in the regression from narcissistic object-choice the object is indeed abolished, but in spite of all it proves itself stronger than the ego's self. In the two contrasting situations of intense love and of suicide the ego is overwhelmed by the object, though in totally different ways.[161]

Freud's concept of narcissism reflects his understanding of it as a tendency toward suffering. This is an important matter because we would be misled if we viewed narcissism as simply synonymous with self-respect or self-regard. It is generally believed–for reasons that are subject to further analysis–that mental health requires this self-confidence or self-approbation. What Freud means is that narcissism is one possibility within the economy of libidinal development, one that is at times productive of neurosis. In his view it is a precise assignment of libido in response to both external and internal conditions which is constantly on the verge of redeployment, or breakdown. The relations of self-regard to libidinal object-cathexis

> may be expressed concisely in the following way. Two cases must be distinguished, according to whether the erotic cathexes are ego-syntonic, or, on the contrary have suffered repression. In the former case (where the use made of libido is ego-syntonic), love is assessed like any other activity of the ego. Loving in itself, in so far as it involves longing and deprivation, lowers self-regard; whereas being loved, having one's love returned, and

---

[160] "Mourning," CP IV, 162-163.
[161] *Ibid.*; *cf.* "Neurosis and Psychosis," SE XIX, 152.

214

possessing the loved object, raises it once more. When libido is repressed, the erotic cathexis is felt as a severe depletion of the ego, the satisfaction of love is impossible, and the re-enrichment of the ego can be effected only by a withdrawal of libido from its objects. The return of the object-libido to the ego and its transformation into narcissism represents, as it were, a happy love once more; and, on the other hand, it is also true that a real happy love corresponds to the primal condition in which object-libido and ego-libido cannot be distinguished.[162]

Narcissism, then, is the response to unrequited love in the conventional sense; but in the psyche love is never unrequited, for it will find its object in the self if not in the world. Freud insists that this activity is always an attempt to recover a primary narcissistic state, whether the love is directed toward the world or the self. The role of the ego-ideal is important as well. If the ego is impoverished in its object-cathexes, it is also impoverished in respect of the ego-ideal. This is true insofar as the ego-ideal is imposed from without. Yet the ego-ideal, unlike the world, is a part of the psyche and though imposed from without, stands as a representative of the primary narcissistic state to which the person wishes to return. The notion of self-regard, then, has three components. The first is primary and unchanging, "the residue of infantile narcissism; another part arises out of the omnipotence which is corroborated by experience (the fulfilment of the ego ideal), whilst a third part proceeds from the satisfaction of object-libido."[163] In the continuous integration and balancing of these libidinal assignments the psyche always strives to achieve, and may be said to achieve, the state of narcissism. The common notion of self-regard as a necessary complement to regard for the world is thus in error; for all "regard," that is, all libidinal attachment, is at bottom narcissistic.[164]

Our love, or hate, of others is narcissistic in essence. This does not mean that we do not love others. It does mean that we love them for motives which are entirely selfish, and that we would not love them otherwise. Freud observes that this is true from the very onset of life, and never ceases to be true. It only becomes more complex as our experience becomes more complicated.[165]

Thus narcissism is the epitome of the human condition for Freud. As we have already seen it was this essential narcissism that came under attack from science, first in the work of Copernicus and Darwin and now

---

[162] "Narcissism," SE XIV, 99-100.
[163] Ibid., 100.
[164] "Supplement," CP IV, 138.
[165] IL, SE XV, 203-204; cf. 211-221, and "Thoughts: I.," SE XIV, 283-284.

in Freud's own contribution.[166] In this understanding of the term, which is not really only clinical anymore but summary–what one might with care call philosophical–Freud explores the quality of egoism, which is the *fons et origo* of human behavior, and the denial of that fact by every person who is asked to examine his own motives. As we have also seen[167] Freud sounds a warning not against narcissism–that would be like attempting to turn back the tide–but against the self-deception which is regularly practiced in the denial of narcissism. It may be true, he argues, that we are not as good as we think we are; but we shall continue to behave in infantile and neurotic ways if we do not begin with a recognition of what we are, and what we can expect from ourselves and the world. An acknowledgment of our true narcissistic motives is the first necessary step, for it is tantamount to reversing the effect of ignorance and self-deception. Further, what one can recognize in narcissism is an essential element in the ideal psychical type. We have already noted Freud's three major libidinal types: the erotic, the obsessional and the narcissistic. They describe the ordering of libido in the psyche, usually with one type dominant. The absolute harmony of the mind is, however, that ideal state, in which each libidinal employment is present and balanced against the others. Narcissism, then, is an essential element in the health of the psyche.[168] The point here, then, is not the denigration of narcissism but the recognition of its truth and the eschewing of self-deception.

In his study of (so-called) group psychology Freud distinguishes narcissism from the other type of libidinal ties, which provides satisfaction of the instincts by anaclitic attachment. This polarity is rooted and grounded in the psychology of the self–and there is no other psychology.[169] Thus the aversion for strangers is an expression of narcissism.[170] However the tie that members of a group share is the attachment they have to a leader, that is, to an ego-ideal; and the ego-ideal is, as we have noted, an extension of the narcissistic desires of the instincts, a deliberate attempt to return to the primary infantile state. Thus that person who represents the ego-ideal, that is to say, the person with whom one is in love, receives the narcissistic libido directed toward the ego-ideal.[171] Thus the binding of groups together, following the primary Oedipal model, is due to narcissism, here expressed in the representative of the ego-ideal.

The importance of the concept of narcissism can hardly be over-

---

[166] *Cf.* "Difficulty," SE XVII, 143-144, IL, SE XVI, 284-285.
[167] *Cf.* "Additional Notes: B.," SE XIX, *e.g.*, 134.
[168] "Libidinal Types," SE XXI, 218-220.
[169] *Group Psychology*, 2.
[170] *Ibid.*, p. 55.
[171] *Cf. Ibid.*, 74.

stated. It denotes a libidinal activity that has the self as its ultimate object. It involves in its working out attachment to external reality for the sake of satisfaction of narcissistic, egoistic desires. It produces an image of the ideal self, in the ego-ideal, which is a significant element in the psychical apparatus and which, under the proper conditions, can be the determining factor in mental health. Of the several theoretical expressions central to Freud's view of the cause of suffering none is more significant; for it identifies the desire for self-satisfaction as the indispensable causal factor in human illness—and, of course, human existence.

Ego

In addressing the causes of suffering one might say that our central theme has been desire, or libido. The power of desire in its drive for satisfaction is unconscious, it seems; for it is certain that our conscious assessment of our actions bears no obvious relation to what Freud tells us is actually happening to us—or what, in that psychoanalytic sense of the term, we are unconsciously doing, thinking and wishing. The very existence of these desires must be inferred from aberrant behavior, from illness, from dreams and other unlikely sources. As we have already seen the reason why lies in the nature of the ego. That is, the obscurity of our libidinal desires must be attributed directly to the operation of the ego; and the illness of the ego indicates the power of these desires and the presence of an elemental conflict which we regularly deny. The ego's mechanisms of defense constitute the substitute formations we call symptoms; it is the ego that represses the timeless desires of the instincts. The ego carries out this dangerous and precarious task because it, alone among the constituent elements, is responsible for the relationship of the self to the external world.

What Freud calls ego is the conscious self as it emerges in the organism's developing contact with the external world. As we have already noted Freud charts a course for the development of the ego which begins with the contact of the desires of the organism with the limitation of external reality.[172] The ego is in fact and substance not a thing at all but precisely that point, an increasingly sophisticated and complex point, but a point nonetheless, of contact. The significance of the ego over against libidinal desires, then, is that the ego is the agency of repression. But it is a very sophisticated agency. It was this sophistication which Freud attempted to represent in the electromagnetic and hydrostatic metaphor of libido. For if we think of libido as a charged volume (mass?) of energy, rather than a temporary force that can evaporate or disappear, the repression of it for the good of the organism implies a redirection of it in some other, acceptable, fashion. This is the other side of the coin of repression, namely, sublimation if one is lucky and symptom formation if

---

[172] *Cf. Civilization*, 14.

217

one is not. The adoption of the metaphor leads at times to some serious literalism in Freud's language. But it is clear that he adopted it in part in order to show that the ego acts over against instinct, or id, but at the same time must effect a compromise with a force it can never defeat. Indeed, the ego is not even separate from the id in a genetic sense, since, as Freud argued in *The Ego and the Id*, it is simply a surface of the id itself. Ego, then, is a necessary concomitant of instinct, libido and id in light of the conflict with reality. The structural theory, the tripartite division of the psyche into ego, super-ego and id, is really a systematic presentation of the conflict, incarnate in the ego, between instinct and the world.

Following the analysis of causes of suffering in terms of libido and desire, in their unconscious forms, we now turn to their conscious forms and ramifications. This is hardly the first mention of ego here. That is instructive; for the whole purpose of psychoanalysis as a therapy could be said to be the strengthening of the ego at every point in its relationship with other elements of the psyche.[173] It is therefore not possible to address any element of the psyche without involving the ego. It is the distress of the ego that attracted the attention of Freud in the first place. Indeed, the entire discussion of psychoanalysis is impossible without the discussion of ego: for it defines the limitations of suffering. Without ego there is no suffering, and without ego there is no end of suffering.

The task of ego is not to eliminate libido, but to successfully repress and redirect it. Further, the challenge to the ego is an economic one; for the issue is always how much libido is being brought to bear on the ego. That is to say, the problems for the ego arise when the demands are too insistent. Thus there is no difference in the conflict of the ego and libido between neurotic and healthy psyches except a quantitative one.[174]

Psychical conflict, then, is characteristic of human life; and we cannot always predict whether this conflict will reach a stage in which the integrity of the mind is threatened. When the integrity of the mind is threatened it is because one part has rejected a development that another encourages.[175] The neurotic is thus one who is incapable of enjoyment and efficiency–"the former because his libido is not directed onto any real object and the latter because he is obliged to employ a great deal of his available energy on keeping his libido under repression and on warding off its assaults."[176] It is the lack of accessibility to the libidinal energy of the mind that deprives the ego of its organizing power. The task of therapy, concludes Freud, is to make that energy available once again to

---

[173] *Cf.*, *e.g.*, "Lay Analysis," SE XX, 205, 242.
[174] "Onset," SE XII, 235-237.
[175] IL, SE XVI, 350.
[176] *Ibid.*, 454-455.

the ego by directing it away from the symptoms which are draining it off. This is the work of transference, as we shall see.[177]

Freud's general treatment of the ego assumed a fairly clear distinction between the conscious operations and the unconscious wishes of the mind.[178] In this view, as we have seen, he distinguished the ego-syntonic, or ego, instincts, from the sexual instincts. One group was preservative, and the latter mindless, in the sense that the consequences of its desires for the organism as an whole were of no concern to it. With the discovery of narcissism, and the further development of the concept of masochism and the revised theory of the instincts, Freud concluded that one could not distinguish between the ego and the sexual instincts as though they were mutually exclusive. Narcissism was too central to the ego's concerns; the ego's interests were just as libidinal as those of the sexual instincts. Further, in elucidating the concept of the id, while Freud held that the unconscious life was coterminous with the id, the interests of the ego were significantly influenced by its original form as part of the id, as well as by the demands of the external world, which it was to represent to the id. In the development of the super-ego this ambivalence of being a representative both of the external world and of the id, filtered through the Oedipal development, became acute. The distinction between the ego and the unconscious could not be maintained any longer as a topographical distinction within the psychical apparatus. Further the notion of a preconscious (the idea of an "antechamber" of the consciousness system where unconscious ideas wait to emerge into the conscious) now was seen to be less important to the structure of the psyche. This notion accorded ill with the dominance of unconscious libidinal wishes revealed in narcissism. "Dynamically" they are unified, but there remains a distinction in their operation. Freud concedes that the ambiguity is unavoidable.[179]

The ego is no longer identified solely with consciousness. Freud now defines the ego as a coherent organization of mental processes. It includes consciousness and "controls the approaches to motility, *i.e.* to the discharge of excitations into the external world." It regulates all its own constituent processes; even in sleep it exercises censorship upon dreams.[180] The function of ego is control of the "approaches to motility,"[181] that is, the approaches to the permissible levels of activity in the world. The ego is not the conscious self, but that function, or process, that makes entrance into and work in the external world possible.

Freud explains the position of the ego with respect to id on the one

---

[177] *Ibid.*; *cf.* 457, and "Articles: (B).," SE XVIII, 250-251.
[178] *Cf.* IL, SE XVI, 360.
[179] *Ego and Id*, 14.
[180] *Ibid.*, 16.
[181] *Cf.* NIL, SE XXII, 75-76.

side and the world on the other in this way:

> Putting ourselves on the footing of everyday knowledge, we recognize in human beings a mental organization which is interpolated between their sensory stimuli and the perception of their somatic needs on the one hand and their motor acts on the other, and which mediates between them for a particular purpose. We call this organization their "Ich" [ego].... ...[P]icture the ego as a kind of facade of the id, as a frontage, like an external cortical layer of it.[182]

We can hold onto this last analogy. We know the cortical layers owe their peculiar characteristics to the modifying influence of the external medium on which they abut. Thus the ego is the layer of the mental apparatus (of the id) that has been altered by the influence of the external, "real," world. It is, then, something superficial and the id something deeper. It lies between reality and the id, which is "truly mental."[183]

The relationship between the ego and the consciousness, then, is not one of identity but of part to whole. Freud uses the term consciousness, or perceptual consciousness, to refer to that part of the ego–not the whole ego–which is in direct contact with the external world.[184] This surface of the ego, originally a surface of the id, can be stimulated from both external and internal sources. Thus even the perceptual consciousness is inherently linked to unconscious forces.[185] In short, the ego is distinguished from the id in this respect, that the contents of the ego are capable of becoming conscious, while those of the id are not. The distinction is economic rather than topographical.[186]

Furthermore, the ego neither responds to nor functions solely in the terms of ego-syntonic, self-preservative desires. The general picture of the psyche is now not one of topographical delineation among certain parts of a machine but rather among certain processes which share the same essential goal–the satisfaction of desire–but respond to the hindrances to that goal in different ways, depending upon their nature and the nature of the hindrances. The clear distinction between consciousness, unconsciousness and preconsciousness breaks down, so that we seem not to know what unconsciousness is, vis-à-vis consciousness.[187]

Thus the ego possesses qualities that are both conscious and unconscious; and we must conclude that while its operations include the organization of conscious behavior it will carry out this task with regard

---

[182] See NIL, SE XXII, 78, for cartoon.
[183] "Lay Analysis," SE XX, 195-196, 198; cf. Outline, 15f., 43-44, 109ff..
[184] NIL, SE XXII, 78-79.
[185] "Lay Analysis," SE XX, 198.
[186] Ibid., 196-198.
[187] Ibid., 118-119; cf. NIL, SE XXII, 68-72.

to motives that are hardly conscious. Moreover, these motives range from the lowest to the very highest activities of the self; the faculties of self-criticism and conscience, "mental activities, that is, that rank as exceptionally high ones," operate unconsciously and produce significant unconscious results as in the case of the "unconscious sense of guilt."[188] It is best therefore to conceive of ego as the opposite end of the mental life from the id, rather than as a discrete entity separate from it. For the ego is in fact that part of the id that is influenced and modified by the influence of the "perceptual system," the representative in the mind of the real external world.[189] Indeed, despite the distinction between ego and id which is presented for the purpose of elucidating more clearly a metapsychology of the self, the separation of the two is both impossible and even nonsensical. In speaking of the moral responsibility of the dreamer Freud argues that although the repressed content of the dream belongs to the id, the ego, while metapsychologically a separate entity, must take responsibility for it.[190] Moreover, the clinical facts suggest that the ego does take responsiblity for the actions of the id, feeling most intensely the pangs of conscience.

The nature of the relationship of the various psychical elements to each other is not really the same as a puzzle which must from time to time be reassembled. In addressing the question of how these elements are related to each other in sickness and in health, Freud states that the neurotic patient "presents us with a torn mind, divided by resistances;" but there is nothing further to be done once the resistances and symptoms related to them are removed. For the mental structure "automatically and inevitably" reunites itself: "the great unity which we call [the patient's] ego fits into itself all the instinctual impulses which before had been split off and held apart from it...." It is not true that something in the patient has been divided into its components and is now quietly waiting for someone to "put it somehow together again."[191] The ego, in short, is an integrating function which will accomplish its task by the nature of its being unless some imbalance in the libidinal life prevents it from doing so. Again, the picture of the mental life in general and of the ego in particular is that of a dynamic set of functions rather than a more or less well-fitted group of parts.[192]

The task of integration is, however, one which the ego hardly accom-

---

[188] *Ego and Id*, 32-33; *cf.* "Lay Analysis," SE XX, 196-198.
[189] *Ibid.*, 34; *cf.* 29-30, 31.
[190] "Additional Notes: B.," SE XIX, 133-134.
[191] "Advance," SE XVII, 161-166.
[192] Freud's own term "apparatus" is suspect under these conditions, and indeed Freud does not use it as blithely after his revision of his ego psychology. For example, in *The Question of Lay Analysis* he attempts to show what he means when he talks about "mental apparatus" in such

plishes at times. Indeed, we can define all the neuroses and psychoses in terms of the state of the ego. For example, Freud makes this two-fold distinction in mental illness (later replaced by a three-fold distinction reflecting the role of narcissistic neuroses), that neurosis is the consequence of conflict between ego and id, while psychosis is the result of conflict between ego and world.[193] The ego serves three masters, the external world, the id, and the super-ego. Any of these relationships can become pathogenic. In "those neuroses capable of transference the ego forbids powerful instinctual impulses. It represses them and substitutes symptoms as a compromise. The symptom serves as the focus of the struggle for ascendancy between the ego and the id. It takes the side of external reality and does not yield to the demands of the id.[194] In psychosis the ego is guided not by memory traces of previous experience of the world nor by fresh knowledge of that world but by a model imposed by the id's wishes, a model bearing no apparent relationship to the external world, which the ego is originally bound to represent. This situation is the result of some overwhelming frustration of a wish by reality.[195] Thus the ego must respond to all of its masters; it cannot ignore any of them, for if it does, in the economic consideration of the psyche, illness is an inevitable consequence.

Even the mechanisms of defense established by the ego will in the end become liabilities in the economy of mental health. The employment of symptoms such as phobias and hysteria serves the purpose of maintaining some sort of balance in the course of critical periods, and may prove indispensable. Indeed, as Freud pointed out, the analyst will serve the patient better by helping the ego sustain neurotic behavior if reality threatens to be fatal. But the mechanisms of defense, which the ego constructs as it resists unpleasure arising from the external world, become dangers.[196] For they are maintained at heavy cost to the psychic economy.[197] The ego, moreover, never abandons these mechanisms of defense, in accordance with the conservative character of libidinal attachment. They become fixated in the ego as regular modes of behavior, repeated whenever a situation analogous to the original trauma occurs.

---

a way that his listener should not attribute too much to it, that is, take it too literally: "The value of a 'fiction' of this kind...depends on how much one can achieve with its help." "Lay Analysis," SE XX, 194; cf. Civilization, 18.

[193] "Neurosis and Psychosis," SE XIX, 149; cf. "Loss of Reality," SE XIX, 183.

[194] Ibid., 149-150.

[195] Ibid., 150-151.

[196] Civilization, 15.

[197] "Analysis," SE XXIII, 237f..

The adult's ego, with its increased strength, continues to defend itself against dangers which no longer exist in reality; indeed, it finds itself compelled to seek out those situations in reality which can serve as an approximate substitute for the original danger, so as to be able to justify...its maintaining its habitual modes of reaction.[198]

The mechanisms contribute to the breaking down of relations with reality by permitting and encouraging behavior alienated from the external world and thus lead to the outbreak of neuroses.[199]

The challenge to the ego is of course enormous; and it is hardly surprising that it fails from time to time. As Freud insists, it is not the fact that the ego yields to pressure from its masters but whether that pressure is too great for it to bear that counts; the pressure is constant. Freud thought he had identified one method adopted by the ego to maintain peace in this boisterous family, through the splitting of the ego, that is, an allowing of encroachments into the unity of the ego itself. In perversions such as fetishism, as well as in what Freud called the "eccentricities and follies of men," there is an indication that by compartmentalizing or splitting the ego can meet the demands of reality on the one hand and the demands of the id on the other, and spare itself at least some of the repressions.[200] Under extreme conditions the ego seems inevitably to tolerate symptom formation and even splitting. In the conflict between the instincts of the id and the world the ego, the child of the unhappy joining of world and self, is less able to control its own instincts than to alter the external conditions.[201]

In order to understand the life of the ego we must begin and conclude with its relationship to the id. Once Freud had shifted from the dualism of ego and unconscious to the dualism of attraction to the world and rejection of the world he saw that the role of the ego was that of organizing its own impulses in light of the world and the super-ego. I say "its own impulses," for the ego is in its primary form the id. The distinction between ego and id is not topographical but structural and economic. It is true that, unlike id, ego learns from the perceptual faculties of its "outmost" surface. But it is not merely its access to this information that distinguishes the ego. Rather, says Freud, "...what distinguishes the ego from the id especially is a tendency to synthesis in its contents, to a combination and identification in its mental processes which are totally lacking in the id."[202] In a popular mode of speaking, ego stands for

---

[198] *Ibid.*, 237-238.
[199] *Ibid.*.
[200] "Neurosis and Psychosis," SE XIX, 152-153.
[201] *Anxiety*, 99-101; *cf. Outline*, 111-112.
[202] NIL, SE XXII, 76.

reason and good sense, id for untamed passion.[203] But its position is precarious.

> From a dynamic point of view [the ego] is weak, it has borrowed its energies from the id....[204]

> The ego must on the whole carry out the id's intentions; it fulfills its task by finding out the circumstances in which those intentions can be best achieved. The ego's relation to the id might be compared with that of a rider to his horse. The horse supplies the locomotive energy, while the rider has the privilege of deciding on the goal and of guiding the powerful animal's movements. But only too often there arises between the ego and the id the not precisely ideal situation of the rider being obliged to guide the horse along the path by which it itself wants to go.[205]

"...[D]riven by the id, confined by the super-ego, repulsed by reality, [it] struggles to master its economic task of bringing about harmony among the forces and influences working in and upon it."[206] Psychoanalysis offers help to the ego and only to the ego. It seeks to make it independent of the super-ego, to "widen its field of perception and enlarge its organization. It is a work of culture—not unlike the draining of the Zuider Zee."[207]

Id

Without the experience of the world, according to Freud, the id is what the self would be. The ego evolves as the part of the id in direct contact with the external world; and it is charged with the task of representing that world to the id. The id is the essence of the self in that all elements of the psyche are modifications of it in light of experience. That the nature of the id is instinctive, that it is utterly mindless of the consequences of its desires, and that its sole intent and goal is satisfaction and gratification of its wishes are eloquent testimony to the truth that desire is the cause of suffering. It is also the cause of human life in that without it the conflict which defines that life simply would not exist. Again, it is misleading to think of the id as a thing, an entity. Freud elected the usage only after he had become convinced that the instinctual life and the life of the ego could not be distinguished solely on the grounds that one was unconscious and the other not. He drew his distinction henceforth on

---

[203] *Ibid.; cf. Ego and Id*, 29-30.
[204] *Ibid.*, 77.
[205] *Ibid.; cf. Ego and Id*, 29-30.
[206] *Ibid.*, 77.
[207] *Ibid.*, 79-80; *cf. Outline*, 62-63, and "Lay Analysis," SE XX, 200-201.

the grounds that some elements of the psyche sought reasonable balance between desire and limitation and others did not.[208]

In identifying psychoanalysis with the psychology of the id Freud was doing no more than restating his original conviction, that it was the unconscious life of man that made him what he was. The introduction of the term "id" to describe the unconscious thoughts, or desires, was required because of his revised understanding on the one hand of the relationship between consciousness and unconsciousness and the nature of the ego on the other. The concept of id allowed him to describe that part of the psyche which was alien to the ego, and therefore that part which cast the longest and darkest shadow upon the ego.

> We perceive that we have no right to name the mental region that is foreign to the ego "the system Ucs.," since the characteristic of being unconscious is not restricted to it. Very well; we will no longer use the term "unconscious" in the systematic sense and we will give what we have hitherto so described a better name and one no longer open to misunderstanding. Following a verbal usage of Neitzsche's and taking up a suggestion by George Groddeck, we will in future call it the "id" [es]. This impersonal pronoun seems particularly well suited for expressing the main characteristic of this province of the mind—the fact of its being alien to the ego.[209]

The alien relationship to the ego implied an even more alien relationship to the external world. As we have already seen the prognosis for mental illness depends upon the orientation of the self to the external world. While the ego's orientation may vary, the id is constantly and, by definition, utterly opposed to the demands of that world. The issue is always whether the ego has joined the id or the world, and also whether the alignment with the world in its struggle with the id is too punishing to bear.[210]

From the point of view of morality, then, says Freud, we may conclude that the id is totally non-moral, over against the ego, which strives to be moral, and the super-ego, which can become hypermorally ruthless. The id has no means of showing the ego either love or hate. It cannot say what it wants.[211] There is, moreover, no indication that the id is in any way affected by the passage of time. It has no recognition of the passage of time, and as a result there is no alleviation or alteration of its processes. It exercises no moral judgement, for it seeks satisfaction only,

---

[208] "Short Account," SE XIX, 209.
[209] NIL, SE XXII, 72; cf. Ego and Id, 27-28.
[210] Cf. "Loss of Reality," SE XIX, 184-185.
[211] Ego and Id, 87.

by whatever means are available.[212]

The id is the reservoir of the libido and the source of the instincts.[213] A cartoon presented in the *New Introductory Lectures*[214] is accompanied by these comments:

> As you see here, the super-ego merges into the id; indeed, as heir to the Oedipus Complex it has intimate relations with the id; it is more remote than the ego from the perceptual system. The id has intercourse with the external world only through the ego–at least according to this diagram. In one respect [the drawing] is undoubtedly not [correct]. The space occupied by the unconscious id ought to have been incomparably greater than that of the ego or the preconscious.[215]

In short, the dominance of the id in the structural representation of the psyche replicates the dominance of desire in human life.

Super-Ego

Like the ego, the super-ego is an extension of the id, emerging out of its struggle with the world; but its role is complex to a degree consistent with its late emergence in the growth of the self. For the super-ego represents both the external world and the id, and presents the ego with the most formidable challenge to its work of harmonization of the conflicting themes of the self. Its unique character arises from the fact that it is what Freud calls an introjection, that is, an incorporation of an external force into the economy of the psyche. A related process takes place in the ego's work of laying down memory traces and in its development of anxiety responses. But in the case of the super-ego what is incorporated is a model, indeed, a person. As we have already noted the super-ego is the heritage of the Oedipal period, and it incorporates the (narcissistic) notion of the ego-ideal. Thus a personality emerges within a personality. The super-ego possesses the qualities of the ego-ideal, in that it serves as a model to emulate for the sole purpose of satisfaction of narcissistic desires, and thus also as a virtually independent force which can bring judgement to bear upon the activities of the ego. In this it operates as a conscience.[216] These functions presume the faculty of self-observation in the structure of the psyche. This is the task of the super-ego.[217]

In describing the origin of the super-ego Freud notes that the ego often substitutes object cathexes for sexual desires. The influence of

---

212 NIL, SE XXII, 74.
213 *Cf.* "Lay Analysis," SE XX, 200f..
214 78-79.
215 *Ibid.*.
216 *Cf. ibid.*, 62-63, and *Outline*, 16.
217 *Ibid.*, 66; *cf.* "Narcissism," SE XIV, 95.

abandoned object cathexes is always significant, but the most influential are the object cathexes of childhood, *i.e.* the identification with the father, in the prehistory of every person.[218]

This object cathexis has two further significant characteristics, those of identification and sexuality. Identification is the process by which the child not only seeks to emulate the parent of the same sex but incorporates the essential sexual nature of that parent, as well as their "otherness," if one may put it so, into his psyche. The sexual aspect of this object cathexis coincides with the emergence of the genital phase. But, as we know, sexuality passes through stages and each stage retains some of the residues of former stages. In the Oedipal period the sexual character of the child is determined in such a way that even the second part of the diphasic onset of sexuality retains the character of this pre-pubescent experience.

The consequence of the Oedipal crisis is, then, the formation of a "precipitate" in the ego, the ego-ideal or super-ego.[219] This precipitate is not simply a residue of perception. Consistent with the ambivalent nature of the instincts and the emerging struggle between the libidinal desires and the limitations of reality, here represented by the parent of the opposite sex, the super-ego is a reaction formation as well as a precipitate.

> Its relation to the ego is not exhausted by the precept: "you *ought to be* such and such (like your father);" it also comprises the prohibition: "you *must not be* such and such (like your father); that is, you may not do all that he does; many things are his prerogative." This double aspect of the ego-ideal derives from the fact that the ego-ideal had the task of effecting the repression of the Oedipus complex, indeed, it is to that revolutionary event that it owes its existence.[220]

As we have already seen Freud's understanding of the "normal" state of development is one in which the Oedipus complex is dissolved, so that the super-ego actually replaces that complex through the sublimation of the sexual energy previously manifested in the complex.[221]

> The super-ego is in fact the heir to the Oedipus complex and only arises after that complex has been disposed of. For that reason its excessive severity does not follow a real prototype but corresponds to the strength which is used in fending off the

---

[218] *Ego and Id*, 39. In a note to this passage Freud suggests that it would be preferable to say "with the parents," since sex differentiation is not recognized by the child at this point. This identification with the father actually takes place before any other object cathexis. *Ibid..*

[219] *Ego and Id*, 44.

[220] *Ibid.*, 44-45.

[221] *Cf., e.g.*, NIL, SE XXII, 64.

temptation of the Oedipus complex. Some suspicion of this state of things lies, no doubt, at the bottom of the assertion made by philosophers and believers that the moral sense is not instilled into men by education or acquired by them in the course of social life, but is implanted in them from a higher source.[222]

As we have also seen the re-sexualization of the super-ego has mental illness, notably melancholia, as its inevitable consequence. But the strength to suppress the sexual desires associated with the Oedipus complex is nevertheless drawn from the ego-ideal. Thus

> the more intense the Oedipus complex was and the more rapidly
> it succumbed to repression...the more exacting later on is the
> domination of the super-ego over the ego—in the form of con-
> scious or perhaps of an unconscious sense of guilt.... [223]

The categorical imperative is thus evidence of the compulsive character of the super-ego.

The super-ego owes its existence to the lengthy period of helplessness in man's childhood and to the Oedipal relations with his parents. Thus one cannot attribute its appearance to chance but to the direct consequences of the most important events in the development both of the individual and of the race; indeed, by giving permanent expression to the influence of the parents it perpetuates the existence of the factors to which it owes its origin.[224] As with the other factors of libidinal development, the super-ego is a case in point of the ontogenetic recapitulation of phylogeny. It is "a reincarnation" of former ego-structures which have left their precipitates behind in the id.[225] There is as it were a guarantee of the continuation of identifiable humanity in the story of the super-ego's rise to power from the ill-defined longing of the child for attention to, for example, the law of Moses. It must not be forgotten either that the original Oedipal source for the super-ego is in Freud's view an historical one. There is a real father over against whom the struggle for liberation is waged, even, as in the case of Leonardo, if it is not the biological father.

The super-ego, like the ego, stands in a relationship of tension with the instincts, and therefore with the id. As noted Freud contrasts the id with the super-ego on the issue of restraint of the instincts in saying that the super-ego can be hypermoral and then becomes as ruthless as only the id can be.[226] The reference to the ruthlessness of the id here means that the super-ego never entirely loses its link to its origin in the

---

[222] *Outline*, 121-122.
[223] *Ego and Id*, 45; *cf.* "Narcissism," SE XIV, 93-94.
[224] *Ibid.*, 46; *cf.* NIL, SE XXII, 62.
[225] *Ego and Id*, 69-70.
[226] *Ibid.*, 79-80.

libidinal cathexes. Freud notes that it cannot be doubted that the super-ego, like the ego, is derived from auditory impressions, but "the cathectic energy" of the contents of the super-ego does not originate from the auditory perceptions, instruction, reading, *etc.*, but from sources in the id.[227] Thus in melancholia the super-ego's function of punishment has been extended and strengthened by the dominance of sadistic drives, and the ego is endangered. A pure culture of the death-instinct now rules in the super-ego, and may drive the ego into death, if the ego does not seek refuge in madness.[228] The super-ego has the task of representing the external world to the ego in a manner directly analogous to the parent's representation to the child of what is acceptable behavior (thus the super-ego's interests may oppose those of the conscious). Its task is not merely to represent but to judge.[229] However it can threaten the ego with great danger, without regard to the consequences of its judgement of the ego, in the manner of the id's disregard for the ego's task. The more a man limits his aggressive behavior toward others, says Freud, the more aggressive does his super-ego become toward the ego. This is the opposite view of things from that held by ordinary morality, that the standard set by the super-ego is the cause for the restraint of aggression. In fact all morality constitutes a harsh view of the activities of the id and ego, and threatens to restrict and press down upon the ego to a point beyond which it can adjust.[230]

In re-examining the phenomenon of masochism Freud realized that the super-ego played an ambivalent role in the psychic economy; for in its origin and nature it represented both sides of the opposition between the instinct and the world. It represented the world through the introjection into the ego of the first objects of the id's libidinal impulses, namely, the two parents.[231] The super-ego retained the characteristics of those parents, their strength, severity and inclination to oversee and judge. They are, in other terms, the most strongly felt representatives of reality. Certainly in this respect the super-ego is closer to the feelings of the person than the memory traces of the external world.[232] Yet precisely because it is invested with perhaps the highest level of libidinal cathexis it remains libidinal in its relationship to the ego. It also acts upon the ego as the id acts upon it, namely, as an alien force. As the maturation of the super-ego takes place, moreover, an investment of the exigencies of life with this libidinal quality is effected. External reality begins to act upon

---

227 *Ibid.*, 77.
228 *Ibid.*.
229 *Cf.* NIL, SE XXII, 68-69.
230 *Ibid.*; *cf.* "Masochism," SE XIX, 170.
231 "Masochism," SE XIX, 166f.; *cf. Civilization*, 70-71.
232 *Ibid.*, 167.

the ego in a manner highly reminiscent of the super-ego and its Oedipal predecessor, that is, as something alien to the ego. Thus last in the series of super-ego figures is Destiny. Most of us insist on personalizing what is an impersonal power in spite of the truth: the notion of a personal power in ultimate control of the universe is simply an expression of our childish desires for love.[233]

> ...[B]ut all who transfer the guidance of the world to Providence, to God, or to God and Nature, arouse a suspicion that they still look upon these ultimate and remotest powers as a parental couple, in the mythological sense, and believe themselves linked to them by libidinal ties.[234]

In arguing that there was no distinction between individual and group psychology Freud observed that what was characteristic of the operation of the super-ego in the individual was identically typical of the group. The issue was important; for the explanation of group behavior required some insight into the role of the element that determined membership and thus identified the members of the group with each other. There is indeed no other authoritative source in culture than the super-ego–that is to say, all authority figures are versions, so to speak, of the super-ego, and of course the super-ego is a version of the parent. Freud defined a group that has a leader but is not yet organized to the point that it acquires the characteristic of an individual as one in which the individuals' ego-ideal is the same.[235]

The group is a group if and only if it shares the same super-ego. This super-ego may be presented in many ways; in the form of primal horde chieftain, the king, the messiah, and so forth. But in no case is his point more obviously taken than in the instance of God the Father. The super-ego figure is not one of the group but the figure who protects and punishes. The leader/god/father is absolutely narcissistic, and utterly independent. He is omnipotent, or appears to be. In short, all the characteristics of the primal father, who persecutes all of his sons equally, and of the immediate father of one's own history, provide the content for the super-ego. What is true of individuals is true of groups; there is but one super-ego, just as there is only one father.[236]

This common identification provides not only identity, as the term rightly implies, but also brings about the transformation of egoism into altruism. This is achieved by the limitation of narcissism through a libidinal tie with other people, accomplished in the sharing of the same

---

[233] *Ibid.*, 166-168.
[234] *Ibid.*; cf. *Civilization*, 73.
[235] *Cf. Group Psychology*, 77ff..
[236] *Cf. Ibid.*, 94-95.

super-ego:[237] "If therefore in groups narcissistic self-love is subject to limitations which do not operate outside them [i.e. the groups], that is cogent evidence that the essence of a group formation consists in a new kind of libidinal tie among the members of the group."[238] Identification, then, is effected both between the individual and the super-ego figure–indeed the super-ego is a result of this identification–and between the individual and other individuals sharing the same figure, or more accurately, the same "local" representation of the original figure. In the individual identification is "the original form of emotional tie with an object." It provides a substitute for the original tie by introjecting the original object into the ego. Finally, it is strengthened "with every new perception of a common quality shared with some other person who is not an object of the sexual instinct."[239] This common quality perceived is the tie with the leader of the group.[240] Thus the super-ego provides the essential bond in all groups in a manner directly analogous to its role in economy of the psyche; and for that reason alone it is clear that there is no group psychology that is not also ego psychology.

In summary, the relationship of the super-ego to the ego is no less libidinal nor less fraught with danger than the relationship between any of the other elements of the psyche. It prevents me in a unique way, however, from doing that which my conscience tells me is wrong or punishes me with remorse and guilt after I have transgressed the boundaries set by my conscience.[241] This restraint and punishment can become so severe that neurosis develops.[242] However, one must beware, as in the case of id and ego, of reifying the super-ego. Freud insists that the notion "really describes a structural relation and is not merely a personification of some abstraction such as that of conscience."[243] In his sketch of the psychic structure Freud depicts the super-ego as merging with the id, to illustrate its libidinal qualities: "as heir to the Oedipus Complex it has intimate relations with the id; it is more remote than the ego from the perceptual system."[244] As in the entire representation of the psychic structure one must think of the whole and all of its parts, including the super-ego, as a series of dynamic relationships arising from and defining the conflict between self and world. It is represented in the form of a cartoon rather than a photograph.

---

[237] Ibid., 56, 57.
[238] Ibid., 58.
[239] Ibid., 65.
[240] Ibid., 66.
[241] NIL, SE XXII, 60.
[242] Ibid., 61, 64-65.
[243] Ibid., 64.
[244] Ibid., 79.

Eros and Thanatos

The conceptualization of the mental life in the structural terms of id, ego and super-ego appears in Freud's writings at a point that suggests that his revision of the theory of the instincts had everything to do with its presentation. The discovery that the ego was also a reservoir of libido led to the notion that the super-ego was a representative of the id as well as of external reality, and that one could no longer simply distinguish between ego or self-preservative instincts and sexual instincts. Ego psychology itself is now seen as libidinal. But Freud never rejected his general dualism; the life of the psyche was a life of conflict. It was not a conflict between ego and sexuality, but rather the tendency of the id toward attaining pleasure by either attaching libido to objects or preserving it entirely for itself and resisting external ties. The super-ego must be understood in the context of the instinctual theory of eros and thanatos.

It was the tendency of some of his patients to repeat unpleasurable experiences that suggested to Freud that a straight-forward (and superficial) distinction between the pleasure principle and the reality principle that assigned restraint to reality and gratification to pleasure was no longer adequate. There was in these patients a drive toward unpleasure which was itself, somehow, pleasurable. Further, it was clear that it was *instinctive.* This compulsion to repeat, Freud said, was an expression of the "unconscious repressed";[245] and thus the explanation for the behavior lay in the unconscious itself. Characteristically, these experiences—caused by the unconscious tendency to repeat—taught no new lessons, that is, no lesson was learned from the fact that these experiences had been unpleasurable in the past, and would continue to be so. The persistence of such evidence both in clinical and literary sources (Freud cites Tancred continually slaying his beloved Clorinda in Torquato Tasso's *Gerusalemma Liberata*) led Freud to conclude that the compulsion to repeat exists even at the expense of the pleasure principle.[246]

In turn, it seemed inescapable to Freud that this compulsion is a convincing indication of an instinctual drive to return to the original state of things. That is the logical implication of a compulsion to repeat, that it is a drive toward prior states; it can only cease, since it is instinctive, *i.e.* bidden to drive towards its end by its very nature, when the last (or first) state is reached, the state of ultimate priority, or non-existence.[247]

The urge inherent in organic life must have an organic base. Freud argues that the cortical layer of the organic structure was altered by the prolonged effect of the impingement of external stimuli upon it.[248]

---

[245] BPP, 41, 44 *et passim.*
[246] *Ibid.,* 46.
[247] *Ibid.,* 67-68; *cf.* IL, SE XV, 22, and *Civilization,* 65.
[248] *Cf.* BPP, 45ff..

The organism responded to this impingement by seeking refuge from it, and over the course of eons of evolution developed an increasingly sophisticated system for returning to its desired state of undisturbed rest. Its life was in fact the working out of an expanding series of detours around unwanted attachments to the world on the way back to a state of morbidity. Furthermore, we see how the germ of a living animal is obliged in the course of its development to recapitulate (even if only in a transient and abbreviated fashion) the structures of all the forms from which it is sprung, instead of proceeding quickly by the shortest path to its final shape. This behavior is only to a very slight degree attributable to mechanical causes, and the historical explanation cannot accordingly be neglected. So too the power of regenerating a lost organ by growing afresh a precisely similar one extends far up into the animal kingdom.[249]

How then shall we understand the basic nature and purpose of organic life? Why and how do organisms acquire their forms and histories? What is their *raison d'être*? Organic development is the consequence of the disturbance of the instinctive movement back to utter morbidity.[250] This is not consistent with the appearance of living things, however, and an explanation is called for. Granting that the instincts are conservative in the most fundamental sense possible, in that they both wish to return to the original state of things and, because of their experience of being disturbed, will trace the paths back to that original state, we now see that the activity, growth and development of organisms are devoted solely to repeating paths and characteristics acquired during their journey back to the undisturbed state.

Those instincts are therefore bound to give a deceptive appearance of being forces tending toward change and progress, whilst in fact they are merely seeking to reach an ancient goal by paths alike old and new.... It would be in contradiction to the conservative nature of the instincts if the goal of life were a state of things which had never yet been attained.[251]

The original instincts were preceded by a state of being which we will

---

[249] *Ibid.*, 68-69.

[250] *Ibid.*, 69-70.

[251] *Ibid.*, 70-71. Freud's felt conflict between his scientific orientation and his view of Jung's concept of instinct is evident in this passage: "...it is tempting to pursue to its logical conclusion the hypothesis that all instincts tend towards the restoration of an earlier state of things. The outcome may give an impression of mysticism or of sham profundity; but we can feel quite innocent of having had any such purpose in view." (BPP, 69; *Cf. Civilization*, 65.)

probably never understand; for the instinct as an attribute of life was provoked from this primordial state by the action of a force "of whose nature we can form no conception."[252] Once provoked, the instinct constituted a tension between the previous inanimate state and the response to the original stimulus. The organism sought to cancel this tension; and the first instinct came into being, "the instinct to return to the inanimate state." In the initial period this resistance to death, which is really now what is meant by life, lasted only a brief time. But the new element of resistance was added to the structure of the inanimate organism; and this resistance would never be abandoned. "Decisive external circumstances" altered so that the return to the inanimate stage became progressively more complex; and with each detour the character of the organism and of its relationship to external reality became more complex.[253]

What of the self-preservative instincts? What is their relationship to the general instinctual tendency to return to the primal inert state? Freud argues that their significance as an independent group of instincts is less than he first thought, for they are simply the guardians of the routes to death, which have already been established. Their function is "to assure that the organism shall follow its own path to death, and to ward off any possible ways of returning to inorganic existence other than those which are immanent in the organism itself."[254] The organism wishes to die, but in its own fashion. A paradox arises, then, in the fact that the self-preservative instincts are originally in the service of the instinct to return to the inert state, the "death" instinct; but in preserving the path already laid down—and they could not preserve any other—they prolong life. They resist any external threat to these circuits that would help the organism to attain its end too quickly, by leaving out any of the established stages.[255]

In one sense, which we might call genetic, the instincts are of but one sort, namely the drive toward the original inert state. But we must bear in mind that an instinct emerges in the first instance only because a situation, the impingement of external stimuli, has arisen which makes necessary a *return*, implying an unwanted departure. The instinct is the drive backwards, the desire to return. All instinctive behavior, Freud now says, is of this type. On the other hand, from what one may call a dynamic perspective, the operations of the instincts prolong life precisely because of their conservative nature. They return to the beginning, but only by routes laid down in their past experience. As external circumstances dictate increasingly complex patterns of avoidance, what we are

---

[252] BPP, 71.
[253] *Ibid.*, 71.
[254] *Ibid.*, 72.
[255] *Ibid.*.

234

accustomed to calling life, the maintenance of the organism's pattern of behavior which enables it to continue to live, comes into being. The self-preservative functions of the instinct, then, are not in opposition to the conservative nature of the instincts or the return to the beginning. On the contrary they are the most significant representatives of the commitment of that organism to return to its original state by its own path.

This particular dualism—which, I think one may say with some justice, is not a dualism in a superficial sense of two opposing forces, but rather one of opposing drives inherent in the nature of the same force—is evident in the critical area of reproduction. (Here of course I mean biological reproduction; but the point Freud wishes to make is a psychological one and therefore brings us to his new understanding of libido, as we shall see.) There are, he says, some organisms living today which recapitulate the whole path of development of the species. These are "elementary entities which compose the complicated body of one of the higher organisms."[256] The germ cells are undoubtedly the most significant of these sorts of organisms. Possessed of their complete inherited traits they make their most significant contribution to the life of the organism when they are separated from that organism. They contain all the inherited characteristics of their parent organism and fulfill their task outside that organism. Under the proper circumstances they repeat the entire series of developments of the characteristics they possess. In this they are simply acting in a manner utterly consistent with the nature of the instincts, but in such a way as to guarantee the repetition of the complex route to death—that is, they are following the instinctual path of life on their way to death. The mortality sought is a postponed mortality. Most significant is the fact that in order to achieve this end the germ cells must leave the organism and join with an external body which, by virtue of its otherness, its externality, is beyond the instinctual base of the organism but, by virtue of its own structure, is similar to that base. The libidinal attachment to the object is thus prefigured; and the importance of this attachment cannot be overstated. We must regard as "in the highest degree significant"

> the fact that this function of the germ-cell is reinforced, or only made possible, if it coalesces with another cell similar to itself and yet differing from it.[257]

The oversight of this function of attachment is the charge of the sexual instincts. We can now begin to understand why, in light of the conservative nature of the instincts, the sexual instincts appear to resist death. They too are conservative; "but they are conservative to a higher degree in that they are peculiarly resistant to external influences; and

---

[256] Ibid., 74.
[257] Ibid..

235

they are conservative too in another sense in that they preserve life itself for a comparatively long period."[258] Yet, says Freud, "it is to them alone that we can attribute an internal impulse towards progress and towards higher development!"[259] Here lies the distinction observed between the sexual instincts and the others, which we can call the death instincts. Both have the same end; but it is the sexual instincts, particularly in their protection of the function of reproduction, which resist the limitations of external reality. Eros, then, is the driving force for life; the sexual instincts disclose themselves in the "clamor for life." Their clamor is in sharp contrast to the mute death instinct. But that does not allow us to conclude that the latter does not exist. We know now that eros and thanatos seek the same conserving end.[260]

But how, in light of the conservative nature of the instincts, shall we explain the apparent drive toward advancement, progress and perfection which seems to characterize, generation after generation, the (by definition) finest efforts of the race? Freud sees no reason to admit such a drive on the same basis as the other instincts, since cultural behavior of whatever sort is based solely on repression. This repression is never wholly successful and it is the difference between the satisfaction demanded and that which is achieved that defines the driving factor of cultural activity. The path backwards to the original state of things is hindered by those resistances which maintain the repressions, that is, the behavior that culture permits. The instinct will nevertheless find some expression in areas in which growth is still free.[261] This flight from repression is of course synonymous with the formation of neurotic symptoms.[262]

We have therefore arrived at the conclusion that dualism is still a proper perspective on the self. It is the dualism of the life and death instincts, "one constructive or assimilatory and the other destructive or dissimilatory."[263] It is necessary now to return to the theory of the instincts, to the notion of libido, and to the nature of the ego. Prior to the revision of the theory of the instincts, Freud held that libido was limited to "the energy of the sexual instincts directed toward an object," and thus not present in the ego, or characteristic of the ego or the self-preservative instincts. This distinction between ego instincts and sexual instincts was challenged when it was discovered that the ego could be an object of the sexual instincts in the narcissistic neuroses. Thus libido could be found in the ego itself. The id was the reservoir of libido; but

---

[258] *Ibid.*, 74-75.
[259] *Ibid.*, 74, note.
[260] *Cf. Ego and Id*, 66.
[261] BPP, 76-77.
[262] *Ibid.*.
[263] *Ibid.*, 88; *cf. Outline*, 20.

this was in principle not different from the idea that the ego too was a reservoir of libido, in light of the nature of its origin.

The ego, therefore, could not be dissociated from libidinal interests, as the presence of narcissistic libido proved. This narcissistic libido was a manifestation of the work of the sexual instincts, and was therefore identified with the self-preservative instincts.[264]

Thus the original opposition between the ego instincts and the sexual instincts proved to be inadequate. A portion of the ego instincts was seen to be libidinal; sexual instincts—probably alongside others—operated in the ego. Nevertheless we are justified in saying that the old formula which lays it down that psychoneuroses are based on a conflict between ego instincts and sexual instincts contains nothing that we need reject today. It is merely that the distinction between the two kinds of instinct, which was originally regarded as in some way *qualitative*, must now be characterized differently—namely as being *topographical*. And in particular it is still true that the transference neuroses, the essential subject of psychoanalytic study, are the result of a conflict between the ego and the libidinal cathexis of objects.[265]

However, as we noted, transference neuroses were but one of three types of mental illness; and in the other two the distinction between ego instincts and sexual instincts also gives way to a distinction between life instincts and death instincts. The "topographical" relevance of the original instinct theory for transference neuroses continues to be admitted, for in those neuroses the struggle is indeed between what the ego will allow and what libido seeks; but what was originally thought to be the fundamental distinction, the essential dualism of mental health, now appears as one facet of the truly primary conflict, between life and death within the life of the organism. Freud rejects the notion that this alteration of the theory of instincts proves what his critics, such as Jung, had argued, namely that there is but one force operating in the self, not two, that is, libido, which is but another name for the instinctual life in general.

---

[264] BPP, 91-92.

[265] *Ibid.*. Freud reviewed much of this argument regarding the emergence of his conviction concerning eros and the death instincts in *Civilization and its Discontents*. (See 64ff..) But whereas there is a more tentative tone in his earlier writings, in the latter he states: "To begin with it was only tentatively that I put forward the views I have developed here, but in the course of time they have gained such a hold upon me that I can no longer think in any other way.... I remember my own defensive attitude when the idea of an instinct of destruction first emerged in psycho-analytic literature, and how long it took before I became receptive to it." (*Civilization*, 66-67.)

Freud insisted that his views had always been dualistic. Now, however, the opposition is seen to be between life and death instincts, rather than between ego and sexual instincts.[266]

Thanatos leads the living creature to death; it expresses its aim in destructive and aggressive impulses toward the external world. It seeks to dissolve the associations, which are multicellular in character, into their constitutional unicellular portions, creating a state of inorganic stability.[267] Eros, on the other hand, seeks the formation of ever greater unities in order to prolong life. These instincts are present in "regular mixtures or fusions." Thus life consists "in the manifestations of the conflict or interaction between the two classes of instincts; death would mean for the individual the victory of the destructive instincts, but reproduction would mean for him the victory of Eros."[268] Finally, the nature of the instincts is irrevocably conservative, the expression of an inertia or elasticity present in what is organic. Both classes of instincts would, on this view, have been in operation and working against each other from the first origin of life.[269]

Granting the dualistic nature of the life of the instincts, it is nevertheless the case that they share a common end; we may think of them in this respect as "fused," a phrase which Freud regularly employed to describe their nominal relationship. There are important implications for the ambivalent nature of the instincts, and particularly for the relationship between sadism and masochism. Freud's earlier view was that sadism was a primal instinct, made evident in the course of the development and transformation of libido, and that masochism was a secondary development, a vicissitude of sadism by inversion. In view of the revised theory of the instincts Freud now held that masochism was an expression in its own right of the death instinct.[270] The phenomenon of the fusion of instincts, however, had obscured the fact of the existence of the death instincts, and thus of masochism as a primal instinct. In psychoanalysis, says Freud, the fusion is extensive, so that the two kinds of instincts seldom appear in distinct forms, and perhaps never in isolation from each other.[271] However, illness is the result of a defusion of the instincts, as in the case of melancholia. Masochism represents the death instincts, and indeed is identical with them. In its primary expression the death instinct is of course sadistic. The issue is how the death instinct comes

---

[266] BPP, 93-94; cf. Ego and Id, 55ff., and "Articles: (B)," SE XVIII, 257-258.

[267] Cf. "Masochism," SE XIX, 163-164.

[268] "Articles: (B)," SE XVIII, 258-259.

[269] Ibid., 259.

[270] "Masochism," SE XIX, 163-164.

[271] Ibid., 164; Cf. Civilization, 66.

to be directed against the self, and thus acquires the masochistic tendencies with which we are already familiar. In the first instance the sadistic expression of the death instinct is directed outwards. Then, if circumstances are right, the sadistic tendency is re-directed toward the self–the ego, in fact–and a secondary masochism is produced as a regression.[272]

The history of the super-ego is, of course, a crucial example of this defusion, as the instances of obsessional neurotic desire for punishment and the melancholic threat to the ego illustrate.[273]

Is it not plausible [Freud wrote] to suppose that this sadism is in fact a death instinct which, under the influence of the narcissistic libido, has been forced away from the ego and has consequently only emerged in relation to the object? It now enters the service of the sexual function. During the oral stage of organization of the libido, the act of obtaining erotic mastery over an object coincides with that object's destruction; later, the sadistic instinct separates off, and finally, at the stage of genital primacy, it takes on, for purposes of reproduction, the function of overpowering the sexual object to the extent necessary for carrying out the sexual act.... Wherever the original sadism has undergone no mitigation or intermixture, we find the familiar ambivalence of love and hate in erotic life.[274]

The usual fate of the death instincts is that they are fused with the erotic components, and appear to be directed against the world in acts of aggression, while for the most part they undoubtedly continue their "inner work" unhindered.[275] Thus the operation of eros is not inconsistent with the sadism present in the ambivalent object-cathexes of libido; for it is not eros but thanatos which is operative. "We identify the characteristics of object love with eros not because they are the only ones but because they are the only ones readily ascertainable. The death instinct is, by definition, silent and buried."[276] It is the libidinal instincts, the life instincts, that break the peace, "constantly producing tensions whose release is felt as pleasure–while the death instincts seem to do their work unobtrusively."[277] The pleasure principle, then, must be in the service of the death instinct–if what we now mean by pleasure is the satisfaction of the conservative instincts in the attainment of their final goal.[278]

---

[272] "Masochism," SE XIX, 164.

[273] Ibid., 165-166; cf. Ego and Id, 55-56.

[274] BPP, 94-95.

[275] Ego and Id, 79.

[276] Cf. BPP, 93-95.

[277] Ibid., 109.

[278] Ibid..

The relationship between the ego, super-ego and id on the one hand and the instinctual forces of eros and thanatos on the other can now be briefly described. The id is the reservoir of all instinctual life; but, as we have seen, it is now understood to be a timeless struggle between eros and thanatos.[279] In striving to recapitulate and protect the path to death the erotic, libidinal components preserve life by attachment to the world in a manner consistent with the organism's past. The death instinct, in the form of aggression against the world and the ego, resists this attachment, but only in the sense that it too maintains the commitment to the original state of things but in a less conservative manner, that is to say, without repeating all the previous steps. The super-ego represents to the ego both the world and the libidinal history of the id. It is nominally the successor to the Oedipus complex, and establishes the "harsh morality" which is characteristic of even the normal conscience. This sublimation of the Oedipal attachments has been accomplished, Freud argues, by the defusion of the erotic from the death instincts. It is this separation that frees thanatos from the limitations imposed by its relationship with eros; therefore "this defusion would be the source of the general character of harshness and cruelty exhibited by the ideal–the dictatorial 'Thou shalt.'"[280]

As for the ego, we know that it is enriched by all contacts with the external world; for it is the function of the ego to arrange the processes of the mind in a "temporal order" and test their "correspondence with reality."[281] On the other hand the ego is committed to the limitation of the effects of libido through its work of identification and sublimation, that is, through repression. It risks some danger here; for through repression it assists the death instinct, but risks becoming an object of that instinct. Its defense lies in loving and being loved, becoming the representative of eros.[282] The ego is truly the abode of anxiety.[283] But it seeks above all the love of others–although as we have seen the ego-libido plays a crucial part in the economy of love.[284] The ego can in fact be a reservoir of libido "from which libido is sent out *to* objects and which is always ready to absorb libido flowing back *from* objects. Thus the instincts of self-preservation were also of a libidinal nature; they were sexual instincts which, instead of external objects, had taken the subject's own ego as an

---

[279] *Ego and Id*, 87.
[280] *Ibid.*, 80.
[281] *Ibid.*, 81.
[282] *Ibid.* 84; *cf. Group Psychology*, 37-39, on the legitimacy of "love" for this trend.
[283] *Ego and Id*, 85ff..
[284] *Group Psychology*, 40.

object."[285]

The ego can survive, then, only when it can serve as the object of libido. The significance of this point must be understood in the context of Freud's notion of the death instinct. The life of the libido is a struggle against the instincts of death, of destruction and inertia. Those instincts of death are—and this is the core of Freud's view on the matter—innate for the individual and the race. Their existence is not evident because they are ordinarily fused to the erotic instincts with which they share a conservative nature. But when they do emerge, notably in the case of neurosis, they are seen immediately to have but one end in view, the circumvention of life. Freud noted that if we take the clinical facts of masochism, the neurotic sense of guilt, and the "negative therapeutic reaction," that is, the resistance to treatment[286] into account, we "shall no longer be able to adhere to the belief that mental events are exclusively governed by the desire for pleasure. These phenomena are unmistakable indications of the presence of a power in mental life which we call the instinct of aggression or of destruction according to its aims, and which we trace back to the original death instinct of living matter."[287]

Highly significant for Freud's view of the cause of suffering are his conclusions concerning the relevance of his new theory of the instincts to what one might call cosmology.[288] He does not espouse either pessimism or optimism. Neither alone explains life: "Only by the concurrent or mutually opposing action of the two primal instincts—Eros and the death-instinct—, never by one or the other alone, can we explain the rich multiplicity of the phenomena of life."[289] Freud turns to the Greek philosopher Empedocles for an illustration of the view he accepts. Freud is, of course (he states), a scientist, a believer in the empirical method, and will not be charged with the crime of cosmic fantasizing; but Empedocles did note the nature of things in terms rather like those of the psychoanalytic theory of the instincts. Empedocles held that the life of the universe and, at the same time and in the same way, the life of the mind were governed by two opposing principles. They were *philia*, love, and *neikos*, strife. They war everlastingly. They were not intelligences, moreover, but behaved in the mindless and irresistible fashion of instincts. One, *philia*, seeks to condense the primal particles of the four elements into a single unity, while *neikos* seeks to separate them from one another. Empedocles's universe was a continuous, unending alternation of periods,

---

[285] "Articles: (B)," SE XVIII, 257-258.
[286] Cf. BPP, 40.
[287] "Analysis," SE XXIII, 243; cf. Outline, 20ff..
[288] Cf., e.g., Ego and Id, 55-56.
[289] "Analysis," SE XXIII, 243.

in which *philia* or *neikos* gains the advantage.[290]

Freud's next comments are very significant with respect to the instinct theory itself but also with respect to the necessary sensitivity to the "guises" in which the truth Freud discovered appears. For it indicates that while Freud believes firmly in the biological and empirical explanation of human behavior he also knows that Empedocles was right, though unscientific; and he knows that he too is right, and perhaps also partial in his knowledge in the eyes of the future.

> We shall not be surprised...to find that, on its re-emergence after two and a half millennia, this theory has been altered in some of its features.... Moreover, we have provided some sort of biological basis for the principle of "strife" by tracing back our instinct of destruction to the death instinct, to the urge of what is living to return to an inanimate state. This is not to deny that an analogous instinct already existed earlier, nor, of course, to assert that an instinct of this sort only came into existence with the emergence of life. And no one can foresee in what guise the nucleus of truth contained in the theory of Empedocles will present itself to later understanding.[291]

Freud's theory of the instincts is both psychological and cosmological. He presents an account of the life of the instincts that describes at once the life of the mind and the innate conflict of existence; they are one and the same thing. The issue of the ontogenetic recapitulation of phylogeny rightly concerns us a good deal; but the cosmological recapitulation of psychology is a still more grand and profound vision of truth.

Perception

Freud's understanding of the mental life could be said, rather simplistically, to rest upon the relation between the self and the world. It was the stimulus of external reality that prompted the inert organism to develop instincts; it is the external reality of *Ananke* against which the desires constituting the id rebel; it is the greatness and tragedy of the ego to be charged with the task of mediating between external reality and the desires of its parent instincts; it is the external world in the form of libidinal objects that makes the evolution of the super-ego necessary and possible; it is the rejection of the external world that constitutes the least remediable form of mental illness, psychosis; and it is the weakness of the ego in coping with the demands of the id to reject the external world's limitations that makes symptoms, repression and fixation necessary. Finally, it is the failure, for obviously selfish, libidinal reasons to understand that the external world is not under the guidance of a projected libidinal figure who is like the father, and who in the psychological

---

[290] *Ibid.*, 245-246.
[291] *Ibid.*, 246-247.

sense is the father, that characterizes religion and the traditional moral demands of civilization. Freud does not believe that anyone can finally live wholly in accordance with the dictates of *Ananke*; indeed the notion of reality as harsh necessity already implies that human life will always be in conflict with reality. The most he hopes for is the replacement of hysterical misery with ordinary unhappiness, that is to say the replacement of the ignorant and self-deceptive substitution of feelings for reality with the comprehension that the self will always be unhappy because in its desiring nature it stands forever against reality.[292] Freud's attitude toward external reality raises the question of how the desiring self comes into touch with this reality, and what mechanisms enable the mental apparatus to know what is real, as opposed to what is felt.

We already know that it is the task of the ego to lay down memory traces which are images, or reports, of the external world. These are essential if the organism is to avoid actions which would be destructive to it. In connection with this work the ego governs the activity of thinking, which is a compromise between full commitment to action in the external world, with all the risks that action entails, and the discharge of the energy dammed up by libidinal impulses which, if not released, can lead to illness. Thinking enables the ego both to postpone the action and to test it to determine whether it is dangerous.[293] We also know that in his depiction of the mental system Freud conceives of the system of perception, or the perceptual consciousness, as the outermost surface of the ego, which is itself the part of the id in direct contact with the external world. Further, when referring to the origins of the super-ego he stated that it arose from auditory impressions; and the ego too arose from auditory impressions—although he goes on to say, significantly, that the operations of the instincts were more consequential for the destiny of both functions. Again, Freud notes that the super-ego and the ego are bodily functions, that is to say, they should be understood as functions of the biological organism, despite their psychological significance.[294]

He does not believe only this of the nature of the psychic structure; but such a conclusion was consistent with his earliest notions of the mental structure, as seen in the unpublished "Project for a Scientific Psychology." At that early point Freud set out to show the biological functions of mental life, and "to discover what form the theory of psychical functioning will take if a quantitative line of approach, a kind of economics of nervous force, is introduced into it...."[295] Psychology could be a natural science, he thought, representing "psychical processes as quantitatively

---

[292] *Cf. Civilization*, 24, 33.
[293] *Cf.* "Project for a Scientific Psychology," SE I, 361.
[294] *Cf. Ego and Id*, 31.
[295] "Project," SE I, 283-284.

determinate states of specifiable material particles, thus making those processes perspicuous and free from contradiction."[296] Two processes were to be demonstrated: the first was inertia, or the primary process of the life of the mind free from external stimulus; the second was the secondary process, or the life of the mind now affected by external stimuli. The difference between the processes was defined in terms of the activity of neurones, as Freud called the ultimate unit of the nervous system. The activity of the mind in these conditions was to be known as Q, which designated the activity of the material particles, the neurones, of which the psychical process was thought to be composed. Q was operative in the activity demanded of the organism in response to external stimulus. However, when the essential inertia of the organism is disturbed from within rather than from without the Q is not available for employment in the usual way, and is then employed, as energy, in another fashion which came to be called repression.

That is to say, Freud set out to develop a homogeneously quantitative expression of mental life–a goal he did not reach, although his quantitative analysis of libido enhanced his earlier program.[297]

But it is Freud the interpreter of dreams, the hermeneut of what was unconscious and emotional in life, with whom we are, rightly, more familiar. In light of the psychoanalytic approach Freud espoused and never departed from what may, then, be said of our perception of and interaction with the external world?

We may begin by pursuing the issue of what it is that becomes conscious. This starting point is implied by all that has gone before; for the perceptual conscious system as Freud denoted it is a function of consciousness over against the rest of the mental apparatus, which is a function of id and the instincts. Our question then really is this: How do the data of the external world become part of our consciousness? The act of perception is tied to consciousness, not unconsciousness. Only that which can be perceived can be rendered conscious; and by implication what is perceived is some element of experience–but we should not, I think, go so far as to say that what is perceived exists in the external world. It is worth bearing in mind that if what we are doing now is epistemology it is also and always psychological epistemology. Thus I prefer to use of the word "experience" with special emphasis upon perception (rather than knowledge of the world *per se*) to distinguish it for the moment from the experience of instinctual drive. Thus what the conscious contains as perception is the result of experienced stimulus from without. In turn, says Freud, all that is conscious must transform itself into external perceptions. That is, what is con-

---

[296] *Ibid.*, 295.
[297] *Ibid.*, 296-297.

scious is perceived as an external entity; this as we shall see does not rule out the possibility that what is conscious may be the result of some internal experience, as in the case of a repression and symptom formation. But it does mean that perceptions must include experience which is not only internal; indeed, as we have learned from the study of the neuroses the pressure imposed by the libido upon the ego is there precisely because of the experienced conflict between the external world and the demands of the instincts. The conscious, then, transforms its contents into external perceptions by building up memory traces in the conscious of something once perceived. These traces may be laid down on the basis of both optical and verbal reception, and auditory impressions.[298]

This function of perception and the establishing of memory traces is the primary function of the ego—despite its own libidinal interests. Perception is the major tool of the ego, or, better, that element which we might call the *sine qua non* of the ego. Perception is to the ego what the instincts are to id.

....[T]he ego has the task of bringing the influence of the external world to bear upon the id and its tendencies, and endeavors to substitute the reality-principle for the pleasure-principle which reigns supreme in the id. In the ego perception plays the part which in the id devolves upon instinct.

The ego represents what we call reason and sanity, in contrast to the id which contains the passion.[299]

The ego is, then, ultimately derived from bodily sensations, a "mental projection" representing the outermost "surface" of the mental apparatus.[300] It is that part of the id which was modified by and adapted for the reception of external stimuli and of which the perceptual system is the chief component with respect to the external world. Yet Freud thinks of it also as a "protective shield" against stimuli, "comparable to the cortical layer by which a small piece of living substance is surrounded."[301]

What do we know of perception? It seems we know what one might call a little about a lot. The most important thing known is that the experience of stimuli transformed into perception constitutes the point at which the ego is born and the conflict of the self begins. What we do not know is whether the experience, the perception and the conscious can tell us what the world really is, *per se*. There is no ontology here, that is, no description of the world as it is. We know nothing of the world save that it is probably the source of those limiting and resisting

---

[298] *Ego and Id*, 21-26; *cf.* above.
[299] *Ibid.*, 29-30.
[300] *Ibid.*, 31.
[301] NIL, SE XXII, 75-76; *cf. Ego and Id*, 29.

ith which the libido collides. We do not even know that it is in a "psychological" sense; that is, it is real only insofar as it (admittedly) crucial part in the dynamic of the self. Perception, not be said to tell us about the world; it tells us some things ι laying down memory traces and performing the subterfuge of thinking, the ego must pay attention to if the mental life is not to lose its balance. Further, by comparison our relationship with those whom we love (and hate) looms with far greater urgency and clarity over our emotional lives than this mere perception. The perception that really makes the difference to our psychical balance is the perception linked to the attachments to those whom we love, that is, our libidinal experience. This is of course perception, and response to stimulus; but it is hardly a subject of epistemology. It tells us not about the world *per se* but about the world as we feel about it, and specifically the world as the persons about whom we feel so strongly. In fact, Freud was not particularly interested in academic psychological questions about how one responds to stimuli, except to say that one does. The emotional effect of that response was much more significant. It is true that in speaking of external reality as *Ananke*, Necessity, he was making a judgement about the world; but it is a purely psychoanalytic one, that is to say, it is the world it is because of its peculiar relationship with our desires, and not for any other reason. Indeed, one probably ought to conclude that for Freud the world does not exist any more than God does, except as an extension of our emotional biography. He is neither an idealist nor a realist; for him perception was significant only insofar as it was a critical element in the cause of suffering, as an experienced foil to our feelings.

Freud himself was not satisfied with his final views of the mental life. I suspect this was true because he never quite gave up the search for the natural science of psychology. This was particularly evident in the stages of his topographical theory. On the one hand he abandoned it when he discovered that the mental life was not simply a conflict between the ego and the sexual instincts. Yet he continued to look for what one might call a material description of empirically verifiable integrity which would meet his natural science requirements. He observed frequently that the knowledge we have of the world cannot have been gained solely by the individual's living experience, or his reception of and reaction to stimuli. Perception is, of course, significant; but it simply does not explain entirely the cause for repression. The issue has nothing to do with the brain's anatomy. It is true that sensations arising from perceptions are conscious entities, *vis-à-vis* the id's thought processes. But we have not accounted for all the individual's perceptions; to do this we must include the archaic heritage he receives at birth, his phylogenetic burden.[302]

---

[302] *Moses*, SE XXIII, 97-98.

This inheritance is not simply biological, although it clearly includes biological dispositions to excitations, impressions, stimuli, *inter alia*. Exactly what constitutes this heritage will concern us in more detail in the discussion of phylogenetic sources for the self, notably the Oedipal issues of libidinal cathexes of the parents. The fact that there is more to our world of external perceptions and to the mental structure in general than what our senses grasp and report to the ego is the significant one here. The point is that, important as the external world as perceived by the self is in its function of limiting libidinal desires, by itself, as an object of the individual's experience, it cannot account for the nature of the conflict within the self.[303]

We may draw some conclusions here. First, Freud does not offer a theory of perception in any complete sense; that is, while he is fully aware of the signal importance of sensation and stimuli in the life of the self, he does not really even raise the question of whether what we experience as external perception corresponds to the external world *per se*. This is not to say that he does not believe in a correspondence theory of truth;[304] but he does not explain how it works. He is only sure that it does; and that one must be committed to the truth of reality rather than fantasy. (I suggest, by the way, that he holds this correspondence view over against religious views, and does so in a notably polemic fashion.) Second, despite the importance of perception it is the internal, instinctual experience that really determines the history of the self, and notably of the ego. Freud includes in this experience inherited libidinal experience of past history; and one is tempted to say that this is the major element in Freud's notion of both external reality and the role of perception. But this sort of perception is not at all what is generally meant when a theory of perception is pursued. Rather, the stimulus-response relationship Freud describes is that of the Oedipus complex; and that is not just any stimulus-response relationship but the most powerful libidinal experience. The mere fact of perception is virtually hidden by the emotional tone of the experience. In short, Freud is not interested in perception except insofar as it is a factor in life and its discontent. In and of itself perception, like the senses and the world, has no significance. It is only in the conflict of the suffering mind that it takes on meaning. In the end Freud is a physician, not a philosopher.

Ananke/Reality

If Freud's theory of perception is peripheral, the question of reality, of what was real, is absolutely central to his entire enterprise. It is not too much of an exaggeration to say that what truly interested Freud was the relationship between what is real and what is imagined. At times they

---

[303] *Ibid.*, 99.
[304] *Cf.*, *e.g.* NIL, SE XXII, 170-171.

seem to him to be mutually exclusive; yet he frequently depicts reality and imagination as living in a sophisticated, complex and interdependent relationship. This double view appears in his treatment of anxiety. The ego is anxious, he says, even when danger and the need for flight are not the results of external circumstances, as in the formation of neurotic phobias. People who have phobias are afraid of something "inside" them, not something in the external world; they are therefore under the rule of their emotions and imagination, and to that extent out of touch with reality. But Freud's conclusion about anxieties is that they indeed have their origin in the external world, for ultimately they are a flight from the threat of castration–and this threat he believes actually was carried out by the enraged father on the son in primaeval times. Moreover, the male child has the evidence of his own eyes to justify his fear of being castrated; for he has only to view the female anatomy to be convinced that it has happened before and can happen again. This view of anxiety as a response to reality is not only not necessarily wrong but is based on Freud's own extension of his conclusions to what in part he guesses to have been actual experience and in part knows to have been actual experience, that is, the primaeval situation and the discovery of the anatomical difference between boys and girls respectively. This is not imagination; and indeed when one says that this account of anxiety is not necessarily wrong, one means that it cannot be disproved, and that opposition to it falls under the rubric of resistance to analysis in general and to the idea of infantile sexuality in particular. Thus a reasonable person might agree with Freud that anxiety is a legitimate response to a real danger. What is strange about it of course is its persistence in the adult; but that problem does not undermine the account of its origin in the child.

Freud strove, overall, to show up illusions and self-deceptions for what they were, that is, to reveal the fundamental nature and cause of the ignorance of real motives which was the cause of all suffering. One had to recognize, first and foremost, that the world itself was neither rational nor sympathetic; attempts to render it so were simply projections of childish wishes. One's fate, he says, may rest upon endowment (he calls it *daimon*); but it rests upon chance (*tuche*) as well.[305] The omnipotence of libidinal desire is an illusion; and it has been the contribution of science to point out man's real situation, of weakness, smallness and mortality.[306] In Leonardo da Vinci Freud espies a hero of science, one who finally recognizes the true meaning of the world of reality as the absence of the father–that is, the absence of supernatural moral order. As we have already seen, Leonardo's childhood enabled him to view the world of nature as something other than the manifestation of the Father's will

---

[305] "Transference," SE XII, 99.
[306] *Totem*, 147.

and power. There was no God to protect or judge, only the workings of nature, which may or may not yield to our probings and testings. What happens to us, what our fate is, lies not in the hands of God but in the hands of Necessity and chance.

If one considers chance to be unworthy of determining our fate, it is simply a relapse into the pious view of the Universe which Leonardo himself was on the way to overcoming when he wrote that the sun does not move. We naturally feel hurt that a just God and kindly providence do not protect us better from such influences during the most defenceless period of our lives. At the same time we are all too ready to forget that in fact everything to do with life is chance, from our origin out of the meeting of spermatazoon and ovum onwards—chance which nevertheless has a share in the law and necessity of nature, and which merely lacks any connection with wishes and illusions.

The world says Freud, is no nursery.[307]

This is the state of things as they really are; and perhaps it is because everyone knows this from the beginning of their existence that they set out to construct a reality that is more conducive to the satisfaction of their wishes. But it is nearer the truth to say that our experience is so overwhelmed by and saturated with libidinal desires and attachments, whether anaclitic or narcissistic, that knowledge of that harsh world is almost entirely prevented. After all, the stages of human growth are emotional, not perceptual, stages. Perception is made to serve libidinal interests. In the clearest Freudian examples of this view of the world, namely the infant, the neurotic, the primitive and the religious person, what one wishes is what exists so far as any action is concerned. This is the notion of the omnipotence of thought, *Die Allmacht der Gedanken.* The wish and the world are one; no distinction exists between psychic and material reality. For normal, ordinary non-neurotic people this collapsed distinction is a regular experience of dreaming—and it is because they must be asleep in order to experience the collapse of the distinction that one may say they are normal. For the neurotic and psychotic, they may be awake and have the same experience. The formation of symptoms constitutes the active step taken by the ego to collapse the distinction between psychic and material reality in such a way as to preserve by substitution the psychic balance. The paraphernalia of religion are created in the same way and for the same reason. Symptom formation becomes necessary when frustration in the real world reaches an unacceptable level.[308]

---

[307] *Leonardo*, 87; NIL, SE XXII, 168-169.

[308] *Cf.* "Onset," SE XII, 231-233, 237-238, "Transference," SE XII, 99-100, and IL, SE XVI, 432.

One may, then, withdraw from the world in two senses: first, one withdraws from the world by substituting one's wishes for the external perceptions and the memory traces of the ego, a condition conducive to psychosis; and second, one withdraws from social intercourse. As to the second withdrawal, Freud notes that the neuroses are asocial in nature. For they arise from a flight away from limiting external reality to the more satisfying world of fantasy, where there is no need for companionship.[309] As for the first withdrawal, the formation of symptoms is related to the abandoning of objects, or the turning of an internal act into an adaptation in place of an action.[310] The external world is a hindrance to the omnipotence of thought; and Freud insists that mental health is the ability to draw the distinction between what is wished and what is real. In the neurotic world, only the neurotic currency of thought counts.[311] The uncanny effect, which Freud finds in several contexts, notably the magical and religious, is a product of the effacement of the distinction between imagination and reality. Like the infantile imagination it over-accentuates the psychical at the expense of the material reality, and is thus an extension of the principle of the omnipotence of thought.[312]

Replacement of attention to the world with attention to the wish is the response of the ego in the work of the formation of symptoms. It is possible that this replacement may become virtually complete, as in psychosis. In psychosis stimuli and memory traces are derived from the id in the form of delusions and hallucinations. What prevents the resolution of psychosis is that the rejected piece of reality is never separated from the psyche. That piece of reality has the same relationship to the mind as the repressed instinct in a neurosis.[313] That is, reality is not lost but transformed; and this suggests that reality in the economy of the mind is whatever contributes memory traces and instincts to the id. Whatever impinges upon the id functions as the "external world" even if it is derived from the id itself. Thus Freud's notion of mental health depends substantially upon the mind's grasp on the external world. The economy of the psyche always has an "external world;" but for health it must be the right external world, the one that has not been transformed into our desires. Eros must be reconciled to Ananke.[314]

In short, the reality Freud intends is opposed to our wishes; and truth is what corresponds to that reality: "This correspondence with the real external world we call 'truth.' " It is the task of science to "arrive

---

309 Totem, 123-124; cf. IL, SE XVI, 359.
310 IL, SE XVI, 366.
311 Totem, 144.
312 "The Uncanny," SE XVII, 244 ff..
313 "Loss of Reality," SE XIX, 185-186.
314 Civilization, 48, 86.

at correspondence with reality–that is to say, with what exists outside us and independently of us and, as experience has taught us, is decisive for the fulfilment or disappointment of our wishes."[315]

When Freud says that the external world is real he means simply that it is beyond our wishes, and that it need not cooperate with those wishes. Further, at some time in each of our lives we must have come to know this truth. That discovery must have been remarkable, even devastating. In fact, it was so devastating that we hid it from ourselves. But we did not forget it; on the contrary, it became the signal event in our development as human beings. It was not henceforth part of our conscious lives but of our unconscious heritage. But that did not mean that it was not a real event. It was real because it did happen, and on the basis of its happening the psychic economy unique to each of us and general to the race took on its shape. The event was not imagined. It happened in time and history. To restate this conclusion as strongly as possible, in saying that it is the conflict between external reality and the libidinal desire that is responsible for the shape of the psychic economy Freud means that a study of the psyche will lead to knowledge of that original event; and that event is as historically and objectively describable as the signing of the *Magna Carta* or the invasion on D-Day: indeed, it may be more so because its traces are *necessarily* present in the analyzed emotional life.

We have already seen one example of this mode of thinking; Freud set out to write the history of Moses and monotheism on the basis of the psychoanalytically revealing data of Judaeo-Christian tradition. One should not underestimate what was being attempted; Freud's reconstruction was for him true in the most empirical sense. Again, Freud attempted to render an account of Leonardo's life and greatness on the basis of a fragment of a childhood fantasy.[316]

What Freud is claiming is that the psychoanalytic truths evident to the analyst lead in the end to the original motive forces and to knowledge of significant emotional events. We have already seen that Freud could tell us with confidence a great deal about Leonardo's relationship with his parents, especially his absent father, and could join that inference of history easily to his assessment of Leonardo's psychic abilities, namely, his extraordinary capacity for sublimating instinctive demands.[317]

It is, then, ever the task of psychoanalysis to demonstrate "the connection along a path of instinctual activity between a person's external experiences and his reactions."[318] Certainly we may see the fulfillment of

---

[315] NIL, SE XXII, 170-171, 171-172; *cf. Moses*, SE XXIII, 76.
[316] *Leonardo*, 84-85.
[317] *Ibid.*, 85-86; *cf.* 33-34.
[318] *Ibid.*, 86.

this promise in the central position assigned to infantile sexual experience, and thus to the significance of infantile experience with the real world in general for the subsequent history of the psyche. The reconstruction of these real events in the life of the individual is of great importance to therapy; and the uncovering of them is one of the most important tasks of analysis.[319] Freud's belief—the word is apt in every respect—in the experience of the external world, a sensuous or sexual experience, as the pivotal factor is patent. While his position is not that of a realist it is certainly not that of an idealist; for the world as experienced is that reality without which the essential conflict between the instinctual desires and their limitations would not have arisen, and there would be no human life.

Ontogeny and Phylogeny

The notion of the historical experience, visible to the archeologist of the mind, is crucial to understanding the individual, but not only the individual. Here we turn to one of the most remarkable aspects of Freud's analysis of suffering: his firm belief in the causal relationship between phylogeny and ontogeny. The events that play a causal role in psychical development (and therefore in the neuroses) happened not only in the life of the patient but in the life of the race. Therefore the suffering of the individual must be said to be a result of his experience not only in his present historical setting but also of his experience as a member of the race; and the latter experience produces racially acquired characteristics. The experience of the race in the past, in other words, added characteristics to the mental structure that were passed on through generations. The question of whether neuroses are caused by disposition or events, and in what degree, is answered in part in Freud's discussion of phylogeny and ontogeny. For the disposition of the individual is caused in large part by the experience of the people who lived long before him, the residues of whose traumas he has inherited.

This conclusion concerning the effect of past generations' actions was meant quite literally by Freud; and it is necessary to understand his attitude in the context of the analysis of suffering. It was as though he had been convinced that human suffering could not be fully explained in terms of either the disposition or the experience of the individual, nor in terms of purely imagined causes of illness, but only in a context of universal psychic conflict in which each individual eventually participates by virtue of being human. Time and history are utterly crucial; but the scope is really that of the history of life, of existence itself, rather than simply, or only, that of the individual.

Freud frequently compared the mental states of the neurotics whom he treated with those whom he called primitive peoples, that is, peoples

---

[319] *Cf.* "Lay Analysis," SE XX, 216.

chronologically at the inception of human social structures. For example, on the question of guilt, we are familiar with Freud's reconstruction of the primitive Oedipal conflict and tragedy. As for the neurotic,

> A compulsive neurotic may be oppressed by a sense of guilt which is appropriate to a wholesale murderer, while at the same time he acts toward his fellow beings in a most considerate and scrupulous manner, a behaviour which he evinced since his childhood. And yet his sense of guilt is justified; it is based upon intensive and frequent death wishes which unconsciously manifest themselves toward his fellow human beings.[320]

The sense of guilt of the neurotic arises not from an act but from a wish—and in the world of neurotics the omnipotence of thought obtains. However, although the guilt of the neurotic may be the result of the omnipotence of thought, the omnipotence of that thought is firmly grounded in a real trauma, in actual events, which were, above all, regretted.[321]

To this understanding of the root of guilt we must add the fact that these neurotics are repressing wishes which they entertained consciously as children, that is, they wished for the same deaths and loves in the course of their own childhood as primitives did in the childhood of man. The latter group actually carried out its wishes; the former repress the thoughts, and feel guilty and thus recapitulate in their minds the historical events of their primitive forebearers.

> A piece of historical reality is also involved; in their childhood these persons had nothing but evil impulses and as far as their childish impotence permitted they put them into action. Each of these over-good persons had a period of badness in his childhood, and a perverse phase as a fore-runner and premise of the latter overt morality. The analogy between primitive men and neurotics is therefore much more fundamentally established if we assume that with the former, too, the psychic reality, concerning whose structure there is no doubt, originally coincided with the actual reality, and that primitive men really did what according to all testimony they intended to do.... "In the beginning was the deed."[322]

Freud noted that the sense of guilt in the child, and the consequent emergence of a conscience, is seemingly out of proportion to the child's actions or even apparent wishes. However, in this the child is responding to an excessively strong aggressiveness in himself; the consequence of this is a correspondingly severe super-ego. The causes of this situation lie

---

[320] *Totem*, 145.
[321] *Ibid.*, 264; *cf. Illusion*, 68ff..
[322] *Totem*, 267-268.

in human phylogeny; "he is following a phylogenetic model and is going beyond the response that would be currently justified; for the father of prehistoric times was undoubtedly terrible, and an extreme amount of aggressiveness may be attributed to him." We cannot escape the fact, Freud argues, that guilt arises not only from wishes but from the primordial deed, the slaying of the father by his sons.[323]

Not only is the act for which the guilt is felt rooted in the real past, but the consequence of that act must be seen, argues Freud, to have actual, as opposed to merely mental, consequences. In discussing the need for repression Freud allows that there are reasons to believe that behavior is brought under self-control not only by virtue of the limitations and threats of society, but also for other, internal, reasons. If instinctual repression occurs, for example, independently of the civilizing forces of upbringing and example, this is explicable on

> a plausible hypothesis...that a primaeval and prehistoric demand has at last become part of the organized and inherited endowment of mankind. A child who produces instinctual repression spontaneously is thus merely repeating a part of the history of civilization.[324]

Thus the experience of the distant past claims a direct result in our psyche; and indeed the psyche of the future may be influenced and molded in the same fashion by the actions of our own civilization. Freud's belief in the real effects of past historical trauma may, then, apply to the future as well, so that he speaks here not simply of the effects of actions upon the structure of the self from the point of view of the present looking backwards, but also of the future, looking forward. It seems, in principle at least, to be an ongoing process, with little reason (as we shall see) to believe that it should stop with us.

Let us return to the implications thrown up by the similarity of our psychic life to the life of primitive peoples. Freud points out that we wish to ignore death, though we cannot in the end; but our ancestors experienced in a much stronger way than we the ambivalence of feelings concerning the death of a loved one. Primitive society, he argues, dealt with the problem by the invention of spirits, totemism, and eventually religion. These artifacts had as their main or, perhaps, sole purpose the denial of death, either one's own or that of a loved one, and thus aided the disguising and forgetting of the pain of truth. Our ambivalent and fearful wishes, which we repress, are simply somewhat weaker versions (weaker because of the inroads of civilization) of the feelings of love and hate that tormented our ancestors. Our dreams and our symptoms, then, are truly common dreams and common symptoms. It was this conclusion

[323] *Civilization*, 78.
[324] "Claims," SE XIII, 188-189.

254

upon which Freud based his defense of psychoanalysis as a general science descriptive of and responsive to the human condition, not simply the condition of an individual. When he concludes that all dreams are children's dreams he concludes also that all children have the same dreams.[325] This is true of symptoms, too. It is scarcely to be assumed that there is any distinction between typical and individual symptoms.[326]

The ego, Freud argues, martials to its aid acquired responses. It is in fact an agency of highly organized mental structures which are "acquisitions of human evolution made under the impact of human history."[327] The unacceptable impulses which lead to the commission of acts that invited a threatening response were gradually repressed as unserviceable. This repression was effected consciously at first, then acquired as a permanent characteristic of ego psychology in the form of substitutive structures. All mental imbalance and all products of civilization may be analyzed in this way.[328] Thus the surface memory of childhood obscures the real events of the past while at the same time hinting strongly at their true nature. A similar activity may be observed in the manner in which civilizations record their history. In *Moses and Monotheism* Freud reflected at length on this question, taking as his starting point the (apparently) distorted report of seminal events in the "official" history.[329] In *Leonardo* Freud begins with an analysis of the vulture fantasy in Da Vinci's painting. The vulture scene is a fantasy as we first approach it, rather than a memory; it has been transposed into Leonardo's childhood memory. Childhood memories are elicited in fact only at a later stage; and at that time, and in the process of eliciting them, they are altered and falsified, and come to serve later concerns. This, it seems to Freud, is directly analogous to the way history is written. In the infancy of a nation no thought is given to the writing of history: it is an age of heroes, not historians. Upon gaining time for and interest in reflection, the need to learn of one's origins and past experiences is felt. Historical writing begins with old legends and tales. This early history is an expression of "present beliefs and wishes rather than a true picture of the past," and thus distortion and displacement occur, in a manner obviously analogous to dream work. Further, the motives for writing the history are not objective but rather instructive and homiletic; so also for childhood memories.[330] Thus not only are the events of the past precisely similar for the individual and the race, but the distortions in the reporting

---

[325] IL, SE XV, 213.

[326] *Ibid.*, 271.

[327] "Preface," SE XVII, 259.

[328] *Ibid.*, 259ff..

[329] *Cf. Moses*, SE XXIII, 7-53.

[330] *Leonardo*, 33-34; *cf. Moses*, SE XXIII, 59-72.

of them to the conscious life, whether individual or collective, are, too, precisely similar.

Further, both reports yield to psychoanalysis; there are real events that the distorted reports reveal to analysis in each case.[331] Finally, then, both cultures and individuals behave as an individual, remembering but distorting the past; both require analysis to trace the truth of the past and the motives that are obscured by our present and conscious versions of ourselves. It is important to recall that when Freud compares the characteristics of individual psychical development with the history of the race there is very little metaphor involved–if metaphor can be quantified in this way. One need only remember that he presents his version of the primordial murder as a real event. Nevertheless we should appreciate the implications of his conclusion in the manner of appreciating a metaphor, that is, we should not fall too far into the valley of literalism. What is clear is that Freud did not limit the causal factors of mental life to the experience of the individual, on the one hand, and on the other he regarded the memories, fantasies, dreams, the imagined fears and happenings of the neurotic, and the rest of us, as the residue of actual, material, historical events the effects of which are, most assuredly, still with us.

We should (if I may digress for a moment) interpret Freud's remarkable hypothesis concerning telepathy in light of these ideas. Freud discounted vigorously any claims on the part of occultists to super-normal powers on the psychologically sound grounds that they represented wish-fulfillment; but he reserves a positive assessment for telepathy. His reservation is based on the observation that, in the proper setting, one person can know another's emotional or mental condition or concerns without being told or informed in any usual way. Freud accepts this as a fact,[332] which can be explained by psychoanalysis: "It would seem to me that psycho-analysis, by inserting the unconscious between what is physical and what was previously called 'psychical', has paved the way for the assumption of such processes as telepathy."[333] He envisions the process as working rather like a telephone; that is, energy is transmitted, converted to another form, and then retransmitted in its original form. The telepathic process "is supposed to consist in a mental act in one person instigating the same mental act in another person. What lies between these two mental acts may easily be a physical process into which the mental one is transformed at one end and which is transformed back once more into the same mental one at the other end."[334] What is inter-

---

[331] Ibid., 34.
[332] Cf. NIL, SE XXII, 31-56.
[333] Ibid., 55f..
[334] Ibid..

esting for the present argument, however, is that one of the main reasons Freud believes that such communication must be possible is that it was, very likely, a form of communication of our antecedents. For example, we do not yet know, he argues, how insects communicate, though they clearly do.[335]

I raise this matter because it is a useful illustration of the strength of Freud's commitment to the idea that past conditions have present results, and that it is very difficult, if not impossible, to explain present situations without comprehending the prior conditions not only of our individual experience but of the experience of the race. This is, of course, what it means to say that ontogeny recapitulates phylogeny; but Darwin is superseded here, since he was simply speaking about physical organs responding to environment; Freud is thinking about destiny and human suffering.

A further theme, not simply an illustration in this instance, is the issue of anxiety. As we have already seen Freud traces anxiety to the ego, the abode of anxiety. He pointed to the similarity between neurotic and real anxiety in that both were attempts to escape an external danger. The difference, he held, was that the neurotic anxiety was a result of the internalization of what was once–but in every psychological sense still is– "real" danger. Further, anxiety is traced to the primordial anxiety, the fear of castration; the little boy has empirical evidence that castration is no empty threat in the anatomy of girls. But–and this is our point here–Freud also believes that in the history of the race the castration threat was probably carried out. Vestiges of that act may be seen in the rites of passage of present day tribesmen, in which the penis is partially mutilated. Therefore, the distinction between neurotic and "real" anxiety is virtually a minor point, hinging entirely upon the strength of the memory of the child and the proximity of events in his childhood to his inborn fear of castration. Anxiety, in short, arises in both the ontogenetic experience, as we expect, and in the phylogenetic. It is otherwise inexplicable.

In treating religion as a neurotic phenomenon Freud assembled his convictions concerning phylogeny and ontogeny, the libidinal struggle of which religion is the chief civilized representative, and the primacy of mental conflict. One must, he says, understand religion in terms of individual neurosis, which nevertheless has its ramifications in social structures. The Freudian assessment of the human condition is not different from its assessment of religion.[336] The compulsive mental conflict which becomes visible to us in the neurotic symptoms arises with the return of the repressed. What is repressed is what is true; it is the emotional

---

[335] *Ibid.*, 55-56.
[336] *Moses*, SE XXIII, 58.

reality of our lives, the quintessence of our feelings, and the cause of our conflict. But, again, what is repressed is not ours alone, as individuals, but ours as the whole of human experience.

One would expect that Freud would not be limited to the appearance of *homo sapiens* in his account of the origins of suffering. We know this already from his treatment of the evolution of the cortical layer. The reference to the manner in which insects communicate is another clue. And, in *Moses and Monotheism* Freud suggests that the diphasic onset of sexuality in human beings shows that the human race had as its immediate ancestor a species of animals which reached sexual maturity in five years. The arresting of sexual development at that point in *homo sapiens sapiens* may well be the result of hominization. It may be a vestige of earlier stages of evolution, even as our anatomy in part is. Further, infantile amnesia occurs at this point. This cannot be mere coincidence.[337]

Also, with respect to the activity of thought and the operation of the unconscious Freud held that the experience of the individual was the same as the group, and that the experience of the group, the human species, was to be traced back to pre-human prototypes. The group, like the individual, retains impressions of the past in unconscious memory-traces.[338] The link between conscious operations and sensory perception is seen originally in the rise of thinking; and in animals the link is also present, though less complex because of the absence of speech.[339]

This concern with the causal role of pre-human conditions serves largely to show that Freud both traces backwards to a prior state and forward to the inheritance of the past. After the animal situation becomes the human situation–specifically, becomes the emotional life of human beings–the inheritance becomes more complex than can be accounted for by biology. Emotional conflicts that are reactions to early traumas can be understood only if both ontogenetic and phylogenetic factors are taken into account. Thus in addition to the animal heritage of the instincts, the senses, and the perceptual operations, we humans have experienced emotional crises of denial and danger that have become as much a part of our phylogenetic inheritance as the opposable thumb. In investigating neuroses, Freud concluded, one can not account for all the characteristics of those neuroses by referring solely to the hidden experiences of the single child. In the reactions to early traumas phylogenetic disposition and content–memory traces–are to be found.[340]

There follows (in *Moses and Monotheism*) a very significant summary

---

[337] *Ibid.*, 71.
[338] *Ibid.*, 94.
[339] *Ibid.*, 97.
[340] *Ibid.*, 99f..

of Freud's view on the nature of the relationship between phylogeny and ontogeny. There is no clearer indication of the depth and fullness of his commitment to this relationship in his writings. What we should understand him to be saying is this: the causes of the mental life are to be found both in the individual experience and in the previous experiences of all our human ancestors, so that by virtue of being a human being, an heir to past experience, one is and feels the life of humanity. It is by virtue of this inheritance, and this experience, that one is what we call human. It is also by virtue of this inheritance and this experience that we suffer. (The reference to biological evolution should be taken as an indication of the level of reality which Freud assigns to the psychological inheritance; that is, as a scientist he means to refer to the most empirical and objective reality.)

On further reflection I must admit that I have behaved for a long time as though the inheritance of memory-traces of the experience of our ancestors, independently of direct communication and of the influence of education by the setting of an example, were established beyond question. When I spoke of the survival of a tradition among a people or of the formation of a people's character, I had mostly in mind an inherited tradition of this kind and not one transmitted by communication.... My position, no doubt, is made more difficult by the present attitude of biological science, which refuses to hear of the inheritance of acquired characters by succeeding generations. I must, however, in all modesty confess that nevertheless I cannot do without this factor in biological evolution. The same thing is not in question, indeed, in the two cases: in the one it is a matter of acquired characters which are hard to grasp, in the other of memory-traces of external events—something tangible, as it were. But it may well be that at bottom we cannot image one without the other. The phylogenetic derivation of neuroses must be asserted. If it is not so, we shall not advance a step further along the path we entered on, either in analysis or in group psychology. The audacity cannot be avoided.[341]

Thus the power of the neuroses in the individual, and the analogous delusions in mankind as an whole, are due to real, remembered, but repressed experiences. It is the memories of those events—and they are real events—which cause so much distress, and the distortion and repression of those memories, and thus those events, by which the ego seeks to preserve the psychic balance. We can only conclude, Freud asserts, that both the individual and the society have developed delusions whose power is due to their historical truth; and their continued power is due to our certain and

---

[341] *Ibid.*, 99-100; *cf.* 101-102.

remembered experience of them.[342] It is now perhaps clearer that Freud's notion of therapy has a universal application. The bringing of what is unconscious into the conscious is a task directed not only at the neurotic individual but at the neurotic society. The deed cannot be undone, of course. But it can be acknowledged, its substitutes unmasked, the guilt accepted for what one is guilty of and not other things, and above all the true nature of our motives known and accepted. Finally, we can (perhaps) leave the past to the past, and cease to continue to impose it upon the present. That, surely, is a measure of freedom.

---

[342] "Construction," SE XXIII, 268-269.

The Origins of *Dukkha*

Anicca

In the teachings of the Buddha those who seek the end of suffering are adjured to seek but one goal, the knowledge of *anicca*, impermanence.

The perceiving of impermanence, brethren, if practised and enlarged, wears out [*pariyādiyati*] all sensual lust [*kāmārago*], all lust of rebirth [*rūparāgaṃ, bhavarāgaṃ*], all ignorance wears out, tears out all conceit of "I am [*asmimānaṃ*]," just as a ploughman cuts through spreading roots or a reed cutter cuts down a reed, as a bunch of mangoes, all joined together, is cut with one blow from the tree.[343]

One must free oneself from the desire for compounded, transient worlds. "Impermanent...[u]nstable... [i]nsecure, monks, are compounded things. So, monks, be ye dissatisfied with all things of this world, be ye repelled by them, be ye utterly free of them!"[344] The compounds are *sankhāras*, those constructions of the mind which are treated as real, and appear as real to the desiring, ignorant self. In truth they are *anicca*, transient.

Eradication of the delusion of permanence is a constant goal for the *Arahant*. The cause of suffering is the failure to know this truth and the resulting self-deception of pursuit of these compounds as though they were real. Suffering is the inevitable result. One must look to the other side of the equation, the desire for transient things. But it is ignorance of the transience of the world we desire and construct that is our concern here. "Transient," says the *Dhammapada*, "is all men think and do." The way to purity is through wisdom. Without this wisdom all is suffering, *dukkha*. What is this wisdom (*paññā*)? It is the wisdom that knows that all that is thought and done is transient.[345]

Thus in order to comprehend the cause of suffering we must understand what is intended by the analysis of thinking and doing, and why they are called transient. What is intended may be stated briefly: the analysis of the causes of all states pertaining to suffering and the analysis of the causes of all states pertaining to the end of suffering. In the Buddhist tradition the comprehension of these causes is formulated in the *paṭiccasamuppāda* series, or the series of co-dependent origination. The transience of all states is the subject of the series. It is frequently thought that this sort of analysis of the causes of suffering should be construed as a causal analysis. This is, strictly speaking, not a true understanding of the nature of the relationship of the elements of the series to each other. A strict causal analysis should follow the Aristotelian model in that one

---

[343] S III, 132.
[344] A IV, 64; *cf.* D II, 118-119.
[345] Dh 277, 27 (9).

must finally arrive at a first or uncaused cause. But the *paṭiccasamuppāda* series has no ultimate or first cause. Rather it presents an analysis of all the parts of the series in relation to each other in such a manner that each is a cause and an effect, like two sheaves leaning against each other. Further, it is more correct to render the verbal root, *paṭicca*, as "give rise to" rather than "cause," for what is meant is that if condition x is present then condition y will follow. The reverse is also true: if condition x is not present, then condition y will not be present. It seems the wisest course to follow those who have translated the phrases in question as the series of "co-dependent origination," in order that we should not be misled. The danger lies not so much in mis-interpreting the relationship between any single condition and its immediate antecedent but rather in our understanding of the nature of the series itself.

Co-dependent Origination

If we bear in mind the central truth of the relationship between *anicca*, transience, and *dukkha*, suffering, we will not be surprised to learn that ultimately all states, positive or negative, are not entities. They are continuing states of transition wholly dependent upon each other for their perceived existence. For example, to begin with a version of the series that leads to release, one who is virtuous has no need of purposeful thought; one who is virtuous has freedom from remorse; one who has freedom from remorse has no need of the purposeful thought, "May joy arise in me"; he who is free from remorse has joy; if joyous he has no need for the purposeful thought, "May rapture come to me"; if one is enraptured there is no need to think, "May body be calm"; if enraptured, body is calm; if body is calm there is no need to purposefully think to attain happiness; for he who is calm in body is happy; if one is happy there is no need for the thought that his mind is concentrated, for if one is happy, then one's mind is concentrated; if it is concentrated, there is no need to think, "I know and see things as they really are"; for if one is concentrated in mind, one sees things as they really are; if one sees things as they really are there is no need to seek to feel revulsion, for interest in things fades; and finally there is no need to think, "I realize release by knowing and seeing"; for it has already happened. The order of causation is then reversed, so that release by knowing and seeing has revulsion and fading interest as cause; seeing and knowing things as they really are have revulsion and fading interest as object and profit, and so forth to the beginning of this version of the series. "Thus, monks, one state just causes another state to swell, one state just causes the fulfilment of another, for the sake of going from the not-beyond to the beyond."[346]

The example shows that the states of the series are interdependent to a radical degree, so that if one state is achieved that which is immedi-

---

[346] A V, 3-4.

ately dependent upon it is also achieved, and if one state is abolished its dependent state is also abolished. What I wish to stress is that at any point in the series the elements are utterly and entirely dependent for their existence upon the other elements. So long as one is present, the others are present; so long as one is absent the others are absent.

Another example, which pertains to causes of suffering rather than release, illustrates the same radical degree of dependency. The matter at issue is the relationship between sensation and contact. The distinction is noteworthy, since sensation applies to the experience known to the self, whereas contact refers to the intersection, as it were, of the external stimulus and the sensory organs, so that contact implies externality but sensation does not. Contact, then, is said to be a cause of sensation. The Buddha relates how this is to be understood.

Were there no contact [phassa] of any sort or kind whatever between any one and anything whatever, that is to say, no reaction of sight, hearing, smell, taste, touch, or imagination [the activity of the mind–mano–is regarded as a sixth sensory activity], then, would there, owing to this cessation of contact, be any appearance of sensation [vedanā]?[347]

The answer is clearly no. Rather,

When the elements of eye and objects that are pleasing and eye-consciousness occur together...owing to the pleasurable contact [sukha, phassa] there arises pleasurable feeling.

This is true also for displeasing and neutral contact and feeling, and for all the senses.[348] Sensation cannot stand on its own for it is utterly dependent upon contact; and contact is equally dependent.

Let us now turn to a classic statement of the paṭiccasamuppāda series, bearing in mind that the truth of anicca as a cause of suffering is what is being explicated. If anicca is a universal cause of suffering, it should be the case that all states are transient–"all men say and do"–and indeed we find that this is so. The following order of co-dependent origination is typical: name-and-form gives rise to cognition (nāmarūpa, viññāṇa); cognition gives rise to name-and-form; name-and-form gives rise to contact (phassa); contact gives rise to grasping (upādāna); grasping gives rise to becoming (bhava); becoming gives rise to birth (jāti); birth gives rise to old age and death; old age and death give rise to grief, lamentation, ill, sorrow, despair; "Such is the coming to pass of this whole body of ill."[349] This is the origin of suffering. The series is then reversed, to show the way in which suffering may be brought to an end. If there is no

---

347 D II, 56; cf. SN 128.
348 S IV, 71.
349 D II, 52.

birth "after the several kinds of every one of these classes of beings [i.e., human, divine, goblins, etc.]" there is no old age and death. Without old age and death there is no becoming. In turn the remainder of the series topples step by step until the entire mass of ill ceases to be.[350]

It is possible to "break into" this series at any point; and it is possible to subject any member of the series to analysis of its characteristics, for no element of existence is unsuited to this analysis. Indeed, the later *Abhidhamma* tradition sought to enumerate and analyze every element of existence; that I shall not attempt here. But I do wish to indicate the general or universal scope of the notion of the transiency of all things, and to show what is meant by the affirmation that all things are transient. This analysis has but one purpose, to point the way to the cause of suffering and to the cause of the end of suffering; this is not "idle speculation," or the consideration of metaphysical truths for the sake of performing mental gymnastics.

Contact, then, can be the point of origination. Contact (*phassa*) is the condition that gives rise to sensation; name and form–by which is meant the psycho-physical entity, the body as individual–give rise to contact; cognition (*viññāṇa*, the general consciousness of the living self) gives rise to name-and-form. The conditions that give rise to our birth are, then, name-and-form together with cognition; if they did not exist, there would be no birth, growth, death, dissolution or reappearance.[351]

Old age and dying (*jarāmaraṇa*) are together an element of the series.

Whatever of various beings in various groups of beings is old age, decrepitude, broken teeth, greying hair, wrinkly skin, the dwindling of the life-space, the collapse of the sense-organs, this...is called old age. Whatever is the falling away, the passing away, the breaking up, the disappearance, the death and dying, the actions of time, the breaking up of the groups (of grasping [khandhas]), the laying down of the body–this...is called dying.[352]

But old-age-and-dying arise because of the arising of birth (*jāti*); and the stopping of birth gives rise to the stopping of old-age-and-dying.[353] Thus one should comprehend birth in order to comprehend old-age-and-dying: "Whatever is the conception, the production, the descent, the coming forth of various beings in various groups of beings, the appearance of the groups (of grasping [khandhas]), the acquiring of the sense bases [saḷāyatana, the six senses], this is birth." From the stopping of becoming

---

[350] *Ibid.*, 52-55.
[351] *Ibid.*, 58-61.
[352] M I, 61-62.
[353] *Ibid.*.

(*bhava*) is the stopping of birth.[354] Becoming is understood thus: there are three kinds of becoming; as to sense pleasures (*kāmabhava*), as to materiality (*rūpabhava*), that is, rebirth in a plane of matter, and the world of matter; and there is becoming as to non-materiality (*arūpabhava*), or the going on to becoming on a non-material plane. In turn, becoming arises on account of grasping (*upādāna*) after new states and after continuing existence. Of grasping it is said that there are four types: grasping after sense pleasures (*kāmupādāna*); after view or beliefs (*diṭṭhupādāna*); after rites and customs (*sīlabbatupādāna*, or the desire for religious performances and obedience as ends in themselves); and after the theory of the self (*attupādāna*). Cessation of grasping leads to the cessation of becoming.

Grasping is in turn the condition that arises because of craving (*taṇhā*). There are six sorts of craving, one each for the five objects of the senses and the objects of the mind. Feeling gives rise to craving; there are six classes of feeling, arising from the sensory impingements upon the five senses and the mind.

Contact gives rise to feeling, with six sorts of contact. The six sense bases, *saḷāyatana*, give rise to contact; and name-and-form in turn give rise to them. *Nāmarūpa*, or name-and-form, are often separated for the purposes of analysis; feeling, perception, volition, sensory impingement, and reflectiveness (*vedanā, saññā, cetanā, phassa, manasikāra*) are mind. The four great elements and the material shape derived from the four great elements are matter. Name-and-form arise because of consciousness (*viññāṇa*). There are six classes of consciousness corresponding to the five senses and the mental sense. In turn the uprising of the mental formations, *sankhāras*, the activities of the self that precede the body of any given birth, give rise to consciousness. The mental formations are of three sorts: formations, or activities, of the body (*kāyasankhāra*), of speech (*vacīsankhāra*) and of mind (*cittasankhāra*).

The uprising of the mental formations is in turn due to the arising of ignorance, *avijjā*. This is ignorance concerning the true nature of things, and upon this ignorance the entire series may be said in part to depend. Ignorance has a special place in the analysis of the nature of suffering; for it would seem to be the *sine qua non* of all the subsequent forms of suffering, which include every element of existence and every stage of life; for ignorance means ignorance of the existence, causes, end and way to the end of *dukkha*.

However, ignorance is identical in respect of its arising to all the other elements of the *paṭiccasamuppāda* series in that its existence is due to another factor, here the *āsavas*, the cankers. Whereas the mental formations pertain to a specific individual's destiny, the cankers are, so to

---

[354] *Ibid.*, 62-63.

speak, principles of continuity, the primordial forces of human activity and desire, which one must challenge in one's own life. There are *āsavas* of sense pleasure (*kāmāsava*), of becoming (*bhavāsava*), of speculation (*diṭṭhāsava*) and of ignorance (*avijjāsava*). As we shall see, the "breaking of the *āsavas*"–with the clear implication that they are "chains"–represents the final stage prior to the release of the monk; that is to say, the *āsavas* represent the most formidable barrier to release from suffering. The Buddha provided a short answer to the question of the source and end of suffering which underscores the significance of the *āsavas*.[355] When the monk has no doubts of the end of the *āsavas*, his task is finished. There is a sense here in which the series may be said to end; for the cessation of ignorance leads to the cessation of the cankers. From the stopping of the cankers arises the cessation of ignorance; from the cessation of ignorances comes the cessation of mental formations, and so forth until the entire series is reversed, and collapses.[356]

The series is expressed frequently in the reverse order, that is beginning with ignorance. Activities arise from ignorance, consciousness from activities, name-and-shape from consciousness, the six senses from name-and-shape, contact from the six senses, feeling from contact, craving from feeling, grasping from craving, becoming from grasping, birth from becoming, and old-age-and-death, suffering, and despair from birth.[357]

The role of the perceiving and desiring self is prominent in the series. So for example the monk Kaccanda explains the arising of ill, beginning with visual consciousness, that is, the experience of sensing through the operation of the eye-shapes and -forms. Visual consciousness, he says, arises from eye and material shapes. There are, then, three operative elements in sensory impingement (*phassa*), namely the consciousness of the eye (*cakkhuviññāṇa*), the material shapes themselves (*rūpa*), and the organ of the eye. From the sensory impingement comes feeling (*vedanā*, that is, the sensation of seeing). From feeling comes perception (*saññā*), which usually means the specific act of realizing the presence of an external shape as an experience. He continues, "...what one feels one perceives; what one perceives one reasons about [*vitakketi*]; what one reasons about obsesses one [*papañceti*]; what obsesses one is the origin of the number of perceptions and obsessions which assail a man in regard to material shapes cognisable by the past, future, present." The same analysis is applied to the other five senses.[358] What one might call the act of perception in general gives rise to a mental state of obsession and compulsion. This relationship between perception and obsession, and therefore suffering,

---

[355] S II, 40; *cf. diṭṭhāsava*, D II, 81, 84, 89 *et passim*.
[356] M I, 63-67, for this version of the series.
[357] S II, 1-2.
[358] M I, 145.

appears regularly in analyses of the series of co-dependent origination. It links the functions of the biological organs to the mental state of suffering; and it serves to point the way to the end of suffering, which leads to controlling of the senses in such a way that they continue to function but do not build up the burden of care, concern and desire which renders their natural operation conducive to suffering.

The relationship among the elements of the series is one of co-dependent origination. If one condition exists another arises; if that condition does not exist the other does not arise. The teaching, or *Dhamma*, is briefly stated thus: "If this is, that comes to be; from the arising of this, that arises; if this is not, that does not come to be; from the stopping of this, that is stopped."[359]

There is another important aspect of the series that must be understood if its nature is to be grasped. It is illustrated in the following exchange (this passage suggests yet another beginning point in the series in its reference to the sustenances, or the fuel, of the series): a disciple asks,

> who now is it, lord, who feeds on the consciousness sustenance [one of the four sustenances or *āhāras*: material food—fine or coarse—, contact, volition—*cetanā*—and consciousness]?
>
> Not a fit question [said the Exalted One]. I am not saying [someone] feeds on it. If I were saying so, to that the question would be a fit one. But I am not saying so. And I not saying so, if you were to ask me "of what now, lord, is consciousness the sustenance?" this were a fit question.[360]

The distinction drawn between the fit and the unfit question is analogous to the distinction between the understanding of the self as a continuing "own-being" and the teaching of *anattā*. In placing the question about the co-dependent origination of suffering in its proper context for the questioner the Buddha denies the implication that there is a self, a being, that is continuously in existence and which forms the central identifying point for the changes described in the series. The reality is the series itself; and it also, therefore, constitutes the analysis of suffering and the truth of *anicca*—and by implication therefore the truth of "no self," *anattā*. Thus the question "who is it who suffers," or, here, "who is it who is sustained by consciousness," is founded upon a fundamental misunderstanding of the nature of the series and cannot be answered without denying the truth of the series itself. The question, in other words, is a manifestation of ignorance and false view.

Having established the proper context for the question, the Buddha proceeds to an analysis of the fit question: "The fit answer is...: the

---

[359] M II, 229-230.
[360] S II, 9ff..

267

consciousness-sustenance is the cause of renewed becoming, of rebirth in the future. When that is come to pass, is present, the sixfold sense-sphere [saḷāyatana]" arises, and from that, contact. Again setting the questioner on the right path in the manner already described, he states that contact is conditioned by the sixfold sense-sphere, and feeling is conditioned by contact. The questioner is again set aright when he asks who it is who feels; for feeling is conditioned by craving. Craving is conditioned by grasping; grasping is conditioned by becoming, and so on to the end of the series.[361]

This revealing formulaic treatment of the series is to be found in a number of other contexts. For example the series itself is seen as the true statement of the middle way between existence and non-existence; and therefore it contains no reference to any continuing or permanent state whatsoever. Indeed, it implies quite clearly that none can exist. It is therefore not a fit question to inquire as to who it is who dies or is born, or whether when the body dies the soul carries on.

[Where there is the view:] "soul and body are one and the same," or the view, "soul and body are different things," then there is no divine life. The Tathāgata teaches neither of these two extremes; he teaches a Middle [Way], and says:–Conditioned by birth is decay-and-dying.... From the utter fading out and ceasing of ignorance these disorders, these disagreements, these distortions, all whatever they be [cease]....[362]

There is no person to whom the series can be related or with whom it is identified.

The truth is co-dependent origination, for this is the nature of transiency, and thus the nature of ill. Dukkha is therefore the essential nature of the elements of the series and as well of transiency and interdependence in both form and substance. Thus Sāriputta declares: "Not any one of these [elements of the series] is, but is conditioned by the succeeding." Like two sheaves of reeds leaning one against the other, name-and-shape arises because of consciousness, consciousness because of name-and-shape, sense because of name-and-shape, etc.. If any sheaf were pulled away, all the others would fall. Just so is the cessation of the series of arisings.[363]

The series of dependency is relevant to elements besides those already mentioned in the "classic" series. For example, an analysis is suggested for the condition of kāma, pleasure. Kāma is a significant condition, as is evident to any reading of the Buddhist texts; for pleasure is conceived of as an object of desire without which desire would not arise. In the

---

[361] Ibid., 9-11; cf. S IV, 71.
[362] S II, 43-44.
[363] Ibid., 79-81.

analysis of pleasure it is said that there is a "cause," that is, conditions from which pleasure arises, for example, *kāmavitakka*, thought of sense desires. In this analysis sense desires are said not to arise without causal basis, and so also for ill-will (*vyāpāda*) and cruelty.[364]

Again, in the discussion of the *khandhas* it was noted that the notion of the "self" as a "heap" of characteristics, *i.e.* body, feeling, perception, activities and consciousness, is intimately linked to the *paṭiccasamuppāda* series. The connection lies in the suffering that results from clinging to any or all of these elements as the self. [365]

In attempting to impart the sense of the *paṭiccasamuppāda* series and the principle of co-dependent origination I have relied upon exemplary material to illustrate the principle of co-dependent origination and to stress the utter absence of any other explanation for suffering. It is essential to an understanding of the teachings to comprehend the fact that there is no other state apart from that of co-dependent origination. It is equally important to realize that the causal roles of desire, of the operations of perception, clinging and grasping are on the same causal level as birth and death. There is no self that desires or grasps, only grasping and desire, which are in turn conditions for the arising and cessation of other conditions.

The statement of this teaching is a supreme challenge. The dialogues of the Buddha and his followers demonstrate that ordinary language is full of assumptions that are called into question by the teachings. But the task of stating the truth was accepted. It was also accepted by Nāgārjuna, whose subtle intellect serves him and us well in summarizing the nature of the teaching of co-dependent origination.

In the dedication of the the the *Mūlamadhyamakakārika*, he pays homage to the "Fully Awakened One," so-called because he taught the doctrine of "relational origination, the blissful cessation of all phenomenal thought constructions.[366] Full enlightenment is his whose understanding of all phenomena is of this sort. We must then understand the relations of the elements of the *paṭiccasamuppāda* series to be of this sort, so that they can best be described negatively.

Nāgārjuna's statement of the series is that of the tradition we have already seen. Thus those who are deluded by ignorance create the three-fold mental configurations, the activities of body, speech and mind, and are reborn in various forms.[367] The configurations give rise to consciousness, consciousness gives rise to name-and-form, name-and-form to the six sense-bases, and touch, or contact, arises from the senses. As we have

---

[364] *Ibid.*, 105-106.
[365] S III, 15-16.
[366] Inada, 39.
[367] *Ibid.*, 106ff..

seen the three conditions of organ, object and consciousness–appropriate to each of the six senses–give rise to touch. From touch, or contact, comes feeling. "Relationally conditioned by feeling, craving arises because it 'thrusts after' the object of feeling. In the process of craving the fourfold clingings are seized." From clinging arises becoming, or being. Becoming (*bhāva*), says Nāgārjuna, is always the five heaps (Sanskrit: *skhandha*; Pāli: *khandha*); and from this birth arises. From birth come old-age-and-death, suffering, misery, grief, despair and mental disturbance. "In this manner the simple suffering attached to the *skhandhas* comes into being;" the ignorant create the mental conformations (*saṁskāras*; Pāli: *sankhāras*) that underlie the life of rebirth. But the wise do not create the mental conformations.[368]

The series, then, in Nāgārjuna's treatment is in essence the classic series; and his exposition of it is helpful, especially on the issue of the relations of what we may call with care cause and effect. All the relations are identical in nature. Nāgārjuna appplies a well-worn but very useful simile to the relationships of the series. Specifically, he responds to the issue of the relationship between the notion of the self, *ātman* (Pāli: *attā*), and clinging, *upādāna*. As we have seen it is at the point of clinging that the *khandhas* come into play in the classic series. Nāgārjuna raises the question of the relationship between grasping and the *khandhas* in response to the issue of the effects of grasping or clinging to any of the *khandhas* as the self. Do the *khandhas* depend upon grasping? What is the nature of the relationship? His answer is applicable to the entire series:

If an entity depends on another entity in order to manifest itself, the latter will also depend on the former for its manifestation. If what is to be depended on for manifestation already exists then (the question is) what depends on what?

Again, fire is not wood nor is it in something else than wood. Fire does not contain wood. There is neither wood in fire nor fire in wood.

The argument, in part, is that fire cannot cause itself, and wood cannot cause itself. If one causes the other then each has been completed previously and there is no necessity for fire, as it would either have gone on for ever or never started. There is relationship, co-origination and dependency, to be sure. But there is nothing that is dependent.[369]

---

[368] *Ibid.*, 160-163.
[369] *Ibid.*, 80-84.

Despite the equality of status of each element of the series of co-dependent origination, desire or craving (*taṇhā*) is of special interest in explicating the causes of suffering. (As the issue of the nature of desire is discussed it should be borne in mind that it is part of a series of origination, that it is dependent upon prior conditions, and that it establishes conditions for the arising of succeeding states. I stress this point as a *caveat* against treating desire itself as a first cause. It is also noteworthy that the English term "desire" is used to translated *chanda* and *rāga* as well as *taṇhā*).

Asked by Ānanda to explain why there is becoming, here meaning rebirth in other worlds, the Buddha responds,

> If there were not worlds of sense-desire [*kāmadhātu*] and no action to ripen therein [*kamma*], Ānanda, would any sensuous becoming be manifested?

> Surely not, Lord.

> In this way, Ānanda, action [*kamma*] is the field, consciousness [*viññāṇa*] the seed, craving [*taṇhā*] the moisture. For beings that are hindered by nescience [*avijjā*], fettered by craving, consciousness is established in lower worlds. Thus in the future there is repeated rebirth. In this way there is becoming, Ānanda.[370]

The analysis is applied then to worlds of form (*rūpadhātu*), and formless worlds (*arūpadhātu*). *Taṇhā* is, then, a necessary condition for rebirth and, therefore, suffering. The metaphor is that of the fertile seed which grows and comes to ripeness, but only when all the conditions required for growth are present. Thus rebirth is the inevitable consequence of the presence of the conditions; and conversely the absence of any one of the conditions brings the process to an end. The role of desire in this metaphor suggests both its importance and its nature. It is called the moisture. It is the consciousness that grows, that is, provides the initial and implied pattern of development. *Kamma*, action, or deeds, provides the setting, the context from which nutriment is derived and in which the growth is rooted. *Taṇhā* provides the crucial element that enables the seed to ripen and the ground, the *kamma*, to provide the driving force–to bend the metaphor somewhat–to the established factors, for the seed and the field precede the moisture, and work together for growth only after it appears. Wherever one pursues the interpretation of the metaphor, however, it is quite clear that there will be no becoming in any of the three worlds–of sense-desire, form and formlessness–that is, no becoming in rebirth at all, without *taṇhā*.

---

[370] A I, 203-204.

Taṇhā is frequently linked directly to *dukkha*, suffering, as a condition for the arising of the latter (this placement differs from the classic series). For example, the analysis of the relationship among the elements of the series, and others not mentioned in the classic series such as *kāma* and *kamma*, proceeds in the following manner. The element, here *kāma*, is examined from six points of view: how it is discerned; its source; the variety of its expression; its fruit, or consequences; its cessation; and the steps leading to its cessation. The role of *taṇhā* in several of these analyses illustrates its central part in the analysis of suffering. With respect to *kāma*, sense-desire, that is, pleasure derived from and sought through the senses, it is said: "In passionate purpose lies man's sense desire–/ The world's gay glitters are not sense-desires,/ In passionate purpose lies man's sense-desire./ The world's gay glitters as they are abide,/ But wise men hold desire therefor in check."[371] The suffering persons, as opposed to the wise, are those who seek gratification of desire, *taṇhā*, through the gratification of senses in external "glitters," objects of desire. The cause of suffering, however, is not the objects but the desire. *Kāma* has as its immediate cause contact, *phassa*, and its manifestations are in its seeking of forms, sounds, smells, tastes, and tactile sensations. Its fruit is that it leads to states of merit or demerit, depending upon what the object of desire is. The ending of *kāma*, in accordance with the fact of co-dependent origination, arises from the ending of contact. But the ultimate cause, as opposed to the material cause, is desire.[372]

Similarly, the analysis of *dukkha*, ill, begins with the concatenation of ill's manifestions: birth is ill, old age, disease, death, grief, sorrow, misery, distress, tribulation, not getting what one wants, "in short, (life's) fivefold bunch of clinging [*upādānakkhandha*] is ill." The source of ill is craving, *taṇhā*; and the cessation of ill arises from the cessation of craving.[373]

Craving is linked not only to becoming but also to annihilation.[374] It is craving that causes being, the frantic scurrying from life to life, the suffering of "life's endless round."[375] Craving drives and assails the world, "the dart where by it's pierced alway," "[b]y itch of pestering desires assailed." "By cords of craving is the world strung up."[376]

The world's situation is bondage; but its nature too is the bondage of desire, from which the *khandhas* arise: "These five grasping groups... have their root in desire.... But where there is desire and lust [*chandarāga*]

---

[371] A III, 291.
[372] *Ibid.*, 292.
[373] *Ibid.*, 291-295; *cf.* M I, 60-61.
[374] M I, 60-61.
[375] S I, 52-53.
[376] *Ibid.*, 54-57.

there also is grasping."[377] The link between desire and the five groups is explained in terms of desire for a future existence, conceived as any or all of the *khandhas*:

> Herein...one thinks thus: "May I be of such a body in future time: may I have such feeling, such perception, such activities, such consciousness in future time." In this way...in the five grasping groups there may be a variety of desire and lust.[378]

The arising of ill is due to the arising of desire. The Buddha teaches that if desire did not arise then there would be no suffering, as he instructed the headman Bhadragaka: "Whatsoever ill," says Bhadragaka, "arising has come upon me in the past,–all that is rooted in desire [*chanda*], is joined to desire." The same is true for the ill that will come in the future. "Desire is the root of ill." This is true, for the headman knows he would suffer at the loss of his wife, an ill which would not have arisen had he not felt "longing or desire or affection" for her.[379] Grief, sorrow and lamentation originate in affection; when there is a change in the beloved the lover grieves, like a young man who committed suicide in order to rejoin his dead beloved one.[380]

The English terms "desire" and "craving" designate a number of Pāli terms, for example, *chanda* and *taṇhā*. However, one of these, *chanda*, occasionally occurs in a unique context, namely the desire for insight or liberation. For example, the Brahman Uṇṇābha questions the Buddha closely concerning the monk's life, and the abandonment of desire which is its presumed goal. Gotama explains that this goal may be accomplished by cultivating the basis of psychic power, of which the features are desire, energy, thought and investigation. Uṇṇābha points to an apparent contradiction: desire seems to play a part in the solution as well as in the problem. How then shall desire (*chanda*) cease? Gotama responds by acknowledging that, indeed, desire plays a very important part in the search for the life without suffering; but it is like the journey Uṇṇābha made to the park where Gotama was teaching. Uṇṇābha made the journey motivated by desire, energy, thought, and investigation, in honest search of the life without suffering. When he arrived at the park, however, these motivations, which were appropriate to his starting, making, and completing the journey, were dissipated for the task was completed. It is so for the monk seeking Arahantship; when it is won the appropriate desires are abated.[381]

This explanation of the place of *chanda* in the search for the end

---

[377] S III, 85f..
[378] *Ibid.*.
[379] S IV, 232-234.
[380] M II, 194-195.
[381] S V, 243-245.

of suffering suggests that it is not something to be opposed but rather something that comes to an end. This conclusion is applicable to co-dependent origination in general; the cause of suffering is in fact a series of relationships and conditions which arise from and give rise to one state after another. What leads to the end of suffering is the reversal of that process; that is, in the elimination of one or more of these elements those that are dependent upon them are eliminated. Desire provides a basis, a root, for ill. Desire, then, is not wrong, evil, or reprehensible in and of itself, any more than any of the elements of the series is. Rather, each gives rise to suffering, inevitably, until the relational chain is broken. What arises is suffering, what passes away is suffering. But suffering is the sum of a series of relationships; thus the cause of suffering and the cause of the end of suffering are inextricable. Desire, while obviously central to the process, is part of a relationship; and thus it is part of both the cause and the end of ill.

Nāgārjuna raised the issue of the role of desire, as passion, *rāga*, by querying the existence of passion and its relationship to the passionate self. In the context of the *paṭiccasamuppāda* series elements are not things, and do not have "own-being," *svabhāva*; therefore they can not be said to exist—or not to exist. Thus one must not be misled into thinking of desire as a thing, an *ens*, or an independent state, but rather as—a poor word—process. So,

> If prior to and separated from the passion [argues Nāgārjuna] the impassioned self is admitted to exist, then the passion will be contingent on the impassioned self. Thus the passion exists only from the fact of the existence of the impassioned self.

The non-existence of the impassioned self is inconceivable; and the simultaneous occurrence of passion and the impassioned self is rejected as absurd. The two entities, passion and the impassioned self, cannot, therefore, be identical in every respect; nor, it is argued, can they be diverse, for there would be no necessary relationship (concomitance). But both concomitance and diversity are desired in the explanation of the relationship between the impassioned self and passion, that is, it is hoped (wrongly, as it happens) that there is an impassioned self, passion, and a joining of the two. What Nāgārjuna argues, however, is the emptiness of the self, of the impassioned self, of passion, and of the relationship between them; for any one of these assertions of being is contrary to the teaching of the Buddha: "Consequently, there is no establishment of passion with or without the accompaniment of the impassioned self."[382]

Yet desire is the moisture which the seed of becoming, and thus suffering, needs. It is the catalyst which brings nutriment from the field to the seed:

---

[382] Inada, 60-62.

Let him by insight break the root of this, "Reckoned as hindrance:"/ All the thoughts "I am":/ Whatever craving there may be within,/ Let him train ever mindful that to oust.[383]

Khandhas

The effects of desire must be understood in terms of a relationship or series of relationships of ignorance. Yet there are antecedent causes of our ignorance concerning the nature of being. They are the constituents of the image of what we misperceive as a fixed and "real" self and world. These are the *khandhas*, the "parts," or "heaps," or constituents which are regularly identified as real, permanent, and the essence of the self. The *khandhas* are body (*rūpa*), perception, feeling, consciousness, and the activities (*sankhāras*). The nature of the activities illustrates the link between ignorance and the *khandhas*. There are three activities, those of body, speech and mind (*kāya, vacī, citta*). Inhalation and exhalation are activities of the body, thought directed and sustained (*vitakka*) is an activity of speech, and perception and feeling are activities of the mind. What draws this analysis into the issue of suffering is the common assumption that these activities of body, speech and mind are activities of a self, an "I." On the contrary, however, the brethren are adjured to reject this assumption. The enlightened monk does not think: "*I* will now emerge, *I* am emerging, *I* have emerged from attaining the ceasing of perception and feeling."[384] For the activities of body, mind and speech do not end, and in this respect the monk is to be distinguished from a dead man, in whom life has run out. Rather, the monk who does not think "I am acting" has his faculties clarified.[385]

The unthinking common folk believe that body is the true self, that feeling, perception, the activities and consciousness are the true self.[386] But the monk who seeks the self is like one who has never heard a lute. He asks for one and is told that it consists of diverse parts. He destroys the lute, and its parts and says: "A poor thing is what you may call a lute, my man, whatever a lute may be. Herein is the world exceeding careless and led astray." Like the lute, body, feeling, perception, the activities, and consciousness have no eternal element; there is no "I" or "I am" or "mine" to be found.[387]

There is, then, no body that "is permanent, stable, by nature lasting, unchanging, like unto the eternal, so that it will stand fast," and so also for the other *khandhas*. Illustrating the idea, Gotama picks up a little

---

[383] SN 134.
[384] S IV, 201f..
[385] *Ibid.*.
[386] S III, 105, 138.
[387] S IV, 129-130; *cf.* S III, 140-141.

pellet of cowdung, and says "[e]ven getting of a selfhood [attabhāva] so small as this...is not permanent, stable, eternal, by nature unchanging, like unto the eternal, so that thus it will stand fast." If this were not so, he concludes, there would be no need for the Ariyan life.[388] This last comment is significant; for the Ariyan life is, above all, devoted to penetrating the misperception of the self, such as that suffered by the ignorant commonfolk. If the true nature of being were immediately evident to our perception, consciousness, feeling, and body the discipline of the Ariyan life would be quite unnecessary. The contrary is true, however; and it is exactly the experience of the Ariyan life that a fixed, stable, eternal essence is not to be found in any of the khandhas, or in them all taken together.[389] Yet in grasping for false reality, in regarding the body, feeling, and so forth as self, the common view is like a man swept away by a mountain stream who clutches at grasses, reeds and creepers, and is destroyed.[390]

This is the "world condition" (lokadhamma), which the Tathāgata has penetrated, realized and declared. The "world condition" here is a reference to the five khandhas which are accepted by the ignorant as the essence of being.[391] This world condition is not the object of the teaching: "I quarrel not with the world, brethren. It is the world that quarrels with me. No preacher of the Norm, brethren, quarrels with anyone in the world."[392] Rather, the Tathāgata upholds that which is upheld in the "world of sages": that body, feeling, perception, the activities and consciousness are impermanent, the activities and consciousness are impermanent and unstable.[393]

The khandhas are commonly referred to as the "five groups of grasping," signifying that the impermanence of the khandhas is not simply a matter of cognition; the real danger lies in grasping after them as the essential self. Thus the monk who simply reflects upon the ontology of the groups has not completed the task of liberation. One may cease to speak of body, perception, and so forth as an expression equivalent to "I am." But there remains "a subtle remnant" from among the five grasping-groups, a subtle remnant of the I-conceit (asmīti māna), of the I-am desire (asmīti chanda), of the unconscious tendency to think "I am" (asmīti anusaya). Only in the contemplation of the rise and fall of the grasping groups, a state transcending the cognizing of their natures, is one then free from the I-conceit, which hangs about the consciousness

---

[388] S III, 122; cf. M I, 281.
[389] Cf. S III, 120.
[390] Ibid., 116.
[391] Ibid., 117-118.
[392] Ibid..
[393] Ibid..

like the smell of soiled linen that has not yet been utterly cleansed.[394]

In truth, then, the body is a compound, as are perception, consciousness, and the activities.[395] Whenever one looks back and remembers different former lives, he thinks, "of such and such a body was I in time past." Another says, "I felt thus and thus"; it is the feeling he remembers, and so also for perception, the activities and consciousness. What is the basis for these "entities"? "Body" is the term used of various states of being affected by cold and heat, hunger and thirst, etc.. "Feeling" is but various feelings, painful, pleasurable and neutral. "Perception" is, for example, perception of various colors. "Activities" are so called because they compose a compound of body, of feeling, of perception, etc.. "Consciousness" is, like the other *khandhas*, a compound, for example, of flavors or odors.[396]

What the monk seeks to escape is the suffering that is an inevitable concomitant of the grasping groups whenever they are identified as the self.[397] The abandonment of the grasping groups proceeds only with the understanding that they are dependent upon one another. Consciousness, for example, has its roots in body, the activities, feeling, and perception. It is impossible to deal with each as an independent entity.[398] But if grasping for the body is ended, then consciousness loses its base, and so also for the other *khandhas*.

The *khandhas* are compounds and therefore are susceptible to analysis. Each must be comprehended in its uprising, its ceasing, the cause of its uprising and the cause of its ceasing. Such comprehension leads and to the supreme enlightenment (*abhisambhodhi*).[399] For example, body is the four elements, air, earth, fire and water. The arising of body is from food (*āhāra*) and from the ceasing of food is the ceasing of body. Again, feeling is born of contact with eye, ear, and so forth. Further, the arising of feeling is due to the arising of contact, and with the ceasing of contact is the ceasing of feeling. From the arising of contact is the arising of perception, and by the cessation of contact perception ceases.

The *sankhāras*, "activities," are the "six seats of will [*cetanā*]: the will for sights, the will for sounds," and so forth. The arising of the activities is due to the arising of contact. Finally, coming full circle, the arising of consciousness, that is, the six seats of consciousness corresponding to the six senses, including mind, comes from the arising of *nāmarūpa*, mind-and-body; and from the ceasing of mind comes the cessation of

---

[394] *Ibid.*, 110; *cf.* M III, 66.
[395] S III, 89.
[396] *Ibid.*, 72-74.
[397] *Ibid.*, 55-57; *cf.* M III, 67-68.
[398] *Ibid.*, 45f..
[399] *Ibid.*, 50ff..

consciousness.[400]

The compounded and dependent nature of the *khandhas* is displayed in the consistent reference of each *khandha* to its constituent parts, as in the role of the five or six senses in the arising of the *khandhas*, and in their dependence upon each other, or, more accurately, their co-dependent origination. Their impermanence is not in and of itself a cause of woe and suffering; for those who do not hold views about the unstable body, impermanent and sorrow-fraught, or about the other *khandhas*, such as "better am I, equal am I, worse am I," see what really is. The body, therefore, is impermanent, impermanence is suffering, and therefore it is not right or fitting to hold "this am I, this is the self of me" about which I am concerned; and so for the other *khandhas*. "[E]very body should be regarded as it really is by right insight. Thus 'this is not mine,' 'this am not I,' 'this of me is not the self,' " (and so forth for the other *khandhas*) is the proper view.[401]

The relationship of co-dependent origination is compared to the striking of sparks. When a contact leads to a pleasant feeling it is

> just as if from the adjusted friction of two sticks, heat is born, a spark is brought forth, but from the separating and withdrawing of those two sticks, the heat which was consequent, that ceases, that is quenched.[402]

Yet our perceiving of body, consciousness, perception, feeling and activities is greatly influenced by "false opinion," that is, the word-concepts we use. In a passage cited above Māra is told that he should not concern himself with the issue of being; among the *khandhas* no being is to be found.[403] With respect to shape, or body, "...just as a space that is enclosed by stakes and creepers and grass and clay is known as a dwelling, so a space that its enclosed by bones and sinews and flesh and skin is known as a material shape."[404]

But in the name there is no being. Rather, name refers to a co-dependent series of origination. Thus the sense of seeing requires a material shape and contact in order that the seeing consciousness may arise. "What has thus come to be," then, is dependent upon eye, material shape and contact in order to produce consciousness. In turn, material shape is, according to the experience in question, "included in the group of grasping after material shape [*rūpupādānakkhandhe*]. What is feeling in what has thus come to be...is included in the group of grasping after feeling [*vedan-*]...whatever is perception in what has thus come to be...whatever

---

[400] *Ibid.*, 50-54.
[401] *Ibid.*, 42-43.
[402] S II, 67.
[403] S I, 169-170.
[404] M I, 236.

278

is habitual tendencies...whatever is consciousness is included in the group of grasping after consciousness."[405] Thus the heaps are not to be dissociated: "...it is not possible to lay down a difference between these states, having analysed them again and again. Your reverence, whatever one feels, that one perceives; whatever one perceives that one discriminates; therefore these states are associated."[406] In this way the five grasping groups come together. The *Tathāgata* said: "Whoever sees conditioned genesis [*paṭiccasamuppāda*] sees *dhammā* [beings, things], whoever sees *dhammā* sees conditioned genesis;" and these are "generated by conditions [*paṭiccasamuppanna*]; that is to say the five groups of grasping."[407] So also the "I am" conceit arises owing to a cause, and that cause, or better, condition, is body, is perception, activities, feeling and consciousness. The seductive and deceptive link between the notion of the self and the five grasping groups is suggestively described: "Suppose, friend Ānanda, that a woman or a man or a young lad fond of self-adornment should gaze at the image of his face in a mirror that is clean and spotless, or in a bowl of clear water,—he would behold it owing to a cause and not otherwise."[408] The love of the self arises out of a desire to see and have a self; but the search leads only to a reflection without substance. A deceived self gazes upon its own image believing it to be real. Narcissus dies of love for this false self; but the self is a nest of diseases, "brittle, a rotting congeries;/ truly a dying end hath (this) life."[409] But one who is freed by insight is like a blind man who was deceived into thinking that a coarse and grimy cloth was finest silk. But when he gained his sight through the application of medicine, he realized he had been defrauded. By insight he knows that he grasped after form, perception, feeling, consciousness, the habitual tendencies; and because of this grasping he was conditioned by becoming, by birth, old age and dying, grief, sorrow, suffering, lamentation and despair. "This is the origin of this whole mass of anguish [*dukkha*]."[410]

Nāgārjuna presses the non-permanence of the *khandhas* to its ultimate logical *reductio*. The truth of the co-dependent origination of the five grasping groups teaches that no ultimate cause or effect can stand on its own. Thus, in discussing the relationship of *rūpa*, or form, to a presumed efficient cause, he concludes that it is equally impossible to separate form from efficient causes and to equate them. If form and cause are separated, "it follows that form will be without a cause. However,

---

[405] *Ibid.*, 236ff..
[406] *Ibid.*, 352.
[407] *Ibid.*.
[408] S III, 89.
[409] Dh N. 148, p. 53.
[410] M II, 190.

nowhere is there a thing existing without a cause." Moreover, if the cause is separated from the effect, or form, then the equally untenable situation of a cause without an effect is proposed. Further, it is untenable that the cause and the effect should be equal, or resemble each other, or not resemble each other, and so forth for the other *skhandhas*.[411] In sum, the proper understanding of the relationship among the *skhandhas* is one that posits neither cause nor effect as separate entities, nor collapses them into an identical state. What remains, as it were, is the true relationship of emptiness, *śūnyata*. Everything is suchness (*tathāyama*), not suchness, both suchness and not suchness, and neither suchness nor not suchness. "This is the Buddha's teaching."[412]

Conceits

Understanding of the true nature of the *khandhas* may be thwarted by what is called conceit, *māna*. The *Dīgha Nikāya* includes three conceits in its "list of threes." The three forms of conceit are "I am better than...," "I am equal to...," "I am worse than...." What is meant is the mistaken notion of self extended into forms of superiority to others, equality to others, or inferiority to others. The issue is not whether one deceives oneself as to superiority, as opposed to equality or inferiority, but that such comparisons yield an idea of a self which, in light of what we have learned of the *khandhas* on the one hand and of desire on the other, can only be false. It is quite common among the unlearned to pursue these comparisons. The term "conceit" is appropriate here because these comparisons are ways of assessing the value of the self, and therefore perpetuate the false notion of the self in one's consciousness and experience.[413] The monk is urged to put away both conceit and wrath, and thus to escape "all the bonds of pris'ners,/ Not cleaving fast unto this mind and body,/ Nowise [by lust, hatred, and dullness] hampered,/ [so that] Sorrow and pain no more may overwhelm ye."[414]

The process prescribed for the rooting out of the conceits reveals their bases. These are found in the individual's belief that his sensory contact with the world, involving his senses, the world of objects, and their coming together to form the consciousness appropriate to any sense, defines the real self. The enlightened brother has no conceit of being the eye or in the eye or coming from the eye or possessing an eye. He has no conceit of objects of eye-consciousness or eye-contact. He has no conceit of himself experiencing pleasant, painful or neutral feelings through eye-

---

[411] Inada, 54-56.
[412] *Ibid.*, 113-116.
[413] D III, 207ff..
[414] S I, 32-33.

contact.[415] The same is true for the other senses.[416]

The conceit of self-hood, founded in the operation of the senses, has no basis in reality at all, but is a powerful deception carried out in the sensing life. Sensation, of course, occurs; but it is a self-deception to believe that because there is sensation or sensing there must be an I (or an eye) underlying and directing the sensing. The truth is otherwise; the *khandhas*, rightly understood, constitute the world and the experiencing of it. Any further conclusion, such as "I am equal," superior or inferior, or "I have an eye," tongue, hearing, *etc.*, that would support the notion of a permanent self is unwarranted in any analysis of perception and arises solely from desire; and desire entangles one in instability.[417]

One must understand how it is that one has a conceit of the world, *lokamāna*: "through the eye, through the ear, nose, tongue, body, through the mind one is conscious of the world." Thus the aim of bringing an end to the world, to which the brethren are committed, is accomplished by understanding that the "world" is a product of conceit of the world, of consciousness of the world. When the conceit of the world is brought to an end by the arising of insight, the world is brought to an end. That is what "world" means, the Buddha tells Ānanda, in the Ariyan discipline.[418]

Rāga, Dosa, Moha/Greed, Hate and Ignorance

In addressing what one might, with some irony, call the Buddhist ontology, that is, the teachings of *anicca*, co-dependent origination and the five *khandhas*, our focus was in fact upon the dialogue between ignorance and knowledge with respect to the relation between the perceiving persons and the world. In discussing *taṇhā*, desire, and *māna*, conceit, the desiring person who is fundamentally in error has been the object of our attention. I want now to shift to the more general theme of causes for action, especially unuseful actions. The Buddhist texts treat the general cause for action under three separate but wholly integrated headings. These are covetousness, *rāga*, malice, *dosa*, and ignorance, *moha*. The Buddhist analysis of suffering turns to these three defilements (*klesas*) for its most general explanation of the origins and end of *dukkha*. They are as it were internal, even "psychological," categories, and that is significant for our understanding. They are also dialectical in their relationship; for they bring together the desire to attract and to repel on the one hand, and also place the entire realm of desire in the context of ignorance. The arising of *rāga*, *dosa* and *moha* is the arising of suffering, and the rooting out of them is regarded as the end of suffering. Their ending, it seems likely, is synonymous with *nibbāna*.

---

[415] S IV, 11-12.
[416] *Ibid.*; *cf.* 13-14.
[417] *Ibid.*, 11-12.
[418] *Ibid.*, 59.

Each unprofitable (*akusala*) act has its roots in lust, *rāga*, in hate, *dosa*, and delusion, *moha*.[419] This is a general truth; but it is a truth that must be experienced in the life of the person. The Buddha warns Sakhā not to be misled by tradition or hearsay concerning lust, malice and delusion: "But when you know for yourself: These things are unprofitable...do you reject them."[420] Evil acts are specifically rooted in these three defilements. For example, one whose life is characterized by lust, malice and ignorance (here *abhijjā, vyāpāda, avijjā*, respectively) "stays a being" (that is, is not reborn in a world higher than one of form), steals, seeks the wife of another, tells lies and misleads others. These states are therefore said to be unprofitable, *akusala*. By contrast, the true Ariyan disciple is one who suffuses the whole world with a heart possessed of widespread equanimity, boundless, and free from enmity and oppression.[421] He is one who can distinguish a mean from an exalted state, who knows there is an escape from consciousness, and is released from the bondage of sensible desire. Such a one reaches the state of knowing that rebirth is ended, the righteous life led, the task done. What distinguishes this knowledge of release is precisely freedom from greed (*lobha*), malice (*dosa*) and delusion (*moha*); and such a one is "cool" (*nibbuta*), a synonym for *nibbāna*. "...[H]e, of himself, abides in experience of bliss, by becoming Brahma."[422] In other words the barrier *par excellence* to release is the three *klesas*. They are replaced by their opposites in the Ariyan life: *lobha* by *alobha, dosa* by *adosa, moha* by *amoha* (here *abhijjā* by *anabhijjā, vyāpāda* by *avyāpāda, avijjā* by *vijjā*).[423]

One who is bound by the three roots of demerit is unaware of his situation. Not only is he unaware of the true roots of his actions, he will actively deny what is true about his motives. Bound by greed, malice and delusion, he is an "inopportune," "untrustful," "irrelevant," speaker, "unjustly causing suffering to another by punishment, imprisonment, loss of wealth, abuse and banishment, on the grounds that 'might is right.' When confronted with the truth he denies it, does not understand it. When confronted with a lie he makes no effort to untangle it, saying, 'this is baseless, this is false.' "[424] His actions are caused by motives he denies; he cannot recognize either the truth or a lie when in this state

---

[419] A I, 118-119. As one expects in an analysis of significant and central ideas, there are a number of Pāli words employed to designate these concepts. It will be made evident what each means in the text. The same procedure will be followed in the case of English translations.

[420] *Ibid.*, 176.

[421] *Ibid.*, 176ff..

[422] *Ibid.*.

[423] *Ibid.*.

[424] *Ibid.*, 183.

of bondage. He is cut off from reality, driven entirely by what in modern jargon we might call his emotional life. Further, unaware of what he is doing, he has devised a complex of explanations with the intention of justifying his actions so as to fulfill the demands of his desires. By contrast one who is not ensnared by his emotions or self-delusion knows the truth when he sees it, and when confronted with a lie searches for its causes and untangles it, concluding: "this is baseless, this is false." Unconscious motives have ceased to exert control; and self-delusion, which preserves the hegemony of the unconscious emotions, has been replaced by recognition of the truth and the desire to get to the bottom of the lie.[425]

The place of the *klesas* of covetousness, malice and delusion in the general scheme of release is a matter of considerable significance. One analysis describes four sorts of progress, beginning with the most difficult and ending with the least difficult and therefore the most efficient. The categories involved are painful and pleasant, sluggish and intuitive. The slowest mode of progress is painful and sluggish, the next painful but intuitive, the third pleasant but sluggish, the fourth pleasant and intuitive. The three defilements are linked directly to the painful category. The slowest mode of progress is assigned to a person of lustful, malicious and deluded nature who is also cursed with dull controlling faculties (these are faith (*saddhā*), energy (*viriya*), mindfulness (*sati*), concentration (*samādhi*) and wisdom (*paññā*)). However in the next category, even if the five controlling faculties are swift and lively rather than dull and sluggish, progress is still painful because of the defiled nature chained by *rāga*, *dosa*, and *moha*.[426]

The inhibition presented by the three *klesas* can be removed only by transforming the nature of action. One bound by the *klesas* performs evil deeds; and evil deeds have their reason and cause in lust, malice and delusion. A "lovely deed" will be performed only by the removal of the defilements.[427]

There can be no freedom of mind for the monk who is not freed from the bonds of greed, malice and delusion. The four freedoms of the mind, in ascending order of freedom, are the immeasurable freedom of mind, the freedom of mind that is "naught," the freedom that is void (*suññatā*) and the freedom that is signless. While there are distinctions to be drawn among these freedoms—for example, the freedom that is signless pays no attention to any signs, while the freedom that is immeasurable is that of the monk whose equanimity suffuses the whole world—they are not different in one significant respect: none of them can be achieved without

---

[425] *Ibid.*, 184.
[426] A II, 153-155.
[427] A V, 61; *cf.* D III, 174, n. 31, and 207-214.

ending the obstructions of attachment, hatred and confusion (*rāga, dosa, moha*). But when these are gone, the mind is "immeasurable, naught, void, and signless."[428]

The monk's happiness is much greater than that of the wealthiest and most powerful princes; for the rulers are still bound by the *klesas*. But those who have renounced their desires are no longer trapped in the current of rebirth. They have not merely rejected the ordinary standard for judging human living; rather they have abandoned both lust and ill-will, desiring neither to collect nor repel; "And no more truck have they with ignorance. These are the Durg-destroyers, *Arahants*. They 'mong all men serene and restful dwell."[429] The hero, the *Arahant*, is not merely one who has abandoned possessions; he has met the final and most serious challenge to liberation from suffering, the self conceived as attracting, repelling and self-deceived. This self lives only for its loves and hates, and deceives itself for the purpose of satisfying its desires to grasp and to destroy. Indeed, the *klesas* define the self, which is a false self, no self at all. Who masters love and hate is free of birth and death.[430]

The serenity achieved in the life of the monk arises not from the absence of objects but from the end of desire's power over him. The end of suffering is that state in which the grounds for attachment no longer exist. As for the objects of perception, in things seen, heard, imagined, and cognizable there is only what is seen, heard, imagined and cognized. From this nothing follows, that is, there is no residual desire to draw the inference of the self. For such a one there is no "here or beyond or midway between." There is no other world to enter into or leave from, and no present world; for there are no grounds for *rāga, dosa,* or *moha*. That is the end of *dukkha*.[431]

Another indication of the high degree of significance and obduracy of the three *klesas* is their position in the shedding of the *sankhāras*, that is the activities, the dynamic factor in attachment to impermanent and compounded things. The ceasing of the *sankhāras* is said to be gradual, to pass through stages. The first four of the classic progression are the four trances in which speech, "initial and sustained thought" (*vitakkavicāra*), zest, and inhalation and exhalation cease in turn. There follows entry into the realm of infinite space, where perception of objects ceases, the realm of infinite consciousness, where perception of the realm of infinite space ceases, the realm of nothingness, where perception of infinite consciousness ceases, the realm of neither-perception-nor-nonperception, where perception of nothingness ceases. "Both perception

---

[428] M I, 358-360.
[429] S I, 23-24.
[430] S IV, 40-41.
[431] *Ibid.*, 42-43.

and feeling have ceased when one has attained the cessation of perception and feeling." It is at this point, when the *āsavas* are destroyed, that "lust [*rāga*] is extinguished, hatred [*dosa*] is extinguished, illusion [*moha*] is extinguished."[432] As the ending of the *sankhāras* is known to be a condition for the attainment of *nibbāna*, the placement of the three *klesas* at the very end of the progression suggests the significance which the Buddhist tradition attached to them. They stand as a major obstacle in the way to the end of suffering, and therefore figure very prominently as causes of suffering.

The heart of the Buddhist treatment of suffering lies in its assignment of causes and effects–if we may use those terms–to the life of the "self," the false self. That self may be comprehended "psychologically." By that I mean that the conditions for suffering are first and foremost conditions of the inner life and not the outer world. The texts repeatedly make the point that the one who is suffering attaches desire or hate to objects and thinks of himself as a continuing self "behind" his perceptions. In his relationship with objects he is deluded to the extent that his own self is seen to exist; and this self is both characterized by and sustained by lust and greed, hate and malice, delusion and ignorance. By contrast the one who is not defined by the three *klesas* is free; in his perceptions there is only perception, in what is imagined, seen or cognized is only that which is imagined, seen or cognized. He has conquered the dominance of his desires, seen the world for what it is and himself for what he is, and is free of illusion and delusion concerning world and self.

The linking of these three "psychological" characteristics, or perhaps one should say emotional drives, is crucial. The life of the self is defined by the dialectic of love and hate, and illusion oversees it and guarantees the continuation of the struggle, protecting the life of desire from the intruding warnings against destruction and a dire fate. Illusion sustains the life of desire, is essential to the love-hate struggle, and is thus a necessary condition of suffering. One cannot succeed in displacing the hegemony of the emotional drives until one is aware of the truth; and it is that awareness, that wisdom which at once removes the roots of greed and malice. Thus the three *klesas* are rightly treated as inseparable. Finally, one cannot discuss love without discussing hate. The desire to attract implies the desire to repel, and *vice versa*. The essential element, desire, is the same in both instances, indeed the "instances" are but two aspects of the same fundamental drive, *taṇhā*. The fundamental elements, then, in the active life of suffering, in the doing of deeds which arise from suffering and are conducive to it, are love, hate, and ignorance.

"Delight in the World"

In reviewing the causes of suffering the early texts are concerned

---

[432] *Ibid.*, 145-146.

with specific obstructions to the end of suffering. Ever present among the causes of *dukkha* is the relationship to the world. There is danger in delight in the world; and a monk who takes delight in the world fashions his own luckless path. Sāriputta advises his listeners to consider the end of one who, "finding delight in the worldly activity, is delighted with worldly activity, gets engrossed in the delight of worldly activity; so too of talk, sleep, company, companionship and vain fancies.... ...[T]he more he so fashions his life, the more he fashions it to a luckless death.... And of this monk it is said: with his bundle of life he is greatly delighted; he has not got rid of his bundle for the utter ending of ill."[433] Engrossment in the world, association with others, and the satisfaction of worldly needs are obstacles to liberation from suffering. The problem is not only human. The *Dīgha Nikāya* describes a class of beings whose attraction for the world was quite literal, and their fate is instructive. These beings were once luminous. Then one of their members tasted the earth and found it savoury, and began to eat. Others followed his example; and their luminous appearance began to fade. The sun, moon and stars became manifest, as well as the night and day, and seasons, months and years. The world came into being again.

> In measure as they thus fed, did their bodies become solid, and did variety in their comeliness become manifest. Some beings were well favored, some were ill favored, thinking: We are more comely than they; they are worse favoured than we. And while they through pride in their beauty thus became vain and conceited, the savoury earth disappeared. At the disappearance of the savoury earth, they gathered themselves together and bewailed it.[434]

The danger of sense-pleasure is an important theme in the treatment of relations with the world, as we have seen. The perils of the five sense-pleasures are frequently described. Mahanama is instructed in the *pañcakāmaguṇā*, the five strands of sense pleasures, and told that they are a stem of ill (*dukkha*).[435] The five strands of pleasure are acknowledged to be kinds of happiness, those of material shapes cognizable by the eye, the ear, the nose, the tongue and the body. Whatever happiness arises from these pleasures is the happiness of that sort. But it is a "vile happiness, the happiness of an average person, an unariyan happiness." Such happiness is to be feared. But in the work of the monk to establish himself aloof even from the pleasures of renunciation is the happiness of tranquility and of self awakening, which is happiness that is not feared.[436]

---

[433] A III, 210-211.
[434] D III, 82-83.
[435] M I, 121.
[436] M III, 281.

The distinction drawn implies the belief that the life of the Ariyan monk is different from that of the householder; and no doubt the path of the monk with respect to aloofness from sense desires is different from that of the average person, who is conceived to be satisfied with the pleasures of the senses. However Ariyan teachings are available to the householder as well. The householder Anāthapiṇḍika complains to Sāriputta of terrible head pains. Sāriputta's response is a compendium of instruction on not grasping after the consciousness, impact, or feeling of the five senses, after the four elements, after shape, feeling, perception, consciousness, the habitual tendencies, and the account of the aloof self progressing through the stages of infinite space, infinite consciousness, emptiness, and neither-perception-nor-non-perception. The grateful householder is told that such truth is not usually laid before householders. Anāthapiṇḍika responds that there are those of his sort who can learn.[437] The episode is significant, for it indicates that within the tradition the analysis of suffering is equally applicable to all despite the presence of different paths, lower and higher, to the final end of liberation. The cause of and the cause of the end of suffering are universal truths.

Clinging to the world, delighting in the world stands, then, in the way of liberation. The well-taught disciple must know well that there is nothing in the world to which he can cling without error. Should he cling to body, to feeling, to perception, etc., then he would be bound to the arising of suffering.[438] With delight in the world comes obsession with it. Obsession is the endless preoccupation with the objects and means of desire, with happiness and sorrow as emotional states, with satisfaction and dissatisfaction of desires. The Sutta Nipāta puts the matter bluntly: "All ill that comes is caused by mind-at-work [viññāṇapaccaya],/ By ending mind-at-work, there comes no ill;/ Knowing this bane: 'Ill's caused by mind-at-work,'/ Becomes from yearning free and wholly cool [nirodhene]."[439] The path to the cessation of obsession is illustrative. Happiness, sorrow and equanimity (somanassama, domanassama, upekhā) are each divided into two sorts, either to be followed or avoided: happiness to be sought is that in which good qualities are increased and bad qualities diminished (kusala, akusala); the happiness not to be followed is the reverse. The same distinctions are drawn with respect to sorrow and equanimity. What distinguishes the desirable happiness, sorrow, and equanimity is the absence of obsession, papañca, "travail of mind."[440] In brief, obsession is characteristic of the suffering self, and its absence of the liberated self.

---

[437] Ibid., 310-313.
[438] S III, 79-80.
[439] SN 110.
[440] D II, 312-314.

Sensation, Objects and the External World

Central to the issue of the causes of suffering is the relationship between what we may provisionally call the world of external objects and the perceiving, sensing, desiring self. The Buddhist view of this matter is that suffering is caused neither by the external world itself nor by the sensing self. Rather it is in the co-dependent origination of their interaction (to put the matter clumsily) that suffering arises. The focus here, as always, is desire and its consequences, rather than a self-existent desiring being or an external source of stimuli.

Koṭṭhita asks whether, after the "passionless ending [*asesavirāga*]," the "six spheres of contact [*phassāyatana*]," that is, the six senses in direct connection with stimuli, remain or are extant at all. We might also put this question by asking whether in the state of *nibbāna* the subject of *nibbāna* has any senses. The response given is that it is not true to say either that the six spheres of contact remain or do not remain; and it is not true to say either that they neither remain nor do not remain. Rather, "...in saying that there is something left one makes difficulty where there is none." "So long...as there is going to the six spheres of contact, for just so long is there a going to difficulty. But...by the passionless ending without remainder of the six spheres of contact there is calming down of difficulty."[441]

The issue is not whether the senses stand in the way of *nibbāna*, that is, cause suffering; for the question is not one which is conducive to the end of suffering. As is evident to a thorough study of the early texts the teachings never opt for either an external or an internal cause of suffering; they never propose realism or idealism. To do so would be radically inconsistent with the understanding of the *paṭiccasamuppāda* series and the nature of the *khandhas*. Neither the world nor the self can be blamed for suffering.

This is not to say that sensation and perception are irrelevant. On the contrary, it is precisely the analysis of the nature of perception and sensation that provides the major clue to the notion of suffering as it occurs in human experience. The emphasis here is not on objects and their relation to a sensing self but upon the changing and impermanent nature of perception itself.

What one perceives, first of all, is controlled by what one wishes to see. This truth is seen in the story of Anuruddha, who was approached by the three fairies of lovely form. These beings could assume any color they desired, any sound, and any happiness. Anuruddha wished that they were blue, and they willingly and instantly obliged; and so for yellow, red and white. All the while they sang and danced in an alluring manner. "But the venerable Anuruddha kept his senses under control. Then thought

---

[441] A II, 168-169.

the fairies: 'Master Anuruddha is not enjoying this,' and immediately vanished."[442] Their power, indeed their very appearance, depended upon the wishes of Anuruddha. Thus, by his control of senses he caused them to disappear.

So also the Brahman is said to be free of the obsession and perception (*papañcasaññāsankhā*) which assail others, for he knows there is nothing to rejoice at, to welcome, to catch hold of. "This is itself an end of a propensity to attachment [*rāgânusaya*]...to a propensity to repugnance [*paṭighânusaya*]...to views [*diṭṭh-*]...to perplexity [*vicikicch-*]...to pride [*mān-*]...to attachment to becoming [*bhavarāg-*]...to ignorance [*avijj-*]."[443] That is, the suffering of attachment, repugnance, ignorance, and so forth has its source not in the objects or the subjects of attachment but in the attachment itself. An anecdote concerning the "former vulture-trainer Ariṭṭha" is illustrative here. This person had been saying that the Buddha taught a view of complete asceticism as the path to release. The Teacher, Ariṭṭha averred, held that sense-pleasures are linked inexorably to pain, and were like a snake's head, which is an extension of the rest of the body. This Ariṭṭha, the Buddha concluded, "...not only misrepresents me, but also injures himself and gives rise to much demerit, this will be for a long time for the woe and sorrow of this foolish man." The truth of the matter is that sense-pleasures are not in themselves causes of suffering or evil; rather "this situation does not occur when one could follow sense-pleasures themselves, apart from perceptions of sense-pleasures [*kāmasaññā*], apart from thoughts of sense-pleasures [*kāmavitakka*]."[444]

That is to say sensation, or sense-pleasures, are not in themselves a cause for suffering. Therefore the ascetic path is useless in the cause of liberation. It is attachment to sense-pleasures, and the loathing of pain, that make the difference between bondage and liberation. The focus is once again upon the desire and the false self, and not upon sensation—which in and of itself is no cause for repugnance or delight. The state of delusion is said to afflict those who are attached to and desirous of sense pleasure, as though it were something good. For example, those bound to sense pleasure, if made to chose between two painful contacts, such as leprosy and fire, may think, if they are leprous, that the fire is pleasant because it is a change in sensation. The truth is that in past, present, and future, sense-pleasure is productive of suffering so long as one desires it, regardless of the nature of the sensation. The issue is then not the sensation, but the manner of understanding its arising and cessation and the presence or absence of grasping for it.[445]

---

[442] A IV, 175-176.
[443] M I, 142-143.
[444] *Ibid.*, 17.
[445] M II, 186-187.

The question of the relation between objects sensed and the subject sensing in the arising and cessation of suffering is relevant to all modes of perception, past, present and future; thus the critique of self-existence is directed to thoughts of a past self and of a future self. One who is not bound reflects about past perception in this manner: "He thinks: 'Such was my vision in the distant past, such were material shapes', but without his consciousness being bound fast there by desire and attachment [chandarāge]; because his consciousness is not bound fast by desire and attachment, he does not delight in it; not delighting in it, he does not follow after the past."[446] The same analysis is applied to the other senses, to the present, and to the future. In the past there were vision, hearing, smelling, tasting, touching—there are and there will be such in the future. And in accordance with the general Buddhist view of perception the objects seen, heard, smelled, tasted and touched are inextricable from the act of perceiving them. But in and of themselves the acts of sensing and perceiving are conducive neither to the arising or the ceasing of suffering, nor, therefore, are the objects on the one hand and the perceiving mechanisms on the other. Rather, the liberated person is one who does not have his consciousness bound fast by attachment and desire, not one who does not sense.

Insight into the true nature of shapes, sounds, smells, tastes, etc., is essential to the release from attachment, just as the ignorance of their true nature is conducive to suffering itself. The truth of anicca, of the impermanence of all states and things, illustrates the true nature of what is perceived as well as the perceptions. "When one knows the impermanency of material shapes themselves, their alteration, disappearance and arrest," through wisdom, then true joy arises. When one knows the true nature of things perceived there arises a longing for perfect wisdom and deliverance. When the uninstructed do not see the peril, their feeling of equanimity does not transcend that which is seen as body, felt, touched, tasted, smelled or thought.[447]

The emergence of dukkha with respect to objects and perception is the subject of the series of co-dependent origination. In the matter of the relationship among the perception of objects, the perceiving senses, and suffering, taṇhā, craving, plays a critical role. Craving works through the senses. Thus there is craving for things seen (rūpataṇhā), for things heard, for odors, for tastes, for tangible things and for ideas. Then feeling arises from eye contact, ear contact, etc. Taken together, feeling, perception, will, contact and work of mind (vedanā, saññā, cetanā, phassa, manasikāra) are called name. Shape (rūpa) and the four great elements are derived from them; and together this is called name-and-

---

446 M III, 241-243; cf. 233-234.
447 Ibid., 265-268.

shape (*nāmarūpa*). From name-and-form arises consciousness at the level of each of the six senses, and the activities of deed, speech and mind. In turn these are dependent upon ignorance. In sum, conditioned by ignorance activities arise, conditioned by activities consciousness arises, and so on to the arising of despair; "such is the uprising of this entire mass of ill."[448]

The relationship between the perceived world and suffering must be seen as a process rather than as that of two opposing entities in conflict. "Because of sight and visible objects visual consciousness arises, contact is the clash of the three; feeling is conditioned by the contact, craving by the feeling. This, brethren, is the arising of ill." This is true for hearing and audible objects, and the other senses. The fading away of ill is the reversal of this process. When craving ceases, grasping ceases, and also, in turn, becoming, birth, decay and death. This is the cessation of *dukkha.* [449]

Again, the crux of the matter lies in the role of craving rather than in the natural operation of the senses *per se* or in the nature of objects of the external world. The natural operations are described in such a way that one may distinguish between a proper and an improper understanding of their nature and work, that is, one that is conducive to suffering and one that is not. The recluse, looking back to past experience–in the sense of past "encounters" with all forms of "stimuli"–, remembers being a certain sort of body, feeling thus-and-thus, perceiving thus-and-thus, and so for all the *khandhas.* The question is put, Why does one say "body"? "One is affected, brethren. That is why the word 'body' is used." It is affected by cold and heat, hunger and thirst, gnats, mosquitoes, wind and sun and snakes. And why is feeling used? Pleasure, pain and neutral feelings are felt; and so also for perceptions, activities and consciousness. There is a body, teaches the Buddha, but it is a body compound which is not I or me or mine, but a compound which may be properly described. There are feelings, but they are a feeling compound, not an I, not belonging to any self or ego. There is a perception compound, an activities compound, a consciousness compound. Each may be observed rightly as functioning, as phenomena.[450] The insight of the recluse is the realization that while there are natural feelings, perceptions, bodies, activities, and consciousness they are not attached to anything but are a process which, when separated from the false self, may be known fully. There is no self.[451]

It is important to understand what is being affirmed and denied. The

---

[448] S II, 1-5.

[449] *Ibid.*, 50-51; *cf.* Inada, 51-53.

[450] S III, 72-74.

[451] S IV, 29. Nāgārjuna approached this question of the relationship between the self and the operations of the senses by arguing that it is illogical to hold that there is a self, *ātman*, antecedent to the functions of

denial of a self that possesses and is affected by the perceiving, sensing conscious operations is clear. This does not mean that those operations do not occur. On the contrary it is an implicit assumption (which is not often discussed) that there are sense objects; and a great deal of care is given to the analysis of sensation. Eye-consciousness, for example, arises because of eye and objects. The eye is impermanent and changing. The objects of the eye are impermanent and changing. The condition of relation between them is permanent and unchanging. It is said that eye, objects, and eye consciousness, have the state of "becoming otherness." Eye contact, which is the coming together of these three–and is therefore a fourth–is also impermanent, changing, and in a state of "becoming-otherness." This is so also for perception, and for the other senses.[452] These conditions of the arising of things are not in and of themselves necessary and sufficient to cause suffering.

The necessary and sufficient condition seems to be the state of being "enamoured." There are "objects cognizable by the eye... desirable, pleasant, delightful and dear, passion-fraught, inciting to lust. If a brother be enamoured of them... dependent on that comes consciousness based on that grasping." It is the grasping, not the sensing, the perceiving, the consciousness or any other *khandha* in itself that prevents liberation. Conversely release in this very life is possible if one does not become enamoured of the pleasing objects.[453]

Objects and their concomitant perceptions may be classified as pleas-

---

seeing, hearing, *etc.*, that the self exists concomitantly with the functions of the senses, or that it exists posterior to the senses' functions. Therefore we have no means of knowing what this entity is.

As for the notion of the self arising out of its functions, this is impossible, since the functions presuppose a self to which they are attached. (Inada, 76-79.) From the viewpoint of rigorous logic the existence and non-existence of the senses are unnecessary to an explanation of the functions of seeing, hearing, and so forth.

The link between the self and the external world in respect of suffering is thus severed. Nāgārjuna rejects all these propositions: that suffering arises by virtue of being self-caused, other caused, both self- and other-caused, or non-caused. If suffering is caused by self, then the self is in some sense separate from the suffering, and of such a one we have no idea. If it is caused by another, that one must also be separated from suffering in order to bring about the cause, and where is he to be found? Neither self nor world causes suffering, for none is separated from it. Suffering, in short, is not an effect at all. One looks in vain, then, for its explication in terms of self-other confrontation.

[452] S IV, 39-40.
[453] *Ibid.*, 62.

ant, painful or neutral. However, these terms are applied to the sensation-objects as descriptive of their nature rather than to the manner in which they are appropriated by the person who experiences them. In other words the elements, *dhātus*, are naturally possessed of diverse qualities which emerge from the operation and process of their arising and ceasing as compounds. Pleasure, pain and neutral feeling (neither pleasurable nor unpleasurable) are qualities which "inhere," so to speak, in the compounds; they become troublesome only when desire and craving and grasping are added. Thus when an object is described as painful or pleasant only, it is a description of things as they really are by virtue of the process of co-dependent origination. No judgement has yet been passed on them and never will be, for they are not conducive to suffering or to release in and of themselves. This is simply the "Diversity of elements" (*dhātunānatta*).[454]

In his useful summary Sāriputta addresses Koṭṭhita on the issue of the true source of the difficulty: "Is the eye of bond of objects, or are the objects the bond of eye? Is the tongue the bond of savours, or are savours the bond of the tongue? Is mind the bond of mind-states, or are mind-states the bond of the mind? Not so, friend Koṭṭhita. The eye is not the bond of objects, nor are objects the bond of eye, but that desire and lust [*chandarāga*] that arise owing to these two. That is the bond." Sāriputta explains the reason for the discipline which the monk undertakes. "If the eye, friend, were the bond of objects, or if objects were the bond of the eye, then this righteous life for the utter destruction of Ill could not be proclaimed." The final model for the successful release from suffering is that of the Exalted one. He has senses, but no desire is attached to them.[455]

The monk who follows this pattern is directed to the four stations of mindfulness: mindfulness of body, of zest for a pleasurable thing, of calmness of body, and of ease. He is free of initial sustained thought. Here it is noteworthy that the goal is not to turn away from objects but to (a) perceive them as they really are and (b) to fully comprehend the mental process by which they are themselves comprehended. The same procedure is followed with respect to feelings and the other *khandhas*. Success in this use of external objects for the purpose of calming is followed by a more advanced state, the non-direction of mind to externals, but addressing the *khandhas* in the same manner. Again the issue is not the external objects, pleasurable or otherwise, in themselves, but the use of them for the purpose of right mindfulness.[456]

---

454 *Ibid.*, 71.
455 *Ibid.*, 101-102.
456 S V, 134-136; *cf.* 159, 161.

False Views

If it is neither the world nor the senses themselves that act as causes of suffering but the grasping, craving and desiring attached to them, it is also true that false views themselves lead to suffering.[457] To perverted view is ascribed all non-meritorious (*akusala* deeds of body, speech, thought, all intention, aspirations and resolves, all activities whatsoever. Perverted view (*micchādiṭṭhi*) is like a tiny seed which, drawing essence from earth and water, grows and flourishes.[458]

Perverted view is, then, one of the essential elements of the arising of suffering. This perverted view is a misunderstanding, a misdirected and corrupted knowledge which, when planted like the seed, yields the fruit of suffering, *dukkha*. It is frequently set in contrast to right view and happy view (*sammādiṭṭhi, diṭṭhi bhaddaka*), which are the true understanding of the successful Ariyan. But the issue here is more than one of ignorance masquerading as truth. Rather, as the Buddha's responses to the questions for which he gives no answers—the so-called unexplained points—show, it is the concern with "view," that is, with belief, that is central to this perspective on the arising of suffering. Thus in replying to the question, Is the *Tathāgata* after death or not, or neither or both, it is said that the Ariyans are not disturbed by doubt about these alternatives because they are view-issues, *diṭṭhigata*. The unlearned do not understand the nature, the arising or the cessation of view or doctrine, opinion or theory. For such a one view grows; he is bound to birth, old age, death and sorrow. The Ariyan, by contrast, is unconcerned about these issues.[459]

This assessment of view as a source of ill applies to all positions that might be designated as philosophical in nature. Thus the Buddha rejects the view of determinism, that is, the view that all actions are caused by prior conditions, and that therefore one is not responsible for those actions. He rejects also the attribution to a Supreme Being of the causes for all actions, so that one holds, falsely, that the necessity for action or inaction is not found to exist in truth and verity. Those who teach this view are said to be bewildered and irresponsible. This is true also for the teaching of indeterminism, the view that all is uncaused.[460]

The *Arahant*'s wisdom has a similar negative relationship to views of any sort, even with respect to his own destiny. It is absurd to say that an *Arahant* believes that he goes on after death, that he does not, that he both does and does not, and that he neither goes on nor does not. It is not by any of those concerns that the *Arahant* is set free:

---

[457] A I, 27-28.
[458] *Ibid.*, 28-29.
[459] A IV, 39-40.
[460] A I, 157-159.

whatever system of verbal expression there is and whatever system of expression, whatever explanation there may be and whatever system of explanation [*adhivacana, nirutti*], whatever communication [*paññatti*]... system of communication, whatever knowledge [*paññā*] there is and whatever sphere of knowledge, whatever round of life [*vatta*] and how far the round is traversed,–by mastery over all this that brother is set free. But to say, of a brother who has been set free [*vimutto*] by insight:– "He knows not, he sees not"–that were absurd![461]

Conversely, the brother who is committed to the view of becoming or to the view of annihilation will fail to know the truth of suffering because his view of one alternative is obscured by his view of the other. For concern with one particular view causes the failure to see that its opposite arises. This happens because one is trapped by the attraction of doctrine, opinion and argument. The fate of the monk who is thus attracted to one view or the other is that he fails to see as they really are the nature, rise, fall, and satisfaction of view, whether of becoming or annihilation.[462]

As is inevitable for the teacher who steers the middle course between opposing doctrines in order to show their emptiness, the Buddha was accused of holding various positions. For example, it was said that he was a nihilist because he laid down "the cutting off, the destruction, the disappearance of the existent entity [*vibhava*]." But he replies that he is not a nihilist, that indeed this is just "what I am not, ...is just what I do not say." His accusers have misrepresented his true teaching. This is: "Formerly I, monks, as well as now, lay down simply anguish and the stopping of anguish [*dukkha*]." Moreover, as the *Tathāgata* finds no joy in the idea that some support him, nor resentment in the idea that some oppose him, so also should the monks feel.[463] He takes no position on nihilism, either for or against. It is not relevant, it is distracting, and it is not the point of suffering.

The same judgement is rendered on the question of the nature of the *Tathāgata*. Whether the *Tathāgata* exists, does not exist, both does and does not, neither does nor does not exist, are not fit questions because the *Tathāgata*-nature precludes the arising of such questions. It is like trying to decide where a fire goes after the fuel is extinguished. When the fuel is gone the debate as to fire's nature is academic only, of no relevance. Thus Vaccha is instructed: "that material shape by which one recognising the *Tathāgata* might recognise him–that material shape has been got rid of by the *Tathāgata*, cut off at the root, made like a palm-tree stump that

---

[461] D II, 65-66.
[462] M I, 87-88.
[463] *Ibid.*, 180.

can come to no further existence and is not liable to arise again in the future." The *Tathāgata* is "deep, immeasurable, unfathomable as is the great ocean." So also is this true for the other four *khandhas* of feeling, perception, habitual tendencies, and consciousness.[464]

The Buddha repeatedly refers to and argues with Jain opponents on the matter of the need for an explanation, a view. They held that pleasure and pain are caused by prior deeds or by some Overlord. If this is true, then the suffering through self-denial which the Jains pursue in their quest for liberation from rebirth must show that their past lives were full of evil deeds. Their quest is fruitless, and they are bound by a false concern with explanation and doctrine. The monk who follows the right path is in fact indifferent to the cause of anguish, to the explanation of its source. This very indifference leads to equanimity, detachment and finally release: "While he is indifferent to that source of anguish, through (his) developing equanimity there is detachment for him. Even so is that anguish also worn away for him."[465]

The Brahmin who casts out speculation concerning the future and the past knows that he is tranquil and without grasping. The one who maintains that course is said to be on the right path to *nibbāna*. By contrast the one who grasps after speculation concerning the future and the past may conclude that he is tranquil and without grasping; but that very realization is itself grasping and not conducive to *nibbāna*.[466] Fretting over the destiny of the self in the future and arguing about the causes of suffering in the past preclude right understanding. The proper view of the past and future is this: of the past one should think "'Such was my material shape in the distant past' and delight therein," and so also for the future, and for the other *khandhas*. As for the present, present things are of concern to those who say that the shape (*rūpa*) is the self or in the self, that self is in the shape or is the shape, and so also for feeling, perception, habitual tendencies and consciousness. But the instructed disciple is not drawn away from his concentration by such unnecessary concerns.[467]

The world's folk are concerned with existence and non-existence (*atthitā, natthitā*). With respect to these, the major alternatives in any philosophical system, the rightly-guided and insightful monk, who sees things as they really are, takes the following positions: he does not accept the non-existence of the world, nor the existence of the world. Why? Because he sees that systems of explanation are irrelevant to things as they really are. They have no basis other than the desire of and for the

---

[464] M II, 165-166.
[465] M III, 10-11; *cf.* A IV, 124.
[466] M III, 23-24.
[467] *Ibid.*.

296

self.[468]

The *Tathāgata* approaches neither the extreme of non-existence nor the extreme of existence, and teaches the doctrine of the middle way, co-dependent origination.[469] The grasping after systems is denied along with the grasping after forms, consciousness, feeling, the activities and perception. "Thus the one who abandons home, who makes no ties, wages wordy warfare no longer. The craving for systems, mental standpoint and dogma will no longer be in him."[470] There is no more guessing at the far-off future. There is no stubborn perversity with respect to doctrines and dogmas pertaining to existence and non-existence, the *khandhas*, the *Tathāgata*, the *āsavas*, or any other element of suffering.[471]

The untaught manyfolk, as we have seen, suffer because they seek a dogma corresponding to an unchanging reality, especially the reality of the self. It is their hope that the self is form or formlessness, consciousness or unconsciousness, or feeling, or another of the *khandhas* and its opposite. Thus from them one hears such pronouncements as "I am," "things will have body," "things will have no body," "things will be conscious," "things will be unconscious," and so forth. They believe these things because they desire to believe them, instead of realizing that the very grasping after views is conducive to the arising of suffering and not to the cessation of suffering.[472] Those who hold the view, for example, that the body is the self are in fact engaging in an activity (*sankhāra*), which is nourished by feeling born of contact with ignorance, and thus does craving arise. Whether one defines self as body or self as possessing body or self as in body, whether one identifies self with feeling, or possessed by feeling or in feeling and so on for the other *khandhas*, makes little difference in the end. For such convictions are activities that arise from craving and are conducive to craving. By contrast the one who knows that these views are arising from desire is able to destroy the *āsavas*, the chains binding him to these processes of deception, ignorance and desire, and to be free.[473]

Among those who pursue philosophical speculation in order to reconcile it with the teachings of the Buddha we find a more sophisticated level of argument and conclusion. But even this professional philosophizing, which amounts to seeking the "irrefutable" formulation of the truth of liberation from suffering, is subject to the same critique as the views of the manyfolk. For example, one Yamaka held the view that when a monk

---

[468] S II, 13.
[469] *Ibid.*.
[470] S III, 10-11.
[471] *Ibid.*, 39-40.
[472] *Ibid.*, 40-41.
[473] *Ibid.*, 80-84.

has destroyed the *āsavas*, after the breaking up of the body he does not become again. In refuting this position Sāriputta inquires whether the body is permanent, is impermanent, whether the *Tathāgata* has a body, is feeling, perception, activities, consciousness, is in any of these things, is possessed by any of these states, and whether the *Tathāgata* is distinct from any of these *khandhas*. The answer given in each instance is no. Sāriputta then concludes that "since in this very life [*diṭṭh' eva dhamme*] a *Tathāgata* is not to be regarded as existing in truth, in reality," it is not proper to assert that when the *āsavas* are destroyed, the body does not become after death. Body is impermanent; what is impermanent is *dukkha*; what is *dukkha*, that has been destroyed.[474] One must abandon the lust, craving, the grasping after systems, dogmas, and mental biases concerning any of the *khandhas*. When that is done, then they are cut off and abandoned, and *dukkha* is overcome. Simply put, the belief in the *khandhas*, according to any philosophical presupposition such as eternalism or nihilism, stands directly in the path of right insight. It is the hardest thing to abandon as well, for it seduces one into thinking that belief will lead to release.[475]

Māra's bondsmen are those who hold fast to belief in propositions, to systems and dogma. They have conceits. There are four conceits; *taṇhā*, *diṭṭhi*, the eternalist view, or *sassatadiṭṭhi*, and the annihilationist view, or *uccedadiṭṭhi*. To believe that "I am," as well as to believe that "I am not," that I shall be or shall not, that I am unconscious, that I am both, that I am neither—all is conceit, and subject to the exploits of Māra. Instead of being irrefutable dogma these views are all subject to guilty waverings and doubtings. To abide fast one must comprehend the irrelevance of belief on the one hand and its seductive nature on the other: " 'I am' is vain imagining.... With heart that has slain conceit will we abide...."[476]

Thus one returns to the ultimate questions but not as one in search of dogma; for the answers are not given. To the question of whether the *Tathāgata* exists there is no answer. As well one might ask how many grains of sand line the Ganges, how many drops are in the ocean. The questions are in principle answerable; but they are also pointless, and yield no insight into the question of suffering.[477] There is always the danger of misunderstanding, for the questioner seeks some clear position to accept or reject, and the respondent is seduced into thinking that what is true is the same as what is believed. Gotama therefore refuses to answer the question of whether there is a self. He explains that if he

---

[474] *Ibid.*, 94-96.
[475] *Ibid.*, 138.
[476] S IV, 134-135.
[477] *Ibid.*, 67.

says yes, he would be counted among the eternalists, and if no, among the annihilationists. If he said yes the principle of *anicca* would be lost; if he said no, his questioner would conclude, "formerly indeed I had a self, but now I have not one anymore." Confusion would be the inevitable result, for the questioner would be utterly misled as to the nature of the *Dhamma*.[478] The concern with views and doctrine leads only to desire and thus to suffering.[479]

The Unguarded Citta

The danger present in the corruption of view, in the concern with *diṭṭhi*, opinion, itself depends upon the failure to guard the central function of understanding, namely the *citta*, translated variously "mind" or "heart." The variety of choice is significant, for it rightly suggests that the *citta* is the most intimate and powerful operation by which one apprehends either the truth of suffering or the world through the senses. The corruption of the heart stems from the desire and lust (*chanda, rāga*) which is in the eye, the ear, the nose, the tongue, the body and the mind. In other words the perceptions constantly threaten the original purity and luminosity of the mind.[480]

Thus the wayward monk Devadatta was bound to hell because he failed to gain control of his *citta* and was thus mastered by eight corrupt states, viz. gain, loss, fame, obscurity, honor, lack of honor, evil intentions and evil friendship. With his mind out of control (*pariyādinnacitta*), he was doomed to irreprievable suffering in hell for a long time. With his mind unmastered the *āsavas*, the cankers, arose. He was full of distress and anguish.[481]

The corruption of the mind is one of the four perversions, along with perversion of perception (*saññā*), thought, and view (*diṭṭhi*). These four perversions indicate the precise failure to comprehend the nature of things as they are, and turn the truth on its head. Thus it is thought that in the impermanent there is permanence (*anicca, nicca*), in the not-ill there is Ill (*adukkha, dukkha*), in the not-self there is self (*anattā, attā*) and in the foul there is fair (*asubha, subha*). Those who are thus distracted are called creatures of unsound mind.[482]

The corruption of the *citta* is counted among the causes of rebirth, along with the failure of morals (*sīla*) and view (*diṭṭhi*). For such persons there is rebirth "in the Waste, the Way of Woe, ...Downfall, ...Purgatory."[483] The depravity of the mind is attributed to greed, aversion and

---

[478] *Ibid.*, 281-282.
[479] SN 128.
[480] S III, 183-185.
[481] A IV, 109-110.
[482] A II, 61.
[483] A I, 247-248.

ignorance, *lobha*, *dosa*, and *moha*. In turn these defilements are related
to the pleasures of the senses, freedom from which is essential to the purity of the *citta*. The unguarded *citta*, then, is an extremely important
condition of suffering. What corrupts the *citta* is sense pleasure, which
arises from sensation.[484] Also, the mind can be overcome with passion
(*rāga*) and one loses control of the *citta*, as happened to Devadatta.[485]
When thought is unguarded, furthermore, bodily action, speech and mental action are out of control. Such a person is a prey to lust, and his will
cannot resist. His mind, words and deeds become "rotten [*pūtika*]," and
his death is unauspicious.[486]

All of the foregoing warnings and analyses presume a state of purity
of *citta* that is constantly threatened by perception, sensation, passion,
aversion and ignorance. The *citta* is "luminous" in essence, that is, transparent, for it has no qualitative characteristics that distort the purity of
truth that shines through it. When unguarded, that is, when susceptible
to the corruption of attachment to perception, sensation, and the other
khandhas, it becomes tainted. Thus the contrast is drawn between the
pure state of the *citta* and its corrupted state. The former has no qualities or characteristics of its own but is simply a conduit through which
the light of liberating truth shines. This is the understanding of the enlightened. But the uneducated common people believe that the mind has
qualities. These qualities are, however, simply the distortions and taints
stemming from perception, sensation and passion. For them "there is no
cultivation of the mind."[487] Rather, their mind, *citta*, is said to run to
and fro.[488] They "scatter thought afar."[489]

Nutriments of Suffering

Another perspective on the causes of suffering is found in the treatment of the nutriments (*āhāras*). As part of the causal nexus of *dukkha* the
nutriments, as their name implies, feed conditions conducive to *dukkha*.
With respect to ignorance and its consequences, for example, it is said
that although there is no initial point prior to which ignorance (*avijjā*)
does not exist, it nevertheless has its nutriment. The five hindrances-
sensuality, ill-will, sloth and torpor, excitement and worry, doubt [490]
-are the nutriments of ignorance. In turn, the five hindrances have their
nutriment, the "three wrong ways of practice."[491] In turn their nutriment

---

[484] M I, 119-120.
[485] A I, 196.
[486] *Ibid.*, 240.
[487] *Ibid.*, 8.
[488] S I, 52.
[489] SN 58.
[490] *Cf.* D III, list of fives, 224-230.
[491] *Cf. Ibid.*, list of threes, 207-214.

is failure to restrain the sense faculties. The series continues through lack of mindfulness and self-composure, lack of thorough work of mind, lack of faith, failure to listen to the true *Dhamma*, and not following the "very man," *i.e.* the *Tathāgata*. The series reversed leads back to ignorance.[492]

The revulsion from nutriment is one of the nine perceptions, together with perception of ugliness, of death, disaffection with everything worldly, impermanence, suffering in impermanence, non-soul in that which suffers, elimination, and passionlessness.[493] The argument here is that a condition requires a nutriment in order to exist. The reversal of the causal series in the direction of liberation and knowledge thus requires the removal of the nutriment. The condition, further, takes its nature and form from its nutriment. Thus when consciousness arises because of eye and material shapes, it is known as visual consciousness, and so forth for other conditions.[494] Thus, for example, perplexity has doubt as its nutriment. When doubt is removed, perplexity loses its nourishment and ceases. The seeing of things as they really are includes the knowledge that perplexity has doubt as its nutriment. The origination of perplexity is thus tied to the presence of doubt; and knowledge of this in itself is sufficient to end the relationship between the nourishing doubt and its effect of perplexity. Thus the monk must think: perplexity has arisen, it has arisen because of the nutriment of doubt, it may cease with the cessation of the nutriment, and by perfect wisdom the nutriment and the state it nourishes cease.[495]

Four sustenances are identified as specific nutriments of the progression toward affliction and despair. These are: (1) solid food, whether coarse or fine; (2) contact; (3) willing of mind (*manosañcetanā*); and (4) consciousness. Thus the desire for food forms the nourishing base for consciousness. Name-and-form follows consciousness, activities follow name-and-form and so forth for the establishment of the *khandhas*. For the future there is only the prospect of renewed becoming and rebirth, decay-and-death, and grief, affliction and despair. The same progression is described in the cause of the other three *āhāras*. This simile is offered:

> Just as if a dyer...or a painter, if...by dye, or lac, or turmeric, or indigo or madder, or a well-polished panel or wall or strip of cloth can fashion a woman's shape or a man's shape complete in all its parts, even so, brethren, if there be passion, delight, craving as to any one of these four foods, there consciousness, being firmly placed, becomes fruitful. Where consciousness is firmly placed and fruitful, there is descent of name-and-shape,

---

[492] A V, 79-80.
[493] D III, 263.
[494] M I, 315f..
[495] *Ibid.*.

etc..[496]

The *āhāras* form the sustaining foundation for beings that have "come to birth or for the forwarding of them that seek to become." In turn, the sustenances are based in craving, craving is based in feeling, feeling in contact, contact in name-and-form, name-and-form in the senses (*saḷāyatana*) and so forth through consciousness of name- and shape-activities and finally to ignorance of the activities. The series is reversed to explain the link between ignorance and the subsequent causal steps. In this particular interpretation, however, the emphasis is placed on the nutriments, which provide the conditions for the maintenance of beings in this and future lives.

The significance of the nutriments, therefore, is two-fold: (a) their role as providing the sustaining power for the conditions they feed; and (b) their role in sustaining beings in their present state, leading to future effects in future births. Thus the Buddhist view is concerned not only with the dynamic aspects of the causal relations of states of being but also with the forces that sustain each of these states. That which provides sustenance is as essential as that which causes the development into the next state. Nevertheless, consistent with all other facets of the analysis of the state of *dukkha*, the nutriments are themselves dependent, for example, upon craving: "From the uprising of craving [*taṇhā*] is the uprising of sustenance, from the stopping of craving is the stopping of sustenance."[497]

"Latent Tendencies"/Anusayas

In the analysis of *dukkha* the Buddhist tradition takes as the field of its concern the dynamic of experience. But experience is not ever construed merely in terms of interaction between a stable subject and the world at large, the manifold external other. Rather, it is the dynamic of the false "self" that constitutes the key to understanding. In discussing nutriments, for example, the nutriments are never conceived of as external but as causal conditions of the experiencing person. In the concept of the latent tendencies, the *anusayas*, the tradition focuses upon "unconscious" tendencies of, among others, attraction, repulsion, and ignorance which characterize the bound self. One must use the term "unconscious" here with care, for it does not imply actual "levels," or even one "level" of the self. Still, the nature of this category of experience is such that it does correspond to what Freud means by "unconscious." The person who is not freed is bound by these tendencies, he is unaware of them, and they are said to be both latent and inherent. Moreover, they constitute a major hindrance to liberation, for they are a major and unacknowledged cause of attachment.

---

[496] S II, 71.
[497] M I, 59.

The *Dīgha Nikāya* lists seven kinds of latent bias or tendencies: "the bias of sensual passion, of enmity, of false opinion, of doubt, of conceit, of lust for rebirth, of ignorance [*kāmânusaya, paṭighânusaya, diṭṭh-*, *vicikicch-*, *mān-*, *bhavarāg-*, *avijj-*]."[498] The significance of these types is that they constitute major causes of suffering and hindrances to cessation of suffering. Let us examine the link between the latent tendencies and feelings. Feelings are said to be expressions of latent tendencies. So it is said: "A tendency to attachment [*rāgânusaya*] lies latent in pleasant feeling; a tendency to repugnance [*paṭighânusaya*] lies latent in painful feeling; a tendency to ignorance [*avijjânusaya*] lies latent in a neutral feeling."[499] The arising of suffering is not a consequence of the feeling itself, it should be understood, but of the "latent bias" present in the feeling. Feeling in and of itself can be freed of the *anusaya*. What the monk must accomplish is the separation or annihilation of the tendency to attachment that is latent in pleasant feelings, the tendency to repulsion inherent in unpleasant feelings, and the tendency to ignorance inherent in neutral feelings. That is, what obstructs the monk in the striving for the cessation of suffering are the unconscious desires to possess, to reject, and to be ignorant which the latent biases represent. That these biases are latent is significant; for only in the alteration of perception and understanding of feelings, which the discipline makes possible, is the fact of the existence of the *anusayas* realized.[500]

These tendencies are said to be rooted in the very nature of being, and to precede experience. It seems strange, one may argue, to attribute to "an innocent baby lying on his back" a state of desire and ignorance. Nevertheless, this baby is bound by the five fetters of false view of own-body, perplexity, clinging to rites and customs, the desire for sense pleasures, and malevolence. The cause is to be found in the latent biases which the baby possesses, bias toward own-body, toward perplexity, and the other fetters.[501] Thus the inherent tendencies are attributed not solely to nurture, but to nature as well. They are innate in the structure of the person, at least from the beginning of a life. Simple experience in the world would not alone cause attachment, repulsion, or ignorance. Rather there must be an inherent tendency toward these states.

Experience, or the consciousness of things, is but one element in the explanation of attachment, repulsion and ignorance. The relationship between sensation and the inherent biases can be expressed in the following way: the experience of pleasure leads to delight in that feeling, because a

---

[498] D III, 237.
[499] M I, 365ff.; *cf.* M III, 334.
[500] M I, 365ff..
[501] M II, 102-103.

latent tendency to attachment exists. Similarly, painful experience leads to repulsion because a latent tendency toward repugnance exists. Finally, an experience that is neither painful nor pleasant produces confusion, because a latent tendency toward ignorance exists.[502] This is true for the other senses of hearing, taste, touch, smell and mind. As we have already seen, attachment, repulsion and ignorance are latent tendencies inherent in the "structure" of the "person," rather than derivatives of the feelings themselves. It is the latent tendencies, not the feelings, that give rise to suffering. The Ariyan disciple may turn from sense objects by acknowledging the feelings of which they are the cause while at the same time rooting out the latent tendencies.[503]

The remarkable story of the death of Upasena illustrates the relationship between feelings and latent tendencies. Upasena, who was bitten by a poisonous snake, asked that his body be removed from the house in which he was to die and be taken outside to be "scattered like chaff." He explained that for one who believes that the eye is "mine" or the tongue, or the mind, etc., the coming of death would cause a change in the body. But for one who had quelled the inherent tendencies that make for I and mine (ahaṃkāra-mamaṃkāra-mānānusaya) the body lacked only the end of this person, Upasena, to become chaff, for it had no constituent parts, that is, the anusayas. Without them there was no body. Accordingly, upon his death, Upasena's body was moved outside and scattered like chaff. It had no substance, for its latent tendencies had been annihilated. This is a dramatic account of the dependency of the belief in body upon the inherent desires; but more, the story illustrates unmistakably the analysis of the body as latent, unconscious desire, and the principle of anattā. When the latent desires no longer work, the body "ceases."[504]

In contrast, the untaught manyfolk think that feeling is reality, and therefore they reject, or are ignorant of, the truth of the nature of feeling. Their entire existence is trapped in the pain-pleasure spectrum. They fail to comprehend that the feelings they experience are of no ultimate value, and are therefore enmeshed in the eternal round of suffering and rebirth. They know no refuge from pain but pleasure.[505] They are in bondage to pain, to pleasure, to neutral feeling, and thus to ignorance; they are bound to birth, death, sorrow and grief, woe, lamentation and despair. In contrast, the disciple knows the reality of feelings, their arising and cessation, and is therefore not trapped into attraction, repulsion, and ignorance.

As with all the other aspects of the causes of suffering the latent

---

[502] M III, 334f..
[503] Ibid., 335-336.
[504] S IV, 20-21.
[505] Ibid., 139-141.

tendencies are not external elements but essential to the dynamic of the person. They are brought into play, as are the other causal factors, in experience; but the mere data of experience do not determine the state of suffering. Rather, the innate "processes" of the self must come into play before bondage is established. The nature of these tendencies is highly significant; they are tendencies of desire, that is, the desires of attachment, of repugnance and of ignorance. These three constitute the entire range of alternatives in the unliberated relationship between the self and the world. One may love in order to be loved, or seek to reject and hate, and be unable to do either because of confusion, failure to comprehend, and reluctance to understand. This view of the self suggests that there is no dichotomy, or dualism, between external and internal life, between subject and object. Thus perception and sensation—that is to say, experience—may be analyzed and understood in precisely the same series of alternatives, as that which exists in the self, even at birth. The dependence between them implies that the distinction between nature and nurture is a false one, and that the nature of suffering is exhausted in the same way in both the "inner" and the "outer" worlds; indeed this inner/outer distinction is academic at best and misleading at worst. The unconscious world of the *anusayas* and the perception world of experience together comprise the reality of suffering. Each is dependent upon the other, and neither may be claimed as self-subsistent (*sva-bhāva*). Thus the monk who asks what knowledge leads to the end of "latent conceits" and their influence in this "consciousness-formed body and all the phenomena external to it" is told that when he thinks of material shape, feeling, perception, the habitual tendencies and consciousness as not mine, not I, not myself, there are no longer any latent conceits.[506]

Will

Complementing the latent tendencies and their role as a cause of *dukkha* is *cetanā*, usually translated "will," in the sense of "volition." In employing these terms the "manifest" (as opposed to latent) quality of this operation of the self is emphasized. Further, will is to be distinguished from the latent *anusayas* in that it is not a tendency but rather a general quality of the nature of *kamma*, or action. For example, the body, while neither one's own nor another's, is said to be caused by four factors: the actions of the past; "plans" (*abhisankhata*); volitions or will; and feeling.[507]

Willing leads to "persistence of consciousness," to the growth of consciousness, to the sense of self, and thus to rebirth, death and decay, grief and suffering. In contrast, by not willing, no object of consciousness,

---

[506] M III, 68.
[507] S II, 44-45.

no persistence of consciousness, no self and no rebirth arise.[508] It is
also true that will (cetanā), rightly employed, may bring about the end
of kamma, in the sense that no action results, no self is sustained, no
rebirth arises. There are four categories of deeds according to the tradition: (1) "dark deeds, dark in result [kammā kaṇhā]"; (2) "bright deeds,
bright in result [kammā sukhā]"; (3) deeds both dark and bright in nature; (4) deeds neither dark nor bright, "the deed that conduces to the
destruction of deeds." Only the fourth category is conducive to the end of
kamma. Cetanā is said to determine success in the desirable fourth type.
"Where...there is the will [cetanā] to get rid of" each of the first three
types, "this...is called the deed that is not dark (and) not bright, neither
dark nor bright in result, the deed that conduces to the destruction of
deeds."[509]

The pivotal nature and significance of will suggests that it is not
will itself that is the cause of dukkha, but rather the object of the will.
Cetanā is, as we have seen, an element of the co-dependent series; that
is, it does not belong outside the general nature of suffering. However,
like all elements of the series it is understood to be subject to and cause
of either suffering or the release from suffering; and in this respect it
participates in the cause of suffering as well as the causes of the cessation
of suffering.

Mind/Mano

Mind, in Buddhist epistemology, is one of the senses. Mind is the
natural capacity for apprehending ideas, in a manner analogous to that
capacity by which the eye apprehends shapes. In this respect especially
mind, mano, should be distinguished from citta. The operation and significance of mind is reminiscent of will/volition, cetanā. Just as one's willing
may lead through action to suffering, mind is said to be the forerunner
of things (dhammā) not conducive to enlightenment (akusalā). The famous first lines of the Dhammapada summarize this teaching: "Things
[dhammā] are forerun by mind [mano], have mind as best, are compounds
of the mind."[510]

Although mano is regarded as one of the six senses, so that this
judgement logically applies also to eye, ear, nose, and so forth, mind
occupies a more exalted and influential position in acknowledgement of
the importance of ideas and consciousness in the scheme of things. The
Dhammapada continues: "If with corrupted mind a man do speak, or act,
therefore ill [dukkha] follows him as shall the foot of drawing (beast)."[511]

---

[508] Ibid., 45.
[509] M II, 57-58.
[510] Dh, 3, n.p.
[511] Ibid..

As mind is inclined, so the consequences follow. Specifically, those consequences are expressed in terms of *dukkha* and *dhammā*. Whether this latter term should be understood in the technical sense of later Buddhists in this passage, that is, as specific beings in themselves, or the *Ding an sich*, or in the sense of entities in general which have potential for corruption is unclear. What does seem clear is that things in the world and the conceiving of them (as ideas) are inseparable, that the resulting being is a consequence of mind's operation, and that from it *dukkha* may arise. This latter interpretation seems to be the proper one for the *Dhammapada* passage cited.[512] Again, the cause of suffering lies not in the things themselves, whatever interpretation of *dhammā* is elected, but in the operation of the mind, *mano*. This understanding of mind should not be construed in the same manner as the more general usage of the term "mind," which may encompass will, thought, conceptualization, brain activities, and other elements. Nevertheless, the locus of interest for the tradition, and for its assessment of the cause of suffering, centers on the "internal" life, here specifically the operation of apprehending ideas.

Kamma and Saṃsāra

In the context of Indian culture the issue of suffering and its cause must, finally, turn to the working out of the effects of past experience—and not merely "acts," as we shall see. As is well known Gotama accepted the traditional notion that one's present status is the consequence of past actions. Suffering, as the definitive characteristic of human life, has causes. It was the purpose of the series of co-dependent origination to explicate the relationship between suffering and the cause of suffering. Physical death did not constitute the end of the series, any more than physical birth constituted its beginning. The self was not body, any more than it was sensation, perception, or any of the five aggregates. Thus traditional inquiries into the possible future consequences of present actions extended into future lives—many thousands of them, indeed, an infinity of them. They extended backwards as well, to search out the past causes of the present situation. Furthermore, however, the causal matrix of suffering—here defined, as everywhere, as life itself—must be comprehended as applicable in the same manner to the question of future and past lives as to any "moment" of the co-dependent series. It is a fallacy to be concerned with the body as the self; and therefore the analysis of *kamma* and its effects has no unique treatment of the physical body.

The Buddha does accept traditional morality. When asked whether it is correct to teach that whatever pleasure, pain or any mental state one experiences is the consequence of a previous act—a matter of considerable concern to his persistent opponents, the Jains—he admits that there is a

---

[512] *Cf.* A I, 9.

measure of truth in this opinion. Suffering has many causes, he agrees: bile, phlegm, wind, union of bodily humors, changes of seasons, stress of untoward happenings, sudden attacks from without, and ripeness of one's *kamma*. This the world holds to be true. But he warns that rigorous correlation between previous acts and present experience is an extreme view.[513]

Immorality in deeds, however, has clear consequences extending beyond this life. Ānanda points out that immorality of deed leads to guilt, to bad repute in the community, and confusion even until death. At the breaking up of the body the immoral one is born in Woe, in Purgatory.[514] Furthermore, deeds sow effects that are reaped according to their nature. Following the four-fold classification of dark deeds, bright deeds, deeds both dark and bright, and deeds neither dark nor bright, it is said that one who performs harmful deeds is born into a harmful world, suffers harmful contact (*phassa*), harmful feelings (*vedanā*), and suffers generally "just as beings do in Purgatory." Those whose deeds are not harmful are born into a world without harmful contact or feeling, one of "utter bliss, such as [that of] the ever radiant devas." He whose deeds are a mixture is born into a world of both pleasure and pain. But he who by proper willing (*cetanā*) wills to abandon dark, bright, and both bright and dark, brings all deeds to an end.[515]

Just as it is equally incorrect to say that the Buddha was a determinist or an indeterminist, the issue of the exact nature of the relationship between deeds and effects turns not upon any system of external cause and effect but upon intention, and upon the presence or absence of the proper goal, that is, whether the act is devoted to release or to bondage, whether it is *kusala* or *akusala*, conducive or non-conducive to release. One may wish to attain a heavenly existence; so the devas encourage the venerable but dying Citta to aspire to a birth as a *rājā*, a world ruler, because in him they (correctly) see a virtuous man. But such a goal, Citta responds, is a transient thing. One must be possessed of an unwavering and certain faith in the Buddha, the *Dhamma* and the *Sangha*. Nothing was more important. The concern for how one will be born, and what past lives led to the present state, is in the Buddha's eyes a dangerous and distracting matter; for while it is undoubtedly true that the flow of co-dependent origination links past, present and future in causal relationship, the truth of *anicca* renders meaningless the questions concerning where the "self" has come from and where it is going. Thus on the one hand the causal connection is accepted, but the mechanical analysis of cause and effect, centered on the supposedly eternal *attā*, the

---

[513] S IV, 155-156.
[514] A I, 57.
[515] A II, 238-239.

308

soul with which so many of his questioners were concerned, is rejected. When a warrior asked the Buddha whether he would be reborn in the company of the devas of passionate delight, the Buddha refuses to answer the question at first–a good indication that the question itself was not a fruitful one.[516] Whereas the traditional morality of the warrior's teachers held that strength in battle would surely be rewarded after death–in the manner of all supernatural justifications of warring–the Buddha knew the situation to be otherwise: "The taking of life...do I know, and the fruits thereof, and how, practising, one who takes life is reborn...in Purgatory, that also do I know."[517] The Buddha's knowledge extends also to the taking of what is not given, of sensual passion, falsehood, backbiting, bitter speech, idle babble, covetousness, hatred and ill-will, and perverted view.[518] In these sources of rebirth it is the absence of moral culture (sīla), of insight (paññā), of the disciplined citta that is the fundamental cause.

What is subject to rebirth? This question is important; for all presumed self-entities, whether body, perception, consciousness, and so forth, are not eternal things that could provide the continuum of rebirth. What is reborn, what is subject to rebirth, is "the all.... What all? The eye, brethren, is subject to rebirth," as are the objects as apprehended by the eye. The same is true for the other five senses, including mano and its objects. That is to say, the whole of the sensing activities, qua activities, are subject to rebirth, as they are impermanent, woeful, void of self. It is the task of the monk to know that the senses are subject to rebirth and impermanent, for in being known they are fully comprehended and the monk's consciousness is conducive to the cessation of suffering.

If we address the question of rebirth in the context not of the individual identity, or body, or any of the other khandhas, but rather in terms of sensation, objects and experience, then we must conclude that rebirth is a "permanent" characteristic of life, from one moment to the next–and, at least according to the following analogy, less than that. The passing away of things, which is tantamount to their death and birth, is as swift as if a man said of four mighty archers, one in each quarter, " 'I will catch and bring the shafts let fly by these four archers mighty with the bow...or ever they reach the ground.' Brethren, as is the speed of that man, as is the speed of moon and sun swifter than he, as is the speed of those spirits who run ahead of moon and sun swifter than he, swifter than them both, so swifter than even these is the passing away of the things of this life."[519] When investigating the matters of death, rebirth, and the effects

---

[516] Cf. S IV, 216-217.
[517] Ibid., 246.
[518] Ibid..
[519] S II, 178.

of actions, thoughts and deeds we find that the analysis of the causes of suffering do not differ in principle between the issues of life after death and life from moment to moment. *Anicca* is the fundamental principle in both instances. It was on the failure to understand this fundamental truth that the Buddha's questioners frequently foundered.

Just as in other metaphysical speculation, concern with the future of the body, its past, and its present, is like worrying about whether the world is or is not eternal, whether it is finite or infinite, whether the *Tathāgata* does or does not exist after death; concern for the body is unprofitable. Such concern does not "conduce to Nibbāna." Thus while the Buddha accepts a relationship between past, present and future, this concern is neither limited to the past, present and future of the physical body nor does it presume a continuous existence which may be said to be the subject of past, present or future. Again and again he urges: "Reason thus: This is Ill, this is the arising of Ill, this is the ceasing of Ill, this is the practice that leads to the ceasing of Ill."[520]

When addressing issues of past causes for present situations Gotama appears actually to reject one or another version of the classic doctrine of *kamma* and its effects in future lives, or *saṃsāra*. For example, in the account of two classes of beings, he denies that he ever taught a doctrine of the "beginning of things" which held that the nature of a past life determined the present situation. What he did not teach is either that self-control in a past life guarantees permanence and eternal uncorrupted life or that debauchery in the past leads, through corruption of self-control, to a transient and impermanent existence, a dying away from the eternal life of the saints. In other words, the present situation—and the situation in this example has specifically to do with release, death and rebirth—is not determined by the previous state. What the Buddha did teach is that whether the being was debauched, release may be seen for what it is: "Whenever one attains to the stage of deliverance [*vimokha*], entitled the Beautiful, one is then aware 'Tis lovely!"[521]

The focus here is not upon a mechanical determinism but upon release, which is, so to speak, where you find it, rather than controlled by an inexorable natural law. Another example of the Buddha's understanding of *kamma* and *saṃsāra* is to be found, by implication, in the remarkable tale of the suicide Channa. Traditional morality condemned suicide, and Gotama himself found the act of laying down one body and taking up another one to be blameworthy. However, Channa, prior to his suicide, having been instructed by the disciple Sāriputta, comprehends that there is only arising and ceasing to be, that there is no self. His enlightenment apparently complete, Channa cuts his windpipe. Responding

---

[520] S V, 354.
[521] D III, 28-32.

to the inquiries of Sāriputta and Cunda, the Buddha holds that Channa is not blameworthy: "For whoso...lays down one body and takes up another body, of him I say 'He is to blame'; but it is not so with brother Channa. Without reproach was the knife used by brother Channa."[522] Once more, what is significant is not the act itself, even if it be suicide, but the disposition of the doer. Furthermore, in the context of the issue of *kamma* and *saṃsāra* Gotama implies that the act will have no deleterious consequences in a future life, contrary to the implied judgement of the contemporary morality. This appears to suggest that the consequences of the acts may be exhausted, although the acts themselves be performed, if the actor is enlightened.

Even for those not enlightened, further, consequences of acts need not be played out in future lives but may be "extinguished," in the sense of the burning out of fuel, in this present moment. The story of Ångulimāla is instructive. On his way to meet the Buddha Ångulimāla suffered numerous injuries from a falling clod of earth, a thrown stick, and thrown gravel, so that he arrived in the Buddha's presence bleeding and tattered, his begging bowl smashed. "Endure this," the Buddha said. "You are experiencing here and now the ripening of that *kamma* through the ripening of which you would (otherwise) boil in Niraya Hell for many years, many hundreds...thousands of years."[523] This teaching was instrumental in Ångulimāla's subsequent experience of the "bliss of freedom [*vimuttisukha*]." Indeed, for those who seek the end of *dukkha*, the wearing out or "experiencing" of a deed's effects takes place in this life. "Some trifling evil deed" may take one to hell to atone for it if one "is careless in culture of body, habits and thought [*sīla, citta, kāya*]. He has not developed insight [*paññā*], he is insignificant, his soul is restricted [*appātumo*], his life is restricted and miserable [*dukkha*]." But for one who is cultured in body, habits and thought, who has developed insight, whose life is "immeasurable," who is great-souled, his small offence will be expiated in experience (*vedanā*) in this very life.[524] In short it is not the deeds that effect results but the nature of the doer.

The difference between the Buddha's understanding of the effects of past actions and that of the Jains, which was in essence deterministic, is evident in a dialogue with the Jain Vappa (who is reported to have subsequently joined the *Sangha*). The question of the effects of the *āsavas* (the persistent effects) of bodily activities, of speech, of vexation and distress arising from ignorance, upon those who follow the Ariyan path is raised. Vappa had argued that these *āsavas* must have effects even upon a monk. But the Buddha argues that for one who abstains from

---

[522] S IV, 32-33.
[523] M II, 289-290.
[524] A I, 228.

bodily activities that cause vexation and distress "these āsavas causing pain do not exist in him. He does no fresh deed; as to his former deed, he wears it out by constant contact [phassa-phassa.]" Though he sees objects, tastes, touches, hears, smells and cognises he "is neither elated nor depressed but rests indifferent, mindful and comprehending." The effects of the āsavas are for him like the stump of a tree which is utterly destroyed, so that it and its shadow utterly disappear, and never arise again. Vappa failed to distinguish between the experience and the nature of him who experiences. For the monk who is indifferent, mindful and comprehending, though there be acts of sensation there is no effect, and the āsavas are utterly destroyed.[525]

Kamma, then, is not necessarily a cause of suffering. The issue is not the deed itself, past, present or future, but the nature of doer.

Nāgārjuna's commentary illustrates the view of karma and saṃsāra from the perspective of emptiness, śūnyata, and suggests the fallacies present in the traditional determinist view. The traditional doctrine of saṃsāra holds that there is an ongoing causal series that determines the nature and state of the soul. Nāgārjuna argues that the teaching of the Tathāgata that the state anterior to saṃsāra, that is, anterior to the life and death cycle, and anterior to the realm of empirical existence, cannot be grasped; for there is no beginning of things. If we should hold that birth is anterior and old age and death posterior, this implies the existence of birth without old age and death, or the existence of a deathless being. If birth is posterior and old age and death anterior, the opposite difficulty arises; for we cannot conceive of a non-existent, unborn being, to whom old age and death do not apply. A simultaneously born and unborn being is an impossible contradiction, as is the idea of one neither born nor unborn. In short, any causal connection between birth and death is inconceivable, and for this reason saṃsāra cannot be explained with respect to origins.[526]

Similar difficulties arise when we ask what it is that is said to transmigrate from existence to existence. For example, if we reject the body, for obvious reasons, could it be said that mental conformations (saṃskāra; Pāli: sankhāra) transmigrate? If we hold that the saṃskāras are permanent entities it cannot be said that they move from one state to another, for this would deny their eternal nature. On the other hand, if we hold that they are impermanent, there is nothing to transmigrate. The same is true for any notion of individuality. "Anything moving from one (sensual) grasping [upādāna] to another will be without a body or form. How does a bodiless or non-grasping thing ever transmigrate?" The same objections apply even with respect to the attainment of nirvāṇa. None of these

---

[525] A II, 208-211.
[526] Inada, 85-87.

supposed elements of transmigration can attain *nirvāṇa* any more than they can be said to transmigrate. The radical conclusion is this: "Where *nirvāṇa* is (subject to) establishment and *saṃsāra* not (subject to) disengagement, how will there by any conception of *nirvāṇa* and *saṃsāra?*"[527]

How, then, are we to understand the nature of *karma*? *Karma* is said to arise from seven activities (here *dharmas*): words, actions, "the indescribable non-abandonment as well as what is asserted to be another form of the indescribable abandonment, virtuous and non-virtuous elements associated with enjoyment of being...and thought itself." In the traditional view *karma* arises for these causes. The Buddha taught, however, that any continuous action is *śūnyata*, which is neither constant nor interrupted. *Karma* has no self-nature, and thus it does not arise. If, to explain, we hold that *karma* has a self-nature, then it must be constant and uncreated. But it can neither create, nor be an initial cause. This contradicts the nature of *karma* as the cause of future states. On the other hand, if *karma* is not possessed of a self-nature (*sva-bhāva*), but void, *śūnya*, as the Master teaches, what could be postulated of it? Further, if *karma* is void in itself, but dependent upon actors, what could we say of the actors, who are themselves thus void? "If there is neither *karman* nor doer, where could the effect arising from the *karman* be?" Where there is no effect, there can be no percipient.

It is as if a master, by his supernormal powers, were to form a figure and this figure, in turn were to form another figure.... In exactly the same way, the doer is like the formed figure and his action...is like the other figure formed by the first. Defilements, *karmans*, bodily entities, doers and effects are all similar to the nature of an imaginary city in the sky, a mirage, and a dream.[528]

Therefore, one's existence in the past, with its attendant concern for the present and future, is unknowable, as is the concomitant of whether the world existed in the past. Nor can it be said that anyone or the world will exist in the future. With respect to one's existence a mistaken certainty with respect to the past and the future is assumed. Neither past nor future is necessary or knowable. It is not reasonable categorically to assert, then, that one existed in the past, any more than it is reasonable to make such an assertion about the future. The crux of the matter is, of course, the nature of *ātman*, or "soul." The *ātman* may, for example, be identified with perceptual clinging, *upādāna*. But such clinging is transitory; with what shall the *ātman* be identified? On the other hand, it cannot be asserted categorically that anyone did not exist in the past and shall exist in the future; for this is tantamount to a claim that one's (present) existence is eternal. It cannot be said, then, that anyone acts

---

[527] *Ibid.*, 101-103.
[528] *Ibid.*, 104-112.

313

or creates, nor that any of one's actions have causes, since there is no anterior (or posterior) state for an eternal being. Views that one did, did not, or both did and did not exist in an anterior state are absurd; and so also is this true for future existence, constancy and non-constancy of self.

What is true of the self is true also for the world. The constancy of the world is as dubious as the non-constancy of the world. Yet if this world is constant, and without limits, what meaning could the distinction between worlds have? On the other hand, if this world is non-constant and limited, how could there be a world at all, much less another one? In sum, the world, the self, *karma*, the doer, and the effects of his deeds are subject to the quatrilemma of the Buddha. All is "void," *śūnya*: it is therefore not true that they do exist, that they do not exist, that they both exist and do not exist, and that they neither exist nor do not exist.[529]

Thus we may not attribute suffering, *dukkha* (as existence), to actions in the past, nor may we postulate future effects of actions—for the whole is void. The cause of suffering lies not in the world, nor in the deed, nor in the doer understood as *ātman*. Rather, the locus of the cause for suffering lies in what we may somewhat misleadingly call the internal life, in feelings, in the perceptions as they exist in states of co-dependent origination, in the *klesas*—in short, in the innermost nature whose transformation was the concern and hope of the Ariyan life. All forms of suffering, as Nāgārjuna argued, are empty. Release is the effect of utter concentration upon arising and cessation rather than upon the world, the self, the actor or the acts.

---

[529] *Ibid.*, 164-171.

III

The Truth of the End of Suffering

Freud and the End of Suffering

Introduction

While it is obvious that Sigmund Freud's insights into the nature of human suffering rest upon his study of psychopathology, and while it is also true, as I have attempted to show, that we must understand the dynamic nature of human experience in terms of conflict and tension, rather than according to some abstract distinction between "normal" and "abnormal," it is apparent that Freud is convinced of what we can call the "Third Noble Truth of the End of Suffering." In this part I shall explore the major elements of this conviction. These are, among others, his commitment to the strengthening of the ego, to the adjustment to the reality principle, the concept of an ideal homeostatic balance among the forces of the psyche, the saving power of love, and—perhaps a *summa* of his most soaring hope–the education to reality and the self's knowledge of its fundamental nature.

It is essential to rightly understand Freud when he argues these matters. They are indicators of the end of suffering, and they are manifestations of the forces of which the human life is comprised. The causes of the end of suffering lie in the causes of suffering themselves. The reality principle and the pleasure principle are interdependent, as are ego and id, thought and instinct, psychical and material reality, phylogeny and ontogeny.

Further, the healthy psyche cannot really be said to be happy; for any notion of happiness is at odds with the reality of the human situation–with one exception, the happiness that is defined as unqualified self-understanding. It is better to say that the end of suffering is not the end of pain, nor the end of pleasure, or joy or of sorrow, and certainly not the end of perception, memory, sensation or thought. Rather, it is the end of bondage to any and all of these things. Finally, it is the end of bondage to the components and combinations of the self; and because there is no other notion of self possible in Freud's understanding of the psyche, it is in the last analysis the end of the suffering self.

The Reality Principle and the Optimum Mental State

Reality

Life lived according to the pleasure principle is untenable; for the self devoted to the pleasure principle risks extinction at the hands of the world's agencies or, indeed, its own. Fortunately, there are tendencies inherent in the evolution of the psyche that impose limitations upon pleasure. These are, so to speak, "natural" tendencies. In fact, the reality principle, which must supersede the pleasure principle for the sake of life, is a version of the pleasure principle; the former is nothing more than the tendency to postpone satisfaction and, if necessary, to abandon satisfaction in acceptable stages. The pleasure principle persists, however, especially among the sexual instincts which, Freud frequently noted, "are so hard to 'educate,' and, starting from those instincts, or in the ego itself, it often succeeds in overcoming the reality principle, to the detriment of the organism as an whole."[1]

Furthermore, the ego has the task of "substituting the reality principle for the pleasure principle." It "represents reason and sanity, in contrast to the id which contains the passions." This distinction is commonly found among people; it is at the same time an "ideal" situation. That is, Freud is quite clear about what he holds to be the ideal situation, namely the dominance of the reality principle maintained by ego functions.[2]

The significance of the reality principle is virtually identical to the significance of the external world for the psyche.[3] The implications of this observation occupied Freud throughout his work. Employing an evolutionary conceptual framework, he argued that the primary process, that is, the unconscious mental processes, preceded the secondary or conscious processes (his concern is not only with phylogenetic but also with ontogenetic development). Pleasure and unpleasure (*Lust-Unlust*) alone dictated the activities of the primary process, which sought to repeat pleasurable activities and to avoid unpleasurable ones. The ultimate or initial state, he thought, was one of psychical rest. This internal existence was disturbed first by internal needs, which were satisfied by hallucination or within the limits of the organism's psychic and physical options.[4] Frequent failure of satisfaction, especially in relation to a discovered external stimulus, led to the introduction of a new principle of mental functioning, in which the determining quality of an experience was not whether it was pleasurable but whether it was "real," that is, determined by forces resisting the control of the primary process and the organism itself. Two principles thus emerged, which from that point on strove against each other perpetually. The secondary process, or consciousness, acquired abilities applicable to the demands of the supreme external world. Freud called these by various names: attention, a system of notation, memory, and most significant, judgement.[5]

---

[1] BPP, 25-26.
[2] *Ego and Id*, 29-30.
[3] NIL, SE XXII, 75-76; *cf.* "Lay Analysis," SE XX, 200f..
[4] *Cf.* IL, SE XVI, 356-357.
[5] "Two Principles," SE XII, 219-221.

He wrote:

The place of repression, which excluded from cathexis as productive of unpleasure some of the emerging ideas, was taken by an *impartial passing of judgement*, which had to decide whether a given idea was true or false[, that is,] whether it was in agreement with reality or not–the decision being determined by making a comparison with memory-traces of reality.

As a consequence, the secondary process came to control motor discharge by guiding activity along lines which would not conflict with what it knew of external reality. That restraint was accomplished specifically by the process of thinking, which Freud thought of as a restraint upon action until the passing of judgement had been completed. Thinking, in turn, "was endowed with characteristics which made it possible for the mental apparatus to tolerate an increased tension of stimuli while the process of discharge was postponed. It is essentially an experimental kind of acting."[6]

The persistence of the primary process, however, required that thinking should be divided into two types. The first was determined directly by the perception and memory of the external world. The second took the form of fantasy, day-dreaming, play, imagination and art. Freud did not regard any of these activities as pathogenic in and of themselves, but rather as essential to the discharge of psychic energy. What was more disturbing to the balance of the mental apparatus was the difficulty in educating the sexual instincts to reality. The sexual instincts are originally auto-erotic, Freud observed; therefore they were unresponsive to the limitations of external reality. However, the onset of sexuality is diphasic in nature; the process of finding an "object" of libidinal cathexis is interrupted very soon after it begins as a consequence of the Oedipal conflict.[7]

Although this account of the evolution of the psyche was later modified by Freud,[8] the two principles of mental functioning were never fully rejected, nor, indeed, was the goal of the ascendancy of the reality principle. But it is important to note just what Freud meant by the reality principle: it was a controlling and safeguarding factor applied to the pleasure principle rather than a substitute for it.[9] Science was the ideal example of this relationship between reality and pleasure; religion, on the other hand taught not reality but myth in its belief in gratification that must be delayed until after death. "It is science which comes nearest to succeeding in that conquest [of the pleasure principle]: science too, how-

---

[6] *Ibid.*.
[7] *Ibid.*, 222.
[8] *Cf. Ego and Id*, BPP.
[9] "Two Principles," SE XII, 223.

ever, offers intellectual pleasure during its work and promises practical gain in the end."[10]

Furthermore, both education and art depend upon the pleasure principle. The former uses the "bait of love of the educator" to accomplish the conquest. Art is peculiar; for it takes the fantasies of pleasure and molds them "into truths of a new kind, which are valued by men as precious reflections of reality." The artist makes no alterations in the external world, but expresses the dissatisfactions generally felt with that world, so that the pleasure principle of the fantasy moves toward the reality principle in expressing the nature of that unsatisfactory world. In short, it becomes part of the world, of reality.[11]

Freud's terminology of the "mental apparatus" frequently set the tone for his discussion of the optimum psychic disposition, so that in expounding the relationship between pleasure and reality he wrote of an economic balance of forces tending toward homeostasis. Pleasure is *"in some way* connected with the diminution, reduction or extinction of the amounts of stimulus prevailing in the mental apparatus, and...similarly unpleasure is connected with their increase."[12] Thus it is the task of the mental apparatus to master and dispose of "the amounts of stimulus and sums of excitation that impinge on it from outside and inside."[13] This calculus of pleasure is, of necessity, significantly modified in the work of the ego. The reality principle is both cause and expression of this modification. Mere maneuvering for the sake of pleasure is replaced by postponement and diminution of satisfaction in light of the inexorable demands of reality. The pleasure principle is never dethroned; the calculus is simply complicated by the addition of the influence of external reality.[14]

There is no reason, so far as I can see, to dispute the conclusion that this situation is optimum for Freud. The problem with it is that, largely because of the reluctance of the sexual instincts to be educated to reality, the balance seems always to be threatened. Symptoms, for example, are elements of the psychic organization that refuse to find their place in the scheme of things, for they are guided by the unmodified pleasure principle and ignore the reality principle. They set an internal act in place of an external one.[15] Fixations draw no distinction between "material" and "psychical" reality. The physician must treat both realities as in principle "real" if he is to be of any help; for what he is trying to overcome is the

---

[10] *Ibid.*, 223-224; *cf. Civilization*, 24ff..
[11] "Two Principles," SE XII, 225.
[12] IL, SE XVI, 356f..
[13] *Ibid.*.
[14] *Ibid.*, 356-357.
[15] *Ibid.*, 366.

neurotic experience of the hegemony of psychic reality and replace it with the supremacy of material reality.[16] But this is a deviation, albeit one potentially present in the optimum state. There is in fact an "original *reality-ego*, which distinguished outer and inner by means of a sound objective criterion." But in the course of development, that is, in the playing out of the vicissitudes of the instinctual life, the organism is subjected to the "*three great polarities that govern mental life.*" These polarities are activity-passivity, which pertains to the biological sphere, pleasure-pain in the economic sphere, and the ego-external world as "*the real.*" If we place this descriptive analysis of the human condition in the context of Freud's notions of health, it is clear that the most significant of the polarities is the last.[17]

But in the course of everyday life the demands of reality must be diluted, just as the demands of pleasure must be restrained. Fantasy can provide the opportunity to achieve satisfaction while bypassing the testing of reality. The chief quality of fantasy that permits this breaking of the rules seems to be the knowledge that it *is* fantasy, not reality–a distinction of paramount importance to the ego. Man cannot live by reality alone. Fantasy is the mid-point between reality and neurosis. It is the stage of the introvert, who is not yet neurotic, and who will not become neurotic as long as the quantity of libido is controlled and controllable.[18] But the line must not be crossed; it is a question of restraint and balance. The aim of all mental activity, seen from the economic point of view, is the mastery of the "mass of stimuli," and the prevention of excessive accumulation of stimuli, which is the cause of unpleasure.[19]

Success in this endeavor is in part dependent upon the healthy expression and satisfaction of narcissistic aims. This is the function of sleep, and probably explains the refreshment we feel after sleeping. Dreaming is narcissistic; it is also harmless to the ego, for it is an activity free of the necessity of reality-testing and it is essential to the balance of the psyche. What distinguishes harmless dreaming sleep from illness is precisely the need for reality-testing in the latter case.

In drawing the most comprehensive picture possible of the psychic life Freud described several syntheses of the forces exerted upon the mental life. Among others (with the biological, economic, and "real" divisions noted already) he included his discovery of the relationship between eros and thanatos, and the nirvana principle. Let us recall that in present-

---

[16] *Ibid.*, 368.
[17] "Instincts," CP IV, 77-78, 83; *cf.* "Neurosis and Psychosis," SE XIX, 152-153.
[18] IL, SE XVI, 373-375.
[19] "Masochism," SE XIX, 159-161.

ing the notion of life and death instincts, he concluded that the fulcrum of the dynamic of this relationship was the disturbance of the state of rest. The life instincts, which he finally equated with libido (as eros), were the watch-guards of life which responded ultimately to the pleasure principle. Thus a distinction was established between the operation of libido and the instinctual drive toward death, or morbidity. Freud also suggested the name "Nirvana Principle" for the tendency toward inertia and resistance to all stimuli. (See the following *Excursus* on Freud's use of the concept of nirvana.) However, a problem arises. The issue is this: the absence of stimulation is itself a state of stability, and in this respect may be seen to be pleasurable, in accordance with the notion that the aim of all living creatures is to return to the state of rest, free of any external stimuli. This conclusion, however, contradicts all other notions of the pleasure principle, which hold that satisfaction of a desire constitutes pleasure. Here it seems that the absence of desire is equated with pleasure; in other words, the distinction between eros and thanatos collapses, and Freud's hard-won dualism fails.[20]

Freud suggests a resolution of this contradiction. In the course of development of the nirvana principle, "belonging as it does to the death instinct, [it] has undergone a modification in living organisms through which it has become the pleasure principle; and we shall henceforward avoid regarding the two principles as one."[21] The modification of the nirvana principle is accomplished through the influence of libido, the life instinct, which has "alongside of the death instinct, seized upon a share in the regulation of the processes of life." Thus, "[T]he *Nirvana* principle expresses the trend of the death instinct; the *pleasure* principle represents the demands of the libido; and the modification of the latter principle, the *reality* principle, represents the influence of the external world."[22] In the life of the psyche none of these principles replaces any of the other two, though conflicts can arise. Thus the pleasure principle, as modified by the reality principle, is "the watchman over our life."[23]

This summary is significant, for it suggests that tripartite division of the psyche whose balance is essential to health, while describing also the nature of the conflicted life of the internal world. The nirvana principle tends toward a reduction of stimuli (an economic consideration, and also a quantitative one); the pleasure principle looks to the satisfaction of desire (a qualitative consideration); and the pleasure principle modified by its contact with external reality, or the reality principle, seeks a postponement of discharge of the stimulus, a "temporary acquiescence in

---

[20] *Ibid.*.
[21] *Ibid.*.
[22] *Ibid.*.
[23] *Ibid.*.

the unpleasure due to tension."[24]

But what is essential is the relationship to the external world, in the sense that if that relationship fails or is weakened, no satisfaction that does not threaten the organization of the psyche and the organism itself is possible. Thus the ego's function of making judgements must never be seriously impaired, for this is the practical application of the reality principle. "Worldly Wisdom" consists precisely in the ego's ability to know the difference between feelings and the worldly situation, and when to side with one or the other.[25]

The task of the physician and psychoanalyst is to convince the patient that it is impossible to conduct life on the pleasure principle; it is the patient who accomplishes the cure.[26] The patient is asked to renounce some pleasures which have detrimental consequences: "...in other words, under the doctor's guidance he is asked to make the advance from the pleasure principle to the reality principle by which the mature human being is distinguished from the child...." It is the "habit of psychoanalysis to replace what is derivative and etiolated by what is original and basic."[27] The doctor helps to bring the unconscious and repressed impulses to which the patient, all unwitting, is bound, to the patient's knowledge, "to induce him to adopt our conviction of the inexpediency of the repressive process established in childhood...."[28] Although as educator the doctor makes use of one of the components of love, his task is to induce the "incomplete human being to respect the decrees of necessity and to spare himself the punishment that follows any infringement of them."[29]

The significance of the reality principle, then, must be understood in terms of its dependent relationship with the pleasure principle. But there can be no doubt that the *sine qua non* of health is the strength of the reality principle, and the concomitant strength of the ego. It is not always the case that the uncovering of resistances and the elevation of the contents of the unconscious into the conscious lead to the recognition of and the embrace of reality; but that is the hope, the *raison d'être*, of psychoanalysis. If it were not possible, it would not be tried. In this regard it may said that Freud regarded the end of suffering as a goal capable of achievement.

Psychosis

The strength of Freud's commitment to the reality principle is further illustrated in his understanding of psychosis, which he regarded as the

---

24 *Ibid..*
25 "Lay Analysis," SE XX, 200-201.
26 "Advance," SE XVII, 159.
27 "Character Types," SE XIV, 312.
28 "Advance," SE XVII, 159.
29 *Ibid..*

only untreatable mental illness. Psychosis is the condition characterized chiefly by the inability of the psyche to respond to the exigencies of external reality; in fact this means that the psyche is unable to attend to external reality. Thus the illness is defined entirely in terms of the reality principle, or more simply and devastatingly, reality.

In both neurosis and psychosis mental illness is in essence a state of rejection, partial or full, of external reality, a struggle against "submitting to the reality of the universe–to Ananke."[30] But while neurotic behavior permits some contact, however slight and threatened, with external reality through the agency of the ego, in psychosis the ego itself functions pathogenically.[31] It rejects external reality and constructs a pathogenic substitute. In a non-psychotic state such activity is restricted to dreaming sleep; in psychosis the dream becomes the reality.[32] The cause of the outbreak of psychosis lies either in an experience of reality that is intolerably painful or in an extraordinary and irresistible intensification of instinctual demands, "both of which, in view of the rival claims made by the id and the external world upon the ego, must produce the same effect upon it."[33] If neurosis is the result of a conflict between the ego and the id, psychosis is the result of a conflict between the ego and the external world.[34]

The ego's relationship with the external world in a state of mental health depends upon two operations, the laying down of memory traces and the reception of current, present and renewable perceptions. In psychosis, especially amentia, neither of these operations occurs; the ego, complying with the id's impulses, creates a new world.[35] This situation arises out of extreme frustration with the external world; but in some instances the power of the super-ego may be joined with the id to overwhelm the ego, as in melancholia.[36]

The distinction between neurosis and psychosis, Freud concludes, lies in whether any relationship at all can be sustained with the external world. In neurosis the ego maintains itself sufficiently through its connection to external stimuli to impose a repression upon the id's desires. Neurosis provides a compensation for the portion of the id that has been damaged.[37] The pathology becomes psychotic whenever the ego yields

---

30 IL, SE XVI, 429-430.
31 Ibid..
32 Outline, 62.
33 Ibid., 114.
34 "Neurosis and Psychosis," SE XIX, 149.
35 Ibid., 150-151.
36 Ibid., 152; cf. Outline, 62.
37 "Loss of Reality," SE XIX, 183.

its allegiance to the id rather than the external world.[38] Neurosis avoids, psychosis remodels; neurosis ignores, psychosis disavows.[39]

The barriers presented to psychoanalysis by neurosis are formidable; but those presented by psychoses are virtually unsurpassable. The ego can be helped to restore its hegemony over the id by strengthening its contact with external reality;[40] but this is an almost impossible task if the patient has constructed a reality wholly from the materials of his own wishes. This patient has no desire to, and sees no reason to, participate in the construction of a healthy relationship between ego and world. He already has a world over which he exercises complete control. The motivation for reconstruction is absent; and before this the analyst is virtually helpless.

In short, so essential and fundamental is the relationship, or the possibility of a relationship, between self and world that no liberation seems possible in its absence. But the role that psychosis plays in the psychoanalytic diagnosis suggests that the end of suffering is a possibility, and that possibility is inexorably linked to the reality principle.

The End of the Neuroses

If the hegemony of the reality principle is a goal capable of achievement, it is also true that the threat represented in the unlimited pleasure principle can be overcome in the experience of the sufferer. In illustration of this point I want to present Freud's conclusions concerning the end of four elements of neurotic suffering: the annihilation of the Oedipus complex; the victory of developmental maturity over regression; the end of repression; and, ironically, the triumph of love.

The Annihilation of the Oedipus Complex

If we were to select but one theme from among the many played by Freud in his analysis of suffering, we could hardly do better than to listen to his work on the Oedipus complex. It is the crisis, the crux, of development, the heart of libido and economic theory, the core of his notion of identity. What I wish to stress here is that, although it is a cause of suffering, in the optimum case it is annihilated. The highest ideals of mankind, which many accused psychoanalysis of ignoring or reducing to relative meaninglessness, are in fact the consequence of the annihilation of the Oedipus complex. In that sense they are dependent upon the complex, in that both its emergence and annihilation are essential to the development of morality and culture. We knew them in connection with our parents, and took them into our natures as the ego-ideal.[41] The

---

[38] *Ibid.*, 186- 187.
[39] *Ibid.*, 184-185.
[40] "Lay Analysis," SE XX, 205.
[41] *Ego and Id*, 47.

ego-ideal is, then, the heir of the Oedipus complex. As such it is the most powerful expression in the economy of the self of the vicissitudes of the instincts. The presence of the ego-ideal means nothing less than the mastery of these instincts based upon the diversion of their power and the exploitation of their force. It also means the subjection of the ego to the id, the ultimate source of the ego-ideal.[42]

This triumph of the super-ego is in turn a consequence of what Freud regards as the natural attrition of the power of the Oedipus complex, and its eventual annihilation. The causes are both ontogenetic–it simply does not happen that the small boy obtains gratification of his desire to possess his mother–and phylogenetic–the complex must yield to next stage of development, that of latency. More specifically, Freud argues that it is the discovery on the part of the boy that girls have no penis that brings home the possible consequences of gratification; for in this discovery the fear of castration finds empirical confirmation. If, on the one hand, the boy behaves in the same manner as a mother does with her husband, he will suffer castration, as he assumes she has. On the other hand, if he acts like his father he will be castrated as punishment for his enjoyment. Whichever view he holds, castration is the feared and anticipated result. Accordingly, the complex disappears and is replaced by the introjection of the father-image into the ego, to become the super-ego. The onset of the latency period follows, marked by inhibition and sublimation of the desires and fears previously associated with the Oedipus complex. These events constitute not merely a regression but an annihilation of a complex. It is an event of the highest significance, Freud insists. For it places the person on the borderline between the normal and the pathological; and its successful conclusion makes it possible to avoid the pathogenic effects of libidinal development.[43]

The End of Repression

The persistence of Oedipal libidinal conflict can be understood in part in terms of repression. The cause of neurotic symptoms, whether for the individual or the race, is the presence of repressed material. But Freud argued that repression can come to an end; and with its end comes the end of neurosis. Repression is replaced by "an *impartial passing of judgement.*"[44] The means for achieving this replacement will be the subject for examination in the treatment of the causes of the end of suffering. Here I will focus on the fact of the end of repression.

The causes for falling ill, according to one of Freud's summaries, are three in number: (1) hereditary factors; (2) the influence of early experiences in childhood; (3) "real frustration," deprivation of love and

---

[42] *Ibid.*, 47-48; *cf. Outline,* 121-122.
[43] "Dissolution," SE XIX, 173-177.
[44] "Two Principles," SE XII, 221.

poverty, "unfavourable social circumstances," and "the strictness of the ethical standards to whose pressure the individual is subject."[45] Therapy, which can do nothing about the first and third causes, must be addressed to the second cause. Some observers held that since it is the repression of libidinal impulses which causes illness, these impulses must be satisfied if health is to be gained; but Freud disagreed strongly with this view, as he did with those who espoused unqualified asceticism. In either case, he argued, symptom-formation would simply be encouraged.[46] The "sole task of our therapy," rather, is to elevate the conflicting forces of the mental life onto equal footing in the conscious. It is the repression of one and the encouragement of the other that constitute the cause of the neurotic's illness.[47] Or, more starkly, he asserts, this "single psychical change" brings the end of repression; and where this is not possible, neither is therapy possible. Thus the patient who undergoes successful treatment is the same person as he was before–but without repression. This is no small advance. What was repressed is now in the realm of the conscious. What is repressed is not annihilated, but removed to the stage of conflict at which it can be admitted to a program of conscious redress. The person "has become what he might have become at best under the most favourable conditions. But that is a very great deal."[48]

This is an extremely important observation, to which we shall return in the discussion of the goals of psychoanalysis. What I wish to emphasize here, however, is that what comes to an end is repression of psychic material rather than, so to speak, the material itself. The patient remains the sum, and more than the sum, of his psychic history. He is now different, and, one is not reluctant to add, free, because repression of part of this material has been replaced by conscious assessment and judgement of it. He understands who he is and how he came to be who he is. For Freud this is tantamount to the optimum state, the highest goal of life. This is liberation. As he pointed out in *Moses and Monotheism*, it is not the repressed material, which is the content of the psychic life, but the fact of its repression that provides the precondition for its perpetual return and the contents of the neuroses. Psychoanalysis finds its ultimate goal in the end of repression. Freud states that psychoanalysis is not true "causal therapy," because it cannot–and indeed, no other field of human endeavor can–offer a chemical agent for the alteration of libidinal conflict. What it does offer is an analysis of the nature and causes of repression; and in that analysis it offers also the cause for the end of

---

[45] IL, SE XVI, 432-433; *cf. Civilization, passim..*
[46] IL, SE XVI, 432-433.
[47] *Ibid.*, 435.
[48] *Ibid..*

repression.[49]   This is the entire purpose of the transference syndrome, psychoanalysis' major tool and hope for success. It is the task of the physician to transform the transferred libidinal desires into memories, and thus accomplishing the movement from unconscious to conscious, ending the repression and removing the resistance.[50]   This goal is capable of accomplishment because it is an inherent possibility in the very structure of psychic development; it is the physician's task to aid the patient in returning control of his life to his conscious by bringing an end to the patient's own activity in causing the illness, that of repression.

The neurotic is "incapable of enjoyment and efficiency." He must devote a great deal of his energy to the repression of his libidinal conflicts. In order to deal with "ordinary unhappiness" this energy must be made available to his conscious processes. By reversing the causal flow, of which repression is the crucial factor, the therapy seeks to make that energy available to the ego, and to restore the mental unity of the person.[51]

If the patient adopts the analyst's conviction that repression established on the basis of childhood experience is inexpedient, he will no longer suffer, or at least, will no longer suffer from the inability to work and enjoy.[52] Thus released, the "torn mind" grows together, healing itself of the divisions that mark the areas of repression. No new synthesis occurs, Freud insists; rather, the end of repression and the defeat of the resistances allow the mind to heal itself.[53] In order to accomplish this, psychoanalysis proposes that the excessive repressions enforced by society be eased, and the repressions, which are radically inefficient, be replaced by other protections.[54] The ego must gain control, lost to earlier repressions, over the id. This restoration is the sole purpose of psychoanalysis. "We have to seek out the repressions which have been set up and to urge the ego to correct them with our help and to deal with conflicts better than by an attempt at flight."[55] The ego must and can learn to tolerate what was repressed rather than fleeing from it. In short, hysterical misery, brought on by repression, can be transformed into ordinary unhappiness.

Developmental Maturity

In what Freud has to say about regression we can also find his notion

---

[49] *Ibid.*, 436.

[50] *Ibid.*, 437ff..

[51] *Ibid.*, 454-455; *cf. Ibid.*, 455: the role of the physician is what enables "the work of interpretation, which transforms what is unconscious into what is conscious;" "the ego is enlarged at the cost of the unconscious."

[52] "Advance," SE XVII, 159; *cf.* "Construction," SE XXIII, 268-269.

[53] "Advance," SE XVII, 161- 166.

[54] "Resistances," SE XIX, 220; *cf.* "Lay Analysis," SE XX, 205.

[55] "Lay Analysis," SE XX, 205.

of the end of suffering; for regression, a neurotic phenonemon, is comprehensible only in terms of a "normal" or optimum progression through successive stages toward maturity. It was through the study of regression to previous stages once left behind that Freud was able to construct his developmental theory of libidinal attachment. We can see in this theory Freud's concept of developmental maturity as a natural progression; its full development constituted mental health, while arrest or regression lay the groundwork for mental illness.

By "developmental theory" I mean here the oral-anal-phallic-genital stage theory.[56] My focus here is not upon the content of the theory but Freud's concept of the full development of the person as a chief mark of the end of suffering.

In Freud's account of "normal" female sexuality he illustrates a contrast between the neurotic complications and the optimal progression in the context of the vicissitudes of the instincts. Despite the wide-spread criticism of this presentation, I think it is important to grasp what Freud intended. He set out to explain the differences between men and women in the area of sexual and libidinal development in order to show the optimum progression of mental development, and to indicate possible points of crisis, leading to neurotic aberration.

Female libidinal development, as we have noted, follows the same progression as the male until the phallic period. At this point the lack of a penis is noted by the female child; the attachment to the similarly incomplete mother ceases, and the female version of the Oedipal relationship is established. The homology between penis and baby supersedes all other images. The resolution of the Oedipus complex for the girl is achieved when a baby, and especially a baby boy, is born to the girl; in Freud's view only at this point is the overpowering sense of incompleteness ("penis envy") overcome. What is important in this account is what Freud thought was normal, and what he thought was neurotic. The progression describes the maturation of the female child through the resolution and annihilation of the Oedipus complex. Neurosis is possible; but we must then speak of deviation, or more specifically, regression, over against the "normal" pattern. Freud described the neurotic possibilities in terms of ambivalence toward the mother manifested in regression to the "masculine" phase of libido attachment, that phase of sexuality centering on the female clitoris prior to the discovery of a lack of a penis. Female neurotics, Freud concluded, tended to be those for whom the pre-Oedipal phase had been traumatic.[57]

However different they appear to be, the successful passage through the crises of libidinal development for male and female is seen to a natural

---

[56] Cf. Outline, 28ff., and "Instincts," CP IV, 78-79.
[57] NIL, SE XXII, 112-135.

and optimum working out of the tension between pleasure and reality; neurosis is the consequence and manifestion of a failure of this process, and of a "defusion of instincts," while passage from an earlier to the definitive genital phase entails acquisition of mature erotic practice.[58] Indeed, it is the final primacy of the genital organization that emerges as the optimum stage of libidinal tension.[59]

We should not underestimate Freud's emphasis upon the necessity of fusion, "intermixture," of the instincts in the service of genital sexuality. This is a temptation, in light of his devastating critique of the traditional identification of sexual activity with this stage only, and its failure to see the entire history of libidinal development. But there is little doubt that the ascendancy of genital organization marks the beginning of the optimum adult sexual, and thus emotional, life, despite the fact that it rests squarely upon pre-Oedipal development stages. The genital stage, when fully developed, marks the end of suffering; it is the goal toward which the psychoanalyst leads his suffering patient.

Love of Self and Love of Others

In his investigations of the economic aspects of the psychical life Freud drew attention to the need to distinguish between pleasure and unpleasure in terms of tension created by the drive for satisfaction of libido. This point has already been raised with respect to the reality and pleasure principles; but it is also significant in Freud's understanding of the ideal balance of love of self and love of others. The issue is not a *"dynamic"* one, so much as an *"economic"* one; that is, the question is whether there is too much libido, whether at any point the economy of the psyche is disrupted.[60] Whether we wish to accept the mechanical symbolism of the mental apparatus, the point for Freud is that some sort of balance must be struck between opposing tendencies in the psyche if it is to be healthy. Among the techniques in the art of living, the most successful is "the way of life which makes love the centre of everything, which looks for all satisfaction in loving and being loved." The pattern for this technique is, of course, sexual love, from which we gain our most intense pleasure. The weakness of the technique is just as obvious; "we are never so defenceless against suffering as when we love, never so helplessly unhappy as when we have lost our loved object or its love."[61]

These tendencies have a number of designations in Freud's writings, including eros and thanatos, reality and pleasure, ego and sexual instincts. Here our interest is in the economic balance between love of the

---

[58] *Ego and Id*, 57-58; *cf.* NIL, SE XXII, 97-102,and IL, SE XVI, 314-315.
[59] BPP, 94-95.
[60] IL, SE XVI, 375; *cf.* 346-347.
[61] *Civilization*, 29.

self and love of others, or ego-libido and object-libido, and their various manifestations. For Freud holds the view that there can be no satisfactory human life unless these two sorts of attachments are possible, despite the fact that each is always satisfied at the expense of the other (hence the "economic" designation).

Freud posits, as we have seen, a primary narcissism or autoerotism. Object love is a secondary development out of this universal and original state; and conversely autoerotism is the cause of the lagging behind of the sexual instincts in the education of the child. In addition, he posits a secondary narcissism, to be distinguished from primary narcissism in that it is a *withdrawal* of libido from objects and a designation of the self as the object of affection. This latter is either very close to, or identical to, a psychotic condition, unless it occurs under the conditions of sleep; in the latter case it is "normal." Further, the emergence of object-attachment implies "that an accumulation of narcissistic libido beyond a certain amount is not tolerated. We may even imagine that it was for that very reason that object-cathexes originally came about, that the ego was obliged to send out its libido so as not to fall ill as a result its being dammed up."[62]

Narcissism may be psychotic; but self-love is an inherent need of the person. It operates at the expense of object-love and object cathexes. If we think of the need to satisfy the desire for the love of self as an inherent quality of the psyche, and of narcissism as not necessarily but rather potentially a psychotic state, we arrive at the conclusion that the life of the psyche is nothing less than a perpetual balancing of love of self and love of others. In an important passage Freud summarizes the economic principle of love:

> Here we may even venture to touch on the question of what makes it necessary at all for our mental life to pass beyond the limits of narcissism and to attach the libido to objects. The answer which would follow from our line of thought would once more be that this necessity arises when the cathexis of the ego with libido exceeds a certain amount. A strong egoism is a protection against falling ill, but in the last resort we must be in love in order not to fall ill, and we are bound to fall ill if, in consequence of frustration, we are unable to love.[63]

Loving is an activity of the ego—indeed, it is the primary activity of the ego. The central issue now is that of the relationship of self-love to the love of others, or, as Freud puts it, the "relations of self-regard to erotism—that is, to libidinal object-cathexis." Loving, he notes, "in so far as it involves longing and deprivation, lowers self-regard; whereas

---

[62] IL, SE XVI, 415-422; *cf.* "Narcissism," SE XIV, 73ff..
[63] "Narcissism," SE XIV, 85.

being loved, having one's love returned, and possessing the loved object, raises it once more."[64] If love is not returned, libido may be withdrawn from objects and taken back into the self. This "happy love" is not true love; on the other hand, a "real happy love" corresponds to the primal state in which no distinction between object- and ego-libido exists.[65] The maintenance of primary narcissism is the responsibility of the ego-ideal. It is a "special psychical agency" which ensures that primary narcissism achieves fulfillment; it fulfills this task by offering itself as a model for that "narcissistic perfection" of childhood.[66] Therefore the ego-ideal makes self-love, in the sense of the return to primitive autoerotism or some acceptable substitute for it, possible.

In the terms of the structural theory, then, the ego's activity of loving is satisfied on the one hand by the fulfillment of the ego-ideal within the structure of the ego and on the other by establishing libidinal object-cathexes. In both actions the ego impoverishes or enriches itself, depending upon the success in finding satisfaction from either attachment.[67] Love is a process, then, by which the ego maintains both self-regard and love for others. That Freud insisted upon both aspects of the process is important; for he conceived of the ego in such a way that it was healthy only when it was nourished from within and without. Conversely the self that is unable to love anything but itself is narcissistic in the psychotic sense; and the self that is unable to love itself risks melancholia and neurotic depression.[68]

Love, then, is universal in scope and import. It is the basis and the expression of all human relations, including those of the psyche to its own being. Freud adopted the term "libido" partly in order to quantify the notion of love, so that he could pursue an economic analysis of the self. He called libido the as yet unmeasurable quantity of energy of all erotic instincts. Language, he said, has quite justifiably identified love of self, of parents and children, of humanity, devotion to things and ideas, friendship for others particular and general, as love. In distinguishing between sexual love and other forms, we need only observe that the same energy, libido, has been desexualized in the latter types, but has maintained enough of its original nature to be recognizable to us. All group ties, then, are libidinal in origin and nature.[69]

Moreover the ties with others are the only hindrances to self-love and to narcissism. Human life understood as a supreme good is possible

---

[64] *Ibid.*, 99-100.
[65] *Ibid.*.
[66] *Cf. ibid.*, 94ff..
[67] *Ibid.*, 100.
[68] *Cf. Group Psychology*, 107, and "Mourning," CP IV, *passim*.
[69] *Group Psychology*, 37-40; *cf. Civilization*, 49.

only when narcissistic impulses—which can be counted upon in any case to find satisfaction—are limited by attachment to others: in the development of mankind as an whole, just as in individuals, "love alone acts as the civilizing factor in the sense that it brings a change from egoism to altruism."[70]

The relationship between object-cathexes, ego-libido and the ego-ideal suggested to Freud a high degree of interdependence, usually expressed in economic terms, between the instinctual tendency toward attachment and resistance, between narcissistic and anaclitic relationship or attachments. But in describing the two great classes of instincts, eros and thanatos, he makes the nature of that relationship clear in a new way by focusing on the fusion of instincts. The importance of the metaphor is this: while there are two opposing developments or expressions of libido, they must be understood not as separate and distinct forces but as tendencies which, in their ideal or healthy states, are fused. In terms of the developmental theory, regression constitutes a "defusion of instincts," just as, conversely, the advance from an earlier to the definitive genital stage would be conditioned by an accession of erotic components. This state of fusion explains the "clamour for life" of eros, and the silence of thanatos. Eros is the driving force of life, moving against its eternal partner, death. If life is governed by a drive for constant equilibrium, the persistent drive toward morbidity is retarded by the claims of eros, expressed in instinctual needs. Death's silence is overwhelming in the life of the thriving ego.

Yet the death instincts must not be seen merely as the opposite number of a dualism, with eros, but, however silent, as essential to the process of life. The lesson may be drawn from biology. Here the pattern of struggle for life is actually an insistence by the organism that it follow its own path to death, resisting any hindrance as a danger.[71] The paradox is heightened when we understand that those biological functions related to procreation, especially in the germ cells, repeat the performance to which they owe their existence. One portion of their substance moves toward death, the other toward a repetition of the inherited cycle. This complete interdependence of life and death is expressed in biological terms; but Freud has a clear view of the nature of the relationships of instinctual and, thus, human life.[72]

The instincts are conservative; and yet to preserve their own path to death they must again and again attach to objects outside of themselves, and thus they perpetuate life through erotic attachment. The truly conservative instincts, then, are of the class of eros. "It is as though the life

---

[70] *Group Psychology*, 57.
[71] BPP, 72.
[72] *Ibid.*, 74.

of the organism moved with a vacillating rhythm. One group of instincts rushes forward so as to reach the final aim of life as swiftly as possible; but when a particular state in the advance has been reached, the other group jerks back to a certain point to make a fresh start and so prolong the journey."[73]

Thus life is the consequence of love; but love is an expression of death. The truly happy self should be understood in terms of this paradox, and in terms that recognize the consequences of defusion. Freud claimed that he had always been a dualist; but in his mature assessment of the life of the instincts he is in fact a mystic—in the precise sense of that term, that is, in his espousal of the truth of the coincidence of opposites as the essential quality of human life. Can we be bold enough to say that there is no life without death, no love without hate, no *nirvāṇa* without *saṃsāra*?

It is, then, Freud's task to show the essential balance of relationship between self-love and love of others. This issue is sufficiently general so that he is able to classify types of personality, under the rubric "libidinal types," in its terms. We have already noted Freud's three general libidinal types: the narcissistic, the erotic, and the obsessional erotic.[74] Each type is clearly valuable for civilization. In compounded types, that value is enhanced. Thus the erotic-obsessional type is exemplary because of its dependence upon the super-ego and the residues of being loved; the erotic-narcissistic type unites opposites, providing new patterns for culture; and the narcissistic-obsessional has a disregard for the external world that makes it heroic. The ideal type, however, is the "supercompound," the erotic-obsessional-narcissistic person, who loves, is loved and is neither bound by the past or anxious about the future.[75]

---

[73] *Ibid.*, 74-75; *cf.* "Articles: (B)," SE XVIII, 258ff..

[74] In *Civilization and its Discontents* Freud suggests a slightly different view and enumeration of libidinal types. He identifies the man who is predominantly erotic, who "will give first preference to his emotional relationships to other people." Second, there is "the narcissistic man, who inclines to be self-sufficient, [and] will seek his main satisfactions in his internal mental processes." Third, there is "the man of action [who] will never give up the external world on which he can try his strength." In this presentation Freud is concerned to demonstrate that reliance upon any one of these typical approaches to life to the exclusion of the others is bound to lead to a situation that is threatening to the health of any person. Further, he adds that one who, by virtue of "a specially unfavourable instinctual constitution" and the failure to transform and rearrange the libidinal components, finds it hard to obtain happiness in the external situation may resort to "flight to neurotic illness...." (30-31.)

[75] "Libidinal Types," SE XXI, 218-220.

As *libidinal* types, these entities serve to illustrate the economy of the libido in Freud's thought; but they also demonstrate his ideal. Suffering has not disappeared in any of these types; but in the ideal type we find what might be called a harmony of sufferings, interdependent and integrated, both world- and self-denying and world- and self-affirming. In the end, love of self and love of the world constitute the humane ideal of liberation from suffering.

But it is worth noting that while the claims of the reality principle and of the external world occupied Freud for so much of his life, he finds that the narcissistic demands with which we began life and whose transformations constitute our growth do achieve a certain grandeur, notably present in humor–the human phenomenon *par excellence*. "Humour is not resigned; it is rebellious." It fends off the possibility of suffering. It is this connection with the human resistance to the compulsion to suffer, rather than simply to single events of unpleasure, that makes humor the great human quality. Without it, there can be no health, despite its continuous link with psychosis. Freud observes that these aspects of humor are apparently due to the similarity between the one with the "sense of humour" and the parent who observes with a condescending but gentle eye the antics of a child. Humor, then, places the accent upon the super-ego and condescends to the ego; or, in the dynamic and quantitative perspective, the super-ego is hypercathected and the ego decathected. Although humor in fact repudiates reality it does so in a manner which we can hardly explain, that we find liberating. It says to us that the world is just worth a jest.[76]

---

[76] "Humour," SE XXI, 162-163, 166.

Cura Animae Psychoanalytica

Freud's goal was the end of suffering. It is important to understand that his program of "cure" rested firmly upon his conviction that "cure" was an achievable end. We must avoid begging the question here; what Freud means by "cure" is, at least, the strengthening of the self–really the ego, as we shall see–so that it can live in the context of reality without self-deception about its motives, and at most–what is not so different–, to enjoy the full development of the self and its living from day to day. Such a purpose explains the emphasis in the present discussion upon reality and the end of the neuroses. Freud's notion of "cure" also provides the proper framework for understanding what he considers to be the goals of psychoanalysis (to which I shall turn presently): the strengthening of the ego, the dictatorship of reason, and the accomplishment of these goals through the purposes and procedures of psychoanalysis. The emphasis here, then, is upon Freud's conviction that all of these issues are comprehensible as attainable goals. How they are to be achieved will be discussed in the final section of this work, Freud's truth of the cause of the end of suffering.

Strengthening The Ego

Although the interpretation of Freud's thought has tended to focus upon his view of the unconscious, Freud himself insisted that the chief task of psychoanalysis was the strengthening of the ego. This is consistent with his other emphases upon the reality principle and the elevation of the unconscious to the conscious.

The ego is that part of the id which, on the one hand, encounters the limitations of the external world and, on the other, brings the influence of that external world to bear upon the id for the purpose of limiting the id's headlong flight toward satisfaction regardless of the consequences. The ego, then, represents reason and sanity. The task of psychoanalysis is to assist the ego in its work. The ego requires assistance; for its work threatens always to overcome its relatively weak position in the struggle of the instincts with the world.[77] Psychoanalysis' link to the external world, to reality, gives it a powerful tool in its task of assisting the ego; for it is the ego's relationship to the external world that determines whether it will succeed or fail in its task of guiding the life of the psyche, and thus of the person. The ego must bring the id into subjection to itself, and must withdraw the libidinal power of the id and transform the id's attachments into "ego-constructions."[78]

As the analysis of the neuroses tells us, the balance among ego, id and external world (and super-ego), with its attendant distinction between the

---

[77] *Ego and Id*, 29-30; *cf.* NIL, SE XXII, 8-10, and *Outline*, 114.
[78] *Ego and Id*, 82.

sanity of the ego and the passions of the id, is an "ideal."[79] Indeed, it is the fragility of the ego and the extreme difficulty of its role that are most striking. The ego is uneasy, aware of alien and powerful guests abroad. It is weak, weaker than its own narcissism allows it to realize, its strength sapped from within by the instinctive drives of the id which threaten to suck dry the reservoir of the ego's own nutriment.[80]

In the end actions are taken of which the ego is unaware. Its only recourse is to look inward, like the ruler who, instead of listening to the paid officials, begins to hear the voice of his people. Then the ego may avoid illness.[81] In other words, egoism will no longer be confused with narcissism. The strengthening of the ego through the infusion of it with libidinal energy will be accomplished at the expense of the narcissistic impulses that are so destructive to the ego's task.[82]

"A person only falls ill of a neurosis if his ego has lost the capacity to allocate his libido in some way. The stronger is his ego, the easier will it be for it carry out that task."[83] The cure for neurosis, whether of future or past occasions, is a strong ego. A strong ego keeps us from falling ill. The neurotic could become healthy again, that is, be capable of enjoyment and efficiency—precisely the traits of which he is incapable by definition—if the conflict between his ego and his libido came to an end and if his libido were again at the ego's disposal.[84]

This is the therapeutic task of psychoanalysis. The "present attachments" of libido that so clearly characterize the neurotic are to be detached and returned to the control and service of the ego. The task of the physician is the stimulation of a transference, in which the old conflicts which produced the detachment of libidinal energy from and the consequent enfeeblement of the ego are revived and redirected back to the ego, and subjected once again to the ego's control. This is a strengthening of the ego for the obvious reason that the psychic energy previously lost to the ego may now nourish it. The conflict, in other words, is elevated to the highest psychical level, as a normal mental conflict, one over which the ego may exert full control. Alienation between ego and libido is brought to an end, no new fresh repression occurs and, —nothing less— the subject's mental unity is restored.[85] The restoration of mental unity, which is tantamount to cure even in the thought of one so reluctant to use the term as Freud, is the direct result and function of the ego's recovery

---

[79] *Ibid.*, 29-30, 82; *cf.* "Analysis," SE XXIII, 235, and *Outline*, 111-112.
[80] "Difficulty," SE XVII, 142; *cf.* "Analysis," SE XXIII, 237.
[81] "Difficulty," SE XVII, 143.
[82] IL, SE XVI, 416-419.
[83] *Ibid.*, 387.
[84] *Ibid.*, 454ff..
[85] *Ibid.*.

335

of lost libidinal power and the consequent reduction of the unconscious control of human life.

The strengthening of the ego is also, Freud argues, an alteration of the ego. From this perspective the ego's reluctance to accept libidinal activity and the consequent repression is replaced by sublimation of a portion of it.[86] Here again what is described is the transformation of what is unconscious into what is conscious, or the establishing of ego control over the content of the unconscious. Practically speaking, while the analytic transference seeks to accomplish a wholesale transfer of all material so detached to the ego, it is frequently satisfied with something less. Yet Freud means to say that the goal of psychoanalysis is the establishment of complete ego control; this is just what he means by "cure."[87] The healthy person is one who is capable of both enjoyment and efficiency, for his ego directs and controls the disposition of libido. This state of affairs is disrupted for the neurotic, and it may be regained.[88]

This last point is significant. As Freud argued throughout his work, the causes of the neuroses are common to all, whether clinically apparent or not. One can distinguish between "healthy" and "neurotic" persons not in terms of their constitutional disposition but in terms of the degree to which the ego disposes of libidinal energy in its attempts to exert mastery over the id. The implication is clear: cure does not mean the end of the disposition, which is constitutional in nature, but the elevation of that disposition to the conscious, to ego control. The healthy person is a neurotic whose mental processes have been set in order under the hegemony of the ego, those very processes that are the cause of neurosis and indeed of mental life itself.

The aim of treatment is to bring about the strengthening of the ego. This does not mean that the patient's world view must eventually conform to that of the physician; it is not the physician's ego that must be strengthened. Rather the focus of treatment is upon the native and natural strengths of the patient; and the goal is to help him "to make the best of him that his inherited capacities will allow and so to make him as efficient and capable of enjoyment as is possible."[89] There is no objective pattern to be matched; rather what is sought is the empowering of the patient's ego in the context of his own biography. It is true that the symptoms should disappear if the "cure" works; but the disappearance of the symptoms is, so to speak, a by-product of the strengthening of the ego.[90] The patient will cure himself, with the aid of the physician, and

---

[86] *Ibid..*
[87] *Ibid.;* *cf.* "Analysis," SE XXIII, 235.
[88] IL, SE XVI, 457.
[89] "Articles: (A)," SE XVIII, 250-251.
[90] *Ibid..*

be able to defend himself against the threats of the instinctual demands of the id and "moral demands of the super-ego," by alliance with the real world.[91] Psychoanalysis tries to restore to the ego the command over the id it lost to its early repressions. This is the sole purpose of analysis.[92] Where id was, there ego shall be.[93]

Finally, we may ask whether psychoanalysis yields a new person. The answer is no; for the cure consists, neither more nor less, in allowing the self to heal itself, to restore the "great unity" which we call the ego. No new synthesis is required or possible.[94]

Cure, then, means the strengthening of an ego weakened by resistances, that is, by the withdrawal of its energy in the struggle against the instincts. But it is useful for us to pause and remind ourselves of the nature of the structure of the ego, its role and function in the psychic economy, lest we misconstrue the nature and possibility of cure. The ego is Freud's term for that part of the psyche established—and caught, so to speak—between the supreme force of external reality, of *Ananke*, and the powerful forces of eros and thanatos, or the id, the unconscious. It is itself related in a fundamental way to both and, indeed, it is most precisely the joining of these two opposing forces. Cure, therefore, means that a *modus vivendi* has been established in the context of the individual's biography, through the making conscious of the forces of the unconscious and of the conflict, once hidden and now revealed to the patient, between them. The cured patient may now proceed in an efficient way to deal with "ordinary unhappiness," that is to say, the natural conflict between world and self, and to find in that life-long work some enjoyment. It is this possibility of enjoyment and efficiency that is really meant by the notion of ego, and it is the relative success or failure of efficiency and enjoyment that Freud means when he refers to a weakened or strengthened ego.

I return to this material because the reader of Freud should be warned lest the ego be construed as a thing, or kind of thing, a conscious soul, a compartment that grows or diminishes in size and importance.[95] Any such conceptualization leads to a misunderstanding of what Freud means by cure. What he understands by cure is the end of inefficient and unnecessary conflict among energies of the psyche. This is the implication of his "economic" terminology. But the strengthened ego, as a goal of psychoanalysis, means simply the ability to live as efficiently and enjoyably as possible. It is also a state to which the psyche will inevitably and automatically return when, with the aid of the physician,

---

91 *Outline*, 63.
92 "Lay Analysis," SE XX. 205.
93 NIL, SE XXII, 79-80.
94 "Advance," SE XVII, 161-166; *cf.* IL, SE XVI, 435.
95 *Cf.*, *e.g.*, "Lay Analysis," SE XX, 194.

the resistances are overcome and the symptoms disappear. The neurotic may heal himself; that is in essence the promise of the strengthening of the ego.

The Goals Of Psychoanalysis

Let us now examine Freud's understanding of the "truth" of the end of suffering in terms of the goals of psychoanalysis. Here the issue is of broader scope than the subject of the preceding section although the goals presuppose the strengthening of the ego.

Let us return to the basic issue, the difference between the mental struggle of the neurotic and that of the "healthy" mind. In either case mental struggle is a given; but the pathogenic struggle between mental impulses is not between two impulses working on the same footing. In the pathogenic case, one "has made its way to the stage of what is pre-conscious or conscious while the other has been held back at the stage of the unconscious...."[96] Therapy seeks not to bring the struggle to an end, a goal unattainable in any case according to Freud's understanding of the nature of human life, but to raise the conflict to the level where the impulses meet on the same ground. This is the sole task of therapy.[97] Only when this is accomplished is a true "decision" possible. What is unconscious must be translated to the conscious; "...we lift the repressions, we remove the preconditions for the formation of symptoms, we transform the pathogenic conflict into a normal one for which it must be possible somehow to find a solution. All that we bring about in a patient is this single psychical change; the length to which it is carried is the measure of the help we provide."[98] It is not the task of psychoanalysis to put an end to mental conflict. The truth of the end of suffering is, rather, that we first realize that we are who we are because of that conflict, and second, we know what that conflict is, for it is not hidden from us by our resistances and defenses.

There will be those, Freud suggests, who may feel some disappointment at this conclusion. They had thought, perhaps, that after "submitting to the tedious labours of a psychoanalysis, [the] patient would become another man; but the total result, so it seems, is that he has rather less that is unconscious and rather more that is conscious in him than he had before. The fact is that you are probably under-estimating the importance of an internal change of this kind. The neurotic who is cured has really become another man, though at bottom, of course, he has remained the same; that is to say, he has become what he might have become under the most favourable conditions. But that is a very great

---

96 IL, SE XVI, 433.
97 Ibid..
98 Ibid., 435.

338

deal."[99]

What these conditions are will concern us shortly; what I stress here is that the creation of a new being is not among the goals of psychoanalysis; rather it seeks to free us from our stubborn resistance to knowing ourselves as we truly are. And yet, ironically and paradoxically, we are different upon achieving that end. Put another way, there is neither the need nor the means to destroy the "old" self; for it possesses all that it needs to be free of suffering, namely, to annihilate the barriers to efficiency and enjoyment.

"Genuine psychoanalysis" has the discovery, or better, the rediscovery, of the transparent self as its goal. Further, true psychoanalysis is the process by which the amnesia that conceals knowledge of his childhood from the patient is removed.[100] As in the analysis of dreams, where it is the task of the analytic process to reverse dream work by making the latent dream manifest,[101] the analysis must liberate the events of childhood from their attachment to the "actual present day" and secure them in the past where they belong.[102] The physician's task is to "bring to the patient's knowledge the unconscious repressed impulses existing in him, and, for that purpose, to uncover the resistances that oppose this extension of his knowledge about himself."[103]

Freud's objection to Jung's views is based in part upon the reality of the amnesia and resistances and, as well, upon the reality of the childhood events that have been repressed. The goal of psychoanalysis as Freud described it is meaningful only if it is clear that the sexuality of infancy is a primary fact. What Jung sought, on the contrary, was to construe sexuality theoretically.[104] In his research on the sexual ideas on which the structure of the family is based, such as the incestuous object choice observed in the context of the Oedipus complex, he eventually departed from the line of logic his research implied, namely, the reality of infantile sexuality, and separated religion and ethics from these sexual sources. "If ethics and religion were not allowed to be sexualized but had to be something other and 'higher' from the start, and if nevertheless the ideas contained in them seemed undeniably to be descended from the Oedipus and family-complex, there could be only one way out: it must be that from the very first these complexes themselves do not mean what they seem to be expressing but bear the higher 'anagogic' meaning (as Silberer calls it) which made it possible for them to be employed in the abstract

---

[99] Ibid..
[100] " 'A Child,' " SE XVII, 183.
[101] Cf. IL, SE XV, 171-180.
[102] "Construction," SE XXIII, 268.
[103] "Advance," SE XVII, 159.
[104] "History," SE XIV, 19.

trains of thought of ethics and religious mysticism."[105]

The truth is otherwise: the patient must deal with his illness. That is "the first piece of reality.... Efforts to spare him that task point to the physician's incapacity to help him to overcome his resistances, or else to the physician's dream of the result of his own work."[106] Jung's fundamental therapeutic error, then, is his resistance (the word is significant) to the fact of the nature of the illness, the repression of infantile sexuality. Unless this reality and the resistances are acknowledged as the fundamental facts of the case, the restoration of the great unity we call the ego will not occur, for the patient will not have been forced to analyze his own torn mind, and thus to bring the amnesia and its protectors, the resistances, to naught.[107]

The removal of the amnesia requires repetition of the original events in the context of analysis. While it is true that, for the most part, Freud despairs of the treatment of narcissistic/psychotic disorders because of their virtually total control of the ego and the concomitant inability of the ego to respond to external reality,[108] the transference neuroses present genuine possibilities for the therapeutic repetition. The path is backwards, to the source of the psychical imbalance. The ego, with the aid of the physician, must seek out the repressions, correct them, and address its conflicts rather than fleeing from them.[109] That correction requires that the analysis return to the earliest period, through the path marked by symptoms, dreams and free associations. The success of analysis depends upon the successful reproduction of the original situation in the patient's memory as a consequence of the backward search, following the signposts of resistance. If successful, the patient's advanced age works in his favor, and his stronger adult ego will not flee the thing that was so frightening to his childish self.[110] Those signposts are crucial; for they are the only sure guarantee that the analysis is proceeding along the right path, backwards over the territory already travelled. Thus may the physician identify that "point of entry into consciousness of the questionable mental process" which, because it was not "brought to an end normally" is the foundation out of which the symptom grows.

The return to the origin—not simply on the part of the physician as he answers for himself the question of whence the symptoms came, but by the patient, who alone can bring the cure to completion—[111] is the way to

---

[105] *Ibid.*, 61-62.
[106] *Ibid.*, 66.
[107] *Cf.* "Advance," SE XVII, 161-166.
[108] *Cf.* IL, SE XVI, 420-422, 437-441.
[109] "Lay Analysis," SE XX, 205.
[110] *Ibid.*.
[111] *Cf.* IL, SE XVI, 437ff..

freeing libido for the service of the ego. We must, Freud argues, become masters of the symptoms, both for the sake of the physician and for the sake of the patient. Indeed, analysis begins with the expressed need of the patient to gain mastery over his symptoms. The original conflict is the cause of the symptoms, and to it both patient and doctor must return: "we must renew the conflict with which [the symptoms] arose, and, with the help of motive forces which were not at the patient's disposal in the past, we must guide it to a different outcome."[112]

Let us return briefly to the issue of the aetiology of neuroses. Freud is concerned chiefly with the neurotic distress caused by the struggles of childhood and their consequences, especially when they have been inefficiently incorporated into the developmental process. Thus repetition and removal of resistances causes the removal of symptoms and elevation of unconscious conflict to the ordinary unhappiness of conscious conflict. But what can be said of the greater "philosophical questions"? Is neurosis to be attributed to nature or to nurture, to environment or endowment, to the self or to the world? In other words, is suffering our doing or the world's?

Freud considers this line of speculation to be pointless, however enticing it appears. He neither favors one option over the other, nor is he willing to go farther than to say that the goals of psychoanalysis are best served when one pays attention to the particular case in hand, acknowledging that both nature and nurture are causal factors—as he states most boldly in his discussion of eros, thanatos and *Ananke*. Illustrative of his attitude in this regard is his understanding of the difference between psychoanalysis and psychiatry. In his *Introductory Lectures* Freud presented the case of a woman who had falsely accused her husband of having an affair. In the course of analysis the accusation was revealed to be a compensation invented by the woman for her wish to have an affair of her own, with a close relation, that is, an incestuous love relationship. Freud pointed out that psychiatry explains such cases in terms of external causes and is thus of necessity unsuccessful in finding the cause for the woman's neurotic behavior.[113] "Psychiatry does not employ the technical methods of psychoanalysis; it omits to make any inferences from the *content* of the delusion, and in pointing to heredity, it gives us a very general and remote aetiology instead of indicating first the more special and proximate causes."[114]

But surely, Freud continues, both constitutional and experiential factors are present. Psychoanalysis does not deny the validity of psychiatric treatment; rather, it undertakes to pay strict attention to both nature

---

[112] *Ibid.*, 454-455.
[113] *Ibid.*, 253ff..
[114] *Ibid.*..

and nurture.[115] It is therefore fallacious and misleading to identify either hereditary and constitutional factors or environment and experience as a final cause of neuroses; the question of whether the neuroses are the result of predisposition or external factors is a false trail. The fixation of libido that determines the neurotic experience may be assigned in part to the "predisposing, internal factor" in the aetiology of the neuroses, while frustration of libidinal expression represents the "accidental, external one."[116] However, it is closer to the reality of psychical disturbance to view the relationship between the contributions of the sexual constitution and external circumstances to neurosis as a "complemental series." At one end there are those people who, because of the path of development their ego has followed were bound to fall ill, and at other end those who would have escaped illness had their circumstances been different."[117]

This conclusion is tantamount to refusing the gambit of opponents and anyone who insisted upon either nature or nurture as the final cause of suffering; furthermore, Freud is in fact refusing to choose a world view, and prefers to concentrate solely upon the suffering patient. In "The Dynamics of Transference" he rejects the criticism that he has ignored constitutional factors in his single-minded attention to infantile impressions. On the contrary, "*Daimon kai tuche* [here, Endowment and Chance] determine man's fate–rarely or ever one of those powers alone. The amount of aetiological effectiveness to be attributed to each of them can only be arrived at in every individual case separately."[118] Thus the goals of psychoanalysis do not include the task of answering the hoary question of nature or nurture. Freud neither chooses one over the other, nor does he collapse the distinction between them. The issue is a false one and not conducive to the end of suffering.

Rather, the focus of psychoanalysis is upon human nature. Nothing else is significant; and whatever is significant is a function of human nature. This means that at times psychoanalysis will succeed in isolating causes for disease, but will be powerless to ameliorate it. Psychoanalysis is, in other words, not merely a therapy. At times it is an unsuccessful therapy. Freud admitted that psychoanalysis, like psychiatry, was powerless against delusions. The patient, he said, cannot be made to understand what has happened to him.[119] Yet the value of psychoanalysis is not to be gainsaid: "We have a right, or rather a duty, to carry on our research without consideration of any immediate beneficial effect." Who can tell when some fragment of knowledge will not be transformed into

---

[115] *Ibid.*; *cf.* IL, SE XV, 20-21.
[116] IL, SE XVI, 346.
[117] *Ibid.*, 339-347.
[118] "Transference," SE XII, 99.
[119] IL, SE XVI, 255-256.

power, into therapeutic power as well? The final justification for psycho-analysis is its contribution to the understanding of human nature, even if it were everywhere as unsuccessful as in cases of psychotic delusion; and, of course, it is not.[120]

This suggests that psychoanalysis is not an appropriate treatment for the so-called "common" (German: *Aktuel*) neuroses, whose symptoms are the result of direct toxic damage. Rather, psychoanalysis begins and ends with the study of the superstructure of the mental life. Thus what it says of the neurotic it may say also, without doing violence to its method, of the history of civilization, of religion and mythology, and of social structures.[121] It is not, as Freud pointed out, true causal therapy, which would rely upon some chemical alteration of the mental system to increase or diminish the amount of libido present at any given time. Indeed, such a panacaea is a chimera. For the cause of the end of suffering is also the cause of suffering, namely, the structure of the mental life.[122]

Psychoanalysis moved away from its origins as a "purely medical technique," from the study of "somatic determinants of nervous disease to an extent that was bewildering to physicians." "Instead, it was brought into contact with the mental substance of human lives—the lives not only of the sick, but of the healthy, the normal and the supernormal.... It learned to recognize the power of memories, the unsuspected importance of the years of childhood in shaping the adult, and the strength of wishes, which falsify human judgements and lay down fixed lines for human endeavour...."[123] The ultimate subject of psychoanalysis was the unstable superstructure of the life of man. The life of the neurotic patient exposes the life of the healthy mind, and of the artifacts and traditions of culture.[124]

Psychoanalysis may be commended, then, not because of its therapeutic value, although that value is enormous precisely because of its true contribution, its account of the information it gives us about what most concerns human beings—their own nature.[125] The account of human nature and the therapeutic contribution of psychoanalysis cannot be separated.[126] Therefore its chief application is in the realm of education, *Erziehung*, the life-long process of growing. Education is the process by which the child learns to control his instincts, and at the same time is a work, indeed, *the* work, of society. Those tasks call upon the very mental

---

[120] *Ibid.*.
[121] *Ibid.*, 389.
[122] *Ibid.*, 436.
[123] "Preface," SE XVII, 259.
[124] *Ibid.*, 259-261.
[125] NIL, SE XXII, 156-157; *cf.* "Articles: (A)," SE XVIII, 248.
[126] *Ibid.*.

forces that can produce neurosis. This is the truth of psychoanalysis, and the truth of suffering, that the analytic work is life-long, an endeavor to convert the causes of suffering into the causes of the end of suffering. In sum, psychoanalysis viewed as a therapy is less important than psychoanalysis understood as the means of discovering the roots of human nature. But that latter knowledge is exactly what Freud always meant by true therapy, the elevation of the unconscious into the conscious, a complete self-understanding, renewed daily.[127]

Whether viewed as therapy or as an understanding of the nature of the self, psychoanalysis is committed to the end of suffering and not to a world view or philosophy. This very important quality of the analytic view of the world is what Freud means to expound in his many comments on the "scientific" nature of psychoanalysis. It is evident in his stout refusal to support either an unqualified program of repression or of satisfaction of libido. He was fully aware of the dangers on either side. Indeed, at times he held that occasionally the physician should retreat before the neurotic symptoms rather than play any part in forcing the patient to live unprotected by his neurosis in the face of genuinely threatening external conditions.[128] The success of analysis must be defined in terms of the illness, not in terms of external factors, social requirements, or preconceived philosophical dogma. Freud insisted that psychoanalysis can not serve any particular philosophy, nor urge it upon a patient. However nobly intentioned, such an approach is "after all only to use violence...."[129] To the consternation of his critics Freud sided neither with repression nor with gratification. This was in part a function of Freud's persistent dualism. The mental life did not seek either simple gratification or simple repression. Just because, for example, ego libido existed did not mean there were no other instincts, as Jung believed.[130] Indeed, contrary to the popular view of psychoanalysis, Freud did not seek to trace the neuroses back to sexuality alone (nor did it seek to "suppress by means of authority any mental phenomenon that may occur in the patient"), but to the "conflict between the sexual impulses and the ego.... To believe that psychoanalysis seeks a cure for neurotic disorders by giving a free rein to sexuality is a serious misunderstanding which can only be excused by ignorance." Quite the contrary; for the "making conscious of repressed sexual desires in analysis" leads not to their fulfillment but to mastery over them "which the previous repression had been unable to achieve."[131]

---

127 NIL, SE XXII, 136-157.
128 IL, SE XVI, 382.
129 "Advance," SE XVII, 165.
130 Cf. "Articles: (A)," SE XVIII, 248.
131 Ibid., 252; cf. IL, SE XVI, 432-433.

This mastery is the sole aim of psychoanalysis. It was objected that such attention to the conflict between sexuality and the ego undermines civilization, that is to say, religion, authority and morals. Such a view of psychoanalysis is quite wrong, Freud insisted. Like all science, psychoanalysis has no such aim in view, for it is quite untendentious and has but a single goal, "namely to arrive at a consistent view of one portion of reality." It is, finally, nothing short of ridiculous to hold that the revelation of the origins of art, love, ethical and social goals, in short the highest goods of humanity, in the life of the instincts will threaten civilization. As we know, it is precisely that knowledge that will strengthen—*Civilization and its Discontents* is, after all, a *defense* of civilization.[132]

Yet Freud had as little truck with conventional morality. The fear evident in Freud's opponents was an infantile one, that if sexuality were acknowledged for the driving power it was society's restrictions on its activity would be threatened. They insisted upon ignoring Freud's lessons about sexuality by limiting their understanding of it (quite willfully) to the genital organization and defending it as procreative only. They care little, Freud repeats, what it costs the individual when society forces the individual "to live psychologically beyond his means, involving him in cultural hypocrisy."[133] Psychoanalysis does not propose that the instincts be gratified at all costs; rather, it urges that instincts be repressed less forcefully and that their power and significance be honestly acknowledged. Repression is important; but the present means are less efficient than what is wanted.[134]

Freud is a moralist; but the morality he defends may not be the conventional morality. For conventional morality, which insists upon a high degree of suppression and willful ignorance of the sexual instincts and their development, is little cause for rejoicing.[135] Morality is among the goals of psychoanalysis; but given its nature and aims this morality will not be the repressive conventional morality of the society (although psychoanalysis explains the sources of this morality). Rather, the morality of which Freud is confident is founded entirely upon an honest self-understanding, utterly free of self-deception. In this and other respects it must be accorded a higher position than the conventional morality. But let us note that it is neither a morality of full gratification nor of full suppression, but of full understanding. It is well said that if we know the truth we shall be free; but Freud insists that we may also be good in the only sense possible, in the sense of being mature.

This is the meaning behind his insistence that psychoanalysis is a

---

[132] "Articles: (A)," SE XVIII, 253-254.
[133] "Resistances," SE XIX, 213-219.
[134] *Ibid.*, 220.
[135] IL, SE XVI, 434-435.

345

science and not a world view, a religion, or a philosophy. It is better to acknowlege and live with ordinary unhappiness than to depend upon illusion.[136] Only then are the twin aims of efficiency and enjoyment capable of achievement. Psychoanalysis promises nothing more–it even acknowledges that at times it cannot deliver even on this promise–and Freud tells us that, in the end, no life can really ask for more without falling into illusions. At least, he notes wryly, psychoanalysis "contains enough revolutionary factors to ensure that no one educated by it will in later life take the side of reaction and repression." More we cannot reasonably expect, or want.[137]

The goals of psychoanalysis are not easily won, for the process demands a recapitulation of the suppressed conflict that defines human life. Resistance during analysis is thus both the surest signpost along the road to and the hindrance to full self-understanding. Resistance, Freud concluded, is not confined to the neurotic under treatment. It is to be found in the opposition to psychoanalytic theory and treatment itself. When the fundamental issue of sexuality was raised it elicited vigorous opposition. Freud pointed out quite cogently that resistance on the part of his critics was neurotic resistance; and this is a fair measure, he noted, of how close neurosis is to normality.[138] "The position was at once alarming and consoling," Freud observed, "alarming because it was no small thing to have the whole human race as one's patient, and consoling because after all everything was taking place as the hypothesis of psychoanalysis declared that it was bound to."[139] It was not the case that psychoanalysis was first to point to the misunderstood power of sexual desire in human life. That prize Freud awards to others, such as the philosopher Schopenhauer. But whereas Schopenhauer came to his conclusions on the strength of abstract considerations–and thereby gained acceptance without threatening his hearers–psychoanalysis showed the power of sexuality to be universal, and sought to press every person toward some informed attitude towards it. Hence, resistance was understandable.[140]

After all, however, the situation was predictable. Resistance is a defense of civilization. Sexual, instinctual, energy is, in other words, sublimated and redirected toward ends deemed acceptable to the purposes of society. But this arrangement is unstable; there is a constant and pervasive risk that the instincts will refuse to be controlled. Society knows no greater threat; and thus it does not wish to be reminded of this precarious portion of its foundation. "It has no interest in the recognition of

---

136 *Cf.* NIL, SE XXII, 158-182.
137 *Ibid.*, 150-151.
138 *Cf.* "Lay Analysis," SE XX, 206-213.
139 "Resistances," SE XIX, 221.
140 "Difficulty," SE XVII, 143-144.

the strength of the sexual instincts or in the demonstration of the importance of sexual life to the individual. On the contrary, it has set about diverting attention from that whole field of ideas. That is why it will not tolerate this outcome of psychoanalytic research...."[141]

In sum, the vigor of the objections to psychoanalysis is rather a confirmation of its truth than an indictment of its procedures. It is as much the confirmation of that truth, and of the legitimacy of the goals of psychoanalysis, as the appearance of resistance in the neurotic patient. Freud does not engage in hyperbole when he speaks of having the whole human race as one's patient.

Yet Freud attempted strenuously to avoid claiming too much for psychoanalysis; for psychoanalysis has to do with human suffering only, that is, the mental conflict that defines the human self. Psychoanalysis "has never claimed to provide a complete theory of human mentality in general, but only expected that what it offered should be applied to supplement and correct the knowledge acquired by other means."[142] In Freud's treatment of Leonardo we can find a good example of those "other means."

Leonardo presents a fascinating example of repression and sublimation of the instincts. That genius sublimated his sexual instincts successfully (and, in view of what we are told about the absence of his father, avoided the neurotic consequences of a dominant super-ego) into a life of research and craving for knowledge. Freud admits that he is at a loss to explain why this is the result of Leonardo's development. It is beyond the scope of psychoanalysis to explain why craving for knowledge was the consequence of sublimation, rather than injury to his intellectual activity or insurmountable disposition to obsessional neurosis. Thus while psychoanalysis can describe the causes and probable effects of mental conflict, it cannot say why, in Leonardo's case, the consequences were ego-syntonic.[143] One might observe that this is but another example of the proximity of neurosis and normality. But Freud goes on to draw the line between the territory of psychoanalysis in general and other methodologies. Instincts and their transformations are at the limit of what psychoanalysis can discern. Biology lies beyond that boundary.[144] Those "other means," then, are biological and somatic explanations. There are, apparently, "organic foundations of character" whose nature is beyond the interest of psychoanalysis. For example, the tendency of biological research of Freud's day was to seek a chemical source for a person's con-

---

[141] IL, SE XV, 22-23.
[142] "History," SE XIV, 49-50.
[143] *Leonardo*, 85-86.
[144] *Ibid.*, 86.

stitution.[145] But these "other means" hold no interest for Freud because they lie outside the chief interest of psychoanalysis, human suffering in the context of the self, where the self is defined as the conflict between the conscious and the unconscious. This, however, is the crux of the human condition; and therefore somatic concerns do not lie properly within the field of the analysis of human suffering, which is concerned with what one does with somatic disturbance, as one deals with the external world.[146]

In short, although the scope of psychoanalysis' interest and competence is limited, it encompasses the heart of human suffering, the issue of the conflict among the ego, id, super-ego and world. From the perspective of the assumption that what is at the heart of the human condition, indeed what defines it, is suffering, everything else is secondary, even insignificant. In limiting the field of psychoanalysis Freud is simply asserting that it is not anything less than a revolutionary re-interpretation of human suffering. He has moved beyond the external analysis and somaticism of the medical profession into the realm of self-knowledge. That knowledge has therapeutic power, of course; but Freud insisted, as we have seen, that psychoanalysis is more valuable as a means of understanding the nature of human life and its structures than as a therapy.

There is, then, a certain irony, and at times understatement, in his delimiting pronouncements about the range of psychoanalysis. Psychoanalysis alone cannot offer a complete *Weltanschauung*.[147] Its contribution lies in its description of a mental apparatus with an ego oriented to the external world and equipped with consciousness, and an unconscious id, dominated by its instinctual needs. These fundamental notions may be employed as contributions to various fields of knowledge. But, Freud says rather disingenuously, "[i]f these contributions often contain the essence of the facts, this only corresponds to the important part which...is played in our lives by the mental unconscious that has so long remained unknown."[148] The scope of psychoanalysis may be limited; but without its insights any other understanding of the human condition is merely superficial.

The Dictatorship Of Reason

Reason, says Freud, stands between normality and neurosis. There is cause for hope; there is a truth of the end of suffering, and it is the "Dictatorship of Reason." In raising this hope Freud moves beyond merely clinical concerns to a kind of soteriology.

We possess in our very mental structure the causes of the end of suffering; they are the same as the causes of suffering, namely, the conflicts

---

[145] *Ibid.*.
[146] *Ibid.*; cf. "Analysis," SE XXIII, 356-357.
[147] "Short Account," SE XIX, 209.
[148] *Ibid.*.

between ego and id, between love and death, in the face of the external world, or *Ananke*. Victory in this conflict means not the end of the conflict (this would be tantamount to the end of human life), but that the conflict is overseen by Logos, the "still small voice" that insists upon the difference between illusion and "reality." It is this sacrifice of emotional satisfaction in favor of mastery by reason that distinguishes the hero of civilization, despite his discontents. So the "Moses" of Michaelangelo, arrested in a moment of heroic control over his anger, stands for the dictatorship of reason over passion.[149]

Leonardo's triumph over emotion displaces obedience to authority. Such obedience is a manifestation of the dominance of the neurotic and emotional conflict of human life. In contrast, Leonardo worked with his reason rather than his memory, and so became the first modern natural scientist, since the Greeks, to rely solely on observation and judgement for an understanding of nature.[150] This triumph of reason is related to his libidinal development. Leonardo accepted nature as the extension of the mother who nourished him, and rejected authority as the father without whom he lived from a very early age.[151]

Free of the need to rely upon authority, Leonardo discovered the truth about the world–that it was "governed" by chance, not by a beneficent Providence. Chance, nevertheless, was not unworthy to determine our fate. We see now the most compelling element in Leonardo's attitude toward the world, according to Freud. Leonardo did not require a kindly Providence, that is, a father who loved him. Thus freed from the bonds of infantile attachment, he could reject religion, God, and authority without penalty. What Leonardo realized was that our fate bore no final relationship to our wishes. Chance takes no notice of narcissistic desires.[152]

Such a realization is liberating. Few of us, says Freud, are able to look upon the "dark power of destiny" as impersonal, as can the Dutch poet Multatuli (E. K. Dekker) who renounces the goddess Moira in favor of Logos and *Ananke*. Yet this is exactly the goal implied in the psychoanalytic understanding of the self's relation to the world, to cut the libidinal ties to a world fashioned out of our infantile wishes.[153] Such liberation is clearly difficult, for it requires that we see that part of ourselves that our very nature allows, even forces, us to deny. Yet it is possible to see in the rise of science, the third of the great cultural stages of human development after magic and religion, just this Leonardian freedom.

---

[149] "Moses," SE XIII, 233.
[150] *Leonardo*, 72-73.
[151] *Ibid.*; *cf.* 85-86.
[152] *Ibid.*, 87.
[153] "Masochism," SE XIX, 166-168; *cf. Illusion, passim.*

In rejecting the omnipotence of thought, and in ceasing to reserve some power for himself while ceding ultimate control cautiously to a divine father–that is, in giving up religion–scientific man has resigned his claim to control of the world.[154] This scientific renunciation of the pleasure principle makes possible the adaption to reality, that is, to the seeking of the object in the external world.[155]

As noted already in the discussion of the causes of suffering and the truth of suffering, Freud's notion of liberation is liberation from any understanding of the universe that rests upon the illusion that there is a connection between our desires and the external world. Philosophy, religion, Marxism, nihilism and their cognates and counterparts are all rejected as based upon illusions emanating out of our own emotional conflicts. Science demands only and always that our knowledge correspond with reality. Science is willing to be corrected in light of the facts of existence even if this means that one must acknowledge and bear pain and suffering. This is better than illusion.[156] In truth, Freud points out, scientific thought is not very different from the normal activity of thought, which all of us–believers and non-believers–employ in looking after our affairs in ordinary life. It is not concerned with affective influences, but rather with trustworthy sense-perceptions, and the conclusions these permit. It seeks truth whether or not it is of practical value.[157]

This encomium to science occurs in the context of the debate with religion, as we have seen. What religion demands, Freud argues, is the renunciation of a scientific spirit which is virtually native to the human endeavor. In contrast,

> Our best hope for the future is that intellect–the scientific spirit, reason–may in process of time establish a dictatorship in the mental life of man. The nature of reason is a guarantee that afterwards it will not fail to give man's emotional impulses and what is determined by them the position they deserve. But the common compulsion exercised by such dominance of reason will prove to be the strongest uniting bond among men and lead the way to further unions. Whatever, like religion's prohibition against thought, opposes such a development, is a danger for the future of mankind.[158]

In fact, we may even now find ourselves in the midst of a phase of development in which the old Oedipal conflict, represented collectively in

---

154 *Totem*, 147.
155 *Ibid.*, 150.
156 NIL, SE XXII, 158-182.
157 *Ibid.*, 170-171.
158 *Ibid.*, 171-172; *Cf. Illusion*, 65ff..

the history of religion, is being succeeded by its dissolution and replacement in the rise of science.[159]

Reason, or, as Freud puts it, "Our God Logos," is insistent and persistent. Its voice is soft but relentless. It succeeds. Here, says Freud, is one of the points about which one may be optimistic in the future of mankind. The primacy of the intellect awaits a distant, but not infinitely distant, future. Its ends are, presumably, the same as those of religion, namely the love of man and the decrease of suffering–insofar as human capacity and external reality, *Ananke*, permit. These wishes will be fulfilled, but not in an illusory manner, with all the cost attached to that kind of satisfaction.[160]

What is promised in this truth of the end of suffering? Not happiness, nor in truth more than an end to ignorance and delusions surrounding suffering through the triumph of intellect, or reason–that, after all, is precisely what Freud means when he paints his picture of the future liberation of humankind. "Our God Logos is perhaps not a very almighty one, and he may only be able to fulfil a small part of what his predecessors have promised."[161] But this realization is not cause for despair, but rather acceptance, or resignation. The world retains its interest; and science may come to know more. This may be illusory; but psychoanalysis is no stranger to illusions, although Freud is hopeful. After all, the very development of our mental organization follows lines laid down by contact with the external world. Further, that organization is an inherent part of the world we investigate scientifically, and, as psychoanalysis has shown, yields knowledge of its own structure and history to such research. Finally, the problem of the external world is not a problem unless it is approached from the direction of our "percipient mental apparatus." Otherwise, it is an empty abstraction, devoid of practical interest.[162]

Among the various possible "cures" of suffering listed in *Civiliza-*

---

159 *Illusion*, 71.
160 *Ibid.*, 87ff..
161 *Ibid.*, 89.
162 *Ibid.*, 87-92. This last observation is one of the surest clues to Freud's attitude toward the external world. While, as he demonstrates massively, he defines the *summum bonum* of human life as living with a clear and unblurred eye to the reality of that world, in and of itself it is meaningless–that is to say, it draws its meaning from the relationship with it created out of human desire. Freud venerates science, especially over against religion; but his admiration stems from what it tells us about our relationship with the world, not about the world itself, considered abstractly. For such an issue, he notes, he has no interest. It is simply a question not worth pursuing. *Cf. Civilization*, 25: "Suffering is nothing other than sensation."

tion and its Discontents, Freud concludes that "one gains the most if one can sufficiently heighten the yield of pleasure from the sources of psychical and intellectual work. When that is so, fate can do little against one."[163] The joy of the artist's creating, of the scientist's unravelling of the mysteries of nature, have a special quality "which we shall certainly one day be able to characterize in metapsychological terms. At present we can only say figuratively that such satisfactions seem 'finer and higher.' " It should not surprise us, I think, to learn that in Freud's view the weak point of this method is that "it is not applicable generally: it is accessible to only a few people," presumbly the Michaelangelo's, the Leonardo's, the Freud's, of this world; and indeed, only those possessed of special dispositions and gifts that are uncommon can follow this path. And even in their lives there is "impenetrable armour against the arrows of fortune, [that] habitually fails when the source of suffering is a person's own body."[164] In a note to this comment, the cause for the rarity of this cure is explored; and Freud suggests that "as a path to happiness, work is not highly prized by men.... The great majority of people only work under the stress of necessity, and this natural human aversion to work raises most difficult social problems."[165] These words are revealing; for, among other things, it shows that what Freud means by science and art is work, a process whose chief psychological significance is this: "the possibility it offers of displacing a large amount of libidinal components, whether narcissistic, aggressive or even erotic, onto professional work and onto the human relations connected with it lends a value by no means second to what it enjoys as something indispensible to the preservation and justification of existence in society."[166]

But for those who can follow the path, fate offers little threat. In fact, for the person whose reason is master of his emotions, this is the closest thing to happiness, to the end of suffering—or more properly to the end of illusion and self-deception—that humankind is ever likely to achieve.

This, then, is the truth of the end of suffering. The conflict of the psychical forces may be directed through psychoanalysis away from neurosis toward health and the dictatorship of reason. Life may be lived without repressions. The energies of the former neurotic may be directed toward living in the world with virtually the full range of his mental and emotional energies at his conscious command. This state of affairs is mature, sober, and subject to constant redress and analysis. It is efficient, and enjoyable. It is life lived in the full light of day, in the *"rosigten*

---

163 *Civilization*, 26.
164 *Ibid.*, 26, 27.
165 *Ibid.*.
166 *Ibid.*.

Licht," the "roseate light" of the conscious world.[167]

Heaven we may leave to the angels and the sparrows.[168] But in one respect nothing has changed; for this truth of the end of suffering is the same as the truth of suffering and its cause. It is only that one knows one's self, and sees clearly what is there, without fear or disappointment, frustration or anxiety.

---

[167] *Ibid.*, 20.
[168] *Illusion*, 82.

The Buddha and the End of Suffering

The truth of suffering and the truth of the end of suffering are both elemental assertions of the nature of human life; but more, they are elementally interdependent. The *paṭiccasamuppāda* series, the series of co-dependent origination, means nothing less. For just as the arising of suffering–from body, sensation, consciousness, rebirth, to suffering–is really a continuous succession of dependent "arisings," so the reversal of that series must be a series of continuous and dependent "cessations." In more general terms, the causes of suffering are precisely the same as the causes of the end of suffering; it is simply that the series of dependency is reversed, either building up or breaking down, as one stands sheaves up against one another or brings them all down by removing any one.

How the arising of suffering is reversed into the series of cessation of suffering will be the concern of the fourth section of this work. It was, however, a matter of enormous significance in the Buddhist tradition that there was a truth of cessation, that suffering did come to an end. This is our present topic. As the tradition insisted, if it were not possible for suffering to come to an end, the Ariyan life would not be proclaimed. This is the counterpart to the assertion that if life were not suffering, the *Dhamma* would not be necessary or possible, nor the *Tathāgata*, nor the *Sangha*, nor the Path. While the *Tathāgata* and the successful *Arahant* know at the end of the path the truth of the cessation of suffering, the beginner, he who has only the faintest glimmering of a suspicion that something is vaguely wrong, must look to the *Tathāgata*, the Teacher and the Enlightened One, for guidance and the guarantee that suffering may indeed be overcome. That is to say, from the very beginning the certainty that suffering can be brought to an end is essential to the Ariyan Truths, the *Dhamma* itself.

But there is more required here than blind trust in the Buddha. The truth of suffering is a truth about the final state itself, the nature of that truth as it is manifest in the *Tathāgata*, the *Arahant*, in the meaning of the end of *dukkha*, and, of course, in the nature of *nibbāna*. Therefore, following the traditional order of the truths, we must first understand the goal before we follow the path. Here our concern is not only with the important question of whether there is an end of suffering, but what it means to say that suffering is at an end. In part, then, the question is answered by examining the characteristics of the *Tathāgata*, in part the characteristics of the *Arahant*/monk–for there is a difference–and in part the nature of *nibbāna* and its relationship to *dukkha*.

In this we will be concerned with the question of the nature of this "final state." Is it a state at all? Is there a person for whom suffering ends? Is there an old person and a new one? What is the relationship of the various arisings discussed earlier to the *khandhas*, the series of co-dependent origination, the inherent tendencies toward love, hate, and

355

ignorance (*rāga-, dosa-, moha-anusayas*), those constitutent parts, as it were, of the human person, to *nibbāna*, to release from suffering? What of the body, and of rebirth? Further, how may we distinguish the monk from the layman, or, more important, the bound from the liberated? How may we distinguish the *Tathāgata*, the one who has achieved his end, from the one who strives? Finally, how shall the liberated one treat his fellow sufferers?

If we are to understand the nature of this discussion we must bear in mind an essential teaching of Gotama, one that has enlightened our thinking already:

...in this very fathom-long body, along with its perception and thoughts, I proclaim the world to be; likewise the origin of the world and the making of the world to end.[169]

The truth of the cessation of suffering is to be found in the same "place" as the truth of the arising of suffering and the truth of suffering–and, as we shall see, as the means of the cessation of suffering, in the nature and experience of human living. In this respect persons are superior to the gods.[170]

The Buddha and the Dhamma as Guarantors

Not only did the Exalted One urge all to work out their own salvation, he also assured them that this task was within their capabilities.[171] The monks can abandon evil (*akusala*), they can cultivate good (*kusala*): "If it were impossible to abandon evil [or to cultivate good] I would not bid you do so...."[172]

But while the capability for bringing suffering to an end lies within the nature of the followers, the Buddha occupies a unique position with

---

[169] A II, 56-57.

[170] As the *Udāna* states, "He hath no branches, how then leaves?/ whose root [*mūlam*] is not in the ground./ Who is worthy to praise that man inspirited, from bondage free?/ Not only devas praise that man; he is also praised by Brahman." U 93.

[171] D II, 173. It is said, for example, that there are three sorts of persons in the world, "[m]aterial [*oḷārika atta-paṭilābha*], immaterial [*manopaṭilābha*], and formless [*arūpa-paṭilābha*]." The first has form, is composed of the four elements and is nourished by solid food. The second has no form, is composed of mind, has all its greater and lesser limbs complete, and all its organs are perfect. The third is without form, and is composed of consciousness only (*saññāmaya*). The *Dhamma* teaches a way with respect to each of these that will allow the three evil dispositions, *rāga, dosa, moha,* that have been acquired in each case to be put away. D I, 259-260.

[172] A I, 3.

356

respect to the arising of the end of suffering; for he proclaimed the Truth "that in this life beareth fruit, that avails not for a time only, that welcometh every one, that leadeth away and onward, that each one who hath intelligence may of and by himself understand...." " 'Wide opened are the portals to Nirvāṇa!' "–so the Enlightened One has said.[173] As proclaimer of this truth Gotama the Buddha has shown the way he himself has followed and has seen through to successful completion. As the pathfinder, then, he is unique. How, it is asked, is the *Tathāgata* to be distinguished from the monk who, because of disgust at body, of the fading out, the ceasing of body (and so also for the other four *khandhas*, perception, feeling, activities, consciousness), is called "freed without grasping, freed by insight?" "He it is," so the answer goes, "who doth cause a way to arise which had not arisen before [*magga*]."[174]

The emphasis of this encomium is not so much upon the dependence of the followers but upon the fact that since the Buddha has already followed this path his wisdom is supreme, for in his own life he has found and known a way not known before.[175] In his recounting to Ānanda of his enlightenment Gotama traces the path he himself followed, which he commends to Ānanda. He recounts his advancement from "awakening...and not wholly awakened," through aloofness from sense desire, through the states of applied and sustained thought, the four *jhānas* of meditation, the spheres of infinite space, infinite consciousness, nothing, of neither-perception-nor-non-perception, the ending of perception and feeling, and then the final emergence, wholly awakened.[176] It is this path that all seekers are to follow. The Buddha's unique place arises from his having trod its entire length to proclaim that "mind's release...is unshakeable, this birth is final, there is now no becoming again."[177] Therefore faith in the Buddha and in the *Dhamma*–and in the *Sangha*, as we shall see–is preferable even to rebirth as a world ruler for any virtuous man, such as

---

[173] D II, 251-252.
[174] This may be the attitude of the monks; but in another passage Gotama asserts that he teaches only what the wise knew. *Cf.* S III, 57-58, 117.
[175] Moreover, the *Tathāgata* may not be ignored. The Jain Sacca is asked three times for a response to a question concerning whether, if material shape is the self, he has the power to elect any particular form or appearance. He refuses to answer, probably because the question can only be answered in such a way as to deny an essential belief of his tradition. For not answering, however, he is threatened with a thunderbolt from the devas that will split his head into seven pieces–this being the penalty for refusing to answer the questions of a *Tathāgata*. M I, 284-285.
[176] A IV, 294-295.
[177] *Ibid.*.

the householder Citta. For that destiny is a transient and wavery thing, while the *Dhamma*, the Buddha and the *Sangha* are not.[178]

What the Buddha guarantees is that the striving can succeed. The seeker learns the *Dhamma* from the teacher, having first established that the teacher is "purified of states of confusion."[179] Hearing, learning and remembering the *Dhamma*, he tests it. Desire to strive arises; and he realizes "with his person the highest truth itself," and is thus awakened to truth. The truth is attained, a higher truth than awakening, "by following, developing and continually practising these things themselves."[180] The truth of the cessation of suffering stated in terms of the relationship between that truth and the seeker is perhaps most clearly portrayed in the metaphor of the refinement of gold. Beginning with the grossest impurities and proceeding to the finest, all taint is removed from the pure metal by the process of refinement. So also the impurities of the self are removed in the process of becoming enlightened, until the pure self is revealed, "pliable, workable, glistening, no longer brittle...capable of perfect workmanship."[181] Just as the refined gold is its own true and purest state, so the refined self is what it has always been in its purest state. The role of the *Tathāgata*, of the Buddha, and of the *Dhamma* is to provide the guidance and means to purification. Their very existence is the guarantee of the truth of the cessation of *dukkha*. But the success in striving is the seeker's, who, guided and encouraged, makes himself his own life's work.

The Tathāgata

The *Tathāgata*, or he who has reached his goal, is the foremost "embodiment"–and the word, even if used in the most provisional sense, is ironic–of the cessation of suffering. As the strict meaning of the term implies, the *Tathāgata* has achieved the end of the path. We shall examine the characteristics of the *Tathāgata*–a task both enlightening and fruitless, for the *Tathāgata* is untraceable.

The *Tathāgata* is one in whom "becoming, cankers [*bhavāsava*], all harsh speech,/ Are quenched, gone to their end, and are no more,/ He, lord-adept, released in every way,/ Oblation worthy is the Man-Thus-Come [*Tathāgata*]!"[182] There is in him complete comprehension and release from the world, from the arising of the world, from the ending of the world.[183]

---

[178] S IV, 210-212.
[179] M II, 363f..
[180] *Ibid.*, 363-365.
[181] A I, 231-232.
[182] SN 69.
[183] A II, 25.

He in whom substance and continuance are no longer [papañca],/
He who has overcome bond and hindrance,–/ That worthy one,
from craving free [nittaṇhā], as he fares onward,/ The world
with its devas knows not.[184]

By insight, paññā, the Tathāgata is said to fully comprehend the
satisfaction of the eye, the misery which is in the eye, the way of escape
from the eye and so also for the other senses.[185] Thus he is not bound
in any way to their operation, to the field of objects, to attachment to
them, to craving, to desire, and so forth. This does not mean, however,
that the Tathāgata does not "have an eye," or any of the other senses. In
these respects the Tathāgata is like any other person. The senses in and
of themselves are not regarded as causes of suffering. For instance, they
are not independent causes any more than any of the other "arisings" of
existence are. Koṭṭhita, speaking with Sāriputta, wondered whether the
eye was bound to the objects of seeing, the ear to objects of hearing, and
so forth. Or was the relationship reversed? As we noted, Sāriputta points
to desire and lust (chandarāga) arising out of sensations as the immediate
source of bondage. Further, if suffering were solely and simply a function
of the physical senses and/or of the objects perceived, there would be
neither need nor possibility of following the Dhamma, since they have
nothing to do, in and of themselves, with striving. But, says Sāriputta,
since it is the desire and lust which are in them that is the bond, the life
of the utter destruction of dukkha may be proclaimed. Possessed fully of
physical senses, the Tathāgata is free of desire, and bound neither by the
senses, by the objects of senses, or by both working together.[186]

The issue, then, is not perception or sensation per se. In character-
izing the Tathāgata it is foolish to ask how his normal physical properties
are altered. They are not altered. So it is said:

[the manifold of objects in the world] in itself is not desires of
sense [kāma],/ Lustful intention [sankapparāga] is man's sense
desires./ That manifold of objects doth endure; the will thereto
[chanda] the wise exterminate.[187]

The problem lies in wrath, conceit (māna), clinging, lust, hatred and
dullness (rāga, dosa, moha), rather than in the body itself, or in the
world itself, the "manifold of objects." The Tathāgata does not set his
mind "to imagine vain things." He has no craving for life in this or
another world. It is this freedom from desire that sets him apart from
the world and its beings; and thus freed, he cannot be found among or

---

[184] U 93.
[185] S IV, 5-6.
[186] Ibid., 101-102.
[187] S I, 32-33.

by men or the gods on this earth or elsewhere.[188]

Just as desire leads to concern for body, for consciousness, for perception, for lingering tendencies, and sensation, so the absence of desire means the end of these as objects of desire. In what sense, then, can the *Tathāgata* be said to exist if he is not bound by the senses or the world, or by the arising of the causes of suffering? The question of the existence of the *Tathāgata* was one of the most important questions thought not to be conducive to the ending of suffering. But, as we have seen, the arising of the question and its concomitant concern was indicative itself of a state of suffering, a concern for false view very like the questions of whether I exist now, did exist in the past, or will exist in the future. Does the *Tathāgata* exist after death, it was asked, or not? Did he neither exist nor not exist? Did he both exist and not exist? These were condemned as mere "view-issues," *diṭṭhigata*. The unlearned person is in fact fearful, and desires desperately to know. But the follower, who understands, is not afraid. He knows these concerns are matters of craving and perception, that they are illusions, vanities, and a source of remorse.[189] As to the question of the *Tathāgata*'s existence, the *Tathāgata* is untraceable; and until men and gods, those devas living with Indra, with Brahma, with Prajāpati, and all others, fully comprehend this, they will fail to be free. Those with freed minds do not concern themselves with such issues.[190]

It is no more proper to concern oneself with the question of whether the *Tathāgata* exists after death, and in what state, than it is to ask whether the *Tathāgata* exists in this life, or existed in any previous life. Sāriputta instructs Yamaka to discard his belief that when a monk has destroyed the *āsavas* he is "broken up and perishes when the body breaks up." The body, and the other "heaps," are impermanent and transient. This is true of the *Tathāgata*, who is not body, nor feeling, nor perception, nor activities, nor consciousness. Neither is he in the body, the feelings, and so forth. Nor is he separate from the body and the other *khandhas*. Thus it is improper to say of the *Tathāgata* that he exists in this very life, or in any other. For the *Tathāgata*, what is impermanent has ceased to arise; *dukkha* has ceased to arise. That is the proper understanding of the state of the *Tathāgata*.[191]

There is, nonetheless, a good deal of interest in the body of the *Tathāgata*. It is truly a remarkable "body"; for when he concentrates "body in mind, and mind in body,"[192] that is "at such time as he enters on and abides in the consciousness of bliss and buoyancy, then it is...that

---

[188] *Ibid.*.

[189] A IV, 39-40.

[190] M II, 179.

[191] S III, 94-96.

[192] I take this to mean that in a state of consciousness characteristic

the *Tathāgata's* body is more buoyant, softer, more plastic and more radiant," like an iron ball heated all day. Thus concentrated he can with little effort rise from the ground into the air. He enjoys magical powers. "From being one he becomes many: from being many he becomes one:...even as far as the Brahma World he has power with his body."[193]

Such powers are typical of one who is not limited by the spatial and temporal restrictions of the body or of physical existence in general.[194] Rather he may have many bodies—this probably means an infinite number of bodies—or one. Dominated by his "one-pointedness" of concentration, the *Tathāgata's* powers appear "magical;" that is, he is free from any limitations except those of his own mind—his *citta*. In other words, the significance of the magical powers of the *Tathāgata* is that they arise from his conquering of the *āsavas*, the bringing to an end of *dukkha*, and becoming a master. These powers are, then, *consequences of liberation*. They are also manifestions of the form of existence, non-existence, neither, and both, of which we have already spoken as being characteristic of the *Tathagāta*. They are, further, the natural concomitants of one who cannot be recognized for what he truly is because of his outward appearance. So Gotama instructs Vaccha, saying that if there were, for example, a fire before him he would recognize it by its parts and elements, be able to say something of its source, and so forth. But what could he say of it after it was extinguished? Just so is the material shape of the *Tathāgata* utterly extinguished.[195]

The *Tathāgata* is no more limited in his knowledge than in his existence. In fully comprehending the arising of suffering the *Tathāgata* knows how arisings existed in the past; and thus his critics concede that he has knowledge of the past. But any learned person may claim the same ability. However, when it is said that the *Tathāgata* knows the past, what is meant is that he knows what is true, what is fact, "and what does redound to your good," and knows also the proper time to reveal this truth. In addition the *Tathāgata*, not bound by time and space, knows the present and the future as well, for he comprehends fully the arising and the end of the arising of suffering. He traverses the world with his thought.[196] His "discriminating consciousness [*viññāṇanidassana*]," furthermore, is said to be impossible to characterize, "unending, lucid in every respect, cannot be reached through the extensity of extension, the

---

of the *Tathāgata* the empirical distinctions between mind and body no longer obtain.
[193] S V, 252-253; *cf.* M I, 92-93, D III, 24; *cf.* also S I, 182-183, M I, 392-393, where it is said that the Buddha disappears at will.
[194] *Cf.* S II 186, on telekinesis.
[195] M II, 165-166.
[196] S I, 101-102.

cohesiveness of cohesion," by examination of any of the four elements, creatures, devas, Prājapati, Brahmas, The Radiant ones, The Lustrous Ones, Vehāpphalas, the Overlord, the All, or the essential qualities of all these things and beings.[197] Thus he declares–literally, is a prophet of–*vadi*–"the hour..., the fact..., the good, the Norm [*Dhamma*]...the Discipline [*vinaya*]. For this is he called *Tathāgata*."[198]

As the *Tathāgata* knows the past, present and future, he knows also what is the mind-state of other beings.[199] Most important is the claim that the *Tathāgata* knows whether a mind (*citta*) is full of attachment, aversion, ignorance and confusion, inferior (*sa-uttara*), distracted, "become great [*mahaggata*]," or composed (*samāhita*). He knows "intuitively of a mind with (some other mental state) superior to it; of a mind with no (other mental state) superior to it"; he knows intuitively of a mind that is composed that it is composed, and that a mind that is not composed is not composed; he knows intuitively of a mind that is freed that it is freed; he knows intuitively of a mind that is not free that it is not freed.[200]

It is important to understand the true point of the *Tathāgata*'s knowledge of other minds. This is not a matter of telepathy, or the simple ability to see or know intuitively or by any other means what is in the mind of other people. Rather, what characterizes especially the *Tathāgata*'s knowledge of other minds is that it is knowledge of the state of the *citta*, and of the state of the *citta* with respect to the liberation from or bondage to suffering. Nothing else is important, after all. Therefore the "supernatural" power of the *Tathāgata* has a very specific nature, as do all the other powers of the *Tathāgata*: its link with the truth of suffering and the truth of the cessation of suffering. It is this knowledge that makes a *Tathāgata* what he is, knowledge of the arising and ending of suffering. And, by implication, we are told that no other "knowledge" is worthy of the name.[201]

In the end, it is said, the *Tathāgata* is "boundless." To describe the *Tathāgata* is a task comparable to counting the sands of the Ganges: both pointless and impossible.[202] As Nāgārjuna concludes, the *Tathāgata* is of the nature of *śūnya*; and of *śūnya* nothing could be asserted–or of *aśūnya*, both *śūnya* and *aśūnya*, or neither *śūnya* and *aśūnya*. For one who is determined to assert the existence of the *Tathāgata* will pursue the

---

[197] M I 392-393.
[198] D III, 126-127.
[199] *Cf.* A III, 286-291, in reference to Devadatta; *cf.* also S I, 224-225, in reference to Pridestiff.
[200] M I, 92-93; *cf.* S III, 80ff., and M II, 217-220.
[201] *Cf.* A I, 155, and D I, 277-278, S IV, 196-919, concerning mystical practices.
[202] S IV, 67.

matter from this world even into the realm of *nirvāṇa*. The *Tathāgata*, therefore, cannot be said to exist either in the *nirvāṇa* realm or in this world; nor can he be said not to exist, both to exist and not to exist, neither to exist and not to exist. And this is the true of the world as well, Nāgārjuna concludes:

...[t]he *Tathāgata's* nature of self-existence is also the nature of this world-existence. The *Tathāgata*, (strictly speaking), is without the nature of self-existence and this world nature is likewise so."[203]

In sum, the nature of the *Tathāgata*, like the nature of *nibbāna*, can not be said to be of this world or another; and indeed, as Nāgārjuna argues–in full agreement with earlier analyses of the nature of suffering– what is true of the world is true of the *Tathāgata* and of *nibbāna*. The truth of the cessation of suffering is the truth of the world and of the *Tathāgata*; for in all three there is neither existence nor non-existence, nor both, nor neither. They are empty, devoid of self-nature (*svabhāva*). But the *Tathāgata* has knowledge, perceives the world, proclaims the truth. He possesses *paññā*, wisdom, he is free of time and space, he is boundless and untraceable. Such, then, is the nature of the end of suffering. Simply put, all of these characteristics are the *Tathāgata's* because he is no longer driven by desire. In consequence, there is no desire for the world or for the self–and he is utterly freed from both. In consequence the distinction between world and self, between emptiness and fullness, between *nibbāna* and *saṃsāra* is meaningless and does not arise. Hence suffering does not arise, rebirth does not arise, existence and non-existence do not arise. All is seen to be what it really is, transparent and empty. It is this seeing from which all the qualities and characteristics of the *Tathāgata* stem.

The Monk/Arahant

We should now inquire of the characteristics of the monk who is grasping the truth of the end of suffering. While these differ hardly at all from those already described in the discussion of the *Tathāgata*, the perspective here is one of progression through a series of ever higher states of release. The general impression is one of process, of the monk *in via*, achieving the goal of Arahantship. The issues here correspond in large part to those raised in the treatment of the arising of suffering; there are others, however, that are peculiar to the truth of the cessation of suffering. The issues of both sorts are as follows: the role of striving, non-attachment, the status of the *paṭiccasamuppāda* series, the *khandhas*, the *anusayas*, the state of the liberated *citta*, *samādhi*, the range of knowledge of the enlightened *Arahant*, the issue of certainty and self-knowledge, and the question of relations to others in the life of the monk.

---

[203] Inada, 131-135.

Striving

There are several indications that release is the work of the monk, whatever the degree of dependence upon the Teacher. Thus striving is essential. In the course of attaining mastery, from the time of his departure from his home the monk is urged constantly to review his thoughts, guard his perceptions, and analyze his motives. It is said that since the *Dhamma* has been made known fully to the monk having left home "through faith," "it is enough [for him]...to stir up energy and vow: Verily let skin and sinews and bones wilt in my body, let flesh and blood dry up, yet shall there be upkeep of energy till I have that which by man's strength, by man's energy, by man's progress may be won."[204] One tradition lists ten conditions of the monk's life that must be perpetually reviewed and contemplated by one who has gone forth.[205] Another places striving at the center of the monk's awakening to truth (*bodhi*).[206] But this striving to gain mastery over one's thoughts, words, deeds, perceptions, sensations, body, and so forth, is preliminary, however difficult and indispensable.

Of seven kinds of persons, we are told, five must be diligent, or strive. There are those who, in differing degrees accounting for the five stages, have not been fully freed from the "cankers" nor have experienced in their person (*kāyena*) the transcendence of "material shapes" (*nāmarūpa*). They are the following: (a) the "mental realiser," who has experienced the transcendence of material stages but for whom only some of the cankers are destroyed; (b) "won to view" (*diṭṭhipatta*), in whom there is no apprehension of the transcendence of material shapes, only some of the cankers destroyed, "and those things proclaimed by the *Tathāgata* are fully seen by him through intuitive wisdom and fully practised"; (c) "freed by faith [*saddhāvimutta*]," in whom there is no apprehension of the transcendence of mental shapes, some of the cankers destroyed, and in whom "faith in the *Tathāgata* is settled, genuine, established;" (d) "striving for *dhamma*," in whom there is no apprehension, the cankers are not yet utterly destroyed, and the *Tathāgata*'s proclamations are "only moderately approved of by means of intuitive wisdom"; (e) "striving after faith," in whom there is no apprehension, the cankers are not utterly destroyed, with enough faith in and regard for the *Tathāgata* that he will receive "the faculty of faith [*saddhindriya*], the faculty of energy, ...mindfulness, ...concentration, ...wisdom." To each of these the charge to be diligent is given.

But the two remaining sorts do not require diligence or striving. One, "freed both ways," has apprehended the transcendence of material shapes

---

[204] S II, 24.
[205] A V, 62-63.
[206] M II, 363-365.

in his own person; and as well has "seen by means of wisdom [*paññā*] his own cankers utterly destroyed." The second, "freed by intuitive wisdom alone," does not apprehend with his person the transcendence of material shapes but has seen the cankers fully destroyed by means of intuitive wisdom. "It has been done by him through diligence, he could not be neglectful."[207] The essential mark, clearly, is the destruction of the *āsavas*, or cankers. For one for whom they are fully destroyed there is no possible arising of desire. Some monks, it is said, must be diligent; but others need not be;

> those monks who are perfected ones, canker-waned, who have lived the life, done what there was to be done, laid down the burden, who have attained their own goal, the fetters of becoming utterly destroyed, who are freed by right profound knowledge, of monks such as these I do not say, monks, that there is something to be done through diligence.... It has (already) been done by these through diligence, these could not become negligent.[208]

For such, brethren, I declare that in respect of the sixfold sphere of sense there is no need to strive earnestly.

These are incapable of "carelessness."[209]

This idea can be set against the view of the Jains, who held that "works" were superior to "faith." In the Buddhist view the Jains sought their salvation solely in terms of the degree of their effort, as though they could achieve a favorable balance in the calculus of good and evil. They were said to have failed to perceive rightly the nature of the problem itself. For actions in and of themselves are neither good nor evil, but are either only insofar as they incorporated desires. In responding to Jain questioners Gotama asks in what way striving or effort is fruitful. The monk, first of all, is mastered neither by anguish nor by happiness. Nor does he disregard happiness. "Thus in the course of striving against the sources of anguish, he is indifferent to that source, he has equanimity, he has detachment. Thus striving, the suffering is worn away."[210]

For him in whom the *āsavas* are destroyed there is no need for a deliberate mental act of effort. He is now incapable of "negligence," that is to say, he will always remain detached from the sources of suffering and is therefore impervious to their seductive powers. In his nature, so to speak, he is diligent without let or qualification. Effort in and of itself determines nothing; striving is necessary only so long as the *āsavas* are not fully destroyed, for diligence has its end in their destruction. Just as one who has crossed the sea of becoming has no further need of the raft of the

---

[207] *Ibid.*, 151-154.
[208] *Ibid.*, 150-151.
[209] S IV, 80.
[210] M III, 10-11.

Dhamma, so he who has conquered the *āsavas*–and, by implication, fully reversed the arising of *dukkha*–has no need of striving. He knows there is no further goal to strive for, nor further hindrance to strive against. Striving is thus empty.

The significance of the question of striving is perhaps more clearly seen if it is interpreted in the context of the monk's aspirations, especially those of the monk equipped already with the basic discipline of the Way. For the progress of the monk depends to a very large extent upon the level to which he aspires: he gets what he asks for, so to speak. Thus a monk endowed with faith, moral habit, learning, relinquishment and wisdom (*saddhā, sīla, suta, cāga, paññā*) may seek rebirth as a rich noble. His desire is conducive to achieving this end. So also is this true for aspirations for rebirth with rich Brahmans, rich householders, in the realms of the devas, in Brahma-realms, in infinite space (*ākāsa*), infinite consciousness, no-thing, and neither perception-nor-non-perception. Finally, the desire to live free of the *āsavas,* by *paññā,* leads to no new state and release from the previous state.[211] The release of the monk is a direct consequence of his aspiration, as much as of his endowment.

Non-Attachment

The consequences of the end of bondage to craving, *taṇhā,* are the destruction of the *āsavas,* the rendering empty of their effects, and the stopping of their "flowing in upon" the monk.[212] He who has transcended both good and evil is a "man of worth."[213] Such a one is indifferent to the work and object of the senses, although it is clear that sensation continues. He abstains from activities of the body, of speech and thought that lead to vexation and distress. At the same time he is said to wear away the effects of past deeds by constant contact with them (*phassa-phassa*), that is, by thorough examination and analysis of their arising and cessation.[214] Thus he whose *citta* is purified creates no new deeds, and wears away the effects of past ones.

The senses of the monk whose *citta* is purified are described as six "constant abiding-states [*satata-vihāra*]." He, seeing an object with the eye, is neither elated nor depressed, but rests indifferent, mindful and comprehending, and so for hearing, smelling, tasting, touching, cogniz-ing, and for the objects of sensations–recalling the earlier definitions of the "sense-fields."[215] He is, in short, indifferent to the operation of the six sense-fields, although they are not annihilated. Again, the issue is

---

[211] *Ibid.,* 139-142.

[212] Th, 246.

[213] Dh, N. 412, p. 133.

[214] At least, this is my interpretation; *cf.* M I, 148-151, and A II, 208-209.

[215] A II, 210-211; *cf.* S I, 156-159.

attachment and non-attachment, desire and absence of desire, in the success of the monk's endeavor, rather than the sensations themselves. Here the Jains failed to draw a distinction and falsely pursued the path of action, with the result that they could not be freed of the *āsavas*.[216] It is the state of the heart (*citta*) that matters, not the state of the world or of a permanent "self" upon which one (falsely) attempts to impose one's will.[217]

Sensation and Perception

How shall we characterize the *Arahant*'s relationship to the world of objects, and the operation of his sense-faculties? We know from the examination of the *paṭiccasamuppāda* series that the arising of suffering is to be understood in terms of dependency among contact, sensation, perception, consciousness, clinging and craving. In an important model biography of a person, Upāli is led to consider, in order, the person as a young boy, lying on his back and playing with his own excrement, playing with the playthings of children, the adult fascination with the "objects cognizable by the eye, objects desirable, agreeable, fascinating, attractive," and so for the other senses, and the wayfaring man. Each stage is more attractive than the last. In the final stage the senses are controlled: "Seeing an object with the eye he is not misled by its outer view nor by its lesser details." Thus seeing and sensing generally he experiences no greed or grasping; he "sets a guard over the faculty of eye and attains control thereof," and so also for the other senses.[218] He may then abandon any hankering after the world, ill-will, sloth and torpor, distraction and flurry, doubt and wavering, and turn his attention fully to the development of right concentration. He enters then the states of knowledge in order of increasing universality, that is, the four musings or levels of meditation, the sphere of unlimited space, of consciousness, of nothingness, of neither-consciousness-nor-unconsciousness—also called the sphere of neither-perception-nor-non-perception—, the sphere of the ending of perception and feeling, and finally the ending, the cool, *nibbāna*. By insight (*paññā*) he knows that in himself the cankers are destroyed.[219]

This, then, is the path to *nibbāna*. Let us note that one of the chief marks—and in some examples it is the only chief mark—of the *Arahant* is the fact that while continuing to sense, perceive and feel, he is indifferent to the sensations, feeling and perceptions and, of course, to the objects of those actions. Mālunkyaputta is instructed that when there is in the seen only the seen, in the heard only the heard, in the tasted only the tasted, there is no cause for the arising of suffering, and thus no arising

---

[216] *Cf.* Dh, N. 383, p. 125.
[217] *Cf.* A IV, 287-289.
[218] A V, 144; *cf.* S IV, 63.
[219] A V, 143-146.

367

of suffering. There will be no "here" or "beyond" or "midway between." This is the end of *dukkha*. For when there is only the seen in what is seen, when there is no desire (that is to say, when there are no grounds for greed, aversion, or confusion, *rāga, dosa, moha*) there is no cause for suffering.[220] The desire for existence, mind-bound by sensation, and the turmoil of feeling cease; and deliverance, freedom and detachment come.[221]

These characteristics pertain also to what is called the end of the world. The world, as noted before, is "that by which one is conscious of the world, by which one has conceit of the world [*loka-saññi, loka-maññi*]." Again, the problem is not with the "external" world, the existence of which is not a significant issue. The cause of suffering lies not in the world as such, but in that by which one experiences, senses, perceives, is conscious of, and thus desires the world. Gotama teaches "the abandoning of the all," which is subject to rebirth, is impermanent, woeful and void of self.[222] He means the abandoning of the eye, of objects pleasing, displeasing, or neutral to the eye, of eye-contact and eye-consciousness, and so for the other senses, including the mind-sense, *mano*. This is accomplished "by fully knowing, by comprehending it."[223] The end of the world is the end of attachment. Things of the world are compounded (*sankhāra*) and thus impermanent (*anicca*), unstable (*adhuva*), and insecure (*anassāsika*). Thus Gotama declares that the end of the world cannot be learned, seen, or gone to by going to the world's end.[224] It is not a question of "going" anywhere; the problem is at home, in the heart. It is through the senses that one has consciousness and conceit of the world. Thus the *Arahant*, who has brought the world to an end, is he over whom the delightful or repulsive objects of the world have no control.[225]

Indeed, it is possible to distinguish between one who is set free in this very life and one who is not in terms of whether, sensing with the six senses, he does or does not cling to the objects cognizable by them. "If he be full of grasping...a brother is not wholly set free." But if one, sensing, does not "persist in clinging [*upādāna*]..." and thus avoids grasping, in this he is fully set free.[226]

We may look to the Buddha's testimony for further clarification of the state of perception and sensation in the experience of the *Arahant*. Af-

---

220 S IV, 42-43.
221 S I, 3.
222 S IV, 13-14.
223 *Ibid.*, 8-9.
224 *Ibid.*, 59.
225 *Ibid.*, 80.
226 *Ibid.*, 62.

ter his temptation by Māra's daughters, Gotama is asked by one daughter, Craving, why he has no friends in the village. The response is illustrative of the manner in which the *Arahant* thinks of sensation: "Now that the host of sweet and pleasant shapes/ Hath been repulsed, I'm seated here alone/ And meditate upon the good I've won,/ The peace of heart, the bliss experienced..../ Thus may impressions of the worlds of sense [*kāmasaññā*]/ Be kept outside of him and catch him not/ Who mainly in rapt meditation bides."[227] The "host of sweet and pleasant shapes" is construed as an army seeking to overwhelm the wayfarer. Repulsed, they retreat; the seeker is one whom they cannot "catch."

The change in the *Arahant* consists in the absence of attraction in the sense and sense-object world. He does not cling to it, grasp it, or desire it. Now if this be true, we may ask whether the senses exist for the *Arahant*, or have they been annihilated. Again, we have uncovered a question not conducive to the end of suffering. Koṭṭhita asks the question in this form: after the "passionless ending" do the "six spheres of contact," that is, the senses and sense-fields understood from the aspect of contact between sense and sense object, or *phassa*, continue to exist, or not? The Buddha responds, "Say not that the six spheres of contact exist after the passionless ending," nor that they do not exist, nor that they both exist and do not exist, nor that they neither exist nor do not exist. "One makes difficulty where there is none." The very question, then, is evidence of obsession, *papañca*.[228]

What is true of the *Arhant* who is, as the expression puts it, "aloof" from sense desires is that he may now enter a series of further states of awareness whose objects—the term must be used rather loosely in light of what we have already seen—are increasingly indistinct. This is a highly desirable progression, since it brings the seeker to the point of destroying any possible source of further grasping, that is, to the point of the destruction of the *āsavas* (but this progression is not the only way to bring about this end, as we shall see). The progression through the *jhāna* states is not hindered by any further temptations from the realm of sensual pleasure; Māra, it is said, loses his ability to see and find the monk, who has "become invisible to the Evil One." The monk is beyond entanglements in the sensual world.[229]

Gotama's progress toward complete release took him beyond aloofness from sense pleasures. He passed through the four *jhāna* states. The state, or "musing," called the musing of discursive thought has its own distractions; and by thinking he entered a higher stage, called the second musing, of meditation without initial and discursive thought. Distrac-

---

[227] S I, 156-159.
[228] A II, 168-169.
[229] A IV, 290-291.

tions of an increasingly diffuse sort impelled him to move into a third stage, which transcends happiness; and then he moved on to a fourth, which transcends both happiness and sorrow. Now transcending all form, he entered the state of formlessness, that is, the sphere of the meditational setting of infinite space. Then, departing from categories of external definition altogether, he entered the sphere of infinite consciousness. There followed the transcendence of both form and formlessness, or the sphere of no-thing, the sphere of neither-perception-nor-non-perception, and finally he entered and abided in the sphere of the stopping of perceiving and feeling. These "spheres" appear not to be places or metaphysical realms in any sense at all. (We shall return to a further investigation of this progression.) Now, having passed through a series culminating in the most universal of all possible states, the stopping of perception and feeling, the Buddha proclaimed that he was not fully enlightened: "And so long...as I attained not to, emerged not from these nine attainments of gradual abidings, both forwards and backwards, I realized not completely, as one wholly awakened, the full perfect awakening; But when I attained to and emerged from these abidings suchwise, then, wholly awakened, I realized completely the full perfect awakening unsurpassed."[230] The passage though these *jhāna* states was not in itself the complete fulfillment of release; and this is of especial importance with respect to perception and sensation.

Thus Ānanda is told that right concentration is of such a sort that "in earth [the monk] is unaware of earth," in water unaware of water, in heat and in air he is unaware of them; that is to say, although the four elements are the context of his existence, in the state of *samādhi* he is unaware of them, not concerned with them. This is expected. But Gotama goes on to say that this detachment is appropriate in the spheres of limitless space, infinite consciousness, nothingness, and neither-perception-nor-non-perception. Or, in brief, right concentration means "that in this world he is unaware of this world, in the world beyond unaware of it." But, strikingly, it is also said, "and yet at the same time he may perceive" this world and the world beyond.[231] Moreover, these states are described as states of happiness, *sukha*, transcending that of the pleasures of the senses.[232]

The monk who moves successfuly through all of the nine states is said to have a mind (*citta*) that "becomes subtle, pliant," capable of "boundless concentration." He "bends the mind to the realization of psychic knowledge of whatever condition is realizable by psychic knowledge and acquires the ability of an eyewitness in every case whatever the range

---

[230] *Ibid.*, 294-295.
[231] A V, 6-7.
[232] M II, 67-69.

may be." Like the *Tathāgata*, he attains what he wishes: he experiences psychic powers in manifold modes—being one he could become many, and many, one; he fares in body even as far as Brahma's world; he hears with the deva-ear all sounds; he knows other beings' minds; he recalls dwelling-places of bygone days; he knows beings' farings according to their deeds.[233] These faculties of the released monk make it clear that, once liberated from desire, from attraction, the monk's knowledge of and relationship with the world have been transformed. No longer blinded by greed, aversion and ignorance, he knows and sees things as they really are, he is unbound by time and space, and he attains what he wishes. Indeed, "should he wish: Having destroyed the cankers...I would enter and abide in mind emancipation," it is done.[234] This appears to mean that, should he desire, the freed monk, who has done what was to be done, may cut himself off from any awareness at all. The point of this passage is, in part, that whichever wish is pursued, either is open to the liberated seeker, that is, either engagement in full knowledge and wisdom of this world, or abiding wholly in the state of mind-emancipation. So significant is the release from the world of sense-pleasure in this scheme that defeat of sense-pleasure can, it seems, lead directly to *nibbāna*, the enlightenment, the passionless ending. A monk who is aloof from sense-desires enters into the first jhanic state, of concentrated thought. Whatever occurs there of form, feeling, perception, mind or consciousness (*rūpa, vedanā, saññā, sankhāra, viññāṇa,* that is the *khandhas*) he knows to be impermanent, hurtful, alien, empty, and not the self. Having rejected the five fetters he thinks: " 'This is the peace [*santaṃ*]...: the stilling of all mind activity [*sabbasaṅkhārasamatho*], the renouncing of all (rebirth) basis [*sabbūpadhipaṭinissaggo*], the destroying of craving [*taṇhākkhayo*], passionless [*virāgo*], ending [*nirodho*], the cool [*nibbānan*].' And steadfast therein he wins to canker destruction."[235] It is possible to interpret this passage to mean that the realization of the nature of sensation, that is of the five *khandhas*, is both necessary and sufficient for release.[236]

The destruction of unskilled (*akusala*) states leaves the monk with something of a choice. Abiding in the first musing, getting rid of unskilled intentions, not producing any more, "his thought is peaceful in its sphere; if he is serene either he comes to imperturbability now or he

---

[233] A IV, 283-284.

[234] *Ibid.*.

[235] *Ibid.*, 284-285.

[236] This passage may mean that success in the first *jhāna* leads to success in all the other stages, but it is simply not spelled out. My interpretation is that sense-aloofness and the first musing are necessary and sufficient for release.

is intent on wisdom."[237] That is to say, he may, by passing through all four jhanic states, win through to imperturbability. But it is, apparently, equally true that one may win through without proceeding through to the fourth jhanic state. For one who does proceed to that state, imperturbability may be won, or, as was the case at the first juncture, one who is intent upon seeking wisdom (*paññā*) may continue to the sphere of infinite space (*ākāsa*), then, if he chooses, to infinite consciousness, and so forth, through to the ninth sphere of the stopping of perception and feeling. As we have seen, this last is not synonymous with *nibbāna*; for it is still possible for the monk to be ensnared in grasping, if he rejoices in his equanimity. "A monk who has grasping, Ānanda, does not attain *nibbāna*."[238]

I have taken some trouble to point out that the *Arahant*'s sensation and perception do not cease;[239] I have stressed especially the point that the mastery over these functions, which is the development of *kusala* states devoid of *taṇhā*, craving, and others, is the goal, rather than the annihilation of perception and sensation. But this conclusion applies also to the monk who has passed through all nine stages of consciousness up to and including the stopping of perception and feeling.

It is asked whether there is any difference between the *Arahant* who has reached the ninth stage of the stopping of perception and feeling and a dead person, or dead body. The answer is couched in terms of the three major activities, bodily, vocal and mental (*kāya, vacī, citta*). In the case of the dead man the bodily activities (*kāyasankhāra*), the vocal activities (*vacīsankhāra*) and the mental activities (*cittasankhāra*) have been stopped, "have subsided, the vitality is entirely destroyed, the heat allayed, the sense-organs are entirely broken asunder." Now for the monk who has attained the sphere of cessation of feeling and perception, the activities have ceased as well; but he has not lost his vitality, his heat (*āyu, usmā*). Nor has he really lost his consciousness–the third major necessity for existence (*viññāṇa*). It is said, rather, that "his sense-organs are purified."[240]

---

[237] M III, 46ff..

[238] *Ibid.*.

[239] The following passage from the *Sutta Nipāta* suggests both this point and as well the freedom from the bondage of perception:

When there is no perceiving of perception,/ Nor the perceiving of things not perceptions [*asaññī, vibhūtassaññī*],/ And there is still no not-perceiving them,/ Nor that perceiving altogether ceased–,/ When thus his state, then form decays for him [*vibhoti rūpaṃ*];/ Reckoned hindrance is perception's source.

SN 129.

[240] M I, 356.

In other descriptions of what is meant by the cessation of perception-and feeling-activities, these functions are said to be mental processes dependent upon mind, and are thus called the "activity of the mind," just as inhalation and exhalation are dependent upon body, and sustained and directed thought is an activity of speech. The cessation of these activities occurs in a specific order, that is, activity of speech, then of body, then of mind. This order follows roughly the progress of the nine states and spheres, and is clearly directed toward the same final stage, the cessation of perception and feeling. What the monk has achieved in the cessation of perception and feeling is that he does not think: "*I* shall attain, *I* am attaining, the ceasing of perception and feeling;" but his mind has been so trained that it leads him on to the state of "being such"–*tathattāya*, a synonym for *nibbāna*.[241] Unlike a dead man, whose activities have also ceased, the monk in whom the end of perception and feeling has been attained has his "faculties...clarified."

Perhaps even more remarkable is the teaching that, unlike the dead man, whose faculties have been broken up, the monk may and must re-emerge from the attainment of the sphere of the cessation of perception and feeling, as we have seen in the case of the Buddha. He does not think, in so emerging, that "*I* am emerging, *I* am now emerged from attaining the ceasing of perception and feeling;" rather his mind is so practiced, his *citta* so disciplined, that "it leads him onto the state of being such." Thinking thus, he re-emerges, and the three activities are regained, in the reverse order in which they were dissipated, beginning with mind and ending with speech. This again recapitulates roughly the nine states and spheres, but in reverse order. Moreover, this process of regaining the world, transformed, accounts for the nature of the released monk's connection with the world. What contacts, for example, may touch him? "...[T]hree contacts touch him: the void, the signless and the aimless contact [*suññatā, animmitta, appaṇihita phassa*]."[242] Finally, a brother re-emerged has his mind inclined toward detachment (*viveka*, a synonym for *nibbāna*).[243]

The released monk is one who has returned transformed to the world, who continues with his sense organs strengthened, his faculties clarified, touched only by *nibbāna*, inclined in his heart/mind only to detachment. He is not dead; he is rather undistracted, alive continually to the nature of things, to the emptiness of things, to *nibbāna* as he goes about the remainder of his life. He does not cease to sense, feel, or perceive; rather, he senses, perceives and feels only that which is sensed, felt and perceived, and nothing else. One who has achieved *nibbāna* experiences

---

[241] S IV, 201f.

[242] *Ibid.*.

[243] *Ibid.*, 201-203.

pleasant feelings, painful feelings, and feelings that are neither pleasant nor painful; and upon having such experiences he "comprehends that it is impermanent...not to be cleaved to...not an object of enjoyment." He experiences any feeling in the manner of detachment from it. Experiencing a feeling that is limited by the body, he comprehends that he is experiencing a feeling limited by the body.[244] This is what is meant by the saying that the brother re-emerged is inclined toward detachment, and is lead to the state of suchness (*viveka, tathattāya*).

The Āsavas

The end of *dukkha*, like its source, must be construed in terms of co-dependent origination. While perception, sensation, consciousness, and contact are dependent elements subject to the Ariyan discipline, control of them must lead to the more inaccessible causes of suffering, and finally to the most deeply rooted cause of all, the *āsavas*–the intoxicants, the floods, the cankers, the last and most pervasive link to the desire for world and self as realities. Their ending is described as a cleaning out of all future causes, whether of rebirth or of desire, and compared to the utter destruction of the stump of the felled palm tree, so that it can never rise again. The Buddha is asked to summarize the question of the source and end of *dukkha*. He replies, "This verily is the way to answer just this matter in brief:–That which the recluse calls intoxicants [*āsava*]– concerning these I have no doubts; they are cleaned out; I am not worried about them."[245] The *āsavas* are the end and substance of *dukkha*. They must be annihilated. The end of the *āsavas* is said to be the "best of sights, sounds, of joys, of conscious states, of becomings."[246] And this is accomplished only when there is no longer any concern for them. The state of the end of suffering is that state in which concern for the *āsavas* has disappeared, along with the causal effects of the cankers themselves.

A seeker complains that, although he has understood by right insight that the ceasing of becoming (*bhavanirodha*) is *nibbāna*, he is not an Arahant because the *āsavas* have not perished. He is like a man who finds a well in the jungle. He is fair gone with thirst and badly needs the water; but there is no way to draw the water out of the well. He has found his goal, but he cannot partake of it.[247] This simile suggests that the annihilation of the *āsavas* must be experienced, and that *paññā* alone, or in and of itself, is not necessarily sufficient for the ending of suffering.

The destruction of the *āsavas* may be accomplished "without delay," that is, without passing through all possible stages, such as the four jhanic

---

[244] M III, 290-291.
[245] S I, I4.
[246] A III, 148-149.
[247] S II, 83.

374

stages, or the nine-fold series of enlightenment, if one can realize that the false views–of body as self, or of self as possessing body, or of body being in the self, of self being in the body, or of any of the other *khandhas* as self in these various ways, of the eternal unchanging nature of the self in the hereafter, or, finally, of the utter annihilation of the self hereafter–are activities "nourished by feeling that is born of contact with ignorance," giving rise to craving, from which is born the activity of believing any of these views. "Thus that activity is impermanent, willed, arisen from a cause.... Thus knowing,...thus seeing, one can without delay destroy the *āsavas*." (This is also the proper analysis for one who is not firmly established in the *Dhamma*, but who lives in doubt, wavering. This too is an activity that is impermanent, willed, arising from a cause.[248]

On the other hand, by giving full attention to "self-training" the *āsavas* are said to be worn away. The recluse who pursues thoroughly and successfully the training upon which he has embarked does not in fact concern himself with the wearing away of the *āsavas*. Rather, it is in their nature to be worn away in that process. The monk does not concern himself, thinking, "O that my heart were freed from the āsavas without grasping!"; and yet his heart (*citta*) is freed of them. The process is compared to a carpenter or apprentice who sees his thumb-print and fingermarks on the handle of his adze. He does not think, "Thus and thus much of my adze-handle has been worn away today." Instead he is simply aware of its gradual shrinking by its being worn down. The process of the end of the *āsavas* is also likened to a stranded sea-going vessel. It rots and spoils until a mild shower is capable of overturning it, and its planks and pegs simply rot away.[249]

The destruction of the *āsavas* means the destruction of the elemental roots of desire. The "compound thing of body and mind" is no more.[250] Lust (*rāga*), hatred (*dosa*) and ignorance (*moha*) are extinguished, "are calmed down."[251] Further, the great classes of *āsavas*, sensuality, becoming, delusion and ignorance, no longer control the "mind set round with intelligence." There no longer exists the flooding surge toward any of these ends.[252] As we have already noted, however, the breaking up of the *āsavas* does not mean that the monk is "broken up and perishes when the body breaks up," or "becomes not after death." Rather, like the *Tathāgata* it cannot be said that in truth in this very life he was body, feeling, perception, activities or consciousness, in or distinct from body or any of the other *khandhas*; and it cannot be said that any of those

---

[248] S III, 80-84.
[249] *Ibid.*, 129-131.
[250] S I, 23.
[251] S IV, 145-146.
[252] D II, 132-3; *cf.* D I, 93-95, where delusion is omitted.

states apply to him after the breaking up of the *āsavas*. Rather, *dukkha* has been destroyed, has ceased.[253]

The "state" of the end of the *āsavas* should be understood to be quite apart from any of the components of existence or any combination of them. What is left? For one who has destroyed the *āsavas* there is no remainder. The mind (*citta*) free of the cankers of sense-pleasure, becoming and ignorance knows that

> Destroyed is birth, brought to a close is the Brahma-faring, done is what was to be done, there is no more being such and such. ...[It] is like a pure, limpid serene pool of water in which a man with vision standing on the bank might see oysters and shells, also gravel and pebbles, and shoals of fish moving about and keeping still. It might occur to him: This pool of water is pure, limpid, serene, here are these oysters and shells, and gravel and pebbles, and shoals of fish are moving about and keeping still. Even so, ...a monk comprehends as it really is: This is anguish [*dukkha*]...he comprehends...: This is the course leading to the stopping of the cankers.[254]

Knowing the arising of the cankers, he knows in the same knowledge the cessation of the *āsavas*, and thus the arising and cessation of *dukkha*. Thus he sees only what is, like the man seeing only what is in the pool, without distortion, as it really is. He knows the *āsavas* for what they are, and is no longer bound by them. Thus freed, the end of suffering has replaced the arising of suffering: "done is what was to be done."

Rebirth and the Body

The end of suffering is repeatedly linked to the question of the destiny of the body in the early literature, if only because of the nature of the questions put to the Buddha and his followers. But as we have seen in the treatment of the *Tathāgata* and the *āsavas* the notion that the body is either annihilated after death in the case of the monk who has broken the *āsavas*, or that the body lives for ever, is clearly denied, as is entirely consistent with the denial of the identity of self and body, and of self and any of the five *khandhas*. It is not correct to affirm of the self after death what was denied of the self before death. Further, obsession (*papañca*) with this question and its variations is a manifestation of the canker of "view," *diṭṭhāsava*, which arises from craving, ignorance, perception, and so forth. In short, body, like any of the *khandhas*, is impermanent, and what is impermanent is woeful.

However, the end of rebirth is a prominent characteristic of the Third Noble Truth. It is helpful, I suggest, to consider this issue in a broader

---

[253] S III, 94-96.
[254] M I, 333; *cf.* D I, 93-95.

context than most Western thinkers are accustomed to; it is typical of their consideration of the question of rebirth that they limit their attention to the context of the physical body which is falsely identified with the self. In the Buddhist tradition the rebirth of the body and rebirth in general are thought of as possible for a virtual infinity of time, space and situations, from the human world to the deva-world, to the Brahma-world, to various hells, to the realm of animals–indeed, in every form, shape and circumstance imaginable. This conception actually means, then, that the Manifold, the Pleroma, is the consequence of the arising of suffering; further, it is the setting for the cessation of suffering. But there is one further and extremely significant point made: the human life provides the opportunity for the cessation of ill. All other forms are merely the consequences of the arising of ill. Therefore, despite the innumerable forms, the Brahma-life is possibly only for the one who seeks discipline and insight, enlightenment and liberation. The human experience is, in short, the All. Further, the presence of many bodies, inhabited and caused by prior action, is a truth no different from the consequences of the arising of suffering in one body. We may, then, regard the truth of the arising of suffering in either a microcosmic or a macrocosmic perspective; but the principle is not affected or altered by our choice. Whether the issue is the arising and cessation of the universe, of countless universes, of any biography, or of any moment, the truth of suffering is inextricably linked to the truths of *anicca* and desire. For this reason questions about whether I or the *Tathāgata* or an *Arahant* or a god will be annihilated or live forever in the next life are rejected in both their positive and negative formulations and responses. They are false questions. The true questions are those of the arising and the cessation of *dukkha*; bodies and rebirth neither are, nor are not, consequences of those truths.

Thus monks are taught that if there were no possibility at all of the consequences of deeds being "worn out" by right thought, right meditation, and right action, there would be no possibility in this life or any other for the end of *dukkha*. If one should think: "Just as this man does a deed [*kamma*] that is to be experienced [*vedanā*], so does he experience its fulfilment," that is the correct view; for in the "interim" between the doing of the deed and the experiencing of it is interposed the *Dhamma*. It is said: "Now, for instance, there may be some trifling evil deed of some person or other which may take him to hell (to atone for it). Or again there may be a like trifling evil deed of some person or other which is to be experienced in this very life. Not much of it, nay not a jot of it is seen (hereafter)."[255] The difference between the two cases is this: in the first, the person is "careless in culture of body, habits and thought [*kāya, sīla, citta*]." He has not developed insight, his soul and life are

---

[255] A I, 227.

restricted and miserable. Even a "trifling deed" will bring him to hell. For him who, on the other hand, is careful of culture of body, habits and thought, who has developed insight, "he is a great soul [jātimahatta], his life is immeasurable." The similar trifling offence has no effect, for it is worn away "in this very life."²⁵⁶

This distinction is evident in the story of Aṅgulimāla, whom we have already encountered. On his way to speak with Gotama a series of disasters befell him, and he arrived tattered and bleeding, with his begging bowl smashed. He is adjured to endure; for the ripening of his kamma here in this body saves him from boiling in Niraya Hell for many, many years. Thus released, Angulimala "experienced the bliss of freedom [vimuttisukha]."²⁵⁷

The arising and cessation of dukkha is not to be understood as though it were solely a function of the external world. This mistaken notion leads to the search in the world for its end, as though this would bring about the end of suffering. So Rohitassa, a hermit with the power of levitation who could move rapidly through the sky, laments his failure to reach the end of the world, "though I traveled a hundred years." But he is told, "in this very fathom-long body, along with its perception and thoughts [saññā], I proclaim the world to be, likewise the origin of the world and making of the world to end, likewise the practice of going to the ending of the world."²⁵⁸ The seeker who is calmed seeks neither this world nor another.²⁵⁹ Those who fully comprehend the Ariyan Truths are freed in this very life from rebirth,²⁶⁰ unlike those who do not understand the suffering nature of existence and delight in activities leading to rebirth.²⁶¹ The difference, already noted, is in the understanding of the suffering nature of existence. But each pursues his path in this life. For those who comprehend the Ariyan Truths there is no cause for continued existence, or annihilation, either in this life or any other. For those who are caught in desire, "existence" has neither beginning nor end. The self must be perpetuated as body, consciousness, perception, feeling and activities.²⁶² But for him who is released, "every body should be regarded as it really is by right insight. Thus 'this is not mine,' 'this am I not,' 'this of me is not the self.' " The same is true for feeling, perception, the activities and consciousness.²⁶³

---

²⁵⁶ *Ibid.*, 228.
²⁵⁷ M II, 289-290.
²⁵⁸ A I, 57.
²⁵⁹ *Ibid.*.
²⁶⁰ S V, 366.
²⁶¹ *Ibid.*, 379.
²⁶² M III, 67.
²⁶³ S III, 42-43.

For one who is freed, then, neither this existence nor any other is meaningful as a locus of the permanent self. There is no worry over whether he is better than he was, equal, or worse than he was, no concern such as this with his future, his present or his past.[264] Nor is there any "here" or "there" or "in between the two," no coming and going, no deceasing and uprising. "This," it is said, "is itself the end of anguish."[265]

The Khandhas

The significance of the khandhas for the truth of the end of suffering can hardly be overstated. If the destruction of the āsavas brings to an end any arising of suffering, the complete understanding of the nature of the khandhas as impermanent and empty means the end of any notion of self as either cause or effect of suffering. It is this understanding that distinguishes the Ariyan from the common and unlearned folk. The latter, believing that body, perception, sensation, the actions or consciousness is the self in any sense are "fettered by the bonds of the body,...bound to the inner and the outer," and go from this world to the world beyond, bound. The Ariyan, because he knows that none of the "heaps" is self or in self, is released from dukkha.[266] The Buddha's testimony underscores the importance of the khandhas for the end of suffering. Only when the five groups of grasping, upādānakhandha, and the "four-fold series," that is, the body, the uprising of the body, the ceasing of body, and the way going to the ceasing of body (and so also for the other khandhas), were "fully understood as they really are,...[only] then...was I assured that about this world, with its devas, its Māras, its Brahmas, in the host of recluses and Brahmins, of devas and men, I was one fully enlightened with the supreme enlightenment [abhisambhuddhoti]."[267]

Like the Buddha, those freed from the view that the body, perception, and so forth, are the self know what each of the khandhas really is, namely impermanent and modes of suffering. Repelled, they are released, and know that they are released.[268] Moreover, the Ariyan is said to be one who, instead of heaping up, reduces the khandhas; instead of

---

[264] Ibid..

[265] M III, 317-318.

[266] S III, 140-141.

[267] S II, 50ff.. In the subsequent sections of this passage each of the khandhas is analyzed with respect to its source, the end of its source, and the way to the end of its source via the Eight-fold Path. From food, āhāra, arises body, from contact with eye, ear, and the other senses arises feeling, perception arises from what is perceived, i.e. sights, sounds, smells, etc., the activities arise from the will, cetanā, for sights, for sounds, etc., consciousness arises in the six seats of consciousness, i.e., eye-consciousness, ear-consciousness, etc., from mind and body, nāmarūpa.

[268] S III, 42-43; cf. SN 80.

grasping he abandons; instead of binding, he scatters; he extinguishes rather than kindles.[269] He is not bound by the *khandhas*; "and so they turn to his bliss and pleasure for many a long day."[270] Constant attention to the true nature of the *khandhas* is an ongoing task for the monk, even for the *Arahant*. This constant contemplation of the true nature of the five grasping-groups eventually destroys the "subtle remnant" of the *anusayas*. For a disciple may be freed from the five fetters; but there is still a lurking tendency of the "I-conceit, of the I-am desire, of the lurking tendency to think 'I am'." If, later, he lives in the contemplation of the five grasping groups, the remnant, the lurking tendency is removed—like a cloth washed and then treated so that no trace of either its former soil or even of those cleaning agents used to make it spotless remains.[271] Obsession with the *khandhas* severally and collectively is replaced with contemplation of their true nature, as impermanent, empty, full of sorrow.

Indeed, it is possible for a monk who ponders, by means of the discipline, the nature of the *khandhas*—and apparently without any other effort—to realize the "fruits of stream-winning [*sotāpanna*]," the first of the four stages of development leading to Arahantship. However, it is also necessary for the achievers of the next three stages, the once-returner, the never-returner, and the *Arahant*, to contemplate the true nature of the *khandhas*.[272] Contemplation of the true nature of the *khandhas*, then, is a necessary stage of release; but it is possible that what is meant is that release is virtually the same thing as contemplation of the *khandhas* as they truly are. Whether this is striving that the *Arahant* is no longer obliged to pursue is not clear. But it seems quite possible that the injunction that the *Arahant* ponder the nature of the *khandhas* implies that, although for him alone there is "nothing more that needs to be done," it is the constant awareness of the nature of the *khandhas* that marks his release. If this interpretation is correct, we can better understand the notion that knowledge of the arising and ending of suffering, here seen in terms of the *khandhas* as the five groups of grasping, are identical. To know the true, empty, nature of the *khandhas* is to know the true nature of the empty self, the "I am" now known as "I am."

As Nāgārjuna argues, the *Tathāgata* can exist only apart from the *skhandhas*; yet existence is possible only in terms of the *skhandhas*. How, then, could the *Tathāgata* be known? Nāgārjuna concludes, as is his custom, that the *skhandhas* are empty, and that the *Tathāgata* is empty. The relationship between the two is therefore that of the four-fold denial

---

[269] *Ibid.*, 75.
[270] *Ibid.*, 98.
[271] *Ibid.*, 110; *cf.* 138.
[272] *Ibid.*, 143-144; *cf.* Th 84c.

of existence, of non-existence, both existence and non-existence, and of neither existence nor non-existence. For our purposes it is important to note that the *khandhas* are never annihilated for there is nothing to annihilate; but knowledge of their true nature is tantamount to release.[273]

The Anusayas

A further consequence of right knowledge is related to the latent conceits or lurking tendencies, the *anusayas*. We have already described these tendencies as inherent and, by their nature, unconscious. We saw also that the end of the *anusayas'* influence arises only when the monk has fully grasped for himself, found in himself, the true nature of the *khandhas*, rather than simply not being bound by them.[274] The latent nature of the *anusayas* renders them particularly inaccessible and powerful. They forge the strongest and most subtle bonds for the senses and sense objects. In turn, they represent perhaps the strongest manifestation of the commitment to the continuing self, and thus constitute the deepest roots of desire, particularly for greed, lust and ignorance.

The one for whom there are no latent conceits that "I am the doer, mine is the doer" (*aham-kāramamamkāramānānusayā*) is he who is freed, thinking of all material shape and the other *khandhas*, "This is not mine, This am I not, This is not my self," who sees it thus as it really is by means of perfect wisdom.[275] He knows that greed, hate and infatuation are profitless and conducive to suffering. He is freed of these conceits, and performs no acts arising from any of them. There are, then, no consequences of acts not based on lust, malice or delusion, and thus they are said to abandoned, "cut off at the root, made like a palm-tree stump, made unable to come again, of a nature not to arise again in future time."[276] The consequences of the end of the *anusayas* are well illustrated in the story of Upasena, whom we have met before. Dying from a snake bite, he asks that his body be scattered like chaff upon his death. Having quelled the *anusayas*, his body would have no further continuing components nor nutriments, and this would be true for any other definitions of self. The story reports, accordingly, that upon his death his body was scattered like a handful of ash.[277]

---

[273] Inada, 131-135.
[274] S III, 110.
[275] M III, 68.
[276] A I, 118-119; *cf.* 176, A III, 253-254.
[277] S IV 20-22. *Cf.* Ānanda's account of the four ways for the successful *Arahant*, each culminating in the coming to an end of the *anusayas*, A II, 162-163; and see the account of Dabba, whose end and consumption through burning of his body is the result of the end of the *khandhas*, U 113.

The Citta

The locus for the discipline and release of the monk with respect to the *anusayas* is the *citta*. It is important to recall the distinction between the *citta* and *mano*, the mind-sense whose proper field is the realm of ideation/imagination. The *citta* is the core of life's enterprise. It is thought of as "unguarded" among the undisciplined, that is, susceptible to and dominated by sensations, emotions and false views and obsessions. The guarding of the *citta*, or the protection of it with thoughtfulness, or right thinking, is a primary task of the monk. But the *citta* is not a continuing self. Rather, it is the heart of the person which, when unguarded, yields to suffering and, when guarded, is supple, pliant and disciplined and is thus impervious to suffering. A monk "has rule over *citta*, he is not under *citta*'s rule."[278]

As Sāriputta said of the teaching of Devadatta, when the *citta* is "heaped round" with thoughtfulness (*cetasā … suparicitaṃ*) it is proper for the monk to assert his knowledge that birth is destroyed, done is what was to be done and there is no more life in these conditions. His *citta* is said to be protected by thoughtfulness, and as a consequence is free of passion, of hatred, and of delusion (*vītarāga, vītadosa, vītamoha*), free of any condition of these sorts, of any condition of return for becoming in the worlds of sense, form and no form (*kāmabhavāyā, rūpabhavāyā, arūpabhavāyā*), that is, in the ninth sphere beyond perception and sense. In this state objects cognizable by the eye and the other senses, when present, do not overwhelm his *citta*, which is unconfused, firm, and composed. He notes the coming and going of objects in the world.[279] He turns his mind away from impermanent phenomena and concentrates wholly upon the "deathless element [*amatāya dhātuyā*]." He thinks, "this is the peace, this is the summit, just this: the stilling of all mind activity, the renouncing of all (rebirth) basis, the destroying of craving, passionless, ending, the cool. And steadfast therein he wins to canker-destruction."[280] The composure and indifference of the *citta* to all forms, then, marks the final release of the monk.

The shift from the unguarded *citta* to the composed *citta* is compared to a cleansing, reminiscent of the gold-refining metaphor we have already met. The introspection of the *citta* leads to its purification and freedom from sense and sense objects. This process is compared, as a way of illustrating its value as a habit of one's own *citta*, to a woman or man or young lad seeing imperfections in his or her face in a reflecting mirror or bowl of clear water. The imperfection, once identified, is removed and cleaned out, to the great pleasure and satisfaction of the person. So the

---

[278] M I, 267.
[279] A IV, 271-272; *cf.* note 1, *Ibid.*.
[280] *Ibid.*, 284-285.

monk is enjoined to reflect upon the image of his own *citta* by asking whether he is covetous, malevolent in heart, slothful, frantic, doubtful, angry, prurient, physically passionate, sluggish or disciplined. If any of these taints is found, he must exert himself for the abandoning of these unprofitable states.[281] Further, he must gain control of his *citta* so that he may concentrate upon the impermanent, the dangerous, the foul, the crooked things of the world, and upon the arising and cessation of the world. And as these matters are comprehended through the disciplined *citta*, so the monk's *citta* shall regard the world as having ceased.[282] With his thought fixed, in the certainty of the *Dhamma*, upon the *citta*, it settles down, becomes one-pointed (*ekodhoti*), and is composed (*samādhi*). When his thought is directed toward the way (*magga*), to abandoning of the fetters, and finally to the ending of the *anusayas*, he is an *Arahant*.[283]

When the *citta* is serene, undisturbed, "made pure, translucent, cultured, devoid of evil, supple, ready to act, firm and imperturbable," the monk is able to make himself the object of his own concentrated thinking:

...he applies and bends down his mind to the calling up of a mental image [*manomayaṃ*]. He calls up from this body another body, having form [*rupiṃ*], made of mind [*manomayaṃ*], having all (his own body's) limbs and parts, not deprived of any organ.

Just, O king, as if a man were to pull a reed from its sheath. He would know "This is the reed, this is the sheath. The reed one thing, the sheath another. It is from the sheath that the reed has been drawn forth."[284]

Another immediate fruit of the serene and supple *citta* is the knowledge of the destruction of the *āsavas*. The image of the man standing on the bank of a pool of clear, transparent water, who sees the shoals and fish within as they really are is, once again, the apt simile.[285]

Finally, the *citta*, when controlled and purified, does not share the destiny of this body "of the four elements compounded, from parents sprung, of a nature to be worn away, pounded away, broken and scattered." For though the body decay, be devoured by crows, kites and dogs, the *citta*, "if longtime practised in faith, virtue, learning, giving up and insight,...soars aloft [and] wins the summit." Like a jar of oil that, plunged into a deep pool of water, breaks, the shards sinking to the bottom and the oil rising to the top, so the *citta* seeks the highest level of release, leaving the empty and broken body behind.[286]

---

[281] A V, 66-67.
[282] *Ibid.*, 73.
[283] A II, 162-163.
[284] D I, 87-89.
[285] *Ibid.*, 93-95.
[286] S V, 320-321.

This purified *citta* is similar to the ego of the Freudian structural theory in at least one important respect: it may be overwhelmed by both external and internal sense-forces. Unguarded it is the locus of the arising of suffering, construed in terms of the experience of the individual. The guarded and purified *citta*, however, resembles the ego that has gained control of the internal forces and is not condemned to distorting its impressions of the external world, but sees them as they are. It is dominated neither by emotion nor sensation; it observes dispassionately the rising and setting of the impermanent forms, on the one hand, and is also the locus of the series of stages leading to the complete cessation of suffering, the end of the *āsavas*, of the *anusayas*, and the attaining of *nibbāna*. The mastery of the *citta* is described as an act of cleansing, of removing taints, and of the seeking of its own highest level. This set of descriptions suggests that the *citta* is "present" whether the situation is one of the truth of the arising of suffering or of the cessation of suffering. It is therefore the "heart" of the human enterprise, the focus of the steps toward complete liberation. It may be free or bound. In essence, it is transparent, supple. The task of the would-be *Arahant* is to remove distortions and taints, to allow it freely to seek its own natural goal of seeing and knowing things as they really are, free of lust, hate and ignorance. The training of the *citta* in truth leads to Arahantship, but that is tantamount to freedom from a distorted knowledge of the self and the world. That is the end of suffering.

Paññā/Wisdom

It is important to have an understanding of the range and depth, as well as the nature, of the *Arahant's* wisdom and insight in the state of the end of suffering. We have pursued this matter from the specific perspective of the *khandhas*, perception and sensation, the *anusayas*, and other issues. Here, however, we note the characteristics of the *Arahant* conceived of as a person who has come to the state of the end of suffering.

Paññā, frequently translated "intuitive wisdom," is of course central to any description of the *Arahant*. *Paññā* is the "tool" with which the clever monk digs up the "burning anthill" of the body.[287] It is by this wisdom that he knows the nature of things, things as they are, knows that he is released, understands that done is what must be done, and knows the "cool." *Paññā* is to be distinguished from *vedanā*, perception, although it is thought to be more like perception than the other *khandhas*, especially feeling or consciousness.[288] It is contrasted with a superficial knowledge of the *Dhamma*, even of the received tradition of the *Sangha*. There are those who are schooled in the prose and versified scriptures, who know "the Expositions, the Verses, the Uplifting Verses, the 'As it

---

[287] M I, 183-186.
[288] *Ibid.*, 352.

was said,' the Birth Stories, the Wonders, the Miscellanies." But, though schooled in the *Dhamma* as a tradition, they are said not to understand it, for they have not tested "the meaning of these things by intuitive wisdom [*paññā*]; and these things whose meaning is untested by intuitive wisdom do not become clear; they master this *Dhamma* simply for the advantage of reproaching others and for the advantage of gossipping, and they do not arrive at that goal for the sake of which they mastered *Dhamma*."[289]

Psychic Powers

By contrast, those who approach and learn the *Dhamma* with intuitive wisdom possess the "seven limbs of wisdom": mindfulness, Norm-investigation, Norm-teaching, zest, tranquillity, concentration, equanimity. For one who has mastered wisdom, then, release in this very life is possible.[290]

The *Arahant* has eliminated the "five mental barrennesses." These are doubts about the Teacher, the *Dhamma* and the *Sangha*, about the training of the Path; and he has eliminated anger. Thus he is zestful and committed. He is also free of the "five mental bondages," that is, he is free of attachment to sense-pleasures, desire, affection, thirst, fever and craving; he is free of attachment to body; he is free of attachment to material shapes; he does not eat as much as his belly will hold; and he does not hope to become a deva in a future life by following the discipline of the *Sangha*.

Thus freed, he has also cultivated the four-fold foundation of psychic power, *iddhipādā*: psychic power possessed of "concentration of intention with activities of striving [*chanda sāmadhi padhānasaṅkhāra samannāgatam*];" the basis of psychic power possessed of energy with activities of striving (*viriya*); the psychic power possessed of consciousness with activities of striving (*cittasa*); psychic power possessed of investigation, etc. (*vīmaṃsa*); and psychic power possessed of exertion, etc. (*ussoḷhi*).[291] Free of the five mental barrennesses and the five bondages, and armed with the four bases of psychic power and exertion, he is said to be possessed of the "fifteen factors." Thus "he becomes one for awakening, he becomes one for winning the incomparable security from the bonds [*yogāni*]." This is synonymous with Arahantship.

The *Arahant* perceives by *paññā* each of the *khandhas* as they really are. He thus disregards shape, feeling, perception, habitual tendencies and consciousness. Disregarding, he is dispassionate; dispassionate, he is freed, and knows that birth is destroyed, done what was to be done. Such a monk is said to have "lifted the barrier," "filled the moat," "pulled up the pillar," and "withdrawn the bolts;" he is said to be "a

---

[289] *Ibid.*, 171.
[290] S V, 55ff..
[291] *Cf. Ibid.*, 225-226.

pure one, the flag laid low, the burden dropped without fetters."[292] He has "lifted the barrier," in that ignorance is got rid of, "made like a palm-tree stump...not liable to rise again." He has "filled the moat," for there is no more again-becoming (*bhava*). He has "pulled up the pillar," for craving is got rid of. He has "withdrawn the bolts," because the "five fetters" (or mental bondages) binding him to the "lower sphere" are broken. Finally, he has "come to be a pure one, the flag laid low, the burden dropped, without fetters," for the fundamental conceit of I-ness (*asmīti anusaya*) has been uprooted.[293] Therefore by insight the faithful Ariyan disciple, striving, recollecting, and composing his mind, and clearly discerning, experiences in his own person the truth he had only heard of previously.[294]

Certainty and Self-knowledge

The four bases of psychic power have formidable potency when applied, even to the point of achieving enlightenment and release in this life. Thus the *Arahant's* success may rest upon his own striving with the aid of intention, energy, consciousness, investigation and exertion and bring him to release by insight.[295] The range of his comprehension is, quite literally, universal. By cultivating the "four arisings of mindfulness" he comprehends the thousandfold world-system, the manifold forms of magic—that is, the truth of the one being many and the many, one—even up to the Brahma world. He has the deva-power of hearing sounds both of devas and of men, both far and near. He is able to read and know the minds of other beings, the lustful as lustful, the liberated as liberated. He knows all causal connections, all arisings and cessations of past, present and future times. He knows the world and all shapes, the characters of beings, the nature of the mind of other beings and other persons. He can remember his past existences in all details and characteristics. With his deva-sight he can discern the comings and goings of beings according to their merits. This monk abides in heart's release, release by insight, who has destroyed the *āsavas*.[296]

Universal knowledge unqualified by time or space is a concomitant and characteristic of the freed heart, released by insight. Knowing all, one is released; released, he knows all. He can, then, distinguish between wise and foolish words, thoughts and deeds—an ability which no unreleased being possesses, for those who are released are not confused or doubtful since they have *paññā*.[297] This person is not susceptible to the wiles of

---

[292] M I, 177-179.
[293] *Ibid.*; *cf.* S III, 98.
[294] S V, 200-202.
[295] *Ibid.*, 253-254.
[296] *Ibid.*, 269-271.
[297] *Cf.* A I, 88-89.

Māra, that is, to sense-impression; for he knows by "superknowledge" (*abhiñña*) the thing itself (*dhamma*), and is a "witness," that is, one who knows things as they really are "now here, now there, whatever may be the plane."[298]

The knowledge of the *Arahant* is unqualified and purified. What he knows is the arising and ceasing of *dukkha*; and there is nothing–in both senses of that term–beyond *dukkha*, and *dukkha* itself is empty. Thus Gotama was fully enlightened when he knew the arising and the cessation of the *khandhas*, for there was nothing else to know.[299] The knowledge and the "mind" of the *Arahant* is limitless, without boundary. The story is told of the monk who seeks to discover where the four elements cease, leaving no trace. After consulting the four great kings, the Gods of the sky, the retinue of Brahma, and Brahma himself with no success, Brahma urged him to seek out Gotama. The Enlightened One altered his question to include all name and form, and answered, "[t]he intellect [*viññāṇa*] of Arahantship, the invisible, the endless, accessible from every side–/ There is it that earth, water, fire, and wind [*etc.*] die out, leaving no trace behind./ When intellection ceases they all also cease."[300] The passage suggests not only the universality and transparency of the *Arahant*'s intellect, but also that in that very intellect there is a form of "knowledge" appropriate to release, although there is neither subject nor object, world nor self.[301]

Is there such a person? The tradition insists not only that there is such a person but that each person is just such a person when he overcomes craving and desire, and comes to know both himself and the world as they truly are, their arising and cessation.

Not only does the *Arahant* know fully and without qualification the truths of the arising and cessation of suffering, he also knows that he knows, that he possesses fully this comprehensive knowledge. He is the man who, standing on the edge of a clear pool, sees all that is there as it truly is. "In freedom the knowledge comes to be that he is freed, and he comprehends: Destroyed is birth, brought to a close is the Brahmafaring, done is what was to be done, there is no more being such and such."[302]

What is it that the *Arahant* knows? He knows fully the arising and cessation of *dukkha*, and knows that he knows. He knows that there is no self in body, in feeling, in perception, in the habitual tendencies or

---

[298] M III, 136. A note identifies "plane" as "meditative plane." *Cf.* S V, 243-245.

[299] S III, 50-54.

[300] D I, 280-284.

[301] *Cf.* D II, 66-68; *cf.* SN 126.

[302] M I, 333; *cf.* D I, 93-95.

activities, or in consciousness: "This is not mine, this am I not, this of me is not the self." He feels disgust at the *khandhas*, and "knows he is released," knows that rebirth is destroyed, that suffering, ignorance, and so forth, are not his any longer.[303] The *Arahant* is no longer bound by the *anusayas*, the fundamental conceits of greed, hatred and ignorance. He has replaced greed with not-greed, hatred with not-hatred, ignorance with knowledge, delusion with non-delusion. The unprofitable (*akusala*) states have been replaced by profitable (*kusala*) states. As well as being freed from these fetters he acquires the knowledge that he is released, "and he is assured: Ended is rebirth; lived is the righteous life; done is my task; there is no more of this state for me." He is assured in and of his knowledge and freedom from greed, hate and delusion.[304] In turn, he is freed from the bondage of the senses. He knows the impermanence of the senses, of sense-consciousness, and of sense-contact. This realization leads to the certain knowledge that there is no continuation of this present state.[305] The disciple who knows that all feelings, whether pleasant, unpleasant, or neutral, are transient grasps after nothing. Then he is confident of the end of rebirth.

> It is just as if a man...were to draw out from a potter's oven a heated jar and were to place it on a smooth portion of earth, so that the heat could there cool off and the sherds dry up. Even so when the brother feels a feeling that his powers have reached their limit, or when he feels a feeling that life has reached its term, he knows that he feels such a feeling. He knows that, at the breaking up of the body, from the end of his life here that he has felt, all that lacked lure for him will grow cold, and bodies will be left on one side.[306]

The destruction of the *āsavas* is, as we have seen, one of the major marks of the *Arahant*'s successful progress towards release. It is also true that the *Arahant* knows they are destroyed. This confidence is exhibited in the fact that the *Arahant*, for whom the cankers are destroyed and who has "lived the life, done what ought to be done," is not concerned about whether there are those who are better than, equal to, or worse than he. In this state he abides in *paññā*;[307] and here no comparisons are useful, since they arise from grasping and desire, but also from doubt and worry. There is neither doubt nor worry for him who is released, and thus he is unconcerned with his standing in the eyes of

---

[303] S III, 42-43.
[304] A I, 176-178.
[305] S IV, 13-14.
[306] S II, 58.
[307] A II, 255.

others. His confidence is utterly untrammeled.[308] This certainty is also characteristic of the *Arahant* who has passed from the nine stages beginning with aloofness from sense desire and culminating in the ending of perception and feeling. He knows by insight that in himself the cankers are destroyed.[309] Concerning the end of the *āsavas* the Buddha asserts summarily: "...concerning these I have no doubts; they are cleaned out; I am not worried about them."[310] Indeed, this certainty is a mark of the *anupādā parinibbāna*, the "completely unattached cool," which the *Arahant* achieves by his own effort: "Destroying the cankers, he enters and abides in the cankerless mind-emancipation, ...here and now, realizing it himself by his own knowledge. This, monks, is called the completely unattached cool."[311] The monk may then be content; for he purifies his mind of weakness and sloth, flurry and worry, fretfulness, irritability and vexation of spirit. "Putting away wavering, he remains as one passed beyond perplexity [*vicikiccā*]; and no longer in suspense as to what is good, he purifies his mind of doubt."[312] The enlightened person has no truck with worry and scurrying of the mind (*mano*), but rests content and sure of his release.[313] He is possessed of a supreme and unassailable confidence. It is not a source a pride—a possibility Gotama pointed out with some asperity.[314] There is no longer an agent of striving in any sense; rather, the work is over. The "cool" of *nibbāna* is the term descriptive of this state; and the supreme confidence, the utter lack of concern, the conviction that the work is done, the life lived, the burden laid down, are central to that notion of extinction, coolness, and release.

Relations with Others

Among the characteristics of the *Arahant*-monk we have explored there is a general emphasis upon freedom from the bondage of attachment to the phenomena of the world, and the liberation of the *citta* through *paññā*, wisdom. This orientation is, as it were, "internal," in contrast with purported relations with the world and with others. We may ask, then, what the ideal relationship with other persons is for one who is freed.

The "Brahman, the man of worth," says the *Dhammapada*, is he who has transcended both good and evil "as bonds, the man selfless,

---

[308] *Ibid.*; *cf.* S III, 42-43.
[309] A V, 143-146.
[310] S II, 40.
[311] A IV, 40-43.
[312] D I, 81-82.
[313] U 44.
[314] A III, 255, where it is said that those who brag about their wisdom will suffer remorse.

dye-faded, purified."[315] Further, in his investigation of things he does not grasp, and is not distracted by attachment to things either internal or external.[316] What is this person's attitude toward others? It is the conclusion of human wisdom that one should be free of evil deeds against others–but should he be free of good ones as well? That latter goal is implied in the foregoing passages, as well as many others. Gotama relates the occasion of temptation by Māra's daughters in which he is asked, cannily, why he has no friends in the village. He responds that in meditation upon the bliss of nibbāna, he requires no friendship.[317] The import of this statement appears to be that friendship is a necessity for the desiring and grasping person who must seek gratification in others' feelings about him, and thus he binds himself to others in a state of friendship. With desire extinguished, Gotama has no need of this sort of relationship.

This does not mean, as our earlier investigations suggest, that the Arahant is careless in his behavior towards others, any more than he is careless in his behavior in general. It is true that he has given total concentration to replacing unskilled with skilled habits. Uggāhamāna says that the one with the highest skills, the unconquerable recluse, has no evil deed in his body, no evil speech, no evil intention, no evil livelihood. The skilled states arise, furthermore, from the mind (citta) that is freed of attachment, aversion and confusion. Among these skilled states are non-malevolence, non-harmful behavior.[318] Evil deeds arise from motives of "partiality [chanda], enmity [dosa], stupidity [moha] and fear [bhaya]." But the Ariyan disciple is free of these motives; and thus he performs no evil deeds in his skilled states.[319] The Arahant has eliminated the foundations of evil action, along with evil thought and speech. He is said to be incapable of nine things: depriving a living creature of life; taking what is not given so that it constitutes theft; sexual impurity; deliberately telling lies; laying up of treasures and indulgence in worldly pleasure as he used to do in the life of the house; taking a wrong course through partiality; taking a wrong course through hate, through cupidity, through fear.[320]

Another aspect of this general ethic of non-violence is the notion of compassion. In the Buddhist tradition both wisdom, paññā, and compassion, karunā, are central to the release of the Arahant. Compassion is probably a consequence of the development of the kusala states. As

---

[315] Dh 133.
[316] M III, 272.
[317] S I, 156-159.
[318] M II, 223-224, 226-227.
[319] D III, 174.
[320] Ibid., 125.

such, it is not a form of attachment but a general attitude or orientation to others based on complete understanding of others and one's own self. Thus Gotama, responding to Queen Mallikā's statement that she loved her soul, notes: "The whole wide world we traverse with our thought [cetasa];/ And nothing find to man more dear than soul [attā]./ Since aye so dear the soul to others is,/ Let the soul-lover harm no other man."[321] This statement suggests that compassion is not to be limited only to fellow *Arahants* but to be extended to all beings regardless of their state of delusion or enlightenment. The *Bhikkhus* are encouraged, furthermore, to show gentleness and patience in their dealings with the common folk. It was said that Sakka, a disciple, was told by the ruler of the Asuras that Sakka should not be so long-suffering of foolish people, for they would never change, and Sakka looked foolish himself in showing sympathy and kindness to them. Sakka's critic here, Vepacitti, was reprimanded for thinking thoughts typical of those who did not understand the *Dhamma* and the *Sangha*.[322]

In the context of relations to others the tradition pays considerable attention to the matter of giving and accepting gifts. Gift-giving has always been a powerful public representation of relations between people, symbolizing obligation, respect and reward. It has usually been thought that the giving of gifts is a worthy and positive act in human relations. It is noteworthy that the tradition is highly critical of gift-giving if it is done for the wrong reasons: motive is everything. There are, it is said, eight grounds for giving. Thése are: giving because of impulse (*chanda*); giving because of exasperation (*dosa*); giving because of misapprehension (*moha*); giving because of fear; or one gives thinking that he must not betray the traditions of his ancestors; or one gives in hopes of being reborn in heavenly bliss; or one gives to attain peace of heart and to gain joy and gladness; or, one gives to enrich and mellow his heart.[323] Each of these motives is selfish, despite the fact that they can be arranged in an order of ascending moral value based on the motives that are at work. The giving of gifts or alms is thus not in itself a necessarily beneficial or skillful act, and may be performed to the detriment of both giver and recipient.

It is again clear that the analysis of suffering and of its cessation is not primarily concerned with any particular act but with the motives and intentions that cause the act. For the *Arahant*, with his purified *citta*, the dominant social characteristic of his existence arises from his freedom from greed, hate and delusion (and fear). Non-hurtfulness is the most significant expression of his relation with others; but it is also the

---

[321] S I, 101-102.
[322] *Ibid.*, 283-286.
[323] A IV, 161.

significant expression of the relationship with the self. Non-hurtfulness is a characteristic, for example, of the monk who has passed through the fourth *jhāna* state. It is described as a feeling (*vedanā*). If that monk "does not strive for his own hurt [*attabyābādha*] or for the hurt of others, if he does not strive for the hurt of both, at that very time he experiences a feeling [*vedanā*] that is not hurtful. I, monks, say that non-hurtfulness is the highest satisfaction among feelings."[324] Non-hurtfulness, rather than being simply an ethical injunction not to harm, is a quality of the monk himself in this liberated state. Ethics, one could say, is not something you do but something you are. This is consistent with the view that actions in and of themselves may be good or evil, but the significant locus is the nature of the desire, or motive, of the "self." Relations to others, then, are the external manifestation of the internal nature. For this reason hurtfulness or non-hurtfulness are qualities of both internal and external relations; they describe both the nature of the "self's internal structure" and of the relationship with others. The principle does not change, in other words, whether we are speaking of the nature of the "self" or of relations with others.

Monks, then, are to train themselves to *be* a certain kind of person; and from this arises their relationship with others.

Neither will our minds become perverted nor will we utter an evil speech, but kindly and compassionate will we dwell, with a mind of friendliness [*mettacitta*], void of hatred; and we will dwell having suffused that person with a mind of friendliness; and, beginning with him, we will dwell having suffused the whole world with a mind of friendliness that is far-reaching, widespread, immeasurable, without enmity, without malevolence....[325]

The mind of friendliness should be distinguished from the friendship of which Gotama had no need. *Mettā* is a quality of the *citta*, just as *paññā* is. Further, it does not imply attachment to others, nor self-satisfaction in the monk. Neither does it imply, obviously, aversion to any other being. It does imply that full knowledge of the *Arahant* which has replaced the usual confusion about the nature and motives of others that is so detrimental to ordinary human relations. *Mettā*, in short, is the non-lustful, non-aversive, non-deluded or non-ignorant state of the *citta* directed toward others. "Friendliness" is based on knowledge and compassion. Compassionate, it is essentially sympathetic to the state of other persons. It is therefore receptive and understanding, completely honest and informed, free of guile or deceit. This is possible because these are precisely the characteristics the *Arahant* possesses with respect to himself;

---

[324] M I, 118.
[325] *Ibid.*, 164.

and in the final analysis complete self-knowledge is complete knowledge of the other. (This is a Buddhist version of the Second Law in Jesus' summary, that you must love others as you love yourself.) Further, *mettā* cannot be limited to a purely individual existence but rather suffuses the whole. It is the monk's task to make this suffusion possible, so that it becomes measureless, like the *citta* of the *Arahant*. This notion of the *mettacitta* forms the basis for the Mahāyāna teaching of the *Bodhisattva* with his or her measureless compassion and friendliness, and of the doctrine that the whole is *mettā*, *karunā* and *paññā*, that is, the *Adhibuddha*.

Within the *Sangha*, there are not many *mettacittas*, so to speak, but only one, encompassing the entire group of individuals. Thus Anuruddha accounts for the harmonious relations within the *Sangha*, so striking in their contrast with ordinary human relations, by saying that there is but one *citta*, characterized by *mettā*, in the brotherhood; "so I, Lord, having surrendered my own mind, am living only according to the mind of these venerable ones. Lord, we have divers bodies, but assuredly only one mind."[326] For those who have destroyed the cankers, lived the life, there is no thought that "There is one better than I," "There is one equal," "There is one worse."[327] Monks do not pray for honor, any more than they pray for long life, beauty, happiness, or the heavenly worlds.[328]

The monks must avail themselves of the "four powers:" the power of wisdom (*paññā*), by which conditions are known as they really are; the power of energy (*viriya*), by which one strives ceaselessly to rid himself of *akusala* states and replace them with *kusala* states; the power of faultlessness (*anavijjā*), by which one renders faultless his thoughts, speech and actions; and finally the power of sympathy (*Sanghabala*), and under this rubric the ideal relations with others are described. Sympathy has four bases: gifts; kindness (*vajjapeyya*); doing good (*atthacariyā*); and equal treatment (*samānattatā*). "Monks," it is said, "that is the best gift: the gift of *Dhamma*." The best kindness is teaching *Dhamma* to the good and attentive listener. The best of good deeds is inciting, instilling, and establishing the ways of faith in an unbeliever, virtue (*sīla*) in the immoral, generosity in the mean, and wisdom in the foolish. The best equality is that which exists between Streamwinner and Streamwinner (*sotāpanna*), between Once-returner and Once-returner (*sakadāgāmin*), between Non-returner and Non-returner (*anāgāmin*), and between Arahant and Arahant. Thus empowered, the monks avoid the fears of livelihood, of ill fame, of embarrassment in assemblies, of death, and of a miserable after-life.[329]

---

[326] *Ibid.*, 258.
[327] A III, 255.
[328] *Cf. ibid.*, 39-40.
[329] A IV, 241-242.

In sum, the true foundation of relations among individuals is sympathy; and sympathy rests in turn upon the *Dhamma*, or, as we should think of it, the truth. Only in this context can the aversion, the greed and the delusion of ordinary human relations be dissolved. That the *Dhamma* is the basis of sympathy is very important for our understanding of the *Arahant*; for, on the one hand, it means that the *Arahant* does engage in such relations, that there is a significant social dimension of the life of the one who is freed; but, on the other hand, it means that relations with others are fulfilled, and ideal, only when they are totally encompassed by the truth of the arising and cessation of suffering—that is, encompassed by the truth, utterly free of delusion and self-deception. Finally, the very existence of this view implies that complete release incorporates a life that is neither solitary nor simply gregarious but communal, based on the love and the knowledge of the *Dhamma*. Such a community is truly called *Sangha*, the community of sympathetic persons, dwelling in compassion, friendliness and wisdom.

Dukkha

Following this discussion of the characteristics of the *Arahant* we must raise the question of the condition of his existence. This leads us to the question of the nature of *nibbāna*; but before addressing that matter we should briefly note the status of the *Arahant* with respect to *dukkha*, and the nature of *dukkha* itself from the perspective of the truth of the end of *dukkha*.

The most important point about *dukkha* from the perspective of this truth is that it is brought to an end. To review briefly, the end of *dukkha* is really the end of an infinite process of ignorance, replaced by wisdom and insight, by knowing things as they truly are without distraction. The monk should investigate the nature of things in such a manner that his consciousness of what is external is undistracted, and his consciousness of what is internal is not disturbed by grasping. Certainly, there must be no confusion between the two forms of consciousness; and when he succeeds in these respects there is no more origination or arising of *dukkha*.[330] The end of *dukkha* is thus synonymous with the clearer vision of what is and the dispassionate assessment of the nature of the self. Thus Mālunkyaputta, that paragon of the liberated person, who is free of lust, aversion and confusion because he senses and perceives only what is there through his senses, has no "therein," that is, no qualification by place and birth or rebirth, no grounds for the future arising of greed, hate and delusion. He is, thus, free of *dukkha*.[331] Again, it is said that the monk who is in complete control of his thinking has made an end of anguish. Pleasure, pain and neutral feelings are known to him as

---

[330] M III, 272.
[331] S IV, 42-43; *cf.* 59.

dukkha.[332] He is called "master in the method and paths of thought; he can think whatever thought he wishes; he will not think any thought that he does not wish; he has cut off craving, done away with fetters, and by fully mastering pride, has made an end of anguish."[333]

It may be said that the end of *dukkha* means the end of acting, thinking or speaking falsely, that is, acting, thinking or speaking out of a false understanding of the self and the world, based on desire, grasping and craving, with all their attendant consequences. The end of *dukkha* does not mean the end of acting, speaking or thinking, as is clear from our previous investigations of the tradition. On the other hand, right thinking, right speaking, right acting arise out of the sure and certain knowledge of the nature of the false bases of these activities, knowledge which in and of itself constitutes release from *dukkha*. The one who stands on the bank of the clear pool at once sees things as they really are, knows he sees things as they really are, and thus forms no continuing basis for *dukkha*. The end of *dukkha* means enlightenment in its literal sense, to see clearly and distinctly and without distortion or qualification, as one looking at something in a clear and unshadowed light. The end of *dukkha*, then, appears precisely to be this "sight" of the self and of the world, in which the world is known to be the work of the senses and their compounds and the self to be the work of desire. There is a world, there is a self, but they are *dukkha*. Knowing they are *dukkha*, the *Arahant* knows they are empty and thus the fetters that bound him to the world and to the self are dropped. He is no longer deceived either about self or world.

Nibbāna

The end of *dukkha* is *nibbāna*. The word means and is translated "The Cool," that is, the consequence of extinguishing the flame of desire, of the end of the *āsavas*, and of the other cessations already described. It is the goal of the Ariyan Path: "...the Brahma-faring is for immergence [*sic*] in nibbāna, for going beyond to nibbāna, for culminating in nibbāna."[334] Several observations may be offered. First, *nibbāna* is not a separate state; on the other hand, it is not the same as *dukkha* if the latter is understood as the fundamentally false "state" of speech, action and thought. It follows that it cannot be said to be both a separate state and *dukkha*; and it cannot be neither that separate state nor *dukkha*. It cannot be said to exist, for existence is qualified by the *khandhas* and the series of co-dependent origination; and *nibbāna* is precisely the absence of bondage to either. Nor can it be said not to exist, when that means

---

[332] *Ibid.*, 139.

[333] M I, 153-156.

[334] *Ibid.*, 367.

the opposite of existence. We have already seen that these and related views are condemned as false.

Second, *nibbāna* is inseparable from the entire series of the arising and cessation of *dukkha*; for it is the designation of the cessation of *dukkha*. When there is no "cool," when, on the contrary, there is "fire with fuel" and other conditions necessary to keep it burning, *nibbāna* is not the state of existence. In every description of the cessation of *dukkha*, especially when it is seen as the reversal of the arising of *dukkha*, the consequence is *nibbāna*. *Nibbāna*, then, cannot be extricated from the arising and cessation of suffering, for it is either implicit or explicit throughout. It is partly for this reason that Nāgārjuna proposes his famous equation of *nirvāṇa* and *saṃsāra*.

Third, it is important, especially for outsiders, to take care not to interpret too literally the tradition of *nibbāna*–here "literally" means both reading into the tradition essentially irrelevant and immaterial interpretations, such as the equation of *nibbāna* with heaven, and taking the term out of its context for the purpose of satisfying just those motives from which false view arises. The "literal" interpretation of *nibbāna* is in fact the consequence of that self-deceiving avoidance of the analysis of the root causes of suffering, namely the desire for I-ness, for continuing existence.

Fourth, *nibbāna* is but one of a number of expressions employed to transmit the truth of the end of suffering. *Vimutti*, "release," is one such expression; the "passionless ending" is another; and extinction, *nirodha*, is a third. The implication is that we are confronted with the end of desire in such a manner that it may be described in quite a number of different ways without losing the essential truth, just as there are quite a number of different ways by which suffering may be brought to an end, quite a number of different paths to follow–they may all be called the *magga*.[335] This view undercuts any notion that *nibbāna* is monolithic, that it is a place, or even that it is a "state of existence."

Fifth, the question is often raised as to whether *nibbāna* has any connection with physical death. As we have seen, the connection is not accidental, but it is secondary. The *Arahant* looked forward to various extensions and limitations of his remaining life, or lives, following the extinction of the *āsavas*. The difference in expectations was based on a type of quantifier effect of past actions, thoughts, and deeds. Death may or may not mark the end of the consequences of the past; but death does not necessarily mean *nibbāna*. *Nibbāna* is always the end of building up of foundations for the arising of suffering. Whether this is an "occasion" is itself not absolutely clear. But the connection with death is, at best, secondary.[336]

---

[335] *Cf.* M III, 46ff..

[336] *Cf. ibid.*, 290-291, where there is a description of one "in" *nibbāna*

In summary, in speaking of *nibbāna* we must recognize its role as term and concept used primarily, but not solely, to decribe a "condition" of the culmination of the cessation of suffering. As such, it never loses its link with the truth of the arising and cessation of suffering, for it is in truth part of the co-dependent origination series leading to the cessation of suffering–of which *nibbāna* itself is a significant descriptive term.

The proclamation "Wide opened are the portals to Nirvāṇa!" suggests that *nibbāna* is a place. Yet *nibbāna* is in fact to be understood as the assertion of the consequence of the *Dhamma* proclaimed by the Buddha "that in this life beareth fruit, that avails not for a time only, that welcometh every one, that leadeth away and onward, that each one who hath intelligence may of and by himself understand!"[337] As a consequence of the proclamation of the *Dhamma* the end of suffering may be anticipated; and thus the "Portals" are the portals to understanding. There is, in other words, an end to the journey of the holy life, or to the effort of abandoning desire. It is like the journey made by the Brahman Uṇṇābha. He asked the Buddha whether it is possible to bring the process of eliminating desire to an end, for the task seemed endless. But, the Buddha pointed out, Uṇṇābha's journey was the consequence of desire, energy, thought, and consideration; and when he reached the park where Gotama was all these motives abated and were still.[338] It is so also for the end of suffering. *Nibbāna*, then, is the end of the struggle and its consequence.[339]

This is the "condition" of the end of *dukkha*:

Monks, there exists that condition wherein is neither earth nor water nor fire nor air; wherein is neither the sphere of infinite space nor of infinite consciousness nor of nothingness nor of neither-consciousness-nor-unconsciousness; where there is neither this world nor a world beyond nor both together nor moon-and-sun. Thence, monks, I declare is no coming to birth; thither is no going (from life); therein is no duration; thence is no falling; there is no arising. It is not something fixed, it moves not on, it is not based on anything. That indeed is the end of Ill.[340]

In saying that the condition exists, the reality of *nibbāna* as the end of suffering is affirmed. It is affirmed, further, in terms of the end of the *jhāna* states, in terms of the end of the arising and cessation of suffering, and it is affirmed as the end of becoming. In short, *nibbāna* is affirmed

---

who continues to perceive.
[337] D II, 251-252.
[338] S V, 243-245.
[339] It should not be confused with the "journey" itself; that is, means and end remain in some sense separate. *Cf. ibid.*, 161.
[340] U 97.

as the extinction of all causes of suffering. It is, of course, a "condition" only in the sense that it is the reality of the end of all conditions; thus it is not fixed, it has no duration, it is neither this world nor another, it has neither life nor death, it has no foundation. Finally, it cannot be said that this is the "condition" of any entity, neither worldly nor of the self. (This is the true condition of emptiness, as we shall see.)

Nibbāna and the ending of suffering are regularly compared to states of existence in which the fire of desire for existence has been extinguished–though existence is neither affirmed nor denied. Thus the one who is free of grasping, and thus of Ill, is compared to a heated jar drawn from a potter's oven and left to cool on a smooth portion of earth.[341] Or, when the monk is released from the bondage of all feelings, it is just as if oil and wick are used up and the lamp goes out, or as if a spark struck from an anvil dies away.[342] The one who is released, whose desire is similarly extinguished, knows that this is so. This certainty is, very probably, one of the reasons for describing the end of suffering as a "condition"; for it may be known.[343]

In the context of this metaphor of the "condition" of *nibbāna*, the notion that there is something left is an unnecessary concern. "In saying that there is something left one makes difficulty [*papañca*] where there is none."[344] Rather, the monk abides in the cankerless mind-emancipation, here and now, realizing it himself by his own knowledge. This is the "completely unattached cool [*anupādā parinibbāna*]."[345] The path to *nibbāna* is followed by him who does not grasp for answers concerning the past, present or future but passes beyond "the rapture of aloofness,...beyond spiritual happiness,...beyond feeling that is neither painful nor pleasant, [who] beholds, 'Tranquil am I, allayed am I, without grasping am I.' As to this, monks, the *Tathāgata* comprehends: This worthy recluse or brahman...beholds...'without grasping am I'–certainly this venerable one maintains the very course that is suitable for nibbāna."[346] The venerable monk is released without further grasping in that he does not concern himself with the future and the past.[347]

Rather, the seeker must emulate the *Tathāgata*, who abides in emptiness; "I, Ānanda, through abiding in...emptiness [*suññatāvihārena*], abide in the fullness thereof."[348] The emptiness of increasingly general states

---

[341] S II, 58.
[342] U 114.
[343] S V, 280-283.
[344] A II, 168-169.
[345] A IV, 40-43.
[346] M III, 23-24.
[347] Cf. ibid., 46-51.
[348] Ibid., 147.

is invoked, beginning with emptiness of Migara's mother's palace—which is empty of elephants, cows, horses, gold and silver, assemblies of men and women—in comparison to the order of monks and its solitude. So the monk, disregarding the village and activities and inhabitants, regards the solitude of the forest, and then the consciousness of earth. In turn, like the palace, the village and the forest, earth-solitude is seen to be empty, and the monk attains to each of the four *jhāna* states, to infinite space, infinite consciousness, no-thing, neither-perception-nor-non-perception. Each, in turn, is found empty. He continues to find, in turn, the "concentration of the mind that is signless," the six sensory fields that, conditioned by life, "are grounded on this body itself." "He regards that which is not there as empty of it." But the concentration of mind that is signless is effected and thought out, "and this is impermanent, liable to stopping." Knowing this, he is freed of the cankers of sense-pleasures, of becoming and of ignorance. In freedom there is the knowledge that he is freed and he comprehends: "Destroyed is birth, brought to a close the Brahma-faring," *etc.*. Further, the very perception of this truth of the emptiness of the six sense-pleasures is itself empty: "This perceiving is empty of the canker of sense-pleasures...of becoming...of ignorance." This is the "utterly purified and incomparably highest realisation of...emptiness."[349] This final stage is devoid, then, of subject or object; the very object of the knowledge sought is empty, as is the knower of the object. Here the emptiness is fully developed; that is to say, the monk moves through a series of increasingly general notions of emptiness, from the emptiness of the palace over against the solitude of the monk of the *Sangha* and his points of concentration, to the end of any object of concentration and any subject of knowledge. Emptiness, which is a central characteristic of *nibbāna*, also suggests that the consequence of the discipline is not a place or thing but the end of the *āsavas* and the meaninglessness of places, things and people with respect to release from suffering. Emptiness, like *nibbāna*, is a condition in the sense that the one who "achieves" it knows that he has been released, that he dwells in the emptiness of all things, free of disturbance. Nothing upsets him, or elicits greed, hatred or delusion, or a desire for becoming.

We may now examine with profit Nāgārjuna's speculations on the nature of *nibbāna/nirvāṇa*, because the notion of emptiness as he proposes it suggests a means of conceptualizing the relationship between *nibbāna* and the arising and cessation of suffering. In reply to his opponent Nāgārjuna asserts that whether things are *śūnya* or *aśūnya*, it is not possible to say to whose abandonment of defilement or to whose extinction of suffering *nirvāṇa* can be attributed. Disposing thus of a rather facile objection, he proceeds to point out that what is never "cast

---

[349] M III, 147-152; *cf.* 154-157.

off, seized, interrupted, constant, extinguished, and produced..." is called *nirvāṇa*. *Nirvāṇa* is not strictly in the nature of ordinary existence for a number of reasons: (1) it does not have the characteristics of suffering; (2) it is not of the created realm (*saṁskṛta*); (3) it is not grasping. On the other hand, what is called non-existence could not be the equivalent of *nirvāṇa*; for where there is no existence, there can be no non-existence (*bhāva, nabhāva*). Further, he argues that since *nirvāṇa* is non-grasping, if it were non-existing it would be a non-existing non-grasping entity; that is, it would be an entity that contradicts its own existence.

What is true of *nirvāṇa* is that it is non-grasping (*anupādāna*) and thus free of the *skhandas*, and not subject to relational and co-dependent causation. Since this is true, the Buddha taught the abandonment of the concepts of being and non-being (*bhāva, vibhāva*); and therefore "*nirvāṇa* is properly neither (in the realm of) existence or non-existence (*bhāvo nabhāvo*)." *Nirvāṇa* is, further and for these reasons, non-grasping, neither created nor uncreated. How, then, shall we understand *nirvāṇa*? For comparison, Nāgārjuna points out that the Blessed One cannot be said to exist after *nirodha* (that is, release from worldly desires), nor can it be said that he does not exist, nor both, nor neither. Further it can not be said that the Blessed One even exists in the present living process (*bhāva*), nor that he does not exist, nor both, nor neither. Nāgārjuna then makes his most dramatic claim about the nature of *nirvāṇa*: "*saṁsāra*...is nothing essentially different from *nirvāṇa*. *Nirvāṇa* is nothing essentially different from *saṁsāra*."

This assertion is, first of all, an answer to an issue implied in the discussion of the relationship between *nirvāṇa* on the one hand and the existence/non-existence states on the other. He argues that if we are to understand the nature of *nirvāṇa* we must also understand the nature of existence and non-existence. The *nirvāṇa/saṁsāra* equation is the blunt and dramatic reply. Thus questions and beliefs concerning such related matters as the life after the end of worldly desires, the limits of the world, the concept of permanence, and so forth, are all based on the concept of *nirvāṇa*, and upon posterior and anterior states of existence. *Nirvāṇa*, simply, defines *saṁsāra*, that is, the world, permanence, anterior and posterior existence and related matters such as the *skhandhas* and the series of co-dependent origination.

Having defined *nirvāṇa* in terms of *saṁsāra*, however, Nāgārjuna comes to his point: since all factors of experience are in the nature of *śūnya*, there is nothing to assert of either *nirvāṇa* or *saṁsāra*; and therefore there is not the slightest difference between them.[350] That is to say, the Buddha never taught that there was any *dhamma*, any "element" or "factor" susceptible to experience for anyone, ever. The whole is empty.

---

[350] Inada, 153-159.

In *śūnyata* it is not possible to draw a distinction between *nirvāṇa* and *saṃsāra*; for each concept is a way of pointing to the truth.

Excursus: Freud and the Nirvana Principle

In his essay "The Economic Problem of Masochism," Freud describes a "principle," that is, an inherent tendency that is part of the primary process—perhaps at the level of the life of the instincts—which he designates the "Nirvana Principle." The relevant passage has been quoted above, but it is useful to have it before us again for the purpose of this brief discussion:

> ...we must perceive that the nirvana principle, belonging as it does to the death instinct, has undergone a modification in living organisms through which it has become the pleasure principle; and we shall henceforward avoid regarding the two principles as one.... ...[T]he life instinct, the libido, has thus, alongside of the death instinct, seized upon a share of the regulation of the processes of life. In this way we obtain a small but interesting set of connections. The *nirvana* principle expresses the trend of the death instinct; the *pleasure* principle represents the demands of the libido; and the modification of the latter principle, the *reality* principle, represents the influence of the external world. None of these three principles is actually put out of action by another. As a rule they are able to tolerate one another, although conflicts are bound to arise occasionally from the fact of the differing aims that are set for each—in one case the quantitative reduction of the load of the stimulus, in another a qualitative characteristic of the stimulus, and lastly [in the third case], a postponement of the discharge of the stimulus and a temporary acquiescence in the unpleasure due to tension.
>
> The conclusion to be drawn from these considerations is that the description of the pleasure principle as the watchman over our life cannot be rejected.[351]

The issue perplexing Freud was the nature and role of masochism in the economy of the human mental life; for he had established that the pleasure principle and its modified form, the reality principle, together were the watchman for any dangers, internal and external. Masochism—and the repetition syndrome—led the way to the notion of *thanatos*, a death instinct, as an inherent principle in the economy of the psyche. As our quotation indicates, Freud decided upon a general dualism, though reformulated from his earlier version, in which the conflict within the mental life is a conflict between eros and thanatos. A crucial element in the reformulation was the tendency of the organism to resist any disturbance, on the one hand, and on the other to incorporate the consequences of disturbance into a newly integrated system.

---

[351] "Masochism," SE XIX, 160-161.

Our interest here is with the principle of stability, or constancy, which Freud dubbed the nirvana principle. What he means by this phrase is clear: it is the principle of stability which operates by seeking an ever greater reduction in the "sums of excitation upon the mental apparatus."[352] It is, therefore, related to the death instinct, which seeks a return to the state of absolute morbidity, utterly undisturbed by stimuli. Thus the nirvana principle is "the trend of the death instinct"; its aim is "the quantitative reduction of the load of stimulus."

My point is that the term "nirvana" is, first, utterly inappropriate as a designation of such a principle, and, second, Freud's use of it is yet another indication of the profundity of his ignorance of religious traditions in general and the Buddhist/Hindu/Indian tradition in particular. What he means by nirvana is clear; it means an absence of stimuli in the economy of the psyche. Thus, as the trend of the death instinct, its aim is a total elimination of stimuli, a state of absolute quiescence from the perspective of perception and sensation. It is opposed, of course, by the principle of eros, which seeks anaclitic attachment.

Yet such a description is virtually a parody of what *nirvāṇa* is and means. If anything, the true *nirvāṇa*, far from being a state of not knowing, of not sensing, of being completely unaware, is a state of knowing the world as it really is, unhindered by delusion and desire. It is a state of seeing, in the manner of the man standing on the edge of the clear pool and seeing all that is within. It is a state of the most remarkably comprehensive awareness, from knowing oneself fully to knowing others fully, those who are released, those who are enmeshed in greed, hatred and delusion, those who are *Arahants*; it is awareness of the past worlds, the present world, the future worlds, and all that is therein. Further, it is a state of compassion and friendliness, as well as wisdom. Far from rejecting others, the *Arahant* neither hates nor grasps after others, anymore than he hates or grasps after his self. He accepts all, knows all, is compassionate and friendly, patient and sympathetic to all.

What the Buddhist tradition has to say about the trend of the death instinct is worth noting; for an understanding of it strengthens the case for Freud's ignorance and for his quite ignorant parodying of the concept. There is in the Buddhist analysis of desire, *taṇhā*, a type of desire that seems to resemble what Freud refers to as the nirvana principle, namely the desire that rejects attachment to the world and to the self–in the sense of finding it repugnant and hateful. I am referring to *vibhava taṇhā*, the so-called desire for non-being, or non-becoming, the antonym of which is *bhavataṇhā*, the desire for becoming. Central to each desire is of course the self, which will either become or not become according to the wishes involved. The logic of the desire for non-being or non-becoming includes

---

[352] *Ibid.*, 159-160.

403

the desire to destroy attachments. Objects of the eye and the rest of senses are found to be hateful; there is an inherent tendency toward rejection or hatred, *paṭighânusaya*, and a fundamental root, or *āsava*, for malice and hatred (*dosāsava*, *inter alia*). It is perhaps the case that this congeries of desire resembles what Freud refers to as the constancy principle, or the nirvana principle.

This matter could be pursued at greater length; my purpose here, however, is simply to show the inadequacy and radical ineptness of using *nirvāṇa* as a term to describe anything like the desire for annihilation or the trend toward the absolute reduction of stimuli. For *vibhavataṇhā* is still *taṇhā*, it is still desire. It rests upon the assumption of an "I" just as much as does *bhavataṇhā*. Eradication of each calls for the same measure, namely the dying down of desire. *Nirvāṇa*, far from being the same thing, or even a related thing, as the desire for destruction, really means that state of the end of the desire for destruction of the self, among all others that obscure true knowledge of the self.

IV

The Cause of the End of Suffering

The Freudian Perspective

Introduction

I have tried to suggest that Freud understood human life in terms of suffering, that he addressed the causes of that suffering, and that he believed that in the understanding of the presence and nature of suffering was also to be found the truth of the end of suffering. My object now is to present what I take to be his view of the way in which suffering is to be brought to an end. Let me stress that the way to the end of suffering is inextricably bound to the arising of suffering. Analysis seeks, in fact, nothing short of the complete comprehension by the one who suffers of the fact of his suffering, and the fact of the cause of his suffering. This truth is a consequence of the nature of suffering itself; in Freud's view suffering is only secondarily a consequence either of external or internal causes. The world is an occasion of suffering; its stimuli, its supreme power are essential characteristics only because of suffering. On the other hand, the nature of the person in Freud's account is irremediably the product of conflict, whether it is construed as internal instinctual conflict between the primary and secondary processes, eros and thanatos, ego and sexual instincts, pressures upon and within the id-ego-superego structure, or in terms of any of the other models of human personality.

Yet the suffering with which Freud is concerned is not primarily the result of the world or of the structure of the self; it is the product of a basic confusion and ignorance of the true nature of these forces, joined to the hegemony of desire. This is clear in Freud's concepts of repression, resistance, symptoms, and of neurosis and psychosis. None of them is caused either by the external world or by the developmental structure or forces of the psyche. Rather, they are the consequences of failure to know one's self and one's history as they really are; they are consequences of the need to construct an endless series of worlds and selves as protection from that knowledge. In the course of that construction of false selves and worlds the true knowledge of the person and the world, which is really a definition of the ego function, is seriously weakened, and perhaps mortally wounded.

Freud understood the task of psychoanalysis to be to encourage the confrontation with the parts of the self and its history that had been hidden, for whatever reason, and to direct life's energies away from the destructive work of repression and resistance, toward the task of dealing with the self in the world—or, as he said, to transform hysterical misery into ordinary unhappiness. This task, as we know, centered upon the individual. Freud rightly concluded that the causes of suffering arise in the individual and therefore could be addressed in their root manifestations only at the individual's own level of crisis. The consequences for both the arising and cessation of the individual's suffering for society were and are enormous. But the social manifestations are just that, manifestations in the social arena of the fundamental suffering of the individual. One could not, after all, address delusions that were purely social, for no such things exist. Ignorance and desire are, first and foremost, individual phenomena, emerging from the biography of the individual. There is no other context for understanding them, despite their significance for social behavior. Indeed, Freud points out in several ways that an analysis of suffering that began and ended with group behavior was skirting the fundamental issues, and seeking to lay the blame for social malaise on supra-personal individuals and institutions–these of course being nothing less than projections of the individual's own psychological biography. Psychoanalysis' procedures for bringing suffering to an end, therefore, arose from roots of suffering in the individual. Those roots were in fact the roots of the individual himself.

That is to say, the analysis of suffering and its end is synonymous with an analysis of the nature of human life. Suffering, I have argued, is the essential human condition, rather than an external or aberrant phenomenon. Its end, therefore, must also be inherent in the human condition, rather than something added on. Freud argued strenuously against any notion that medicine cured mankind of its suffering; only individuals could restore themselves, with the aid of the analyst or, indeed, anyone who would act in such a role. This is the significance of transference, of the "fundamental method" of free association, of asceticism, and of "working through." The patient, who is the cause of his own illness, is also his own physician. His task, if he decides to accept it, is not so much to eliminate an ailment as it is to search for his true nature, which he pursues through the tangled pathos of his own protective and defensive artifices, laid down by no one other than himself, though all unwitting. What he discovers is that he has been suffering, that, in a most fundamental sense, he is suffering–that is, this is his state of being. He has denied it; he has denied it all of his life, and his denial has taken the form of the myriad devices, protective and destructive, that constitute his symptoms, his neurotic behavior, his failure to come to terms either with himself or the world. Instead of fleeing from one self to another, he learns to stop and look, and see what he was and what he truly is. Seeing that, he is freed. His suffering comes to an end only when he knows he has been, and is, suffering, and that the suffering is who and what he is.

The task of psychoanalysis, however it attacks this problem, is to help the person see all of this; and that means he must learn to look beyond his defenses. Psychoanalysis aids this work. It strengthens the ego, or seeks to strengthen it, in the work of freeing a person from delusion and desire. It helps the patient see what part of his past he has refused to remember, and why. In short, it helps to make what is unconscious conscious. To this end it must follow the method of the archeologist, moving backwards, piecing together the clues and hints at the site, and reconstructing what really happened. But this is done not simply in order to tell the patient what has happened. That effort is of academic importance only. Rather, the archeological work has a deeper purpose: the removal of the amnesia and the remembering of what happened, but this time in the context of full and conscious awareness of the nature of the event. Once known, that event loses its power to control and corrupt, and becomes a full-fledged episode in the acknowledged history of the person, a "past life" that he knows fully and fully comprehends. This cure, if that is what it is to be called, does not make any person better or worse by any accepted canons of social behavior—although that may be a secondary consequence. Rather, the person becomes his own person, conscious, capable of enjoyment and efficiency, free of delusion, and knowing that he knows.

The topic of this section, then, is the way in which psychoanalysis seeks to bring the suffering described to an end; but it should always be remembered that psychoanalysis is a therapy, and the cure is the work of the suffering self.

Strengthening the Ego

Let us recall how important Freud considered the task of strengthening the ego to be. The ego-functions with respect to the external world were, as we have seen, both especially important and especially vulnerable. The "natural" function of the ego, Freud argued, is to incorporate the experience of the id, or the organism, with external stimuli into the economy of the psyche. In general terms Freud thought of this task as a moving from the pleasure principle to the reality principle, of replacing what was "derivative and etiolated" in the history of the emotional development by what is "original and basic"[1] –in short, as dealing with reality. This task is specifically the work of the conscious.[2] As noted earlier, the conscious learned to address elements of the external world without respect to their pleasure or unpleasure value by developing the function of *attention*, and by introducing a system of *notation* which could "lay down the results of this periodical activity of consciousness." Repression, in this case, could be replaced by "an *impartial passing of judgement*," and the psyche was thus able to distinguish among actions with respect to whether they were in agreement with reality, rather than simply in terms of their pleasure-unpleasure content, with the aid of memory-traces.[3] This developed function was constantly threatened by the power of the pleasure principle; and it was the task of the analyst to aid the ego-consciousness in maintaining the reality-testing function of the ego.

The physician's task, when he was confronted with a breakdown of this function of assessing reality because of the interposition of symptoms, is to join with the weakened ego of the patient, and "basing themselves upon the real external world,...to combine against the enemies, the instinctual demands of the id, and the moral demands of the super-ego."[4] There is a "kernel of truth" in the patient's delusions; and, rather than attempting to deny the delusion, the analyst, together with the patient, must uncover that "fragment of historical truth" and separate it from "its distortions and its attachments to the actual present day" and lead it back to its true position in the patient's emotional history.[5] The success of this operation frees the ego for effective relations with external reality.

But the analyst must not become a fanatic in favor of health. For,

---

[1] "Character Types," SE XIV, 312.
[2] In his earlier works, *e.g.* "Two Principles," ego and consciousness were equated; in later works, *e.g. Ego and Id*, the roots of the ego in the id were recognized. The distinction is not significant in this particular discussion of consciousness.
[3] "Two Principles," SE XII, 220-221.
[4] *Outline*, 63.
[5] "Construction," SE XXIII, 268.

as Freud observes, there is not only neurotic misery in the world but real, irremovable suffering as well. And in exceptional cases only a symptom stands between the patient and his destruction; at times, the flight of the neurotic into illness is fully justified.[6]

But in the main the analyst's task is the strengthening of the ego at the expense of the pleasure principle. That effort does not always meet with success; for the analyst has no means of forcing the patient to understand the roots of his neurosis.[7] Nevertheless, as Freud tells his questioner in "The Question of Lay Analysis," the aim of analytic therapy is to strengthen the ego, "to restore the ego, to free it from its restrictions, and to give it back the command over the id which it has lost owing to its early repressions. It is for this one purpose that we carry out analysis, our whole technique is directed to this aim."[8]

With this fundamental goal of psychoanalysis before us again, we may now ask, what is it about the nature and method of psychoanalysis that leads to its success in bringing suffering to an end?

Amnesia and Archaic Origins

Freud insisted that analytic work deserves to be recognized as "genuine psycho-analysis" only when it has succeeded in removing the amnesia which surrounds the patient's knowledge of his childhood.[9] Whatever else may be asserted of the nature of psychoanalysis it is committed to removing the amnesia that prevents the adult from knowing his past, and thus himself. We have seen that the neurotic is a person whose energy is displaced from efficient and enjoyable endeavors to the area of unconscious conflict, of which he is quite literally unconscious and from which, in a profound sense, he is protecting himself. So long as this situation obtains he will be unable to live a free and mature life.

It is the task of analysis, argues Freud, to remove this amnesia. By breaking down the resistances, and passing the repressions in review, the strengthened ego can live efficiently and expect some measure of enjoyment.[10] In short, the analyst seeks to lead the patient *ad fontes*, to the sources of his malaise, and encourage him to confront them directly rather than hiding behind the barrier of symptoms. Of course the analyst by himself cannot accomplish this confrontation. He can only endeavor to trace the causation and to remove it by bringing about a "permanent modification" in the causal conditions.[11]

---

6 IL, SE XVI, 382.
7 *Cf. ibid.*, 255-256.
8 "Lay Analysis," SE XX, 205.
9 " 'A Child,' " SE XVII, 183.
10 "Articles: (A)," SE XVIII, 250-251.
11 *Ibid.*.

If we are to understand the psychoanalytic concept of cure of suffering, we must begin and end with the notion that cure is a reversal of a process of causation. We noted, for example, that in the analysis of dreams Freud identified an activity of the psyche which he labelled "dream work." Dream work is an unconscious activity devoted to transforming the actual content of the dream so that it becomes latent; but it could be known to the conscious of the dreamer in a modified and censored form. The reported dream is, then, the manifest dream; but the actual dream is different, having been distorted by the dream work for reasons we have already explored, namely the denial of certain contents of the dream to the conscious. Psychoanalysis seeks to reverse this process with respect to dreams, that is, to discover the latent, real dream, and to bring it into consciousness by cutting through the distortions.[12]

The reversal of the process of symptom formation is identical to dream interpretation in intention and procedure. Psychoanalysis seeks this reversal by moving from the present neurotic situation back to the emotional causal facts that have been obscured. The contents of delusions, themselves symptoms, are among the most important clues to the nature of the causation at work. This method gives psychoanalysis the appearance of archeology, a point to which we shall return. But its archeological research is devoted to uncovering the psychological causes of psychological effects. Illness is defined as the illness of the self, of the mental life, of the psyche, of the instinctual structure, and so forth. In this respect, as Freud argued, psychoanalysis must be distinguished from other methods and disciplines concerned with human illness. Psychiatry, he noted, is concerned with mental illness; but it tended to look to biological causes and effects. We may recall the case of the woman who claimed her husband was having an affair when the statement was patently untrue. Psychiatry has nothing to say about this case. But it is a form of mental illness, and its origins lie in the development, or the causal series, of her own emotional history. Psychoanalysis understands this case very well; and because it understands it, it knows exactly how to treat it. The "law" of psychoanalysis might be said to be this: emotional illness has emotional causes, and when the power of the causes is eliminated, the illness is eliminated.[13]

The energy of the neurotic is attached to his symptoms. We must, says Freud, make ourselves masters of the symptoms and resolve them. To this end we must return to their origin, renew the conflict from which they arise, and, with the help of adult strength, guide it to a different outcome. Through transference the patient is enabled to repeat the events which constitute the cause of his illness; but with the aid of the analyst

---

[12] IL, SE XV, 171ff..
[13] IL, SE XVI, 254-255.

and the adult strength of the neurotic, those events will be brought to a different conclusion, that is, as a "normal mental conflict" occurring in the full light of consciousness. There it may be resolved and the patient's mental unity restored.[14] My point here, however, is that this therapeutic development begins with the primary events of conflict which have been hidden from the patient by his own symptoms and their development. The direction of cure is backward before it is forward.

These events occurred during childhood, and are sexual in nature and consequence.[15] The work of analysis leads, then, back to the earliest situations of conflict, "which have for the most part been forgotten and which we try to revive in the patient's memory." The symptoms, dreams and free associations, and especially the points of resistance encountered in the analysis, are the material with which the analyst and the patient work; for they are precisely the residues and the defense mechanisms of that hidden conflict.[16]

Analysis is a work of both interpretation and construction. The analyst must interpret and present the material the patient gives him. He is thus also engaged in the work of construction, or of reconstructing the truth of the past, which is buried but extant in the patient's own memory and obscured by his symptoms. Freud points out that in the task of construction success is not indicated by whether the patient agrees with the construction presented, but rather by what effect the construction has on the analysis, that is, whether the construction presented is met with refusal or resistance. For, having reconstructed the past events, the analyst must now allow and encourage the patient to relive them with, it is to be hoped, a different and more syntonic resolution than in the original instance.[17] Again, in this work of construction the analyst must not ignore the delusions presented by the patient, for these are fundamental clues to a piece of historical reality. Construction in psychoanalysis is effective only when the "historical truth" of the past is discovered. In this it shares its power with delusions, which are puissant precisely because they, too, present the element of historical truth, and insert it in the place of the "rejected reality." This is true for delusions of the race of mankind as an whole in precisely the same manner that it is true for the individual. Delusions of the race, like delusions of the individual, are able to conquer reality because the more powerful but repressed reality of the forgotten and primaeval past has been substituted for knowledge of external reality.[18] It is the work of analysis to lead this historical reality

---

[14] IL, SE XVI, 454-455.
[15] Cf. "Lay Analysis," SE XX, 216.
[16] Ibid., 205.
[17] "Construction," SE XXIII, 257-265.
[18] Ibid., 268-269.

from its dominant position in the present economy of the mental life back to its real locus in the individual's experience, thus freeing him from its power.[19]

This backward therapy is tantamount to a reversal of the process by which the neurotic's suffering arose. Freud chooses not regard this return to the beginning as "true causal therapy," by which he means the application of chemical or mechanical means to reduce and control the quantity of libido, so that at a given time one instinct would dominate another. He makes this point in the *Introductory Lectures* in the process of explicating the unique qualities of psychoanalysis, and it is useful to recall his determination to, on the one hand, distinguish psychoanalysis from biological therapies and, on the other, to insist that psychoanalysis is scientific. In this context his notion of "causal therapy" tends to be presented as biological therapy, which, he insists, psychoanalysis does not concern itself with. However, I think we may with confidence set aside this prejudice of his times and assert, as Freud might have in other circumstances, that his therapy is true causal therapy in that the causes for illness are inherent in the nature of the illness itself, a point he made time and again. If it is true that neurosis is the consequence of flight from past realities, then the return to those realities must constitute therapy and, possibly, cure.[20]

While the issue of the outcome of therapy in its reconstruction stage is clear in an ontogenetic context, it is important to note again that Freud saw no difference in principle in the explanation for the aetiology of neurosis in individuals and in the race as an whole. He recognized no separate psychology for groups that was not individual psychology writ large. Thus in *Totem and Taboo* and in *Moses and Monotheism* he proposed to explain the origins of religion in terms of the aetiology of the neuroses. Specifically, the aetiology and development of childhood trauma, founded upon the conflicts inherent in the sexual development of the child, may be applied to the race as an whole. Trauma happens before the age of five, is sexual-aggressive in nature, is subject to amnesia, and is the originating point of the emergence of symptoms. The effects of trauma may be positive or negative, that is, a fixation or desire to repeat may emerge, or it may be rejected totally in the form of inhibitions or phobias. A compulsion frequently appears that threatens the entire psychic structure and especially its relationship to reality. Neurosis is the consequence. Further, the trauma and its effects enter a period of latency; but at puberty the effects return in the form of psychopathic behavior, that is, the return of the repressed is experienced. The defensive mechanisms of latency may break down, or may become symptomatic

---

[19] *Ibid.*.
[20] *Cf.* IL, SE XVI, 436.

of illness. If the dominant mechanism of defense directly linked to the trauma is not moderated by other experience with reality, psychosis is a probable consequence.[21]

The rise of religion is explained as a universal development of this traumatic-neurotic type;[22] the basic pattern is that of trauma, repression, latency, and partial return of the repressed. The initial trauma, the killing of the father in the context of sexual conflict of the Oedipal type, is repressed and re-emerges in a distorted form, such as the projection of the real father into the form of a spiritual being bearing the characteristics of the original father with useful modifications, who demands and receives the appropriate responses from his worshipers/children.[23]

As we have already noted, the tale is that of the murder of Moses- itself an historical event homologous to the murder of God the Father-, the emergence of Hebrew monotheism, the Prophets and the Law, the reformer Paul who confesses the original sin of killing the father–a crime for which the Son paid the price–, and the paralysis of Judaism in its inability to confess to the deed.[24]

Further, the phylogeny of neuroses has a direct effect upon its on- togeny, as we have seen. The contents of the mental life are attributable at least in part to an archaic heritage shared by all; the content of neu- roses may not be derivable, in the case of the individual, solely from a particular trauma in that person's life, but neurosis is nevertheless the consequence of that original trauma, the effects of which have be- come part of our inheritance.[25] Group neuroses and individual neuroses are thus *in origine* indistinguishable. Ontogeny recapitulates phylogeny, in this case. "In his mental development the child would be repeating the history of his race in an abbreviated form, just as embryology long since recognized was the case with somatic development."[26] Therapy prescribed for the neurosis of the individual is, it follows, also therapy for the race. It is clear that Freud promoted an understanding of the true origins of religion, that is, the displacement of the religion-neurosis and its symptoms back to its origins in the development of both the individ- ual and the race, as the *sine qua non* of the restoration of mental unity. It is, I think, this that he means when he speaks of *logos*, of science, of the orientation to reality and the conquering of the pleasure principle, and of a correspondence theory of reality. It is equally necessary, equally applicable and equally successful in the individual and the race. Both the

---

[21] *Moses*, SE XXIII, 72-78.

[22] *Ibid.*, 80-84.

[23] *Ibid.*, 80.

[24] *Ibid.*, 86-92.

[25] *Ibid.*, 92-102.

[26] "Lay Analysis," SE XX, 212; *cf.* "Articles: (A)," SE XVIII, 253.

person and the race, following this confrontation with their past, the re-living of their past and the coming to different and syntonic conclusions, transform hysterical misery into ordinary unhappiness. While Freud is hopeful of the possibilities for the individual, it is worth noting that he is not sanguine with respect to mankind as an whole.[27]

Finally, one may ask whether the events to which the analyst (and archeologist) returns are "real." Freud insisted upon the "historical" reality of the scenes in the earliest act of human civilization, such as the killing and eating of the father. This "historical" reality has significance, it should be recalled, because of the mental consequences and causes of the event. That those mental consequences and causes are real in the most compelling sense of the term is, it seems to me, indisputable. It is therefore certain that the traumatic events are at least real in that sense as well. But are they objectively, historically verifiable? With respect to the individual Freud insisted that the wishes of the neurotic were the causes of neurosis; and in the neurotic's own delusions he sought "real events" to explain what he already felt so powerfully. On the other hand, with respect to the race Freud insisted that those traumatic events were pieces of historical reality, discoverable by the same constructive method applied to the delusions, dreams, and distorted reports of the patient. He says, for example, that the inhibitions to satisfaction of desire which appear to be internal in the patient are residues of real, that is external, frustrations in the prehistoric period of human development.[28]

One observation is quite important. Freud is an archeologist; he re-constructs the past as best he can from the available evidence. He knows whether he is successful only at that point at which the patient's response is appropriate, typically in the form of resistance and transference. But in this he is more than an archeologist—for the latter has only the data and his own logic with which to work. No one from the age and place with which he is concerned can tell him whether his reconstruction is correct. If we bear in mind that Freud's explanation for the history of the race is identical to his account of the history of the individual, we see that what he knows of the origins of neurosis in the latter must be analogous to what he knows about the neurosis of the former. He speaks, then, not with the confidence of the ethnologist (he was fully aware of the absence of any ethnographic evidence for his account of the origins of religion), but of the psychoanalyst. Thus, by extension from his basic premises, the truth of the patient's past is known through symptoms, and therefore the truth of the race's history must also be known through symptoms. Symptoms do not convey what is not true, but reveal what is true, only in their own way.

---

[27] Cf. *Illusion*, 87ff..
[28] IL, SE XVI, 350.

In conclusion, since there are real events–real in the sense I have indicated–in the past of the individual, there must be events at least as real in the past of the race. To ask whether they really happened is to ask, what does the symptomatic structure reveal of the past? That there is a past is beyond question in the analytic context. The issue is, how may we understand the relationship between past trauma, present symptoms, and future resolution of the symptoms? In the end no one but the patient can tell us whether our knowledge of his past is correct. That such a response is hard to elicit from the race (for reasons that are themselves part of the syndrome) does not make the point any less valid. Freud is simply extending what he has learned from the individual to the collection of all individuals. We may ask, then: Was there a trauma in the past? The answer, indubitably, is yes. It is in this sense, and in this sense only, that the events of the past "really happened." This is the historical truth of which Freud speaks so frequently, namely the historical truth of the origins of neurosis.

Remembering, Repetition and Working Through

As already noted, Freud is adamant in his view that it is not enough simply to return to the root events, or causes of neurosis. Nor is it enough that the analyst present to his patient an account, or reconstruction, of what the analyst believes happened. This is of academic interest only; and however essential the archeological reconstruction is, only the re-membering, repetition and working through to different conclusions of the same occluded material can rightly be called analysis–as Freud said, the amnesia must be removed.

Freud's imaginary–and imaginative–questioner in "The Question of Lay Analysis," having heard his instructor's brief outline of psychoanalysis, objects that it sounds both over-complicated and inefficient; for surely hypnosis would get to the heart of the problem, that is, the repressed trauma, and suggestion would bring the matter to a swift and easy resolution. This seems to be a much more efficient treatment.[29] But the questioner has not yet got the point of psychoanalysis. Its purpose is not simply to uncover and present the facts of the past, but to enforce the remembering, the living through again–the *anamnesis*–of the past *in the mind of the patient.* That the patient does not want to do this at first is both the most obvious characteristic of the beginning of an analysis and a sure indication that there is a cause for the neurosis. When the patient is first told the fundamental rule of psychoanalysis, free association and the saying of whatever is present in his consciousness, the response, Freud noted, is silence. This is in fact a repetition syndrome. "As long as the patient is in the treatment he cannot escape from this compulsion to

---

[29] "Lay Analysis," SE XX, 193.

repeat; and in the end we understand that this is his way of remembering."[30] This repetition has the effect, furthermore, of bringing symptoms of the illness, and thus the illness itself, into the arena of the treatment.

In this characteristic psychoanalysis is both different from and superior to hypnosis. The causal events are, of course, "remembered" under hypnosis. But "[r]emembering as it was induced in hypnosis, could not but give the impression of an experiment carried out in the laboratory."[31]

Repeating, as it is induced in analytic treatment, on the other hand, implies conjuring up a piece of real life; for that reason it cannot ("alas") be harmless and unobjectionable.[32] In other words, analysis seeks not only to recover the forgotten past, but to encourage the patient to repeat the past in the context of the treatment. Remembering, then, becomes an activity of the conscious and increasingly free mind rather than an activity limited to technically manipulable circumstances. The patient himself must remember, as well as repeat, in the clear and honest light of self-scrutiny. This repetition, as Freud puts it, must be kept under control in the analysis; and this means that the patient learns to keep "in the psychical sphere all the impulses which [he] would like to direct into the motor sphere; and [the analyst] celebrates it as a triumph that something that the patient wishes to discharge in action is disposed of through the work of remembering." The energy committed to repetition may be freed from the "motor sphere," that is, physical action, and engaged in the work of searching out the causes of the illness. This, it must be remembered, is the work of the patient in the end.[33]

The role of the analyst, then, is not limited to simply telling the patient what he has forgotten, and why he is distorting his reporting of the past. That, says Freud, explains things to the analyst—which is useful but not therapeutic. The analyst's task is to locate the point of repression of past events. We shall see that Freud discovered that point at the locus of greatest resistance; and the analysis cannot proceed until the resistance is discovered and pursued. The physician is rather like a man who gives directions by pointing to signposts along a road; but it is the patient who must complete the journey. The signs are the points of resistance; the journey is the patient's repetition and remembering of the events and causes about which he refuses to think and upon which he has imposed a very successful amnesia.[34] The work of interpretation is carried out by both doctor and patient. If they are successful, what has

---

[30] "Remembering," SE XII, 150-151.
[31] *Cf.* "Articles: (A)," SE XVIII, 247, and "Further Recommendations in the Technique of Psychoanalysis," CP II, 362ff..
[32] "Remembering," SE XII, 151-152.
[33] *Ibid.*, 153; *cf.* 155-156.
[34] *Cf.* IL, SE XVI, 437-447.

hitherto been locked up and protected in the unconscious is accessible to conscious judgement. In terms of the economy of the psyche we may say that libido is now freed for the ego's disposition. The ego no longer rejects the libido or its attachments to symptoms. The closer the treatment comes to this resolution, Freud concludes, the more successful it will be.[35] However this is an alteration in the state of affairs which must be carried out by the patient, with the doctor as his ally. Thus the questioner's concept of psychoanalysis is seen to be inadequate; for simple knowledge of the past does not have any therapeutic value. Freud does not seek explanation only but cure. It is highly significant that the alteration of the neurotic state of affairs is presented solely in terms of the patient's working through. For in a successful treatment what has happened is that the patient comes to know himself and his whole history, and his mental unity is restored. This is the difference between historical and saving knowledge.[36]

The Techniques of Psychoanalysis

Freud identifies the "fundamental rule," or "fundamental method," of psychoanalysis as "free association," that is, the association of value with everything said to the analyst by the patient and the need to say everything that comes into the patient's mind. Absolutely everything must be told the analyst, he explains to his questioner; and the result entails an enormous burden of interpretation.[37] As we noted, the patient greets this invitation with silence; and the analyst must understand this response to be a form of repetition syndrome. It is the initial stage of remembering; but remembering is an activity in which the patient will be engaged against his own initial inclination. In short, the fundamental rule is the direct assault on resistance and the repression it is guarding.

As anyone who has ever tried it knows, this seemingly simple request is very difficult to fulfill. After all, while the patient knows something is wrong, he does not want to find out what it is–that is precisely and succinctly the state of neurosis. Yet he is asked, indeed it is demanded of him, that he say everything that is in his mind, and say it without pre-judgement, judgement or reservation. It goes almost without saying that these activities are forbidden to the analyst with respect to any pre-conceived social or philosophical or religious standards, as we have seen. It soon becomes clear to the physician that the patient is resisting, perhaps even refusing to relate whole areas of obvious significance in his life, present and past. If those areas are eventually uncovered he, the patient, will then take refuge in intellectual "objectivity," perhaps

---

[35] *Ibid.*, 455.

[36] See below, *Excursus*: **Self Analysis.**

[37] *Cf.* "Articles: (A)," SE XVIII, 247, and "Lay Analysis," SE XX, 206ff..

turning his attention to the content of psychoanalytic theories and their possible relevance to life in general.[38] But the fundamental rule never varies: everything and anything must be reported. Together with dream analysis, these "sayings" constitute the clues offered by and through the conscious mind with which the analyst will begin to piece together the events of the past and form a history of the neurosis and an aetiology of its symptoms.

As for the proper orientation and attitude of the analyst, a matter of no mean consequence, Freud described his mental ambiance in this way:

> Experience [with free association] soon showed that the attitude which the analytic physician could most advantageously adopt was to surrender himself to his own unconscious mental activity, in a state of *evenly suspended attention*, to avoid as far as possible reflection and the construction of conscious expectations, not to try to fix anything that he heard particularly in his memory, and by these means to catch the drift of the patient's unconscious with his own unconscious. It was found then that, except under conditions that were too unfavourable, the patient's associations emerged like allusion, as it were, to one particular theme and that it was only necessary for the physician to go a step further in order to guess the material which was concealed from the patient himself and to be able to communicate it to him.[39]

The significance of the training analysis now becomes clearer; for in effect the analyst, in his state of evenly suspended attention, has allowed the reportage of the patient's unconscious to mesh with his own, of which he is, in this state, helpfully aware. The consequence is an understanding of the patient's meaning based upon the analyst's sense of the contents and development of his own unconscious, to which he has a degree of access not yet attained by the patient. Such understanding implies knowledge of the associations presented in the patient's talking, assocations with the significant but still obscured—at least at this point in the analysis—pieces of "real life," for which the analyst and, eventually, the patient, search.

Asceticism

We know from Freud's case histories and many of his general writings that this is very hard work. It is hard because it must be conducted

---

[38] IL, SE XVI, 286-292. *Cf.* "Case Histories: Fräulein Anna O.," SE II, 21-47; "Notes upon a Case of Obsessional Neurosis," (1909), SE X, 153-249; "From the History of an Infantile Neurosis," (1918[1914]), SE XVII, 7-122.

[39] "Articles: (A)," SE XVIII, 239.

with a minimum of distraction from less essential activities and respon-sibilities. It is hard also because it is not harmless, like hypnosis. It demands, then, both enormous mental discipline, exacting honesty, and much courage. After all, what is being attempted is the discovery of the nature of this person's experience, only part of which he is willing to recognize. Therefore Freud demands that the analytic task be carried out within the boundaries of a stringent ascetic self-denial, so that the requisite attention, concentration, energy, discipline and courage not be sapped and misdirected to less important—and rather tempting, for that reason—matters.

This state of self-denial must, of course, be distinguished from neu-rotic asceticism. On this latter point we have already noted Freud's insis-tence that the analyst is no proponent of either sexual license or celibacy for the neurotic. Either course serves the neurosis.[40] The issue is not gratification *versus* repression but rather the integration of sexuality into the conscious control of the ego.

What Freud has in mind is that the patient's treatment will be suc-cessful only if he postpones for the duration of the treatment any signif-icant decisions about his future, such as the choice of a profession, new business undertakings, marriage or divorce.[41] That is to say, the patient under analysis must withdraw as far as he can from engagement in tasks of either fulfillment or denial, so that he is, so far as possible, neutral in his feelings toward the world, so that his illness is as clearly limned as pos-sible, and so that he is not distracted from the task of self-examination. The analyst desires, as we have seen, that, above all, the patient should decide for himself what his destiny shall be; but in the state of neurotic self-deception his decisions are driven by irrelevant and distorting issues. Analysis seeks to transform the task of making decisions from one that is dominated by neurotic concerns to one that addresses only the matter in hand. Since the neurotic is incapable of doing this—this is at the very least what his inability to be efficient means—he is asked to postpone any significant actions until he can address them directly and with a single mind.

Further, there is the danger that decisions made under the influence of neurotic concerns will simply perpetuate the illness, since they will be made not in terms of their own merits but in terms of their possible ser-vice to the symptoms. Thus the analyst must, in so far as he can, prevent the patient from finding new substitute satisfactions as his symptoms are displaced and more libidinal energy is available for cathexis. Common routes followed are physical infirmity, bad marriages, disastrous profes-sional choices. What the still sick patient seeks is a cause for his guilt,

---

[40] IL, SE XVI, 432-433.
[41] *Ibid.*, 433-434.

an event which explains his need to be punished.[42]

"*Analytic treatment*," says Freud, "*should be carried through, as far as possible, under privation—in a state of abstinence.*" By abstinence "is not to be understood doing without any and every satisfaction—that would of course not be practicable; nor do we mean what it popularly connotes, refraining from sexual intercourse; it means something else which has far more to do with the dynamics of falling ill and recovering."[43] If we recall that the patient cures himself, it is clear that what Freud means by abstinence and privation is that nothing must interfere with the full running out of the course of the analysis. The analyst must prevent as far as possible any distraction lest the task of freeing all of the libidinal energy from the control of symptoms into the control of the ego be thwarted. It is "*frustration*" that made the patient ill; as this frustration is gradually reduced the force impelling the patient toward recovery is reduced. "It is possible to observe during the treatment that every improvement in his condition reduces the rate at which he recovers and diminishes the instinctual force impelling him towards recovery. But this instinctual force is indispensable; reduction of it endangers our aim—the patient's restoration to health." It is, ironically, the task of the doctor both to reduce the effects of neurotic symptoms by leading the patient to breaking them down analytically and also to ensure that the level of energy embodied in frustration is not reduced beyond a useful point. He does this by reinstating the suffering of the patient "in the form of some appreciable privation; otherwise we run the danger of never achieving any improvements except quite insignificant and transitory ones."[44] This privation, incidentally, is relative not only to the world beyond the analysis but to the analyst as well. The patient gets no satisfaction from the doctor, especially in the course of a successful transference (see below). "As far as his relations with the physician are concerned, the patient must be left with unfulfilled wishes in abundance. It is expedient to deny him precisely those satisfactions which he desires most intensely and expresses most importunately."[45]

One final observation is that in the course of such treatment it is very likely that the level of abstinence becomes higher, that is, more difficult of achievement and more general in focus. Indeed, it is not until all actions are understood solely in terms of their own natures and consequences, undistorted by neurotic concerns and distractions, that the analysis is complete, and the patient/doctor ready to see the world in terms of ordinary unhappiness. The thrust of the analysis is toward

---

[42] "Advance," SE XVII, 164.
[43] *Ibid.*.
[44] *Ibid.*, 162-163.
[45] *Ibid.*, 164; *cf.* "Analysis," SE XXIII, 353.

an understanding of the self, out of whom an understanding of the world can emerge. This follows from the nature of the extent of the privation Freud demands. It is not until the symptoms are torn apart that the patient may address the major and minor issues of his life and of the world. And of course, finally, it is the intention of psychoanalysis that he do so address them.[46]

Resistance

In his review of the fundamental concepts of psychoanalysis in the *New Introductory Lectures* Freud reminded his audience that it was the discovery of resistances and the repressions they protect that provided the key to unlocking the unconscious elements of the ego.[47] In his earlier "History" he placed resistances, with transference, at the heart of psychoanalysis. Whenever, he noted, an attempt was made to trace the sources of neurosis in the events of the past, blocked by amnesia, two "striking and unexpected facts" emerged, resistance and transference. Indeed, any "investigation which recognizes these two facts and takes them as the starting point of its work has a right to call itself psychoanalysis...."[48] Further, Freud insisted that resistances and transference were not "*premisses*" but "*findings*" of psychoanalysis; that is, they were drawn solely and directly from observation of the patient's behavior.

As the "fundamental rule" of telling all "without pre-judgement, judgement or reservation" is applied, the analyst soon notes that the patient becomes increasingly reluctant to pursue certain lines of reporting; he is resisting the material of his report. When the initial resistance is overcome a secondary line of defense emerges, taking the form of intellectual argument, discussion about the means and methods of treatment—anything but the material the patient refuses, unwittingly, to confront. In the course of this resistance the repressed material is transferred to the physician; this is the phenomenon of transference. As with resistance, transference is, despite its apparent irrationality, the most hopeful sign in the analysis. Resistance is not fixed at one point only, but is dynamic in quality. For the closer the analysis comes to the unconscious material, and the event of which it is a consequence, the more powerful the resistance. Conversely, resistance weakens in proportion to the increase of "distance" from that material. This empirical characteristic provides an invaluable and indispensable clue to the doctor. Resistance marks that point of entry into consciousness of the questionable mental process which, because it was not brought to an end normally, is the basis of the symptoms. Resistance, then, points to a repression; and repression must be replaced by judgement. In larger terms, resistance is the

---

[46] *Cf.* IL, SE XVI, 433-434.
[47] NIL, SE XXII, 57-80.
[48] "History," SE XIV, 16-17.

clinical opening through which that which is unconscious may be made conscious.[49]

But resistance is what its name means, an opposition to analysis. Freud points out that analysis may be seen as the process by which libido is tracked down to its hiding place and brought into the service of the ego. Libido attached to symptoms represents a balanced state of affairs whose disruption is resisted vigorously. If frustration engenders symptoms of neurosis, the neurotic libidinal economy nevertheless has established a balance of power not only with respect to reality but with respect to the economy of the psyche of the neurotic in which frustration has been redistributed rather than resolved. This work is not lightly undone; for resistance occurs in order to maintain this "new state of affairs," that is, the state engendered by a frustration of satisfaction. Analysis seeks to overcome the attraction of the unconscious, to enhance the power of reality, and thus to remove the "repression of unconscious instincts and productions, which has...been set up in the subject."[50]

Resistance weakens as the analysis moves away from the repressed material; and in the course of treatment the analyst may be seduced by his apparently good relations with his patient into thinking that all is going well. The true mark of development, however, is the moment when the resistance becomes so persistent that relations between analyst and patient threaten to break down completely because of conflict between the demands of the analyst and the patient's resistance. It is at this point that transference is initiated.[51]

But it is not the physician alone for whom resistances are both problems and possibilities. As in the general case of the archeological function of the analysis, it is highly important but not sufficient for the therapist to have uncovered the probable cause of the disease. Merely telling the patient what is wrong with him is not a cure. Indeed, the explanation offered may provide highly useful material for further resistance. The doctor may tell the patient that he is resisting, and may even tell him why. But giving the resistance a name, says Freud, does not bring the symptoms to an end. "One must allow the patient time to become more conversant with his resistance with which he has not become acquainted, to *work through* it, to overcome it, by continuing, in defiance of it, the analytic work according to the fundamental rule of analysis...." This working through of the resistances is in practice an "arduous task for the subject of the analysis and a trial of patience for the analyst." Nevertheless, "it is a part of the work which effects the greatest changes in the patient and which distinguishes analytic treatment from any kind of

---

[49] IL, SE XVI, 286-91, 294.
[50] "Transference," SE XII, 103.
[51] *Ibid.*.

treatment by suggestion."[52]

Freud describes his task not merely as that of explaining what has happened in the past which forms the traumatic foundation of neurosis, but rather of convincing the patient to adopt the analyst's conviction that life based on the pleasure principle is inexpedient and, finally, impossible.[53] The breaking down of the resistances after they have been located is, in the end, the work of the patient who has a sympathetic, patient and undeceived physican as an ally. Having said that simply recounting the resistances to the patient does not constitute cure, we can note the other side of the therapeutic coin, namely that when the patient has broken down the resistances, he is in fact cured; there is no need for a succeeding "synthesis." The breaking down of the resistances is, in short, *per se* the means but also the end of the therapeutic process. What remains is what has always been there, the unity of the self. But its divisions are healed, for the barriers have been taken away, once it is seen that they are no longer needed to support the edifice of the self.[54]

Transference

Resistances draw their power from the repressed material, the heart of the disease. When that heart is closely approached, the resistance grows strong enough that a new phase of the disease is encountered, the transference of the hidden emotional "charge" that is the core of the neurosis onto the doctor. This stage constitutes the last and most powerful form of resistance, and at that same time offers an opportunity for the re-assignment of libido and the restructuring of the symptoms of such a magnitude that it can be said to be the *sine qua non* of successful analysis. Even as he considered the implications of his revised theory of the instincts in *Beyond the Pleasure Principle* Freud believed that "it is still true that the transference neuroses, the essential subject of psychoanalytic study," were the essential concern of analysts.[55]

The importance of transference lies chiefly in its role as the re-enactment of the constituent causal events of neurosis in the course of the analysis, not simply in the memory of the patient. Transference is a neurotic phenomenon, and this should not be forgotten. Just as resistance, however significant for *therapeutic* technique it may be, is still a resistance to health, so transference is a neurotic condition. It is a recapitulation of the causal matrix of neurosis. In his later years Freud described the transference "neurosis" as an "after-education" of the patient in the experiences of childhood; but the analyst takes on the role of

---

[52] "Remembering," SE XII, 155-156.
[53] "Advance," SE XVII, 159.
[54] *Ibid.*, 161-166.
[55] BPP, 91-92.

the crucial parent, with the attendant ambivalence. Further, the transference situation is not an experience of reality, and eventually the patient must be made to realize this fact. Rather, it is a replay of childhood, with the analyst acting as a substitute for the parent. In other words, transference is a repetition of the acts leading to the formation of the internal reality which is governing, in a malevolent fashion, the psyche of the patient.[56]

The physician, like every new acquaintance in the experience of the patient, will be the object of a cathexis which is held ready in anticipation. For the neurotic is one for whom the need for love has not been entirely satisfied by the experience with reality but rather subsists in the unconscious, prevented from further expansion. Thus he is "bound to approach every new person whom he meets with libidinal anticipatory ideas." Further, these ideas are greatly influenced by—one may even say formed in the image of—earlier prototypes of libidinal attachment.[57] But the physician's interests differ from those of other newly-met persons; for his task is to discover and challenge the resistances protecting the repressed material. He can, then, use the "cathexes" directed toward him to advantage in the treatment by pressing them to their strongest point. That point is the stage of transference. "When anything in the complexive material (in the subject matter of the complex) is suitable for being transferred on to the figure of the doctor, that transference is called out; it produces the next association, and announces itself by indications of a resistance—by a stoppage, for instance. We infer from this experience that the transference-idea has penetrated into consciousness in front of any other possible associations *because* it satisfies the resistance."[58]

In less formal terms, drawn directly from Freud's analytic work (and not merely from speculation),[59] in transference the doctor is imputed with the patient's feelings about the major figures in his past, and thus made responsible for past relations. The beginnings of a repetition of those past emotional events are now glimpsed, with the doctor taking the role of the primary subject in the patient's life.[60] Freud presents a "text-book" account of the emergence of the transference phenomenon and therefore of the transference neurosis. Typically in the group of neuroses Freud designated "transference neuroses"—that is, for example, hysteria, anxiety hysteria and obsessional neurosis—, the initial stages of the analysis proceed smoothly. The patient is willing to enter into the work of analysis, realizing that he is ill. He employs his intellect to ad-

---

56 *Outline*, 66-70.
57 "Transference," SE XII, 99-100.
58 *Ibid.*, 103.
59 *Cf.* "History," SE XIV, 16-17.
60 IL, SE XVI, 286-291.

vantage. Remembering comes relatively easily. Then a change occurs; the patient's interest in the doctor, in his personal life, indeed in everything about him increasingly dominates the analytic meetings. It seems as though the patient talks incessantly about the doctor. The doctor may take these developments as a sign of improvement, perhaps as signifying the imminent and successful resolution of the analysis. But after a time these positive feelings are replaced by a negative attitude. Upon examination it becomes clear that the physician himself is not the true object of this feeling. Further scrutiny reveals that this is true for the earlier positive feelings as well. In fact, the expressed feelings attached to the physician have no real direct connection with what has been remembered in the analytic work. The truth emerges: the emotional, libidinal experience of the patient has been transferred onto the doctor, whether he likes it or not.

In female patients this transference phenomenon may have the appearance of falling in love with the male physician, and have a largely positive expression–though this is not invariably the case. As for male patients the transference feelings are largely negative, possibly as a defense in fear of homosexual attraction. In either case the transference is libidinal. The patient has transferred to the analyst a substantial portion of his or her libidinal attachment. But the nature of this attachment indicates that the experience is a repetition of past relationships, rooted in the course of earlier libidinal development. Of course the patient is unaware that the attachment to the doctor has nothing to do with the doctor himself but with a forgotten past.

The transference phenomenon provides the analyst with the access to the unconscious for which he has been seeking. It is now his task to transform the transference experience from an unconscious cathexis to a part of the patient's conscious memory. This is tantamount to "raising" what is unconscious and the cause of the neurosis and its symptoms into the conscious. That task, if successful, is synonymous with the removing of resistance and the ending of repression. However, what transpires in the course of the elevation of the unconscious material is not only a remembering and repeating of the past experience. The neurosis is now traced back to its origins, and those origins are revived, lived through again, in the conscious of the patient. He feels the emotions of the primary experience. However, what is remarkable about the transference neurosis is that it is played out in conjunction with a different sort of object, the doctor, who is an ally of the ego, and who can act both as the object of transference and the agent of the end of the resistance. The hidden conflict, in other words, now becomes manifest, and may be addressed with the aid of an ego-consciousness hitherto restricted in its dealings with the unresolved struggle.

Indeed, the primary motive force in the therapy is the patient's neurosis itself. Unless this is brought fully into play the treatment is merely suggestion; and Freud's clinical experience convinced him that such an approach was fruitless. Rather, the power of the neurosis must be maintained until the end of the treatment; "every improvement effects a diminution of it." Two other elements are required in addition, however: "the knowledge of the paths by which the desired end may be reached, and the amount of energy needed to oppose the resistances."

The analytic treatment helps to supply both these deficiencies. The accumulation of energy necessary to overcome the resistances is supplied by analytic utilization of the energies which are always ready to be "transferred;" and by timely communications to the patient at the right moment analysis points out the direction in which these energies should be employed. The transference alone frequently suffices to bring about a disappearance of the symptoms of the disease, but this is merely temporary and lasts only as long as the transference itself is maintained. The treatment then is nothing more than suggestion, not a psycho-analysis. It deserves the latter name only when the intensity of the transference has been utilized to overcome the resistances; only then does illness become impossible, even though the transference is again dissolved as its function in the treatment requires.[61]

The transference stage is possible and evident in the transference neuroses, and is what distinguishes them from other types.[62] Freud points out that transference is an essential stage in the development of the neurosis; for in each case there is a very high degree of object cathexis—one might say too high a degree, for that is the cause of the neurotic symptoms. Object-cathexis is directed by neurotic longings. On the other hand, it is over-determined object-cathexis that constitutes the fundamental opportunity for the cure of the neurosis. The disease itself, carried toward the stage of transference, is the best ally of the analyst and most effective tool for cure; for this reason Freud insists upon drawing the whole of the disease out into the light of conscious analysis, even at the risk of prolonging the neurotic symptoms.[63] However, those mental illnesses that hinder object-cathexis, psychosis or narcissistic neurosis, are not susceptible to transference, and Freud accordingly considered them beyond the abilities of analytic cure. Unless libido is available for direction toward the physician or some other person, transference cannot occur; and this is the case in narcissism, in which libido takes the self

---

[61] "Further Recommendations," CP II, 364.
[62] Cf. IL, SE XVI, 299.
[63] See the section on abstinence, above.

alone as its object.[64]

In his description of the course of transference Freud stressed the significant negative stage. If we recall that transference is a resistance of very high magnitude, it must be true that the negative transference has greater revelatory significance than the positive transference; for the patient's rejection of the doctor—really of the person/event now imputed to the doctor—constitutes a refusal of the true emotional conflict. In addition, there is a kind of positive transference that has value as a resistance, namely the "positive transference of repressed erotic impulses." These may be distinguished from feelings ("friendly and affectionate feelings") that are readily admissible to the conscious and therefore do not constitute materials of resistance. But the positive feelings in the transference function as expressions of repressed sexual longings. The transference reveals that, like the feelings of hostility, these positive feelings rest upon sources not admissible to the conscious and thus function as a resistance. The positive transference phenomenon reveals that our sense of sympathy, friendship, trust and so forth, are linked with sexuality, however noble and unsensual they may seem.[65] In treating the transference neurosis, therefore, the doctor may "remove" the transference by making conscious these two "components of the emotional act from the person of the doctor; the other component, which is admissible to consciousness and unobjectionable, persists and is the vehicle of success in psychoanalysis exactly as it is in other methods of treatment."[66] For it is in making conscious the hostile and erotic transference that the entire conflict is raised to the surface, along with the clue to its existence already present in the conscious life.

This is not what the patient wants to do, of course; and thus the context of the transference is one of struggle. The patient's impulses, arising from his emotional conflict, seek expression in the immediate present; thus emotions that are properly directed toward a primary person in the past with whom relations were never successfully worked through are now directed toward the doctor. The doctor wishes to enlist the patient in his conviction that such activity is irrational, inefficient, and conducive to his further suffering. The doctor seeks to convince the patient that what is bothering him is directly related to a part of his past which he refuses to acknowledge—"refuses" meaning that a part of him refuses, and that part is not admissible to his conscious life. Because the patient insists upon treating the doctor in this inappropriate manner, the struggle between doctor and patient becomes the struggle between the patient and his own past, played out exclusively and, it is to be hoped, completely, on

---

[64] IL, SE XVI, 437-447.
[65] "Transference," SE XII, 105.
[66] *Ibid.*.

the field of the transference. "It is on that field," Freud concludes, "that the victory must be won–the victory whose expression is the permanent cure of the neurosis." The hidden and repressed impulses must be made manifest if cure is to be achieved. "It cannot be disputed that controlling the phenomena of transference presents the psychoanalyst with the greatest difficulties. But it should not be forgotten that it is precisely they that do us the inestimable service of making the patient's hidden and forgotten erotic impulses immediate and manifest. For when all is said and done, it is impossible to destroy anyone *in absentia* or *in effigie*."[67]

The last comment is revealing; transference onto the doctor of the libidinal conflict makes it possible, on the one hand, to have the object of love and hate present before the patient, not merely an image of it. The destruction of the person, that is, the destruction of repression, is possible only when the issues are played out fully. The doctor serves the invaluable role of responding to the charges of the patient. On the other hand, what is destroyed is not, of course, either the doctor or the person/event that constitutes the foundation of the neurosis, but the patient's attachment to it, his frustration. In transference, then, the original situation happens again, with all the force and fury of its primary occasion. Only then, as an older generation might have said, can the demon be exorcised.

What happens may be described in this way: the original neurosis is replaced by an artificial one, the transference, which has all the characteristics of the original disease. All the libido, as well as everything opposing it, is, in the context of the transference, withdrawn from the symptoms and directed toward the person of the doctor.[68] However, the transference "creates an intermediate region between illness and real life through which the transition from one to the other is made." This illness has a remarkable quality which distinguishes it most obviously from the original neurosis–that in every respect it is manifest and visible, first to the doctor and then, with good analytic work, to the patient. "It is a piece of real experience," Freud notes, "but one which has been made possible by especially favourable conditions, and it is of a provisional nature."[69] With the help of the doctor, then, the new struggle around the doctor as libidinal object is lifted to the highest psychical level, as a normal mental conflict. There is no fresh repression; and thus the former alienation between ego and libido comes to an end, and mental unity is

---

[67] *Ibid.*, 108. *Cf.* IL, SE XVI, 444-445, 451, where Freud asserts that cure is effected when unconscious material is brought into the conscious through transference; but *ct.* SE XXIII, 211ff. for a more pessimistic view.

[68] IL, SE XVI, 454-455.

[69] "Remembering," SE XII, 154.

restored.[70] The repeated struggle is thus brought to a different outcome; the analyst seeks to compel the patient to bring the conflict to a different conclusion.[71]

The successful transference syndrome is achieved only when certain pitfalls are avoided, and certain precautions taken. We have already remarked that Freud argues the importance of preventing the patient from finding intermediate substitutive satisfactions as his symptoms are displaced. The analyst must detect and prohibit these intermediate regressions. Second, the doctor must avoid responding to the patient in the manner the patient desires. Unless the strain between the patient's longing for satisfaction and the doctor's rigorous searching out of resistances is maintained, the patient will lose the energy necessary for a complete analysis. The transference situation is, for obvious reasons, fraught with temptations for the doctor to act in a manner consistent with the patient's image of him. But it is his task to bring the patient to the knowledge that the transference is neurotic, is taking place, and must be brought to an end.[72] As with all aspects of analysis, the physician's viewpoint must be one of equanimity and self-abnegation.[73] In addition, there is the constant danger of counter-transference, the phenomenon in which the analyst in the transference setting imputes to the patient his own libidinal cathexes. Despite Jung's positive views of it[74] Freud regarded counter-transference as a threat to the analysis because the so-called "analytic distance" necessary to maintain the strain and tension required for the continuation of the analysis is lost. The one sure defense, if such a thing exist, against counter-transference is the training analysis.[75] In looking to the future of psychoanalytic therapy in 1910, Freud noted the phenomenon "which arises in the physician as a result of the patient's influence on his unconscious feelings." He argued strongly for requiring a training analysis in order that the physician recognize and overcome the counter-transference. He had observed that "every analyst's achievement is limited by what his own complexes and resistances permit, and consequently we require that he should begin his practice with a self-analysis [training analysis] and should extend and deepen this constantly while making his observations on his patients. Anyone who cannot succeed in this self-analysis may without more ado regard himself as unable to treat

---

[70] IL, SE XVI, 454-455.

[71] *Ibid..*

[72] "Advance," SE XVII, 164.

[73] *Cf.* "Lay Analysis," SE XX, 225-228.

[74] *Cf.*, *e.g.*, "Problems of Psychotherapy," *Modern Man in Search of a Soul*, tr. W. S. Dell and Cary F. Baynes (New York: Harcourt, Brace and World, 1933).

[75] *Cf.* "Future Aspects of Psychoanalytic Therapy," CP II.

neurotics by analysis."[76]

Transference offered the best hope for the cure of neurosis precisely because of the central role of libidinal objects in the disease. Freud observed on several occasions that the success achieved in analysis had been almost solely with the transference neuroses. The others "have been far from thoroughly studied by psychoanalysis...."[77] Thus, he notes, "we have good reason to recognize and to dread in the amount of his narcissism a barrier against the possibility of [the patient's] being influenced by even the best analytic technique."[78] In the transference neuroses the struggle is between the ego, directed by the super-ego and, ultimately, by the forces of the external world, and the impulses of the id. The neurosis consists of the structure of defense established for the purpose of repressing unacceptable material. Transference is simply the extension of that struggle through the identification with the doctor as an actor in the repressed experience and thus brings control of the ego into the area that was hitherto repressed. The ego, in other words, continues to function in its attention to external reality throughout the life of the neurosis–and it is this connection that the analysis exploits in working through the neurosis.[79]

However, in the case of narcissistic neuroses, for example, the ego's link with its origins in external reality is broken. Freud designates a category of illness of this type, such as melancholia, as "narcissistic psychoneuroses." In addition there may also arise a conflict between the ego and the external world itself. This is psychosis *purex*. However, from the point of view of the transference the difficulties are identical; in neither case is the ego representing the interests of forces other than the id.[80] In the case of schizophrenia, after repression is accomplished no new object is sought by the withdrawn libido. Rather, the libido retreats to the ego; for the object cathexes are given up and the primitive narcissism is re-established. Patients who suffer from this and related disturbances are incapable of transference; consequently they are inaccessible to therapeutic efforts. They repudiate external reality, their ego becomes hyper-cathected with libido, so that the ego is both source and object of libido and is to all intents and purposes indistinguishable from the id. Their general psychic life is apathetic. They are, in short beyond the reach of analytic cure as Freud understood it.

But they are not beyond analysis, in the sense that analysis provides an examination of the cause of their illness. What is missing is precisely

---

[76] *Ibid.*, 289.

[77] IL, SE XVI, 299 *et passim*.

[78] *Ibid.*, 446.

[79] "Neurosis and Psychosis," SE XIX, 149-150.

[80] *Ibid.*, 152; *cf.* "Articles: (A)," SE XVIII, 250-251.

the desire to engage in the cure. Analysts since Freud have expressed repeatedly their frustration with narcissistic disorders, for the reasons described. But the frustration with narcissism suggests something significant about the nature of psychoanalysis, namely, its commitment to the idea that once a patient senses that something is wrong, he will not finally avoid attempts to resolve the issue. It also suggests the significance of consciousness, ego-control and the external world for the world view of psychoanalysis. If the psychotic will not participate in the attempt to bring what is unconscious into the conscious it is because there is no distinction between them, no ego or world that is not id. On the other hand, psychoanalytic therapy insists upon the distinction between self and world; the healthy person is one whose cares are ordinary, the inevitable but not neurotic consequence of the ego making its way in the world free of confusion between its wishes and what is "the case." The significance of transference is clear; for it depends upon the disease as a condition in which the distinction between wish and world is warped and distorted. But in the narcissistic disorder there is no distinction at all, and thus no possibility for transference.

Is Life Analysis?

And, as Peter's grandfather said in *Peter and the Wolf*, what then? How shall we distinguish between the patient whose transference therapy has gone well and the neurotic? We can begin by recalling the characteristics of the healthy person over against the neurotic, the goal of the treatment, and therefore the ideal person as described by Freud. First, the aim of the treatment is to restore to the ego its control over the id, which it had lost to earlier repressions; psychoanalysis has this single aim.[81] Restating this summary in a slightly different form, Freud distinguishes between the struggle between mental impulses both of which are on the same psychological footing and the pathogenic conflict in neurotics, and concludes that the transformation of the latter conflict to the same status as the former, that is, to make it possible for a true decision of the conflict to be reached on the same ground, is the sole task of therapy.[82]

The goal of therapy is the translating of what is unconscious into what is conscious. The repressions are lifted, the preconditions for the formation of symptoms disappear, and the pathogenic conflict is transformed into a normal one for which some solution must be possible.[83] We must not underestimate the depth and power of this change; for the patient is both the old patient, the old person, the one he has always been, and is also transformed: he has become another person. This means

---

[81] "Lay Analysis," SE XX, 205.
[82] IL, SE XVI, 433.
[83] *Ibid.*, 435.

that, on the one hand, he like all of us healthy people is "virtually a neurotic." But the new man, unlike the old, is capable of efficiency and enjoyment.[84] Moreover, in the normative analytic situation, and before and after, he lives in the condition in which he must struggle with tasks that face him.[85]

What has happened–a question tantamount to asking after the state into which the former neurotic incapable of efficiency and enjoyment has passed–is that in analysis the patient becomes aware of the unconscious and repressed impulses in himself. This fundamental enlightenment about his own nature removes the foundation for repression and thus for resistance, and convinces him of the impossibility of living life according to the pleasure principle.[86] And when the resistances are removed, what is the result? The torn mind, no longer riven by resistances, grows together. It is whole and entire.[87]

It is of crucial importance that Freud's notion of analysis and its goals centers upon the manner in which the ego, or the person, deals with ordinary experience. What he does not guarantee is happiness, but rather seeks the triumph of ordinary unhappiness over neurotic misery. An essential element of his notion of ordinary unhappiness is the fundamental metaphysics of struggle which he finds, for the same reasons, in the individual, the community and the universe. Existence is suffering. Analysis reveals just that truth, and no more; for that knowledge is precisely what brings resistance to an end. In raising the question of whether analysis is terminable or interminable Freud discloses the true scope of his concerns, the assessment not only of the nature of the neurotic self but of the nature of life at all its levels.

The "end of an analysis" seen from a practical point of view is a relatively simply matter; it is that point at which the analyst and the patient cease to meet. The reasons may be circumstantial as well as therapeutic. In a more ambitious sense, the end of the analysis may be said to be that point at which the patient is no longer dominated by neurotic symptoms. But difficulties immediately arise: is this the consequence of real control of instinctual conflict or the subsidence of external contributing factors? Freud cites several cases, deliberately representative of many others, in which analytic therapy had been terminated, only for the patient's symptoms to arise years later under the stress of events. Or perhaps it was not the events themselves that functioned as primary cause but rather an–in truth–unresolved instinctual conflict which simply took a much later oc-

---

[84] Ibid., 461.
[85] Ibid..
[86] "Advance," SE XVII, 159.
[87] Ibid., 161-166.

casion to reappear.[88] So much for the *patient's* experience in termination of analysis.

The other central concern here is the psychical state of the analyst. We noted Freud's insistence upon a training analysis as a prerequisite for a career in psychoanalysis. Yet it can only be "short and incomplete;" "the main object of it is to enable the instructor to form an opinion whether the candidate should be accepted for further training." Its purpose, further, is to "impart to the learner a sincere conviction of the existence of the unconscious" to enable him "through the emergence of repressed material in his own mind to perceive in himself processes which otherwise he would have regarded as incredible and gives him a first sample of the technique which has proved to be the only correct method in conducting analysis."[89] However, one observed consequence of this training analysis is that it seems to encourage defensive mechanisms in the response of the analysts "which enable them to evade the conclusion and requirements of analysis themselves, probably by applying it to others." Here is the phenomenon of counter-transference re-encountered.[90]

In practice, analysis may be, and regularly is, terminated. This means that a particular analytic treatment has a beginning and an end. The question remains, however, when one considers the nature of analysis *per se*, whether it is terminable or interminable. Freud's observations of both patients and analysts suggested to him that from this "theoretical" perspective analysis is interminable.

The reasons are to be found at the heart of the analytic notion of suffering. While a particular set of neurotic symptoms may be overcome in the course of analysis, the fundamental causes are synonymous with the causes of human life itself. Freud's thoughts on this matter may be found in his comments on what he calls "character-analysis."

> So not only the patient's analysis but that of the analyst himself has ceased to be a terminable and become an interminable task.

> At this point we must guard against a mistaken conception; it is not my intention to assert that analysis in general is an endless business. Whatever our theoretical view may be, I believe that in practice analyses do come to an end. Every analyst of experience will be able to think of a number of cases in which he has taken leave of the patient *rebus bene gestis*. There is a far smaller discrepancy between theory and practice in cases of so-called character-analysis. Here it is not easy to predict a natural end to the process, even if we do not look for impossibilities or ask too much of analysis. Our object will not be to

---

[88] "A Note on the Prehistory of the Teaching of Analysis," CP V, 320ff..
[89] *Ibid.*, 352.
[90] *Ibid.*, 353.

rub off all the corners of the human character so as to produce "normality" according to schedule, nor yet to demand that the person who has been "thoroughly analyzed" shall never again feel the stirrings of passion in himself or become involved in any internal conflict. The business of analysis is to secure the best possible psychological conditions for the functioning of the ego; when this has been done, analysis has accomplished its task....[91]

The farther psychoanalysis drives toward the heart of the structure of human experience the more prolonged the analysis. What is more significant is the nature of analysis as it is viewed from this perspective. As Freud reiterated frequently, the task of analysis is the restoration of the unity of the ego. The restored ego is able to address the conditions of the world as they are, without distortion; but more, it is able to experience internal struggle, the "stirrings of passion," in their proper place, and perspective, without confusing passions with experience of the world. The task of analysis is the restoration of such a functioning unity; but the functioning unity, the ego, will perpetually employ the lessons learned in analysis in order to accomplish its diurnal aims. And surely, in this sense, analysis is interminable. It was, after all, the accomplishment of the analysis to enable the patient to distinguish between his own desires and "reality." His continued "health" is nothing more nor less than his continued ability to do just that.

This view of analysis implies, furthermore, a metapsychological perspective that threatens, some would say, to become cosmic. For it holds that life is struggle, that conflict is not only inevitable but definitive of human existence. Freud turns his attention to the question of "analysis terminable or interminable" in this more embracing direction in his comments on the similarity between the philosophy of Empedocles and his own conclusions concerning the conflict between love and death, eros and thanatos. We can, he recalls, only explain the "rich multiplicity" of the phenomena of life "by the concurrent or mutually opposing action of the two primal instincts–Eros and the death instinct–, never by one or the other alone."[92] In Empedocles' "cosmic-phantasying" about the two great forces of the universe, Love and Strife, Freud finds a theme common to his own analytic theory of the instincts. He is not even particularly concerned that Empedocles is a philosopher in the older, nobler Greek sense while he, Freud, is "content to claim biological validity." True, in the intervening millenia a biological language has been constructed, largely replacing the mythology of Empedocles. Still, "[t]his is not to deny that an analogous instinct already existed earlier, nor, of course to assert that an instinct of this sort only came into existence with the

---

[91] *Ibid.*, 353-354.
[92] "Analysis," SE XXIII, 243.

emergence of life. And no one can foresee in what guise the nucleus of truth contained in the theory of Empedocles will present itself to later understanding."[93]

While we should take Freud at his word in his vacillating attempts to put distance between himself as a scientist and the older mythological views, in these words he nevertheless asserts rather plainly something approaching a cosmological source of the interminable nature of analysis. The forces with which the ego must deal, with the aid of analysis and, initially, with the aid of an ally, are continuous with the fundamental principles of existence. He means nothing less, it seems to me; and in this context the notion of an interminable analysis is tantamount to a notion of the nature of existence. If that be so, then to have the wisdom of Empedocles is very like having the wisdom of analysis—and that, after all, is what was always meant by healing and the end of suffering.[94]

---

[93] *Ibid.*, 245-247.

[94] I wish to make a further observation on this treatment of Empedocles, and Freud's use of sources from non-scientific traditions, such as literature, as well. Despite his stout and persistent defense of science Freud only rarely fell into the trap of literalism, of naive realism, or of the worst excesses of the "correspondence theory of reality." He was almost always able to see the analytic, therapeutic and psychological truths inherent in all of humane expression. Yet, as he observes with respect to Empedocles' truth, no one can be certain in what form it will next appear. The implication is truly liberating; for Freud is not so closely wedded to his own expression, that is, his neuro-biological/psychological expression, that he could not foresee the fundamental truths seeking new and differing forms. He understood his work, in short, as part of a continuum inherited from the past and inherited by the future, transformed, altered and restated in the context of other historical and cultural settings. It may be that "no one can foresee in what guise the nucleus of truth contained in the theory of Empedocles will present itself to later understanding"; but there can be no doubt of three things: (1) there is a "nucleus of truth"; (2) Empedocles—and many others—expressed it before Freud in their own language; (3) it will find a new guise.

I point this out not only to underscore Freud's inheritance but also to stress his own sense of standing in a tradition which, on the one hand, expresses the truth, and on the other regularly alters the means of its expression of that truth in light of experience and history. The reverse is also true: that the experience and the history are consequences of that truth, known and loved. Freud, then, is a man of faith, as was Empedocles, and as I am: and like Empedocles and I (I hope!), that profound sense of the truth that transcends any particular expression of it drives Freud to make it known as fully as possible. Perhaps ironically,

Excursus: **Self Analysis**

If the work of the patient is as crucial as we have seen it to be, we may ask whether analytic treatment might not be carried out without the aid of the physician. Freud experimented with self-analysis–in the sense just mentioned, although the term has another meaning in his later writings–early in his career. In recounting his own development as an analyst Freud pointed to the significance of dream interpretation as the pivotal issue in his departure from reliance upon hypnosis and his future commitment to psychoanalysis. He began to see in the technique of free association in the analytic meetings and in dream analysis a way to bring the hidden past into the conscious of the patient. He notes, further: "Moreover, I soon saw the necessity of carrying out a self-analysis, and this I did with the help of a series of my own dreams which led me back through all the events of my childhood; and I am still of the opinion to-day that this kind of analysis may suffice for anyone who is a good dreamer and not too abnormal."* This confidence was not sustained. For although the interpretation of one's own dreams may be revealing, it is no guarantee against resistance. In his correspondence with Fliess (especially letters 70, 71, (October, 1897)), he wrote: "My self-analysis is still interrupted and I have realized the reason. I can only analyse myself with the help of knowledge obtained objectively (like an outsider). Genuine self-analysis is impossible; otherwise there would be no [neurotic] illness. Since I still find some puzzles in my patients, they are bound to help me up in my self-analysis." Again, in a short note on parapraxes (1935), he remarked: "In self-analysis the danger of incompleteness is particularly great. One is too soon satisfied with a partial explanation, behind which resistance may easily be keeping back something that is more important perhaps." Despite a further reference to self-analysis, this one favorable (*cf.* preface to E. Pickworth Farrow's paper, 1926), we may take the preceding statements to be indicative of Freud's view of the matter. It is of course consistent with his clinical observations in that his patients do not want to pursue the road to its end, and have built up resistances for that reasons. This is, he implies, no less true of the doctor than of the patient, or of any one else. As the saying goes, the doctor who treats himself has a fool for a patient; and this is true of psychoanalytic treatment to a final degree.**

---

this is what we mean when we speak of *homo religiosus*–he who has the courage to give a name to that which transcends his understanding, to know that it has been done before, and because it has been done before he may continue in this courageous effort, and to know that it will be done again, in part because he did it.

* "History," SE XIV, 20.

** *Ibid.*, 20-21; *cf.* editor's note 2.

On the other hand, Freud takes a strong stand on the need for another kind of self-analysis for the physician, that which came to be called the training analysis. The point is clear and important: no doctor can be of any help whatever to his patients if he has not undergone a thorough analysis himself. No one can be an analyst without first being analyzed: "It is only in the course of this 'self-analysis' [training analysis] (as it is misleadingly termed)," he says to his questioner, "when they actually experience as affecting their own person—or rather, their own mind—the processes asserted by analysis that they acquire the conviction by which they are later guided as analysts."*** This very important observation reveals not only that Freud regarded the causes and effects of neuroses as universal human phenomena, but that their nature is such that the doctor passes on, so to speak, the knowledge and even wisdom that he has acquired and, hopefully, goes on acquiring about his own nature. The doctor becomes the patient; and the patient, at least according to the principles of psychoanalysis, may become the doctor, both to himself and, if he chooses, to others. It is for this reason that I believe we may speak of psychoanalysis as a tradition, complete with a kind of apostolic succession (Freud, Anna Freud, Kris, et al.), committed to the transmission of the way to the end of neurotic suffering. In the context of this discussion, such a tradition is tantamount to one of human self-understanding.

*** "Lay Analysis," SE XX, 198-199; cf. "Analysis," CP V, 352.

The Fourth Noble Truth of the Buddha

Introduction

The truth of the end of suffering is inherent in the truth of the arising of suffering. This conclusion has important consequences for the truth of the cause of the end of suffering; for the cause of the cessation of suffering is to be found in the cause of the arising of suffering. The chief characteristics of this Fourth Truth have the qualities of substitution and reversal of those characteristics of existence that lead to suffering. The most obvious example is the place of the *paṭiccasamuppāda* series in the Fourth Truth. Just as the arising of suffering is a series of dependent "causes," so the end of the series is a series of dependent causes, moving in the opposite direction (to employ a spatial metaphor). No new element is added; rather, the nature of the relationship of the causes is radically transformed. The principle of dependent causation, which is a fundamental insight of each of three principle concepts of Buddhist "ontology," *dukkha*, *anicca* and *anattā*–suffering, transience and the emptiness of the "self"–, is affirmed in both truths of arising and cessation of suffering. This is a further and insightful meaning of the oft-repeated statement that *dukkha* is the only reality, and that life is *dukkha* in its most specific and most general facets.

The Fourth Truth constitutes the way that leads to the radical alteration of the causes and effects. The Eight-fold Path is of course the classic doctrinal formulation of this way, and the equation of the Path with the Fourth Noble Truth is virtually complete. Effort is required, as we have already seen; and the effort is directed toward the self in its manifold aspects. The discipline of the self is a formidable undertaking; the early Buddhist tradition takes that discipline seriously enough to stress the advantage of the monk over the layperson. For the layperson lives in a world of constant distraction, so that the goal of one-pointedness of the mind (*ekodhoti*) is very hard to achieve. The discipline begins with the usual expectations in the realm of behavior which a society imposes upon its members. But it does not stop there; for to be a good person in the commonly accepted sense of the phrase is not, in the Buddhist tradition, the same as being enlightened–as C.S. Lewis once said, there is a difference between being nice and being saved. The goal lies at the end of the path of the command of the senses, not only in that their work ceases to be a distraction but also in that they become an effect rather than a cause, directed by the insightful, wise *Arahant* who sees and knows things as they really are.

It is not the purpose of this section to present a manual [95] but rather an understanding of the Fourth Noble Truth of the way of cessation. In

---

[95] For a useful and concise example of a systematic method for the cessation of suffering, see the "Method of 108," S IV, 156-157.

439

this task the most important quality to be grasped is its relationship to the truth of the arising of suffering. Since suffering is the only reality, the only release from suffering must lie in that realm of reality: it cannot be introduced from "outside," for as we have learned the notion of an "outside," a fixed point not inherent in the sway of *dukkha*, is an illusion, itself a construct of the series of co-dependent origination. Nāgārjuna puts this in his usual radical form by asserting that *saṃsāra* is *nirvāṇa*. Further, in an important sense the Fourth Noble Truth asserts neither an old person destroyed and replaced by a new one, nor a continuation of the same person unchanged. The metaphors, such as the refinement of gold,[96] the replacing of a large peg by driving it out with a smaller one, the extinction, the cool, the wearing away, all suggest the reversal of a process of growth and, perhaps, corruption. What has been growing is illusion, seizing more and more of the energy needed for a free and productive life unfettered by ignorance, greed and hate. What is left–if any object or subject is at all appropriate here–is pure, clear, transparent.

The Fourth Noble Truth is the culmination of the *Dhamma*, the Truth. It is integral to all the other Truths, and to the *Dhamma* itself– and the same must be said of each of the other three Truths. There are no "other" truths. As we have seen, monks are urged not to waste their time and energy speculating on insignificant questions: whether the world is finite or infinite, whether the body is the essence of existence, whether the *Tathāgata* exists after death, or not, or both, or neither. Rather, they must give their entire effort to working though the four-fold Noble Truth of *dukkha*, its arising, its cessation and the causes for both.[97] For those who understand "as it really is" the four-fold Truth, there is release; "They, able to end all, go not to birth and eld."[98] By contrast any who are distracted from this truth are like "a stick, thrown into the air, that falls now on its tip, now its middle, now its butt," wandering hither and yon, "hindered by ignorance, fettered by craving."[99] The prolongation of suffering is a consequence of not grasping the four-fold Ariyan Truth– there is no middle, neutral ground, no other truth. For those to whom the truth is clear, there is no more birth, and thus no more ignorance, suffering, and so forth.[100] In addressing the Fourth Noble Truth I wish to stress, then, that the Truth is the nature of things, and that if it is understood "as it really is" the nature of things is known, and this understanding is tantamount to release. The opposite result is just as certain for those who are blind to the truth. There are no alternatives.

---

96 *Cf.* M III, 290-291.
97 S V, 354.
98 *Ibid.*, 366.
99 *Ibid.*, 371-372; *cf.* 379.
100 D II, 96.

The Eight-fold Path

The cause of the end of suffering is to be understood in the same manner as the arising of suffering. Thus the Eight-fold Path is to be grasped sequentially, in a manner exactly analogous to any of the series of co-dependent origination. The positive statement of the Path is best known; there is, however, a converse statement. It is said, "[w]hen ignorance leads the way, by reaching of states unprofitable, shamelessness and recklessness follow in its train. In one who is swayed by ignorance, is void of sense, wrong view has scope [micchādiṭṭhi]." Wrong view gives rise to wrong aim, wrong aim to wrong speech, wrong speech to wrong action, wrong action to wrong living, wrong living to wrong effort, wrong effort to wrong mindfulness, and wrong mindfulness to wrong concentration. In contrast, knowledge leads to right view, right purpose, right speech, and so forth.[101] Ignorance has its eight-fold path, just as knowledge does.

In its positive formulation the Eight-Fold Path is divided into three classes: (1) right speech, right action and right livelihood constitute the class of moral habit; (2) right endeavor, right mindfulness and right concentration are members of the class of concentration; (3) intuitive wisdom is a class containing right view and right thought.[102] It is probably correct to conceive of this ranking as one of increasing merit and difficulty, although achievement of the final class has the result of producing the effects mentioned in the earlier and, in some respects, "lower" classes.[103]

For example, the eight stages are presented as interdependent in the order in which they sustain the final stage of right meditation—which is the crux of the second class—, or samādhi. There are, it is said, seven requisites for the practice of samādhi: "right views [diṭṭhi], right intention [saṃkappa], right speech [vacī], right action [kamma], right livelihood [ājiva], right effort [vāyāma], right mindfulness [sati]. That concentration of thought [citta ekodhoti], Sirs, which is prepared by these seven factors, is called Noble Right Rapture [samādhi] together with its bases, together with its requisites. Right intention suffices to maintain right views, right speech suffices to maintain right intention, right action suffices to maintain right speech, right livelihood suffices to maintain right action, right effort suffices to maintain right livelihood, right mindfulness suffices to maintain right effort, right rapture suffices to maintain right mindfulness, right knowledge suffices to maintain right rapture, right freedom suffices to maintain right knowledge."[104]

---

[101] S V, 1-2.

[102] M I, 363.

[103] One summary lists these three elements and a fourth, vimutti, release, in the form of four Noble Truths, i.e., sīla, samādhi, paññā and vimutti. D II, 122.

[104] Ibid., 250.

The application of the Eight-fold Path is presented, as we expect, in direct relation to the major elements of the analysis of suffering, the five *khandhas* and the *paṭiccasamuppāda* series. In the analysis of the *khandhas* it is repeatedly stated that when one achieves an understanding of them "as they really are," like the Buddha one is assured that in this world he is "fully enlightened with the supreme enlightenment [*abhisambhuddoti*]." One who is released understands the body, the arising of body, the ceasing of body, and the way of going to the ceasing of body. As with the Four-fold Truth of *dukkha*, the fourth understanding is the Eight-fold Path for body (*rūpa*) and for the other four *khandhas* (perception, feeling, activities and consciousness). Body is understood to be based on the four elements, feeling upon the contact with eye, ear, *etc.*, perception upon the "six seats of perception," of sights, sounds, *etc.*, the activities upon the "six seats of will [*cetanā*]," the will for sights, for sounds, *etc.*, and consciousness upon the "six seats of consciousness," that is, eye-consciousness, ear-consciousness, *etc.*. For each of these the Four-fold Truth is the path to understanding and release; and the fourth is the Eight-fold Path.[105]

The method described is that of the application of the Eight-fold Path to each of the *khandhas*. This suggests that the Path is both the specific and the general remedy of suffering, since it is to be used with respect to each of the elements of suffering as well as for suffering broadly conceived, just as the Four-fold Truth applies to each instance of suffering by the process of first recognizing its existence, understanding its causes, knowing that there is an end to suffering, and understanding the way to that end. So, for example, the Eight-fold Path leads to the cessation of bondage to feelings.[106] Or again, it is the Eight-fold Path that, when followed, leads to the abandoning of greed, hatred and delusion, and so to the end of *dukkha*.[107]

The Eight-fold Path may be followed with respect to any facet of the truth of suffering; for the culmination of that path is "perfect view [*sammādiṭṭhi*]" of things as they really are. Sāriputta presents several options, each leading through the Eight-fold Path to perfect view. Perfect view, he notes, is achieved "when a disciple of the ariyans comprehends unskill and unskill's root." "Unskill's root" is the "onslaught on creatures," taking what is not given, sexual misconduct, lying speech, slanderous speech, harsh speech, gossip, covetousness, and confusions. The skillful activities are the opposites of these. The disciple, "having got rid of all addiction to attachment [*rāgânusaya*], having dispelled addiction to shunning [*paṭighânusaya*], having abolished addiction to the

---

[105] S III, 50-54; *cf.* 54-57.
[106] S IV, 157.
[107] A I, 196.

442

latent view 'I am' [diṭṭhi mānānusaya], having got rid of ignorance, having made knowledge arise, is here and now an end-maker of anguish." This is perfect view.[108]

The Eight-fold Path is the way to this goal, regardless of the occasion for investigation. For example, Sāriputta says that one may begin with the investigation of sustenance (āhāra), its uprising, its stopping and the means of its stopping. Sustenance for creatures who are becoming, have become, or will become is of four kinds: material food (coarse or fine); sense-impingement (phassa); volition (manosañcetanā); and consciousness (viññāṇa). Now sustenance arises because of craving, as is explained in the series of co-dependent origination. From the uprising of craving comes the uprising of sustenance, from the stopping of craving is the stopping of sustenance (and thus of the body, and so forth, in a reversal of the paṭiccasamuppāda series). The course leading to the stopping of sustenance is the Eight-fold Path:[109] perfect view, perfect thought, perfect speech, perfect action, perfect way of living, perfect endeavor, perfect mindfulness, perfect concentration. One who, following this path, wins through to perfect view, comes into the truth, Dhamma.[110]

The Eight-fold Path leads to the end of dukkha, as it does to the end of sustenance. "...[B]irth is anguish, and old age...and disease...and dying,...grief, lamentation,...suffering...tribulation...despair...if one does not get what one wants...; in short, the five groups of grasping are anguish." The arising of dukkha is dependent upon the arising of the desire for delight in sense pleasures, the desire for becoming, and the desire of annihilation (kāmataṇhā, bhavataṇhā, vibhavataṇhā). The stopping of dukkha is, therefore, the stopping of taṇhā, craving. That cessation follows the course of the Eight-fold Path, as above.[111] The application is analogous for old age and dying (jarāmaraṇa), where the arising of birth is the cause of the arising of old age and dying.[112]

The content of the series of co-dependent origination now emerges, and in each instance the "course" to the cessation of the issue in question is the Eight-fold Path. Thus birth arises because of the arising of becoming (bhava), and the course leading to the end of birth is the Eight-fold Path, leading to perfect view.[113] The pursuit of becoming is attributed to grasping, grasping is attributed to craving, craving to feeling, feeling to contact, contact to the sense impressions (saḷāyatana), sense impressions to name-and-form (here mind, defined as feeling, perception, voli-

---

[108] M I, 58.
[109] Note the difference in order of stages.
[110] Ibid., 59; cf. S II, 8-9.
[111] Ibid., 60-61.
[112] Ibid., 61-62.
[113] Ibid., 62-63.

tion, sensory impingement, reflectiveness–*vedanā, saññā, cetanā, phassa,* and *manasikāra;* body is the four great elements of extension, cohesion, heat and mobility). Name-and-form (*nāmarūpa*) are attributed to consciousness (*viññāṇa*), consciousness to the "formations" (*sankhāras*), and the formations (here three formations, the activities of the body, speech and the mind–*kāya, vacī,* and *citta*) are attributed to ignorance (*avijjā,* here "whatever...is not knowing in regard to anguish [*dukkha*],...the uprising...the stopping...the course leading to the stopping of dukkha....."). Finally, so to speak, the uprising of ignorance is attributed to the uprising of the *āsavas,* the cankers, of sense pleasure, becoming and ignorance. "From the uprising of ignorance is the uprising of the cankers, from the stopping of ignorance is the stopping of the cankers," Sāriputta concludes, thus reversing the series at the point of the interdependence of ignorance and the cankers.[114]

In sum, the Eight-fold Path serves to bring an end to any of the arisings in the series of co-dependent origination. It follows, given the nature of the series, that the end of any one of the arisings leads to the end of the arising that depends up it, and of the next, and so forth until the series is not a series of arisings but of cessations leading to the utter extinction of arisings, that is, to *nibbāna.* It is for this reason that Sāriputta presents his analysis in terms of a series of alternative occasions of suffering, whether sustenance, craving, becoming, or others. The Path, once fully travelled, leads to the end of the entire series; it is not necessary to repeat it for each arising in the series. Again, this is a result of the dependent nature of the series. The same is true also of the relationship between the Eight-fold Path and the *khandhas.*

In the hierarchy of the Eight-fold Path perfect view, *sammādiṭṭhi,* comes first. The monks are asked why this is so. With respect to right purpose, for example, right view enables the monk to distinguish between wrong and right purpose. "Wrong purpose" is defined as a purpose of sense pleasures, for ill-will, for harming. "Right purpose" is of two sorts: (1) "the right purpose that has cankers, is on the side of merit, and ripens unto cleaving (to new birth)"; (2) there is right purpose that is Ariyan, cankerless, supramundane, a factor of the Way. The first is purpose for renunciation, non-ill-will, non-harming. It gives rise to cleaving. The second right purpose is reasoning (*takka*), initial thought (*vitakka*), purpose, and the speech of one learned in the Ariyan Way. This knowledge is attained through right view. So also the correlative distinctions are the same with respect to the other elements of the Path, right speech, action, livelihood, endeavor, mindfulness, and concentration, namely that right

---

[114] *Ibid.,* 59-67. For a duplicate presentation of the relationship between the Eight-fold Path and the *paṭiccasamuppāda* series, *cf.* A II, 291-295.

view is first because all the others are known through it.[115] Right view is contrasted with the false views present in dogmas and teachings concerning the existence or non-existence of the world; in contrast, one knows "that which arises is Ill, that which passes away is Ill." He knows the truth of the arising and cessation of ill (through the *paṭiccasamuppāda* series) and is not in doubt, not perplexed, does not have knowledge merely learned from another. This is right view; and one who has attained to it may be said to be free.[116] He does not wonder what his life was in the past, or what he shall be in the future, or what is the nature of his present existence.[117]

The application of the Eight-fold Path is described as the replacement of "unprofitable," *akusala*, states with "profitable," *kusala*, states. Evil or unprofitable acts, words and thoughts are eliminated by replacing them with good deeds, thoughts and words. This is necessary for the development of right thought, action, livelihood and the other elements of the Path.[118] A monk is urged to reflect upon his own desires, for example: "'Now, am I of evil desires, in thrall of evil desires?' If...while the monk is reflecting he knows thus: 'I am of evil desires, *etc.*' then,...that monk should strive to get rid of those evil unskilled [*akusala*] states."[119]

If a monk is afflicted by the five mental barrennesses (*cetakhīla*), namely, doubts about the teacher, doubts about the *Dhamma*, doubts about the order, doubts about the path of training, and anger, he must strive to replace the doubts with certainty and replace anger with equanimity. He must root out the five mental bondages, which are dependent upon the five mental barrennesses: attachment to sense-pleasures, to body, to material shapes, eating as much as his belly will hold and being intent on the ease of comfort, and the hope of becoming a deva in a future life. He may accomplish this by cultivating "that basis of psychic power that is possessed of concentration of intention with activities of striving [*chanda-samādhipadhānasaṅkhārasamannāgataṃ*], the basis of energy...with activities of striving [*viriya-*]; he cultivates...consciousness; ...concentration of investigation ..., ...exertion ...." The result is the replacement of the unskilled with the skilled state rather than simply the annihilation of the *akusala* states.[120]

Perfect view arises when the roots of both skilled and unskilled states are understood. Unskilled roots are seen in theft, sexual misconduct, lying speech, slander, gossip, harsh speech, greed and confusion. The oppo-

---

[115] M III, 113-121.
[116] S II, 13.
[117] *Ibid.*, 22.
[118] *Cf.* A III, 311.
[119] M I, 129; *cf.* S I, 259.
[120] M I, 135; *cf.* A V, 13-16.

site is evidence of the *kusala* root. Having comprehended both, and thus ending the "addiction to attachment...to shunning...to the latent view 'I am' [*rāgānusaya, paṭighānusaya, diṭṭhi mānānusaya,* respectively]," and thus replacing ignorance with knowledge, the monk brings suffering to an end. This is perfect view.[121] The skilled states, furthermore, bring an end to the effects of the unskilled states, for the latter are "stopped without remainder."[122]

The replacement of the unskilled states is effected by reflecting upon them as unskilled. Thus Gotama recalls his experience as a *Bodhisattva* "not fully awakened." He thought in this manner: he separated his thoughts into parts, one of thoughts of sense-pleasure, malevolence, and harm, the other of thoughts of renunciation, non-malevolence, and non-harmfulness. As each element of the first part arose in his mind, he reflected upon it; and as he reflected, it subsided. By contrast, in reflecting upon renunciation, non-malevolence and non-harmfulness he saw that they were conducive to release. These thoughts replaced the thoughts of sense-pleasure, malevolence and harm. Now his mind (*citta*) was calmed and focused.[123]

While following the path, then, the monk is advised to attend to "five characteristics," which are five stages leading to the elimination of unprofitable thoughts. If a monk is intent upon "higher thought [*adhicitta*]," that is, determined to bring his *citta* under control so that it is free of attachment, regardless of any state, element, or characteristic to which his attention is given, and if *akusala* thoughts arise linked to desire (*chanda*), aversion (*dosa*) or confusion (*moha*), "that monk should attend, instead of to that characteristic, to another characteristic which is associated with what is skilled." In so doing, the unskilled thoughts came to an end. Success in this endeavor leads to a mind that is "one-pointed," concentrated. It is like the carpenter's technique of knocking out a large peg with a smaller one. Thus concentrated, if, in the second stage, unskillful thoughts still arise he should think: "Indeed these are unskilled thoughts." So doing, these thoughts may come to an end. If, in the third stage, the unskilled thoughts persist, the monk "should bring about forgetfulness of and lack of attention to these thoughts." They may come to an end. In the fourth stage, if the evil thoughts persist, the monk "should attend to the thought function and form of those thoughts." While he is attending to the thought function and form they will come to an end. But if they persist, the monk, "his teeth clenched, his tongue pressed against his palate, should by his mind subdue, restrain and then dominate the mind." One who succeeds in this is master in the method and paths of

---

[121] *Ibid.*, 58; *cf.* 142-143.
[122] *Ibid.*.
[123] *Ibid.*, 148-151.

446

thought. He can think whatever thought he wishes; he will not think any thought that he does not wish.[124] The basic method, then, is the replacement of attention to unskilled thoughts with attention to skilled thoughts, and the development of concentration. As a result, the monk becomes complete master of his own thought, indeed, master of his own *citta*.

The fundamental method, if it may be so described, for the Buddhist pursuit of the Path is the replacement of evil with good thought. Unskilled thoughts are conducive to harm, attachment, and not conducive to release or *nibbāna*, to intuitive wisdom, or to virtue. The discipline undertaken is intended to replace one destructive set of thoughts with another that is liberating. Thus the monk must undertake to fulfill five conditions. He must become virtuous, diligent in the training, serious in his speech and conversation, concentrated in mind, looking for the "insight of release, penetrating to the perfect ending of Ill." To fulfill these obligations four other conditions must be cultivated: from the abandoning of lust (*rāga*) grows the idea of the "unlovely"–that is, detachment; from the abandoning of malice (*byāpāda*) grows amity (*mettā*); from the suppression of discursive thought (*vitakka*) grows mindfulness (*sati*) of in-breathing and out-breathing; from the uprooting of the pride of egoism grows the consciousness of impermanence. Thus "[i]n him...who is conscious of impermanence the consciousness of what is not self is established [*aniccasaññā, anattāsaññā*]. He who is conscious of what is not the self wins the uprooting of the pride of egoism in this very life [*asmimānasamugghātaṃ...diṭṭhe 'va dhamme*], namely, he wins nibbāna."[125]

The task of the monk is to cultivate those powers by which he may replace what is not conducive to release, and thus evil, with those states that are. We know already that this task involves recognition of the true nature of both the *akusala* and *kusala* states, which he pursues by means of rigorous mental discipline. The monk may be said to seek a stage of being reliant upon himself. By faith (*saddhā*), the monk may put away evil and make good arise in its stead; and then, it is said, the evil is truly gone. So also if by conscientiousness (*hiri*) a monk reject evil and cause good, that evil is rejected. The result is the same if the monk rejects evil by fear of blame (*ottappa*), by energy (*viriya*), and by wisdom (*paññā*).[126] And when the monk has achieved the replacement of the *akusala* states with the *kusala* states, he follows what ought to be followed, attends to what ought to be attended to, avoids what ought to be avoided, and expels what ought to be expelled.[127] In short, he is wholly self-reliant,

---

[124] M I 153-156.
[125] U 44.
[126] A IV, 233-234.
[127] *Ibid.*.

not distracted, completely concentrated.

The successful monk, then, is characterized not as one who ceases to act, speak or think; rather he is one whose words, deeds and thoughts reflect skill, profit, and good without exception, and not profitless, unskillful or evil concerns. The former have replaced the latter. Just this replacement is the goal of the Ariyan Path. The Eight-fold Path seeks to substitute right action, right thought, right concentration, and so forth, for wrong. This suggests that there is not an end to thought or deed but a transformation brought about by right view, by wisdom (*paññā*), by the control of the *citta*. It is important to realize that the nature of the *kusala* states is positive in the sense that reflection or concentration upon them is an action conducive to the cessation of ill. The monk does not stop doing or thinking so much as he stops doing or thinking that which is not conducive to the end of suffering and does or thinks that which is conducive, by reflecting upon the nature and uprising of the unskilled states and thus causing them to subside. This observation is consistent with our understanding of *nibbāna* as a positive freedom to think, act and speak in a manner that does not give rise to suffering, in a manner that is *kusala*. Thus he who gains the level of mastery of thought continues to think, but is the master of, and not mastered by, his thought. His life, in short, is conducive to the end of suffering and not to its uprising; and there is no more doubt.[128]

Samādhi, the States of Jhāna and the Four Spheres

One of the most important elements in the training and experience of the monk is the development of right concentration. It is, as we know, the failure to guard the senses that contributes most effectively to the loss of mastery of the *citta*, and blocks the attainment and implementation of intuitive wisdom. The task of the monk is, on the one hand, to gain mastery of his senses so that he directs them, not they him. On the other hand the mastery of the senses leads to the seeing of things as they really are. To achieve this end diligence, effort and training are essential, as is the preliminary cultivation of virtuous habit and moral life. Only when the monk has learned to refrain from those vices we have already listed is he thought to be ready for the more difficult task of training himself in the mastery of the senses, in the seeing of things as they truly are, and in the freeing of himself from the *āsavas* and the cessation of *dukkha*.

Samādhi, the practice of concentration, is the task to which the monk must now devote himself; for in this practice he knows as they really are the arising and cessation of the five *khandhas*, of body, feeling, perception, the activities and consciousness. He knows further the arising and cessation of the series of co-dependent origination; and in knowing he is

---

[128] *Cf.* D III, 78, 108, 274ff..

released.[129] Achieving the state of perfect or right concentration, he has no notion of "I" or "mine" or any tendency to conceit. How, it is asked, is this *samādhi* acquired? The monk thinks: "This is the calm [*santa*], this is the excellent state, to wit–rest from all activities [*sankhāra*], the forsaking of all substrate (of rebirth) [*sabbhupadhi*], the destruction of craving [*taṇhā*], passionlessness [*virāga*], making to cease [*nirodha*], nibbāna."[130] In this state he performs no action leading to further effects. Cultivating virtuous habits (*sīla*), "restrained with restraint of the obligations," he passes through the four "musings" or jhanic states and the four spheres (see below), thus achieving *samādhi*. The *āsavas* are destroyed; and he attains release by insight (*paññā vimutti*). There are, then, three ways of "cleansing by wearing out" and attaining to release, says Ānanda: (1) *sīla*, or virtue, followed by (2) *samādhi*, followed by (3) *paññā*.[131] *Samādhi*, right concentration, is a crucial stage in the monk's passage from the fundamental moral virtue to release from suffering.

As noted in the earlier discussion of the truth of the end of suffering, the monk, like the *Tathāgata*, moves through a series of stages of consciousness, each replacing the preceding, in an ascending order of increasing abstraction. While this is an ascending order it is ultimately an order of renunciation, first of the realm of sense, then of the realm of form, then of the realm of formlessness, in which each step of renunciation is essential to its successor and which leads to emptiness and then release. The *Dīgha Nikāya* lists nine successive states, to wit, the four *jhānas*, or meditation states, of the consciousness of the world of form (*rūpa*), the four states of the consciousness of formless worlds (*arūpa*), and finally the state beyond perception and feeling, meaning (perhaps) complete trance, or *samādhi* (see below). These states are identified as follows: (1) the state of sensuous perception (*kāma*); (2) the state of applied thought (*vitakka*); (3) the state of ardour, or zest (for the *Dhamma*); (4) the state of respiration, that is, inhalation and exhalation; (5) the state of the perception of infinite space; (6) the state of the perception of infinite consciousness; (7) the state of perception of nothingness; (8) the state of the perception that is neither conscious nor unconscious; (9) the state of the cessation of perception and feeling.

In fact, the *Dīgha*'s recitation of this nine-fold progression takes the form of an order of the *cessation* of each of these states. It should, then, be read in the following manner: (1) the First *jhāna*, sensuous perceptions cease (*kāma-saññā*); (2) Second *jhāna*, applied and sustained thought ceases (*vitakka-vicāra*); (3) Third *jhāna*, zest ceases; (4) Fourth *jhāna*, (unmindful) respiration ceases; (5) the Fifth Sphere, by the perception of

---

[129] S III, 15-16.
[130] A I, 115-116.
[131] *Ibid.*, 197-200.

infinite space, perception of material things ceases; (6) the Sixth Sphere, by the perception of infinite consciousness, perception of infinite space ceases; (7) the Seventh Sphere, by perception of nothingness, perception of infinite consciousness ceases; (8) the Eighth Sphere, by the perception that is neither conscious nor yet unconscious, perception of nothingness ceases; (9) the Ninth Sphere, by the cessation of perception and feeling, perception that is neither conscious nor yet unconscious ceases.[132]

This account of the role of *samādhi* strongly suggests that the monk passes through a succession of increasingly abstract states of awareness until awareness itself is transformed into *samādhi*. Ānanda is told: "A monk's winning of concentration [*samādhi*] may be of such a sort that in earth he is unaware of earth, in water unaware of water, in heat unaware of heat, in air unaware of air." Further, "in the sphere of unbounded space [he is] unaware of it, in the sphere of infinite intellection [consciousness], in the sphere of nothingness,...in the sphere of neither-perception-nor-non-perception [he is] unaware of it." This, however, is not the end of the story; for though successively "unaware" of these jhanic states, and "in this world...unaware of this world, in the world beyond unaware of it," yet "at the same time he may perceive [*saññā*].... Herein, Ānanda, a monk has this perception: This is the real, this the best, namely, the calming of all activities [*sankhāra*], the rejection of all substrate [*sabbūpadhipaṭinissaggo*], the ending of craving, the fading of interest, stopping, nibbāna."[133] This is the nature and goal of *samādhi*.

The process may be characterized as a gradual calming. Thus it is said that the ceasing of activities (*sankhāra*) is gradual, the ending of "whatsoever is experienced [*vedayita*]" and joined with *dukkha*. There are said to be six calmings (*nirodha*). In the first *jhāna* speech is calmed, in the second thought is calmed, in the third, zest is calmed, and in the fourth inbreathing and outbreathing. In the trance where perception and feeling have ceased, perception and feeling are calmed down. And for the monk who has destroyed the *āsavas*, lust, hatred and illusion are calmed down.[134] Thus the aim of *samādhi* is a cessation of the activities conducive to *dukkha*. Having become equable (*upekkhā*), a *Bhikkhu* is mindful and self-possessed, and experiences the joy (*sukha*) of one who is mindful and self-possessed. As he enters the third *jhāna*, "that subtle, but yet actual, consciousness, that he just had, of the joy and peace born of concentration [*samādhi*], passes away. And thereupon there arises a subtle, but yet actual, consciousness of the bliss of equanimity. And he becomes a person conscious of that...." Through training the *Bhikkhu* replaces one sort of consciousness with another (*saññā*) until the point of

---

[132] D III, 245.
[133] A V, 6-7.
[134] S IV, 145-146.

consciousness passes away.[135]

With respect to feelings, it is said that in entering the fourth *jhāna* the monk has got rid of joy and sorrow, has dispensed with the effects of his former joys and sorrows (*somanna, domanna*). Thus he enters the fourth *jhāna*; and if he does not strive for his own hurt or for the hurt of others or both, he experiences the feeling of non-hurtfulness, the highest satisfaction of all feeling.[136] Thus in the context of *samādhi* the virtue of *ahimsā* is a fruit and a characteristic.

The nine states are attained by meditation, as the central role given to the discipline of breathing, *pāṇayāma*, indicates. The monk is instructed to remain concentrated upon his inhalation and exhalation. The intent concentration upon the act of breathing serves to aid him in abandoning attachment to worldly life. It helps him to reject both what is repugnant and what is not, so that he may become and remain indifferent.

At this stage in his meditation the monk may enter into the first jhanic state. He may then enter into the second, third and fourth *jhānas*, and in doing so must give strict attention to the inhalation and exhalation of his breath. Thus entering the second trance thought directed and sustained is calmed, one-pointedness of mind achieved. Entering the third trance, zest is abandoned and he becomes indifferent and mindful. Abandoning both joy and sorrow, he enters the fourth trance, by means of attention to the *pāṇayāma* discipline.

If the monk desires to enter the succeeding sphere of infinite space, passing utterly beyond all consciousness of objects, he must give attention to in-breathing and out-breathing. This is commended also for reaching the spheres of infinite consciousness, nothingness and the sphere of neither-perception-nor-non-perception (or neither-consciousness-nor-unconsciousness). Last, he may pass into the sphere of the cessation of consciousness and sensation (*saññā, vedanā*). How may we understand his state at this point? It is said: "Now...if intent concentration of this sort be cultivated and made much of, when he feels a pleasant feeling he understands: This is impermanent. He understands: I do not cling to it." And so also for painful and neutral feelings. He feels released from bondage to all feelings. Just as oil and wick are used up and the lamp goes out, so all experiences lose their lure and grow cold; and the monk is aware that this is what he knows and feels.[137]

I want to stress the following point: the consequence of this meditational journey is the absence of attraction to and for all feelings, not the end of feelings. The monk is indifferent to his feelings, knows he is indifferent, and this is true even as he continues to feel. He achieves

---

[135] D I, 249-251.
[136] M I, 118.
[137] S V, 280-283.

451

this state of release only *after* passing through the increasingly abstract stages of consciousness, indeed, through stages of emptiness, neither-consciousness-nor-unconsciousness, and through the stage of the cessation of consciousness and sensation. None of these stages is the final goal of the *samādhi* traning; that final state is described in terms of the end of attachment rather than the end of feeling. It is possible, for example, to interpret this meditational/*samādhi* training as the passing through stages leading to the utter cessation of feeling and sensation on to the recovery of them in a vitally different form, the form of sensations and perceptions known to the monk but now fully understood as they really are, and thus devoid of the power to entrap.

A further characteristic of the knowledge associated with passing through the latter spheres, moreover, is *mano viññāṇa*, "purified mental consciousness." What is knowable by the purified mental consciousness, separated from the other five sense organs? it is asked. This purified mental consciousness arises consequent to "aloofness from sense desires," that is, by having successfully passed through the lower four jhanic states of the cessation of applied and sustained thought, zest, sorrow and joy, and respiration. No longer devoted to the five senses and their operation, the sixth organ, *mano*, now comes into play. This mental consciousness, now purified, is an agent of knowing at each of the subsequent stages. Thus "the plane of infinite ether [space, *ākāsa*] is knowable by pure mental consciousness [*manoviññāṇa*] isolated from the five sense-organs; ...the plane of infinite consciousness is knowable; ...the plane of nothing is knowable."[138]

Mano viññāṇa is not an aspect of the subsequent stages. Rather, the question is asked, "[by] what means does one comprehend a knowable mental object?" The answer is that a knowable mental object is comprehended by "intuitive wisdom [*paññā*]." Whether this means that the subsequent spheres of neither-perception-nor-non-perception and the cessation of perception and feeling are not accessible as knowable to the *mano viññāṇa* is not clear. However the fact that the progression of *samādhi* moves beyond any conceivable object, even nothingness, before it reaches its final end suggests that even the purified mental consciousness gives way to *paññā*. So the "seven resting places of cognition [*viññāṇa*]," which correspond (roughly) to the first eight stages and spheres, are known "as they really are, [that is, their] coming to be and the passing away, the pleasures and the misery of, and the way of escape from," by the monk. Then, "that brother by being purged of grasping [*anupādāna*], becomes free. And then, Ānanda, he is called Freed-by-Reason [*paññā-vimutti*]."[139]

---

[138] M I, 352-353.
[139] D II, 66-68.

We know that *paññā* is the *summum bonum* with respect to knowledge; and it would be logical to conclude that in the latter jhanic spheres through to the superknowledge of release (*paññā-vimutti*) we see the arising and utter dominance of *paññā*, beyond even the most abstract realm of meditation. Finally, it is said that by means of intuitive wisdom knowable mental objects are comprehended. This suggests that while the *mano viññāṇa* is operative in the mediate ranges of the *samādhi* discipline the final, only and ultimate means of wisdom is *paññā* , while *mano*, like the other senses, is an operation that must be refined of impurities, made transparent with the clarity of *paññā* itself. The freed monk knows all by *paññā*; and it is toward this state of knowing that the *samādhi* discipline aspires.

The pivotal stage in the *samādhi* discipline is the point between the fourth *jhāna* and the abiding in the sphere of infinite space; for here the chief obstacle to liberation—devotion to the desires of the senses—is overcome. The defeat of the senses, or the achievement of aloofness from sense desires, is frequently described as the defeat of Māra and Māra's realm. As the monk makes his way through the first four jhanic states he is said to be fleeing Māra. But upon entering the sphere of infinite space the monk is said to have surrounded Māra with a cloak of darkness; and Māra, his own vision blotted out and obscured, loses his range of power. The monk has become "invisible to the Evil One." This freedom is sustained though the remaining spheres, "and by wisdom [the monk] sees that the cankers are completely destroyed." He is invisible to Māra and Māra's force and thus beyond entanglements. Māra, of course, stands for the world of sense-pleasures, as in the story of the Buddha's enlightenment. It is important to remember that neither Māra nor the world of sense-pleasure is annihilated or disappears; the metaphor of invisibility points to the dissociation of the monk from the attraction and temptation of sense-pleasures rather than their extirpation. The world and Māra continue to do their work; but the monk is free of them in his pursuit of *samādhi*.[140]

Let us return to the question of how we may understand the nature of the monk who has achieved *samādhi*, and who has reached the stage of the stopping of perception and feeling. As we have already seen, in response to the question of how one who has achieved this state of existence differs from a corpse—a not unnatural question, given the stages involved in the *samādhi* discipline, but one that runs the risk of accepting the annihilation of sensation and perception as the final goal of the Buddhist discipline—it is said that the corpse has lost its bodily, vocal and mental activities. They have been destroyed and the organs are entirely disintegrated. The monk, on the other hand, retains his bodily, mental

---

[140] A IV, 290-291.

and vocal activities; but his sense organs have been purified.[141]

This contrast suggests the real goal of *samādhi*, namely, purification and refinement of the functions of the self. The other stages of the progression must therefore be seen as preparatory to the end. Indeed, each is necessary both of attainment and of cessation. Thus canker-destruction is said to be dependent upon each of the jhanic stages and spheres in turn. But it is dependent on the cessation of each of these stages as well. The monk enters and abides in the first *jhāna*. Whatever occurs there of form, feeling, perception, minding or consciousness (*rūpagata, vedanāgata, saññā-, sankhāra-, viññāṇa-*, in short, the *khandhas*), he sees as impermanent, hurtful, alien, not the self, as ill, as a disease. He may then direct his mind, *citta*, towards the *amata dhātu*, the "deathless element," with the thought of the peace, the end of all mental activity, all basis for rebirth, the destruction of craving, the passionless ending, and *nibbāna*. Thus he gains the destruction of the *āsavas*.[142] Passing through all the jhanic states and spheres, he achieves and surpasses the sphere of the ending of perception and feeling. His mind becomes subtle and pliant; he attains boundless concentration. He acquires psychic knowledge and the "ability of an eyewitness in every case, whatever the range may be." He attains now whatever he wishes. He may experience psychic powers in manifold modes; being one he can become many, and many one; he can range in body even as far as Brahma's world, hear with the deva's hearing all sounds, know other beings' minds, recall dwelling places of bygone days, and know beings' lives according to their deeds. Or, if he wishes, having destroyed the cankers, he may enter and abide in mind-emancipation.[143] This goal is beyond the jhanic states and spheres.

Again, if we return to the persistent questioning of the Buddha concerning the "end of the world," let us recall that the "end of the world," which is in fact the end of attachment to the world and thus the end of *dukkha*, is not to be found by an external journey, and thus by implication not by any self-denying discipline such as the Jains pursue. The Buddha describes the discipline of the monk, aloof from sense-desires, as he enters the first, second, third and fourth *jhānas*, the spheres of infinite space, infinite consciousness, nothingness, neither-perception-nor-non-perception. Yet this monk has not reached the "end of the world," he is still "world bound." Then he asks his questioners to consider the monk who, transcending the sphere of neither-perception-nor-non-perception, enters and abides in the ending of perception and feeling [*saññāvedayitanirodha*] and by wisdom sees that the cankers are completely destroyed; "that monk is said to have come to the world's end and abide at the world's end, to

---

[141] M I, 356.
[142] A IV, 284-285.
[143] *Ibid.*, 283-284.

have passed through the world's entanglements."[144]

Gotama's own progress took him not only through all the jhanic states and spheres but beyond them. As he recounts it, having withdrawn from the world his mind was not yet calm, steadfast. He recounts his discovery that the peril of pleasure was not yet understood, not enjoyed. Following this thought he became aloof from sense desires. "And presently, Ānanda, aloof from sense desires, ...I entered and abode in the first musing [jhāna]; but as I abode in this abiding, thoughts and distractions of a sensuous kind beset me; and it was for me a disease." He suppressed applied and sustained thought, passing into the second musing, but found that unsatisfactory. This was so for his passage into the third and fourth jhānas and the spheres of infinite space, infinite consciousness, nothingness, neither-perception-nor-non-perception, to the ending of perception and feeling. By wisdom (paññā) he saw that the āsavas were destroyed. Yet his final judgment on the jhanic states and spheres, and by implication the samādhi discipline, is this: "And so long, Ānanda, as I attained not to, emerged not from these nine attainments of gradual abidings, both backwards and forwards, I realized not completely, as one wholly awakened, the full perfect awakening...; but when I attained to and emerged from these abidings suchwise, then, wholly awakened, I realized completely the full perfect awakening unsurpassed.... [T]his birth is final, there is now no becoming again."[145]

We may think of the samādhi discipline, then, as the passage through and beyond three worlds: the world of sense-becoming, kāmabhava; the world of form-becoming, rūpabhava; and the world of formless-becoming, arūpabhava. For one who has renounced all three worlds, being no part of any, he has brought suffering to an end.[146] Each of the stages is said to be the "product of higher [thought] [abhisañcetayitaṃ]." The monk, realizing this, thinks: "Now even that which is a higher product, produced by higher thought is impermanent, of a nature to end."[147] So the monk presses on to the end of the jhanic states, rejecting each in turn for the next higher state.

Some accounts of the ascent through the jhanic states suggest the possibility of attaining a degree of success without moving onto the next state.[148] It is said, for example, that the one who dwells in the first jhanic state, aloof from the pleasures of the senses, will get rid of unskilled (akusala) intentions; and "if he is serene either he comes to imperturbability now or if he is intent on wisdom," he may achieve the

---

[144] *Ibid.*, 287-289.
[145] A IV, 294-295.
[146] A III, 309-310.
[147] A V, 220-223.
[148] *Cf.*, *e.g.*, *ibid.*.

status of *Arahant* or enter the subsequent *jhānas*. In the latter case, "[a]t the breaking up of the body after dying this situation exists, that that evolving consciousness [*viññāṇa*] may accordingly reach imperturbability." The same options exist for infinite space, for infinite consciousness, for the plane of no-thing, and for neither-perception-nor-non-perception. It is noteworthy, however, that the monk who has moved to the equanimity of mind characteristic of one who has attained and departed from the realm of neither-perception-nor-non-perception has not necessarily achieved *nibbāna*. When this issue was raised the Buddha replied that some attain it and others do not. The difference lay in whether the monk desired to grasp the state of neither-perception-nor-non-perception. The monk who has grasping, the Buddha says, does not attain *nibbāna*, even if it is grasping after the highest jhanic sphere.[149]

One may, then, traverse the jhanic states and spheres without attaining the goal, if one remains entranced, if I may so term it, with them. It is only when that grasping is wholly given up that the mind is delivered. The issue of the final freedom of mind is relevant to this point. There are four descriptions of freedom of mind; they are said to be "different in connotation as well as being different in denotation," and to be identical in connotation as well as being different in denotation. These descriptions apply to the four types of freedom of mind, which are immeasurable freedom of mind, freedom of mind that is naught (*ākiñcañña*), freedom of mind that is void (*suññatā*), and freedom of mind that is signless. Immeasurable freedom of mind refers to the mind of the monk abiding having suffused the whole world, "everywhere, in every way with a mind of equanimity that is far-reaching, wide-spread, immeasurable, without enmity, without malevolence." These are characteristics usually associated with the fourth *jhāna* and the realm of infinite space. Freedom of mind that is naught, "passing quite beyond the plane of infinite consciousness, thinking, 'There is not anything', enters in and abides in the plane of no-thing." The monk possessed of freedom of mind that is void reflects thus: " 'This is void of self or of what pertains to self.' " Finally, the freedom of mind that is signless is possessed by the monk who, "paying no attention to any signs, entering on the concentration of mind that is signless, abides therein." The differences among the states with respect to both connotation and denotation arise from their achievement at the different respective jhanic levels. Their identity in connotation and difference in denotation is seen in that all of them are obstructed by greed, hate and delusion; and when the cankers are destroyed these are wholly rooted out and cannot return. The mind that is freed of greed, hate and delusion (*rāga, dosa, moha*), and in which the cankers are destroyed is immeasurable, naught, void and signless.[150]

---

[149] M III, 46-51.

[150] M I, 358-360; *cf.* 357, a reference to "emerging from freedom of mind

Conjointly with the destruction of the *āsavas*, the successful passage through and beyond the jhanic states and spheres effects the end of the *anusayas* latent in the three classes of feelings, *i.e.* pleasant (*sukha*), painful (*dukkha*) and neutral (*adukkhamasukha*) (the last means feeling that is pleasant "as to knowing, painful as to not knowing.") The "latent tendencies" in each, *rāgānusaya, paṭighānusaya,* and *avijjānusaya,* are tendencies toward greed, toward aversion, and toward ignorance that are deeply rooted. The monk who is free from the pleasures of the senses and unskilled states may enter the first meditation "which is accompanied by initial thought [*vitakka, viveka*], is born of aloofness, and is rapturous and joyful." Here he gets rid of attachment, and the latent tendency toward attachment (*rāgānusaya*) is not any longer extant. Then, "from setting up a yearning for the incomparable Deliverance," he feels a distress, presumably brought on by the tension between his present state and the Deliverance. The result is the end of the tendency toward aversion (*paṭighānusaya*). Thus "...a monk, by getting rid of joy [*sukha*] and, by getting rid of anguish, by the going down of his former pleasures and sorrows, enters on and abides in the fourth meditation which has neither anguish nor joy and which is entirely purified by equanimity and mindfulness." Here he disposes of ignorance and the tendency toward ignorance (*avijjānusaya*).[151]

It is consistent with the ending of the *āsavas* and the passing away of the latent tendencies that the monk does not conceive of an agent, himself, as the doer in the *samādhi* discipline. The question of "who" is passing though these states is subject to the quatrilemma imposed upon all such questions as whether the *Tathāgata* exists after the breaking up of the body, and so forth. The layman Visākhā is assured that it does not occur to a monk who is attaining the stopping of perception and feeling: " 'I will attain the stopping of perception and feeling,' or 'I have attained the stopping of perception and feeling.' For, his mind has been previously so developed in that way that it leads him onto the state of being such."[152] As, for example, the gradual destruction of the *anusayas* of greed, aversion and ignorance is achieved there can be no thought of one who so grasps, hates, and is ignorant.

The *Tathāgata* is said, furthermore, to distinguish between the monk who pursues his goal by grasping after it (*upādāna*) and the one who does not. The former is inferior. He grasps after speculation concerning the past and future, after the control of the senses, after the rapture of aloofness, after spiritual happiness, after the feeling that is neither painful nor pleasant. He may declare: " 'Tranquil am I, allayed am I, with-

---

that is signless."
[151] M I, 365-367. Here the second and third jhanic states are omitted.
[152] *Ibid.*, 365.

out grasping am I.' " But, contrary to his own beliefs, he still grasps and will not achieve release despite his efforts, though they are prosecuted along the same path as the monk who proceeds without grasping. The superior monk is not concerned with speculation, does not seek to concentrate solely upon the fetters of the senses, and passes beyond the rapture of coolness, beyond spiritual happiness, beyond the feeling that is neither pleasant nor painful. His declaration, " 'Tranquil am I, allayed am I, without grasping am I,' " is that of one whose course is bound for *nibbāna.*[153]

This distinction is important because it clarifies the very nature of the *samādhi* discipline. The monk who seeks to attain each step and rejoices in it thinks of himself as the doer, the attainer, and, on the other hand, does not comprehend that the discipline is intended as a median way, a path, and is not itself the goal. The great error is that the monk who rejoiced in his attainments, formidable though they were, was by his very attention to the means preventing his attainment of the end. For the task of the monk is to complete, to bring to an end, to move beyond all of the states of the discipline, to *nibbāna.* No intermediate goal has merit unless seen in this context.

The full range of the discipline is usefully presented in the discussion of emptiness, beginning with emptiness in the most obvious and ordinary sense and culminating in emptiness as the truth of *nibbāna.* It is useful because the place of the meditation states, spheres and the discipline of *samādhi* is clearly seen at the upper reaches of the Path, but by no means as synonymous with the end.

Speaking to Ānanda, Gotama summarizes: "I, Ānanda, though abiding in (the concept of)[154] emptiness [*suññatāvihārena*], abide in the fulness thereof." He sets out to explain what he means. He begins with the notion that the place where they are, the palace of Migara's mother, is empty of elephants, cows, horses and mares, gold and silver, and groups of men and women. Indeed, despite its emptiness in this ordinary sense, and while empty with respect to its *former* function—a metaphorical nicety worth noting—"there is this that is not emptiness, that is to say the solitude grounded on the Order of monks." In the same way, a monk must think of the village and its perceptions, or of human beings, as empty, *i.e.,* "not attending" to them, and must think and attend to the "solitude grounded on the perception of the forest," or in other words he must withdraw in body and mind from the concerns of secular life. In the "forest," the situation is empty of the concerns of the village; it is not empty only with respect to the "solitude grounded on the perception

---

[153] M III, 23-24; *cf. ibid.,* 310-313.

[154] I am not in agreement with the narrowly intellectualist connotation of this translation of *suññatāvihārena* as "the *concept* of emptiness."

458

of the forest." This is a proper understanding of emptiness.[155]

However the monk is then to direct his attention to the "perception of the earth, earth solitude," and in this perception the perception of the forest is gone, or, in other words, earth-solitude, earth-perception, is empty of forest-solitude and forest-perception. The monk has now directed his attention away from his immediate solitary surroundings, however free from the life of the village and the concerns of human beings he may be, to the broader and more abstract perspective of the earth itself, of which the forest is simply a small part. His concentration works in such a way that earth-perception replaces forest-perception, and the former is said to be empty of the latter.

The next step is the perception of infinite ākāsa, infinite space, which is said to be empty of earth-perception; and so forth through the spheres of infinite consciousness, of no-thing, of the realm of neither-perception-nor-non-perception, with each latter stage replacing the former, each latter stage said to be empty of the former. In this account the realm of neither-perception-nor-non-perception is replaced by "solitude" grounded in the "the concentration of the mind that is signless [animittaṁ cetosamādhiṁ].... And there is only this that is not emptiness, that is to say the six sensory fields that, conditioned by life, are grounded on this body itself." He may then establish his attention on the foundation of the mind that is signless. His mind is satisfied with, pleased with, set on and freed in the concentration of the mind that is signless. But whatever is effected and thought out, like the signless mind, is impermanent. Knowing this the monk's thought is free of the āsavas of kāma, bhava, and avijjā (sense-pleasure, becoming and ignorance). Only the six sensory fields, then, are not empty.[156]

There is at least one striking conclusion to be drawn from this description of emptiness, that the full understanding of emptiness stops short of a state in which the senses are not extant, a state empty of senses. That is, the pursuit of emptiness eliminates, through gradual development of states of emptiness beginning with the most obvious, all the causes of suffering. The meditation states do not, however, lead to the end of the six sense-fields. It clearly does lead to the end of the arising and the satisfaction and the peril of the six sense-fields. But the discipline frees the monk from bondage in body and mind; it is this freedom which constitutes emptiness. The monk is empty of, that is, free from disturbance by, the realms of sense, of form and of formlessness. But he is still very much alive.[157]

Finally, let us return to a point raised earlier. Gotama's account

---

155 *Ibid.*, 147-148.
156 *Ibid.*, 147-152; *cf.* 154-155.
157 *Cf. ibid.*, 23-24.

of his own enlightenment refers to passing through all the meditation states "forward and backward" as a crucial characteristic of his release. This suggests that the states represent an intermediate stage in enlightenment, as we have seen. The goal is not reached until they are left behind. In the account of the Buddha's *parinibbāna* the events related confirm this view. Following his reknowned final words, "Decay is inherent in all component things! Work out your salvation with diligence! [*Vayadhammā saṃkhāra, appamādena sampādethāti*]," he passed through the four first *jhānas*, through the spheres of infinite space, infinite consciousness, no-thing, neither-perception-nor-non-perception, and the state of the cessation of feelings and thought (or feelings and perception). At this point Ānanda is said to have remarked that he had died. Anuruddha dissented, and was correct. For the Buddha then passed back through the spheres of neither-perception-nor-non-perception, of no-thing, of infinite consciousness, or infinite space, through the fourth, third, second and first *jhānas*. Only then did he expire (*parinibbāyi*).[158] This final recapitulation of his enlightenment, from aloofness of the senses to the cessation of feeling and perception, back to sense-aloofness and beyond, is a dramatic and convincing account of the course of enlightenment, and a revealing description of the role of the jhanic states and *samādhi*. It suggests that true release is achieved through the development of the *samādhi* discipline; but it also suggests that the goal of the disciple is a return to the world, with the *citta* purified, transformed in the sense of refined, and transparent. Things will now be seen as they really are through the senses, now fully controlled by the I-less person that has put away all causes of *dukkha*. Having now fully understood the Ariyan truths of suffering, the arising of suffering, the end of suffering and the arising of the end of suffering, one is free to go about the task of living and dying.

Monk and Layperson

The literature with which we are concerned is devoted largely to the life and training of individuals who have taken the pursuit of the Ariyan Path seriously enough to step apart from the mainstream of common life. For example, we have seen that the distinction between the Ariyan follower and the ordinary or untaught masses is a persistent theme and a framework on which to place various expositions concerning the Ariyan life. The conclusion that may reasonably be drawn from these and many other themes is that it is necessary to become a monk in order to follow the Ariyan Path to its successful conclusion. Certainly, Gotama thought that because of the inevitable distractions of the life of the householder it was harder for him to follow the Path; and in this sense his "kingdom was not of this world." But we should be clear on the nature of the distinction.

---

[158] D II, 173-175.

First, the analysis of the nature and arising of suffering is, of course, universal and therefore identical for the monk and the layperson. Second, what distinguishes the layperson from the monk is not any difference with respect to the truths of suffering, but rather the greater efficiency offered by the monastic discipline in moving along the way to the cessation of suffering. Third, at least according to the interpretation of the *summum bonum* I have offered, the monastic life is truly a means and not an end. The "state" of *nibbāna*, for example, is one of absolute transparency and clarity of understanding leading to the end of suffering. The attainment of this goal, or the goal of Arahantship, is facilitated by the monastic disciple, but is by no means identical with it. The *Arahant* seems to be one who may follow any particular path he chooses; and it is important to note that he is recognizable only by another *Arahant*, or by the *Tathāgata*. The implication is that he or she is not in principle restricted from or to any community, although he or she may be "invisible" to some or even all of its members. Thus the *Arahant* may in fact be indistinguishable from the "ordinary person" except to other *Arahants* or the *Tathāgata*.

The *Dhamma* is, nevertheless, directed toward those who have taken refuge in it, along with the Buddha and the *Sangha*. [159] Willingly, they have become subject to the discipline of body, thoughts and speech for the purpose of conquering the *āsavas*; and in this respect they are to be distinguished from others. While they do not separate themselves entirely from the world at large–there would be no teaching if this were so–their sensing and perceiving in and of the world is governed by the *Dhamma* and their "zest" for the *Dhamma*.

That the vast majority of men and women are not disciplined in their actions, thoughts and words is a fundamental observation of the tradition. The epithet "untaught manyfolk," *puthujjana*, describes the group that is as yet unable to recognize the truth of suffering. They think, as we have seen, that the self is body, or that feeling is self, or perception is self, and so forth. Thus ignorant, they are naturally unaware of the impermanent nature of any and all of the *khandhas*, and suffer the consequences of their ignorance.[160] They, "fettered by the bonds of body, ...bound to the inner and the outer," move from this world to another.[161]

Among those who live and die, who have freed themselves from the envy of others' goods, from sense desires, from greed, those who have abandoned home, family, wealth, lust, ill-will, and ignorance are the serene *Arahants*.[162] Those who have left home have found a way to live free of greed, aversion and ignorance. The suppliant Mahānāma asks

---

159 *Cf.* S II, 24.
160 S III, 138.
161 *Ibid.*, 140-141.
162 S I, 23-24; *cf.* D I, 81-82.

what conditions must exist for the breaking of these fetters. He is told that if he did not dwell in a house and enjoy the pleasures of the senses he would be able to put away greed, aversion and confusions.[163] To the lay king Pasenadi Gotama declares, "Hard it is, sire, for you who are a layman, holding worldly possessions, dwelling amidst the encumbrances of children, accustomed to Benares sandalwood, arrayed in garlands and perfumed unguents, using gold and silver, to know whether those are Arahants, or are in the Path of Arahantship,"–as he points to a group of Jains.[164] The distractions of the king's daily life prevent him from recognizing an *Arahant.* This is virtually the same thing as saying that because of his entrapment in the life of sense-pleasures of the home he is incapable of knowing one who has found the truth, and, by extension, the truth itself. The life of the householder, while not condemned, stands as an obstacle to following the *Dhamma,* or even to recognizing it.

Both the life of the householder and of the wayfarer move through stages of development. However in an important summary of the Ariyan life, addressed to Upāli in response to his expressed desire to join the *Sangha,* the life of the householder is said to precede in all its stages the life of the wayfarer. The ordinary person, as a small child, enjoys lying on his back, and playing with his own excrement. This gives way, as a source of satisfaction, to other games, in which his sense-faculties are employed in playing with the playthings of children. That is a higher stage: "Does not this game come to be finer and more valued than the former...?" Growing older, the ordinary person becomes "a prey" to his senses, "to objects cognizable by the eye, objects desirable, agreeable, fascinating, attracting: to sounds, cognizable..., to odors...tastes...touches...things concerned with sensual desires and passionate. Now what think you, Upāli? Does not this game come to be finer and more valuable than the former?"[165]

The stages of the wayfarer lie beyond the possibilities of development for the householder. Thus the ordinary person may be attracted as a disciple to an *Arahant.*[166] He leaves home, practices *ahimsā,* and delights in harmony. He sets a guard over his sense-faculties: "Seeing an object with the eye he is not misled by its outer view nor by its lesser details," and so also for the other senses. This is a "finer game" than the former. He continues in growth and development, retiring to the forest, passes through the jhanic states and spheres, and by insight knows that the

---

[163] M I, 119-120.
[164] S I, 105.
[165] A V, 141-143.
[166] There is said to be great benefit for anyone even in the mere sight and sound of a monk. The mere presence of the successful monk is cause for the pursuit of the Path. S V, 55.

cankers are destroyed.[167]

The relationship between the two styles of development is revealing; for the life of the wayfarer succeeds and is indeed dependent upon the life of the householder. It is not until dependence upon the sense-faculties emerges as the dominant aspect of the householder's life that the possibility of the wayfarer's style emerges. Further, taken together, the two constitute an unbroken continuum moving toward release, so that the wayfaring life and the goal of the end of suffering are both clearly fixed in the general context of human development from childhood forward.[168] Furthermore, it is strongly suggested that among householders there are those who can apprehend (or learn) the truth of the cause and the end of suffering. The householder Anāthapiṇḍika comes to Sāriputta with a complaint of dreadful pain in his head. Sāriputta advises him to bring to an end his grasping after vision and so be freed from consciousness dependent upon vision—and so also for the other five senses. He must not grasp after contact, feeling, nor after the elements of extension, liquidness, radiation, motion, space or consciousness, nor after the five *khandhas*, nor after the jhanic states and spheres, nor after this world. He will then have no consciousness dependent either on this world or the world beyond. The householder weeps and thanks Sāriputta for putting the matter so clearly, in a way not usually employed for laymen. There are others, he concludes, who can learn these truths.[169]

What constrains the layperson is not his lay status so much as the distractions of the lay life that are so great in number and so entrancing in nature that he has less of a chance of success in bringing suffering to an end than the monk. That is not to say, as we have already seen, that the monk's life is not beset with its own enticements.[170] For in both one must abandon concern for what one shall eat, and where, or for sleep. "Whosoe'er trains and leads the homeless life, /Must oust these thoughts that lead to discontent."[171] "Self-training" is the essential point of the Path.[172]

But the farther along the Path one has travelled the greater the benefit; and in this respect the *Arahant* has clearly gone well beyond the ordinary person, even if the latter achieves a degree of discipline. The Master Kassapa, speaking of Brahmins and wanderers, points out that

---

[167] A V, 143-146.

[168] *Cf.* M I, 119-120.

[169] M III, 310-313. Anāthapiṇḍika was neither encouraged to leave his state as householder nor did he choose to do so. That is, the *Dhamma* was told to him in his role as layman to good effect.

[170] *Cf.* S I, 259.

[171] SN 141.

[172] S III, 129-131.

they have a different power of perception from that of ordinary people:

> those Wanderers and Brahmins who haunt the lonely and re-
> mote recesses of the forest where voice, where sound there hardly
> is, they there abiding strenuous, ardent, aloof, purify the eye di-
> vine; they by that purified eye divine, passing the vision of men,
> see both this world and that other world [here, of the gods], and
> beings reborn not of parents. In this way...is the other world to
> be seen, and not...by this fleshly eye.[173]

Thus it is said that there are three sorts of persons found in the world, each sort further divided into two other classes, those of the ordinary person and the follower of the *Tathāgata*. First, by transcending consciousness of form (*rūpasaññā*), by the "disappearance of consciousness of resistance" (*paṭighasaññā*), by paying no heed to the "diversity of consciousness" (*nānattasaññā*), and regarding space as infinite, a person attains and abides in the sphere of infinite space. There he remains; and when he dies he is reborn among the devas who reached the sphere of infinite space. He remains among them for a life-time of 20,000 cycles. At the end of this time the ordinary man (*puthujjana*) goes to purgatory, or the world of an animal or the Realm of Ghosts. But one who has been a disciple of the Exalted One, having reached this realm of the devas and having remained there, finally passes away in that very state (*parinibbāyati*).[174]

The second sort of person is like the first except that he abides in the sphere of infinite consciousness among the devas whose life-time is 40,000 cycles. The ordinary person then returns to another life-time while the disciple passes away there. The third sort attains the sphere of no-thing (*ākiñcañña*), remaining there for 60,000 cycles; and the same distinction between the ordinary person and the disciple obtains. Thus while both a disciple and an ordinary person may attain these jhanic states, what distinguishes the fates of the two is whether one has been a follower of the Exalted One.[175] The point here is that the attainment of the higher meditative states is not in and of itself the chief and unique mark of the disciple, by which he is distinguished from the layperson. Rather, it is his freedom from grasping and desire, even, as we have already seen in the case of Anāthapiṇḍika, the desire for the higher meditative states. "Who lives not by his wits, lightsome, fain for his weal,/ In sense controlled [*yatindriyo*],/ In every way at liberty,/ Homeless, without thoughts of self, nor hungering,/ When he has banished pride [*Māram*], that monk fares on alone."[176]

---

[173] D II, 355-357.
[174] A I, 245-246.
[175] *Ibid.*.
[176] U 39; *cf.* U 44.

The expectations laid down for the life of the monk are such that the discipline constitutes a challenge to the householder's life only in the sense that the hindrances and distractions lying in the path of enlightenment are more easily addressed by the monk than the householder. The problem is not with being a householder but with the hindrances that, depending upon the attention to them, serve as obstacles. The faithful Ariyan disciple is: (1) "utterly devoted to the *Tathāgata*," with faith, without doubt, and thus "he will dwell resolute in energy," ever striving to abandon bad qualities and to acquire good qualities; (2) he is "mindful, possessed of supreme discrimination," and calls to mind and remembers things said long ago; (3) he will lay hold of concentration, one-pointedness of mind; (4) thus equipped, he will by insight see the arising and cessation of ignorance, craving, suffering and rebirth; (5) finally, he knows that he is aware of the truth, "having experienced it in his own person."[177]

This monk is not seized by lust, hatred or confusion upon seeing, hearing, touching, tasting, smelling or cognizing any object. He knows that desire and lust are the cause of the arising of bondage and suffering, not the objects or the senses themselves. It is precisely in this respect that one who is enlightened is different from one who is not.[178] It is, furthermore, this truth upon which the proclamation of the righteous life is founded.[179] The end of bondage to desire is the goal of the Ariyan task. [180] The layperson is not prevented from entering upon that task because he is a layperson but because anyone who does not understand as yet the truth of suffering, its arising, its cessation and the nature of its cessation will continue to look elsewhere for an explanation. There is a sense in which anyone who perceives this truth of desire as the cause of suffering is not any longer an ordinary person—whether he dons the saffron robe or not. But in taking the robe, by taking refuge in the *Sangha*, he becomes more efficient in his pursuit of release. But this is true simply because he has taken as his task that goal and that goal alone, and thus gradually defeats the distractions of ordinary life. Success in this pursuit, furthermore, finally obliterates the distinction between monk and layperson. One is not freed because he becomes a monk and leaves the home life behind; he is freed because he has conquered the *āsavas*, done what has had to be done, possesses a *citta* of utter transparency, and is an adamantine plane of unshakeable strength in the Truth.

The social distinction between layperson and monk is not a primary cause of liberation, but a secondary effect; and it is important that we keep that distinction in mind. Gotama directs his words to, among oth-

---

[177] S V, 200-202.
[178] *Cf.* S V, 60-63.
[179] *Cf.* S IV, 101-102.
[180] *Cf.* S V, 243-245.

ers, those who elected to follow him and the *Dhamma*, and to live together as the *Sangha* for the purpose of facilitating their release from suffering. It was, clearly, never the intention of Gotama to found another order of monks; rather, he sought to "turn the wheel of the *Dhamma*"–again, it should be noted. He made this proclamation to any who would listen; and he did not discourage any who wished to follow the path if their intention was of the same serious purpose as his own (there are several accounts of his ability to discriminate beween those who were intent upon the end of suffering and those who were simply impressed with his powers and rhetoric). One consequence of his work, as is common in the history of civilization, was the appearance of a sub-group within the society based upon its allegiance to its present leader, its teachings, and its rules for behavior. But it is a consequence, and a secondary one at that. The primary consequence of the Buddha's proclamation was the reversal of the *paṭiccasamuppāda* series, the breaking down of the *khandhas*, and the destruction of the *āsavas*. We know that the emergence in the latter periods of the tradition of a critique of the necessity of monastic seclusion arose–again a common occurrence in the history of civilization–founded on the belief that Gotama did not demand that one become a monk in order to gain release, regardless of how much more efficient, at least in principle, the secluded life might be in the pursuit of the end of suffering. There was nothing to suggest that the *Arahant* was of necessity a monk; what was indisputable was that the *Arahant* had achieved *vimutti*, *nibbāna*.

Thus the significance of the monastic movement in the early Buddhist tradition is sociological; and it is a consequence of the primary teaching, that one must devote one's energies to the highest possible degree to tracing the roots of suffering in one's own life. There is no end of suffering until this is done. This truth is proclaimed to laymen, to Jains, to *Bhikkhus*–to all. The *Dhamma*, then, is not a monastic but a human discipline.

Furthermore, according to the development of a monk he may attain a stage in the four-fold hierarchy of release. The listing of "fours" in the *Dīgha Nikāya* includes the four fruits of the life of a recluse, the "fruit," that is, benefit, "of the level of Stream-Entrant [*sotāpatti-phala*], of Once-Returner [*sakadāgāmi-phala*], of Never-Returner [*anāgāmi-phala*], and of Arahant [*arahatta-phala*]."[181] The distinction refers to the time it takes to wear out the effects of past action after he has gained mastery and thus produces no new effects or states of bondage in his life.[182] The difference is compared to an iron slab, "heated and beaten all day." A bit may detach itself and cool down immediately. So the Non-Returner,

---

[181] D III, 214ff.; *cf.* S V, 351.
[182] *Cf.*, *e.g.*, S V, 159.

who knows by intuitive wisdom that there is peace (*santa*), who has abandoned concern about the past, present and future, has acquired equanimity, but who has not completely overcome the tendencies toward conceit, toward the desire for becoming, nor toward ignorance (*mānānusaya, bhavarāgānusaya, avijjānusaya*), "when the lower five fetters are destroyed, he becomes completely cool after an interval [*antara parinibbāyi*]." The Non-Returner may be contrasted with the Stream-Entrant, for example, who is said to be like a bit from such an iron slab that may fly off, ignite a fire which consumes a heap of grass and sticks, sets fire to the shrubland and woodland, comes to the edge of a green cornfield, upland, rock, water or lush countryside and there dies down from lack of fuel. The *Arahant*, however, knowing the end of the lurking tendencies, having destroyed the cankers, "enters and abides in the cankerless mind-emancipation, wisdom emancipation, here and now, realizing it himself by his own knowledge." This is called the *anupādā parinibbāna*, the completely unattached cool.[183]

While each of these stages indicates the end of the arising of *dukkha* they differ with respect to the playing out of the effects of earlier actions. Each is enjoined to contemplate the same causes and effects of suffering, such as the five *khandhas*. By so pondering each realizes the fruits of the appropriate stage. A virtuous brother so pondering will realize the fruits of entering the stream, and so for a Once-Returner and a Non-Returner. The *Arahant*, who is also enjoined to reflect upon the five grasping groups is, however, different. "For the arahant...there is nothing further to be done, nor is there return to the upheaping of what is done."[184]

Thus the primary distinction among the four stages is not in the level of knowledge of the *Dhamma* but in the level of success in removing the same obstacles and unskilled states. The distinction illustrates development and maturity along the path. The *Arahant* stage, furthermore, is placed above the state of Never-Returner, although it includes the characteristics of the goals achieved at that and previous stages. This suggests that the state of *Arahant* is not identical to any of the previous states, nor to the state of rebirth or non-rebirth, but is a state surpassing both, and in fact renders both irrelevant. If we recall the impossibility of answering the question of whether the *Tathāgata* exists after death—impossible because irrelevant to release and the end of suffering—we have a deliberately exact analogy to the state of the *Arahant*. It is absurd to say than an *Arahant* believes that he goes on after death, that he does not, or both, or neither. For "whatever verbal expression there is or whatever system of verbal expression, whatever explanation there may be and whatever system of explanation, whatever communication is pos-

---

[183] A IV, 40-43.
[184] S III, 143-144.

sible and whatever system of communication, whatever knowledge there is and whatever sphere of knowledge, whatever round of life and how far the round is traversed,–by mastery over all this that brother is set free. But to say, of a brother who has been so set free by insight:–'He knows not, he sees not,'–that were absurd!"[185]

Diversity of Ways and Means

In fact, the way to the end of suffering is impressive for its diversity. The tradition has paid attention to the relationship between the type and level of suffering, the state of abilities of the person struggling with the suffering, and the nature of the release–although of course there is but one release, just as there is but one *Dhamma*.

In general, a distinction appears to be drawn between the pursuit of release by insight and by calming of the senses. Obviously the difference is one of emphasis; for in the final analysis both are required for release. For example, we are told that two conditions exist that have a part in knowledge, calm (*samatha*) and introspection (*vipasaññā*). If calm is cultivated, all lust (*rāga*) is abandoned. If introspection is cultivated, all ignorance is abandoned. "A mind defiled by lust is not set free; nor can insight defiled by ignorance be cultivated." The presentation implies two distinct lines of approach to the question of suffering, one leading toward insight, the other toward absolute mastery of the senses. "Indeed, monks, this ceasing of lust is the heart's release, this ceasing of ignorance is the release by insight [*paññā*]."[186]

Again, we may observe a rough equality among diverse appoaches to release in a passage in which Gotama is asked to decide among three ideals of release. Kotthita held that one who has "testified to the Truth with [his] body" was superior, because the "faculty of concentration is most developed." Sāriputta preferred one "who has won view," because in him the faculty of insight (*paññā*) was most developed, and as well one "who is released by faith [*saddhā*]," because the faculty of faith was most developed. Gotama's judgement is revealing: "It is no easy thing, Sāriputta, to decide off-hand this matter. It may well be that the person who is released by faith is on the path to Arahantship: that this one who has testified to the truth of the body is a once-returner or a non-returner: that this one who has won view is also a once-returner or a non-returner," and so forth for the other possible combinations. "Indeed," says Gotama, "it is no easy task, Sāriputta, to decide off-hand which of these three persons is most excellent and choice."[187]

The distinction is extended to the movement through the jhanic spheres, in the exposition of the state of "freed both ways." The two ways

---

[185] D II, 65-66.
[186] A I, 55-56.
[187] *Ibid.*, 102-103.

describe, first, the seer-in-body (*kāyasakkhin*), and second, the wisdom-freed (*paññā-vimutta*). The seer-in-body, aloof from sense-desires, enters the first sphere of jhanic contemplation, and dwells there, and so forth for the remaining states and spheres. The wisdom-freed, aloof from sense-desires, enters and abides in the first sphere and by wisdom understands it, and so forth for the remaining musings and spheres. But the one who is said to be freed-both-ways, that is by wisdom and "in body"–which I take to mean by mastery of the senses–abides in the first musing with body attuned to it and by wisdom understands it, and so on through to the last sphere and the destruction of the cankers.[188]

While the one who is freed-both-ways seems superior, that freedom is offered to each of the other approaches. At times it seems that while one may be successful in one way, he may be something of a novice in the other. For example, Gotama says of Ānanda, "Monks, Ānanda is a learner [*sekha*]. Yet it would not be easy to find his equal in insight [*paññā*]."[189] Or, more frequently, success may be gained although the full discipline of the jhanic states is not completed.[190]

Apart from the distinction between the path of wisdom and the path of meditative discipline and introspection, the texts distinguish among strengths and weakness with respect to progress towards release. As we have seen, one such series of distinctions plays on the relationship between the relative strength of the three major *klesas*, lust, hate and ignorance and the five controlling faculties, namely faith (*saddhā*), energy (*viriya*), mindfulness (*satī*), concentration (*samādhi*), and wisdom (*paññā*). The slowest sort of progress is that hindered both by the power of the *klesas* and the dullness of the faculties, called painful and sluggish. Next in ascending order toward ease of progress is that situation (called "painful but of swift intuition") in which the *klesas* are powerful but the faculties, especially intuition–said to be swift here–are strong. The third mode of progress, called "pleasant," is that in which the nature of the person is not overwhelmed by the *klesas*, however he is possessed of a sluggish intuition and his controlling faculties are dull. The final and most rapid mode of progress is one in which the *klesas* are weak and the controlling faculties swift and strong.[191] Each of these types is successful; the distinction in mode and rate of progress is a function of the nature of the person.

A very similar analysis is offered in a discussion of four types of release from the *sankhāras*, or activities, habitual tendencies. This follows a very similar pattern to the ones just described, so that one may gain his release in this very life, but with some effort. Here, possessed of the

---

188 A IV, 297.
189 A I, 205.
190 *Cf.* A IV, 284-285.
191 A II, 153-155.

five controlling faculties in strength and abundance, one contemplates the ugliness of the body, the repulsiveness of food, becomes aware of a distaste for the world, and knows the impermanence of all activities. Such a one is released in this life, but without effort. For him who contemplates the ugliness of the body and the impermanence of *sankhāras*, but whose controlling faculties are dull, he is released when this body is broken up, with some effort. Third, moving to the stage of jhanic meditation, a monk who, aloof from sense desires, enters and abides in the first, second, third and fourth musings, and who manifests the five controlling faculties, attains release in this life without effort. Finally, the monk who, entering the *jhānas* in order, abiding in the fourth *jhāna*, but whose controlling faculties are dull, attains release when the body is broken up, without effort.[192]

But the *Arahant* is described as having won through in one or all four ways; that is to say, by winnning through in any or all of the following ways one may be said to be an *Arahant*. First, by cultivating calm (*samatha*), he is established in it, with fetters abandoned. The "lurking tendencies [*anusaya*]" come to an end. Second, he may begin with insight, cultivate calm, follow and establish himself in the Way, and the fetters are abandoned, the tendencies allayed. Third, by calm and insight joined, he may win through, following the stages mentioned, to the end of the *anusayas*. Fourth, established without doubt in the truth of *Dhamma*, "...his thought stands fixed in the very self [*cittaṃ ajjhattaṃ*], settles down [*santi*], becomes one-pointed [*ekodihoti*], is composed [*samādhi*];" and this leads to the end of the fetters and the lurking tendencies.[193]

Thus while one may conclude that there are various paths to *nibbāna*, to *vimutti*, at the same time there is an ideal that incorporates them all. It may be summarized thus: There is no more craving, no future suffering, nor more rebirth when these four Ariyan truths are realized, namely, "[t]he noble conduct of life [*sīla*], the noble earnestness in meditation [*samādhi*], the noble kind of wisdom [*paññā*], and the noble salvation of freedom [*vimutti*]." Each of these aids and assists the others. "Great becomes the fruit, great the advantage of earnest contemplation [*samādhi*], when it is set round with upright conduct. Great becomes the fruit...of intellect [*paññā*] when it is set round with earnest contemplation. The mind [*citta*] set round with intelligence [*paññā*] is set quite free from the Intoxications [*āsavas*], that is to say, from the intoxication of Sensuality [*kāmāsava*]...of Becoming [*bhavāsava*], ...of Delusion [*diṭṭhāsava*], ...of Ignorance [*avijjāsava*]."[194] Final release, in short, is guaranteed to one whose mind is governed by insight, whose actions are governed by virtue,

---

[192] *Ibid.*, 160-162.
[193] *Ibid.*, 162-163.
[194] D II, 132-133.

whose knowledge is governed by discipline.

The Unitary Vision of Sigmund Freud and Gotama the Buddha

The distinguished and venerable Buddhologist Edward Conze once wrote that Buddhism has nothing at all to do with psychoanalysis or psychotherapy. We should agree, however surprising that agreement may seem in light of the foregoing pages. "Buddhism," if that is the proper term, has nothing to do with psychoanalysis and everything to do with suffering. Conversely, psychoanalysis has everything to do with suffering. The issue in this work is not whether Gotama was a great psychoanalyst and therefore right; nor is it that Sigmund Freud was a great Buddhist and therefore right. To put the matter thus is in some sense to trivialize it, as though the truth were psychoanalysis or some such thing as Buddhism. The truth is the truth. That is the context in which we should understand the contributions of our two traditions to human life. Of course, in a rather literal sense, Freud is a "Buddhist" in that he seeks enlightenment about the nature of suffering. There can, I think, be no doubt on this point. And Gotama provides us with one of the most profound and thorough analyses of the nature of human experience, its sources and consequences.

The point of this work is neither Buddhism nor psychoanalysis but suffering. The fact, at least as I see it, that both traditions turn to suffering as the central issue of human life suggests that it is central and therefore that its nature is the most important subject of understanding to which we may devote ourselves. It is the human study *par excellence*.

Let me offer some summary observations on the first truth, the truth of suffering. Despite its ancient Indian origin, the presentation of the question of suffering in the classic form of the Four Ariyan Truths has universal application. This is true for a reason both obvious and fundamental, namely, that the question of whether there is suffering, especially suffering at the level of human experience with which we have been concerned—the "deepest" level, so to speak—is not easily answered in the affirmative. Indeed, the refusal to acknowledge the truth of suffering is tantamount to the cause of its continuation, and thus is critical for the truth of the cause of suffering.

When we have spoken of suffering we have not meant the suffering caused solely by external forces, but rather the suffering that involves external forces but exists in our experience. Indeed, suffering cannot be understood apart from our experience, and thus it is that both Freud and Gotama begin and end their analysis of suffering with the nature of our experience. The suffering whose truth we are concerned with, then, is in ourselves.

Thus the analysis of the world is of little significance to this first truth, and, indeed, to any of the others. The truth of suffering is a truth of the suffering in our experience. What is striking, of course, is that we largely refuse to acknowledge the locus of suffering in the self and its nature. Thus the neurotic is incapable of enjoyment and efficiency because he is denying the reality of his suffering, that is, the conflict between his desires for satisfaction and the barriers that prevent that satisfaction. That is the truth of suffering, the link between desire and ignorance, or, as we can say, repression. Symptoms are the consequences of this link. Furthermore, the truth of suffering is precisely the conflict, represented by Freud in the form of narcissistic neuroses, masochism and sadism, the perversions, psychosis and melancholia, that finds its expression in distorting, obscuring (and revealing) manifestations, just as dreams both reveal and obscure these conflicts in the life of every person.

While it is clear, as Freud pointed out on several occasions, that the study of pathology is essential, his purpose in doing so gradually became that of discovering the nature of human experience; for pathology simply revealed in a rather evident way the conflict that defined human experience after that conflict had transcended the mechanisms of control and defense that were in place in so-called "healthy" people. But the truth was not that those who were ill were aberrant in their suffering; rather, the truth was that the very nature of human experience tended toward suffering. Suffering was not simply one possibility among others in human life, it was the definition of the human experience. All is *dukkha*, the *Āgamas* report, from birth to ignorance to discomfort to death. *Dukkha* was not a deviant experience but the most common, because fundamental, one.

The suffering of which we speak here both is and depends upon illusion. This illusion is evident in the individual's concept of the self. Thus the *puthujjana*, the "ordinary person," desiring mightily a core of continuing existence, mistakenly believes that his body, his consciousness, his sensation, his continuing activities, his feelings, or any one of them is his true self. Thus deluded, he has a care for these things, wonders what has happened to him in the past, what his status is in the present, and what his future destiny will be. This worry is neurotic, for on the one hand it prevents his enjoyment and efficiency and on the other obscures the true nature of his experience.

The illusion based on desire is not limited to the individual's worry about his own destiny but constitutes the foundations of all cultural forms as well. Philosophy, religion, art, indeed, civilization in general all rest upon a profound illusion about the nature of the world and the self. The very existence of "view issues," religious beliefs and world-views is proof of the truth of suffering as illusion. For the fundamental roots of all these are wishes and desires. In fact, say Freud and Gotama, the world is not like the one depicted in the cultural artifacts. That, however, makes no difference to the neurotic, the ordinary person; for what is driving him is the very profound desire that the world be thus and such. Thought, or wish, is omnipotent.

Life cannot be lived well on the foundation of the pleasure principle. Pleasure is, as we have seen, complex. It can drive toward attraction of others to ourselves; but it can also drive toward repulsion of others. On the other hand it both heightens our sense of self-worth and inflicts sometimes irreparable damage upon ourselves and others. Furthermore, of its influences we are unconsciously, but willfully, ignorant. The tendencies toward lust, or aggrandizement, toward repulsions or destruction—toward cathexis of objects with libido and toward rejection of all relationships—are wholly integrated with our ignorance and delusion about what is actually happening to us. The pleasure principle sustains suffering because, in the last analysis, it is suffering. The realm of Māra is a burning, blazing realm whose fire feeds upon itself.

What is the cause of suffering? Briefly, no single concrete element may be identified as the cause of suffering. Rather we must speak in metaphors of development, motion, drive, process, or a cause-and-effect loop that has no single and first cause. Each of these metaphors does nevertheless have a focus—it is desire. For the cause of suffering is inseparable from desire. Without desire there is no suffering.

But this desire is, as we have seen, a complex thing. It arises from causes, it passes through vicissitudes, it advances and regresses. Moreover, it is never destroyed, though it may be transformed. The ontological status of desire is such that it cannot be said to be a quality or characteristic of anything, that is, of a person. Rather, what we mean by "person" is a consequence of desire. Both Gotama and Freud approach the question of being a person, or a self, from an analytic perspective, and discover that there is no reason to believe in a continuous, unaltered, essential *res* or *ens* which we may rightly designate as a self. This is true, both insist, despite the obvious and almost irresistible urge to find that part of our experience, our feelings, our emotions, our sensations, our physical organisms, that would be the self. That desire, furthermore, is itself a fact of the complex of suffering. On the contrary, the analysis of the self reveals that there is only a complex process of desire which throws up causes and effects we identify as these various candidates for selfhood. This is the import of the doctrine of the five grasping groups (*khandhas*), the concept of libido, the developmental theory of libido, and the vicissitudes of the instincts. The Freudian analysis of the self tells us that it "has" a structure—id, ego, super-ego. But these are simply functions of desire whose relationship is one of conflict, tension, and, possibly, balance.

Moreover, desire is, as it were, multi-directional. It is its nature to seek satisfaction, and it will do so whether in attachments to objects or in the rejection of objects. Desire is in conflict with itself, taking both sides (and at times more than one) as its manifestation. Thus desire is known in forms of love and hate, attraction and repulsion. This is the explanation for the nature of human life as conflict. Both Freud and Gotama transcend the rather simplistic proposition that suffering is the result of conflict between external world and the desire of the person, and find the conflict not only there but in the nature of the self as well. The analysis of suffering, in other words, leads ultimately to the analysis of desire. It is worth pointing out again that when we speak of desire we do not mean only sexuality in the sense that civilization understands it. The issue here is with Freud; and when Freud spoke of sexuality he meant the entire scope of libidinal development. In the context of his economy of the psyche this development is identical to the entire range of desire, through the vicissitudes of the instincts, narcissism, sadism and masochism, being in love, the emotional foundation of all social relationships, eros and thanatos. The vocabulary he employs, including the notion of sexual development, vicissitudes of forces he called instincts, the concept of ego libido, of object-cathexis, and others, should not mislead us; for his task is to explain human suffering as a consequence of desire in all its forms and transformations. This is the insight of Gotama as well. The fundamental insight of both traditions is identical—that the cause of suffering is desire, and that desire and nothing else determines the form and content of our suffering lives.

Desire is, of course, not merely conscious desire. As we have seen in some detail, in rejecting the common notion that the self is identical with our conscious self-perception at any given moment, both traditions look to a fundamental process, of which the momentary self-consciousness is but an effect, for their understanding of desire and its link with suffering. Freud speaks of the unconscious, the most important insight he has to offer. Gotama, who finds consciousness to be but one part of the co-dependent series of origination and one of the khandhas, points to the "latent tendencies" (anusayas) of desire, which play a very significant role in the vicissitudes of desire. He also understands the āsavas, the persistent tendencies, to be so deeply rooted that even the most disciplined persons find them an almost insuperable barrier to complete self-understanding. Desire is not, then, simply conscious desire—indeed, the notion of the "conscious" is an effect of desire. To speak of desire as unconscious, to speak of latent tendencies, is only to speak of desire seen in a broader context than that of consciousness. Indeed, it is to speak of desire in its fullest sense, and to relegate conscious desire to a secondary if revealing role in the economy of desire.

Whatever we call the self, whether we speak of ego or attā, is desire in its manifestations and process. In order to understand suffering, there-fore, we must understand the entire realm of the conflict of desire, not simply that of which we are conscious. As we understand more fully the implications of this truth it becomes clear, furthermore, that conscious desire is determined in its nature just as much by "ignorance," that is to say, distortion, repression and resistance, as by the full ramifications of the conflict of desire. Conscious desire obscures as much as it reveals. This, argues Freud, is the function of the "mechanisms of defense" in the ego.

Desire is multifarious, supremely so. It takes the forms that it does, however, not because of any external controlling factor. Given the onto-logical status of desire there can be no external controlling factor. The whole of the arising and the cessation of suffering is to be found in the economy of desire. This is the essential message of the teaching of the series of co-dependent origination. There is no causal factor nor any ef-fect extraneous to that series. Furthermore, the process of analysis may be initiated at any point in the series, although some points are favored over others in the tradition. Contrary to our own usual "false views" the world, or external reality, or even stimulus, is not a cause of suffering. As Freud pointed out the significance of the world (as *Ananke*, harsh reality) lies solely in our experience of it, not in its own nature. It is the conflict we experience, not the world; and that conflict is a function of desire, an element of the economy of attraction and rejection. Gotama's analysis of the world begins and ends with the power of our sensory experience in the context of desire; and thus the world is in fact the world as we experience it, compelled by our craving and grasping. The end of the world means the end of our sensations within the economy of *dukkha*.

Only those who are imprisoned by false views are concerned about the existence, the arising, the future of the world, just as the concern for God or Providence and its nature rests solely upon an illusion arising out of our wishes. The reality lies not beyond us in a world or in heaven but in the nature and conflict of desire. It is a hallmark of human suffering that this truth is rejected in favor of more palliating beliefs. The analysis of desire implies, then, an understanding of the relationship beween causes and effects. Both traditions reject any "misplaced concretions;" both hold to the doctrines of *anicca* and *anattā*. There is no "First Cause" in the analysis of suffering and its links with desire, for desire is, on the one hand, the fundamental reality and, on the other, not a thing at all. Freud may search for the biological origins of the instincts; but his concern is with human suffering, and in that context there is no first cause, only the vicissitudes of instincts. In the analysis of desire there is no Kantian principle of causality; there are only causes and effects of desire. Nothing arises without a cause, says Gotama; and there is no cause that is not also an effect in the economy of desire. This, both argue, is our experience, rightly understood. Philosophical issues of causality are irrelevant and misleading. For the belief in an uncaused cause is simply an exercise in illusion, a childish desire for a universe in which it is not necessary to face the reality of desire and of suffering. Further, if this understanding of desire threatens our hopes for permanent stability in our experience—

and in the world—that is simply because there is nothing in the analysis of desire to suggest that such a state is a reasonable expectation. Rather, we know, because of that analysis, that such an expectation is, again, an illusion, the desire for the fulfillment of a wish. And, as with all other illusions, so long as we maintain our commitment to it we shall suffer precisely because it is an illusion, that is, inconsistent with an intractable reality. The dynamic nature of desire can never be denied; and, strangely, once this is understood, there is calm.

If the momentary self-consciousness is but a ramification of the dynamic of desire, what is the scope, the range of desire's cause-effect relationship? In apparently different ways, both traditions come finally to the conclusion that the range is not limited to an individual—a suspiciously convenient fiction—and therefore extends infinitely forward and backward. Gotama, using the vocabulary of *kamma/karma* and *saṃsāra*, of the continuous working out of effects, was more comfortable with this conclusion than Freud, it appears. This is not difficult to understand, given the two views of history operative in the different traditions. It was already evident to Gotama that one's existence could not be limited to one's direct experience or even memory of it. But Freud comes to a conclusion in his own analysis of suffering that at the very least is analogous. If the notion of the unconscious, or at least the notion of the limitations of consciousness, were to be taken seriously, then one could not explain the suffering of neurotics—and by extension all persons—by any one event or any series of events and wishes that was limited to the experience of an individual. The evidence suggested that only by the introduction of the notion of a racial memory of events in a "suspiciously distant" past could events in the present be explained. The concept of the ontogenetic recapitulation of phylogeny, or the integration of a racial with an individual memory, extended Freud's analysis of desire to a very distant past. It is remarkable, at least at first, to confront Freud's vigorous insistence on the events of that distant past; and one only comprehends what he means when it is understood that psychic events are real events whose consequences never disappear. Thus he challenges the notion of history of his time. In so doing he shares the insight of Gotama, namely, that the dynamic of desire transcends any concepts of merely external history in its comprehensive power over human life. Further, this infinite temporal scale of desire is consonant with the position in both traditions—more evident in Freud's thought but clearly implied in the Pāli tradition—that the analysis of desire is neither psychology nor sociology. That is, it is an analysis that does not distinguish between individual and group behavior. Further, it recognizes the individual as neither more nor less than a locus, or loci, in a series of co-dependent origination, susceptible to infinite analysis. In other terms, neither explains individuals as opposed to groups, nor *vice versa*, but rather desire, of which individuals and groups are consequences and manifestations. The individual is, of course, the most significant manifestation. No attempts to describe a separate ontology for groups can succeed, for groups and their behavior are simply variations on the fundamental theme of the conflict of desire.

Finally, while desire is a cause of suffering, the most significant quality of that suffering, from the point of view of one who suffers, is ignorance. Ignorance means not only not knowing in some intellectual sense that suffering rests upon desire, but also doing the work of obscuring that truth. There is, as both Freud and Gotama point out, a deliberate activity devoted to this end, or, we should say, a multitude of deliberate activities. These activities, which include dream work, distortion, repression, resistance, confusion, *moha*, are not at all confined to deliberate conscious choice—an activity of which we may now be rightly suspicious if some "pure" form of it devoid of unconscious forces is meant. Gotama speaks of latent tendencies toward confusion as well as toward love and hate; Freud speaks of resistance, repression, regression, and symptom formation. All of these are consequences of desire. That is to say, the ignorance concerning the truth of suffering and its link with desire is itself a consequence of desire.

The unguarded *citta*, like the ego, is drawn toward false goals, and thus rejects the truth of suffering. The ego itself prefers, even wishes mightily, not to confront its own sources, found in the desires of the id; and the unguarded *citta* allows corrupting attachments and repulsion to render ineffective its pristine and clear role as conduit to the nature of things as they are, and functions as a barrier. Both unguarded *citta* and ego obscure even as they reveal. Objects of desire, whether noble in the eye of civilization or not, loom as attractions toward which the individual struggles. Each struggle serves only to perpetuate the ignorance of the nature of desire. We can neither enjoy nor work efficiently; our energies are sapped and our understanding disintegrates in the struggle for these empty, illusory, attainments. This ignorance is "deliberate," for it is in the nature of desire and its internal conflict that one side will seek to overcome the other; and in the process we do not know what is happening. The penalty for this ignorance is suffering.

The truth of the end of suffering is the guarantee that there is an end to suffering. Both Freud and Gotama find in their analysis of the arising of suffering the promise of its end. Gotama's frequently stated declaration that if suffering did not arise from the human experience, but lay somehow and somewhere beyond it, the Path, the Life would be proclaimed in vain, illustrates very well how dependent the two truths of the arising and the cessation of suffering are. Freud's apparently minimalist assertion that the task of analysis is to raise what is unconscious into the conscious, to replace repression with judgement, and to convert neurotic misery into ordinary unhappiness rests upon the same basis, that suffering arises from the nature of the human life and experience—not from anywhere else—and for that reason it is susceptible to "cure." Just what cure means in this context is a question we should pursue.

The most revealing metaphors from the Buddhist tradition regarding the truth of the end of suffering are, first, that of the man standing on the edge of the clear pool in which he can see everything within clearly and without distortion—the shoals of fish, the rocks and shells—, and second, the metaphor of the refining of gold by removing all of its impurities, gross and fine, and heating it so that it becomes supple and pliant. The major points of interpretation are, respectively for the two metaphors: (1) the absence of any distortion in our vision—indeed, our sensing—of reality, and thus the absence of any sources of distortion, with the result that we see, absolutely clearly, things as they really are, not as we wish them to be (with all the consequences of that desire); (2) the notion of "cure" as refinement, cleansing and freeing from any particular form the quintessential nature of humankind.

The truth of the end of suffering, in other words, means in essence that we are cured when nothing of our desires stands between us and seeing things as they really are, on the one hand, and on the other when our essential nature is free of all distortions and particularities and is simply there, supple and pliant. There is a sense in which, then, suffering really means our (self-imposed) and willful failure to see that we are transparent, like the water of the pool. The end of suffering, therefore, is this end of that willful failure to understand our true selves. As Freud expressed this truth, it is not as though a patient is waiting for the analyst to put him back together again, like Humpty-Dumpty. Rather, once repression is ended and the resistances removed—and in those very accomplishments—the person is whole again, precisely by virtue of the end of repression and resistance, of distortion of self-understanding and understanding of the world arising from the conflict of his desire. The truth of the end of suffering means the restoration of the original state of things, so to speak, that is, the original ideal of the person.

We may say what is probably not true of such a state, as well as what is true. Despite what is commonly thought about the state of *nibbāna*, for example, the Buddhist tradition does not say that one who has attained the Cool ceases to sense, perceive, think, act, or enter into relations with people. Nor, obviously, can it be said that death is the ideal state, or some state beyond death. Rather, as the Buddhist tradition puts it, one who is released knows that he senses, knows what it is that he perceives, and only that. In the seen there is only the seen, in what is heard only that which is heard, and so also for the other senses. One ceases to be a patient afflicted with symptoms, bound by repressions, enervated by resistance, and becomes one who fully understands the nature and source of his feelings. This knowledge is not some arcane or "mystic"

wisdom, but knowledge of the self. One continues to have feelings, ev
to experience pain and pleasure; but one knows that the experience
of pain and pleasure and no more. Obsession with pain and pleasure
exists no longer; it is replaced by judgement. The ordinary conflicts of
life are faced clearly and without illusion, set on a plane where they can
be addressed.

One who is freed, according to both traditions, knows that he is
freed, is no longer beset by doubt, no longer wondering what happened
to him in the past, and what will happen to him in the future. He is not
arrogant, or even necessarily omniscient (although both the Buddhist and
Freudian traditions admit that a person who is sensitive to the nature of
suffering and to the conflict of desire may recognize the state of release
or bondage in another person, just as the analyst is able to comprehend
the difficulties in which his patient finds himself by virtue of his own
self-understanding of the conflict of desire.) Rather, he knows his own
motives, he does not confuse his wishes with what is true of his experience
in the world. In knowing this, and in knowing that he knows, he is
freed. In other words, both traditions identify the enlightened person, the
person enlightened about his own nature, with the happy person—although
happiness here does not mean the absence of pain and the presence of
pleasure; that is precisely the illusion upon which the neurotic and the
"ordinary" person builds his life, with the results now familiar to us.

It is said that we need illusion to help us through life. This means,
in both traditions, that we need to believe that, to some minimal extent,
life is consistent with our wishes regardless of whether this is in fact
true. Religion, for example, is an illusion that has therapeutic value at
times. But both traditions insist that the truth of the end of suffering
moves beyond this compromise with the truth, insisting that human life
is not fully and finally complete until even those therapeutic illusions are
seen for what they are, expressions of what we wish were true. Neither
tradition denies the reality of wishes or their power, nor does either call
for the end of wishing. What is demanded is the knowledge of the nature
of a wish, the end of confusion about what is a wish and what is reality.
One must not only see only what is there, one must also be able to
distinguish between what is there and what it is that is wished to be
there. Only then can one be called free.

What sort of person are we describing? It is a person without illusions. (How revealing it is that most of us think of such a person as
cynical, thus illustrating the depth of commitment to illusions in the
quest for happiness!) Such a person's relationship with other people is
distorted neither by love nor hate; for other people are no longer regarded
as occasions for the fulfillment of desire, whether that desire be aggressive
or affectionate. On the other hand such a person's self-understanding is
clear-sighted and not determined by the dominance of one side or the

other in the conflict of desire. Such a person is not pathologically narcissistic. Rather, in relations with others he knows who and what they are, and treats them with sympathy and compassion. He does not use them to fulfill his own obscure desires but regards them as worthy in and of themselves. He does not make them into more or less than they are in his knowledge of and experience with them. Relations with others, then, are not refused; indeed, it is in the relations with others that the self finds one part of its balance. The other part is the relationship with what we may call the self, for the moment. One's relationship with the self is neither narcissistic nor melancholic. One's relationship with others is neither aggressive or dependent. It is, rather, "friendly," that is, full of sympathy and compassion, but not lust, and is consistent with the full understanding of the nature of the self and thus of all selves. One is equable, serene, and undeceived about himself and others. He does not injure by word, thought or deed. He does not seek preference. He does not hold views simply because others hold them. He is not afraid, either of life or death.

This state of release–although one may rightly object, I think, to calling it a "state"–may be described as that which follows the end of confusion of feelings or emotions concerning what is real with that which is real. Neither Freud nor Gotama is particularly interested in metaphysics. Gotama says that there is no difference among the many manifestations of existence since they are all *anicca*, impermanent. Freud speaks of reality in terms of *Ananke*, harsh reality, thereby designating reality as that which by nature comes into conflict with our wishes eventually. More than that does not interest him. The implication for both is that knowing the true nature of human desire is tantamount to knowing the difference between one's feelings and anything else one perceives–the end of illusion. To know fully this difference is to know fully and at the same time the self and the world. Speculation about the nature of world is pointless. It always arises out of wishes; and when the true nature is known, the world is instantly known for what it is, directly and without distortion, as the metaphor of the clear pool teaches. But the chief issue here is that one is freed precisely because he is no longer deceived about the true nature of his wishes, or about the conflict and economy of desire. That is exactly what the "Truth of the End of Suffering" means.

Thus *nibbāna* is not a place and, in Nāgārjuna's thought, not a place any different from the turning of life's wheel, *saṃsāra*. *Nibbāna* is that "point" at which the confusion about the depth and nature of desire ends, when the *āsavas* are worn away, when the resistances are removed. The physical, sensing, thinking, perceiving and acting elements of experience are recognized for what they are. None is grasped as the "essential self," in the false hope for continuing existence.

The unconscious, or "latent conceits," *anusayas*, lose their power because they cease to be latent, or unconscious. One who is freed realizes that he has wished for things and wished in ways of which he was ignorant, and over which he had no control. Now, knowing, he is no longer bound to them. Furthermore the piling up of consequences of blind and ignorant desire of all kinds is reversed. Now the consequence is emptiness, *suññatā*, the absence of any remainder of the consequences of ignorant desire, of the *āsavas*, and all the characteristics of the series of co-dependent origination. In other words, knowing the origins of all things he knows also the origins of the end of all things. All things are, inevitably, *dukkha*; thus the enlightened person, the free person, is one empty of the consequences of *dukkha*, who has experienced *dukkhanirodha*, the annihilation of the arising of suffering. For him there are no more consequences; and, like the *Tathāgata*, it cannot be said that he exists, that he does not exist, that he both exists and does not exist, and that he neither exists nor does not exist. The question of what happens to him is, no more than the question of what happens to one who has successfully brought what is unconscious into the conscious, not a "fit" question, for it is mere speculation, a "view issue" (*diṭṭhigata*).

The person who is freed transcends the scope of any psychological theories, any systems, whether freely accepted or imposed by civilization. His behavior is governed by his nature and not by any external force. In this he is no longer a child but an adult. He is, very likely, a threat to civilization, for he has seen the shaky foundations, forged out of compromise in the conflict of desire, upon which civilization, conventional morality, and accepted definitions of truth are constructed. He is the *Tathāgata*, the One with the Nature of Suchness, whose knowledge and love of the truth about himself and the world must perforce overwhelm the usual illusions, lies and compromises of culture. He is neither good nor bad; he is neither happy nor unhappy, in any conventional sense; he simply knows, and knows that he knows. The core of his being is an adamantine plane, eternal and unconquerable.

The truth of the cause of the end of suffering is the reverse of the truth of the cause of the arising of suffering. This is the insight offered by Freud in his archeological investigation of the origins of neurosis for both individual and society. It is the insight offered by the Buddha in the investigation of the origins of suffering in the series of co-dependent origination and its reversal. One must return to the origins, one must analyze all causes. In so doing suffering is replaced with knowledge. Further, there is no other path, no other way to be pursued; nothing is added, nothing taken away. The cause of the end of suffering is exactly the cause of the end of suffering, but with a reversed casual flow.

The way or passage to the end of suffering is that by which this reversal is achieved. Success means, as both traditions insist, not merely to know in some informational or objective sense the facts of the cause of suffering. This is, in Freud's terms, merely a resistance in which the patient becomes engrossed in psychoanalytic theory and technique; or, in Gotama's terms, it means to accept a statement as true simply because some one else says that it is true. Such a method is no more productive than hypnosis, by which the analyst is able to uncover the traumatic events central to the arising of the patient's suffering that are hidden first from the patient himself and then from the analyst. It is useful to the analyst, not to the patient. The *Arahant* or the *Tathāgata* may know the state of bondage of an ordinary person–but this is of no use to the ordinary person, even were the *Arahant* to tell him what is true.

The method must be one in which the patient, the one who does not yet know, confronts the truth about himself *in his own experience.* He must experience joy and know that it is joy, experience pain and know that it is pain, must know objects seen, heard, touched, smelled, tasted and imagined, and know that they are such objects and nothing more. He must know that he has desired the destruction or building up of objects. He must look to his past moments and know what happened, know who and how he was. He must confront his own motives, and his attempts to hide them, as well as his repressions of his deeds and wishes. And he must bring to an end the resistances to this understanding of his past. He must come to know what he did not want to know. All of this must happen to him, must become a part of his own biography.

The experience of the analyst, the Buddha, the *Arahant,* or any other person has no ultimate significance in the truth of the cause of the end of suffering. The analyst, the Buddha, the *Dhamma* simply insist upon the truth of the Path, which leads along the series of causal links in the individual's experience. That truth is that the end of suffering can be found only in the context of the arising of suffering. Both Freud and Gotama followed that path; and that is what each individual must do for himself. Both traditions teach, on the basis of experience, that there is a need for another, whether analyst or traditional techniques, to reduce the risk of self-deception as much as possible. But in the end the patient cures himself.

The stages of the path, or the techniques of the ending of suffering are, of necessity, drawn from the nature of suffering. One begins with the fact of ignorance, indeed, of amnesia, whether with respect to traumatic events and wishes of childhood or of the link between desire, behavior and suffering (for this link is "forgotten" too). There is a need to uncover the causal relations to which we are willingly blind in our desire to live according to the pleasure principle. The initial and fundamental method in both traditions is to regard with utterly uncommitted attention, with a complete absence of prejudice and willfulness, the content of our sensations, memories, actions, motives–indeed the whole of the content of our "selves." As is the case with the "fundamental method" of psychoanaly-

sis, this is both straightforward and exceptionally difficult. How di
it is is clear in the dialogues of both traditions. It is immediately (
that, on the one hand, the ordinary person regards as true only wha.
he wishes to be true, and on the other that his interlocutor steadfastly
refuses to allow such self-deception to continue unopposed. The agony of
the conflict between what is and what is wished instantly arises—and the
agony persists until there is no longer any reason for it to persist, that
is, until the conflict no longer exists. But what a difficult passage!

The disease itself is the cause of the cure. No compromise is permitted along the way, no minor victories of battle in this great war. Freud
and Gotama find in the frustration of the one *in via* the energy to bring
the work of cure to fruition. Therefore the privation, or asceticism of
denial of mediate fruits, is itself the driving force leading to the goal.
One must refuse the satisfactions inherent in the pleasure principle up
to the very end; and in so doing he is drawn along the path toward full
understanding. However heroic the achievements of self-understanding,
so long as the monk believes that he has achieved them the goal has not
been reached; only when the resistances are encountered in their fullest
and most mature force can the patient realize the true nature and depth
of his willful self-deception. Until that point is reached, until the *āsavas*
are worn down, until the resistances are broken, the frustration and privation inherent in the discipline of the path must be borne and employed.
The power to stay the course is drawn from the disease itself, until its
ultimate depths are plumbed. The end of the cause of suffering is reached
when those causes no longer have any power. That is the same thing as
saying that their true nature is known. The consequence of this discovery is, to employ the Buddhist terminology, that useful and constructive
motives replace unuseful and destructive motives, or, to use Freud's terminology, that the energy devoted to the formation of symptoms and the
mechanisms of defense now become available to the ego for the purpose
of establishing a stable and integrated organization of the person. It is
not the case that the patient awaits some new principle, force, or external
power, to be made available by the analyst. Rather, by experiencing in
a conscious mode the causes of suffering, by placing the conflict of desire
and all its elements on the equal footing of conscious choice the causes of
suffering are replaced by the causes of the end of suffering. As the carpenter knocks out a larger peg with a smaller one, so the causes are reversed;
and now the commitment is to the end of suffering and not its building up.

Going through to the end of suffering does not mean that minor
victories are not achieved along the way. The Eight-fold Path holds out
possibilities for those who seek to correct their behavior in their own
society. One may learn not to steal, not to kill, not to eat too much,
not to depend upon magical and mystical devices, and to think, act and
speak clearly and morally. Analyses do come to termination when the

patient no longer insists upon anti- social or asocial behavior. But that is not the end of suffering for either tradition. In addressing the question of whether analysis was interminable Freud suggests that the root causes of suffering lay in character, or rather, in the nature of the self. While particular symptoms may be allayed by analysis, the fundamental causes of suffering itself require an "interminable" analysis. Eschewing cheap solutions, Freud insisted that, consistent with his analysis of the nature of human life, the end of suffering lies in nothing less than a complete understanding by the individual concerned of the whole of his nature. This task requires the complete attention of a mature person, who is free of self-deception. Analysis is indeed interminable if it is to be understood in terms of the full implications for the end of suffering.

The Buddhist tradition, too, finds right concentration and wisdom (pañña) to be essential to full enlightenment. Thus the monk, having freed himself from desires conducive to suffering, must devote an increasing share of his energies to understanding the nature of his life. This task is expressed in the traditional Indian terms of meditation, the jhanic states and spheres, from aloofness from sense desire to the cessation of both perception and non-perception. But Western and modern readers should not be misled by the unfamiliar terminology. The goal is the same as that of Freud—namely, the full and complete understanding of the nature of the self. Moreover, although in both traditions the "emptiness" or process or impermanence of that self is to be plumbed to its depths, even to the point of denying the denial of perception and non-perception, its return to the full experience of life in its most ordinary sense—in Freud's terms, ordinary unhappiness—is the mark of full liberation. Here we understand Nāgārjuna's equation of saṃsāra and nirvāṇa. No "other world" can be the aim, for no end of suffering may be separated from the cause of suffering. In the end neither religion nor the highest stages of meditation constitutes an ultimate goal. The goal is to replace neurotic misery with ordinary unhappiness, to see in the seen only what is seen.

One may ask whether the ordinary person is capable of this. The answer, despite millenia of tradition, must be yes. This must be so, since the origins of the end of suffering lie in the origins of the arising of suffering, since the arising and the cessation of suffering are the definitive, whole and complete truths of human life. No one is exempt, no one is unqualified. Some, it would seem, have no sense of suffering; and for them the task seems insuperable. There are Jains, who are convinced that by their own actions they can annihilate their desires, rather than converting them into the desire for truth, reversing the series of co-dependent origination; there is the psychotic, for whom the world is fully a construct of his own wishes in the context of the conflict of desire. The rest know something is wrong—that is to say, they are aware of suffering that no amount of alteration of external circumstances can cure.

486

That knowledge, however misguided (as in the case of symptoms) is the key to the end of suffering. This is, then, the most general sense in which the truth of the end of suffering is the truth of suffering itself.

It must be asked whether there is really the same message to be found in the two traditions, since the Buddhist tradition in the texts we have examined is eminently a monastic tradition. In response, on the one hand, the advantage the monk has over the layperson in the Buddhist tradition has nothing to do with the truth of the arising of suffering, or indeed with any of the other truths. Those truths exist for all. Further, the monk is simply one who has learned to devote more of his energy to pursuing the Four Truths than the layperson. The path is no different; and it is by no means limited to monks. One does not attain *nibbāna* because he is a monk but because the causes of suffering have been reversed. That is, of course, the goal of the monk as well. But, as we have seen, withdrawal from ordinary social intercourse constitutes no guarantee of success. Indeed, it is possible to pass through all the stages or the succession of stages leading to *samādhi* and fail because of thinking that "I" have performed all of these heroic spiritual deeds.

On the other hand, the psychoanalytic tradition calls for privation and sustaining of ever higher levels of frustration (or self-denial) in order to learn that life may not be fully lived in obedience to the pleasure principle. Freud's warnings against asceticism apply generally. Asceticism as a *Weltanschauung* may be neurotic in nature; and, perhaps, here is a parallel with the Buddha's warnings against the pursuit of *samādhi* itself as an end, with its concomitant failure to distinguish between it and true release. Any goal, that is to say, that is less than full understanding, full raising of the unconscious to the conscious, less than the end of any "latent" conceits, possessed of any blindness to the consequences of the principle of self-satisfaction, is intermediate and preliminary. Confusion on this issue is a danger in both traditions.

In short, the monk's life is beset with as many perils as the layperson's, even if they are apparently more sophisticated. We must take care not to confuse the sociological consequences of the routinization of charisma (in Max Weber's terms) with the real point of the teaching about the difficulties attendant upon the householder's life; that point is the dangers of desire for pleasure, for pain, for delusion. Those dangers are present also for the monk. But the monk and the psychoanalytic patient have, for reasons unique to each individual (and that idiosyncrasy of motive is very clear in both traditions), turned to a life of abstinence and privation–whether it entails living in a monastic setting or devoting five or so hours a week to a rigorous and painful examination of his or her feelings and their origins and a suspension of some ordinary relationships (and, incidentally, at some material cost to both).

Finally, the relationship between the truth of the arising of suffering and the cessation of suffering cannot be exaggerated. From the perspective of the Fourth Noble Truth this means, at the very least, that, although there is a path, each must follow it in his own way; for the origins of suffering are personal, and the end of suffering is personal. Both traditions are highly suspicious of methods, mechanics, and medicines—to say nothing of mysticism. One must confront oneself—only there are the four truths known. To be able to recite the poetry, the prose, the "Thus have I Heard's," and so forth, means nothing in the end. To have read and recited the whole history of psychoanalysis has merely academic significance. It is of the highest significance that there exists a tradition that holds up the truths of suffering, of which most of us are wilfully ignorant. But we must, as the Buddhist tradition insists, cross the Stream of Becoming ourselves, even if we ride the raft of the *Dhamma*; and once on the other side, the raft is of no further use. Or, as Freud says, the patient is not waiting for the analyst to put him back together again; he will accomplish that task himself. Who else could do it for him?

Yet there is but one mind in the *Sangha*; and ontogeny recapitulates phylogeny. The Four Truths apply to the individual and the group. Here a number of observations are in order. First, suffering is not atomistic, any more than existence is atomistic in the sense of the materialist philosophers. The Four Truths are universal; and in that alone atomism is denied. "Personal" is not a synonym for "atomistic." Nor, on the other hand, do we need to believe in an Over-Soul, or a Universal Monad; both traditions deny such a conclusion outright as having no basis in experience. Third, however, the continuity of which we speak in the analysis of suffering is of cause and effect, of process, of co-dependent origination. It has already been said that, given this truth of suffering, there is no such entity as an eternal, continuing *res* or *ens*; the belief in such is clearly the consequence of illusion. The conclusion applies equally to both individual and collective entitities, to an individual/collective entity, or to a Nothingness, a Void that is not also a Pleroma (Nāgārjuna's analysis of emptiness makes this point clear). This is true; and therefore the distinction between individual and collective fails in light of the analysis of suffering. The truths of suffering are neither psychological nor sociological truths—that distinction is in fact a consequence of wishful thinking (contrast Voltaire and Marx for an exercise in such thinking). Gotama expresses this insight in terms of *kamma* and *saṃsāra*, Freud in terms of ontogeny and phylogeny. But the fundamental truth is the same; the nature of suffering is the fundamental truth, and whether it is approached from the preconceptions about individual suffering or collective suffering makes no difference; and the distinction is, indeed, merely a matter of speculation, *diṭṭhigata*.

Thus we return to the statement that suffering is personal and therefore the end of suffering is personal. There is no me, no mine, no I—there is only suffering and the end of suffering. The I, me, mine, ego, id, super-ego, and their social manifestations, are consequences of suffering, and the knowledge of their true nature has the end of suffering as its consequence.

The only reality is the arising and the cessation of suffering. *Nirvāṇa* is *saṃsāra*.

GLOSSARY OF SELECTED PĀLI TERMS

Abhijjā, covetousness
Abhisambodhi, The Highest Enlightenment
Āhāra, food, nutriment
Ahiṃsā, non-hurtfulness, kindness
Ājiva, livelihood, means of subsistence
Ākāsa, sky; space
Ākiñcañña, nothingness, *i.e.* neither-perception-nor-non-perception
Akusala, non-useful, non-helpful
Anāgāmi, Never-returner; third of four stages of breaking through to Arahantship
Anattā, not a soul, without a soul
Anicca, impermanence
Anusaya, latent proclivity
Arahant, one who has attained *Nibbāna*
Ariya, noble, distinguished
Āsava, barrier to highest understanding, *e.g.* greed, hatred and ignorance
Asmimāna, pride of self, egoism
Attā, soul (Sanskrit: *Ātman*)
Avijjā, ignorance

Bhava, becoming, *i.e.* a life
Bhavataṇhā, desire for becoming in a life
Bhikkhu, monk, ascetic; fem. *Bhikkhunī*
Bodhi, supreme knowledge of a *Buddha*
Buddha, One who has attained enlightenment and is superior to all other beings in this respect

Cakkhu, eye, both as sense-organ and as faculty of normal and supersensory perception
Cetanā, will, intention
Chanda, desire
Chandarāga, exciting desire
Citta, mind, heart; the center of emotion and intellect

Deva, God
Dhātu, form of being; condition
Dhamma, The Norm; the Truth
Diṭṭhi, view, belief, dogma
Diṭṭhigata, false opinion or belief; sophistical speculation
Dosa, hatred
Dukkha, suffering

491

Ekodhoti, one-pointedness (of thought)

Jarāmaraṇa, old age and death
Jāti, birth, rebirth, former life
Jhāna, one of a series of stages of increasing enhancement of awareness, leading to release

Kāma, pleasure
Kāmataṇhā, desire for pleasure
Kamma, an action; action in general as productive of consequences (Sanskrit: *Karma*)
Karuṇā, compassion
Kāya, body, especially seen as it truly is
Khandha, a collection or mass, usually one of five, *i.e.* name-and-form, consciousness, feeling, sensation and perception
Kilesa/Klesa, taint; vice
Kusala, useful, helpful

Lobha, greed
Loka, a world; a division of the world

Magga, path, way; The Path
Mahāyāna, Buddhist movement distinguished by denial that only ascetics could attain *Nibbāna*
Māna, conceit, pride
Mano, mind as one of six senses; the activity of thinking
Māra, The Tempter; world of rebirth as opposed to *Nibbāna*
Mettā, friendliness
Mettacitta, a friendly and sympatethic heart
Moha, delusion, bewilderment

Nāmarūpa, name-and-shape; the individual as an whole
Nibbāna, extinction, as of a flame, of all causes of hindrance to the end of *dukkha* (Sanskrit: *Nirvāṇa*)
Nirodha, cessation; annihilation

Paññā, wisdom, insight
Papañca, obstacle, impediment; obsession
Parinibbāna, "complete" *Nibbāna*, with no further bases for rebirth (Sanskrit: *Parinirvāṇa*)
Paṭiccasamuppāda, (series of) co-dependent origination
Paṭigha, repugnance, anger
Phassa, contact, especially among object, sense and perception

492

Puthujjana, ordinary unlearned person

Rāga, excitement, passion
Rūpa, material form

Saḷāyatana, the six organs of sense and their objects (including mind and ideas)
Samādhi, a concentrated, intent state of mind
Saṃsāra, transmigration
Sangha, The Community of followers of the *Dhamma* and the *Buddha*
Sankhāra, activity; all action, as part of the *paṭiccasamuppāda* series
Saññā, sense perception, consciousness
Satī, mindfulness
Sīla, good character, virtue
Sīlabbatupādāna, grasping after works and rites
Sotāpanna, stream-entrant; first of four stages to Arahantship
Sukha, pleasant; joy (n)
Suññatā, emptiness (Sanskrit: *Śūnyata*)

Taṇhā, craving, desire
Tathāgata, one who has attained the Truth
Theravāda, early Buddhist movement (originally called *Hīnayāna*) that insisted upon ascetic practices to attain *Nibbāna*

Upādāna, grasping after, holding onto

Vacī, speech
Vedanā, feeling, sensation
Vibhava, power, prosperity
Vibhavataṇhā, desire for power and prosperity; desire for annihilation
Vihāra, staying in a place, living
Vimutti, release, deliverance
Viññāṇa, general consciousness, animation
Virāga, indifference
Viriya, vigor, energy
Vitakka, reflection, thought, thinking

Index

Cakkhu (*cf.* Eye), 139, 267.

Canker (*cf. Āsava*), 160, 265, 266, 299, 358, 364, 365, 367, 371, 374-376, 382, 388, 389, 393, 399, 444, 453-457, 463, 467, 469.

Case Histories, 26, 73, 86, 174, 184, 418, 418n.

Castration, 28, 40-41, 43, 51, 57, 104, 109, 115, 179, 208-210, 248, 257, 324.

Categorical Imperative, 84, 88, 213, 228.

Cathexis, 47, 60, 174, 175, 189, 199, 203, 214, 215, 226, 227, 229, 237, 239, 247, 317, 329-331, 419, 424-426, 429, 430, 475, 476.

Censor, 19, 24, 25, 30, 50, 168, 206, 219.

Cetanā (*cf.* Will), 160, 265, 267, 277, 290, 301, 305-306, 308, 379, 442, 444.

Chanda (*cf.* Desire), 140, 141, 271, 273, 299, 359, 390, 391, 446.

Chandarāga, 139, 146, 162, 272, 290, 293, 299, 359.

Character (Analysis), 433, 486.

Christianity, 103, 125.

Church, 68, 71, 122, 123, 126.

Circumcision, 41, 99, 100, 102, 104.

Citta (Heart/Mind), 131-133, 136, 138, 141-143, 160, 275, 299-300, 361-363, 366, 367, 370, 372, 373, 375, 376, 382-384, 389-393, 441, 444, 446-448, 454, 460, 465, 470, 479.

Civilization, 16, 17, 32, 35, 36, 52, 55, 59, 66, 67, 71, 71-82, 82-85, 90, 94, 97-99, 101, 108, 112, 115, 116, 119, 171, 172, 175, 176, 180, 185-187, 190, 192, 193, 200, 206, 207, 210, 243, 254, 255, 332n, 343-346, 349, 414, 474, 476, 479, 483.

Clitoral (Clitoris), 201, 202, 327.

Co-Dependent Origination (*cf. Paṭiccasamuppāda*), 9, 134, 145, 147, 159-163, 261, 262, 262-270, 271, 272, 274, 278, 279, 281, 288, 290, 293, 297, 306-308, 314, 355, 373, 395, 397, 400, 440, 441, 443, 444, 448, 476-478, 483, 486, 488.

Comic, 49.

Compassion (*Karuṇā*), 389-394, 403, 482.

Complemental Series, 34, 115, 179-181, 342.

Compulsive (Compulsion), 28, 49, 77, 101, 102, 105, 172, 228, 232, 253, 258, 333, 350, 412, 415.

Conceit (Pride; *cf. Māna*), 136, 139, 147, 155, 261, 279, 280-281, 303, 305, 359, 368, 380, 381, 449, 467.

Condemnation, 30, 31, 173, 209.

Conscious, 8, 20-22, 26, 28, 30, 31, 33, 36, 46, 50, 60, 63, 64, 66, 81, 82, 89, 99, 101, 111, 118, 120, 165-170, 173, 175, 176, 185, 188, 194, 195, 219, 220, 229, 244-246, 256, 258, 260, 316, 321, 325, 326, 334, 336, 338, 344, 348, 352, 353, 407, 408-409, 410, 416, 418, 425, 427, 428, 431, 436, 476, 479, 483, 485, 487.

Consciousness, 18, 25, 30, 62, 63, 81, 165-170, 189, 190, 197, 205, 210, 219, 220, 225, 243, 244, 316, 340, 348, 408, 410, 411, 415, 421, 424, 427, 431, 478.

Consciousness (*cf. Viññāṇa*), 8, 142, 144-148, 157, 159-163, 264-271, 273, 275-280, 287, 291, 292, 296-298, 301, 305, 306, 309, 355, 357, 360, 361, 367-374, 375, 378, 379-381, 384, 385, 388, 442-444, 448, 452, 454, 456, 463, 473, 475.

Constitution (-al), 35, 67, 74, 102, 191, 238, 332, 336, 341, 342, 348.

Construction (Re-, in Psychoanalysis), 33, 56, 411, 414, 415.

Contact (*cf. Phassa*), 146, 147, 154, 160-162, 260-270, 272, 277, 278, 280, 281, 288-293, 301, 302, 308, 312, 366, 367-374, 379, 388, 442, 443, 463.

Covetousness (*cf. Rāga, et. al*), 136, 281, 283, 309, 442.

Culture, 2, 4, 5, 9, 22, 24, 33, 36, 37, 48, 70, 72, 80, 90, 111, 112, 224, 230, 236, 256, 323, 332, 343, 483.

Cure, 8, 15n, 27, 62, 64, 78, 89, 114, 120, 169, 170, 193, 202, 211, 321, 334-338, 340, 344, 351, 352n, 407, 410-412, 417, 422, 423, 426, 428, 430, 431, 480, 484-486.

Death, 8, 10, 58-60, 61, 90, 93, 108, 130, 131, 135, 140, 146, 147, 152, 153, 156-159, 161-164, 167, 254, 317, 332, 349.

Death Instinct (*cf. Thanatos*), 51, 53, 75, 79, 80, 86, 194-196, 210, 229, 232-242, 319, 320, 331, 434.

Defense (Defence) Mechanism(s), 28, 39, 42, 43, 56, 62, 67, 70, 72, 103, 177, 198, 213, 217, 222, 240, 338, 346, 406, 411, 413, 421, 425, 430, 474, 477, 485.

Deliverance (*cf. Vimutti*), 132, 151, 290, 310, 368, 457.

Delusion (*cf. Moha, Avijjā*), 134, 140, 141, 148, 158, 261, 282, 283, 285, 289, 375, 381, 382, 388, 391, 394, 399, 403, 442, 456, 457, 470.

Delusion(s), 33, 34, 48, 56, 58, 61, 63, 71, 94, 106, 250, 259, 341-343, 351, 406-408, 410, 411, 414, 475, 487.

Dementia Praecox, 54, 165, 213.

Desire (*cf. Taṇhā*), 129, 135-137, 138-140, 141, 142, 146, 150, 152, 155, 162, 261, 266-269, 271-275, 275, 280, 281, 284, 285, 287-290, 293, 297, 299, 303-305, 359, 360, 363, 365-369, 371, 374, 375, 377, 378, 381, 385, 387, 388, 390, 395-398, 403, 445, 453, 464, 465, 474-479.

Desire for Becoming (*cf. Bhavataṇhā*), 129, 399, 403, 443, 467.

Destiny, 52, 88, 167, 230, 257, 349, 419, 474.

Developmental Theory (*cf. Libido*), 182, 187, 200, 326-328, 331, 341, 475.

Dhamma, 7n, 129, 133, 141, 148, 149, 151, 152, 155-157, 158n, 159, 267, 299, 301, 308, 355, 356-358, 359, 362, 364, 366, 375, 377, 383-385, 391, 393, 394, 397, 440, 443, 445, 449, 461-463, 466-468, 470, 484, 488.

Diphasic Onset (of sexual development), 42, 102, 227, 258.

Dissolution (of Oedipus Complex), 82, 184, 201, 207, 209, 210, 351.

Distortion, 19, 20, 24-26, 38, 39, 57, 69, 70, 73, 80, 100, 105, 106, 116,

118, 120, 167, 168, 182, 183, 255, 259, 408, 410, 434.

Diṭṭhi (*cf.* False Views), 148-159, 160, 294-299, 441.

Diṭṭhigata (*cf.* False Views), 148-159, 294-299, 360, 483, 488.

Dosa (*cf.* Hatred), 141, 144, 281-285, 300, 356, 359, 368, 375, 390, 391, 446, 457.

Dream Interpretation, 15, 25, 28, 206, 410, 436.

Dream Work, 19-22, 14, 26, 28, 37, 116, 168, 182, 255, 339, 410, 479.

Dreams, 15, 18-26, 28, 30, 35, 38, 43, 44, 55, 77, 109, 110, 165, 167, 168, 179, 182, 183, 188, 204, 206, 217, 219, 244, 254-256, 319, 322, 339, 340, 410, 411, 414, 436, 474.

Dualism, 194, 203, 210, 223, 232, 235-238, 320, 331, 344.

Dukkha (*cf.* Ill), 8, 10, 129, 130, 132, 139, 140, 144, 156, 157, 159-163, 261, 262, 265, 268, 272, 279, 281, 284, 286, 290, 291, 294, 295, 298-300, 302, 305-307, 311, 314, 355, 358-361, 366, 368, 374, 376-379, 387, 394-395, 396, 397, 439, 440, 442-444, 448, 450, 454, 457, 460, 467, 474, 477, 483.

Economic(s), 36, 55, 60, 109, 243, 318-320, 328-331, 337.

Economic Theory (Principle), 113, 173, 175, 193, 194, 197, 202, 212, 218, 220, 222-224, 323.

Education (*Erziehung*), 35, 75, 76, 78, 177, 191, 192, 208, 209, 228, 259, 315, 318, 329, 343, 423.

Ego-Ideal, 38, 45, 50, 68-70, 82, 184, 206, 212, 213, 215-217, 226-231, 323, 324, 330, 331.

Ekodhoti (One-pointedness of Thought), 383, 439, 441, 470.

Empedocles, 32n, 241, 242, 434, 435n.

Emptiness (*cf.* *Suññatā, Śūnya, Śūnyata*), 7n, 159, 274, 280, 287, 295, 312, 363, 366, 371, 373, 379, 380, 387, 395, 398-400, 439, 449, 452, 458, 459, 483, 486, 488.

Energy (Instinctual), 15, 20, 31, 32, 46, 113, 173-175, 185, 186, 189, 193-195, 198, 199, 217, 218, 229, 236, 243, 244, 256, 317, 326, 330, 335-337, 346, 409, 410, 416, 419, 420, 426, 485.

Eros, 50, 51, 53, 75, 79, 86, 167, 173, 186, 187, 194-196, 203, 232-242, 250, 319, 320, 328, 331, 337, 341, 405, 434, 476.

Erotic (-ism), 46, 54, 57, 63, 64, 74, 77, 83, 84, 111, 116, 172, 183, 185-187, 200n, 214-216, 239-242, 328-334, 352, 427, 428.

Ethics, 53, 66, 97, 175, 186, 178, 179, 339, 340.

Evolution, 21, 48, 73, 75, 97, 233, 255, 258, 259, 315, 317.

Eye (*cf.* *Cakkhu*), 132, 139, 144, 160, 263, 266, 277, 278, 280, 281, 286, 290, 292, 293, 299, 301, 304, 306, 309, 359, 366, 367-374, 379, 382, 404, 442, 462.

Faith, 2, 3, 6, 97, 105, 283, 301, 308, 435n.

False View(s) (*cf.* *Diṭṭhi, -gata*), 148-159, 161, 267, 278, 294-299, 303,

360, 375, 376, 379, 382, 396, 445, 477.

Family, 73, 179, 339.

Fantasy (Phantasy), 35, 38, 56, 58, 111, 112, 113, 113-118, 182, 183, 190, 208, 247, 250, 251, 255, 317-319, 347, 349, 350.

Father, 3, 31, 40, 41, 47, 52, 57, 68, 70, 74, 85-87, 89, 92-94, 98, 102-104, 106, 108, 110, 117, 122, 180, 183, 201, 202, 205-210, 227, 228, 230, 242, 243, 248, 251, 254, 324, 413, 414.

Feeling (cf. Vedanā), 8, 262-270, 273, 275-280, 287, 288, 293, 296-298, 302-305, 308, 314, 357, 360, 367-374, 375, 378, 379-381, 384, 385, 387-389, 392, 394, 398, 442, 443, 448-450, 454, 461, 463, 474, 475.

Female Sexuality, 46, 117, 200, 202, 327.

Fetish (-ism), 43-44, 55, 57, 209, 223.

Fixation, 26, 30, 34, 35, 39, 101, 114, 116, 119, 168, 173, 177, 199, 204, 242, 318, 342, 412.

Foreconscious (cf. Preconscious), 166.

Four Noble Truths, 7, 7n, 142, 163, 355, 378, 442, 460, 470.

Free Association, 31, 340, 406, 411, 415, 417, 418, 424, 436.

Frustration, 13-15, 22, 27, 28, 34, 35, 39, 48, 49, 55, 87, 137, 178, 222, 249, 322, 324, 329, 342, 353, 414, 420, 422, 428, 431, 485, 487.

Fundamental Method (of Psychoanalysis), 62, 406, 417.

Fusion (of Instincts), 60, 184n, 238, 328, 331.

God, 33, 88-90, 92-94, 97, 99, 100, 102-106, 108, 111, 122, 124, 126, 208, 210, 230, 246, 249, 349, 413, 477.

Gods, 19, 60, 73, 90, 93, 102.

Gratification, 43, 79, 91, 92, 104, 113, 120, 176, 182, 194, 224, 232, 317, 324, 344, 345, 419.

Greed (cf. Rāga, et. al.), 140-142, 281-286, 299, 367, 368, 371, 381, 388, 391, 394, 399, 403, 440, 442, 445, 456, 457, 461, 462.

Group Psychology (cf. Social Psychology), 33, 67, 198, 211, 216, 230, 231, 259, 330, 406, 412, 413, 478, 479.

Guilt, 38, 51-53, 60, 73, 74, 84-88, 92, 102-105, 111, 116, 122, 208, 209, 221, 228, 231, 241, 253, 254, 260, 419.

Hallucination, 23, 33, 56, 60, 61, 250, 316.

Hate, 51, 59, 76, 86, 105, 116, 171, 180, 182, 194, 195, 215, 225, 239, 246, 254, 332, 428, 475, 479, 481.

Hatred (cf. Dosa, Paṭigha), 280, 281-286, 309, 359, 375, 382, 388, 392, 399, 403, 404, 442, 450, 465.

Health, 9, 13, 15, 16, 21, 38, 45-47, 52, 78, 83, 84, 168-170, 172, 189, 193, 209, 214, 217, 218, 221, 222, 237, 250, 319-322, 325, 327, 332n, 333, 352, 408, 420, 423, 434.

Heap (Group; cf. Khandha), 8, 129, 142, 148, 269, 270, 275-281, 360,

379-381, 475.
Heart/Mind (see *Citta*).
Heaven, 75, 93, 353, 477.
Heredity, 35, 77, 324, 341, 342.
Hindrances (to Release), 134, 152, 300, 303, 465.
History, 13, 17, 21, 33, 36, 39, 41, 59, 69-72, 77, 90, 101, 102, 114, 115, 117-120, 127, 179, 187, 192, 205, 251, 252, 254-256, 413, 414, 478.
Homeostasis (-tic), 120, 175, 315, 318.
Homosexual, 44, 117, 194, 202, 207, 212, 213, 425.
Horde (Primal Human), 85, 92, 102, 230.
Humor (Humour), 48, 49, 333.
Hypnosis, 69, 165-167, 200n, 415, 416, 419, 436, 484.
Hypocrisy (Psychological), 26, 77, 172, 345.
Hysteria, 28n, 31, 32, 35, 39, 50, 53, 165, 174, 203, 222, 326, 424.

Ibsen, Henrik, 87, 205, 206.
Id, 9, 25, 42, 45, 50, 52, 55, 57, 81, 82, 88, 120, 173, 185, 195, 197, 198, 213, 217-231, 232, 236, 240, 242-245, 250, 315, 316, 322-324, 334-338, 348, 349, 405, 408-409, 430, 431, 475.
Ideal, The, 125-126.
Identification, 50, 61, 68, 69, 86, 184, 194, 207, 227-231, 240.
Ignorance (*cf. Avijjā, Moha*), 130, 131, 133, 134, 136, 137, 138n, 140-142, 144, 146-148, 159, 160, 163, 261, 265-269, 275, 281-286, 289-291, 194, 297, 300, 301, 302-305, 311, 356, 362, 371, 375, 376, 381, 384, 386, 388, 394, 440, 441, 443, 444, 446, 457, 459, 461, 462, 465, 467-469, 470, 474, 476, 479.
Ignorance (of Unconscious), 9-11, 21, 27, 35, 48, 94, 98, 120, 167, 205, 216, 248, 345, 351, 405, 406, 475, 476, 479, 484.
Ill (*cf. Dukkha*), 7, 9, 10, 11, 129, 130, 139, 140, 146, 148, 150, 153, 154, 158, 161, 162, 263, 264, 266, 268, 272-274, 286, 287, 291, 293, 294, 299, 306, 310, 377, 398, 445, 448, 454.
Illness, 8, 9, 14-17, 21, 24, 26, 27, 33, 35, 50, 52, 58, 61, 62, 66, 67, 73, 78, 79, 84, 87, 89, 102, 103, 130, 172, 185, 193, 204, 209, 210, 217, 222, 225, 237, 319, 322, 325, 327, 332, 335, 340, 342, 344, 406, 409, 410, 412, 413, 416, 419, 426, 428, 430, 436.
Illusion(s), 1, 3, 59, 60, 68, 77, 80, 91-96, 105-107, 111, 120, 126, 133, 140-142, 153, 248, 249, 285, 346, 349-352, 474, 477, 478, 481-483, 488.
Imagination (and Reality), 101, 102, 205, 248, 250, 317.
Immortality, 58, 60, 108.
Impermanence (*cf. Anicca*), 132, 133, 149, 159, 261-262, 276, 278, 290, 301, 388, 447, 470, 486.
Indifference (*cf. Virāga*), 296, 382.
Infantile (Narcissism), 9, 22, 34, 38, 46, 47, 50, 70, 89, 93, 98, 109, 111, 120, 212, 215, 216, 250, 252, 342, 345, 349.

Injustice, 74n.
Insight (*cf. Paññā*), 134, 137, 156, 275, 278, 279, 281, 290, 291, 295, 298, 309, 311, 357, 359, 367, 374, 377, 378, 383, 384-385, 386, 389, 394, 447, 449, 463, 465, 468-471.
Instinct(s), 17, 25, 26, 30, 32n, 35, 40, 42, 48, 50, 51, 53, 55, 56, 64, 66, 68, 74-77, 79, 80, 82, 84, 86, 92, 104, 115, 121, 166, 170-204, 206, 216, 217-231, 232-243, 243-247, 250-252, 258, 315-321, 324, 326-328, 329-334, 334-338, 338-353, 405, 412, 422, 423, 434, 475-477.
Introjection, 77, 184, 201, 226, 229, 324.

Jain(s), 296, 307, 311, 357, 365, 367, 454, 462, 466, 486.
Jarāmaraṇa (*cf.* Old-Age-and-Dying), 10, 264, 443.
Jāti (*cf.* Birth, Rebirth, Former Life), 263, 264.
Jesus, 101, 103, 105.
Jethro (the Midianite), 99.
Jew(s), 103-105, 126.
Jewish, 70, 104, 106.
Jhāna, 357, 369-371, 392, 397, 399, 448-460, 470.
Jokes, 21, 31, 48, 49, 165.
Judaism, 103-106, 125, 413.
Judgement, 19, 31, 79, 120, 173, 189, 209, 212, 225, 226, 316, 317, 321, 324, 325, 343, 349, 408, 417, 421, 479, 481.
Jung, Carl, 203, 233n, 237, 339, 340, 344, 429.
Justice, 16, 93, 94, 100, 103, 202.

Kāma (*cf.* Pleasure), 138-140, 160, 265, 268, 269, 271, 272, 289, 359, 369, 382, 449, 459.
Kāmataṇhā, 129, 443.
Kamma (*cf.* Action), 150, 151, 271, 272, 305, 306, 307-314, 377, 378, 441, 478, 488.
Karma (*cf.* Action), 150, 312-314, 478.
Kāya, 160, 275, 311, 372, 377, 444.
Khandha (*cf.* Heap), 8, 129, 142, 143, 145-148, 152, 157, 159, 160, 264, 269, 270, 272, 273, 275-290, 281, 288, 291, 292, 293, 296-298, 300, 301, 309, 355, 357, 360, 363, 371, 375, 376, 379-381, 384, 385, 387, 388, 395, 400, 442, 444, 448, 454, 461, 463, 466, 467, 475, 476.
Killing (the Father), 85, 86, 98, 103, 104, 210, 413, 414.
Kissing, 36.
Klesa (*cf. Dosa, Moha, Paṭigha, Rāga et. al.*), 281-285, 314, 469.
Kusala (Useful), 153, 287, 308, 356, 372, 388, 390, 393, 445-448.

Latency, 46, 101-103, 190, 324, 412, 413.
Latent Disposition (*cf. Anusaya*), 144, 381, 476, 479, 482, 487.

Leonardo da Vinci, 112, 117, 118n, 207, 208, 228, 248, 249, 251, 255, 347, 349, 352.
Libidinal Types, 82-84, 209, 216, 332, 333.
Libido, 15, 18, 22, 31, 39, 40, 45-47, 49-51, 54, 59-62, 68-70, 74, 81, 84, 174, 182, 183, 193, 196, 198-204, 206, 211-217, 217-224, 226, 232-242, 244-246, 319, 320, 323, 327, 328-334, 334-338, 341-348, 412, 417, 422, 423, 426, 428, 430, 475, 476.
Livelihood (cf. Ājīva), 390, 393, 441, 444, 445.
Lobha (cf. Greed), 141, 144, 281-285, 300.
Loka (cf. World), 276, 281, 368.
Love (cf. Eros, Libido), 13, 22, 31, 38, 40, 44-47, 50, 51, 58-61, 67, 69, 70, 74, 76, 77, 79, 83, 86, 87, 91, 95, 105, 113, 116, 117, 171, 172, 180, 182, 192, 194, 195, 198, 199, 200n, 203, 204, 206, 211, 212, 214, 215, 230, 232-242, 246, 254, 315, 321, 323, 324, 328-334, 345, 349, 351, 424, 428, 434, 474, 476, 479, 481.

Magga (cf. Path), 357, 383, 396.
Mahāyāna, 7, 393.
Māna (cf. Conceit, Pride), 280-281, 359.
Mano (cf. Mind), 132, 263, 301, 306-307, 309, 368, 382, 389, 452, 453.
Māra, 129, 132, 138, 155, 278, 298, 369, 387, 390, 453, 475.
Marxism, 95, 96, 350.
Masochism (-tic), 38, 51-53, 67, 116, 182, 183, 187, 196, 219, 229, 238, 239, 241, 474, 476.
Masturbation, 41, 57, 116, 208.
Melancholia, 58-61, 66, 82, 84, 120, 172, 183, 184, 199, 209, 214, 228, 229, 238, 322, 330, 430, 474, 482.
Memory, 29, 71, 117, 118, 189, 255, 257, 316, 317, 478.
Memory Traces, 71, 197, 222, 226, 229, 243, 245, 246, 250, 258, 259, 317, 322, 408.
Mental Unity, 24, 55, 81, 221, 223, 326, 335, 337, 340, 411, 413, 417, 423, 428, 434.
Mettā, 389-394, 447.
Mettacitta, 389-394.
Michaelangelo, 71-73, 349, 352.
Mind, 17-22, 28, 30, 31, 33, 48, 49, 55-57, 64, 84, 91, 115, 165, 167, 177, 180, 185, 188, 193, 196, 204, 216, 218, 219, 240, 241, 244, 250, 326, 338, 340, 343, 415, 416, 418, 419, 432, 433, 437.
Mind (cf. Mano), 131, 132, 138, 139, 142, 146, 160, 263, 265, 269, 275, 277, 281, 291, 293, 301, 304, 306-307, 368, 373, 382, 389.
Mnemic (Residues), 20, 197.
Moha (cf. Ignorance), 141, 144, 281-285, 300, 356, 359, 368, 375, 382, 390, 391, 446, 457, 479.
Monk, 146, 157, 160, 266, 273, 275, 276, 277, 280, 283, 284, 286, 287,

112, 124, 126, 181, 204, 209, 249, 252-254, 330.

Projection, 1, 3, 40, 69, 95, 210, 245, 248, 406, 413.

Providence, 88, 91, 93, 94, 230, 249, 350, 477.

Psyche, 31, 48, 54, 94, 114, 166, 172, 174-176, 181, 184, 185, 194, 195, 202, 211-231, 232, 250-252, 254, 405, 408, 410, 417, 422, 424, 476.

Psychiatry, 17, 168, 341, 410.

Psychoanalysis, 1, 15, 17, 25, 28, 29, 35, 36, 48, 50, 54, 64, 66, 74, 78, 79, 91, 112, 169, 170, 175, 179, 183, 185, 218, 224, 225, 238, 251, 255, 256, 321, 323, 325, 326, 334-338, 338-348, 351, 352, 405-407, 409-412, 415-417, 421, 426, 427, 430, 431, 433, 434, 436, 437, 473, 485, 488.

Psychology (*cf.* Group Psychology, Social Psychology), 11, 20, 66, 101, 115, 185, 198, 201, 202, 213, 216, 221, 225, 232, 242, 243, 246, 255, 412, 478.

Psychosis, 8, 23, 44, 49, 53-58, 102, 120, 175, 185, 190, 211, 222, 242, 250, 321-323, 333, 405, 413, 426, 430, 431, 474.

Psychotic(s), 11, 17, 22-24, 28, 44, 45, 47, 53-58, 84, 167, 172, 199, 249, 321-323, 329, 330, 340, 343, 486.

Puberty, 14, 35, 41, 46, 102, 190, 412.

Punishment, 23, 40-42, 51-53, 57, 86, 95, 116, 201, 205, 209, 210, 229, 231, 239, 321, 324.

Puthujjana ("Ordinary Person"), 11, 142-145, 162, 461, 464, 474.

Q, 244.

Rāga (*cf.* Passion), 136, 141, 261, 271, 274, 281-285, 299, 300, 356, 359, 368, 375, 447, 457, 468.

Reality Principle, 90, 91, 112, 114, 175, 188-198, 203, 232, 245, 315-321, 322, 323, 328, 333, 334, 408.

Reality Testing, 114, 190, 191, 197, 319, 408.

Regression, 20, 22, 38, 50, 91, 116, 183, 184, 202, 204, 207, 211, 214, 239, 323, 324, 326-328, 331, 429, 479.

Religion, 1-4, 6, 16, 17, 22, 25, 33, 58, 70, 73, 74n, 88-108, 109, 111, 120, 122-127, 175, 179, 186, 192, 208, 210, 243, 249, 254, 257, 317, 339, 343, 345, 346, 349-351, 412-414, 474, 481, 486.

Remembering, Repeating and Working Through, 27, 62, 407, 415-417, 425.

Remorse, 85, 86, 111, 231.

Repetition (Syndrome), 62, 80, 195, 331, 417, 424, 425.

Repression, 16, 28, 29, 30-35, 38, 39, 41, 43, 46, 47, 55, 56, 60, 64, 66, 67, 70, 72, 74, 78, 80-83, 87, 98-102, 104, 108, 112, 113, 119, 166-169, 171, 173-177, 180, 183, 192, 203, 214, 217, 218, 223, 228, 236, 240, 244-246, 254, 255, 259, 317, 322, 323, 324-326, 335, 337, 338-348, 352, 405, 408, 409, 413, 416, 417, 419, 421, 422, 425, 428, 430-432, 474, 477, 479, 484.

Resistance, 16, 31, 62-64, 81, 119, 166, 221, 236, 321, 326, 337, 338-348, 405, 409, 411, 414, 416, 417, 421-423, 424-427, 429, 432, 436n, 477, 479, 480, 482, 484, 485.
Ritual (and Rites, Grasping After; *cf. Sīlabbatupādāna*), 135, 136, 160, 265, 303.
Rūpa (*cf.* Body), 131, 136, 144, 265, 266, 275, 279, 290, 296, 371, 442, 449.

Sadism (-tic), 32, 38, 51, 52, 60, 67, 116, 182, 183, 238, 239, 474, 476.
Saḷāyatana (*cf.* Six Senses, the), 159, 264, 265, 268, 302, 443.
Samādhi, 283, 363, 370, 383, 441, 448-460, 469, 470, 487.
Saṃsāra, 7n, 131, 150, 151, 159, 307-314, 363, 396, 400, 401, 440, 478, 482, 486, 488, 489.
Sangha, 308, 355, 357, 358, 384, 385, 389-394, 399, 461, 465, 466, 488.
Sankhāra (*cf.* Activity (-ies)), 8, 130, 131, 142, 147, 159, 261, 265, 279, 275-280, 284, 285, 297, 312, 368, 371, 372, 444, 449, 450, 470.
Saññā (Sense Perception), 160, 265, 266, 290, 299, 356, 369, 371, 378, 444, 450, 451.
Satī (Mindfulness), 283, 441, 447, 469.
Schizophrenic (Schizophrenia), 47, 430.
Schopenhauer, Arthur, 32n, 48, 346.
Science(s), 1-3, 17, 66, 73, 96, 109, 123, 126, 169n, 180, 192, 215, 243, 246, 248, 250, 255, 259, 317, 345, 346, 349-352, 413, 435.
Seduction (Fantasies), 35, 114, 115, 179.
Sexuality, 36, 37, 42, 48, 66, 102, 116, 171, 175-187, 188, 200, 208, 227, 232, 317, 327, 328, 339, 344-346, 419, 427, 476.
Sexuality, Infantile, 16, 35-37, 41, 42, 64, 82, 101, 104, 111, 113, 248, 258, 339, 340.
Shakespeare, William, 86-87.
Sīla, 299, 309, 366, 377, 393, 441, 449, 470.
Sīlabbatupādāna (*cf.* Ritual and Rites, Grasping After), 160, 265.
Six Senses, the (*cf. Saḷāyatana*), 10, 132, 138, 159, 160, 264-266, 268-270, 272, 278, 288, 291, 306, 365, 366, 368, 399, 442, 452.
Sleep, 18, 21, 23, 24, 44, 49, 55, 168, 204, 206, 219, 249, 319, 322, 329.
Slips of the Tongue, 21, 30, 31, 43, 44, 165.
Social Psychology, 20, 66-68, 71, 90, 95, 119, 478.
Society, 16, 32, 36, 64, 66, 67, 71, 77, 79, 81, 97, 176, 201, 202, 254, 259, 260, 326, 343, 345, 346, 352, 406, 483.
Sotāpanna (Stream-Entrant), 380, 393, 466.
Soul, 60, 90, 337.
Soul (*cf. Attā, Ātman*), 268, 308, 312, 313, 391.
Space (*cf. Ākāsa*), 144, 145, 284, 287, 357, 366, 370, 372, 377, 397, 399, 449-456, 459, 460, 464.
Speech (*cf. Vacī*), 134, 265, 269, 275, 284, 291, 294, 300, 311, 366, 373, 390, 392, 393, 395, 441, 443, 444, 461.

Splitting of the Ego, 23n, 44, 55, 57, 223.

Structural Theory (*cf.* Id, Super-Ego), 79, 166, 180, 218, 232, 330, 405.

Sublimation, 74-76, 80, 169, 177, 192, 217, 227, 240, 324, 336, 347.

Substitution (*re:* Symptoms), 27, 42, 55, 56, 92, 168, 209, 222, 249.

Sukha (Pleasant), 263, 370, 378, 450, 457.

Suññatā (*cf.* Emptiness), 283, 373, 398, 456, 483.

Śūnya (*cf.* Emptiness), 313, 314, 362, 399, 400.

Śūnyata (*cf.* Emptiness), 7n, 280, 312, 313, 401.

Super-Ego, 28, 38, 41, 42, 45, 52, 53, 66, 67, 79, 81-83, 86, 88, 104, 172, 183-185, 195, 201, 206, 209, 212-214, 218, 219, 222-226, 227-231, 232, 239, 240, 242, 243, 253, 322, 324, 332-334, 337, 347, 348, 405, 408, 430, 475, 489.

Sustained Thought (*cf.* Vitakka), 275, 284, 293, 357, 373, 444, 447, 449, 452, 457.

Symptoms, 1, 14, 15, 26-29, 30, 32, 35-39, 42-45, 48, 51, 57, 58, 60, 62, 64-66, 78-80, 89, 96, 99, 101, 103, 105, 108, 114, 116, 119, 122, 167-169, 173-175, 183, 201-203, 217, 219, 221-223, 236, 242, 245, 249, 250, 254, 255, 257, 318, 324, 336, 338-348, 405, 406, 408-423, 425, 426-431, 431-433, 474, 479, 480, 485.

Taṇhā (*cf.* Desire), 131, 135-137, 138-140, 155, 265, 271-275, 281, 285, 290, 298, 302, 366, 372, 403, 404, 443, 449.

Tathāgata, 8, 139, 152, 153, 156, 157, 268, 276, 279, 294-299, 301, 310, 312, 355-357, 358, 363, 364, 371, 375-377, 380, 398, 440, 449, 457, 461, 464, 465, 467, 483, 484.

Telepathy, 108, 110-111, 169n, 256.

Thanatos (*cf.* Death Instinct), 50, 77, 79, 167, 173, 174, 186, 187, 194-196, 203, 232-242, 319, 320, 328, 331, 337, 341, 405, 434, 476.

Therapy (-eutic), 15n, 21, 29, 31, 33, 36, 44, 62-64, 71, 78, 111, 218, 252, 260, 325, 326, 338, 340, 342-344, 348, 407, 409, 411-413, 416, 417, 423, 425, 429-432, 435n, 481.

Theravāda, 7n.

Thinking, 20, 20n, 317, 482.

Totem (-ism), 85, 92, 102, 104, 254.

Transference, 47, 62-65, 187, 211, 213, 219, 222, 237, 326, 335, 336, 340, 406, 410, 414, 420-422, 423-431.

Trauma, 21, 26, 27, 34, 41, 43, 49, 71, 101-104, 115, 121, 180, 181, 222, 252-254, 258, 412-415, 423, 484.

Uncanny, 108, 109, 250.

Unconscious, the, 8, 17, 18, 20-22, 25, 28, 30, 31, 34, 36, 38, 50, 60, 66, 81, 108, 111, 120, 121, 165, 165-170, 171, 176, 195, 196, 205, 219, 232, 256, 258, 316, 321, 326n, 334, 336-339, 344, 348, 417, 421, 422, 424, 425,

432, 433, 476, 478, 482, 487.

Unhappiness, Ordinary, 8, 185, 243, 326, 337, 341, 346, 405, 414, 420, 432, 479, 486.

Upādāna (Grasping), 147, 159, 263, 265, 270, 312, 313, 368, 457.

Vacī (*cf.* Speech), 160, 265, 275, 372, 441, 444.

Vedanā (*cf.* Feeling), 160, 263, 265, 266, 278, 290, 308, 311, 371, 377, 384, 392, 444, 451.

Vibhava (*cf.* Annihilation (-ism)), 138, 156, 295, 403.

Vibhavataṇhā (Desire for Annihilation), 129, 403, 404, 443.

Vicissitudes (of Instincts), 53, 82, 84, 170-175, 182, 185, 187, 194, 201, 238, 319, 324, 327, 475-477.

Vihāra (Staying in a Place), 366.

Vimutti (*cf.* Deliverance), 295, 311, 378, 396, 441, 449, 453, 466, 470.

Viññāṇa (*cf.* Consciousness), 162, 263-265, 271, 287, 371, 372, 387, 443, 444, 452-454, 456.

Virāga (*cf.* Indifference), 288, 449.

Viriya (Vigor), 283, 385, 393, 445, 447, 469.

Vitakka (*cf.* Sustained Thought), 266, 269, 275, 284, 289, 444, 447, 449, 457.

Weltanschauung, 95, 348, 487.

Will (*cf.* *Cetanā*), 160, 161, 277, 290, 301, 305-306, 379, 442.

World (*cf.* *Loka*), 3, 129, 130, 135, 136, 142, 144, 149, 153, 156, 160, 261, 265, 271, 272, 276, 280-282, 284, 285-299, 303, 305, 307, 308, 310, 313, 314, 449, 453-455, 464.

Yoga, 91, 92.

Gordon E. Pruett holds a B.A. from Yale University, M.A.'s from Oxford University and Princeton University, and the Ph.D. in Religion from Princeton University. He is the author of a number of articles and reviews in the area of Religious Studies. He has taught at Westminster Choir College, Princeton, N. J., at Lehigh University, and has been a member of the Department of Philosophy and Religion at Northeastern University, Boston, MA, since 1969.

'illusin of, niversality'
permanence. etc.

tanha - grasping - we can't hold on to everything
because everything is impermanent,
in a state of flux + change.

The pleasure principle - clinging to pleasures, averting
displeasures -
The development of equanimity.